P9-CNB-773

On China

Also by Henry Kissinger

A World Restored: Metternich, Castlereagh, and the Problems of Peace: 1812–22

Nuclear Weapons and Foreign Policy

The Necessity for Choice: Prospects of American Foreign Policy

The Troubled Partnership: A Reappraisal of the Atlantic Alliance

American Foreign Policy

White House Years

Years of Upheaval

Diplomacy

Years of Renewal

Does America Need a Foreign Policy? Toward a Diplomacy for the 21st Century

Ending the Vietnam War: A History of America's Involvement in and Extrication from the Vietnam War

Crisis: The Anatomy of Two Major Foreign Policy Crises

On China

Henry Kissinger

THE PENGUIN PRESS

New York

2011

THE PENGUIN PRESS
Published by the Penguin Group • Penguin Group (USA) Inc.,
375 Hudson Street, New York, New York 10014, U.S.A. • Penguin Group (Canada),
90 Eglinton Avenue East, Suite 700, Toronto, Ontario, Canada M4P 2Y3 (a division of
Pearson Penguin Canada Inc.) • Penguin Books Ltd, 80 Strand, London WC2R 0RL,
England • Penguin Ireland, 25 St. Stephen's Green, Dublin 2, Ireland (a division of
Penguin Books Ltd) • Penguin Books Australia Ltd, 250 Camberwell Road,
Camberwell, Victoria 3124, Australia (a division of Pearson Australia Group Pty Ltd) •
Penguin Books India Pvt Ltd, 11 Community Centre, Panchsheel Park,
New Delhi—110 017, India • Penguin Group (NZ), 67 Apollo Drive, Rosedale,
Auckland 0632, New Zealand (a division of Pearson New Zealand Ltd) • Penguin Books
(South Africa) (Pty) Ltd, 24 Sturdee Avenue, Rosebank, Johannesburg 2196, South Africa

Penguin Books Ltd, Registered Offices: 80 Strand, London WC2R 0RL, England

First published in 2011 by The Penguin Press, a member of Penguin Group (USA) Inc.

Library of Congress Cataloging-in-Publication Data

Kissinger, Henry, 1923–
On China / Henry Kissinger.
p. cm.
Includes bibliographical references and index.
ISBN 978-1-59420-271-1 (hardback)
1. China—Foreign relations—20th century. 2. China—Foreign relations—21st century.
3. World politics—21st century. I. Title.
DS775.8.K47 2011
327.51—dc22
2011009265

Printed in the United States of America
1 3 5 7 9 10 8 6 4 2

DESIGNED BY MARYSARAH QUINN
MAP BY JEFFREY L. WARD

To Annette and Oscar de la Renta

Contents

CHINA AND ITS NEIGHBORS
KAZAKHSTAN
L. Balkhash
Almaty
Bishkek
KYRGYZSTAN
Tianshan Range
Urumqi
MONGOLIA
Kashgar
TAJIKISTAN
Taklamakan Desert
XINJIANG
Great Wall
AFGHANISTAN
PAKISTAN
Kunlun Mountains
Islamabad
Rawalpindi
LADAKH
JAMMU AND KASHMIR
Lahore
QINGHAI
NINGXIA
Yellow R.
GANSU
TIBET
New Delhi
Himalayas
CHINA
NEPAL
Lhasa
SICHUAN
Kathmandu
Thimphu
BHUTAN
Yangtze (Yangzi) R.
Ganges R.
INDIA
BANGLADESH
Dhaka
Calcutta
YUNNAN
MYANMAR
VIETNAM
Hanoi
Bay of Bengal
LAOS
0 Miles 500
0 Kilometers 500
Vientiane
Yangon
THAILAND
© 2011 Jeffrey L. Ward

RUSSIA
L. Baikal
Amur R.
Ussuri R.
Zhenbao Island
Heilongjiang
Ulan Bator
Jilin
Manchuria
Vladivostok
Inner Mongolia
Gobi Desert
Shenyang
Liaoning
North Korea
Sea of Japan
Beijing
Liaodong Peninsula
Wonsan
Tianjin
Dalian
Pyongyang
Panmunjom
Tokyo
Beihe/Hai R.
Dagu Forts
Lushun (Port Arthur)
Seoul
Japan
Inchon
Kyoto
Great Wall
Hebei
South Korea
Yellow R.
Shanxi
Pusan
Shandong
Yan'an
Yellow Sea
Grand Canal
Xi'an
Shaanxi
Henan
Jiangsu
Pacific Ocean
Nanjing
Suzhou
Shanghai
Anhui
Hubei
Chongqing
Wuhan
Zhoushan Islands
Hangzhou
East China Sea
Ningbo
Yijiangshan
Ryukyu Islands
Zhejiang
Dachen
Jiangxi
Okinawa
Hunan
Fuzhou
Taipei
Fujian
Taiwan Strait
Guizhou
Xiamen
Guangdong
Taiwan
Area of detail
Guangzhou (Canton)
Shenzhen
Guangxi
Hong Kong
Zhuhai
Hainan
South China Sea
Philippines
Manila
Matsu
Quemoy
Pescadores/ Penghu Islands
0 Mi.
100
0 Km.
100

Preface

FORTY YEARS AGO almost to the day, President Richard Nixon did me the honor of sending me to Beijing to reestablish contact with a country central to the history of Asia with which America had had no high-level contact for over twenty years. The American motive for the opening was to put before our people a vision of peace transcending the travail of the Vietnam War and the ominous vistas of the Cold War. China, though technically an ally of the Soviet Union, was in quest of maneuvering room to resist a threatened attack from Moscow.

In the interval I have been to China more than fifty times. Like many visitors over the centuries, I have come to admire the Chinese people, their endurance, their subtlety, their family sense, and the culture they represent. At the same time, all my life I have reflected on the building of peace, largely from an American perspective. I have had the good luck of being able to pursue these two strands of thinking simultaneously as a senior official, as a carrier of messages, and as a scholar.

This book is an effort, based in part on conversations with Chinese leaders, to explain the conceptual way the Chinese think about problems of peace and war and international order, and its relationship to the more pragmatic, case-by-case American approach. Different histories and cultures produce occasionally divergent conclusions. I do not always agree with the Chinese perspective, nor will every reader. But it is necessary to understand it, since China will play such a big role in the world that is emerging in the twenty-first century.

Since my first visit, China has become an economic superpower and a major factor in shaping the global political order. The United States has prevailed in the Cold War. The relationship between China and the United States has become a central element in the quest for world peace and global well-being.

Eight American presidents and four generations of Chinese leaders have managed this delicate relationship in an astonishingly consistent manner, considering the difference in starting points. Both sides have refused to permit historic legacies or different conceptions of domestic order to interrupt their essentially cooperative relationship.

It has been a complex journey, for both societies believe they represent unique values. American exceptionalism is missionary. It holds that the United States has an obligation to spread its values to every part of the world. China's exceptionalism is cultural. China does not proselytize; it does not claim that its contemporary institutions are relevant outside China. But it is the heir of the Middle Kingdom tradition, which formally graded all other states as various levels of tributaries based on their approximation to Chinese cultural and political forms; in other words, a kind of cultural universality.

A primary focus of this book is the interaction between Chinese and American leaders since the People's Republic of China was founded in 1949. Both in and out of government, I have kept records of my conversations with four generations of Chinese leaders and have drawn on them as a primary source in writing this book.

This book could not have been written without the dedicated and able assistance of associates and of friends who permitted me to impose on them for help.

Schuyler Schouten was indispensable. He came to my attention eight years ago when Professor John Gaddis of Yale recommended him as one of his ablest students. When I started this project I asked him to take a two-month leave from his law firm. He did so, and in the process became so involved that he saw the effort through to its end a year later. Schuyler undertook much of the basic research. He helped with the translation of Chinese texts and even more with penetrating the implications of some of the subtler ones. He was indefatigable during the editing and proofreading phase. I have never had a better research associate and very rarely one as good.

It has been my good fortune to have Stephanie Junger-Moat work with me for a decade across the gamut of my activities. She was what in baseball they would call the essential utility player. She did research and some editing, and was the principal liaison with the publisher. She checked all the endnotes. She helped coordinate the typing and never hesitated to pitch in when deadlines approached. Her crucial contribution was reinforced by her charm and diplomatic skill.

Harry Evans edited *White House Years* thirty years ago. He permitted me to impose on our friendship to go over the entire manuscript. His editorial and structural suggestions were numerous and wise.

Theresa Amantea and Jody Williams typed the manuscript many times over and spent many evenings and weekends helping meet deadlines. Their good cheer, efficiency, and sharp eye for detail were vital.

Stapleton Roy, former ambassador to China and distinguished China scholar; Winston Lord, my associate during the opening to China and later ambassador to China; and Dick Viets, my literary executor, read several chapters and made insightful comments. Jon Vanden Heuvel provided helpful research on several chapters.

Publishing with The Penguin Press was a happy experience. Ann Godoff was always available, ever insightful, never harassing, and fun to be with. Bruce Giffords, Noirin Lucas, and Tory Klose expertly shepherded the book through the editorial production process. Fred Chase copyedited the manuscript with care and efficiency. Laura Stickney was the book's principal editor. Young enough to be my granddaughter, she was in no way intimidated by the author. She overcame her reservations about my political views sufficiently that I came to look forward to her occasionally acerbic and always incisive comments in the margins of the manuscript. She was indefatigable, perceptive, and vastly helpful.

To all these people I am immensely grateful.

The governmental papers on which I drew have all been declassified for some time. I would like to thank in particular the Woodrow Wilson International Center for Scholars Cold War International History Project for permission to use extended excerpts from their archive of declassified Russian and Chinese documents. The Carter Library helpfully made available many of the transcripts of meetings with Chinese leaders during the Carter presidency, and the Reagan Library provided numerous useful documents from their files.

Needless to say, the shortcomings of the book are my own.

As always over half a century, my wife, Nancy, provided her staunch moral and intellectual support amidst the solitude authors (or at least this author) generate around themselves when writing. She read most of the chapters and made innumerable important suggestions.

I have dedicated *On China* to Annette and Oscar de la Renta. I started the book in their home in Punta Cana and finished it there. Their hospitality has been only one facet of a friendship that has added joy and depth to my life.

Henry A. Kissinger
New York, January 2011

Note on Chinese Spellings

THIS BOOK MAKES frequent reference to Chinese names and terms. Well-known alternative spellings exist for many Chinese words, based on two particularly widespread methods of transliterating Chinese characters into the Roman alphabet: the Wade-Giles method, prevalent through much of the world until the 1980s, and the pinyin method, adopted officially in the People's Republic of China in 1979 and increasingly common in Western and other Asian publications thereafter.

For the most part, this book employs pinyin spellings. For example, the pinyin spelling "Deng Xiaoping" is used rather than the Wade-Giles spelling "Teng H'siao-ping." Where other, non-pinyin spellings remain significantly more familiar, they are retained for the reader's convenience. For example, for the name of the ancient military theorist "Sun Tzu," the traditional spelling is used, rather than the newer pinyin spelling "Sunzi."

Occasionally, in the interest of achieving consistency throughout the book's text, quoted references to names originally listed in the Wade-Giles format have been rendered in their pinyin spellings. Such changes are further noted in the endnotes. In each case, the underlying Chinese word remains the same; the difference is in the method of rendering the word in the Roman alphabet.

On China

Prologue

IN OCTOBER 1962, China's revolutionary leader Mao Zedong summoned his top military and political commanders to meet with him in Beijing. Two thousand miles to the west, in the forbidding and sparsely populated terrain of the Himalayas, Chinese and Indian troops were locked in a standoff over the two countries' disputed border. The dispute arose over different versions of history: India claimed the frontier demarcated during British rule, China the limits of imperial China. India had deployed its outposts to the edge of its conception of the border; China had surrounded the Indian positions. Attempts to negotiate a territorial settlement had foundered.

Mao had decided to break the stalemate. He reached far back into the classical Chinese tradition that he was otherwise in the process of dismantling. China and India, Mao told his commanders, had previously fought "one and a half" wars. Beijing could draw operational lessons from each. The first war had occurred over 1,300 years earlier, during the Tang Dynasty (618–907), when China dispatched troops to support an Indian kingdom against an illegitimate and aggressive rival. After China's intervention, the two countries had enjoyed centuries of flourishing religious and economic exchange. The lesson learned from the ancient campaign, as Mao described it, was that China and India were not doomed to perpetual enmity. They could enjoy a long period of peace again, but to do so, China had to use force to "knock" India back "to the negotiating table." The "half war," in Mao's mind, had taken place seven hundred years later, when the Mongol ruler Timurlane sacked Delhi. (Mao reasoned that since Mongolia and China were then part of the same political entity, this was a "half" Sino-Indian war.) Timurlane had won a significant victory, but once in India his army had killed over 100,000 prisoners. This time, Mao enjoined his Chinese forces to be "restrained and principled."[1]

No one in Mao's audience—the Communist Party leadership of a revolutionary "New China" proclaiming its intent to remake the international order and abolish China's own feudal past—seems to have questioned the relevance of these ancient precedents to China's current strategic imperatives. Planning for an attack continued on the basis of the principles Mao had outlined. Weeks later the offensive proceeded much as he described: China executed a sudden, devastating blow on the Indian positions and then retreated to the previous line of control, even going so far as to return the captured Indian heavy weaponry.

In no other country is it conceivable that a modern leader would initiate a major national undertaking by invoking strategic principles from a millennium-old event—nor that he could confidently expect his colleagues to understand the significance of his allusions. Yet China is singular. No other country can claim so long a continuous civilization, or such an intimate link to its ancient past and classical principles of strategy and statesmanship.

Other societies, the United States included, have claimed universal applicability for their values and institutions. Still, none equals China in persisting—and persuading its neighbors to acquiesce—in such an elevated conception of its world role for so long, and in the face of so many historical vicissitudes. From the emergence of China as a unified state in the third century B.C. until the collapse of the Qing Dynasty in 1912, China stood at the center of an East Asian international system of remarkable durability. The Chinese Emperor was conceived of (and recognized by most neighboring states) as the pinnacle of a universal political hierarchy, with all other states' rulers theoretically serving as vassals. Chinese language, culture, and political institutions were the hallmarks of civilization, such that even regional rivals and foreign conquerors adopted them to varying degrees as a sign of their own legitimacy (often as a first step to being subsumed within China).

The traditional cosmology endured despite catastrophes and centuries-long periods of political decay. Even when China was weak or divided, its centrality remained the touchstone of regional legitimacy; aspirants, both Chinese and foreign, vied to unify or conquer it, then ruled from the Chinese capital without challenging the basic premise that it was the center of the universe. While other countries were named after ethnic groups or geographical landmarks, China called itself *zhongguo*—the "Middle Kingdom" or the "Central Country."[2] Any attempt to understand China's twentieth-century diplomacy or its twenty-first-century world role must begin—even at the cost of some potential oversimplification—with a basic appreciation of the traditional context.

CHAPTER 1

The Singularity of China

SOCIETIES AND NATIONS tend to think of themselves as eternal. They also cherish a tale of their origin. A special feature of Chinese civilization is that it seems to have no beginning. It appears in history less as a conventional nation-state than a permanent natural phenomenon. In the tale of the Yellow Emperor, revered by many Chinese as the legendary founding ruler, China seems already to exist. When the Yellow Emperor appears in myth, Chinese civilization has fallen into chaos. Competing princes harass each other and the people, yet an enfeebled ruler fails to maintain order. Levying an army, the new hero pacifies the realm and is acclaimed as emperor.[1]

The Yellow Emperor has gone down in history as a founding hero; yet in the founding myth, he is reestablishing, not creating, an empire. China predated him; it strides into the historical consciousness as an established state requiring only restoration, not creation. This paradox of Chinese history recurs with the ancient sage Confucius: again, he is seen as the "founder" of a culture although he stressed that he had invented nothing, that he was merely trying to reinvigorate the principles of harmony which had once existed in the golden age but had been lost in Confucius's own era of political chaos.

Reflecting on the paradox of China's origins, the nineteenth-century missionary and traveler, the Abbé Régis-Evariste Huc, observed:

> Chinese civilization originates in an antiquity so remote that we vainly endeavor to discover its commencement. There are no traces of the state of infancy among this people. This is a very peculiar fact respecting China. We are accustomed in the history of nations to find some well-defined point of departure, and the historic documents, traditions, and monuments that remain to us generally permit us to follow, almost step by step, the progress of civilization, to be present at its birth, to watch its development, its onward march, and in many cases, its subsequent decay and fall. But it is not thus with the Chinese. They seem to have been always living in the same stage of advancement as in the present day; and the data of antiquity are such as to confirm that opinion.[2]

When Chinese written characters first evolved, during the Shang Dynasty in the second millennium B.C., ancient Egypt was at the height of its glory. The great city-states of classical Greece had not yet emerged, and Rome was millennia away. Yet the direct descendant of the Shang writing system is still used by well over a billion people today. Chinese today can understand inscriptions written in the age of Confucius; contemporary Chinese books and conversations are enriched by centuries-old aphorisms citing ancient battles and court intrigues.

At the same time, Chinese history featured many periods of civil war, interregnum, and chaos. After each collapse, the Chinese state reconstituted itself as if by some immutable law of nature. At each stage, a new uniting figure emerged, following essentially the precedent of the Yellow Emperor, to subdue his rivals and reunify China (and sometimes enlarge its bounds). The famous opening of *The Romance of the Three Kingdoms*, a fourteenth-century epic novel treasured by centuries of Chinese (including Mao, who is said to have pored over it almost obsessively in his youth), evokes this continuous rhythm: "The empire, long divided, must unite; long united, must divide. Thus it has ever been."[3] Each period of disunity was viewed as an aberration. Each new dynasty reached back to the previous dynasty's principles of governance in order to reestablish continuity. The fundamental precepts of Chinese culture endured, tested by the strain of periodic calamity.

Before the seminal event of Chinese unification in 221 B.C., there had been a millennium of dynastic rule that gradually disintegrated as the feudal subdivisions evolved from autonomy to independence. The culmination was two and a half centuries of turmoil recorded in history as the Warring States period (475–221 B.C.). Its European equivalent would be the interregnum between the Treaty of Westphalia in 1648 and the end of the Second World War, when a multiplicity of European states was struggling for preeminence within the framework of the balance of power. After 221 B.C., China maintained the ideal of empire and unity but followed the practice of fracturing, then reuniting, in cycles sometimes lasting several hundred years.

When the state fractured, wars between the various components were fought savagely. Mao once claimed that the population of China declined from fifty million to ten million during the so-called Three Kingdoms period (A.D. 220–80),[4] and the conflict among the contending groups between the two world wars of the twentieth century was extremely bloody as well.

At its ultimate extent, the Chinese cultural sphere stretched over a continental area much larger than any European state, indeed about the size of continental Europe. Chinese language and culture, and the Emperor's political writ, expanded to every known terrain: from the steppelands and pine forests in the north shading into Siberia, to the tropical jungles and terraced rice farms in the south; from the east coast with its canals, ports, and fishing villages, to the stark deserts of Central Asia and the ice-capped peaks of the Himalayan frontier. The extent and variety of this territory bolstered the sense that China was a world unto itself. It supported a conception of the Emperor as a figure of universal consequence, presiding over *tian xia*, or "All Under Heaven."

The Era of Chinese Preeminence

Through many millennia of Chinese civilization, China was never obliged to deal with other countries or civilizations that were comparable to it in scale and sophistication. India was known to the Chinese, as Mao later noted, but for much of history it was divided into separate kingdoms. The two civilizations exchanged goods and Buddhist influences along the Silk Road but were elsewhere walled off from casual contact by the almost impenetrable Himalayas and the Tibetan Plateau. The massive and forbidding deserts of Central Asia separated China from the Near Eastern cultures of Persia and Babylonia and even more from the Roman Empire. Trade caravans undertook intermittent journeys, but China as a society did not engage societies of comparable scale and achievement. Though China and Japan shared a number of core cultural and political institutions, neither was prepared to recognize the other's superiority; their solution was to curtail contact for centuries at a time. Europe was even further away in what the Chinese considered the Western Oceans, by definition inaccessible to Chinese culture and pitiably incapable of acquiring it—as the Emperor told a British envoy in 1793.

The territorial claims of the Chinese Empire stopped at the water's edge. As early as the Song Dynasty (960–1279), China led the world in nautical technology; its fleets could have carried the empire into an era of conquest and exploration.[5] Yet China acquired no overseas colonies and showed relatively little interest in the countries beyond its coast. It developed no rationale for venturing abroad to convert the barbarians to Confucian principles or Buddhist virtues. When the conquering Mongols commandeered the Song fleet and its experienced captains, they mounted two attempted invasions of Japan. Both were turned back by inclement weather—the *kamikaze* (or "Divine Wind") of Japanese lore.[6] Yet when the Mongol Dynasty collapsed, the expeditions, though technically feasible, were never again attempted. No Chinese leader ever articulated a rationale for why China would want to control the Japanese archipelago.

But in the early years of the Ming Dynasty, between 1405 and 1433, China launched one of history's most remarkable and mysterious naval enterprises: Admiral Zheng He set out in fleets of technologically unparalleled "treasure ships" to destinations as far as Java, India, the Horn of Africa, and the Strait of Hormuz. At the time of Zheng's voyages, the European age of exploration had not yet begun. China's fleet possessed what would have seemed an unbridgeable technological advantage: in the size, sophistication, and number of its vessels, it dwarfed the Spanish Armada (which was still 150 years away).

Historians still debate the actual purpose of these missions. Zheng He was a singular figure in the age of exploration: a Chinese Muslim eunuch conscripted into imperial service as a child, he fits no obvious historical precedent. At each stop on his journeys, he formally proclaimed the magnificence of China's new Emperor, bestowed lavish gifts on the rulers he encountered, and invited them to travel in person or send envoys to China. There, they were to acknowledge their place in the Sinocentric world order by performing the ritual "kowtow" to acknowledge the Emperor's superiority. Yet beyond declaring China's greatness and issuing invitations to portentous ritual, Zheng He displayed no territorial ambition. He brought back only gifts, or "tribute"; he claimed no colonies or resources for China beyond the metaphysical bounty of extending the limits of All Under Heaven. At most he can be said to have created favorable conditions for Chinese merchants, through a kind of early exercise of Chinese "soft power."[7]

Zheng He's expeditions stopped abruptly in 1433, coincident with the recurrence of threats along China's northern land frontier. The next Emperor ordered the fleet dismantled and the records of Zheng He's voyages destroyed. The expeditions were never repeated. Though Chinese traders continued to ply the routes Zheng He sailed, China's naval abilities faded—so much so that the Ming rulers' response to the subsequent menace of piracy off China's southeast coast was to attempt a forced migration of the coastal population ten miles inland. China's naval history was thus a hinge that failed to swing: technically capable of dominance, China retired voluntarily from the field of naval exploration just as Western interest was beginning to take hold.

China's splendid isolation nurtured a particular Chinese self-perception. Chinese elites grew accustomed to the notion that China was unique—not just "a great civilization" among others, but civilization itself. A British translator wrote in 1850:

> An intelligent European, accustomed to reflect on the state of a number of countries enjoying a variety of different advantages, and laboring each under peculiar disadvantages, could, by a few well directed questions, and from very little data, form a tolerably correct notion of the state of a people hitherto unknown to him; but it would be a great error to suppose that this is the case with the Chinese. Their exclusion of foreigners and confinement to their own country has, by depriving them of all opportunities of making comparisons, sadly circumscribed their ideas; they are thus totally unable to free themselves from the dominion of association, and judge everything by rules of purely Chinese convention.[8]

China knew, of course, of different societies around its periphery in Korea, Vietnam, Thailand, Burma; but in the Chinese perception, China was considered the center of the world, the "Middle Kingdom," and other societies were assessed as gradations from it. As the Chinese saw it, a host of lesser states that imbibed Chinese culture and paid tribute to China's greatness constituted the natural order of the universe. The borders between China and the surrounding peoples were not so much political and territorial demarcations as cultural differentiations. The outward radiance of Chinese culture throughout East

Asia led the American political scientist Lucian Pye to comment famously that, in the modern age, China remains a "civilization pretending to be a nation-state."[9]

The pretensions underlying this traditional Chinese world order endured well into the modern era. As late as 1863, China's Emperor (himself a member of a "foreign" Manchu Dynasty that had conquered China two centuries earlier) dispatched a letter informing Abraham Lincoln of China's commitment to good relations with the United States. The Emperor based his communication on the grandiloquent assurance that, "[h]aving, with reverence, received the commission from Heaven to rule the universe, we regard both the middle empire [China] and the outside countries as constituting one family, without any distinction."[10] When the letter was dispatched, China had already lost two wars with the Western powers, which were busy staking out spheres of interest in Chinese territory. The Emperor seems to have treated these catastrophes as similar to other barbarian invasions that were overcome, in the end, by China's endurance and superior culture.

For most of history, there was, in fact, nothing particularly fanciful about Chinese claims. With each generation, the Han Chinese had expanded from their original base in the Yellow River valley, gradually drawing neighboring societies into various stages of approximation of Chinese patterns. Chinese scientific and technological achievements equaled, and frequently outstripped, those of their Western European, Indian, and Arab counterparts.[11]

Not only was the scale of China traditionally far beyond that of the European states in population and in territory; until the Industrial Revolution, China was far richer. United by a vast system of canals connecting the great rivers and population centers, China was for centuries the world's most productive economy and most populous trading area.[12] But since it was largely self-sufficient, other regions had only peripheral comprehension of its vastness and its wealth. In fact, China produced a greater share of total world GDP than any Western society in eighteen of the last twenty centuries. As late as 1820, it produced over 30 percent of world GDP—an amount exceeding the GDP of Western Europe, Eastern Europe, and the United States combined.[13]

Western observers encountering China in the early modern era were stunned by its vitality and material prosperity. Writing in 1736, the French Jesuit Jean-Baptiste Du Halde summed up the awestruck reactions of Western visitors to China:

> The riches peculiar to each province, and the facility of conveying merchandise, by means of rivers and canals, have rendered the domestic trade of the empire always very flourishing. . . . The inland trade of China is so great that the commerce of all Europe is not to be compared therewith; the provinces being like so many kingdoms, which communicate to each other their respective productions.[14]

Thirty years later, the French political economist François Quesnay went even further:

> [N]o one can deny that this state is the most beautiful in the world, the most densely populated, and the most flourishing kingdom known. Such an empire as that of China is equal to what all Europe would be if the latter were united under a single sovereign.[15]

China traded with foreigners and occasionally adopted ideas and inventions from abroad. But more often the Chinese believed that the most valuable possessions and intellectual achievements were to be found within China. Trade with China was so prized that it was with only partial exaggeration that Chinese elites described it not as ordinary economic exchange but as "tribute" to China's superiority.

Confucianism

Almost all empires were created by force, but none can be sustained by it. Universal rule, to last, needs to translate force into obligation. Otherwise, the energies of the rulers will be exhausted in maintaining their dominance at the expense of their ability to shape the future, which is the ultimate task of statesmanship. Empires persist if repression gives way to consensus.

So it was with China. The methods by which it was unified, and periodically overturned and reunified again, were occasionally brutal. Chinese history witnessed its share of sanguinary rebellions and dynastic tyrants. Yet China owed its millennial survival far less to the punishments meted out by its Emperors than to the community of values fostered among its population and its government of scholar-officials.

Not the least exceptional aspect of Chinese culture is that these values were essentially secular in nature. At the time when Buddhism appeared in Indian culture stressing contemplation and inner peace, and monotheism was proclaimed by the Jewish—and, later, Christian and Islamic—prophets with an evocation of a life after death, China produced no religious themes in the Western sense at all. The Chinese never generated a myth of cosmic creation. Their universe was created by the Chinese themselves, whose values, even when declared of universal applicability, were conceived of as Chinese in origin.

The predominant values of Chinese society were derived from the prescriptions of an ancient philosopher known to posterity as Kong Fu-zi (or "Confucius" in the Latinized version). Confucius (551–479 B.C.) lived at the end of the so-called Spring and Autumn period (770–476 B.C.), a time of political upheaval that led to the brutal struggles of the Warring States period (475–221 B.C.). The ruling House of Zhou was in decline, unable to exert its authority over rebellious princes competing for political power. Greed and violence went unchecked. All Under Heaven was again in disarray.

Like Machiavelli, Confucius was an itinerant in his country, hoping to be retained as an advisor to one of the princes then contending for survival. But unlike Machiavelli, Confucius was concerned more with the cultivation of social harmony than with the machinations of power. His themes were the principles of compassionate rule, the performance of correct rituals, and the inculcation of filial piety. Perhaps because he offered his prospective employers no short-term route to wealth or power, Confucius died without achieving his goal: he never found a prince to implement his maxims, and China continued its slide toward political collapse and war.[16]

But Confucius's teachings, recorded by his disciples, survived. When the bloodletting ended and China again stood unified, the Han Dynasty (206 B.C.–A.D. 220) adopted Confucian thought as an official state philosophy. Compiled into a central collection of Confucius's sayings (the *Analects*) and subsequent books of learned commentary, the Confucian canon would evolve into something akin to China's Bible and its Constitution combined. Expertise in these texts became the central qualification for service in China's imperial bureaucracy—a priesthood of literary scholar-officials selected by nationwide competitive examinations and charged with maintaining harmony in the Emperor's vast realms.

Confucius's answer to the chaos of his era was the "Way" of the just and harmonious society, which, he taught, had once been realized before—in a distant Chinese golden age. Mankind's central spiritual task was to re-create this proper order already on the verge of being lost. Spiritual fulfillment was a task not so much of revelation or liberation but patient recovery of forgotten principles of self-restraint. The goal was rectification, not progress.[17] Learning was the key to advancement in a Confucian society. Thus Confucius taught that

> [l]ove of kindness, without a love to learn, finds itself obscured by foolishness. Love of knowledge, without a love to learn,

> finds itself obscured by loose speculation. Love of honesty, without a love to learn, finds itself obscured by harmful candour. Love of straightforwardness, without a love to learn, finds itself obscured by misdirected judgment. Love of daring, without a love to learn, finds itself obscured by insubordination. And love for strength of character, without a love to learn, finds itself obscured by intractability.[18]

Confucius preached a hierarchical social creed: the fundamental duty was to "Know thy place." To its adherents the Confucian order offered the inspiration of service in pursuit of a greater harmony. Unlike the prophets of monotheistic religions, Confucius preached no teleology of history pointing mankind to personal redemption. His philosophy sought the redemption of the state through righteous individual behavior. Oriented toward this world, his thinking affirmed a code of social conduct, not a roadmap to the afterlife.

At the pinnacle of the Chinese order stood the Emperor, a figure with no parallels in the Western experience. He combined the spiritual as well as the secular claims of the social order. The Chinese Emperor was both a political ruler and a metaphysical concept. In his political role, the Emperor was conceived as mankind's supreme sovereign—the Emperor of Humanity, standing atop a world political hierarchy that mirrored China's hierarchical Confucian social structure. Chinese protocol insisted on recognizing his overlordship via the kowtow—the act of complete prostration, with the forehead touching the ground three times on each prostration.

The Emperor's second, metaphysical, role was his status as the "Son of Heaven," the symbolic intermediary between Heaven, Earth, and humanity. This role also implied moral obligation on the Emperor's part. Through humane conduct, performance of correct rituals, and occasional stern punishments, the Emperor was perceived as the linchpin of the "Great Harmony" of all things great and small. If the

Emperor strayed from the path of virtue, All Under Heaven would fall into chaos. Even natural catastrophes might signify that disharmony had beset the universe. The existing dynasty would be seen to have lost the "Mandate of Heaven" by which it possessed the right to govern: rebellions would break out, and a new dynasty would restore the Great Harmony of the universe.[19]

Concepts of International Relations: Impartiality or Equality?

Just as there are no great cathedrals in China, there are no Blenheim Palaces. Aristocratic political grandees like the Duke of Marlborough, who built Blenheim, did not come into being. Europe entered the modern age a welter of political diversity—independent princes and dukes and counts, cities that governed themselves, the Roman Catholic Church, which claimed an authority outside of state purview, and Protestant groups, which aspired to building their own self-governing civil societies. By contrast, when it entered the modern period, China had for well over one thousand years a fully formed imperial bureaucracy recruited by competitive examination, permeating and regulating all aspects of the economy and society.

The Chinese approach to world order was thus vastly different from the system that took hold in the West. The modern Western conception of international relations emerged in the sixteenth and seventeenth centuries, when the medieval structure of Europe dissolved into a group of states of approximately equal strength, and the Catholic Church split into various denominations. Balance-of-power diplomacy was less a choice than an inevitability. No state was strong enough to impose its will; no religion retained sufficient authority to sustain universality. The concept of sovereignty and the legal equality of states became the basis of international law and diplomacy.

China, by contrast, was never engaged in sustained contact with another country on the basis of equality for the simple reason that it never encountered societies of comparable culture or magnitude. That the Chinese Empire should tower over its geographical sphere was taken virtually as a law of nature, an expression of the Mandate of Heaven. For Chinese Emperors, the mandate did not necessarily imply an adversarial relationship with neighboring peoples; preferably it did not. Like the United States, China thought of itself as playing a special role. But it never espoused the American notion of universalism to spread its values around the world. It confined itself to controlling the barbarians immediately at its doorstep. It strove for tributary states like Korea to recognize China's special status, and in return, it conferred benefits such as trading rights. As for the remote barbarians such as Europeans, about whom they knew little, the Chinese maintained a friendly, if condescending, aloofness. They had little interest in converting them to Chinese ways. The founding Emperor of the Ming Dynasty expressed this view in 1372: "Countries of the western ocean are rightly called distant regions. They come [to us] across the seas. And it is difficult for them to calculate the year and month [of arrival]. Regardless of their numbers, we treat them [on the principle of] 'those who come modestly are sent off generously.'"[20]

The Chinese Emperors felt it was impractical to contemplate influencing countries that nature had given the misfortune of locating at such a great distance from China. In the Chinese version of exceptionalism, China did not export its ideas but let others come to seek them. Neighboring peoples, the Chinese believed, benefited from contact with China and civilization so long as they acknowledged the suzerainty of the Chinese government. Those who did not were barbarian. Subservience to the Emperor and observance of imperial rituals was the core of culture.[21] When the empire was strong, this cultural sphere expanded: All Under Heaven was a multinational entity comprising the ethnic Han Chinese majority and numerous non-Han Chinese ethnic groups.

In official Chinese records, foreign envoys did not come to the imperial court to engage in negotiations or affairs of state; they "came to be transformed" by the Emperor's civilizing influence. The Emperor did not hold "summit meetings" with other heads of state; instead, audiences with him represented the "tender cherishing of men from afar," who brought tribute to recognize his overlordship. When the Chinese court deigned to send envoys abroad, they were not diplomats, but "Heavenly Envoys" from the Celestial Court.

The organization of the Chinese government reflected the hierarchical approach to world order. China handled ties with tribute-paying states such as Korea, Thailand, and Vietnam through the Ministry of Rituals, implying that diplomacy with these peoples was but one aspect of the larger metaphysical task of administering the Great Harmony. With less Sinicized mounted tribes to the north and west, China came to rely on a "Court of Dependencies," analogous to a colonial office, whose mission was to invest vassal princes with titles and maintain peace on the frontier.[22]

Only under the pressure of Western incursions in the nineteenth century did China establish something analogous to a foreign ministry to manage diplomacy as an independent function of government, in 1861 after the defeat in two wars with the Western powers. It was considered a temporary necessity, to be abolished once the immediate crisis subsided. The new ministry was deliberately located in an old and undistinguished building previously used by the Department of Iron Coins, to convey, in the words of the leading Qing Dynasty statesman, Prince Gong, "the hidden meaning that it cannot have a standing equal to that of other traditional government offices, thus preserving the distinction between China and foreign countries."[23]

European-style ideas of interstate politics and diplomacy were not unknown in the Chinese experience; rather, they existed as a kind of countertradition taking place within China in times of disunity. But as if by some unwritten law, these periods of division ended with the reunification of All Under Heaven, and the reassertion of Chinese centrality by a new dynasty.

In its imperial role, China offered surrounding foreign peoples impartiality, not equality: it would treat them humanely and compassionately in proportion to their attainment of Chinese culture and their observance of rituals connoting submission to China.

What was most remarkable about the Chinese approach to international affairs was less its monumental formal pretensions than its underlying strategic acumen and longevity. For during most of Chinese history, the numerous "lesser" peoples along China's long and shifting frontiers were often better armed and more mobile than the Chinese. To China's north and west were seminomadic peoples—the Manchus, Mongols, Uighurs, Tibetans, and eventually the expansionist Russian Empire—whose mounted cavalry could launch raids across its extended frontiers on China's agricultural heartland with relative impunity. Retaliatory expeditions faced inhospitable terrain and extended supply lines. To China's south and east were peoples who, though nominally subordinate in the Chinese cosmology, possessed significant martial traditions and national identities. The most tenacious of them, the Vietnamese, had fiercely resisted Chinese claims of superiority and could claim to have bested China in battle.

China was in no position to conquer all of its neighbors. Its population consisted mainly of farmers bound to their ancestral plots. Its mandarin elite earned their positions not through displays of martial valor but by way of mastery of the Confucian classics and refined arts such as calligraphy and poetry. Individually, neighboring peoples could pose formidable threats; with any degree of unity, they would be overwhelming. The historian Owen Lattimore wrote, "Barbarian invasion therefore hung over China as a permanent threat. . . . Any barbarian nation that could guard its own rear and flanks against the other barbarians could set out confidently to invade China."[24] China's vaunted centrality and material wealth would turn on itself and into an invitation for invasion from all sides.

The Great Wall, so prominent in Western iconography of China, was a reflection of this basic vulnerability, though rarely a successful solution to it. Instead, Chinese statesmen relied on a rich array of diplomatic and economic instruments to draw potentially hostile foreigners into relationships the Chinese could manage. The highest aspiration was less to conquer (though China occasionally mounted major military campaigns) than to deter invasion and prevent the formation of barbarian coalitions.

Through trade incentives and skillful use of political theater, China coaxed neighboring peoples into observing the norms of Chinese centrality while projecting an image of awesome majesty to deter potential invaders from testing China's strength. Its goal was not to conquer and subjugate the barbarians but to "rule [them] with a loose rein" (*ji mi*). For those who would not obey, China would exploit divisions among them, famously "using barbarians to check barbarians" and, when necessary, "using barbarians to attack barbarians."[25] For as a Ming Dynasty official wrote of the potentially threatening tribes on China's northeastern frontier:

> [I]f the tribes are divided among themselves they [will remain] weak and [it will be] easy to hold them in subjection; if the tribes are separated they shun each other and readily obey. We favor one or other [of their chieftains] and permit them to fight each other. This is a principle of political action which asserts: "Wars between the 'barbarians' are auspicious for China."[26]

The goal of this system was essentially defensive: to prevent the formation of coalitions on China's borders. The principles of barbarian management became so ingrained in Chinese official thought that when the European "barbarians" arrived on China's shores in force in the nineteenth century, Chinese officials described their challenge with the same phrases used by their dynastic predecessors: they would "use barbarians against barbarians" until they could be soothed and subdued. And they applied a traditional strategy to answer the initial British attack. They invited other European countries in for the purpose of first stimulating and then manipulating their rivalry.

In pursuit of these aims, the Chinese court was remarkably pragmatic about the means it employed. The Chinese bribed the barbarians, or used Han demographic superiority to dilute them; when defeated, they submitted to them, as in the beginning of the Yuan and Qing Dynasties, as a prelude to Sinicizing them. The Chinese court regularly practiced what in other contexts would be considered appeasement, albeit through an elaborate filter of protocol that allowed the Chinese elites to claim it was an assertion of benevolent superiority. Thus a Han Dynasty minister described the "five baits" with which he proposed to manage the mounted Xiongnu tribes to China's northwestern frontier:

> To give them . . . elaborate clothes and carriages in order to corrupt their eyes; to give them fine food in order to corrupt their mouth; to give them music and women in order to corrupt their ears; to provide them with lofty buildings, granaries and slaves in order to corrupt their stomach . . . and, as for those who come to surrender, the emperor [should] show them favor by honoring them with an imperial reception party in which the emperor should personally serve them wine and food so as to corrupt their mind. These are what may be called the five baits.[27]

In periods of strength, the diplomacy of the Middle Kingdom was an ideological rationalization for imperial power. During periods of decline, it served to mask weakness and helped China manipulate contending forces.

In comparison to more recent regional contenders for power, China was a satisfied empire with limited territorial ambition. As a scholar during the Han Dynasty (A.D. 25–220) put it, "the emperor does not govern the barbarians. Those who come to him will not be rejected, and those who leave will not be pursued."[28] The objective was a compliant, divided periphery, rather than one directly under Chinese control.

The most remarkable expression of China's fundamental pragmatism was its reaction to conquerors. When foreign dynasts prevailed in battle, the Chinese bureaucratic elite would offer their services and appeal to their conquerors on the premise that so vast and unique a land as they had just overrun could be ruled only by use of Chinese methods, Chinese language, and the existing Chinese bureaucracy. With each generation, the conquerors would find themselves increasingly assimilated into the order they had sought to dominate. Eventually their own home territories—the launching points for their invasions—would come to be regarded as part of China itself. They would find themselves pursuing traditional Chinese national interests, with the project of conquest effectively turned on its head.[29]

Chinese *Realpolitik* and Sun Tzu's *Art of War*

The Chinese have been shrewd practitioners of *Realpolitik* and students of a strategic doctrine distinctly different from the strategy and diplomacy that found favor in the West. A turbulent history has taught Chinese leaders that not every problem has a solution and that too great an emphasis on total mastery over specific events could upset the harmony of the universe. There were too many potential enemies for the empire ever to live in total security. If China's fate was relative security, it also implied relative insecurity—the need to learn the grammar of over a dozen neighboring states with significantly different histories and aspirations. Rarely did Chinese statesmen risk the outcome of a conflict on a single all-or-nothing clash; elaborate multiyear maneuvers were closer to their style. Where the Western tradition prized the decisive clash of forces emphasizing feats of heroism, the Chinese ideal stressed subtlety, indirection, and the patient accumulation of relative advantage.

This contrast is reflected in the respective intellectual games favored by each civilization. China's most enduring game is *wei qi* (pronounced roughly "way chee," and often known in the West by a variation of its Japanese name, *go*). *Wei qi* translates as "a game of surrounding pieces"; it implies a concept of strategic encirclement. The board, a grid of nineteen-by-nineteen lines, begins empty. Each player has 180 pieces, or stones, at his disposal, each of equal value with the others. The players take turns placing stones at any point on the board, building up positions of strength while working to encircle and capture the opponent's stones. Multiple contests take place simultaneously in different regions of the board. The balance of forces shifts incrementally with each move, as the players implement strategic plans and react to each other's initiatives. At the end of a well-played game, the board is filled by partially interlocking areas of strength. The margin of advantage is often slim, and to the untrained eye, the identity of the winner is not always immediately obvious.[30]

Chess, on the other hand, is about total victory. The purpose of the game is checkmate, to put the opposing king into a position where he cannot move without being destroyed. The vast majority of games end in total victory achieved by attrition or, more rarely, a dramatic, skillful maneuver. The only other possible outcome is a draw, meaning the abandonment of the hope for victory by both parties.

If chess is about the decisive battle, *wei qi* is about the protracted campaign. The chess player aims for total victory. The *wei qi* player seeks relative advantage. In chess, the player always has the capability of the adversary in front of him; all the pieces are always fully deployed.

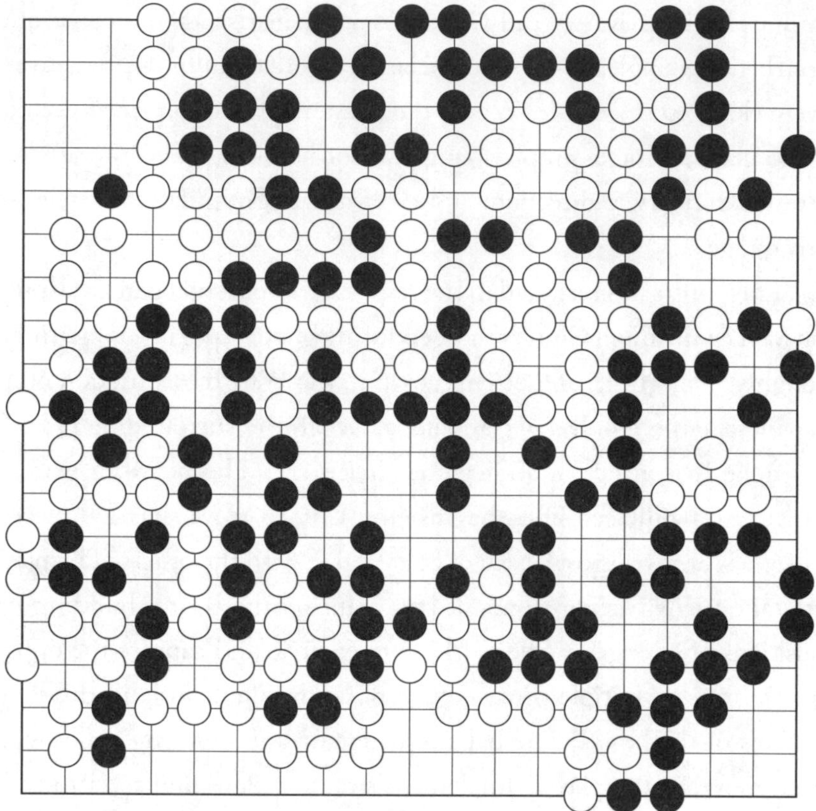

THE OUTCOME OF A *WEI QI* GAME BETWEEN TWO EXPERT PLAYERS.
BLACK HAS WON BY A SLIGHT MARGIN.

Source: David Lai, "Learning from the Stones: A Go *Approach to Mastering China's Strategic Concept,* Shi*" (Carlisle, PA: U.S. Army War College Strategic Studies Institute, 2004).*

The *wei qi* player needs to assess not only the pieces on the board but the reinforcements the adversary is in a position to deploy. Chess teaches the Clausewitzian concepts of "center of gravity" and the "decisive point"—the game usually beginning as a struggle for the center of the board. *Wei qi* teaches the art of strategic encirclement. Where the skillful chess player aims to eliminate his opponent's pieces in a series of head-on clashes, a talented *wei qi* player moves into "empty" spaces on the board, gradually mitigating the strategic potential of his opponent's pieces. Chess produces single-mindedness; *wei qi* generates strategic flexibility.

A similar contrast exists in the case of China's distinctive military theory. Its foundations were laid during a period of upheaval, when ruthless struggles between rival kingdoms decimated China's population. Reacting to this slaughter (and seeking to emerge victorious from it), Chinese thinkers developed strategic thought that placed a premium on victory through psychological advantage and preached the avoidance of direct conflict.

The seminal figure in this tradition is known to history as Sun Tzu (or "Master Sun"), author of the famed treatise *The Art of War*. Intriguingly, no one is sure exactly who he was. Since ancient times, scholars have debated the identity of *The Art of War*'s author and the date of its composition. The book presents itself as a collection of sayings by one Sun Wu, a general and wandering military advisor from the Spring and Autumn period of Chinese history (770–476 B.C.), as recorded by his disciples. Some Chinese and later Western scholars have questioned whether such a Master Sun existed or, if he did, whether he was in fact responsible for *The Art of War*'s contents.[31]

Well over two thousand years after its composition, this volume of epigrammatic observations on strategy, diplomacy, and war—written in classical Chinese, halfway between poetry and prose—remains a central text of military thought. Its maxims found vivid expression in the twentieth-century Chinese civil war at the hands of Sun Tzu's student Mao Zedong, and in the Vietnam wars, as Ho Chi Minh and Vo Nguyen Giap employed Sun Tzu's principles of indirect attack and psychological combat against France and then the United States. (Sun Tzu has also achieved a second career of sorts in the West, with popular editions of *The Art of War* recasting him as a modern business management guru.) Even today Sun Tzu's text reads with a degree of immediacy and insight that places him among the ranks of the world's foremost strategic thinkers. One could argue that the disregard of his precepts was importantly responsible for America's frustration in its Asian wars.

What distinguishes Sun Tzu from Western writers on strategy is the emphasis on the psychological and political elements over the purely military. The great European military theorists Carl von Clausewitz and Antoine-Henri Jomini treat strategy as an activity in its own right, separate from politics. Even Clausewitz's famous dictum that war is the continuation of politics by other means implies that with war the statesman enters a new and distinct phase.

Sun Tzu merges the two fields. Where Western strategists reflect on the means to assemble superior power at the decisive point, Sun Tzu addresses the means of building a dominant political and psychological position, such that the outcome of a conflict becomes a foregone conclusion. Western strategists test their maxims by victories in battles; Sun Tzu tests by victories where battles have become unnecessary.

Sun Tzu's text on war does not have the quality of exaltation of some European literature on the subject, nor does it appeal to personal heroism. Its somber quality is reflected in the portentous opening of *The Art of War:*

> *War is*
> *A grave affair of the state;*
> *It is a place*
> *Of life and death,*
> *A road*
> *To survival and extinction,*
> *A matter*
> *To be pondered carefully.*[32]

And because the consequences of war are so grave, prudence is the value most to be cherished:

A ruler
Must never
Mobilize his men
Out of anger;
A general must never
Engage [in] battle
Out of spite . . .

Anger
Can turn to
Pleasure;
Spite
Can turn to
Joy.
But a nation destroyed
Cannot be
Put back together again;
A dead man
Cannot be
Brought back to life.

So the enlightened ruler
Is prudent;
The effective general
Is cautious.
This is the Way
To keep a nation
At peace
And an army
Intact.[33]

What should a statesman be prudent about? For Sun Tzu, victory is not simply the triumph of armed forces. Instead, it is the achievement of the ultimate political objectives that the military clash was intended to secure. Far better than challenging the enemy on the field of battle is undermining an enemy's morale or maneuvering him into an unfavorable position from which escape is impossible. Because war is a desperate and complex enterprise, self-knowledge is crucial. Strategy resolves itself into a psychological contest:

Ultimate excellence lies
Not in winning
Every battle
But in defeating the enemy
Without ever fighting.
The highest form of warfare
Is to attack [the enemy's]
Strategy itself;
The next,
To attack [his]
Alliances.
The next,
To attack
Armies;
The lowest form of war is
To attack
Cities.
Siege warfare
Is a last resort . . .

The Skillful Strategist
Defeats the enemy
Without doing battle,

Captures the city
Without laying siege,
Overthrows the enemy state
Without protracted war.[34]

Ideally, the commander would achieve a position of such dominance that he could avoid battle entirely. Or else he would use arms to deliver a coup de grâce after extensive analysis and logistical, diplomatic, and psychological preparation. Thus Sun Tzu's counsel that

The victorious army
Is victorious first
And seeks battle later;
The defeated army
Does battle first
And seeks victory later.[35]

Because attacks on an opponent's strategy and his alliances involve psychology and perception, Sun Tzu places considerable emphasis on the use of subterfuge and misinformation. "When able," he counseled,

Feign inability;
When deploying troops,
Appear not to be.
When near,
Appear far;
When far,
Appear near.[36]

To the commander following Sun Tzu's precepts, a victory achieved indirectly through deception or manipulation is more humane (and surely more economical) than a triumph by superior force. *The Art of*

War advises the commander to induce his opponent into accomplishing the commander's own aims or force him into a position so impossible that he opts to surrender his army or state unharmed.

Perhaps Sun Tzu's most important insight was that in a military or strategic contest, everything is relevant and connected: weather, terrain, diplomacy, the reports of spies and double agents, supplies and logistics, the balance of forces, historic perceptions, the intangibles of surprise and morale. Each factor influences the others, giving rise to subtle shifts in momentum and relative advantage. There are no isolated events.

Hence the task of a strategist is less to analyze a particular situation than to determine its relationship to the context in which it occurs. No particular constellation is ever static; any pattern is temporary and in essence evolving. The strategist must capture the direction of that evolution and make it serve his ends. Sun Tzu uses the word "*shi*" for that quality, a concept with no direct Western counterpart.[37] In the military context, *shi* connotes the strategic trend and "potential energy" of a developing situation, "the power inherent in the particular arrangement of elements and . . . its developmental tendency."[38] In *The Art of War,* the word connotes the ever-changing configuration of forces as well as their general trend.

To Sun Tzu, the strategist mastering *shi* is akin to water flowing downhill, automatically finding the swiftest and easiest course. A successful commander waits before charging headlong into battle. He shies away from an enemy's strength; he spends his time observing and cultivating changes in the strategic landscape. He studies the enemy's preparations and his morale, husbands resources and defines them carefully, and plays on his opponent's psychological weaknesses—until at last he perceives the opportune moment to strike the enemy at his weakest point. He then deploys his resources swiftly and suddenly, rushing "downhill" along the path of least resistance, in an assertion of superiority that careful timing and preparation have rendered a fait accompli.[39] *The Art of War* articulates a doctrine less of territorial conquest than of psychological dominance; it was the way the North Vietnamese fought America (though Hanoi usually translated its psychological gains into actual territorial conquests as well).

In general, Chinese statesmanship exhibits a tendency to view the entire strategic landscape as part of a single whole: good and evil, near and far, strength and weakness, past and future all interrelated. In contrast to the Western approach of treating history as a process of modernity achieving a series of absolute victories over evil and backwardness, the traditional Chinese view of history emphasized a cyclical process of decay and rectification, in which nature and the world can be understood but not completely mastered. The best that can be accomplished is to grow into harmony with it. Strategy and statecraft become means of "combative coexistence" with opponents. The goal is to maneuver them into weakness while building up one's own *shi*, or strategic position.[40]

This "maneuvering" approach is, of course, the ideal and not always the reality. Throughout their history, the Chinese have had their share of "unsubtle" and brutal conflicts, both at home and occasionally abroad. Once these conflicts erupted, such as during the unification of China under the Qin Dynasty, the clashes of the Three Kingdoms period, the quelling of the Taiping Rebellion, and the twentieth-century civil war, China was subjected to wholesale loss of life on a level comparable to the European world wars. The bloodiest conflicts occurred as a result of the breakdown of the internal Chinese system—in other words, as an aspect of internal adjustments of a state for which domestic stability and protection against looming foreign invasion are equal concerns.

For China's classical sages, the world could never be conquered; wise rulers could hope only to harmonize with its trends. There was no New World to populate, no redemption awaiting mankind on distant shores. The promised land was China, and the Chinese were already there. The blessings of the Middle Kingdom's culture might theoretically be extended, by China's superior example, to the foreigners on the empire's periphery. But there was no glory to be found in venturing across the seas to convert "heathens" to Chinese ways; the customs of the Celestial Dynasty were plainly beyond the attainment of the far barbarians.

This may be the deeper meaning of China's abandonment of its naval tradition. Lecturing in the 1820s on his philosophy of history, the German philosopher Hegel described the Chinese tendency to see the huge Pacific Ocean to their east as a barren waste. He noted that China, by and large, did not venture to the seas and instead depended on its great landmass. The land imposed "an infinite multitude of dependencies," whereas the sea propelled people "beyond these limited circles of thought and action": "This stretching out of the sea beyond the limitations of the land, is wanting to the splendid political edifices of Asiatic States, although they themselves border on the sea—as for example, China. For them the sea is only the limit, the ceasing of the land; they have no positive relations to it." The West had set sail to spread its trade and values throughout the world. In this respect, Hegel argued, landbound China—which in fact had once been the world's greatest naval power—was "severed from the general historical development."[41]

With these distinctive traditions and millennial habits of superiority, China entered the modern age a singular kind of empire: a state claiming universal relevance for its culture and institutions but making few efforts to proselytize; the wealthiest country in the world but one that was indifferent to foreign trade and technological innovation; a culture of cosmopolitanism overseen by a political elite oblivious to the onset of the Western age of exploration; and a political unit of unparalleled geographic extent that was unaware of the technological and historical currents that would soon threaten its existence.

CHAPTER 2

The Kowtow Question and the Opium War

AT THE CLOSE of the eighteenth century, China stood at the height of its imperial greatness. The Qing Dynasty, established in 1644 by Manchu tribes riding into China from the northeast, had turned China into a major military power. Fusing Manchu and Mongol military prowess with the cultural and governmental prowess of the Han Chinese, it embarked on a program of territorial expansion to the north and west, establishing a Chinese sphere of influence deep into Mongolia, Tibet, and modern-day Xinjiang. China stood predominant in Asia; it was at least the rival of any empire on earth.[1]

Yet the high point of the Qing Dynasty also turned into the turning point of its destiny. For China's wealth and expanse attracted the attention of Western empires and trading companies operating far outside the bounds and conceptual apparatus of the traditional Chinese world order. For the first time in its history, China faced "barbarians" who no longer sought to displace the Chinese dynasty and claim the Mandate of Heaven for themselves; instead, they proposed to replace the Sinocentric system with an entirely new vision of world order—with free trade rather than tribute, resident embassies in the Chinese capital, and a system of diplomatic exchange that did not refer to non-Chinese heads of state as "honorable barbarians" pledging fealty to their Emperor in Beijing.

Unbeknownst to Chinese elites, these foreign societies had developed new industrial and scientific methods that, for the first time in centuries—or perhaps ever—surpassed China's own. Steam power, railways, and new methods of manufacturing and capital formation enabled enormous advances in productivity in the West. Imbued with a conquering impulse that propelled them into China's traditional sphere of dominance, the Western powers considered Chinese claims of universal overlordship over Europe and Asia risible. They were determined to impose on China their own standards of international conduct, by force if necessary. The resulting confrontation challenged the basic Chinese cosmology and left wounds still festering over a century later in an age of restored Chinese eminence.

Beginning in the seventeenth century, Chinese authorities had noted the increasing numbers of European traders on the southeast China coast. They saw little to differentiate the Europeans from other foreigners operating at the fringes of the empire, save perhaps their particularly glaring lack of Chinese cultural attainments. In the official Chinese view, these "West Sea barbarians" were classified as "tribute envoys" or "barbarian merchants." On rare occasions, some were permitted to travel to Beijing, where—if admitted into the presence of the Emperor—they were expected to perform the ritual kowtow: the act of prostration, with the forehead touching the ground three times.

For foreign representatives the points of entry into China and routes to the capital were strictly circumscribed. Access to the Chinese market was limited to a tightly regulated seasonal trade at Guangzhou (then known as Canton). Each winter foreign merchants were required to sail home. They were not permitted to venture further into China. Regulations deliberately held them at bay. It was unlawful to teach the Chinese language to these barbarians or to sell them books on Chinese history or culture. Their communications were to take place through specially licensed local merchants.[2]

The notion of free trade, resident embassies, and sovereign equality—by this point, the minimum rights enjoyed by Europeans in almost every other corner of the world—were unheard of in China. One tacit exception had been made for Russia. Its rapid eastward expansion (the Czar's domains now abutted Qing territories in Xinjiang, Mongolia, and Manchuria) placed it in a unique position to threaten China. The Qing Dynasty, in 1715, permitted Moscow to establish a Russian Orthodox mission in Beijing; it eventually took on the role of a de facto embassy, the only foreign mission of its kind in China for over a century.

The contacts extended to Western European traders, limited as they were, were seen by the Qing as a considerable indulgence. The Son of Heaven had, in the Chinese view, shown his benevolence by allowing them to partake in Chinese trade—particularly in tea, silk, lacquerware, and rhubarb, for which the West Sea barbarians had developed a voracious appetite. Europe was too far from the Middle Kingdom ever to become Sinicized along Korean or Vietnamese lines.

Initially, the Europeans accepted the role of supplicants in the Chinese tributary order, in which they were labeled as "barbarians" and their trade as "tribute." But as the Western powers grew in wealth and conviction, this state of affairs grew untenable.

The Macartney Mission

The assumptions of the Chinese world order were particularly offensive to Britain (the "red-haired barbarians" in some Chinese records). As the premier Western commercial and naval power, Britain bridled at its assigned role in the cosmology of the Middle Kingdom, whose army, the British noted, still primarily used bows and arrows and whose navy was practically nonexistent. British traders resented the increasing amount of "squeeze" extracted by the designated Chinese merchants at Guangzhou, through which Chinese regulations required that all Western trade be conducted. They sought access to the rest of the Chinese market beyond the southeast coast.

The first major British attempt to remedy the situation was the 1793–94 mission of Lord George Macartney to China. It was the most notable, best-conceived, and least "militaristic" European effort to alter the prevailing format of Sino-Western relations and to achieve free trade and diplomatic representation on equal terms. It failed completely.

The Macartney mission is instructive to examine in some detail. The diary of the envoy illustrates how the Chinese perception of its role operated in practice—and the gulf existing between Western and Chinese perceptions of diplomacy. Macartney was a distinguished public servant with years of international experience and a keen sense of "Oriental" diplomacy. He was a man of notable cultural achievements. He had served three years as envoy-extraordinary to the court of Catherine the Great in St. Petersburg, where he negotiated a treaty of amity and commerce. Upon his return, he published a well-received volume of observations on Russian history and culture. He had subsequently served as Governor of Madras. He was as well equipped as any of his contemporaries to inaugurate a new diplomacy across civilizations.

The aims of the Macartney mission to China would have seemed modest to any educated Briton of the time—especially compared with the recently established British dominion over the neighboring giant, India. Home Secretary Henry Dundas framed the Macartney instructions as an attempt to achieve "a free communication with a people, perhaps the most singular on the Globe." Its principal aims were the establishment of reciprocal embassies in Beijing and London and commercial access to other ports along the Chinese coast. On the latter point, Dundas charged Macartney to draw attention to the "discouraging" and "arbitrary" system of regulations at Guangzhou that prevented British merchants from engaging in the "fair competition of the Market" (a concept with no direct counterpart in Confucian China). He was, Dundas stressed, to disclaim any territorial ambitions in China—an assurance bound to be considered as an insult by the recipient because it implied that Britain had the option to entertain such ambitions.[3]

The British government addressed the Chinese court on equal terms, which would have struck the British ruling group as affording a non-Western country an uncommon degree of dignity, while being treated in China as insubordinate insolence. Dundas instructed Macartney to take the "earliest opportunity" to impress upon the Chinese court that King George III saw Macartney's mission as "an embassy to the most civilized as well as most ancient and populous Nation in the World in order to observe its celebrated institutions, and to communicate and receive the benefits which must result from an unreserved and friendly intercourse between that Country and his own." Dundas instructed Macartney to comply with "all ceremonials of that Court, which may not commit the honour of your Sovereign, or lessen your own dignity, so as to endanger the success of your negotiation." He should not, Dundas stressed, "let any trifling punctilio stand in the way of the important benefits which may be obtained" by success in his mission.[4]

To help further his aims, Macartney brought with him numerous examples of British scientific and industrial prowess. Macartney's entourage included a surgeon, a physician, a mechanic, a metallurgist, a watchmaker, a mathematical instrument maker, and "Five German Musicians" who were to perform nightly. (These latter performances were one of the more successful aspects of the embassy.) His gifts to the Emperor included manufactures designed at least in part to show the fabulous benefits China might obtain by trading with Britain: artillery pieces, a chariot, diamond-studded wristwatches, British porcelain (copied, Qing officials noted approvingly, from the Chinese art form), and portraits of the King and Queen painted by Joshua Reynolds.

Macartney even brought a deflated hot-air balloon and planned, without success, to have members of his mission fly it over Beijing by way of demonstration.

The Macartney mission accomplished none of its specific objectives; the gap in perceptions was simply too wide. Macartney had intended to demonstrate the benefits of industrialization, but the Emperor understood his gifts as tribute. The British envoy expected his Chinese hosts to recognize that they had been hopelessly left behind by the progress of technological civilization and to seek a special relationship with Britain to rectify their backwardness. In fact, the Chinese treated the British as an arrogant and uninformed barbarian tribe seeking special favor from the Son of Heaven. China remained wedded to its agrarian ways, with its burgeoning population making food production more urgent than ever, and its Confucian bureaucracy ignorant of the key elements of industrialization: steam power, credit and capital, private property, and public education.

The first discordant note came as Macartney and his entourage made their way to Jehol, the summer capital northeast of Beijing, traveling up the coast in Chinese yachts laden with generous gifts and delicacies but carrying Chinese signs proclaiming, "The English Ambassador bringing tribute to the Emperor of China." Macartney resolved, in keeping with Dundas's instructions, to make "no complaint of it, reserving myself to notice it if a proper opportunity occurs."[5] As he approached Beijing, however, the chief mandarins charged with administering the mission opened a negotiation that put the gap in perceptions in sharper light. The issue was whether Macartney would kowtow to the Emperor or whether, as he insisted, he could follow the British custom of kneeling on one knee.

The Chinese side opened the discussions in a circuitous manner by remarking on, as Macartney recalled in his diary, "the different modes of dress that prevailed among different nations." The mandarins concluded that Chinese clothes were, in the end, superior, since they allowed the wearer to perform with greater ease "the genuflexions and prostrations which were, they said, customary to be made by all persons whenever the Emperor appeared in public." Would the British delegation not find it easier to free itself of its cumbersome knee-buckles and garters before approaching the Emperor's august presence? Macartney countered by suggesting that the Emperor would likely appreciate if Macartney paid him "the same obeisance which I did to my own Sovereign."[6]

The discussions over the "kowtow question" continued intermittently for several more weeks. The mandarins suggested that Macartney's options were to kowtow or to return home empty-handed; Macartney resisted. Eventually it was agreed that Macartney could follow the European custom and kneel on one knee. It proved to be the only point Macartney won (at least as to actual conduct; the official Chinese report stated that Macartney, overwhelmed by the Emperor's awesome majesty, had performed the kowtow after all).[7]

All of this took place within the intricate framework of Chinese protocol, which showed Macartney the most considerate treatment in foiling and rejecting his proposals. Enveloped in all-encompassing protocol and assured that each aspect had a cosmically ordained and unalterable purpose, Macartney found himself scarcely able to begin his negotiations. Meanwhile he noted with a mixture of respect and unease the efficiency of China's vast bureaucracy, assessing that "every circumstance concerning us and every word that falls from our lips is minutely reported and remembered."[8]

To Macartney's consternation, the technological wonders of Europe left no visible impression on his handlers. When his party demonstrated their mounted cannons, "our conductor pretended to think lightly of them, and spoke to us as if such things were no novelties in China."[9] His lenses, chariot, and hot-air balloon were brushed aside with polite condescension.

A month and a half later, the ambassador was still waiting for an audience with the Emperor, the interval having been consumed by banquets, entertainment, and discussions about the appropriate protocol for a possible imperial audience. Finally, he was summoned at four o'clock in the morning to "a large, handsome tent" to await the Emperor, who presently appeared with great ceremony, borne in a palanquin. Macartney wondered at the magnificence of Chinese protocol, in which "every function of the ceremony was performed with such silence and solemnity as in some measure to resemble the celebration of a religious mystery."[10] After bestowing gifts on Macartney and his party, the Emperor flattered the British party by "sen[ding] us several dishes from his own table" and then giving "to each of us, with his own hands, a cup of warm wine, which we immediately drank in his presence."[11] (Note that having the Emperor personally serve wine to foreign envoys was specifically mentioned among the Han Dynasty's five baits for barbarian management.)[12]

The next day, Macartney and party attended a convocation to celebrate the Emperor's birthday. Finally, the Emperor summoned Macartney to his box at a theater performance. Now, Macartney assumed, he could transact the business of his embassy. Instead, the Emperor rebuffed him with another gift, a box of precious stones and, Macartney recorded, "a small book, written and painted by his own hand, which he desired me to present to the King, my master, as a token of his friendship, saying that the box had been eight hundred years in his family."[13]

Now that these tokens of imperial benevolence had been bestowed, the Chinese officials suggested that in view of the approaching cold winter, the time for Macartney's departure had arrived. Macartney protested that the two sides had yet to "enter into negotiation" on the items in his official instructions; he had "barely opened his commission." It was King George's wish, Macartney stressed, that he be allowed to reside at the Chinese court as a permanent British ambassador.

Early in the morning of October 3, 1793, a mandarin awoke

Macartney and summoned him in full ceremonial dress to the Forbidden City, where he was to receive the answer to his petition. After a wait of several hours, he was ushered up a staircase to a silk-covered chair, upon which sat not the Emperor, but a letter from the Emperor to King George. The Chinese officials kowtowed to the letter, leaving Macartney to kneel to the letter on one knee. Finally, the imperial communication was transported back to Macartney's chambers with full ceremony. It proved to be one of the most humiliating communications in the annals of British diplomacy.

The edict began by remarking on King George's "respectful humility" in sending a tribute mission to China:

> You, O King, live beyond the confines of many seas, nevertheless, impelled by your humble desire to partake of the benefits of our civilization, you have dispatched a mission respectfully bearing your memorial.

The Emperor then dismissed every substantive request that Macartney had made, including the proposal that Macartney be permitted to reside in Beijing as a diplomat:

> As to your entreaty to send one of your nationals to be accredited to my Celestial Court and to be in control of your country's trade with China, this request is contrary to all usage of my dynasty and cannot possibly be entertained. . . . [He could not] be allowed liberty of movement and the privilege of corresponding with his own country; so that you would gain nothing by his residence in our midst.

The proposal that China send its own ambassador to London, the edict continued, was even more absurd:

> [S]upposing I sent an Ambassador to reside in your country, how could you possibly make for him the requisite arrangements? Europe consists of many other nations besides your own: if each and all demanded to be represented at our Court, how could we possibly consent? The thing is utterly impracticable.

Perhaps, the Emperor ascertained, King George had sent Macartney to learn the blessings of civilization from China. But this, too, was out of the question:

> If you assert that your reverence for Our Celestial Dynasty fills you with a desire to acquire our civilization, our ceremonies and code of laws differ so completely from your own that, even if your Envoy were able to acquire the rudiments of our civilization, you could not possibly transplant our manners and customs to your alien soil.

As for Macartney's proposals regarding the benefits of trade between Britain and China, the Celestial Court had already shown the British great favor allowing them "full liberty to trade at Canton for many a year"; anything more was "utterly unreasonable." As for the supposed benefits of British trade to China, Macartney was sadly mistaken:

> [S]trange and costly objects do not interest me. If I have commanded that the tribute offerings sent by you, O King, are to be accepted, this was solely in consideration for the spirit which prompted you to dispatch them from afar. . . . As your Ambassador can see for himself, we possess all things.[14]

Given this state of affairs, trade beyond what was already taking place was impossible. Britain had nothing to offer that China wanted, and China had already given Britain all that its divine regulations permitted.

Since it appeared that there was nothing more to be done, Macartney decided to return to England via Guangzhou. As he prepared to depart, he observed that after the Emperor's sweeping rejection of Britain's requests, the mandarins were, if anything, more attentive, causing Macartney to reflect that perhaps the court had had second thoughts. He inquired to that effect, but the Chinese were done with diplomatic courtesy. Since the barbarian supplicant did not seem to understand subtlety, he was treated to an imperial edict verging on the threatening. The Emperor assured King George that he was aware of "the lonely remoteness of your island, cut off from the world by intervening wastes of sea." But the Chinese capital was "the hub and center about which all quarters of the globe revolve. . . . The subjects of our dependencies have never been allowed to open places of business in Peking [Beijing]." He concluded with an admonition:

> I have accordingly stated the facts to you in detail, and it is your bounden duty to reverently appreciate my feelings and to obey these instructions henceforward for all time, so that you may enjoy the blessings of perpetual peace.[15]

The Emperor, clearly unfamiliar with the capacity of Western leaders for violent rapaciousness, was playing with fire, though he did not know it. The assessment with which Macartney left China was ominous:

> [A] couple of English frigates would be an overmatch for the whole naval force of their empire . . . in half a summer they could totally destroy all the navigation of their coasts and reduce the inhabitants of the maritime provinces, who subsist chiefly on fish, to absolute famine.[16]

However overbearing the Chinese conduct may seem now, one must remember that it had worked for centuries in organizing and sustaining a major international order. In Macartney's era, the blessings of trade with the West were far from self-evident: since China's GDP was still roughly seven times that of Britain's, the Emperor could perhaps be forgiven for thinking that it was London that needed Beijing's assistance and not the other way around.[17]

No doubt the imperial court congratulated itself on deft handling of this barbarian mission, which was not repeated for over twenty years. But the reason for this respite was less the skill of Chinese diplomacy than the Napoleonic Wars, which consumed the resources of the European states. No sooner was Napoleon disposed of than a new British mission appeared off China's coasts in 1816, led by Lord Amherst. This time the standoff over protocol devolved into a physical brawl between the British envoys and the court mandarins assembled outside the throne room. When Amherst refused to kowtow to the Emperor, whom the Chinese insisted on referring to as "the universal sovereign," his mission was dismissed abruptly. Britain's Prince Regent was commanded to endeavor with "obedience" to "make progress towards civilized transformation"; in the meantime, no further ambassadors were necessary "to prove that you are indeed our vassal."[18]

In 1834, the British Foreign Secretary Lord Palmerston sent another mission to attempt a grand resolution. Palmerston, not known for his expertise in Qing dynastic regulations, dispatched the Scottish naval officer Lord Napier with the contradictory instructions to "conform to the laws and usages of China" while, at the same time, requesting permanent diplomatic relations and a resident British embassy in Beijing, access to further ports along the Chinese coast, and, for good measure, free trade with Japan.[19]

Upon Napier's arrival in Guangzhou, he and the local governor settled into an impasse: each refused to receive the other's letters on the basis that it would be demeaning to treat with a figure of such low station. Napier, whom the local authorities had, by this point, christened with a Chinese name translating as "Laboriously Vile," took to posting belligerent broadsheets around Guangzhou using the services of a local translator. Fate finally solved this vexing barbarian problem for the Chinese when both Napier and his translator contracted malarial fever and departed this world. Before expiring, however, Napier did note the existence of Hong Kong, a sparsely populated rocky outcropping that he assessed would provide an excellent natural harbor.

The Chinese could take satisfaction in having forced another round of rebellious barbarians into compliance. But it was the last time the British would accept rejection. With every year, British insistence grew more threatening. The French historian Alain Peyrefitte summed up the reaction in Britain in the aftermath of the Macartney mission: "If China remained closed, then the doors would have to be battered down."[20] All of China's diplomatic maneuvers and abrupt rejections only delayed an inevitable reckoning with the modern international system, designed as it was along European and American lines. This reckoning would impose one of the most wrenching social, intellectual, and moral strains on Chinese society in its long history.

The Clash of Two World Orders: The Opium War

The ascendant Western industrial powers would clearly not abide for long a diplomatic mechanism that referred to them as "barbarians" presenting "tribute" or a tightly regulated seasonal trade at a single Chinese port city. For their part, the Chinese were willing to make limited concessions to Western merchants' appetite for "profit" (a vaguely immoral concept in Confucian thought); but they were appalled by the Western envoys' suggestions that China might be simply one state among many, or that it should have to live with permanent daily contact with barbarian envoys in the Chinese capital.

To the modern eye, none of the Western envoys' initial proposals were particularly outrageous by the standards of the West: the goals of free trade, regular diplomatic contacts, and resident embassies offend few contemporary sensibilities and are treated as a standard way to conduct diplomacy. But the ultimate showdown occurred over one of the more shameful aspects of Western intrusion: the insistence on the unrestricted importation of opium into China.

In the mid-nineteenth century, opium was tolerated in Britain and banned in China, though consumed by an increasing number of Chinese. British India was the center of much of the world's opium poppy growth, and British and American merchants, working in concert with Chinese smugglers, did a brisk business. Opium was, in fact, one of the few foreign products that made any headway in the Chinese market; Britain's famed manufactures were dismissed as novelties or inferior to Chinese products. Polite Western opinion viewed the opium trade as an embarrassment. However, merchants were reluctant to forfeit the lucrative trade.

The Qing court debated legalizing opium and managing its sale; it ultimately decided to crack down and eradicate the trade altogether. In 1839, Beijing dispatched Lin Zexu, an official of considerable demonstrated skill, to shut down the trade in Guangzhou and force Western merchants to comply with the official ban. A traditional Confucian mandarin, Lin dealt with the problem as he would with any particularly stubborn barbarian issue: through a mixture of force and moral suasion. Upon arriving in Guangzhou, he demanded that the Western trade missions forfeit all of their opium chests for destruction. When that failed, he blockaded all of the foreigners—including those having nothing to do with the opium trade—in their factories, announcing that they would be released only on the surrender of their contraband.

Lin next dispatched a letter to Queen Victoria, praising, with what deference the traditional protocol allowed, the "politeness and submissiveness" of her predecessors in sending "tribute" to China. The crux of his missive was the demand that Queen Victoria take charge of the eradication of opium in Britain's Indian territories:

> [I]n several places of India under your control such as Bengal, Madras, Bombay, Patna, Benares and Malwa . . . opium [has] been planted from hill to hill, and ponds have been opened for its manufacture. . . . The obnoxious odor ascends, irritating heaven and frightening the spirits. Indeed you, O King, can eradicate the opium plant in these places, hoe over the fields entirely, and sow in its stead the five grains. Anyone who dares again attempt to plant and manufacture opium should be severely punished.[21]

The request was reasonable, even when couched in the traditional assumption of Chinese overlordship:

> Suppose a man of another country comes to England to trade, he still has to obey the English laws; how much more should he obey in China the laws of the Celestial Dynasty? . . . The barbarian merchants of your country, if they wish to do business for a prolonged period, are required to obey our statutes respectfully and to cut off permanently the source of opium. . . .
>
> May you, O King, check your wicked and sift your vicious people before they come to China, in order to guarantee the peace of your nation, to show further the sincerity of your politeness and submissiveness, and to let the two countries enjoy together the blessings of peace. How fortunate, how fortunate indeed! After receiving this dispatch will you immediately give us a prompt reply regarding the details and circumstances of your cutting off the opium traffic. Be sure not to put this off.[22]

Overestimating Chinese leverage, Lin's ultimatum threatened to cut off the export of Chinese products, which he supposed were existential necessities for the Western barbarians: "If China cuts off these benefits with no sympathy for those who are to suffer, then what can the barbarians rely upon to keep themselves alive?" China had nothing to fear from retaliation: "[A]rticles coming from the outside to China can only be used as toys. We can take them or get along without them."[23]

Lin's letter seems never to have reached Victoria. In the meantime, British opinion treated Lin's siege of the British community in Guangzhou as an unacceptable affront. Lobbyists for the "China trade" petitioned Parliament for a declaration of war. Palmerston dispatched a letter to Beijing demanding "satisfaction and redress for injuries inflicted by Chinese Authorities upon British Subjects resident in China, and for insults offered by those same Authorities to the British Crown," as well as the permanent cession of "one or more sufficiently large and properly situated Islands on the Coast of China" as a depot for British trade.[24]

In his letter Palmerston acknowledged that opium was "contraband" under Chinese law, but he stooped to a legalistic defense of the trade, arguing that the Chinese ban had, under Western legal principles, lapsed due to the connivance of corrupt officials. This casuistry was unlikely to convince anybody and Palmerston did not allow it to delay his fixed determination to bring matters to a head: in light of the "urgent importance" of the matter and the great distance separating England from China, the British government was ordering a fleet immediately to "blockade the principal Chinese ports," seize "all Chinese Vessels which [it] may meet with," and seize "some convenient part of Chinese territory" until London obtained satisfaction.[25] The Opium War had begun.

Initial Chinese reactions rated the prospect of a British offensive as a baseless threat. One official argued to the Emperor that the vast distance between China and England would render the English impotent:

"The English barbarians are an insignificant and detestable race, trusting entirely to their strong ships and large guns; but the immense distance they have traversed will render the arrival of seasonable supplies impossible, and their soldiers, after a single defeat, being deprived of provisions, will become dispirited and lost."[26] Even after the British blockaded the Pearl River and seized several islands opposite the port city of Ningbo as a show of force, Lin wrote indignantly to Queen Victoria: "You savages of the further seas have waxed so bold, it seems, as to defy and insult our mighty Empire. Of a truth it is high time for you to 'flay the face and cleanse the heart,' and to amend your ways. If you submit humbly to the Celestial dynasty and tender your allegiance, it may give you a chance to purge yourselves of your past sins."[27]

Centuries of predominance had warped the Celestial Court's sense of reality. Pretension of superiority only accentuated the inevitable humiliation. British ships swiftly bypassed the Chinese coastal defenses and blockaded the main Chinese ports. The cannons once dismissed by Macartney's mandarin handlers operated with brutal effect.

One Chinese official, Qishan, the Viceroy of Zhili (the administrative division then encompassing Beijing and the surrounding provinces), came to understand China's vulnerability when he was sent to make preliminary contact with a British fleet that had sailed north to Tianjin. He recognized that the Chinese could not counter British seaborne firepower: "Without any wind, or even a favorable tide, they [steam vessels] glide along against the current and are capable of fantastic speed. . . . Their carriages are mounted on swivels, enabling the guns to be turned and aimed in any direction." By contrast, Qishan assessed that China's guns were left over from the Ming Dynasty, and that "[t]hose who are in charge of military affairs are all literary officials . . . they have no knowledge of armaments."[28]

Concluding that the city was defenseless before British naval power, Qishan opted to soothe and divert the British by assuring them that the imbroglio in Guangzhou had been a misunderstanding, and did not reflect the "temperate and just intentions of the Emperor." Chinese officials would "investigate and handle the matter fairly," but first it was "imperative that [the British fleet] set sail for the South" and await Chinese inspectors there. Somewhat remarkably, this maneuver worked. The British force sailed back to the southern ports, leaving China's exposed northern cities undamaged.[29]

Based on this success, Qishan was now sent to Guangzhou to replace Lin Zexu and to manage the barbarians once again. The Emperor, who seems not to have grasped the extent of the British technological advantage, instructed Qishan to engage the British representatives in drawn-out discussions while China gathered its forces: "After prolonged negotiation has made the Barbarians weary and exhausted," he noted in the vermilion imperial pen, "we can suddenly attack them and thereby subdue them."[30] Lin Zexu was dismissed in disgrace for having provoked a barbarian attack. He set off for internal exile in far western China, reflecting on the superiority of Western weaponry and drafting secret memorials advising that China develop its own.[31]

Once at his post in southern China, however, Qishan confronted a more challenging situation. The British demanded territorial concessions and an indemnity. They had come south to obtain satisfaction; they would no longer be deferred by procrastinating tactics. After British forces opened fire on several sites on the coast, Qishan and his British counterpart, Captain Charles Elliot, negotiated a draft agreement, the Chuan-pi Convention, which granted the British special rights on Hong Kong, promised an indemnity of $6 million, and allowed that future dealings between Chinese and British officials would take place on equal terms (that is, the British would be spared the protocol normally reserved for barbarian supplicants).

This deal was rejected by both the Chinese and the British governments, each of whom saw its terms as a humiliation. For having exceeded his instructions and conceded too much to the barbarians, the Emperor had Qishan recalled in chains and then sentenced to death (later commuted to exile). The British negotiator, Charles Elliot, faced a somewhat gentler fate, although Palmerston rebuked him in the harshest terms for having gained far too little: "Throughout the whole course of your proceedings," Palmerston complained, "you seemed to have considered that my instructions were waste paper." Hong Kong was "a barren island with hardly a house upon it"; Elliot had been far too conciliatory in not holding on to more valuable territory or pressing for harsher terms.[32]

Palmerston appointed a new envoy, Sir Henry Pottinger, whom he instructed to take a harder line, for "Her Majesty's Government cannot allow that, in a transaction between Great Britain and China, the unreasonable practice of the Chinese should supersede the reasonable practice of all the rest of mankind."[33] Arriving in China, Pottinger pressed Britain's military advantage, blockading further ports and cutting traffic along the Grand Canal and lower Yangtze River. With the British poised to attack the ancient capital Nanjing, the Chinese sued for peace.

Qiying's Diplomacy: Soothing the Barbarians

Pottinger now faced yet another Chinese negotiator, the third to be sent on this supremely unpromising assignment by a court still fancying itself supreme in the universe, the Manchu prince Qiying. Qiying's method for handling the British was a traditional Chinese strategy when confronted with defeat. Having tried defiance and diplomacy, China would seek to wear the barbarians down by seeming compliance. Negotiating under the shadow of the British fleet, Qiying judged that it befell the court's ministers to repeat what the Middle Kingdom's elites had done so often before: through a combination of delay, circumlocution, and carefully apportioned favors, they would soothe and tame the barbarians while buying time for China to outlast their assault.

Qiying fixed his focus on establishing a personal relationship with the "barbarian headman" Pottinger. He showered Pottinger with gifts and took to addressing him as his cherished friend and "intimate" (a word specially transliterated into Chinese for this express purpose). As an expression of the deep friendship between them, Qiying went so far as to propose exchanging portraits of their wives and even proclaimed his wish to adopt Pottinger's son (who remained in England, but was henceforth known as "Frederick Keying Pottinger").[34]

In one remarkable dispatch, Qiying explained the approach to a Celestial Court that found the seduction process difficult to comprehend. He described the ways he had aspired to appease the British barbarians: "With this type of people from outside the bounds of civilization, who are blind and unawakened in styles of address and forms of ceremony . . . even though our tongues were dry and our throats parched (from urging them to follow our way), still they could not avoid closing their ears and acting as if deaf."[35]

Therefore, Qiying's banquets and his extravagant warmth toward Pottinger and his family had served an essentially strategic design, in which Chinese conduct was calculated in specific doses and in which such qualities as trust and sincerity were weapons; whether they reflected convictions or not was secondary. He continued:

> Certainly we have to curb them by sincerity, but it has been even more necessary to control them by skillful methods. There are times when it is possible to have them follow our directions but not let them understand the reasons. Sometimes we expose everything so that they will not be suspicious, whereupon we can dissipate their rebellious restlessness. Sometimes we have given them receptions and entertainment, after which they have had a feeling of appreciation. And at still other times we have shown trust in them in a broad-minded way and deemed it unnecessary to go deeply into minute discussions

> with them, whereupon we have been able to get their help in the business at hand.[36]

The results of this interplay between Western overwhelming force and Chinese psychological management were two treaties negotiated by Qiying and Pottinger, the Treaty of Nanjing and the supplementary Treaty of the Bogue. The settlement conceded more than the Chuan-pi Convention. It was essentially humiliating, though the terms were less harsh than the military situation would have allowed Britain to impose. It provided for payment of a $6 million indemnity by China, the cession of Hong Kong, and the opening of five coastal "treaty ports" in which Western residence and trade would be permitted. This effectively dismantled the "Canton System" by which the Chinese court had regulated trade with the West and confined it to licensed merchants. Ningbo, Shanghai, Xiamen, and Fuzhou were added to the list of treaty ports. The British secured the right to maintain permanent missions in the port cities and to negotiate directly with local officials, bypassing the court in Beijing.

The British also obtained the right to exercise jurisdiction over their nationals residing in the Chinese treaty ports. Operationally, this meant that foreign opium traders would be subject to their own countries' laws and regulations, not China's. This principle of "extraterritoriality," among the less controversial provisions of the treaty at the time, would eventually come to be treated as a major infringement of Chinese sovereignty. Since the European concept of sovereignty was unknown, however, in China extraterritoriality came to be a symbol at the time, not so much of the violation of a legal norm as of declining imperial power. The resulting diminution of the Mandate of Heaven led to the eruption of a flurry of domestic rebellion.

The nineteenth-century English translator Thomas Meadows observed that most Chinese did not at first appreciate the lasting repercussions of the Opium War. They treated the concessions as an application of the traditional method of absorbing the barbarians and wearing them down. "[T]he great body of the nation," he surmised, "can only look on the late war as a rebellious irruption of a tribe of barbarians, who, secure in their strong ships, attacked and took some places along the coast, and even managed to get into their possession an important point of the grand canal, whereby they forced the Emperor to make certain concessions."[37]

But the Western powers were not so easily soothed. Every Chinese concession tended to generate additional Western demands. The treaties, conceived at first as a temporary concession, instead inaugurated a process by which the Qing court lost control of much of China's commercial and foreign policy. Following the British treaty, U.S. President John Tyler promptly sent a mission to China to gain similar concessions for the Americans, the forerunner of the later "Open Door" policy. The French negotiated their own treaty with analogous terms. Each of these countries in turn included a "Most Favored Nation" clause that stipulated that any concession offered by China to other countries must also be given to the signatory. (Chinese diplomacy later used this clause to limit exactions by stimulating competition between the various claimants for special privilege.)

These treaties are justly infamous in Chinese history as the first in a string of "unequal treaties" conducted under the shadow of foreign military force. At the time, the most bitterly contested provisions were their stipulations of equality of status. China had until this point insisted on the superior position ingrained in its national identity and reflected in the tributary system. Now it faced a foreign power determined to erase its name from the roll of Chinese "tribute states" under threat of force and to prove itself the sovereign equal of the Celestial Dynasty.

The leaders on both sides understood that this was a dispute about far more than protocol or opium. The Qing court was willing to appease avaricious foreigners with money and trade; but if the principle of barbarian political equality to the Son of Heaven was established, the entire Chinese world order would be threatened; the dynasty risked the loss of the Mandate of Heaven. Palmerston, in his frequently caustic communications to his negotiators, treated the amount of the indemnity as partly symbolic; but he devoted great attention to berating them for acquiescing to Chinese communications whose language revealed "assumptions of superiority on the part of China" or implied that Britain, victorious in war, remained a supplicant asking for the Emperor's divine favor.[38] Eventually, Palmerston's view prevailed, and the Treaty of Nanjing included a clause explicitly ensuring that Chinese and British officials would henceforth "correspond . . . on a footing of perfect equality"; it went so far as to list specific written Chinese characters in the text with acceptably neutral connotations. Chinese records (or at least those to which foreigners had access) would no longer describe the British as "begging" Chinese authorities or "tremblingly obeying" their "orders."[39]

The Celestial Court had come to understand the military inferiority of China but not yet the appropriate method for dealing with it. At first, it applied the traditional methods of barbarian management. Defeat was not unknown in the course of China's long history. China's rulers had dealt with it by applying the five baits described in the previous chapter. They saw the common characteristic of these invaders as being their desire to partake of Chinese culture; they wished to settle on Chinese soil and partake of its civilization. They could therefore gradually be tamed by some of the psychological methods illustrated by Prince Qiying and, in time, become part of Chinese life.

But the European invaders had no such aspiration nor limited goals. Deeming themselves more advanced societies, their goal was to exploit China for economic gain, not to join its way of life. Their demands were therefore limited only by their resources and their greed. Personal relationships could not be decisive, because the chiefs of the invaders were not neighbors but lived thousands of miles away, where they were governed by motivations obtuse to the subtleness and indirection of the Qiying type of strategy.

Within the space of a decade, the Middle Kingdom had gone from preeminence to being an object of contending colonial forces. Poised between two eras and two different conceptions of international relations, China strove for a new identity, and above all, to reconcile the values that marked its greatness with the technology and commerce on which it would have to base its security.

CHAPTER 3

From Preeminence to Decline

As the nineteenth century progressed, China experienced almost every imaginable shock to its historic image of itself. Before the Opium War, it conceived of diplomacy and international trade mainly as forms of recognition of China's preeminence. Now, even as it entered a period of domestic turmoil, it faced three foreign challenges, any one of which could be enough to overturn a dynasty. These threats came from every direction and in heretofore barely conceivable incarnations.

From across the oceans in the West came the European nations. They raised not so much the challenge of territorial defense as of irreconcilable conceptions of world order. For the most part, the Western powers limited themselves to extracting economic concessions on the Chinese coast and demanding rights to free trade and missionary activity. Paradoxically this was threatening because the Europeans did not view it as a conquest at all. They were not seeking to replace the existing dynasty—they simply imposed an entirely new world order essentially incompatible with the Chinese one.

From the north and west, an expansionist and militarily dominant Russia sought to pry loose China's vast hinterland. Russia's cooperation could be purchased temporarily, but it recognized no boundaries between its own domains and the Chinese outer dominions. And unlike previous conquerors, Russia did not become part of the Chinese culture; the territories it penetrated were permanently lost to the empire.

Still, neither the Western powers nor Russia had any ambition to displace the Qing and claim the Mandate of Heaven; ultimately they reached the conclusion that they had much to lose from the Qing's fall. Japan, by contrast, had no vested interest in the survival of China's ancient institutions or the Sinocentric world order. From the east it set out not only to occupy significant portions of Chinese territory, but to supplant Beijing as the center of a new East Asian international order.

The ensuing catastrophes are viewed with considerable dismay in contemporary China, as part of an infamous "century of humiliation" that ended only by the reunification of the country under an assertively nationalist form of Communism. At the same time, the era of China's hobbling stands in many ways as a testimony to its remarkable abilities to surmount strains that might break other societies.

While foreign armies were marching across China and extorting humiliating terms, the Celestial Court never stopped asserting its claim to central authority and managed to implement it over most of China's territory. The invaders were treated as other invaders had been in previous centuries, as a nuisance, an unwelcome interruption of the eternal rhythm of Chinese life. The court in Beijing could act in this manner because the foreign depredations were mostly on the periphery of China and because the invaders had come for commerce; as such it was in the interest of the invaders that the vast central regions, including most of the population, remain quiescent. The government in Beijing thereby achieved a margin of maneuver. All the exactions had to be negotiated with the imperial court, which was therefore in a position to play off the invaders against one another.

Chinese statesmen played their weak hand with considerable skill and forestalled what could have been an even worse catastrophe. From the point of view of the balance of power, the objective configuration of forces would have suggested the impossibility of China's survival as a unitary, continent-sized state. But with the traditional vision of Chinese preeminence under often violent challenge and the country lashed by waves of colonial depredation and domestic upheaval, China eventually overcame its travails by its own efforts. Through a painful and often humiliating process, China's statesmen in the end preserved the moral and territorial claims of their disintegrating world order.

Perhaps most remarkably, they did so using almost entirely traditional methods. A segment of the Qing ruling class wrote eloquent memorials in the classical style about the challenges posed by the West, Russia, and a rising Japan, and the resulting need for China to practice "self-strengthening" and improve its own technological capabilities. But China's Confucian elite and its generally conservative populace remained deeply ambivalent about such advice. Many perceived the importation of foreign-language texts and Western technology as endangering China's cultural essence and social order. After sometimes bruising battles, the prevailing faction decided that to modernize along Western lines was to cease to be Chinese, and that nothing could justify abandoning this unique heritage. So China faced the era of imperial expansion without the benefit of a modern military apparatus on any national scale, and with only piecemeal adaptations to foreign financial and political innovations.

To weather the storm, China relied not on technology or military power but instead on two deeply traditional resources: the analytical abilities of its diplomats, and the endurance and cultural confidence of its people. It developed ingenious strategies for playing off the new barbarians against one another. Officials charged with managing China's foreign relations offered concessions in various cities—but they deliberately invited multiple sets of foreigners to share in the spoils, so that they could "use barbarians against barbarians" and avoid dominance by any one power. They eventually insisted on scrupulous adherence to the "unequal treaties" with the West and to foreign principles of international law, not because Chinese officials believed them to be valid, but because such conduct provided a means to circumscribe foreign ambitions. Faced with two potentially overwhelming contenders for dominance in northeast China, and possessing almost no force with which to repulse them, China's diplomats set Russia and Japan against each other, mitigating to some degree the scope and permanence of the encroachments by each of them.

In light of the contrast between China's military near impotence and its expansively articulated vision of its world role, the rearguard defense to maintain an independent Chinese government was a remarkable achievement. No victory celebration attended this accomplishment; it was an incomplete, decades-long endeavor marked by numerous reversals and internal opponents, outlasting and occasionally ruining its proponents. This struggle came at considerable cost to the Chinese people—whose patience and endurance served, for neither the first nor the last time, as the ultimate line of defense. But it preserved the ideal of China as a continental reality in charge of its own destiny. With great discipline and self-confidence, it kept the door open for the later era of Chinese resurgence.

Wei Yuan's Blueprint: "Using Barbarians Against Barbarians," Learning Their Techniques

In navigating the treacherous passage of assaults by the Western European nations with their superior technology and the new ambitions of both Russia and Japan, China was well served by its cultural cohesion and the extraordinary skill of its diplomats—all the more remarkable in the face of the general obtuseness of the imperial court. By the middle of the nineteenth century, only a few members of the Chinese elite had begun to understand that China no longer lived in a system marked by its predominance and that China had to learn the grammar of a system of competing power blocs.

One such official was Wei Yuan (1794–1856), a midranking Confucian mandarin and associate of Lin Zexu, the Guangzhou governor whose crackdown on the opium trade had triggered British intervention and eventually forced him into exile. While loyal to the Qing Dynasty, Wei Yuan was deeply concerned about its complacency. He wrote a pioneering study of foreign geography using materials collected and translated from foreign traders and missionaries. Its purpose was to encourage China to set its sights beyond the tributary countries on its immediate borders.

Wei Yuan's 1842 "Plans for a Maritime Defense," in essence a study of China's failures in the Opium War, proposed to apply the lessons of European balance-of-power diplomacy to China's contemporary problems. Recognizing China's material weakness vis-à-vis the foreign powers—a premise that his contemporaries generally did not accept—Wei Yuan proposed methods by which China might gain a margin for maneuver. Wei Yuan proposed a multipronged strategy:

> There are two methods of attacking the barbarians, namely, to stimulate countries unfriendly to the barbarians to make an attack on them, and to learn the superior skills of the barbarians in order to control them. There are two methods of making peace with the barbarians, namely, to let the various trading nations conduct their trade so as to maintain peace with the barbarians, and to support the first treaty of the Opium War so as to maintain international trade.[1]

It was a demonstration of the analytical skill of Chinese diplomacy that, faced with a superior foe and potentially escalating demands, it understood that holding fast to even a humiliating treaty set a limit to further exactions.

In the meantime, Wei Yuan reviewed the countries that, based on European principles of equilibrium, could conceivably put pressure on Britain. Citing ancient precedents in which the Han, Tang, and early Qing Dynasties had managed the ambitions of aggressive tribes, Wei Yuan surveyed the globe, reviewing the "enemy countries of which the British barbarians are afraid." Writing as if the slogan "let barbarians fight barbarians" were self-implementing, Wei Yuan pointed to "Russia, France, and America" in the West, and "the Gurkhas [of Nepal], Burma, Siam [Thailand], and Annam [northern Vietnam]" in the East as conceivable candidates. Wei Yuan imagined a two-pronged Russian and Gurkha attack on Britain's most distant and poorly defended interests, its Indian empire. Stimulating long-running French and American animosities toward Britain, causing them to attack Britain by sea, was another weapon in Wei Yuan's analysis.

It was a highly original solution hampered only by the fact that the Chinese government had not the slightest idea how to implement it. It had only limited knowledge of the potential allied countries in question and no representation in any of their capitals. Wei Yuan came to understand China's limits. In an age of global politics, he asserted, the issue was not that "the outer barbarians cannot be used"; rather, "we need personnel who are capable of making arrangements with them" and who knew "their locations [and] their interrelations of friendship or enmity."[2]

Having failed to stop the British advance, Wei Yuan continued, Beijing needed to weaken London's relative position in the world and in China. He came up with another original idea: to invite other barbarians into China and to set up a contest between their greed and Britain's, so that China could emerge as the balancer in effect over the division of its own substance. Wei Yuan continued:

> Today the British barbarians not only have occupied Hongkong and accumulated a great deal of wealth as well as a

> proud face among the other barbarians, but also have opened the ports and cut down the various charges so as to grant favor to other barbarians. Rather than let the British barbarians be good to them in order to enlarge their following, would it not be better for us ourselves to be good to them, in order to get them under control like fingers on the arm?[3]

In other words, China should offer concessions to all rapacious nations rather than let Britain exact them and benefit itself by offering to share the spoils with other countries. The mechanism for achieving this objective was the Most Favored Nation principle—that any privilege granted one power should be automatically extended to all others.[4]

Time is not neutral. The benefit of Wei Yuan's subtle maneuvers would have to be measured by China's ability to arm itself using "the superior techniques of the barbarians." China, Wei Yuan advised, should "bring Western craftsmen to Canton" from France or the United States "to take charge of building ships and making arms." Wei Yuan summed up the new strategy with the proposition that "before the peace settlement, it behooves us to use barbarians against barbarians. After the settlement, it is proper for us to learn their superior techniques in order to control them."[5]

Though initially dismissive of calls for technological modernization, the Celestial Court did adopt the strategy of adhering to the letter of the Opium War treaties in order to establish a ceiling on Western demands. It would, a leading official later wrote, "act according to the treaties and not allow the foreigners to go even slightly beyond them"; thus Chinese officials should "be sincere and amicable but quietly try to keep them in line."[6]

The Erosion of Authority: Domestic Upheavals and the Challenge of Foreign Encroachments

The Western treaty powers, of course, had no intention of being kept in line—and in the aftermath of the Qiying-Pottinger negotiations, a new gap in expectations began to appear. For the Chinese court, the treaties were a temporary concession to barbarian force, to be followed to the degree necessary but never voluntarily broadened. For the West, the treaties were the beginning of a long-term process by which China would be steadily drawn into Western norms of political and economic exchange. But what the West conceived of as a process of enlightenment was seen by some in China as a philosophical assault.

This is why the Chinese refused to submit to foreign demands to broaden the treaties to include free trade throughout China and permanent diplomatic representation in the Chinese capital. Beijing understood—despite its extremely limited knowledge about the West—that the combination of the foreigners' superior force, unfettered foreign activity within China, and multiple Western missions in Beijing would seriously undermine the assumptions of the Chinese world order. Once China became a "normal" state, it would lose its historic unique moral authority; it would simply be another weak country beset by invaders. In this context, seemingly minor disputes over diplomatic and economic prerogatives turned into a major clash.

All of this took place against a backdrop of massive Chinese domestic upheaval, masked to a large degree by the imperturbable self-confidence projected by Chinese officials charged with managing contacts with foreigners—a trait unchanged in the modern period. Macartney had already remarked in 1793 on the uneasy accommodation between the Qing's Manchu ruling class, Han Chinese bureaucratic elite, and mostly Han general population. "Scarcely a year now passes," he noted, "without an insurrection in some of the provinces."[7]

The dynasty's Mandate of Heaven having been put into question, domestic opponents escalated the scope of their defiance. Their challenges were both religious and ethnic, providing the basis for conflicts of encompassing brutality. The far western reaches of the empire witnessed Muslim rebellions and the declaration of short-lived separatist khanates, suppressed only at a major financial and human cost. In central China, an uprising known as the Nian Rebellion drew considerable support from Han Chinese laboring classes and, beginning in 1851, conducted a nearly two-decades-long insurgency.

The most serious challenge came from the Taiping Rebellion (1850–64), mounted by a Chinese Christian sect in the south. Missionaries had existed for centuries, though severely circumscribed. They began to enter the country in larger numbers after the Opium War. Led by a charismatic Chinese mystic claiming to be Jesus's younger brother and an associate asserting telepathic powers, the Taiping Rebellion aimed to replace the Qing with a new "Heavenly Kingdom of Great Peace" ruled by its leaders' bizarre interpretation of imported missionary texts. Taiping forces succeeded in wresting control of Nanjing and much of south and central China from the Qing, ruling in the mode of a nascent dynasty. Though little known in Western historiography, the conflict between the Taiping and the Qing ranks as one of history's most devastating conflicts, with casualties estimated in the tens of millions. While no official figures exist, it is estimated that during the Taiping, Muslim, and Nian upheavals China's population declined from roughly 410 million in 1850 to roughly 350 million in 1873.[8]

The Treaty of Nanjing and its French and American counterparts came up for renegotiation in the 1850s, while China was torn by these civil conflicts. The treaty powers insisted that their diplomats be permitted to reside year-round in the Chinese capital, signifying that they were not tributary envoys but the representatives of equal sovereign states. The Chinese deployed their wide array of delaying tactics with the added incentive that given the fate of preceding negotiators, no Qing official could possibly have wanted to concede the point of permanent diplomatic representation.

In 1856, an intrusive Chinese inspection of a British-registered Chinese ship, the *Arrow*, and the alleged desecration of its British flag, provided a pretext for the renewal of hostilities. As in the 1840 conflict, the casus belli was not entirely heroic (the ship's registration, it was later discovered, had technically lapsed); but both sides understood that they were playing for higher stakes. With China's defenses still in an inchoate state of development, British forces seized Guangzhou and the Dagu Forts in northern China, from which they could easily march on Beijing.

During the negotiations that followed, the gap in perceptions was as wide as ever. The British pressed on with missionary conviction, presenting their negotiating positions as a public service that would at last bring China up to speed with the modern world. Thus London's assistant negotiator Horatio Lay summed up the prevailing Western view: "[D]iplomatic representation will be for your good as well as ours, as you will surely see. The medicine may be unpleasant but the aftereffects will be grand."[9]

Qing authorities were not nearly so enthusiastic. They acceded to the treaty terms only after a flurry of anguished internal communications between the imperial court and its negotiator and another British threat to march on Beijing.[10]

The centerpiece of the resulting 1858 Treaty of Tianjin was the concession that London had sought in vain for over six decades—the right to a permanent embassy in Beijing. The treaty further permitted foreign travel on the Yangtze River, opened additional "treaty ports" to Western trade, and protected Chinese Christian converts and Western proselytizing in China (a prospect particularly difficult for the Qing given the Taiping Rebellion). The French and Americans concluded their own treaties on similar terms under their Most Favored Nation clauses.

The treaty powers now applied their attention to establishing resident embassies in a clearly unwelcoming capital. In May 1859, Britain's new envoy, Frederick Bruce, arrived in China to exchange ratifications of the treaty that would grant him the right to take up residence in Beijing. Finding the main river route to the capital blocked with chains and spikes, he ordered a contingent of British marines to clear the obstacles. But Chinese forces shocked Bruce's party by opening fire from the newly fortified Dagu Forts. The ensuing battle resulted in 519 British troops killed and 456 wounded.[11]

It was the first Chinese victory in battle against modern Western forces, and shattered, at least temporarily, the image of Chinese military impotence. Yet it could only stall the British ambassador's advance temporarily. Palmerston dispatched Lord Elgin to lead a joint British and French march on Beijing, with orders to occupy the capital and "bring the Emperor to reason." As retaliation for the "Dagu Repulse" and a symbolic show of Western power, Elgin ordered the burning of the Emperor's Summer Palace, destroying invaluable art treasures in the process—an act still resented in China a century and a half later.

China's seventy-year campaign of resistance against Western norms of interstate relations had now reached undeniable crisis. Efforts at diplomatic delay had run their course; force had been met with superior force. Barbarian claims of sovereign equality, once dismissed in Beijing as risible, shaded into ominous demonstrations of military dominance. Foreign armies occupied China's capital and enforced the Western interpretation of political equality and ambassadorial privileges.

At this point, another claimant to China's patrimony stepped into the fray. By 1860, the Russians had been represented in Beijing for over 150 years—with an ecclesiastical mission, they were the only European country permitted to establish a residence. Russia's interests had in some ways trailed those of the other European powers; it had gained all the benefits extended to the treaty powers without joining the British in the periodic exercises of force. On the other hand, Moscow's overall objective went much further than religious proselytizing or commerce along the coast. It perceived in the Qing's decline an opportunity to dismember the Chinese Empire and reattach its "outer dominions" to Russia. It set its sights in particular on the lightly administered and ambiguously demarcated expanses of Manchuria (the Manchu heartland in northeast China), Mongolia (the then quasi-autonomous tribal steppe at China's north), and Xinjiang (the expanse of mountains and deserts in the far west, then populated mostly by Muslim peoples). To that end, Russia had moved gradually and deliberately to expand its presence along these inland frontiers, poaching the loyalties of local princes through offers of rank and material benefit, underscored by a menacing cavalry.[12]

At the moment of China's maximum peril Moscow surfaced as a colonial power, offering to mediate in the 1860 conflict—which was, in fact, a way of threatening to intervene. Artful—others might argue duplicitous—diplomacy was underpinned by the implicit threat of force. Count Nikolai Ignatieff, the Czar's brilliant and devious young plenipotentiary in Beijing, managed to convince the Chinese court that only Russia could secure the evacuation of the Western occupying powers from the Chinese capital, and to convince the Western powers that only Russia could secure Chinese compliance with the treaties. Having facilitated the Anglo-French march on Beijing with detailed maps and intelligence, Ignatieff turned and convinced the occupying forces that with the approaching winter the Beihe, the river route in and out of Beijing, would freeze, leaving them surrounded by hostile Chinese mobs.[13]

For these services Moscow exacted a staggering territorial price: a broad swath of territory in so-called Outer Manchuria along the Pacific coast, including the port city now called Vladivostok.[14] In a stroke, Russia had gained a major new naval base, a foothold in the Sea of Japan, and 350,000 square miles of territory once considered Chinese.

Ignatieff also negotiated a provision opening Urga (now Ulan Bator) in Mongolia and the far western city of Kashgar to Russian trade and consulates. To compound the humiliation, Elgin secured for Britain an expansion of its Hong Kong colony into the adjacent territory of Kowloon. China had enlisted Russia to forestall what it believed to be a further assault by the treaty powers dominating China's capital and its coast; but in an era of Chinese weakness, "using barbarians against barbarians" was not without its costs.

Managing Decline

China had not survived for four thousand years as a unique civilization and for two millennia as a united state by remaining passive to near-rampant foreign intrusions. For all that period, conquerors had been obliged either to adopt Chinese culture or to be gradually engulfed by their subjects, who masked their practicality by patience. Another such period of trial was at hand.

In the aftermath of the 1860 conflict, the Emperor and the court faction that had urged resistance to the British mission fled the capital. Prince Gong, the Emperor's half brother, assumed the role of de facto head of government. Having negotiated the conclusion of hostilities, Prince Gong summed up, in a memorial to the Emperor in 1861, the appalling strategic choices:

> Now the Nian rebellion is ablaze in the north and the Taiping in the south, our military supplies are exhausted and our troops are worn out. The barbarians take advantage of our weak position and try to control us. If we do not restrain our rage but continue the hostilities, we are liable to sudden catastrophe. On the other hand, if we overlook the way they have harmed us and do not make any preparations against them,

> then we shall be bequeathing a source of grief to our sons and grandsons.[15]

It was the classic dilemma of the defeated: can a society maintain its cohesion while seeming to adapt to the conqueror—and how to build up the capacity to reverse the unfavorable balance of forces? Prince Gong invoked an ancient Chinese saying: "Resort to peace and friendship when temporarily obliged to do so; use war and defense as your actual policy."[16]

Since no grand resolution was available, the Gong memorial established a priority among the dangers, in effect based on the principle of defeating the near barbarians with the assistance of the far barbarians. It was a classical Chinese strategy that would be revisited roughly a hundred years later by Mao. The Gong memorial demonstrated great geopolitical acumen in its assessment of the kind of threat represented by the various invaders. Despite the imminent and actual threat from Britain, the Gong memorial put Britain last in the order of the long-range danger to the cohesion of the Chinese state and Russia first:

> Both the Taiping and Nian are gaining victories and constitute an organic disease. Russia, with her territory adjoining ours, aiming to nibble away our territory like a silk worm, may be considered a threat at our bosom. As to England, her purpose is to trade but she acts violently, without regard for human decency. If she is not kept within limits, we shall not be able to stand on our feet. Hence she may be compared to an affliction of our limbs. Therefore we should suppress the Taiping and Nian first, get the Russians under control next, and attend to the British last.[17]

To accomplish his long-range aims toward the foreign powers, Prince Gong proposed the establishment of a new government office—an embryonic foreign ministry—to manage affairs with the Western powers and analyze foreign newspapers for information on developments beyond China's borders. He hopefully predicted that this would be a temporary necessity, to be abolished "[a]s soon as the military campaigns are concluded and the affairs of the various countries are simplified."[18] This new department was not listed in the official record of metropolitan and state offices until 1890. Its officials tended to be seconded from other, more important departments as a kind of temporary assignment. They were rotated frequently. Though some of its cities were occupied by foreign forces, China treated foreign policy as a temporary expedient rather than a permanent feature of China's future.[19] The new ministry's full name was the Zongli Geguo Shiwu Yamen ("Office for the General Management of the Affairs of All Nations"), an ambiguous phrasing open to the interpretation that China was not engaging in diplomacy with foreign peoples at all, but rather ordering their affairs as part of its universal empire.[20]

The implementation of Prince Gong's policy fell into the hands of Li Hongzhang, a top-ranking mandarin who had risen to prominence commanding forces in the Qing campaigns against the Taiping Rebellion. Ambitious, urbane, impassive in the face of humiliation, supremely well versed in China's classical tradition but uncommonly attuned to its peril, Li served for nearly four decades as China's face to the outside world. He cast himself as the intermediary between the foreign powers' insistent demands for territorial and economic concessions and the Chinese court's expansive claims of political superiority. By definition his policies could never meet with either side's complete approbation. Within China in particular Li left a controversial legacy, especially among those urging a more confrontational course. Yet his efforts—rendered infinitely more complex by the belligerence of the traditionalist faction of the Chinese court, which periodically insisted on meeting the foreign powers in battle with minimal preparation—demonstrate a remarkable ability to navigate between, and usually mitigate, late-Qing China's severely unattractive alternatives.

Li made his reputation in crisis, emerging as an expert in military affairs and "barbarian management" during China's midcentury rebellions. In 1862 Li was sent to administer the wealthy eastern province of Jiangsu, where he found its main cities besieged by Taiping rebels but secured by Western-led armies determined to defend their new commercial privileges. Applying the maxims of the Gong memorandum, Li allied himself with—and established himself as the ultimate authority over—the Western forces in order to destroy their common foe. During what was effectively a joint Chinese-Western counterinsurgency campaign, Li forged a working relationship with Charles "Chinese" Gordon, the famous British adventurer later killed by the Mahdi in the siege of Khartoum in the Sudan. (Li and Gordon eventually fell out when Li ordered the execution of captured rebel leaders to whom Gordon had promised clemency.) With the Taiping threat quelled in 1864, Li was promoted to a series of increasingly prominent positions, emerging as China's de facto foreign minister and the chief negotiator in its frequent foreign crises.[21]

The representative of a society under siege by vastly more powerful countries and significantly different cultures has two choices. He can attempt to close the cultural gap, adopt the manners of the militarily stronger and thereby reduce the pressures resulting from the temptation to discriminate against the culturally strange. Or he can insist on the validity of his own culture by flaunting its special characteristics and gain respect for the strength of its convictions.

In the nineteenth century Japanese leaders took the first course, aided by the fact that when they encountered the West their country was already well on the way to industrialization and had demonstrated its social cohesion. Li, representing a country wracked by rebellion for whose defeat he needed foreign help, did not have that option. Nor would he have shed his Confucian provenance, whatever the benefits of such a course.

An account of Li Hongzhang's travels within China serves as a grim record of China's turmoil: within one fairly representative two-year period in 1869–71, he was catapulted between southwest China, where French representatives had raised a protest over anti-Christian riots; to the north, where a new set of riots had broken out; back to the far southwest, where a minority tribe on the Vietnamese border was in revolt; then to the northwest to address a major Muslim rebellion; from there to the port of Tianjin in the northeast, where a massacre of Christians had drawn French warships and a threat of military intervention; and finally to the southeast, where a new crisis was brewing on the island of Taiwan (then known in the West as Formosa).[22]

Li cut a distinctive figure on a diplomatic stage dominated by Western-defined codes of conduct. He wore the flowing robes of a Confucian mandarin and proudly sported ancient designations of rank, such as the "Double-Eyed Peacock Feather" and the "Yellow Jacket," that his Western counterparts could only observe with bewilderment. His head was shaved—in the Qing style—except for a long braided ponytail, and covered by an oblong official's cap. He spoke epigrammatically in a language that only a handful of foreigners understood. He carried himself with such otherworldly serenity that one British contemporary compared him, with a mixture of awe and incomprehension, to a visitor from another planet. China's travails and concessions, his demeanor seemed to suggest, were but temporary obstacles on the route to the ultimate triumph of Chinese civilization. His mentor, Zeng Guofan, a top-ranking Confucian scholar and veteran commander of the Taiping campaigns, had advised Li in 1862 how to use the basic Confucian value of self-restraint as a diplomatic tool: "In your association with foreigners, your manner and deportment should not be too lofty, and you should have a slightly vague, casual appearance. Let their insults, deceitfulness, and contempt for everything appear to be understood by you and yet seem not understood, for you should look somewhat stupid."[23]

Like every other Chinese high official of his era, Li believed in the superiority of China's moral values and the justness of its traditional imperial prerogatives. Where he differed was less in his assessment of China's superiority than in his diagnosis that it lacked, for the time being, a material or military basis. Having studied Western weaponry during the Taiping conflict and sought out information on foreign economic trends, he realized that China was falling dangerously out of phase with the rest of the world. As he warned the Emperor in a bluntly worded 1872 policy memorial: "To live today and still say 'reject the barbarians' and 'drive them out of our territory' is certainly superficial and absurd talk. . . . They are daily producing their weapons to strive with us for supremacy and victory, pitting their superior techniques against our inadequacies."[24]

Li had reached a conclusion similar to Wei Yuan's—though by now the problem of reform was exponentially more urgent than in Wei Yuan's time. Thus Li warned:

> The present situation is one in which, externally, it is necessary for us to be harmonious with the barbarians, and internally, it is necessary for us to reform our institutions. If we remain conservative, without making any change, the nation will be daily reduced and weakened. . . . Now all the foreign countries are having one reform after another, and progressing every day like the ascending of steam. Only China continues to preserve her traditional institutions so cautiously that even though she be ruined and extinguished, the conservatives will not regret it.[25]

During a series of landmark Chinese policy debates in the 1860s, Li and his bureaucratic allies outlined a course of action they named "self-strengthening." In one 1863 memorandum, Li took as his starting point (and as a means of softening the blow for his imperial readership) that "[e]verything in China's civil and military system is far superior to that in the West. Only in firearms is it absolutely impossible to catch up with them."[26] But in light of its recent catastrophes, Li counseled, China's elite could no longer afford to look down on foreign innovations, "sneer[ing] at the sharp weapons of foreign countries as things produced by strange techniques and tricky craft, which they consider it unnecessary to learn."[27] What China needed was firearms, steamships, and heavy machinery, as well as the knowledge and the techniques to produce them.

In order to enhance Chinese capacity to study foreign texts and blueprints and converse with foreign experts, young Chinese needed to be trained in foreign languages (an undertaking heretofore dismissed as unnecessary, since all foreigners presumably aspired to become Chinese). Li argued that China should open schools in its major cities—including its capital, which it had fought so long to safeguard from foreign influence—to teach foreign languages and engineering techniques. Li framed the project as a challenge: "Are Chinese wisdom and intelligence inferior to those of Westerners? If we have really mastered the Western languages and, in turn, teach one another, then all their clever techniques of steamships and firearms can be gradually and thoroughly learned."[28]

Prince Gong struck a similar note in an 1866 proposal urging that the Emperor support the study of Western scientific innovations:

> What we desire is that our students shall get to the bottom of these subjects . . . for we are firmly convinced that if we are able to master the mysteries of mathematical calculation, physical investigation, astronomical observation, construction of engines, engineering of water-courses, this, and this only, will assure the steady growth of the power of the empire.[29]

China needed to open up to the outside world—and to learn from countries heretofore considered vassals and barbarians—first to strengthen its traditional structure and then to regain its preeminence.

This would have been a heroic task had the Chinese court been unified behind Prince Gong's foreign policy concept and Li Hongzhang's execution of it. In fact, a vast gulf separated these more outward-looking officials from the more insular traditionalist faction. The latter adhered to the classical view that China had nothing to learn from foreigners, as given voice by the ancient philosopher Mencius in Confucius's era: "I have heard of men using the doctrines of our great land to change barbarians, but I have never yet heard of any being changed by the barbarians."[30] In the same vein Wo-ren, the chancellor of the prestigious Hanlin Academy of Confucian scholarship, assailed Prince Gong's plans to hire foreign instructors in Chinese schools:

> The foundation of an empire rests on propriety and righteousness, not on schemes and stratagems. Its roots lie in the hearts of men, not skills and crafts. Now for the sake of a trivial knack, we are to honor barbarians as our masters. . . . The empire is vast and abundant in human talents. If astronomy and mathematics must be studied, there are bound to be some Chinese who are well-versed in them.[31]

The belief in China's self-sufficiency represented the combined experience of millennia. Yet it supplied no answer to how China was to confront its immediate peril, especially how to catch up with Western technology. Many of China's top-ranking officials still seemed to assume that the solution to China's foreign problems lay in executing or exiling its negotiators. Li Hongzhang was stripped of his rank in disgrace three times while Beijing challenged the foreign powers; but each time he was recalled because his opponents could find no better alternative than to rely on his diplomatic skills to solve the crises they had generated.

Torn between the compulsions of a weak state and the claims of a universal empire, China's reforms proceeded haltingly. Eventually a palace coup forced the abdication of a reform-leaning Emperor and returned the traditionalists, headed by the Empress Dowager Cixi, to a predominant position. In the absence of fundamental internal modernization and reform, China's diplomats were, in effect, asked to limit the damage to China's territorial integrity and to stem further erosions in its sovereignty without being supplied the means to alter China's basic weakness. They were to gain time without a plan for using the time they gained. And nowhere was this challenge more acute than in the rise of a new entrant into the balance of power in Northeast Asia—a rapidly industrializing Japan.

The Challenge of Japan

Unlike most of China's neighbors, Japan had for centuries resisted incorporation into the Sinocentric world order. Situated on an archipelago some one hundred miles off the Asian mainland at the closest crossing, Japan long cultivated its traditions and distinctive culture in isolation. Possessed of ethnic and linguistic near homogeneity and an official ideology that stressed the Japanese people's divine ancestry, Japan nurtured an almost religious commitment to its unique identity.

At the apex of Japan's society and its own world order stood the Japanese Emperor, a figure conceived, like the Chinese Son of Heaven, as an intermediary between the human and the divine. Taken literally, Japan's traditional political philosophy posited that Japanese Emperors were deities descended from the Sun Goddess, who gave birth to the first Emperor and endowed his descendants with an eternal right to rule. Thus Japan, like China, conceived of itself as far more than an ordinary state.[32] The title "Emperor" itself—insistently displayed on Japanese diplomatic dispatches to the Chinese court—was a direct challenge to the Chinese world order. In China's cosmology, mankind had only one Emperor, and his throne was in China.[33]

If Chinese exceptionalism represented the claims of a universal empire, Japanese exceptionalism sprang from the insecurities of an island nation borrowing heavily from its neighbor, but fearful of being dominated by it. The Chinese sense of uniqueness asserted that China was the one true civilization, and invited barbarians to the Middle Kingdom to "come and be transformed." The Japanese attitude assumed a unique Japanese racial and cultural purity, and declined to extend its benefits or even explain itself to those born outside its sacred ancestral bonds.[34]

For long periods, Japan had withdrawn from foreign affairs almost entirely, as if even intermittent contacts with outsiders would compromise Japan's unique identity. To the extent that Japan participated in an international order, it did so by means of its own tribute system in the Ryukyu Islands (modern-day Okinawa and the surrounding islands) and various kingdoms on the Korean Peninsula. With a certain irony, Japan's leaders borrowed this most Chinese of institutions as a means of asserting their independence from China.[35]

Other Asian peoples accepted the protocol of the Chinese tribute system, labeling their trade as "tribute" to gain access to Chinese markets. Japan refused to conduct its trade with China in the guise of tribute. It insisted on at least equality to China, if not superiority. Despite the natural ties of trade between China and Japan, seventeenth-century discussions over bilateral trade deadlocked because neither side would honor the protocol required by the other's pretensions of world-centrality.[36]

If China's sphere of influence waxed and waned along its long frontiers in accordance with the power of the empire and the surrounding tribes, Japan's leaders came to conceive of their security dilemma as a much starker choice. Possessing a sense of superiority as pronounced as the Chinese court's but perceiving their margin of error as far smaller, Japanese statesmen looked warily west—to a continent dominated by a succession of Chinese dynasties, some of which extended their writ into Japan's closest neighbor, Korea—and tended to see an existential challenge. Japanese foreign policy thus alternated, at times with startling suddenness, between aloofness from the Asian mainland and audacious attempts at conquest geared toward supplanting the Sinocentric order.

Japan, like China, encountered Western ships wielding unfamiliar technology and overwhelming force in the mid-nineteenth century—in Japan's case, the 1853 landing of the American Commodore Matthew Perry's "black ships." But Japan drew from the challenge the opposite conclusion as China: it threw open its doors to foreign technology and overhauled its institutions in an attempt to replicate the Western powers' rise. (In Japan, this conclusion may have been assisted by the fact that foreign ideas were not seen as connected to the question of opium addiction, which Japan largely managed to avoid.) In 1868, the Meiji Emperor, in his charter oath, announced Japan's resolve: "Knowledge shall be sought from all over the world, and thereby the foundations of the imperial rule shall be strengthened."[37]

Japan's Meiji Restoration and drive to master Western technology opened the door to stunning economic progress. As Japan developed a modern economy and a formidable military apparatus, it began to insist on the prerogatives afforded the Western great powers. Its governing elite concluded that, in the words of Shimazu Nariakira, a nineteenth-century lord and leading advocate of technological modernization, "If we take the initiative, we can dominate; if we do not, we will be dominated."[38]

As early as 1863, Li Hongzhang concluded that Japan would become China's principal security threat. Even before the Meiji Restoration, Li wrote of the Japanese response to the Western challenge. In 1874, after Japan seized on an incident between Taiwanese tribesmen and a shipwrecked Ryukyu Islands crew to mount a punitive expedition,[39] he wrote of Japan:

> Her power is daily expanding, and her ambition is not small. Therefore she dares to display her strength in eastern lands, despises China, and takes action by invading Taiwan. Although the various European powers are strong, they are still 70,000 li away from us, whereas Japan is as near as the courtyard or the threshold and is prying into our emptiness and solitude. Undoubtedly, she will become China's permanent and great anxiety.[40]

Viewing the lumbering giant to its west with its increasingly hollow pretensions to world supremacy, the Japanese had begun to conceive of supplanting China as the predominant Asian power. The struggle between these competing claims came to a head in a country at the intersection of its larger neighbors' ambitions—Korea.

Korea

The Chinese Empire was extensive but not intrusive. It demanded tribute and the recognition of the Emperor's suzerainty. But the tribute was more symbolic than substantive, and suzerainty was exercised in a way that allowed for autonomy almost indistinguishable from independence. By the nineteenth century the fiercely independent Koreans had reached a practical accommodation with the Chinese giant to their north and west. Korea was technically a tributary state and Korean Kings regularly sent tribute to Beijing. Korea had adopted Confucian moral codes and Chinese written characters for formal correspondence. Beijing, in turn, had a strong interest in developments on the peninsula, whose geographic position established it as a potential invasion corridor to China from the sea.

Korea played in some ways a mirror-image role in Japan's conception of its strategic imperatives. Japan, too, saw foreign dominance of Korea as a potential threat. The peninsula's position jutting out from the Asian mainland toward Japan had tempted the Mongols to use it as a launching point for two attempted invasions of the Japanese archipelago. Now with Chinese imperial influence waning, Japan sought to secure a dominant position on the Korean Peninsula, and began asserting its own economic and political claims.

Throughout the 1870s and 1880s, China and Japan engaged in a series of court intrigues in Seoul, sparring for predominance amongst royal factions. As Korea found itself beset by foreign ambitions, Li Hongzhang advised the Korean rulers to learn from the Chinese experiences with the invaders. It was to organize a competition among potential colonizers by inviting them in. In an October 1879 letter to a high Korean official, Li counseled that Korea should seek a supporter among the far barbarians, especially the United States:

> You may say that the simplest way to avoid trouble would be to shut oneself in and be at peace. Alas, as far as the East is concerned, this is not possible. There is no human agency capable of putting a stop to the expansionist movement of Japan: has not your government been compelled to inaugurate a new era by making a Treaty of Commerce with them? As matters stand, therefore, is not our best course to neutralize one poison by another, to set one energy against another?[41]

On this basis, Li proposed that Korea "seize every opportunity to establish treaty relations with Western nations, of which you would make use to check Japan." Western trade, he warned, would bring "corrupting influences" such as opium and Christianity; but in contrast to Japan and Russia, which sought territorial gains, the Western powers' "only object would be to trade with your kingdom." The goal should be to balance the dangers from each outside power, allowing none to predominate: "Since you are aware of the strength of your adversaries, use all possible means to divide them; go warily, use cunning—thus will you prove yourselves good strategists."[42] Li left unstated the Chinese interest in Korea—either because he took for granted that Chinese overlordship was not a threat of the same nature as other foreign influences, or because he had concluded that China had no practical means to secure a Korea free from foreign influence.

Inevitably Chinese and Japanese claims to a special relationship with Korea grew incompatible. In 1894, both Japan and China dispatched troops in response to a Korean rebellion. Japan eventually seized the Korean King and installed a pro-Japanese government. Nationalists in both Beijing and Tokyo called for war; only Japan, however, had the benefit of a modern naval force, funds initially levied for the modernization of the Chinese navy having been requisitioned for improvements to the Summer Palace.

Within hours of the outbreak of war, Japan destroyed China's poorly funded naval forces, the ostensible achievement of decades of self-strengthening. Li Hongzhang was recalled from one of his periodic forced retirements to go to the Japanese city of Shimonoseki to negotiate a peace treaty, with the almost impossible mission of salvaging Chinese dignity from the military catastrophe. The side that has the upper hand in war often has an incentive to delay a settlement, especially if every passing day improves its bargaining position. This is why Japan had deepened China's humiliation by rejecting a string of proposed Chinese negotiators as having insufficient protocol rank—a deliberate insult to an empire that had heretofore presented its diplomats as embodiments of heavenly prerogatives and therefore outranking all others, whatever their Chinese rank.

The terms under discussion at Shimonoseki were a brutal shock to the Chinese vision of preeminence. China was obliged to cede Taiwan to Japan; to desist from tributary ceremony with Korea and recognize its independence (in practice opening it up to further Japanese influence); to pay a significant war indemnity; and to cede to Japan the Liaodong Peninsula in Manchuria, including the strategically located harbors of Dalian and Lushun (Port Arthur). Only a would-be assassin's bullet from a Japanese nationalist spared China an even more demeaning outcome. Grazing Li's face at the scene of the negotiations, it shamed the Japanese government into dropping a few of its more sweeping demands.

Li continued to negotiate from his hospital bed, to show that he was unbowed in humiliation. His stoicism may have been influenced by the fact that he knew that, even as the negotiations proceeded, Chinese diplomats were approaching other powers with interests in China, in particular Russia, whose expansion to the Pacific had needed to be dealt with by Chinese diplomacy since the end of the 1860 war. Li had foreseen the rivalry of Japan and Russia in Korea and Manchuria, and he had instructed his diplomats, in 1894, to treat Russia with the utmost sensitivity. No sooner had Li returned from Shimonoseki than he secured Moscow's leadership of a "Triple Intervention" by Russia, France, and Germany that forced Japan to return the Liaodong Peninsula to China.

It was a maneuver with far-reaching consequences. For once again, Moscow practiced its by now well-established interpretation of Sino-Russian friendship. For its services, it extracted special rights in another huge swath of Chinese territory. This time it was subtle enough not to do so outright. Rather, in the wake of the Triple Intervention it summoned Li to Moscow to sign a secret treaty containing an ingenious and transparently acquisitive clause stipulating that in order to guarantee China's security against potential further Japanese attacks, Russia would construct an extension of the Trans-Siberian Railway across Manchuria. In the secret agreement, Moscow pledged not to use the railway as a "pretext for the infringement of Chinese territory, or for encroachment on the lawful rights and privileges of H[is] I[mperial]

M[ajesty] the Emperor of China"[43]—which was, however, exactly what Moscow now proceeded to do. Inevitably, once the railway was constructed, Moscow insisted that the territory adjoining it would require Russian forces to protect the investment. Within a few years, Russia had acquired control over the area Japan had been forced to relinquish, and significantly more.

It proved to be Li's most controversial legacy. The intervention had forestalled the advances of Japan, at least temporarily, but at the cost of establishing Russia as a dominant influence in Manchuria. The Czar's establishment of a sphere of influence in Manchuria precipitated a scramble for comparable concessions by all the established powers. Each country responded to the advances of the others. Germany occupied Qingdao in the Shandong Peninsula. France obtained an enclave in Guangdong and solidified its hold over Vietnam. Britain expanded its presence in the New Territories across from Hong Kong and acquired a naval base opposite Port Arthur.

The strategy of balancing the barbarians had worked to a degree. None had become totally predominant in China, and in that margin, the Beijing government could operate. But the clever maneuver of saving the essence of China by bringing in outside powers to conduct their balance-of-power machinations on Chinese territory could function in the long run only if China remained strong enough to be taken seriously. And China's claim to central control was disintegrating.

Appeasement has become an epithet in the aftermath of the conduct of the Western democracies toward Hitler in the 1930s. But confrontation can be safely pursued only if the weaker is in a position to make its defeat costly beyond the tolerance of the stronger. Otherwise, some degree of conciliation is the only prudent course. The democracies unfortunately practiced it when they were militarily stronger. But appeasement is also politically risky and stakes social cohesion. For it requires the public to retain confidence in its leaders even as they appear to yield to the victors' demands.

Such was Li's dilemma through the decades he sought to navigate China between European, Russian, and Japanese rapaciousness and the intransigent obtuseness of his own court. Later Chinese generations have acknowledged Li Hongzhang's skill but have been ambivalent or hostile about the concessions to which he lent his signature, most notably to Russia and Japan, as well as ceding Taiwan to Japan. Such a policy grated at the dignity of a proud society. Nevertheless, it enabled China to preserve the elements of sovereignty, however attenuated, through a century of colonial expansion in which every other targeted country lost its independence altogether. It transcended humiliation by seeming to adapt to it.

Li summed up the impetus of his diplomacy in a mournful memorial to the Empress Dowager shortly before his death in 1901:

> Needless for me to say how greatly I would rejoice were it possible for China to enter upon a glorious and triumphant war; it would be the joy of my closing days to see the barbarian nations subjugated at last in submissive allegiance, respectfully making obeisance to the Dragon Throne. Unfortunately, however, I cannot but recognize the melancholy fact that China is unequal to such an enterprise, and that our forces are in no way competent to undertake it. Looking at the question as one affecting chiefly the integrity of our Empire, who would be so foolish as to cast missiles at a rat in the vicinity of a priceless piece of porcelain?[44]

The strategy of pitting Russia against Japan in Manchuria produced a rivalry in which both powers progressively tested each other. In its relentless expansion, Russia jettisoned the tacit agreement among the exploiters of China to maintain some balance between their respective claims and a degree of continuing Chinese sovereignty.

The competing claims of Japan and Russia in northeast China led to a war for preeminence in 1904, ending in Japanese victory. The 1905 Treaty of Portsmouth gave Japan the dominant position in Korea and potentially in Manchuria, though less than what its victory might have made possible, due to the intervention of the American President, Theodore Roosevelt. His mediations of the end of the Russo-Japanese War based on principles of balance of power, rare in American diplomacy, kept Japan from seizing Manchuria and preserved an equilibrium in Asia. Stymied in Asia, Russia returned its strategic priorities to Europe, a process that accelerated the outbreak of the First World War.

The Boxer Uprising and the New Era of Warring States

By the end of the nineteenth century, the Chinese world order was totally out of joint; the court in Beijing no longer functioned as a meaningful factor in protecting either Chinese culture or autonomy. Popular frustration boiled to the surface in 1898, in the so-called Boxer Uprising. Practicing a form of ancient mysticism and claiming magical immunity to foreign bullets, the Boxers—so called because of their traditional martial arts exercises—mounted a campaign of violent agitation against foreigners and the symbols of the new order they had imposed. Diplomats, Chinese Christians, railroads, telegraph lines, and Western schools all came under attack. Perhaps judging that the Manchu court (itself a "foreign" imposition, and no longer a particularly effective one) risked becoming the next target, the Empress Dowager embraced the Boxers, praising their attacks. The epicenter of the conflict was once again the long-contested foreign embassies in Beijing—which the Boxers besieged in the spring of 1900. After a century of vacillating between haughty disdain, defiance, and anguished conciliation, China now entered a state of war against all of the foreign powers simultaneously.[45]

The consequence was another harsh blow. An Eight-Power allied expeditionary force—consisting of France, Britain, the United States,

Japan, Russia, Germany, Austria-Hungary, and Italy—arrived in Beijing in August 1900 to relieve the embassies. After suppressing the Boxers and allied Qing troops (and laying waste to much of the capital in the process), they dictated another "unequal treaty" imposing a cash indemnity and granting further occupation rights to the foreign powers.[46]

A dynasty unable to prevent repeated foreign marches on the Chinese capital or to forestall foreign exactions from Chinese territory had plainly lost the Mandate of Heaven. The Qing Dynasty, having prolonged its existence for a remarkable seven decades since the initial clash with the West, collapsed in 1912.

China's central authority was again fractured, and it entered another period of warring states. A Chinese Republic, deeply divided from its birth, emerged into a dangerous international environment. But it never had the opportunity to practice democratic virtues. The nationalist leader Sun Yat-sen was proclaimed president of the new republic in January 1912. As if by some mysterious law commanding imperial unity, Sun, after just six weeks in office, deferred to Yuan Shikai, commander of the only military force capable of unifying the country. After the failure of Yuan's abortive declaration of a new imperial dynasty in 1916, political power devolved into the hands of regional governors and military commanders. Meanwhile in the Chinese heartland, the new Chinese Communist Party, established in 1921, administered a kind of shadow government and parallel social order loosely aligned with the world Communist movement. Each of these aspirants claimed the right to rule, but none was strong enough to prevail over the others.

Left without a universally acknowledged central authority, China lacked the instrument for the conduct of its traditional diplomacy. By the end of the 1920s the Nationalist Party, led by Chiang Kai-shek, exercised nominal control over the entirety of the ancient Qing Empire. In practice, however, China's traditional territorial prerogatives were increasingly challenged.

Exhausted by their exertions in the war and in a world influenced by Wilsonian principles of self-determination, the Western powers were no longer in a position to extend their spheres of influence in China; they were barely able to sustain them. Russia was consolidating its internal revolution and in no position to undertake further expansion. Germany was deprived of its colonies altogether.

Of the former contestants for dominance in China, only one was left, albeit the most dangerous to China's independence: Japan. China was not strong enough to defend itself. And no other country was available to balance Japan militarily. After the defeat of Germany in the First World War, Japan occupied the former German concessions in Shandong. In 1932, Tokyo engineered the creation of a secessionist Japanese-dominated state of Manchukuo in Manchuria. In 1937, it embarked on a program of conquest across much of eastern China.

Japan now found itself in the position of previous conquerors. It was difficult enough to conquer such a vast country; it was impossible to administer it without relying on some of its cultural precepts, which Japan, prizing the uniqueness of its own institutions, was never prepared to do. Gradually, its erstwhile partners—the European powers backed by the United States—began to move into opposition to Japan, first politically and eventually militarily. It was a kind of culmination of the policy of the self-strengthening diplomacy, with the former colonialists now cooperating to vindicate the integrity of China.

The leader of this effort was the United States, and its instrument was the Open Door policy proclaimed by Secretary of State John Hay in 1899. Originally intended to claim for the United States the benefits of other countries' individual imperialism, it was transformed in the 1930s into a way to preserve China's independence. The Western powers joined the effort. China would now be able to overcome the imperialist phase, provided it could survive the Second World War and once again forge its unity.

With the Japanese surrender in 1945, China was left devastated and divided. The Nationalists and Communists both aspired to central authority. Two million Japanese soldiers remained on Chinese territory for repatriation. The Soviet Union recognized the Nationalist government but had kept its options open by supplying arms to the Communist Party; at the same time, it had rushed a massive and uninvited Soviet military force into northeast China to restore some of their erstwhile colonial claims. Beijing's tenuous control of Xinjiang had eroded further. Tibet and Mongolia had gravitated into quasi-autonomy, aligned with the respective orbits of the British Empire and the Soviet Union.

United States public opinion sympathized with Chiang Kai-shek as a wartime ally. But Chiang Kai-shek was governing a fragment of a country already fragmented by foreign occupation. China was treated as one of the "Big Five" who would organize the postwar world and were granted a veto in the United Nations Security Council. Of the five, only the United States and the Soviet Union possessed the power to carry out this mission.

A renewal of the Chinese civil war followed. Washington sought to apply its standard solution to such civil conflict, which has failed time after time then and in the decades afterward. It urged a coalition between the Nationalists and Communists, who had been battling each other for two decades. U.S. Ambassador Patrick Hurley convened a meeting between Chiang Kai-shek and Communist Party leader Mao Zedong in September 1945 at Chiang's capital in Chongqing. Both leaders dutifully attended while preparing for a final showdown.

No sooner had the Hurley meeting concluded than the two sides recommenced hostilities. Chiang's Nationalist forces opted for a strategy of holding cities, while Mao's guerrilla armies based themselves in the countryside; each sought to surround the other using *wei qi* strategies of encirclement.[47] Amidst clamor for American intervention in support of the Nationalists, President Harry Truman sent General George Marshall to China for a yearlong effort to encourage the two sides to agree to work together. During that time, the Nationalist military position was collapsing.

Defeated by the Communists on the mainland, Nationalist troops retreated to the island of Taiwan in 1949. The Nationalists brought with them their military apparatus, political class, and remnants of national authority (including Chinese artistic and cultural treasures from the Imperial Palace collection).[48] They declared the relocation of the Republic of China's capital to Taipei, and maintained that they would husband their strength and someday return to the mainland. They retained the Chinese seat in the United Nations Security Council.

Meanwhile, China was uniting again, under the newly proclaimed People's Republic of China. Communist China launched itself into a new world: in structure, a new dynasty; in substance, a new ideology for the first time in Chinese history. Strategically, it abutted over a dozen neighbors, with open frontiers and inadequate means to deal simultaneously with each potential threat—the same challenge that had confronted Chinese governments throughout history. Overarching all these concerns, the new leaders of China faced the involvement in Asian affairs of the United States, which had emerged from the Second World War as a confident superpower, with second thoughts about its passivity when confronted with the Communist victory in the Chinese civil war. Every statesman needs to balance the experience of the past against the claims of the future. Nowhere was this more true than in the China that Mao and the Communist Party had just taken over.

CHAPTER 4

Mao's Continuous Revolution

THE ADVENT OF a new dynasty in China had, over the millennia, developed a distinct rhythm. The old dynasty would begin to be perceived as failing in its mission of protecting the security of the Chinese population or fulfilling its fundamental aspirations. Rarely as the result of a single catastrophe, most frequently through the cumulative impact of a series of disasters, the ruling dynasty would, in the view of the Chinese people, lose the Mandate of Heaven. The new dynasty would be seen as having achieved it, in part by the mere fact of having established itself.

This kind of upheaval had happened many times in China's dramatic history. But no new ruler had ever proposed to overthrow the value system of the entire society. Previous claimants to the Mandate of Heaven—even, and perhaps especially, foreign conquerors—had legitimized themselves by affirming the ancient values of the society they took over and governing by its maxims. They maintained the bureaucracy they inherited, if only to be able to govern a country more populous and richer than any other. This tradition was the mechanism of the process of Sinification. It established Confucianism as the governing doctrine of China.

At the head of the new dynasty that, in 1949, poured out of the countryside to take over the cities stood a colossus: Mao Zedong.

Domineering and overwhelming in his influence, ruthless and aloof, poet and warrior, prophet and scourge, he unified China and launched it on a journey that nearly wrecked its civil society. By the end of this searing process, China stood as one of the world's major powers and the only Communist country except Cuba, North Korea, and Vietnam whose political structure survived the collapse of Communism everywhere else.

Mao and the Great Harmony

Revolutionaries are, by their nature, powerful and single-minded personalities. Almost invariably they start from a position of weakness vis-à-vis the political environment and rely for their success on charisma and on an ability to mobilize resentment and to capitalize on the psychological weakness of adversaries in decline.

Most revolutions have been on behalf of a specific cause. Once successful, they have been institutionalized into a new system of order. Mao's revolution had no final resting place; the ultimate goal of "Great Harmony" that he proclaimed was a vague vision, more akin to spiritual exaltation than political reconstruction. Cadres of the Communist Party were its priesthood, except their task was crusading, not fulfilling a defined program. Under Mao, cadres also led a life at the edge of perdition. For them, there was always the danger—over time the near certainty—of being engulfed in the very upheavals they were incited to promote. The roster of leaders of the second generation (that of Deng Xiaoping) had almost all suffered that fate, returning to power only after periods of great personal trial. Every close associate of Mao during the revolutionary period—including in the end his long-serving Premier and chief diplomat Zhou Enlai—was eventually purged.

It was no accident that the Chinese ruler whom Mao most admired was the founding Emperor Qin Shihuang, who ended the Period of the Warring States by triumphing over all other rivals and unifying them into a single polity in 221 B.C. Qin Shihuang is generally considered the founder of China as a unified state. Yet he has never been afforded ultimate respect in Chinese history because he burned books and persecuted traditional Confucian scholars (burying 460 of them alive). Mao once remarked that China's governance required a combination of Marx's methods and Qin Shihuang's, and he eulogized the Emperor in a poem:

> *Please don't slander Emperor Qin Shihuang, Sir*
> *For the burning of the books should be thought through again.*
> *Our ancestral dragon, though dead, lives on in spirit,*
> *While Confucius, though renowned, was really no one.*
> *The Qin order has survived from age to age.*[1]

Mao's China was, by design, a country in permanent crisis; from the earliest days of Communist governance, Mao unleashed wave after wave of struggle. The Chinese people would not be permitted ever to rest on their achievements. The destiny Mao prescribed for them was to purify their society and themselves through virtuous exertion.

Mao was the first ruler since the unification of China to tear apart Chinese traditions as a deliberate act of state policy. He conceived of himself as rejuvenating China by dismantling, at times violently, its ancient heritage. As he proclaimed to the French philosopher André Malraux in 1965:

> The thought, culture, and customs which brought China to where we found her must disappear, and the thought, customs, and culture of proletarian China, which does not yet exist, must appear. . . . Thought, culture, customs must be born of struggle, and the struggle must continue for as long as there is still danger of a return to the past.[2]

China, Mao once vowed, was to be "smashed" like an atom, in order to destroy the old order but, at the same time, produce an explosion of popular energy to lift it to ever greater heights of achievement:

> Now our enthusiasm has been aroused. Ours is an ardent nation, now swept by a burning tide. There is a good metaphor for this: our nation is like an atom. . . . When this atom's nucleus is smashed the thermal energy released will have really tremendous power. We shall be able to do things which we could not do before.[3]

As part of this process, Mao generated a pervasive assault on traditional Chinese political thought: where the Confucian tradition prized universal harmony, Mao idealized upheaval and the clash of opposing forces, in both domestic and foreign affairs (and, indeed, he saw the two as connected—regularly pairing foreign crises with domestic purges or ideological campaigns). The Confucian tradition prized the doctrine of the mean and the cultivation of balance and moderation; when reform occurred, it was incremental and put forward as the "restoration" of previously held values. Mao, by contrast, sought radical and instant transformation and a total break with the past. Traditional Chinese political theory held military force in relative disesteem and insisted that Chinese rulers achieved stability at home and influence abroad through their virtue and compassion. Mao, driven by his ideology and his anguish over China's century of humiliation, produced an unprecedented militarization of Chinese life. Where traditional China revered the past and cherished a rich literary culture, Mao declared war on China's traditional art, culture, and modes of thought.

In many ways, however, Mao incarnated the dialectic contradictions that he claimed to be manipulating. He was passionately and publicly anti-Confucian, yet he read widely in Chinese classics and was wont to quote from the ancient texts. Mao enunciated the doctrine of "continuous revolution," but when the Chinese national interest required it, he could be patient and take the long view. The manipulation of "contradictions" was his proclaimed strategy, yet it was in the service of an ultimate goal drawn from the Confucian concept of *da tong,* or the Great Harmony.

Maoist governance thus turned into a version of the Confucian tradition through the looking glass, proclaiming a total break with the past while relying on many of China's traditional institutions, including an imperial style of governance; the state as an ethical project; and a mandarin bureaucracy that Mao loathed, periodically destroyed, and, in the end, equally periodically was obliged to re-create.

Mao's ultimate objectives could not be expressed in a single organizational structure or be fulfilled by realizing a specific set of political objectives. His goal was to sustain the process of revolution itself, which he felt it was his special mission to carry on through ever greater upheavals, never permitting a resting point until his people emerged from the ordeal purified and transformed:

> To be overthrown is painful and is unbearable to contemplate for those overthrown, for example, for the Kuomintang [Nationalist Party] reactionaries whom we are now overthrowing and for Japanese imperialism which we together with other peoples overthrew some time ago. But for the working class, the labouring people and the Communist Party the question is not one of being overthrown, but of working hard to create the conditions in which classes, state power and political parties will die out very naturally and mankind will enter the realm of Great Harmony.[4]

In traditional China, the Emperor had been the linchpin of the Great Harmony of all living things. By his virtuous example, he was perceived to keep the existing cosmic order in joint and maintain the equilibrium between heaven, man, and nature. In the Chinese view, the Emperor "transformed" rebellious barbarians and brought them to heel; he was the pinnacle of the Confucian hierarchy, assigning to all people their proper place in society.

This is why, until the modern period, China did not pursue the ideal of "progress" in the Western sense. The Chinese impetus for public service was the concept of rectification—the bringing of order to a society that had been allowed to fall into dangerous imbalance. Confucius declared as his mission to try to *recover* profound truths that his society had neglected, thereby restoring it to a golden age.

Mao saw his role as diametrically the opposite. The Great Harmony came at the end of a painful process likely to claim as victims all who traversed it. In Mao's interpretation of history, the Confucian order had kept China weak; its "harmony" was a form of subjugation. Progress would come only through a series of brutal tests pitting contradictory forces against each other both domestically as well as internationally. And if these contradictions did not appear by themselves, it was the obligation of the Communist Party and its leader to keep a permanent upheaval going, against itself if necessary.

In 1958, at the outset of the nationwide program of economic collectivization known as the Great Leap Forward, Mao outlined his vision of China in perpetual motion. Each wave of revolutionary exertion, he proclaimed, was organically a precursor to a new upheaval whose beginning needed to be hastened lest the revolutionaries became indolent and start resting on their laurels:

> Our revolutions are like battles. After a victory, we must at once put forward a new task. In this way, cadres and the masses will forever be filled with revolutionary fervour, instead of conceit. Indeed, they will have no time for conceit, even if they like to feel conceited. With new tasks on their

> shoulders, they are totally preoccupied with the problems for their fulfillment.[5]

The cadres of the revolution were to be tested by ever more difficult challenges at shorter and shorter intervals. "Disequilibrium is a general, objective rule," wrote Mao:

> The cycle, which is endless, evolves from disequilibrium to equilibrium and then to disequilibrium again. Each cycle, however, brings us to a higher level of development. Disequilibrium is normal and absolute whereas equilibrium is temporary and relative.[6]

But how can a state in permanent upheaval participate in the international system? If it applies the doctrine of continuous revolution literally, it will be involved in constant turmoil and, likely, in war. The states that prize stability will unite against it. But if it tries to shape an international order open to others, a clash with the votaries of continuous revolution is inevitable. This dilemma beset Mao all his life and was never finally resolved.

Mao and International Relations: The Empty City Stratagem, Chinese Deterrence, and the Quest for Psychological Advantage

Mao proclaimed his basic attitude toward international affairs on the eve of taking power. Before the newly assembled People's Political Consultative Conference, he summed up China's attitude toward the prevailing international order in the phrase "The Chinese people have stood up":

> We have a common feeling that our work will be recorded in the history of mankind, and that it will clearly demonstrate that the Chinese, who comprise one quarter of humanity, have begun to stand up. The Chinese have always been a great, courageous and industrious people. It was only in modern times that they have fallen behind, and this was due solely to the oppression and exploitation of foreign imperialism and the domestic reactionary government. . . . Our predecessors instructed us to carry their work to completion. We are doing this now. We have united ourselves and defeated both our foreign and domestic oppressors by means of the people's liberation war and the people's great revolution, and we proclaim the establishment of the People's Republic of China.[7]

To stand up to the world was a daunting prospect for China in 1949. The country was underdeveloped, without the military capacity to impose its own preferences on a world that vastly outmatched it in resources and, above all, in technology. When the People's Republic emerged on the world stage, the United States was the principal nuclear superpower (the Soviet Union having just exploded its first nuclear weapon). The United States had supported Chiang Kai-shek during the Chinese civil war, transporting Nationalist troops to northern Chinese cities after the Japanese surrender in World War II to preempt the Communist armies. Mao Zedong's victory was greeted with dismay in Washington and triggered a debate over who had "lost" China. That implied, at least in Beijing, an eventual attempt to reverse the outcome—a conviction reinforced when in 1950, upon the North Korean invasion of the South, President Truman moved the Seventh Fleet into the Taiwan Strait, forestalling an attempt by the new government on the mainland to reconquer Taiwan.

The Soviet Union was an ideological ally and was needed initially as a strategic partner to balance the United States. But China's leaders had not forgotten the series of "unequal treaties" extorted for a century to establish the Russian possession of its Far East maritime provinces and a zone of special influence in Manchuria and Xinjiang, nor that the Soviet Union was still claiming the validity of concessions in northern China extracted from Chiang Kai-shek in wartime agreements in 1945. Stalin took for granted Soviet dominance in the Communist world, a stance incompatible in the long run with Mao's fierce nationalism and claim to ideological importance.

China was also involved in a border dispute with India in the Himalayas, over the territory known as Aksai Chin in the west and over the so-called McMahon Line in the east. The disputed region was no small matter: at roughly 125,000 square kilometers, the total contested area was approximately the size of Pennsylvania or, as Mao later noted to his top commanders, the Chinese province of Fujian.[8]

Mao divided these challenges into two categories. At home, he proclaimed continuous revolution and was able to implement it because he increasingly exercised total control. Abroad, world revolution was a slogan, perhaps a long-range objective, but China's leaders were sufficiently realistic to recognize that they lacked the means to challenge the prevailing international order except by ideological means. Within China, Mao recognized few objective limits to his philosophic visions other than the ingrained attitudes of the Chinese people, which he struggled to overwhelm. In the realm of foreign policy, he was substantially more circumspect.

When the Communist Party seized power in 1949, substantial regions had broken away from the historic Chinese Empire, notably Tibet, parts of Xinjiang, parts of Mongolia, and the border areas of Burma. The Soviet Union maintained a sphere of influence in the northeast, including an occupation force and a fleet in the strategically located Lushun harbor. Mao, like several founders of dynasties before him, claimed the frontiers of China that the empire had established at its maximum historic extent. To territories Mao considered part of that historic China—Taiwan, Tibet, Xinjiang, Mongolia, border regions in the Himalayas or the north—he applied the maxim of domestic politics: he was implacable; he sought to impose China's governance and generally succeeded. As soon as the civil war ended, Mao set out to reoccupy the secessionist regions, such as Xinjiang, Inner Mongolia, and eventually Tibet. In that context, Taiwan was not so much a test of Communist ideology as a demand to respect Chinese history. Even when he refrained from military measures, Mao would put forward claims to territories given up in the "unequal treaties" of the nineteenth century—for example, claims to territory lost in the Russian Far East in the settlements of 1860 and 1895.

With respect to the rest of the world, Mao introduced a special style that substituted ideological militancy and psychological perception for physical strength. It was composed of a Sinocentric view of the world, a touch of world revolution, and a diplomacy using the Chinese tradition of manipulating the barbarians, with great attention paid to meticulous planning and the psychological domination of the other side.

Mao eschewed what Western diplomats viewed as the commonsense dictum that to recover from the decades of upheaval China should conciliate the major powers. He refused to convey any appearance of weakness, chose defiance over accommodation, and avoided contact with Western countries after establishing the People's Republic of China.

Zhou Enlai, the first Foreign Minister of the People's Republic of China, summed up this attitude of aloofness in a series of aphorisms. The new China would not simply slip into existing diplomatic relationships. It would set up "a separate kitchen." Relations with the new regime would have to be negotiated from case to case. The new China would "sweep the house clean before inviting the guests"—in other words, it would clean up lingering colonial influences before establishing diplomatic relations with Western "imperialist" countries. It would use its influence to "unite the world's people"—in other words, encourage revolution in the developing world.[9]

Diplomatic traditionalists would have rejected this attitude of aloof challenge as unfeasible. But Mao believed in the objective impact of ideological and, above all, psychological factors. He proposed to achieve psychological equivalence to the superpowers by calculated indifference to their military capabilities.

One of the classic tales of the Chinese strategic tradition was that of Zhuge Liang's "Empty City Stratagem" from *The Romance of the Three Kingdoms.* In it, a commander notices an approaching army far superior to his own. Since resistance guarantees destruction, and surrender would bring about loss of control over the future, the commander opts for a stratagem. He opens the gates of his city, places himself there in a posture of repose, playing a lute, and behind him shows normal life without any sign of panic or concern. The general of the invading army interprets this sangfroid as a sign of the existence of hidden reserves, stops his advance, and withdraws.

Mao's avowed indifference to the threat of nuclear war surely owed something to that tradition. From the very beginning, the People's Republic of China had to maneuver in a triangular relationship with the two nuclear powers, each of which was individually capable of posing a great threat and, together, were in a position to overwhelm China. Mao dealt with this endemic state of affairs by pretending it did not exist. He claimed to be impervious to nuclear threats; indeed, he developed a public posture of being willing to accept hundreds of millions of casualties, even welcoming it as a guarantee for the more rapid victory of Communist ideology. Whether Mao believed his own pronouncements on nuclear war it is impossible to say. But he clearly succeeded in making much of the rest of the world believe that he meant it—an ultimate test of credibility. (Of course in China's case, the city was not entirely "empty." China eventually developed its own nuclear weapons capability, though on a much smaller scale than that of the Soviet Union or the United States.)

Mao was able to draw on a long tradition in Chinese statecraft of accomplishing long-term goals from a position of relative weakness. For centuries, Chinese statesmen enmeshed the "barbarians" in relationships that kept them at bay and studiously maintained the political fiction of superiority through diplomatic stagecraft. From the beginning of the People's Republic, China played a world role surpassing its objective strength. By consequence of its fierce defense of its definition of its national patrimony, the People's Republic of China became an influential force in the Non-Aligned Movement—the grouping of newly independent countries seeking to position themselves between the superpowers. China established itself as a great power not to be trifled with while conducting a redefinition of the Chinese identity at home and challenging the nuclear powers diplomatically, sometimes concurrently, sometimes sequentially.

In pursuit of this foreign policy agenda, Mao owed more to Sun Tzu than to Lenin. He drew inspiration from his reading of the Chinese classics and the tradition he outwardly disdained. In charting foreign policy initiatives he was less likely to refer to Marxist doctrine than to traditional Chinese works: Confucian texts; the canonical "24 Dynastic Histories" recounting the rise and fall of China's imperial dynasties; Sun Tzu, *The Romance of the Three Kingdoms,* and other texts on warfare and strategy; tales of adventure and rebellion such as *Outlaws of the Marsh*; and the novel of romance and courtly intrigue, *Dream of the Red Chamber*, which Mao claimed to have read five times.[10] In an echo of the traditional Confucian scholar-officials whom he denounced as oppressors and parasites, Mao wrote poetry and philosophical essays and took great pride in his unorthodox calligraphy. These literary and artistic elements were not a refuge from his political labors but an integral part of them. When Mao, after a thirty-two-year absence, returned to his native village in 1959, he wrote a poem not of Marxism or materialism but of romantic sweep: "It is the bitter sacrifices that strengthen our firm resolve, and which give us the courage to dare to change heavens and skies, to change the sun, and to make a new world."[11]

So ingrained was this literary tradition that, in 1969, at a turning point in Mao's foreign policy, four marshals assigned by Mao to outline his strategic options illustrated their recommendations of the need to open relations with the then archenemy America by citing *The Romance of the Three Kingdoms*, which was banned in China but which they could be certain Mao had read. So, too, even in the midst of his most sweeping assaults on China's ancient heritage, Mao framed his foreign policy doctrines in terms of analogies with highly traditional Chinese games of the intellect. He described the opening maneuvers in the Sino-Indian War as "crossing the Han-Chu boundary," an ancient metaphor drawn from the Chinese version of chess.[12] He held up the traditional gambling game of mahjong as a school for strategic thought: "If you knew how to play the game," he told his doctor, "you would also understand the relationship between the principle of probability and the principle of certainty."[13] And in China's conflicts with both the United States and the Soviet Union, Mao and his top associates conceived of the threat in terms of a *wei qi* concept—that of preventing strategic encirclement.

It was in precisely these most traditional aspects that the superpowers had the most difficulty comprehending Mao's strategic motives. Through the lens of Western strategic analysis, most of Beijing's military undertakings in the first three decades of the Cold War were improbable and, on paper at least, impossible affairs. Setting China against usually far stronger powers and occurring in territories previously deemed of secondary strategic importance—North Korea, the offshore islands of the Taiwan Strait, sparsely populated tracts of the Himalayas, frozen swatches of territory in the Ussuri River—these Chinese interventions and offensives caught almost all foreign observers—and each of the adversaries—by surprise. Mao was determined to prevent encirclement by any power or combination of powers, regardless of ideology, that he perceived as securing too many *wei qi* "stones" surrounding China, by disrupting their calculations.

This was the catalyst that led China into the Korean War despite its relative weakness—and that, in the aftermath of Mao's death, would lead Beijing to war with Vietnam, a recent ally, in defiance of a mutual defense treaty between Hanoi and Moscow and while the Soviet Union maintained a million troops on China's northern borders. Long-range calculations of the configuration of forces around China's periphery were considered more significant than a literal calculus of the immediate balance of power. This combination of the long-range and the psychological also came to expression in Mao's approach to deterring perceived military threats.

However much Mao absorbed from China's history, no previous Chinese ruler combined traditional elements with the same mix of authority and ruthlessness and global sweep as Mao: ferocity in the face of challenge and skillful diplomacy when circumstances prevented his preference for drastic overpowering initiatives. His vast and daring foreign policy initiatives, however traditional his tactics, were carried out amidst a violent churning of Chinese society. The whole world, he promised, would be transformed, and things turned into their opposites:

> Of all the classes in the world the proletariat is the one which is most eager to change its position, and next comes the semi-proletariat, for the former possesses nothing at all while the latter is hardly any better off. The United States now controls a majority in the United Nations and dominates many parts of the world—this state of affairs is temporary and will be changed one of these days. China's position as a poor country denied its rights in international affairs will also be changed—the poor country will change into a rich one, the country

> denied its rights into one enjoying them—a transformation of things into their opposites.[14]

Mao was too much of a realist, however, to pursue world revolution as a practical goal. As a result, the tangible impact of China on world revolution was largely ideological and consisted of intelligence support for local Communist parties. Mao explained this attitude in an interview with Edgar Snow, the first American journalist to describe the Chinese Communist base in Yan'an during the civil war, in 1965: "China supported revolutionary movements, but not by invading countries. Of course, whenever a liberation struggle existed China would publish statements and called demonstrations to support it."[15]

In the same vein, *Long Live the Victory of People's War,* a 1965 pamphlet by Lin Biao, then Mao's presumptive successor, argued that the countryside of the world (that is, the developing countries) would defeat the cities of the world (that is, the advanced countries) much as the People's Liberation Army (PLA) had defeated Chiang Kai-shek. The administration of Lyndon Johnson read these lines as a Chinese blueprint for support for—and probably outright participation in—Communist subversion all around the world and especially in Indochina. Lin's pamphlet was a contributing factor in the decision to send American forces to Vietnam. Contemporary scholarship, however, treats his document as a statement of the limits of Chinese military support for Vietnam and other revolutionary movements. For, in fact, Lin was proclaiming that "[t]he liberation of the masses is accomplished by the masses themselves—this is a basic principle of Marxism-Leninism. Revolution or people's war in any country is the business of the masses in that country and should be carried out primarily by their own efforts; there is no other way."[16]

This restraint reflected a realistic appreciation of the real balance of forces. We cannot know what Mao might have decided if the equilibrium had been tilted in favor of the Communist power. But whether as a reflection of realism or philosophical motivation, revolutionary ideology was a means to transform the world by performance rather than war, much as the traditional emperors had perceived their role.

A team of Chinese scholars with access to Beijing's Central Archives has written a fascinating account of Mao's ambivalence: dedicated to world revolution, ready to encourage it wherever possible, yet also protective of the necessities of China's survival.[17] This ambivalence came to expression in a conversation with the head of the Australian Communist Party, E. F. Hill, in 1969, while Mao was considering the opening with the United States, with which China had been locked in an adversarial relationship for two decades. He put a question to his interlocutor: Are we heading into a revolution that will prevent war? Or into a war that will produce revolution?[18] If the former, the rapprochement with the United States would be improvident; if the latter, it would be imperative, to prevent an attack on China. In the end, after some hesitation, Mao chose the option of rapprochement with America. The prevention of war (which, by this point, would most likely involve a Soviet attack on China) was more important than the encouragement of global revolution.

The Continuous Revolution and the Chinese People

Mao's opening to the United States was a major ideological as well as strategic decision. But it did not alter his commitment to the concept of continuous revolution at home. Even in 1972, the year of President Richard Nixon's visit to China, he caused to be distributed nationwide a letter he had sent to his wife, Jiang Qing, at the beginning of the Cultural Revolution six years earlier:

> The situation changes from a great upheaval to a great peace once every seven or eight years. Ghosts and monsters jump out

> by themselves. . . . Our current task is to sweep out the Rightists in all the Party and throughout the country. We shall launch another movement for sweeping up the ghosts and monsters after seven or eight years, and will launch more of this movement later.[19]

This call to ideological commitment also epitomized Mao's dilemma as that of any victorious revolution: once revolutionaries seize power, they are obliged to govern hierarchically if they want to avoid either paralysis or chaos. The more sweeping the overthrow, the more hierarchy has to substitute for the consensus that holds a functioning society together. The more elaborate the hierarchy, the more likely it is to turn into another even more elaborate version of the replaced oppressive Establishment.

Thus from the beginning Mao was engaged in a quest whose logical end could only be an attack on Communism's own institutions, even those he had created himself. Where Leninism had asserted that the advent of Communism would solve the "contradictions" of society, Mao's philosophy knew no resting place. It was not enough to industrialize the country as the Soviet Union had done. In the quest for the historic Chinese uniqueness, the social order needed to be in constant flux to prevent the sin of "revisionism," of which Mao increasingly accused post-Stalin Russia. A Communist state, according to Mao, must not turn into a bureaucratic society; the motivating force must be ideology rather than hierarchy.

In this manner, Mao generated a series of built-in contradictions. In pursuit of the Great Harmony, Mao launched the Hundred Flowers Campaign in 1956, which invited public debate and then turned on those intellectuals who practiced it; the Great Leap Forward in 1958, designed to catch up with the West industrially in a three-year period but which led to one of the most pervasive famines in modern history and produced a split in the Communist Party; and the Cultural

Revolution in 1966, in which a generation of trained leaders, professors, diplomats, and experts were sent to the countryside to work on farms to learn from the masses.

Millions died to implement the Chairman's quest for egalitarian virtue. Yet in his rebellion against China's pervasive bureaucracy, he kept coming up against the dilemma that the campaign to save his people from themselves generated ever larger bureaucracies. In the end, destroying his own disciples turned into Mao's vast enterprise.

Mao's faith in the ultimate success of his continuous revolution had three sources: ideology, tradition, and Chinese nationalism. The single most important one was his faith in the resilience, capabilities, and cohesion of the Chinese people. And in truth, it is impossible to think of another people who could have sustained the relentless turmoil that Mao imposed on his society. Or whose leader could have made credible Mao's oft-repeated threat that the Chinese people would prevail, even if it retreated from all its cities against a foreign invader or suffered tens of millions of casualties in a nuclear war. Mao could do so because of a profound faith in the Chinese people's ability to retain its essence amidst all vicissitudes.

This was a fundamental difference with the Russian Revolution a generation earlier. Lenin and Trotsky viewed their revolution as a triggering event for world revolution. Convinced that world revolution was imminent, they agreed to cede a third of European Russia to German control in the Treaty of Brest-Litovsk of 1918. Whatever happened to Russia would be subsumed by the imminent revolution in the rest of Europe, which, Lenin and Trotsky assumed, would sweep away the existing political order.

Such an approach would have been unthinkable for Mao, whose revolution was largely Sinocentric. China's revolution might have an impact on world revolution but, if so, through the efforts and sacrifice and example of the Chinese people. With Mao, the greatness of the

Chinese people was always the organizing principle. In an early essay in 1919, he stressed the unique qualities of the Chinese people:

> I venture to make a singular assertion: one day, the reform of the Chinese people will be more profound than that of any other people, and the society of the Chinese people will be more radiant than that of any other people. The great union of the Chinese people will be achieved earlier than that of any other place or people.[20]

Twenty years later, amidst Japanese invasion and the Chinese civil war, Mao extolled the historic achievements of the Chinese nation in a way that the dynastic rulers could have shared:

> Throughout the history of Chinese civilization its agriculture and handicrafts have been renowned for their high level of development; there have been many great thinkers, scientists, inventors, statesmen, soldiers, men of letters and artists, and we have a rich store of classical works. The compass was invented in China very long ago. The art of paper-making was discovered as early as 1,800 years ago. Block-printing was invented 1,300 years ago, and movable type 800 years ago. The use of gunpowder was known in China before the Europeans. Thus China has one of the oldest civilizations in the world; she has a recorded history of nearly 4,000 years.[21]

Mao kept circling back to a dilemma as ancient as China itself. Intrinsically universal, modern technology poses a threat to any society's claims to uniqueness. And uniqueness had always been the distinctive claim of Chinese society. To preserve that uniqueness, China had refused to imitate the West in the nineteenth century, risking colonization and incurring humiliation. A century later, one objective of Mao's Cultural Revolution—from which indeed it derived its name—had been to eradicate precisely those elements of modernization that threatened to involve China in a universal culture.

By 1968, Mao had come full circle. Driven by a mixture of ideological fervor and a premonition of mortality, he had turned to the youth to cleanse the military and the Communist Party and bring into office a new generation of ideologically pure Communists. But reality disappointed the aging leader. It proved impossible to run a country by ideological exaltation. The youths who had heeded Mao's instructions created chaos rather than commitment and were now in their turn sent to the remote countryside; some of the leaders initially targeted for purification were brought back to reestablish order—especially in the military. By April 1969, nearly half of the Party's Central Committee—45 percent—were members of the military, compared with 19 percent in 1956; the average age of new members was sixty.[22]

A poignant reminder of this dilemma came up in the first conversation between Mao and President Nixon in February 1972. Nixon complimented Mao on having transformed an ancient civilization, to which Mao replied: "I haven't been able to change it. I've only been able to change a few places in the vicinity of Beijing."[23]

After a lifetime of titanic struggle to uproot Chinese society, there was not a little pathos in Mao's resigned recognition of the pervasiveness of Chinese culture and the Chinese people. One of the historically most powerful Chinese rulers had run up against this paradoxical mass—at once obedient and independent, submissive and self-reliant, imposing limits less by direct challenges than by hesitance in executing orders they considered incompatible with the future of their family.

Therefore, in the end, Mao appealed not so much to the material aspects of his Marxist revolution as to its faith. One of Mao's favorite tales drawn from classical Chinese lore was the story of the "foolish old man" who believed he could move mountains with his bare hands. Mao related the story at a Communist Party conference as follows:

> There is an ancient Chinese fable called "The Foolish Old Man Who Removed the Mountains." It tells of an old man who lived in northern China long, long ago and was known as the Foolish Old Man of North Mountain. His house faced south and beyond his doorway stood the two great peaks, Taihang and Wangwu, obstructing the way. He called his sons, and hoe in hand they began to dig up these mountains with great determination. Another greybeard, known as the Wise Old Man, saw them and said derisively, "How silly of you to do this! It is quite impossible for you to dig up these two huge mountains." The Foolish Old Man replied, "When I die my sons will carry on; when they die, there will be my grandsons, and then their sons and grandsons, and so on to infinity. High as they are, the mountains cannot grow any higher and with every bit we dig, they will be that much lower. Why can't we clear them away?" Having refuted the Wise Old Man's wrong view, he went on digging every day, unshaken in his conviction. God was moved by this, and he sent down two angels, who carried the mountains away on their backs. Today, two big mountains lie like a dead weight on the Chinese people. One is imperialism, the other is feudalism. The Chinese Communist Party had long made up its mind to dig them up. We must persevere and work unceasingly, and we, too, will touch God's heart.[24]

An ambivalent combination of faith in the Chinese people and disdain for its traditions enabled Mao to carry out an astonishing tour de force: an impoverished society just emerging from a rending civil war tore itself apart at ever shorter intervals and, during that process, fought wars with the United States and India; challenged the Soviet Union; and restored the frontiers of the Chinese state to nearly their maximum historic extent.

Emerging into a world of two nuclear superpowers, China managed, despite its insistent Communist propaganda, to conduct itself as essentially a geopolitical "free agent" of the Cold War. In the face of its relative weakness, it played a fully independent and highly influential role. China moved from hostility to near alliance with the United States and in the opposite direction with the Soviet Union—from alliance to confrontation. Perhaps most remarkably, China managed, in the end, to break free of the Soviet Union and come out on the "winning" side of the Cold War.

Still, with all its achievements, Mao's insistence on turning the ancient system upside down could not escape the eternal rhythm of Chinese life. Forty years after his death, after a journey violent, dramatic, and searing, his successors again described their now increasingly well-off society as Confucian. In 2011, a statue of Confucius was placed in Tiananmen Square within sight of Mao's mausoleum—the only other personality so honored. Only a people as resilient and patient as the Chinese could emerge unified and dynamic after such a roller coaster ride through history.

CHAPTER 5

Triangular Diplomacy and the Korean War

IN HIS FIRST MAJOR ACT of foreign policy, Mao Zedong traveled to Moscow on December 16, 1949, barely two months after having proclaimed the People's Republic of China. It was his first trip outside China. His purpose was to form an alliance with the Communist superpower, the Soviet Union. Instead, the meeting inaugurated a series of moves that would culminate in transforming the hoped-for alliance into a triangular diplomacy by which the United States, China, and the Soviet Union maneuvered with and against each other.

In his first meeting with Stalin, which took place on the day of his arrival, Mao stressed China's need for "a period of 3–5 years of peace, which would be used to bring the economy back to pre-war levels and to stabilize the country in general."[1] Yet within less than a year of Mao's trip, the United States and China would be at war with each other.

It all came about through the machinations of a seemingly minor player: Kim Il-sung, the ambitious Soviet-installed ruler of North Korea, a state that had been created only two years earlier by agreement between the United States and the Soviet Union based on the zones of liberated Korea each had occupied at the end of the war against Japan.

As it happened, Stalin had little interest in helping China recover. He had not forgotten the defection of Josip Broz Tito, the leader of Yugoslavia and the only European Communist leader to have achieved power by his own efforts and not as the result of Soviet occupation. Tito had broken with the Soviet Union during the preceding year. Stalin was determined to avoid a similar outcome in Asia. He understood the geopolitical significance of the Communist victory in China; his strategic goal was to manipulate its consequences and benefit from its impact.

Stalin could have little doubt that, in Mao, he was dealing with a formidable figure. The Chinese Communists had prevailed in the Chinese civil war against Soviet expectations and by ignoring Soviet advice. Though Mao had announced China's intent to "lean to one side"—Moscow's—in international affairs, of all Communist leaders he was among the least beholden to Moscow for his position, and he now governed the most populous Communist country. Thus the encounter between the two Communist giants led to an intricate minuet culminating, six months later, with the Korean War, which involved China and the United States directly and the Soviet Union by proxy.

Convinced that the raging American debate over who "lost" China augured an eventual American attempt to reverse the outcome—a view to which Communist ideology led him, in any event—Mao strove for the greatest possible material and military support from the Soviet Union. A formal alliance was his objective.

But the two Communist autocrats were not destined to cooperate easily. Stalin had, by that time, been in power for nearly thirty years. He had triumphed over all domestic opposition and led his country to victory against the Nazi invaders at horrific cost in human life. The organizer of periodic purges involving millions of victims and, even then, in the process of starting a new set of purges, Stalin was by now beyond ideology. His leadership was instead marked by a ruthless, cynical Machiavellianism based on his brutal interpretation of Russian national history.

During China's long struggles with Japan in the 1930s and 1940s, Stalin had deprecated the potential of the Communist forces and disparaged Mao's rural, peasant-based strategy. Throughout, Moscow had maintained official ties with the Nationalist government. At the end of the war against Japan in 1945, Stalin had obliged Chiang Kai-shek to grant the Soviet Union privileges in Manchuria and Xinjiang comparable to those achieved by the czarist regime, and to recognize Outer Mongolia as a nominally independent People's Republic under Soviet control. Stalin actively encouraged separatist forces in Xinjiang.

At Yalta that same year, Stalin insisted to his colleagues, Franklin D. Roosevelt and Winston Churchill, on international recognition for Soviet special rights in Manchuria, including a naval base at Lushun (the old Port Arthur) and a harbor in Dalian, as a condition for entering the war against Japan. In August 1945, Moscow and the Nationalist authorities signed a treaty affirming the Yalta agreements.

In these circumstances, the meeting of the two Communist titans in Moscow could not possibly be the warm embrace shared ideology called for. As Nikita Khrushchev, then a member of Stalin's Politburo, recalled:

> Stalin loved to show off his hospitality to his esteemed guests, and he knew how to do it very well. But during Mao's stay, Stalin would sometimes not lay eyes on him for days at a time—and since Stalin neither saw Mao nor ordered anyone else to entertain him, *no* one dared go see him. . . . Mao let it be known that if the situation continued, he would leave. When Stalin heard about Mao's complaints, I think he had another dinner for him.[2]

It was clear from the outset that Stalin did not consider the Communist victory a reason for giving up the gains he had made for the Soviet Union as a price for entering the war against Japan. Mao began the conversation by stressing his need for peace, telling Stalin: "Decisions on the most important questions in China hinge on the prospects for a peaceful future. With this in mind the [Central Committee of the Communist Party of China] entrusted me to ascertain from you, comr[ade] Stalin, in what way and for how long will international peace be preserved."[3]

Stalin was reassuring about prospects for peace, perhaps to slow down any request for emergency assistance and to minimize the urgency of rushing into an alliance:

> The question of peace greatly occupies the Soviet Union as well, though we have already had peace for the past four years. With regards to China, there is no immediate threat at the present time: Japan has yet to stand up on its feet and is thus not ready for war; America, though it screams war, is actually afraid of war more than anything; Europe is afraid of war; in essence, there is no one to fight with China, not unless Kim Il Sung decides to invade China? Peace will depend on our efforts. If we continue to be friendly, peace can last not only 5–10 years, but 20–25 years and perhaps even longer.[4]

If that was the case, a military alliance was really not needed. Stalin made his reserve explicit when Mao formally raised the issue. He made the stunning assertion that a new treaty of alliance was superfluous; the existing treaty, which had been signed with Chiang Kai-shek in quite different circumstances, would suffice. Stalin buttressed this argument with the claim that the Soviet position was designed to avoid giving "America and England the legal grounds to raise questions about modifying" the Yalta agreements.[5]

In effect, Stalin was arguing that Communism in China was best protected by a Russian agreement made with the government Mao had just overthrown. Stalin liked this argument so much that he also applied it to the concessions the Soviet Union had extracted from Chiang

Kai-shek with respect to Xinjiang and Manchuria, which, in his view, should now be continued at Mao's request. Mao, ever the fervent nationalist, rejected these ideas by redefining Stalin's request. The present arrangements along the Manchurian railroad, he argued, corresponded to "Chinese interests" insofar as they provided "a training school for the preparation of Chinese cadres in railroad and industry."[6] Chinese personnel needed to take over as soon as they could be trained. Soviet advisors could stay until this training was completed.

Amidst protestations of amity and affirmations of ideological solidarity, two major Machiavellians were maneuvering over ultimate predominance (and over sizeable tracts of territory around China's periphery). Stalin was the senior and, for a time, more powerful; Mao, in a geopolitical sense, the more self-confident. Both were superior strategists and therefore understood that, on the course they were formally charting, their interests were almost bound to clash eventually.

After a month of haggling, Stalin yielded and agreed to a treaty of alliance. However, he insisted Dalian and Lushun would remain Soviet bases until a peace treaty with Japan was signed. Moscow and Beijing finally concluded a Treaty of Friendship, Alliance and Mutual Assistance on February 14, 1950. It provided what Mao had sought and Stalin had tried to avoid: an obligation of mutual assistance in case of conflict with a third power. Theoretically, it obliged China to come to the assistance of the Soviet Union globally. Operationally, it gave Mao a safety net if the various looming crises around China's borders were to escalate.

The price China had to pay was steep: mining, railroad, and other concessions in Manchuria and Xinjiang; the recognition of the independence of Outer Mongolia; Soviet use of Dalian harbor; and the use, until 1952, of the Lushun naval base. Years later, Mao would still complain bitterly to Khrushchev about Stalin's attempt to establish "semicolonies" in China by means of these concessions.[7]

As for Stalin, the emergence of a potentially powerful eastern neighbor presented a geopolitical nightmare. No Russian ruler could ignore the extraordinary demographic disparity between China and Russia along a two-thousand-mile frontier: a Chinese population of over five hundred million adjoined a Russian total of less than forty million in Siberia. At what point in China's development would numbers begin to matter? Seeming consensus on ideology emphasized, rather than diminished, the concern. Stalin was too cynical to doubt that when powerful men achieve eminence by what they consider their own efforts, they resist the claim of superior orthodoxy by an ally, however close. Stalin, having taken the measure of Mao, must have known that he would never concede doctrinal preeminence.

Acheson and the Lure of Chinese Titoism

An episode that occurred during Mao's stay in Moscow was symptomatic of both the fraught relations within the Communist world as well as the potential and looming role of the United States in that emerging triangle. The occasion was an attempt by Secretary of State Dean Acheson to answer the chorus of domestic critics on who had "lost" China. Under his instructions, the State Department had issued a White Paper in August 1949 addressing the collapse of the Nationalists. Though the United States still recognized the Nationalists as the legitimate government for all of China, the White Paper described them as "corrupt, reactionary and inefficient."[8] Acheson had therefore concluded, and he advised Truman in the White Paper's letter of transmittal, that

> [t]he unfortunate but inescapable fact is that the ominous result of the civil war in China was beyond the control of the government of the United States. Nothing that this country did or could have done within the reasonable limits of its

> capabilities could have changed that result. . . . It was the product of internal Chinese forces, forces which this country tried to influence but could not.[9]

In a speech to the National Press Club on January 12, 1950, Acheson reinforced the White Paper's message and put forward a sweeping new Asia policy. His speech contained three points of fundamental importance. The first was that Washington was washing its hands of the Chinese civil war. The Nationalists, Acheson proclaimed, had displayed both political inadequacy as well as "the grossest incompetence ever experienced by any military command." The Communists, Acheson reasoned, "did not create this condition," but had skillfully exploited the opening it provided. Chiang Kai-shek was now "a refugee on a small island off the coast of China with the remnants of his forces."[10]

Having conceded the mainland to Communist control and whatever geopolitical impact this might have, it made no sense to resist Communist attempts to occupy Taiwan. This was in fact the judgment of NSC-48/2, a document reflecting national policy prepared by the National Security Council staff and approved by the President. Adopted on December 30, 1949, it concluded that "the strategic importance of Formosa [Taiwan] does not justify overt military action." Truman had made a similar point at a press conference on January 5: "The United States Government will not provide military aid or advice to Chinese forces on Formosa."[11]

Second and even more significantly, Acheson left no doubt about who was threatening China's independence in the long run:

> This Communistic concept and techniques have armed Russian imperialism with a new and most insidious weapon of penetration. Armed with these new powers, what is

> happening in China is that the Soviet Union is detaching the northern provinces [areas] of China from China and is attaching them to the Soviet Union. This process is complete in outer Mongolia. It is nearly complete in Manchuria, and I am sure that in inner Mongolia and in Sinkiang there are very happy reports coming from Soviet agents to Moscow. This is what is going on.[12]

The final new point in Acheson's speech was even more profound in its implications for the future. For it did nothing less than suggest an explicit Titoist option for China. Proposing to base relations with China on national interest, Acheson asserted that the integrity of China was an American national interest regardless of China's domestic ideology: "We must take the position we have always taken—that anyone who violates the integrity of China is the enemy of China and is acting contrary to our own interest."[13]

Acheson was laying out a prospect for a new Sino-American relationship based on national interest, not ideology:

> [Today] is a day in which the old relationships between east and west are gone, relationships which at their worst were exploitation, and which at their best were paternalism. That relationship is over, and the relationship of east and west must now be in the Far East one of mutual respect and mutual helpfulness.[14]

Such a view toward Communist China would not be put forward again by a senior American official for another two decades, when Richard Nixon advanced similar propositions to his Cabinet.

Acheson's speech was brilliantly crafted to touch most of Stalin's raw nerves. And Stalin was in fact lured into trying to do something about it. He dispatched his foreign minister, Andrey Vyshinsky, and his senior minister, Vyacheslav Molotov, to call on Mao, still in Moscow for the alliance negotiations, to warn him of the "slander" being spread by Acheson and, in effect, inviting reassurance. It was a somewhat frantic gesture, not in keeping with Stalin's usual perspicacity. For the very request for reassurance defines the potential capacity for unreliability of the other side. If a partner is thought capable of desertion, why would reassurance be credible? If not, why would it be necessary? Moreover, both Mao and Stalin knew that Acheson's "slander" was an accurate description of the current Sino-Soviet relationship.[15]

The Soviet pair asked Mao to disavow Acheson's accusations that the Soviet Union might seek to detach parts of China, or a dominant position in them, and recommended that he describe it as an insult to China. Mao did not comment to Stalin's emissaries except to ask for a copy of the speech and inquire about Acheson's possible motives. After a few days, Mao approved a statement sarcastically attacking Acheson—but in contrast to Moscow's response, which was issued in the name of the Soviet foreign minister, Beijing left it to the head of the People's Republic of China's official news bureau to reject Acheson's overtures.[16] The language of the statement decried Washington's "slander" but its relatively low protocol level kept China's options open. Mao chose not to address the full implications of his view while he was in Moscow, trying to construct a safety net for his still isolated country.

Mao revealed his true feelings about the possibility of separating from Moscow later, in December 1956, with characteristic complexity, in the guise of rejecting the option once again albeit in a more muted way:

> China and the Soviet Union stand together. . . . [T]here are still people who have doubts about this policy. . . . They think China should take a middle course and be a bridge between the Soviet Union and the United States. . . . If China stands between the Soviet Union and the United States, she appears

> to be in a favorable position, and to be independent, but actually she cannot be independent. The United States is not reliable, she would give you a little something, but not much. How could imperialism give you a full meal? It won't.[17]

But what if the United States were ready to offer what Mao called "a full meal"? That question would not be answered until 1972, when President Nixon began his overtures to China.

Kim Il-sung and the Outbreak of War

Matters could have proceeded as a kind of shadowboxing for several, perhaps many, years as the two morbidly suspicious absolute rulers were calibrating each other by ascribing their own motives to their counterpart. Instead Kim Il-sung, the North Korean leader whom Stalin had ridiculed in his first meeting with Mao in December 1949, entered the geopolitical fray with startling results. In their Moscow meeting, Stalin had fended off a military alliance between China and the Soviet Union by mockingly suggesting that the only threat to peace would come from North Korea, if "Kim Il Sung decides to invade China."[18]

That is not what Kim Il-sung decided. Instead, he chose to invade South Korea and, in the process, brought the major countries to the edge of a global war and China and the United States into actual military confrontation.

Before the North Korean invasion of the South, it would have seemed inconceivable that a China barely emerging from civil war would go to war against a nuclear-armed America. That the war broke out is due to the suspicions the two Communist giants had of each other and to Kim Il-sung's ability, though wholly dependent on his incomparably more powerful allies, to manipulate their mutual suspicions.

Korea had been incorporated into imperial Japan in 1910 and quickly became the jumping-off point for Japanese incursions into China. In 1945, after Japan's defeat, Korea was occupied in the North by Soviet armies, in the South by American forces. The dividing line between them, the 38th parallel, was arbitrary. It simply reflected the limits their armies had reached at the end of the war.[19]

When the occupying powers withdrew in 1949 and the hitherto occupied zones became fully sovereign states, neither felt comfortable within its boundaries. Their rulers, Kim Il-sung in the North and Syngman Rhee in the South, had spent their lives fighting for their national causes. They saw no reason to abandon them now, and both claimed the leadership for all of the country. Military clashes along the dividing line were frequent.

Starting with the withdrawal of American forces from South Korea in June 1949, Kim Il-sung had throughout 1949 and 1950 tried to convince both Stalin and Mao to acquiesce in a full-scale invasion of the South. Both at first rejected the proposal. During Mao's visit to Moscow, Stalin asked Mao's opinion of such an invasion, and Mao, though favorable to the objective, judged the risk of American intervention as too high.[20] He thought any project to conquer South Korea should be deferred until the completion of the Chinese civil war through the conquest of Taiwan.

It was precisely this Chinese aim that provided one of the incentives for Kim Il-sung's project. However ambiguous American statements, Kim Il-sung was convinced that the United States was unlikely to accept two Communist military conquests. He was therefore impatient to achieve his objectives in South Korea before Washington had second thoughts should China succeed in occupying Taiwan.

A few months later, in April 1950, Stalin reversed his previous position. During a visit by Kim Il-sung in Moscow, Stalin gave the green light to Kim's request. Stalin stressed his conviction that the United

States would not intervene. A Soviet diplomatic document recounted that

> Comrade Stalin confirmed to Kim Il Sung that the international environment has sufficiently changed to permit a more active stance on the unification of Korea. . . . Now that China has signed a treaty of alliance with the USSR, Americans will be even more hesitant to challenge the Communists in Asia. According to information coming from the United States, it is really so. The prevailing mood is not to interfere. Such a mood is reinforced by the fact that the USSR now has the atomic bomb and that our positions are solidified in Pyongyang.[21]

Thereafter there is no record of a direct Chinese-Soviet dialogue on the subject. Kim Il-sung and his envoys became the vehicle through which the two Communist giants communicated with each other on Korea. Both Stalin and Mao were maneuvering for dominant influence in Korea or, at a minimum, to keep the other partner from achieving it. During that process, Mao agreed to transfer up to fifty thousand ethnic Korean troops who served in the People's Liberation Army units to North Korea with their weapons. Was his motive to encourage Kim Il-sung's design or to prove his ideological support while limiting a final Chinese military commitment? Whatever Mao's ultimate intentions, the practical result was to leave Pyongyang in a significantly strengthened military position.

In the American domestic debate about the Korean War, Dean Acheson's speech on Asia policy in January 1950 came to be widely criticized for placing Korea outside the American "defensive perimeter" in the Pacific, thereby allegedly giving a "green light" to the North Korean invasion. In its account of American commitments in the Pacific, Acheson's speech was not an innovation. General Douglas MacArthur, Commander-in-Chief of the U.S. Far East Command, had similarly placed Korea outside the American defense perimeter in a March 1949 interview in Tokyo:

> Now the Pacific has become an Anglo-Saxon lake and our line of defense runs through the chain of islands fringing the coast of Asia.
>
> It starts from the Philippines and continues through the Ryukyu Archipelago, which includes its main bastion, Okinawa. Then it bends back through Japan and the Aleutian Island chain to Alaska.[22]

Since then, the United States had withdrawn the majority of its forces from Korea. A Korean aid bill was currently before Congress, where it faced considerable resistance. Acheson was left to repeat MacArthur's sketch, stating that the "military security of the Pacific area" involved a "defensive perimeter [that] runs along the Aleutians to Japan and then goes to the Ryukyus . . . [and] runs from the Ryukyus to the Philippine Islands."[23]

On the specific question of Korea, Acheson presented an ambiguous account reflecting the current state of American indecision. Now that South Korea was "an independent and sovereign country recognized by nearly all the rest of the world," Acheson reasoned that "our responsibilities are more direct and our opportunities more clear" (though what these responsibilities and opportunities were, Acheson did not explain—specifically whether they included defense against invasion). If an armed attack were to occur in an area of the Pacific not explicitly to the south or east of the American defensive perimeter, Acheson suggested that "[t]he initial reliance must be on the people attacked to resist it and then upon the commitments of the entire civilized world under the Charter of the United Nations."[24] To the extent deterrence requires clarity about a country's intention, Acheson's speech missed the mark.

No specific reference to this aspect of Acheson's speech has so far emerged in any Chinese or Soviet documents. Recently available diplomatic documents do suggest, however, that Stalin based his reversal in part on access to NSC-48/2, which his spy network, probably through the British turncoat Donald Maclean, had uncovered. This report also specifically placed Korea outside the U.S. defense perimeter. Since it was highly classified, the document would have seemed particularly credible to Soviet analysts.[25]

Another element in Stalin's reversal may have been his disenchantment with Mao stemming from the negotiations leading to the Sino-Soviet Treaty of Friendship described earlier. Mao had made it abundantly clear that Russian special privileges in China would not last long. Russian control of the warm-water port of Dalian was bound to be temporary. Stalin may well have concluded that a unified Communist Korea might prove more accommodating to Soviet naval needs.

Ever devious and complex, Stalin urged Kim to speak about this subject with Mao, noting that he had "a good understanding of Oriental matters."[26] In reality, Stalin was shifting as much responsibility as he could to Chinese shoulders. He told Kim not to "expect great assistance and support from the Soviet Union," explaining that Moscow was concerned and preoccupied with "the situation in the West."[27] And he warned Kim: "If you should get kicked in the teeth, I shall not lift a finger. You have to ask Mao for all the help."[28] It was authentically Stalin: haughty, long-range, manipulative, cautious, and crass, producing a geopolitical benefit for the Soviet Union while shifting the risks of the effort to China.

Stalin, who had encouraged the outbreak of the Second World War by freeing Hitler's rear through the Nazi-Soviet pact, applied his practiced skill in hedging his bets. If the United States did intervene, the threat to China would increase as would China's dependence on the Soviet Union. If China responded to the American challenge, it would require massive Soviet assistance, achieving the same result. If China stayed out, Moscow's influence in a disillusioned North Korea would grow.

Kim next flew to Beijing for a secret visit with Mao on May 13–16, 1950. In a meeting on the night of his arrival, Kim recounted to Mao Stalin's approval of the invasion plan and asked Mao to confirm his support.

To limit his risks even further, Stalin, shortly before the attack he had encouraged, added reinsurance by withdrawing all Soviet advisors from North Korean units. When that hamstrung the performance of the North Korean army, he returned Soviet advisors, albeit under the cover of their being correspondents from TASS, the Soviet press agency.

How a minor ally of both Communist giants unleashed a war of major global consequences was summed up by Mao's translator Shi Zhe to the historian Chen Jian, who paraphrased the content of the key conversation between Mao and Kim Il-sung:

> [Kim] told Mao that Stalin had approved his plans to attack the South. Mao solicited Kim's opinions of possible American response if North Korea attacked the South, stressing that as the Syngman Rhee regime had been propped up by the United States and that as Korea was close to Japan the possibility of an American intervention could not be totally excluded. Kim, however, seemed confident that the United States would not commit its troops, or at least, it would have no time to dispatch them, because the North Koreans would be able to finish fighting in two to three weeks. Mao did ask Kim if North Korea needed China's military support, and offered to deploy three Chinese armies along the Chinese-Korean border. Kim responded "arrogantly" (in Mao's own words, according to Shi Zhe) that with the North Koreans' own forces and the

> cooperation of Communist guerillas in the South, they could solve the problem by themselves, and China's military involvement was therefore unnecessary.[29]

Kim's presentation apparently shook Mao sufficiently that he ended the meeting early and ordered Zhou Enlai to cable Moscow requesting an "urgent answer" and "personal clarification" from Stalin.[30] The next day the reply arrived from Moscow, with Stalin again shifting the onus back to Mao. The cable explained that

> [i]n his talks with the Korean comrades, [Stalin] and his friends . . . agreed with the Koreans regarding the plan to move toward reunification. In this regard a qualification was made, that the issue should be decided finally by the Chinese and Korean comrades together, and in case of disagreement by the Chinese comrades the decision on the issue should be postponed pending further discussion.[31]

This, of course, placed the blame for vetoing the project entirely on Mao. Further disassociating himself from the outcome (and providing Kim with an additional opportunity for exaggeration and misrepresentation), Stalin preempted a return telegram from Beijing by explaining that "[t]he Korean comrades can tell you the details of the conversation."[32]

No records of Mao and Kim's subsequent conversation have yet been made available. Kim returned to Pyongyang on May 16 with Mao's blessing for an invasion of South Korea—or at least that is how he described it to Moscow. Mao may well have also calculated that acquiescence in the conquest of South Korea might establish a premise for Soviet military assistance for a subsequent Chinese attack on Taiwan. If so, it was a grievous miscalculation. Because even had the United States stood aloof from the conquest of South Korea, American public opinion would not have allowed the Truman administration to ignore another Communist military move in the Taiwan Strait.

Ten years later, Moscow and Beijing still could not agree on which side had actually given Kim the final green light to launch his invasion. Meeting in Bucharest in June 1960, Khrushchev, who was by then Soviet General Secretary, insisted to Chinese Politburo member Peng Zhen that "if Mao Zedong had not agreed, Stalin would not have done what he did." Peng retorted that this was "totally wrong" and that "Mao Zedong was against the war. . . . [I]t was Stalin who agreed."[33]

The two Communist giants thus slid into a war without addressing the global implications should Kim Il-sung's and Stalin's optimistic forecasts prove to be erroneous. Once the United States entered the war, they would be forced to consider them.

American Intervention: Resisting Aggression

The trouble with policy planning is that its analyses cannot foresee the mood of the moment when a decision has to be made. The various statements of Truman, Acheson, and MacArthur had correctly reflected American thinking when they were made. The nature of American commitment to international security was a subject of domestic controversy and had not ever considered the defense of Korea. NATO was still in the process of being formed. But when American policymakers came face-to-face with an actual Communist invasion, they ignored their policy papers.

The United States surprised the Communist leaders after Kim Il-sung's attack on June 25, not only by intervening but by linking the Korean War to the Chinese civil war. American ground forces were sent to Korea to establish a defensive perimeter around Pusan, the port city in the south. That decision was supported by a U.N. Security Council resolution made possible because the Soviet Union absented itself from the vote in protest against the fact that the Chinese seat in the Security Council was still occupied by Taipei. Two days later, President Truman ordered the U.S. Pacific Fleet to "neutralize" the Taiwan Strait by preventing military attacks in either direction across it. The motive was to obtain the widest congressional and public support for the Korean War; there is no evidence that Washington considered that it was, in fact, expanding the war into a confrontation with China.

Until that decision, Mao had planned to attack Taiwan as his next military move and had assembled major forces in southeast China's Fujian province to that end. The United States had conveyed in many statements—including a press conference by Truman on January 5—that it would not block such an effort.

Truman's decision to send the Seventh Fleet to the Taiwan Strait was intended to placate public opinion and to limit American risk in Korea. In announcing the fleet's dispatch, Truman cited the importance of Taiwan's defense but also called on "the Chinese Government on Formosa to cease all air and sea operations against the mainland." Truman further warned: "The Seventh Fleet will see that this is done."[34]

To Mao, an evenhanded gesture was unimaginable; he interpreted the assurances as hypocrisy. As far as Mao was concerned, the United States was reentering the Chinese civil war. The day after Truman's announcement, on June 28, 1950, Mao addressed the Eighth Session of the Central People's Government Committee, during which he described the American moves as an invasion of Asia:

> The U.S. invasion in Asia can only arouse broad and determined resistance among the people of Asia. Truman said on January 5 that the United States would not intervene in Taiwan. Now he himself has proved he was simply lying. He has also torn up all international agreements guaranteeing that the United States would not interfere in China's internal affairs.[35]

In China, *wei qi* instincts sprang into action. By sending troops to Korea and the fleet to the Taiwan Strait, the United States had, in Chinese eyes, placed two stones on the *wei qi* board, both of which menaced China with the dreaded encirclement.

The United States had no military plan for Korea when the war broke out. The American purpose in the Korean War was declared to be to defeat "aggression," a legal concept denoting the unauthorized use of force against a sovereign entity. How would success be defined? Was it a return to the status quo ante along the 38th parallel, in which case the aggressor would learn that the worst outcome was that he did not win—possibly encouraging another attempt? Or did it require the destruction of North Korea's military capacity to undertake aggression? There is no evidence that this question was ever addressed in the early stages of America's military commitment, partly because all governmental attention was needed to defend the perimeter around Pusan. The practical result was to let military operations determine political decisions.

After MacArthur's stunning September 1950 victory at Inchon—where a surprise amphibious landing far from the Pusan front halted North Korean momentum and opened a route to the recapture of the South Korean capital of Seoul—the Truman administration opted for continuing military operations until Korea was reunified. It assumed that Beijing would accept the presence of American forces along the traditional invasion route into China.

The decision to press forward with operations inside North Korean territory was formally authorized by a United Nations resolution on October 7, this time by the General Assembly under a recently adopted parliamentary device, the Uniting for Peace Resolution, which allowed the General Assembly to make decisions on international security by a two-thirds vote. It authorized "[a]ll constituent acts" to bring about "a unified, independent and democratic government in the sovereign

State of Korea."[36] Chinese intervention against U.S. forces was believed to be beyond Chinese capabilities.

None of these views remotely coincided with the way Beijing regarded international affairs. As soon as American forces intervened in the Taiwan Strait, Mao treated the Seventh Fleet's deployment as an "invasion" of Asia. China and the United States were approaching a clash by misinterpreting each other's strategic design. The United States strove to oblige China to accept its concept for international order, based on international organizations like the United Nations, to which it could not imagine an alternative. From the outset, Mao had no intention to accept an international system in the design of which China had no voice. As a result, the outcome of the American military strategy was inevitably going to be at best an armistice along whatever dividing line emerged—along the Yalu River, which denoted the border between North Korea and China, if the American design prevailed; along some other agreed line if China intervened or the United States stopped unilaterally short of Korea's northern frontier (for example, at the 38th parallel or at a line, Pyongyang to Wonsan, which emerged later in a Mao message to Zhou).

What was most unlikely was Chinese acquiescence in an American presence at a border that was a traditional invasion route into China and specifically the base from which Japan had undertaken the occupation of Manchuria and the invasion of northern China. China was all the less likely to be passive when such a posture involved a strategic setback on two fronts: the Taiwan Strait and Korea—partly because Mao had, to some extent, lost control over events in the prelude to Korea. The misconceptions of both sides compounded each other. The United States did not expect the invasion; China did not expect the reaction. Each side reinforced the other's misconceptions by its own actions. At the end of the process stood two years of war and twenty years of alienation.

Chinese Reactions: Another Approach to Deterrence

No student of military affairs would have thought it conceivable that the People's Liberation Army, barely finished with the civil war and largely equipped with captured Nationalist weapons, would take on a modern army backed up by nuclear weapons. But Mao was not a conventional military strategist. Mao's actions in the Korean War require an understanding of how he viewed what, in Western strategy, would be called deterrence or even preemption and which, in Chinese thinking, combines the long-range, strategic, and psychological elements.

In the West, the Cold War and the destructiveness of nuclear weapons have produced the concept of deterrence: to pose risks of destruction to a potential aggressor out of proportion to any possible gain. The efficacy of the threat is measured by things that do not happen, that is, the wars being avoided.

For Mao, the Western concept of deterrence was too passive. He rejected a posture in which China was obliged to wait for an attack. Wherever possible, he strove for the initiative. On one level, this was similar to the Western concept of preemption—anticipating an attack by launching the first blow. But in the Western doctrine, preemption seeks victory and a military advantage. Mao's approach to preemption differed in the extraordinary attention he paid to psychological elements. His motivating force was less to inflict a decisive military first blow than to change the psychological balance, not so much to defeat the enemy as to alter his calculus of risks. As we shall see in the later chapters, Chinese actions in the Taiwan Strait Crises of 1954–58, the Indian border clash of 1962, the conflict with the Soviets along the Ussuri River in 1969–71, and the Sino-Vietnam War of 1979 all had the common feature of a sudden blow followed quickly by a political phase. Having restored the psychological equation, in Chinese eyes, genuine deterrence has been achieved.[37]

When the Chinese view of preemption encounters the Western concept of deterrence, a vicious circle can result: acts conceived as defensive in China may be treated as aggressive by the outside world; deterrent moves by the West may be interpreted in China as encirclement. The United States and China wrestled with this dilemma repeatedly during the Cold War; to some extent they have not yet found a way to transcend it.

Conventional wisdom has ascribed the Chinese decision to enter the Korean War to the American decision to cross the 38th parallel in early October 1950 and the advance of U.N. forces to the Yalu River, the Chinese-Korean border. Another theory was innate Communist aggressiveness on the model of the European dictators a decade earlier. Recent scholarship demonstrates that neither theory was correct. Mao and his colleagues had no strategic designs on Korea in the sense of challenging its sovereignty; before the war they were more concerned about balancing Russia there. Nor did they expect to challenge the United States militarily. They entered the war only after long deliberations and much hesitation as a kind of preemptive move.

The triggering event for planning was the initial dispatch of American troops to Korea coupled with the neutralization of the Taiwan Strait. From that moment, Mao ordered planning for Chinese entry into the Korean War for the purpose, at a minimum, of preventing the collapse of North Korea—and occasionally for the maximal revolutionary aim of expelling American forces from the peninsula entirely.[38] He assumed—well before American or South Korean forces had moved north of the 38th parallel—that, unless China intervened, North Korea would be overwhelmed. Stopping the American advance to the Yalu was a subsidiary element. It created, in Mao's mind, an opportunity for a surprise attack and a chance to mobilize public opinion; it was not the principal motivating factor. Once the United States repelled the initial North Korean advance in August 1950, Chinese intervention became highly probable; when it turned the tide of battle by outflanking the North Korean army at Inchon and then crossed the 38th parallel, it grew inevitable.

China's strategy generally exhibits three characteristics: meticulous analysis of long-term trends, careful study of tactical options, and detached exploration of operational decisions. Zhou Enlai started that process by chairing conferences of Chinese leaders on July 7 and July 10—two weeks after the American deployment in Korea—to analyze the impact on China of American actions. The participants agreed to redeploy troops originally intended for the invasion of Taiwan to the Korean border and to constitute them as the Northeast Border Defense Army with the mission "to defend the borders of the Northeast, and to prepare to support the war operations of the Korean People's Army if necessary." By the end of July—or more than two months before U.S. forces crossed the 38th parallel—over 250,000 Chinese troops had been assembled on the Korean border.[39]

The Politburo and Central Military Commission meetings continued through August. On August 4, six weeks before the Inchon landing, when the military situation was still favorable to the invading North Korean forces and the front was still deep in South Korea around the city of Pusan, Mao, skeptical about North Korea's capabilities, told the Politburo: "If the American imperialists are victorious, they will become dizzy with success, and then be in a position to threaten us. We have to help Korea; we have to assist them. This can be in the form of a volunteer force, and be at a time of our choosing, but we must start to prepare."[40] At the same meeting, Zhou made the same basic analysis: "If the American imperialists crush North Korea, they will be swollen with arrogance, and peace will be threatened. If we want to assure victory, we must increase the China factor; this may produce a change in the international situation. We must take a long-range view."[41] In other words, it was the defeat of the still advancing North Korea, not the particular location of American forces, that China needed to resist. The next day, Mao ordered his top commanders to "complete their preparations within this month and be ready for orders to carry out war operations."[42]

On August 13, China's 13th Army Corps held a conference of senior military leaders to discuss this mission. Though expressing reservations about the August deadline, the conference participants concluded that China "should take the initiative, cooperate with the Korean People's Army, march forward without reluctance, and break up the enemy's dream of aggression."[43]

In the meantime, staff analysis and map exercises were taking place. They led the Chinese to conclusions Westerners would have considered counterintuitive, to the effect that China could win a war against the American armed forces. American commitments around the world, so the argument ran, would limit U.S. deployment to a maximum of 500,000, while China had an army of four million to draw on. China's proximity to the battlefield gave it a logistical advantage. Chinese planners thought they would have a psychological advantage too because most of the world's people would support China.[44]

Not even the possibility of a nuclear strike daunted the Chinese planners—probably because they had no firsthand experience with nuclear weapons and no means of acquiring them. They concluded (though not without some prominent dissenters) that an American nuclear response was unlikely in the face of the Soviet nuclear capacity, as well as the risk, due to the "jigsaw pattern" of troops on the peninsula, that an American nuclear strike on Chinese troops advancing into Korea might destroy U.S. forces as well.[45]

On August 26, Zhou, in a talk to the Central Military Commission, summed up the Chinese strategy. Beijing should "not treat the Korean problem merely as one of concerning a brother country or as one related to the interests of the Northeast." Instead Korea "should be regarded as an important international issue." Korea, Zhou argued, "is indeed the focus of the struggles in the world. . . . After conquering Korea, the United States will certainly turn to Vietnam and other colonial countries. Therefore the Korean problem is at least the key to the East."[46] Zhou concluded that due to recent North Korean reversals, "Our duty is now much heavier . . . and we should prepare for the worst and prepare quickly." Zhou stressed the need for secrecy, so that "we could enter the war and give the enemy a sudden blow."[47]

All of this was taking place weeks before MacArthur's amphibious landing at Inchon (which a Chinese study group had predicted) and well over a month before U.N. forces crossed the 38th parallel. In short, China entered the war based on a carefully considered assessment of strategic trends, not as a reaction to an American tactical maneuver—nor out of a legalistic determination to defend the sanctity of the 38th parallel. A Chinese offensive was a preemptive strategy against dangers that had not yet materialized and based on judgments about ultimate American purposes toward China that were misapprehended. It was also an expression of the crucial role Korea played in China's long-range calculations—a condition perhaps even more relevant in the contemporary world. Mao's insistence on his course was also probably influenced by a belief that it was the only way to remedy his acquiescence in the Kim Il-sung and Stalin strategy of invasion. Otherwise he might have been blamed by other leaders for the worsening of China's strategic situation by the presence of the Seventh Fleet in the Taiwan Strait and of American forces on China's borders.

The obstacles to Chinese intervention were so daunting that all of Mao's leadership was needed to achieve the approval of his colleagues. Two major commanders, including Lin Biao, refused the command of the Northeast Border Defense Army on various pretexts before Mao found in Peng Dehuai a commander prepared to undertake the assignment.

Mao prevailed, as he had in all key decisions, and preparations for the entry of Chinese forces into Korea went inexorably forward. October saw American and allied forces moving toward the Yalu, determined to unify Korea and to shelter it under a U.N. resolution. Their purpose was to defend the new status quo with these forces, technically constituting a U.N. command. The movement of the two armies toward each other thus acquired a foreordained quality about it; the Chinese were preparing a blow while the Americans and their allies remained oblivious to the challenge waiting for them at the end of their march north.

Zhou was careful to set the diplomatic stage. On September 24 he protested to the United Nations what he characterized as American efforts to "extend the war of aggression against Korea, to carry out armed aggression on Taiwan, and to extend further its aggression against China."[48] On October 3, he warned the Indian Ambassador K. M. Panikkar, that U.S. troops would cross the 38th parallel and that "[i]f the U.S. troops really do so, we cannot sit by idly and remain indifferent. We will intervene. Please report this to the Prime Minister of your country."[49] Panikkar replied that he expected the crossing to occur within the next twelve hours, but that the Indian government would "not be able to take any effective action" until eighteen hours after the receipt of his cable.[50] Zhou responded: "That is the Americans' business. The purpose of this evening's talk is to let you know our attitude toward one of the questions raised by Prime Minister Nehru in his letter."[51] The talk was more making a record for what was already decided than a last plea for peace, as it is so often treated.

At that point, Stalin reentered the scene as the deus ex machina for the continuation of the conflict he had encouraged and which he did not want to see ended. The North Korean army was collapsing, and another American landing on the opposite coast was expected by Soviet intelligence near Wonsan (wrongly). Chinese preparations for intervention were far advanced but as yet not irrevocable. Stalin therefore decided, in a message on October 1 to Mao, to demand Chinese intervention. After Mao deferred a decision, citing the danger of American intervention, Stalin sent a follow-up telegram. He was prepared, he insisted, to pledge Soviet military support in an all-out war should the United States react to Chinese intervention:

> Of course, I took into account also [the possibility] that the USA, despite its unreadiness for a big war, could still be drawn into a big war out of [considerations of] prestige, which, in turn, would drag China into the war, and along with this draw into the war the USSR, which is bound with China by the Mutual Assistance Pact. Should we fear this? In my opinion, we should not, because together we will be stronger than the USA and England, while the other European capitalist states (with the exception of Germany which is unable to provide any assistance to the United States now) do not present serious military forces. If a war is inevitable, then let it be waged now, and not in a few years when Japanese militarism will be restored as an ally of the USA and when the USA and Japan will have a ready-made bridgehead on the continent in a form of the entire Korea run by Syngman Rhee.[52]

At its face value, this extraordinary communication seemed to assert that Stalin was ready to go to war with the United States to prevent Korea from becoming part of America's strategic sphere. A united, pro-American Korea—to which, in Stalin's eyes, sooner or later a resurgent Japan would become a partner—presented, in that analysis, the same threat in Asia as the emerging NATO in Europe. The two together might be more than the Soviet Union could handle.

In the event, when put to the test, Stalin proved unwilling to undertake the all-out commitment he had pledged to Mao—or even any aspect of direct confrontation with the United States. He knew that the balance of power was too unfavorable for a showdown, much less a two-front war. He sought to tie down the American military potential in Asia and to involve China in enterprises that magnified its dependence on Soviet support. What Stalin's letter does demonstrate is how seriously Soviet and Chinese strategists assessed the strategic importance of Korea, if for quite different reasons.

Stalin's letter placed Mao in a predicament. It was one thing to plan intervention in the abstract partly as an exercise in revolutionary solidarity. It was another actually to carry it out, especially when the North Korean army was on the verge of disintegrating. Chinese intervention made imperative Soviet supplies and, above all, Soviet air cover, since the PLA had no modern air force to speak of. Thus when the issue of intervention was put before the Politburo, Mao received an unusually ambivalent response, causing him to pause before giving the final answer. Instead, Mao dispatched Lin Biao (who had refused the command of the Chinese forces, citing health problems) and Zhou to Russia to discuss the prospects of Soviet assistance. Stalin was in the Caucasus on vacation but saw no reason to alter his schedule. He obliged Zhou to come to his retreat even though (or, perhaps, because) Zhou would have no means of communication with Beijing from Stalin's dacha except through Soviet channels.

Zhou and Lin Biao had been instructed to warn Stalin that, without assurances of guaranteed supplies, China might not, in the end, carry out what it had been preparing for two months. For China would be the principal theater of the conflict Stalin was promoting. Its prospects would depend on the supplies and direct support Stalin would make available. When faced with this reality, Mao's colleagues reacted ambivalently. Some opponents even went so far as to argue that priority should be given to domestic development. For once Mao seemed to hesitate, if only for a moment. Was it a maneuver to obtain a guarantee of support from Stalin before Chinese forces were irrevocably committed? Or was he truly undecided?

A symptom of internal Chinese divisions is the mysterious case of a telegram from Mao to Stalin sent on the night of October 2, of which two contradictory versions are held in the archives of Beijing and Moscow.

In one version of Mao's telegram—drafted in Mao's handwriting, filed in the archives in Beijing, published in a *neibu* ("internal circulation only") Chinese collection of Mao's manuscripts, but likely never actually dispatched to Moscow—Mao wrote that Beijing had "decided to send some of our troops to Korea under the name of [Chinese People's] Volunteers to fight the United States and its lackey Syngman Rhee and to aid our Korean comrades."[53] Mao cited the danger that absent Chinese intervention, "the Korean revolutionary force will meet with a fundamental defeat, and the American aggressors will rampage unchecked once they occupy the whole of Korea. This will be unfavorable to the entire East."[54] Mao noted that "we must be prepared for a declaration of war by the United States and for the subsequent use of the U.S. air force to bomb many of China's main cities and industrial bases, as well as an attack by the U.S. navy on [our] coastal areas." The Chinese plan was to send twelve divisions from south Manchuria on October 15. "At the initial stage," Mao wrote, they would deploy north of the 38th parallel and "will merely engage in defensive warfare" against enemy troops that cross the parallel. In the meantime, "they will wait for the delivery of Soviet weapons. Once they are [well] equipped, they will cooperate with the Korean comrades in counterattacks to annihilate American aggressor troops."[55]

In a different version of Mao's October 2 telegram—sent via the Soviet ambassador in Beijing, received in Moscow, and filed in the Russian presidential archives—Mao informed Stalin that Beijing was *not* prepared to send troops. He held out the possibility that after further consultations with Moscow (and, he implied, pledges of additional Soviet military support), Beijing would be willing to join the conflict.

For years, scholars analyzed the first version of the telegram as if it were the sole operative version; when the second version emerged, some wondered whether one of the documents might be a fabrication. Most plausible is the explanation put forth by the Chinese scholar Shen Zhihua: that Mao drafted the first version of the telegram intending to send it, but that the Chinese leadership was so divided that a more equivocal telegram was substituted. The discrepancy suggests that even as Chinese troops advanced toward Korea, the Chinese leadership was still debating about how long to hold out for a definitive commitment of support from its Soviet ally before taking the last irrevocable step.[56]

The two Communist autocrats had been trained in a hard school of power politics, which they were now applying to each other. In this case, Stalin proved the quintessential hardball player. He coolly informed Mao (via a joint telegram with Zhou) that, in view of China's hesitation, the best option would be to withdraw the remnants of the North Korean forces into China, where Kim Il-sung could form a provisional government-in-exile. The sick and disabled could go to the Soviet Union. He did not mind Americans on his Asian border, said Stalin, since he already faced them along the European dividing lines.

Stalin knew that the only outcome Mao wanted less than American forces at China's borders was a provisional Korean government in Manchuria in contact with the Korean minority living there, claiming some kind of sovereignty and constantly pressing military adventures into Korea. And he must have sensed that Mao had passed the point of no return. China's choice, at this point, was between an American army on the Yalu, directly threatening the half of Chinese industry within easy reach, and a disgruntled Soviet Union, holding back on supplies, perhaps reinvoking its "rights" in Manchuria. Or else China would proceed along the course Mao had continued to pursue even while bargaining with Stalin. He was in a position where he had to intervene, paradoxically in part to protect himself against Soviet designs.

On October 19, after several days of delay to await a guarantee of Soviet supplies, Mao ordered the army to cross into Korea. Stalin pledged substantial logistical support, provided only that it involved no direct confrontation with the United States (for example, air cover over Manchuria but not over Korea).

Mutual suspicion was so rampant that Zhou had no sooner returned to Moscow, from where he could communicate with Beijing, than Stalin seemingly reversed himself. To prevent Mao from maneuvering the Soviet Union into bearing the brunt of equipping the PLA without getting the benefit of its tying down American forces in combat in Korea, Stalin informed Zhou that no supplies would start moving until Chinese forces had, in fact, entered Korea. Mao issued the order on October 19, in effect without an assurance of Soviet support. After that, the originally promised Soviet support was reinstated, though the ever cautious Stalin confined Soviet air support to Chinese territory. So much for the readiness expressed in his earlier letter to Mao to risk a general war over Korea.

Both Communist leaders had exploited each other's necessities and insecurities. Mao had succeeded in obtaining Soviet military supplies to modernize his army—some Chinese sources claim that during the Korean War he received equipment for sixty-four infantry divisions and twenty-two air divisions[57]—and Stalin had tied down China into a conflict with the United States in Korea.

Sino-American Confrontation

The United States was a passive observer to these internal Communist machinations. It explored no middle ground between stopping at the 38th parallel and the unification of Korea, and ignored the series of Chinese warnings about the consequences of crossing that line. Acheson puzzlingly did not consider them official communications and thought they could be ignored. He probably thought he could face Mao down.

None of the many documents published to date by all sides reveals any serious discussion of a diplomatic option by any of the parties. The many meetings of Zhou with the Central Military Commission or the Politburo reveal no such intent. Contrary to popular perception, Beijing's "warning" to Washington not to cross the 38th parallel was almost certainly a diversionary tactic. By that point, Mao had already sent ethnic-Korean PLA troops from Manchuria to Korea to assist the North Koreans, moved a significant military force away from Taiwan and toward the Korean border, and promised Chinese support to Stalin and Kim.

The only chance that might have existed to avoid immediate U.S.-China combat can be found in instructions Mao sent in a message to Zhou, still in Moscow, about his strategic design on October 14, as Chinese troops were preparing to cross the Korean border:

> Our troops will continue improving [their] defense works if they have enough time. If the enemy tenaciously defends Pyongyang and Wonsan and does not advance [north] in the next six months, our troops will not attack Pyongyang and Wonsan. Our troops will attack Pyongyang and Wonsan only when they are well equipped and trained, and have clear superiority over the enemy in both air and ground forces. In short, we will not talk about waging offensives for six months.[58]

There was no chance, of course, that in six months China could have achieved clear superiority in either category.

Had American forces stopped at the line, from Pyongyang to Wonsan (the narrow neck of the Korean Peninsula), would that have created a buffer zone to meet Mao's strategic concern? Would some American diplomatic move toward Beijing have made any difference? Would Mao have been satisfied with using his presence in Korea to reequip his forces? Perhaps the six-month pause Mao mentioned to Zhou would have provided an occasion for diplomatic contact, for military warnings, or for Mao or Stalin to change his mind. On the other hand, a buffer zone on hitherto Communist territory was almost certainly not Mao's idea of his revolutionary or strategic duty. Still he was enough of a Sun Tzu disciple to pursue seemingly contradictory strategies simultaneously. The United States, in any event, had no such capacity. It opted for a U.N.-endorsed demarcation line along the Yalu over what it could protect with its own forces and its own diplomacy along the narrow neck of the Korean Peninsula.

In this manner, each side of the triangular relationship moved toward a war with the makings of a global conflict. The battle lines moved back and forth. Chinese forces took Seoul but were driven back until a military stalemate settled over the combat zone within the framework of armistice negotiations lasting nearly two years, during which American forces refrained from offensive operations—the almost ideal outcome from the Soviet point of view. The Soviet advice throughout was to drag out the negotiations, and therefore the war, as long as possible. An armistice agreement emerged on July 27, 1953, settling essentially along the prewar line of the 38th parallel.

None of the participants achieved all of its aims. For the United States, the armistice agreement realized the purpose for which it had entered the war: it denied success to the North Korean aggression; but it had, at the same time, enabled China, at a moment of great weakness, to fight the nuclear superpower to a standstill and oblige it to retreat from its furthest advance. It preserved American credibility in protecting allies but at the cost of incipient allied revolt and domestic discord. Observers could not fail to remember the debate that had developed in the United States over war aims. General MacArthur, applying traditional maxims, sought victory; the administration, interpreting the war as a feint to lure America into Asia—which was surely Stalin's strategy—was prepared to settle for a military draw (and probably a long-term political setback), the first such outcome in a war fought by America. The inability to harmonize political and military goals may have tempted other Asian challengers to believe in America's domestic vulnerability to wars without clear-cut military outcomes—a dilemma that reappeared with a vengeance in the vortex of Vietnam a decade later.

Nor can Beijing be said to have achieved all its objectives, at least in conventional military terms. Mao did not succeed in liberating all of Korea from "American imperialism," as Chinese propaganda claimed initially. But he had gone to war for larger and in some ways more abstract, even romantic, aims: to test the "New China" with a trial by fire and to purge what Mao perceived as China's historic softness and passivity; to prove to the West (and, to some extent, the Soviet Union) that China was now a military power and would use force to vindicate its interests; to secure China's leadership of the Communist movement in Asia; and to strike at the United States (which Mao believed was planning an eventual invasion of China) at a moment he perceived as opportune. The principal contribution of the new ideology was not its strategic concepts so much as the willpower to defy the strongest nations and to chart its own course.

In that broader sense, the Korean War was something more than a draw. It established the newly founded People's Republic of China as a military power and center of Asian revolution. It also built up military credibility that China, as an adversary worthy of fear and respect, would draw on through the next several decades. The memory of Chinese intervention in Korea would later restrain U.S. strategy significantly in Vietnam. Beijing succeeded in using the war and the accompanying "Resist America, Aid Korea" propaganda and purge campaign to accomplish two central aims of Mao's: to eliminate domestic opposition to Party rule, and to instill "revolutionary enthusiasm" and national pride in the population. Nourishing resentment of Western exploitation, Mao framed the war as a struggle to "defeat American arrogance"; battlefield accomplishments were treated as a form of spiritual rejuvenation after decades of Chinese weakness and abuse. China emerged from the war exhausted but redefined in both its own eyes and the world's.

Ironically, the biggest loser in the Korean War was Stalin, who had given the green light to Kim Il-sung to start and had urged, even blackmailed, Mao to intervene massively. Encouraged by America's acquiescence in the Communist victory in China, he had calculated that Kim Il-sung could repeat the pattern in Korea. The American intervention thwarted that objective. He urged Mao to intervene, expecting that such an act would create a lasting hostility between China and the United States and increase China's dependence on Moscow.

Stalin was right in his strategic prediction but erred grievously in assessing the consequences. Chinese dependence on the Soviet Union was double-edged. The rearmament of China that the Soviet Union undertook, in the end, shortened the time until China would be able to act on its own. The Sino-American schism Stalin was promoting did not lead to an improvement of Sino-Soviet relations, nor did it reduce China's Titoist option. On the contrary, Mao calculated that he could defy both superpowers simultaneously. American conflicts with the Soviet Union were so profound that Mao judged he needed to pay no price for Soviet backing in the Cold War, indeed that he could use it as a threat even without its approval, as he did in a number of subsequent crises. Starting with the end of the Korean War, Soviet relations with China deteriorated, caused in no small part by the opaqueness with which Stalin had encouraged Kim Il-sung's adventure, the brutality with which he had pressed China toward intervention, and, above all, the grudging manner of Soviet support, all of which was in the form of repayable loans. Within a decade, the Soviet Union would become China's principal adversary. And before another decade had passed, another reversal of alliance would take place.

CHAPTER 6

China Confronts Both Superpowers

OTTO VON BISMARCK, probably the greatest diplomat of the second half of the nineteenth century, once said that in a world order of five states, it is always desirable to be part of a group of three. Applied to the interplay of three countries, one would therefore think that it is always desirable to be in a group of two.

That truth escaped the chief actors of the China-Soviet-U.S. triangle for a decade and a half—partly because of the unprecedented maneuvers of Mao. In foreign policy, statesmen often serve their objectives by bringing about a confluence of interests. Mao's policy was based on the opposite. He learned to exploit overlapping hostilities. The conflict between Moscow and Washington was the strategic essence of the Cold War; the hostility between Washington and Beijing dominated Asian diplomacy. But the two Communist states could never merge their respective hostility toward the United States—except briefly and incompletely in the Korean War—because of Mao's evolving rivalry with Moscow over ideological primacy and geostrategic analysis.

From the point of view of traditional power politics, Mao, of course, was in no position to act as an equal member of the triangular relationship. He was by far the weakest and most vulnerable. But by playing on the mutual hostility of the nuclear superpowers and creating the impression of being impervious to nuclear devastation, he managed to bring about a kind of diplomatic sanctuary for China. Mao added a novel dimension to power politics, one for which I know of no precedent. Far from seeking the support of either superpower—as traditional balance-of-power theory would have counseled—he exploited the Soviet-U.S. fear of each other by challenging each of the rivals simultaneously.

Within a year of the end of the Korean War, Mao confronted America militarily in a crisis in the Taiwan Strait. Almost simultaneously, he began to confront the Soviet Union ideologically. He felt confident in pursuing both courses because he calculated that neither superpower would permit his defeat by the other. It was a brilliant application of the Zhuge Liang Empty City Stratagem described in an earlier chapter, which turns material weakness into a psychological asset.

At the end of the Korean War, traditional students of international affairs—especially Western scholars—expected that Mao would seek a period of respite. Since the victory of the Communists, there had been nary a month of even apparent tranquility. Land reform, the implementation of the Soviet economic model, and the destruction of the domestic opposition had constituted a packed and dramatic domestic agenda. Simultaneously the still quite underdeveloped country was engaged in a war with a nuclear superpower in possession of advanced military technology.

Mao had no intention to enter history for the respites he availed to his society. Instead, he launched China into a set of new upheavals: two conflicts with the United States in the Taiwan Strait, the beginning of conflict with India, and a growing ideological and geopolitical controversy with the Soviet Union.

For the United States, by contrast, the end of the Korean War and the advent of the administration of Dwight Eisenhower marked the return to domestic "normalcy" that would last for the rest of the decade. Internationally, the Korean War became a template for Communism's commitment to expansion by political subversion or military aggression wherever possible. Other parts of Asia supplied corroborating evidence: the guerrilla war in Malaysia; the violent bid for power by leftists in Singapore; and, increasingly, in the wars in Indochina. Where the American perception went partially awry was in thinking of Communism as a monolith and failing to understand the depth of suspicion, even at this early stage, between the two Communist giants.

The Eisenhower administration dealt with the threat of aggression by methods borrowed from America's European experience. It tried to shore up the viability of countries bordering the Communist world following the example of the Marshall Plan, and it constructed military alliances in the style of NATO, such as the Southeast Asia Treaty Organization (SEATO) between the new nations bordering China in Southeast Asia. It did not fully consider the essential difference between European conditions and those at the fringe of Asia. The postwar European countries were established states with elaborated institutions. Their viability depended on closing the gap between expectation and reality, caused by the depredations of the Second World War—an expansive project that proved manageable, however, in a relatively brief period of time as history is measured. With domestic stability substantially assured, the security problem turned into defense against a potential military attack across established international frontiers.

In Asia around the rim of China, however, the states were still in the process of formation. The challenge was to create political institutions and a political consensus out of ethnic and religious divisions. This was less a military, more a conceptual, task; the security threat was domestic insurrection or guerrilla warfare rather than organized units crossing military frontiers. This was a particular challenge in Indochina, where the end of the French colonial project left four countries (North Vietnam, South Vietnam, Cambodia, and Laos) with contested borders and weak independent national traditions. These conflicts had their own dynamism not controllable in detail from Beijing or Moscow or Washington, yet influenced by the policies of the strategic triangle. In Asia, therefore, there were very few, if any, purely military challenges. Military strategy and political and social reform were inextricably linked.

The First Taiwan Strait Crisis

Beijing and Taipei proclaimed what amounted to two competing versions of the same Chinese national identity. In the Nationalist view, Taiwan was not an independent state: it was the home of the Republic of China's government-in-exile, which had been temporarily displaced by Communist usurpers, but which—as Nationalist propaganda insistently proclaimed—would return to assume its rightful place on the mainland. In Beijing's conception, Taiwan was a renegade province whose separation from the mainland and alliance with foreign powers represented the last vestige of China's "century of humiliation." Both Chinese sides agreed that Taiwan and the mainland were part of the same political entity. The disagreement was about *which* Chinese government was the rightful ruler.

Washington and its allies periodically floated the idea of recognizing the Republic of China and the People's Republic of China as separate states—the so-called two China solution. Both Chinese sides vociferously rejected this proposal on the ground that it would prevent them from fulfilling a sacred national obligation to liberate the other. Against its initial judgment, Washington affirmed Taipei's stance that the Republic of China was the "real" Chinese government, entitled to China's seat in the United Nations and other international institutions. Assistant Secretary of State for Eastern Affairs Dean Rusk—later to become Secretary of State—articulated this stance for the Truman administration in 1951, stating that, despite appearances to the contrary, "The Peiping [then the Nationalist appellation for Beijing] . . . regime is not the Government of China. . . . It is not Chinese. It is not entitled to speak for China in the community of nations."[1] The People's Republic of China with its capital in Beijing was, for Washington, a legal and diplomatic nonentity, despite its actual control over the world's largest population. This would remain, with only minor variations, the official American position for the next two decades.

The unintended consequence was American involvement in the Chinese civil war. It cast the United States, in Beijing's conception of international affairs, as the latest in a string of foreign powers perceived as conspiring for a century to divide and dominate China. In Beijing's view, so long as Taiwan remained under a separate administrative authority receiving foreign political and military assistance, the project of founding a "New China" would remain incomplete.

The United States, Chiang's primary ally, had little appetite for a Nationalist reconquest of the mainland. Though Taipei's supporters in Congress periodically called on the White House to "unleash Chiang," no American President seriously considered a campaign to reverse the Communist victory in the Chinese civil war—a source of profound misapprehension on the Communist side.

The first direct Taiwan crisis erupted in August 1954, little more than a year after the end of active hostilities in the Korean War. The pretext for it was a territorial quirk of the Nationalist retreat from the mainland: the remaining presence of Nationalist forces on several heavily fortified islands hugging the Chinese coast. These offshore islands, which were much closer to the mainland than to Taiwan, included Quemoy, Matsu, and several smaller outcroppings of land.[2] Depending on one's view, the offshore islands were either Taiwan's first line of defense or, as Nationalist propaganda proclaimed, its forward operating base for an eventual reconquest of the mainland.

The offshore islands were an odd location for what turned into two major crises within a decade in which, at one point, both the Soviet

Union and the United States implied a readiness to use nuclear weapons. Neither the Soviet Union nor the United States had any strategic interest in the offshore islands. Neither, as it turned out, did China. Instead, Mao used them to make a general point about international relations: as part of his grand strategy against the United States in the first crisis and against the Soviet Union—especially Khrushchev—in the second.

At the closest point, Quemoy was roughly two miles from the major Chinese port city of Xiamen; Matsu was similarly close to the city of Fuzhou.[3] The islands were visible with the naked eye from the mainland and within easy artillery range. Taiwan was well over a hundred miles away. PLA forays against the offshore islands in 1949 were turned back by strong Nationalist resistance. Truman's dispatch of the Seventh Fleet to the Taiwan Strait at the outset of the Korean War forced Mao to postpone the planned invasion of Taiwan indefinitely and Beijing's appeals to Moscow for support in the full "liberation" of Taiwan were met by evasions—a first stage toward the ultimate estrangement.

The situation grew more complex when Eisenhower succeeded Truman as President. In his first State of the Union address on February 2, 1953, Eisenhower announced an end to the Seventh Fleet's patrol in the Taiwan Strait. Because the fleet had prevented attacks in both directions, Eisenhower reasoned that the mission had "meant, in effect, that the U.S. Navy was required to serve as a defensive arm of Communist China" even while Chinese forces were killing American troops in Korea. Now he was ordering it out of the strait, since Americans "certainly have no obligation to protect a nation fighting us in Korea."[4]

In China, the Seventh Fleet's deployment to the strait had been seen as a major American offensive move. Now, paradoxically, its redeployment set the stage for a new crisis. Taipei began reinforcing Quemoy and Matsu with thousands of additional troops and a significant store of military hardware.

Both sides now faced a dilemma. China would never abandon

its commitment to the return of Taiwan, but it could postpone its implementation in the face of overwhelming obstacles such as the presence of the Seventh Fleet. After the fleet's withdrawal, it faced no comparable obstacle vis-à-vis the offshore islands. For its part, America had committed itself to the defense of Taiwan, but a war over offshore islands that Secretary of State John Foster Dulles described as "a bunch of rocks" was another matter.[5] The confrontation became more acute when the Eisenhower administration began negotiating a formal mutual defense treaty with Taiwan, followed by the creation of the Southeast Asia Treaty Organization.

When faced with a challenge, Mao generally took the most unexpected and most intricate course. While Secretary of State John Dulles was flying to Manila for the formation of SEATO Mao ordered a massive shelling of Quemoy and Matsu—a shot across the bow of Taiwan's increasing autonomy and a test of Washington's commitment to multilateral defense of Asia.

The initial artillery barrage on Quemoy claimed the lives of two American military officers and prompted the immediate redeployment of three U.S. carrier battle groups to the vicinity of the Taiwan Strait. Keeping to its pledge to no longer serve as a "defensive arm" of the People's Republic of China, Washington now approved retaliatory artillery and aircraft strikes by Nationalist forces against the mainland.[6] In the meantime, members of the Joint Chiefs of Staff began developing plans for the possible use of tactical nuclear weapons should the crisis escalate. Eisenhower demurred for the moment at least, and approved a plan to seek a cease-fire resolution at the U.N. Security Council. The crisis over territory nobody wanted had become global.

The crisis had, however, no obvious political objective. China was not threatening Taiwan directly; the United States did not want a change in the status of the strait. The crisis became less a rush to confrontation—as the media presented it—than a subtle exercise in crisis management. Both sides maneuvered toward intricate rules designed to *prevent* the military confrontation they were proclaiming on the political level. Sun Tzu was alive and well in the diplomacy of the Taiwan Strait.

The outcome was "combative coexistence," not war. To deter an attack caused by a misapprehension as to American resolve—as in Korea—Dulles and the Taiwanese ambassador in Washington, on November 23, 1954, initialed the text of the long-planned defense treaty between the United States and Taiwan. However, on the matter of the territory that had just come under actual attack, the American commitment was ambiguous: the treaty applied specifically only to Taiwan and the Pescadores Islands (a larger group of islands about twenty-five miles from Taiwan). It made no mention of Quemoy, Matsu, and other territories close to the Chinese mainland, leaving them to be defined later, "as may be determined by mutual consent."[7]

For his part, Mao prohibited his commanders from attacking American forces, while laying down a marker to blunt America's most intimidating weapon. China, he proclaimed, in the incongruous setting of a meeting with the new Finnish ambassador in Beijing, was impervious to the threat of nuclear war:

> The Chinese people are not to be cowed by U.S. atomic blackmail. Our country has a population of 600 million and an area of 9,600,000 square kilometres. The United States cannot annihilate the Chinese nation with its small stack of atom bombs. Even if the U.S. atom bombs were so powerful that, when dropped on China, they would make a hole right through the earth, or even blow it up, that would hardly mean anything to the universe as a whole, though it might be a major event for the solar system . . . if the United States with its planes plus the A-bomb is to launch a war of aggression against China, then China with its millet plus rifles is sure to emerge the victor. The people of the whole world will support us.[8]

Since both Chinese sides were playing by *wei qi* rules, the mainland began moving into the gap left by the treaty's omissions. On January 18, it invaded the Dachen and Yijiangshan Islands, two smaller island groups not specifically covered by the treaty. Both sides continued to carefully define their limits. The United States did not attempt to defend the small islands; the Seventh Fleet, in fact, assisted with the evacuation of Nationalist forces. PLA forces were prohibited to fire on American armed forces.

As it turned out, Mao's rhetoric had a greater impact on his Soviet allies than on the United States. For it confronted Khrushchev with the dilemma of supporting his ally for a cause that reflected no Russian strategic interest but involved risks of nuclear war, which Khrushchev increasingly described as unacceptable. The Soviet Union's European allies with their tiny populations were even more terrified of Mao's utterances about China's capacity to lose half its population in a war and eventually prevail.

As for the United States, Eisenhower and Dulles matched Mao's dexterity. They had no intention to test Mao's endurance with respect to nuclear warfare. But neither were they prepared to abandon the option of defending the national interest. In the last week of January, they arranged for the passage of a resolution of both houses of the United States Congress authorizing Eisenhower to use U.S. forces to defend Taiwan, the Pescadores Islands, and "related positions and territories" in the Taiwan Strait.[9] The art of crisis management is to raise the stakes to where the adversary will not follow, but in a manner that avoids a tit for tat. On that principle Dulles, at a press conference on March 15, 1955, announced that the United States was prepared to meet any major new Communist offensive with tactical nuclear weapons, which China did not have. The next day, Eisenhower confirmed the warning, observing that so long as civilians were not in harm's way, he saw no reason the United States could not use tactical nuclear weapons "just exactly as you would use a bullet or anything else."[10] It was the first time the United States had made a specific nuclear threat in an ongoing crisis.

Mao proved more willing to announce China's imperviousness to nuclear war than to practice it. He ordered Zhou Enlai, then at the Asian-African Conference of Non-Aligned countries in Bandung, Indonesia, to sound the retreat. On April 23, 1955, Zhou extended the olive branch: "[T]he Chinese people do not want to have a war with the United States of America. The Chinese government is willing to sit down and enter into negotiations with the U.S. government to discuss the question of relaxing tension in the Far East, and especially the question of relaxing tension in the Taiwan area."[11] The next week China ended the shelling campaign in the Taiwan Strait.

The outcome, like that of the Korean War, was a draw, in which each side achieved its short-term objectives. The United States faced down a military threat. Mao, aware that mainland forces did not have the capacity to occupy Quemoy and Matsu in the face of concerted opposition, later explained his strategy as having been much more complex. Far from seeking to occupy the offshore islands, he told Khrushchev that he had used the threat against them to keep Taiwan from breaking its link to the mainland:

> All we wanted to do was show our potential. We don't want Chiang to be too far away from us. We want to keep him within our reach. Having him [on Quemoy and Matsu] means we can get at him with our shore batteries as well as our air force. If we'd occupied the islands, we would have lost the ability to cause him discomfort any time we want.[12]

In that version, Beijing shelled Quemoy to reaffirm its claim to "one China" but restrained its action to prevent a "two China solution" from emerging.

Moscow, with a more literal approach to strategy and actual

knowledge of nuclear weapons, found it incomprehensible that a leader might go to the brink of nuclear war to make a largely symbolic point. As Khrushchev complained to Mao: "If you shoot, then you ought to capture these islands, and if you do not consider necessary capturing these islands, then there is no use in firing. I do not understand this policy of yours."[13] It has even been claimed, in a one-sided but often thought-provoking biography of Mao, that Mao's real motive in the crisis had been to create a risk of nuclear war so acute that Moscow would be obliged to assist Beijing's fledgling nuclear weapons program to ease the pressure for Soviet assistance.[14] Among the many counter-intuitive aspects of the crisis was the apparent Soviet decision—later revoked as a result of the second offshore islands crisis—to help Beijing's nuclear program in order to put a distance between itself and its troublesome ally in any future crisis by leaving the nuclear defense of China in China's hands.

Diplomatic Interlude with the United States

One result of the crisis was the resumption of a formal dialogue between the United States and China. At the Geneva Conference of 1954 to settle the first Vietnam War between France and the Communist-led independence movement, Beijing and Washington had grudgingly agreed to maintain contacts through consular-level officials based in Geneva.

The arrangement provided a framework for a kind of safety net to avoid confrontations because of misapprehensions. But neither side did so with any conviction. Or rather, their convictions ran in opposite directions. The Korean War had put an end to all diplomatic initiatives toward China in the Truman administration. The Eisenhower administration—coming into office with the war in Korea not yet ended—considered China the most intransigent and revolutionary of the Communist powers. Hence its primary strategic goal was the construction of a security system in Asia to contain potential Chinese aggression. Diplomatic overtures to China were avoided lest they jeopardize still fragile security systems such as SEATO and the emerging alliances with Japan and South Korea. Dulles's refusal to shake hands with Zhou Enlai at the Geneva Conference reflected both moral rejection and strategic design.

Mao's attitude was the mirror image of Dulles's and Eisenhower's. The Taiwan issue created a permanent cause of confrontation especially so long as the United States treated the Taiwan authorities as the legitimate government of all of China. Deadlock was inherent in Sino-U.S. diplomacy because China would discuss no other subject until the United States agreed to withdraw from Taiwan, and the United States would not talk about withdrawing from Taiwan until China had renounced the use of force to solve the Taiwan question.

By the same token, the Sino-U.S. dialogue, after the first Taiwan Strait Crisis, ran into the ground because so long as each side maintained its basic position, there was nothing to talk about. The United States reiterated that the status of Taiwan should be settled through negotiations between Beijing and Taipei, which should also involve the United States and Japan. Beijing interpreted this proposal as an attempt to reopen the Cairo Conference decision that, during the Second World War, declared Taiwan part of China. It refused as well to renounce the use of force as an infringement of China's sovereign right to establish control over its own national territory. Ambassador Wang Bingnan, the principal Chinese negotiator for a decade, summed up the deadlock in his memoirs: "In retrospect, it was impossible for the US to change its China policy at the time. Under the circumstances, we went directly at the Taiwan question, which was the most difficult, least likely to be resolved, and most emotional. It was only natural that talks could not get anywhere."[15]

Only two agreements resulted from these discussions. The first was procedural: to upgrade existing contacts at Geneva, which had been held at the consular level, to ambassadorial rank. (The significance of the ambassadorial designation is that ambassadors are technically personal representatives of their head of state and presumably have somewhat greater latitude and influence.) This only served to institutionalize paralysis. One hundred thirty-six meetings were held over a period of sixteen years from 1955 until 1971 between the local U.S. and Chinese ambassadors (most of them in Warsaw, which became the venue for the talks in 1958). The only substantive agreement reached was in September 1955, when China and the United States permitted citizens trapped in each country by the civil war to return home.[16]

Thereafter, for a decade and a half, American policy remained focused on eliciting a formal renunciation of the use of force from China. "We have searched year after year," Secretary of State Dean Rusk testified before the House Foreign Affairs Committee in March 1966, "for some sign that Communist China was ready to renounce the use of force to resolve disputes. We have also searched for some indication that it was ready to abandon its premise that the United States is its prime enemy. The Chinese Communist attitudes and actions have been hostile and rigid."[17]

American foreign policy toward no other country had ever been submitted to such a stringent precondition for negotiation as a blanket renunciation of the use of force. Rusk did take note of the gap between the fierce Chinese rhetoric and its relatively restrained international performance in the 1960s. Still, he argued that American policy, in effect, should be based on the rhetoric—that ideology was more significant than conduct:

> Some say we should ignore what the Chinese Communist leaders say and judge them only by what they do. It is true that they have been more cautious in action than in words—more cautious in what they do themselves than in what they have urged the Soviet Union to do. . . . But it does not follow that

> we should disregard the intentions and plans for the future which they have proclaimed.[18]

Based on these attitudes, in 1957, using the Chinese refusal to renounce the use of force over Taiwan as a pretext, the United States downgraded the Geneva talks from the ambassador to the first secretary level. China withdrew its delegation, and the talks were suspended. The second Taiwan Strait Crisis followed soon after—though ostensibly for another reason.

Mao, Khrushchev, and the Sino-Soviet Split

In 1953, Stalin died after more than three decades in power. His successor—after a brief transitional period—was Nikita Khrushchev. The terror of Stalin's rule had left its mark on Khrushchev's generation. They had made their big step up the ladder in the purges of the 1930s when an entire generation of leaders was wiped out. They had purchased the sudden rise to eminence at the cost of permanent emotional insecurity. They had witnessed—and participated in—the wholesale decapitation of a ruling group, and they knew that the same fate might await them; indeed Stalin was in the process of beginning another purge as he was dying. They were not yet ready to modify the system that had generated institutionalized terror. Rather they attempted to alter some of its practices while reaffirming the core beliefs to which they had devoted their lives, blaming the failures on the abuse of power by Stalin. (This was the psychological basis of what came to be known as Khrushchev's Secret Speech, to be discussed below.)

With all their posturing, the new leaders knew deep down that the Soviet Union was not competitive in an ultimate sense. Much of Khrushchev's foreign policy can be described as a quest to achieve a "quick fix": the explosion of a super-high-yield thermonuclear device in 1961; the succession of Berlin ultimatums; the Cuban Missile Crisis in 1962. With the perspective of the intervening decades, these steps can be considered a quest for a kind of psychological equilibrium permitting a negotiation with a country that Khrushchev deep down understood was considerably stronger.

Toward China, Khrushchev's posture was condescension tinged with frustration that the self-confident Chinese leaders presumed to challenge Moscow's ideological predominance. He grasped the strategic benefit of the Chinese alliance, but he feared the implications of the Chinese version of ideology. He tried to impress Mao but never learned the grammar of what Mao might have taken seriously. Mao used the Soviet threat without paying attention to Soviet priorities. In the end, Khrushchev withdrew from his initial commitment to the alliance with China into a sulky aloofness while gradually increasing Soviet military strength along the Chinese frontier, tempting his successor, Leonid Brezhnev, into exploring the prospects of preemptive action against China.

Ideology had brought Beijing and Moscow together, and ideology drove them apart again. There was too much shared history raising question marks. Chinese leaders could not forget the territorial exactions of the Czars nor Stalin's willingness, during the Second World War, to settle with Chiang Kai-shek at the expense of the Chinese Communist Party. The first meeting between Stalin and Mao had not gone well. When Mao came to put himself under Moscow's security umbrella, it took him two months to convince Stalin, and he had to pay for the alliance with major economic concessions in Manchuria and Xinjiang impairing the unity of China.

History was the starting point, but contemporary experience supplied seemingly endless frictions. The Soviet Union regarded the Communist world as a single strategic entity whose leadership was in Moscow. It had established satellite regimes in Eastern Europe that were dependent on Soviet military and, to some extent, economic support. It seemed natural to the Soviet Politburo that the same pattern of dominance should prevail in Asia.

In terms of Chinese history, his own Sinocentric view, and his own definition of Communist ideology, nothing could have been more repugnant to Mao. Cultural differences exacerbated latent tensions—especially since the Soviet leaders were generally oblivious of Chinese historic sensitivities. A good example is Khrushchev's request that China supply workers for logging projects in Siberia. He struck a raw nerve in Mao, who told him in 1958:

> You know, Comrade Khrushchev, for years it's been a widely held view that because China is an underdeveloped and overpopulated country, with widespread unemployment, it represents a good source of cheap labor. But you know, we Chinese find this attitude very offensive. Coming from you, it's rather embarrassing. If we were to accept your proposal, others . . . might think that the Soviet Union has the same image of China that the capitalist West has.[19]

Mao's passionate Sinocentrism prevented him from participating in the basic premises of the Moscow-run Soviet empire. The focal point of that empire's security and political efforts was in Europe, which was of secondary concern to Mao. When, in 1955, the Soviet Union created the Warsaw Pact of Communist countries as a counterweight to NATO, Mao refused to join. China would not subordinate the defense of its national interests to a coalition.

Instead, Zhou Enlai was sent to the 1955 Asian-African Conference in Bandung. The conference created a novel and paradoxical grouping: the alignment of the Non-Aligned. Mao had sought Soviet support as a counterweight to potential American pressure on China in pursuit of American hegemony in Asia. But concurrently he tried to organize the Non-Aligned into a safety net against Soviet hegemony. In that sense, almost from the beginning, the two Communist giants were competing with each other.

The fundamental differences went to the essence of the two societies' images of themselves. Russia, salvaged from foreign invaders by brute force and endurance, had never claimed to be a universal inspiration to other societies. A significant part of its population was non-Russian. Its greatest rulers, like Peter the Great and Catherine the Great, had brought foreign thinkers and experts to their courts to learn from more advanced foreigners—an unthinkable concept in the Chinese imperial court. Russian rulers appealed to their people on the basis of their endurance, not their greatness. Russian diplomacy relied, to an extraordinary extent, on superior power. Russia rarely had allies among countries where it had not stationed military forces. Russian diplomacy tended to be power-oriented, tenaciously holding on to fixed positions and transforming foreign policy into trench warfare.

Mao represented a society that, over the centuries, had been the largest, best-organized, and, in the Chinese view at least, most beneficent political institution in the world. That its performance would have a vast international impact was received wisdom. When a Chinese ruler appealed to his people to work hard so that they could become the greatest people in the world, he was exhorting them to reclaim a preeminence that, in the Chinese interpretation of history, had been only recently and temporarily misplaced. Such a country inevitably found it impossible to play the role of junior partner.

In societies based on ideology, the right to define legitimacy becomes crucial. Mao, who described himself as a teacher to the journalist Edgar Snow and thought of himself as a significant philosopher, would never concede intellectual leadership of the Communist world. China's claim to a right to define orthodoxy threatened the cohesion of Moscow's empire and opened the door to other largely national interpretations of Marxism. What started as irritations over nuances of interpretation transformed into disputes over practice and theory and eventually turned into actual military clashes.

The People's Republic began by modeling its economy on Soviet economic policies of the 1930s and 1940s. In 1952, Zhou went so far as to visit Moscow for advice regarding the first Chinese Five-Year Plan. Stalin sent his comments in early 1953, urging Beijing to adopt a more balanced approach and temper its planned rate of economic growth to no more than 13–14 percent annually.[20]

But by December 1955, Mao openly distinguished the Chinese economy from its Soviet counterpart and enumerated the "unique" and "great" challenges that the Chinese had faced and overcome in contrast to their Soviet allies:

> We had twenty years' experience in the base areas, and were trained in three revolutionary wars; our experience [on coming to power] was exceedingly rich. . . . Therefore, we were able to set up a state very quickly, and complete the tasks of the revolution. (The Soviet Union was a newly established state; at the time of the October Revolution,[21] they had neither army nor government apparatus, and there were very few party members.) . . . Our population is very numerous, and our position is excellent. [Our people] work industriously and bear much hardship. . . . Consequently, we can reach socialism more, better, and faster.[22]

In an April 1956 speech on economic policy, Mao transformed a practical difference into a philosophical one. He defined China's path to socialism as unique and superior to that of the Soviet Union:

> We have done better than the Soviet Union and a number of Eastern European countries. The prolonged failure of the

> Soviet Union to reach the highest pre-October Revolution level in grain output, the grave problems arising from the glaring disequilibrium between the development of heavy industry and that of light industry in some Eastern European countries—such problems do not exist in our country.[23]

Differences between Chinese and Soviet conceptions of their practical imperatives turned into an ideological clash when, in February 1956, Khrushchev addressed the Twentieth Congress of the Communist Party of the Soviet Union and denounced Stalin for a series of crimes, several of which he detailed. Khrushchev's speech convulsed the Communist world. Decades of experience had been based on ritualistic affirmations of Stalin's infallibility, including in China, where, whatever qualms Mao may have had about Stalin's conduct as an ally, he formally acknowledged his special ideological contribution. Deepening the insult, non-Soviet delegates—including Chinese delegates—were not permitted in the hall when Khrushchev delivered his speech, and Moscow declined to provide even its fraternal allies with an authoritative text. Beijing cobbled together its initial response based on Chinese delegates' incomplete notes of a secondhand version of Khrushchev's remarks; eventually the Chinese leadership was forced to rely on Chinese translations of reports from the *New York Times*.[24]

Beijing lost little time in assailing Moscow for having "discarded" the "sword of Stalin." The Chinese Titoism that Stalin had feared from the beginning raised its head in the form of a Chinese defense of the ideological importance of Stalin's legacy. Mao branded Khrushchev's de-Stalinization initiative a form of "revisionism"—a new ideological insult—which implied that the Soviet Union was moving away from Communism and back toward its bourgeois past.[25]

To restore a measure of unity, Khrushchev assembled a conference of socialist countries in Moscow in 1957. Mao attended; it was only the second time that he had left China, and it was to be his last sojourn abroad. The Soviet Union had just launched Sputnik—the first orbiting satellite—and the meeting was dominated by the belief, shared then by many in the West, that Soviet technology and power were ascendant. Mao adopted this notion, declaring pungently that the "East Wind" now prevailed over the "West Wind." But he drew from the apparent relative decline of American power a conclusion uncomfortable for his Soviet allies, namely that China was in an increasingly strong position to assert its autonomy: "Their real purpose," Mao later told his doctor, "is to control us. They're trying to tie our hands and feet. But they're full of wishful thinking, like idiots talking about their dreams."[26]

In the meantime, the 1957 conference in Moscow reaffirmed Khrushchev's call for the socialist bloc to strive for "peaceful coexistence" with the capitalist world, a goal first adopted at the same 1956 congress at which Khrushchev delivered his Secret Speech criticizing Stalin. In a startling rebuke to Khrushchev's policy, Mao used the occasion to call his socialist colleagues to arms in the struggle against imperialism, including his standard speech on China's imperviousness to nuclear destruction. "We shouldn't fear war," he declared:

> We shouldn't be afraid of atomic bombs and missiles. No matter what kind of war breaks out—conventional or thermonuclear—we'll win. As for China, if the imperialists unleash war on us, we may lose more than three hundred million people. So what? War is war. The years will pass, and we'll get to work producing more babies than ever before.[27]

Khrushchev found the speech "deeply disturbing," and he recalled the audience's strained and nervous laughter as Mao described nuclear Armageddon in whimsical and earthy language. After the speech, the Czechoslovak Communist leader Antonin Novotny complained, "What about us? We have only twelve million people in Czechoslovakia. We'd lose every last soul in a war. There wouldn't be anyone left to start over again."[28]

China and the Soviet Union now were engaged in constant, frequently public controversies, yet they were also still formal allies. Khrushchev seemed convinced that the restoration of comradely relations awaited only some new Soviet initiative. He did not understand—or, if he did, would not admit to himself—that his policy of peaceful coexistence—especially when coupled with pronouncements of the fear of nuclear war—was, in Mao's eyes, incompatible with the Sino-Soviet alliance. For Mao was convinced that, in a crisis, fear of nuclear war would trump loyalty to the ally.

In these circumstances, Mao missed no opportunity to assert Chinese autonomy. In 1958, Khrushchev proposed, via the Soviet ambassador in Beijing, the building of a radio station in China to communicate with Soviet submarines, and to help build submarines for China in return for the use of Chinese ports by the Soviet navy. Since China was a formal ally, and the Soviet Union had supplied it with much of the technology to improve its own military capacities, Khrushchev apparently thought Mao would welcome the offer. He was proved disastrously wrong. Mao reacted furiously to the initial Soviet proposals, berating the Soviet ambassador in Beijing and causing such alarm in Moscow that Khrushchev traveled to Beijing to assuage his ally's wounded pride.

Once in Beijing, however, Khrushchev made an even less appealing follow-up proposal, which was to offer China special access to Soviet submarine bases in the Arctic Ocean—in exchange for Soviet use of China's warm-water ports in the Pacific. "No," Mao replied, "we won't agree to that either. Every country should keep its armed forces on its own territory and on no one else's."[29] As the Chairman recalled, "We've had the British and other foreigners on our territory for years now, and we're not ever going to let anyone use our land for their own purposes again."[30]

In a normal alliance, disagreements on a specific issue would usually lead to increased efforts to settle differences on the remaining agenda. During Khrushchev's calamitous 1958 visit to Beijing, it provided an occasion for a seemingly endless catalogue of complaints by both sides.

Khrushchev put himself at a disadvantage to begin with by blaming the dispute about naval bases on an unauthorized demarche by his ambassador. Mao, only too familiar with the way Communist states were organized, with a strict separation of military and civilian channels, easily saw through the utter inconceivability of that proposition. The recital of the sequence of events led to an extended dialogue in which Mao lured Khrushchev into ever more humiliating and absurd propositions—the point probably being made to demonstrate for Chinese cadres the unreliability of the leader who had presumed to challenge Stalin's image.

It also provided Mao with an opportunity to convey how deeply Moscow's overbearing conduct had cut. Mao complained about Stalin's condescending behavior during his visit to Moscow in the winter of 1949–50:

> MAO: . . . After the victory of our Revolution, Stalin had doubts about its character. He believed that China was another Yugoslavia.
>
> KHRUSHCHEV: Yes, he considered it possible.
>
> MAO: When I came to Moscow [in December 1949], he did not want to conclude a treaty of friendship with us and did not want to annul the old treaty with the Guomindang.[31] I recall that [Soviet interpreter Nikolai] Fedorenko and [Stalin's emissary to the People's Republic Ivan] Kovalev passed me his [Stalin's] advice to take a trip around the country, to look around. But I told them that I have only three tasks: eat, sleep and shit. I did not come to Moscow only to

> congratulate Stalin on his birthday. Therefore I said that if you do not want to conclude a treaty of friendship, so be it. I will fulfill my three tasks.[32]

The mutual needling quickly went beyond history into contemporary disputes. When Khrushchev asked Mao if the Chinese really considered the Soviets "red imperialists," Mao made clear how much the quid pro quo for the alliance had rankled: "It is not a matter of red or white imperialists. There was a man by the name of Stalin, who took Port Arthur and turned Xinjiang and Manchuria into semi-colonies, and he also created four joint companies. These were all his good deeds."[33]

Still, whatever Mao's complaints on a national basis, he respected Stalin's ideological contribution:

> KHRUSHCHEV: You defended Stalin. And you criticized me for criticizing Stalin. And now vice versa.
>
> MAO: You criticized [him] for different matters.
>
> KHRUSHCHEV: At the Party Congress I spoke about this as well.
>
> MAO: I always said, now, and then in Moscow, that the criticism of Stalin's mistakes is justified. We only disagree with the lack of strict limits to criticism. We believe that out of Stalin's 10 fingers, 3 were rotten ones.[34]

Mao set the tone of the next day's meeting by receiving Khrushchev not in a ceremonial room but in his swimming pool. Khrushchev, who could not swim, was obliged to wear water wings. The two statesmen conversed while swimming, with the interpreters following them up and down the side of the pool. Khrushchev would later complain: "It was Mao's way of putting himself in an advantageous position. Well, I

Two world orders meet:
China's Emperor prepares to receive the British ambassador in 1793.

GETTY IMAGES

Li Hongzhang, China's chief diplomat in the late nineteenth century. CORBIS

Mao Zedong addressing troops in 1938.

GETTY IMAGES

Chinese, Soviet, and Eastern European leaders convene for a conference of Communist parties in Moscow in 1957. GETTY IMAGES

Mao receives his Soviet counterpart Nikita Khrushchev in Beijing in August 1958, during a period of great strain in their relations. GETTY IMAGES

Chinese Premier Zhou Enlai and Indian Prime Minister Jawaharlal Nehru in Beijing in October 1954. CORBIS

Indian troops patrolling Ladakh in 1962: Competing Indian and Chinese claims in the Himalayas led to a series of border clashes. CORBIS

The Cultural Revolution: Red Guards wave the "Little Red Book" of Mao quotations in front of the Soviet Embassy in Beijing in August 1966. AP

A scene from Guangzhou: "Big character posters" proclaim China's military and ideological vigilance.

GETTY IMAGES

Zhou Enlai and the author in Beijing:
After more than two decades of Sino-American hostility,
our task was to explore avenues for cooperation.

LIBRARY OF CONGRESS, HENRY KISSINGER ARCHIVES

Zhou and the author in Beijing: During the secret visit of 1971, Zhou combined modern ideological commitment with a long tradition of Chinese diplomacy. LIBRARY OF CONGRESS, HENRY KISSINGER ARCHIVES

The author and his aide Winston Lord take a break from negotiating the text of the Shanghai Communiqué on an October 1971 visit to Beijing.

WHITE HOUSE PHOTO OFFICE COLLECTION

President Richard Nixon arrives at the Beijing airport in February 1972.

LIBRARY OF CONGRESS, HENRY KISSINGER ARCHIVES

Mao and Nixon in 1972.

LIBRARY OF CONGRESS, HENRY KISSINGER ARCHIVES

President Gerald Ford confers with the newly rehabilitated Deng Xiaoping in December 1975. Nancy Tang translates. GETTY IMAGES

Deng Xiaoping and President Jimmy Carter in January 1979 in Washington, D.C. GETTY IMAGES

Treasury Secretary Michael Blumenthal and Acting Chief of Mission J. Stapleton Roy convert the American Liaison Office in Beijing into an embassy in March 1979. AP

Deng tours a Texas rodeo during his 1979 U.S. trip.
GETTY IMAGES

Deng Xiaoping and the author in the 1980s. Deng's reforms opened the door to stunning economic growth. AUTHOR'S PERSONAL COLLECTION

President Ronald Reagan and Nancy Reagan tour the terra-cotta warriors in Xi'an in April 1984. GETTY IMAGES

British Governor Chris Patten receives the British flag on June 30, 1997, after it is lowered for the last time in Hong Kong.

GETTY IMAGES

President Jiang Zemin and the author in the 1990s.
AUTHOR'S PERSONAL COLLECTION

President Bill Clinton signs a bill granting China Most Favored Nation trade status in 2000. GETTY IMAGES

Jiang Zemin and the author enjoying a moment of levity in Washington, D.C., in 1997.

GETTY IMAGES

U.S. President George W. Bush, Russian President Vladimir Putin, and Chinese President Hu Jintao at a November 2006 Asia-Pacific Economic Cooperation summit in Vietnam.

GETTY IMAGES

Inaugurating a new era:
The opening ceremonies at the 2008 Summer Olympics in Beijing. GETTY IMAGES

The author and Chinese President Hu Jintao in Beijing.

AUTHOR'S PERSONAL COLLECTION

President Barack Obama at the Forbidden City during a November 2009 state visit to China.

GETTY IMAGES

got sick of it. . . . I crawled out, sat on the edge, and dangled my legs in the pool. Now I was on top and he was swimming below."[35]

Relations had deteriorated even further a year later when Khrushchev stopped in Beijing, on his return trip from the United States, to brief his fractious ally on October 3, 1959, on his summit with Eisenhower. The Chinese leaders, already highly suspicious about Khrushchev's American sojourn, were further agitated when Khrushchev took the side of India with respect to the first border clashes in the Himalayas between Indian and Chinese forces that had just occurred.

Khrushchev, whose strong suit was not diplomacy, managed to raise the sensitive issue of the Dalai Lama; few topics could generate a more hair-trigger Chinese response. He criticized Mao for not having been tough enough during the uprisings in Tibet earlier that year, which had culminated in the Dalai Lama's flight to northern India: "I will tell you what a guest should not say[:] the events in Tibet are your fault. You ruled in Tibet, you should have had your intelligence there and should have known about the plans and intentions of the Dalai Lama."[36] After Mao objected, Khrushchev insisted on pursuing the subject by suggesting that the Chinese should have eliminated the Dalai Lama rather than let him escape:

> KHRUSHCHEV: . . . As to the escape of the Dalai Lama from Tibet, if we had been in your place, we would not have let him escape. It would be better if he was in a coffin. And now he is in India, and perhaps will go to the USA. Is this to the advantage of the socialist countries?
>
> MAO: This is impossible; we could not arrest him then. We could not bar him from leaving, since the border with India is very extended, and he could cross it at any point.
>
> KHRUSHCHEV: It's not a matter of arrest; I am just saying that you were wrong to let him go. If you allow him an

> opportunity to flee to India, then what has Nehru to do with it? We believe that the events in Tibet are the fault of the Communist Party of China, not Nehru's fault.[37]

It was the last time Mao and Khrushchev were to meet. What is amazing is that for another ten years the world treated Sino-Soviet tensions as a kind of family quarrel between the two Communist giants rather than the existential battle into which it was turning. Amidst these mounting tensions with the Soviet Union, Mao initiated another crisis with the United States.

The Second Taiwan Strait Crisis

On August 23, 1958, the People's Liberation Army began another massive shelling campaign of the offshore islands, accompanying its bombardment with propaganda salvos calling for the liberation of Taiwan. After two weeks, it paused, and then resumed the shelling for a further twenty-nine days. Finally, it settled into an almost whimsical pattern of shelling the islands on odd-numbered days of the month, with explicit warnings to their inhabitants and often avoiding sites of military significance—a maneuver Mao described to his senior associates as an act of "political battle" rather than conventional military strategy.[38]

Some of the factors at work in this crisis were familiar. Beijing again sought to test the limits of the American commitment to defend Taiwan. The shelling was also partly a reaction to American downgrading of the U.S.-China talks that had resumed after the last offshore island crisis. But the dominant impetus seems to have been a desire to stake a global role for China. Mao explained to his colleagues at a leadership retreat held at the outset of the crisis that the shelling of Quemoy and Matsu was China's reaction to American intervention in

Lebanon, where American and British troops had been landed during the summer:

> [T]he bombardment of Jinmen [Quemoy], frankly speaking, was our turn to create international tension for a purpose. We intended to teach the Americans a lesson. America had bullied us for many years, so now that we had a chance, why not give it a hard time? . . . Americans started a fire in the Middle East, and we started another in the Far East. We would see what they would do with it.[39]

In that sense the shelling of the offshore islands was a blow in the contest with the Soviet Union. Soviet quiescence in the face of a strategic American move in the Middle East was being contrasted with Chinese ideological and strategic vigilance.

Having demonstrated its military resolve, Mao explained, China would now rejoin the talks with the United States and have available "both an action arena and a talk arena"[40]—an application of the Sun Tzu principle of combative coexistence in its modern version of offensive deterrence.

The most significant dimension of the shelling was not the taunting of the American superpower so much as the challenge to China's formal ally, the Soviet Union. Khrushchev's policy of peaceful coexistence had made the Soviet Union, in Mao's eyes, a problematical ally and perhaps even a potential adversary. Thus, Mao seems to have reasoned, if the Taiwan Strait Crisis were pushed to the brink of war, Khrushchev might have to choose between his new policy of peaceful coexistence and his alliance with China.

In a sense Mao succeeded. What conferred a special edge to Mao's maneuvers was that the Chinese policy in the Strait was being carried out ostensibly with the blessing of Moscow so far as the world was concerned. For Khrushchev had visited Beijing three weeks before the second Taiwan Strait Crisis—for the disastrous encounters over the submarine base issues—much as he had been there in the opening weeks of the first crisis four years earlier. In neither case had Mao revealed his intentions to the Soviets either before or during the visit. In each instance Washington assumed—and Eisenhower alleged as much in a letter to Khrushchev—that Mao was acting not only with Moscow's support but at its behest. Beijing was adding its Soviet ally to its diplomatic lineup against its will and indeed without Moscow realizing that it was being used. (A school of thought even holds that Mao invented the "submarine base crisis" to induce Khrushchev to come to Beijing to play his assigned role in that design.)

The second Taiwan Strait Crisis paralleled the first with the principal difference being that the Soviet Union participated in issuing nuclear threats on behalf of an ally that was in the process of humiliating it.

Roughly one thousand people were killed or wounded in the 1958 bombardment. As in the first Taiwan Strait Crisis, Beijing combined provocative evocations of nuclear war with a carefully calibrated operational strategy. Mao initially asked his commanders to conduct the shelling in such a way as to avoid American fatalities. When they responded that no such guarantee was possible, he ordered them not to cross into the airspace over the offshore islands, to fire only on Nationalist vessels, and not to return fire even if fired on by U.S. ships.[41] Both before and during the crisis, PRC propaganda trumpeted the slogan "We must liberate Taiwan." But when the PLA's radio station undertook a broadcast announcing that a Chinese landing was "imminent" and inviting Nationalist forces to change sides and "join the great cause of liberating Taiwan," Mao declared it a "serious mistake."[42]

In John Foster Dulles, Mao met an adversary who knew how to play the game of combative coexistence. On September 4, 1958, Dulles reiterated the U.S. commitment to the defense of Taiwan, including "related positions such as Quemoy and Matsu." Dulles intuited China's limited aims and in effect signaled American willingness to keep the crisis limited: "Despite, however, what the Chinese Communists say, and so far have done, it is not yet certain that their purpose is in fact to make an all-out effort to conquer by force Taiwan (Formosa) and the offshore islands."[43] On September 5, Zhou Enlai confirmed China's limited aims when he announced that Beijing's goal in the conflict was the resumption of U.S.-China talks at the ambassadorial level. On September 6, the White House released a statement taking note of Zhou's remarks and indicating that the United States ambassador at Warsaw stood ready to represent the United States at resumed talks.

With this exchange, the crisis should have been over. As if they were rehearsing a by-now familiar play, the two sides had repeated timeworn threats and had arrived at a familiar deus ex machina, the resumption of ambassadorial talks.

The only party in the triangular relationship who did not grasp what was taking place was Khrushchev. Having heard Mao proclaim his imperviousness to nuclear war in Moscow the year previously and recently in Beijing, he was torn between contradictory fears of nuclear war and of the potential loss of an important ally if he failed to stand by China. His dedicated Marxism made it impossible for him to understand that his ideological ally had become a strategic adversary, yet his knowledge of nuclear weapons was too great to integrate them comfortably into a diplomacy that constantly relied on threatening their use.

When a rattled statesman confronts a dilemma, he is sometimes tempted to pursue every course of action simultaneously. Khrushchev sent his foreign minister, Andrei Gromyko, to Beijing to urge restraint, which he knew would not be well received, and, to balance it, to show the Chinese leaders a draft letter he proposed to send Eisenhower, threatening full support—implying nuclear support—for China should the Taiwan Strait Crisis escalate. The letter stressed that "an attack on the

Chinese People's Republic, which is a great friend, ally and neighbor of our country, is an attack on the Soviet Union" and warned that the Soviet Union "will do everything . . . to defend the security of both states."[44]

The initiative failed with both addressees. Khrushchev's letter was politely rejected by Eisenhower on September 12. Welcoming the Chinese willingness to rejoin ambassadorial talks and repeating Washington's insistence that Beijing renounce the use of force over Taiwan, Eisenhower urged Khrushchev to recommend restraint to Beijing. Oblivious to the reality that Khrushchev was an actor in a play written by others, Eisenhower implied collusion between Moscow and Beijing, noting that "[t]his intense military activity was begun on August twenty-third—some three weeks after your visit to Peiping."[45]

In a public address delivered roughly simultaneously on September 11, 1958, Eisenhower justified American involvement in the offshore islands in sweeping terms. The shelling of Quemoy and Matsu, he warned, was analogous to Hitler's occupation of the Rhineland, Mussolini's occupation of Ethiopia, or (in a comparison that must have particularly vexed the Chinese) the Japanese conquest of Manchuria in the 1930s.

Gromyko fared no better in Beijing. Mao responded to the draft letter by speaking openly of the possibility of nuclear war and the conditions under which the Soviets should retaliate with nuclear weapons against America. The threats were all the safer to make because Mao knew the danger of war had already passed. In his memoirs, Gromyko recounts being "flabbergasted" by Mao's bravado and quoted the Chinese leader as telling him:

> I suppose the Americans might go so far as to unleash a war against China. China must reckon with this possibility, and we do. But we have no intention of capitulating! If the USA

> attacks China with nuclear weapons, the Chinese armies must retreat from the border regions into the depths of the country. They must draw the enemy in deep so as to grip US forces in a pincer inside China. . . . Only when the Americans are right in the central provinces should you give them everything you've got.[46]

Mao was not asking for Soviet help until American forces had been drawn deep into China—which he knew was not going to happen in the already completed scenario. Gromyko's report from Beijing seems to have shocked Khrushchev. Though ambassadorial talks had already been agreed between Washington and Beijing, Khrushchev undertook two more steps to prevent nuclear war. To calm what he understood to be Beijing's fear of American invasion, he offered to send Soviet anti-aircraft units to Fujian.[47] Beijing delayed a response and then accepted when the crisis was already over, provided that Soviet troops were placed under Chinese command—an improbable outcome.[48] In a further demonstration of his nervousness, Khrushchev sent another letter to Eisenhower on September 19, urging restraint but warning of the imminence of nuclear war.[49] Except that China and the United States had, in fact, already settled the issue before Khrushchev's second letter arrived.

In their meeting on October 3, 1959, Khrushchev had summed up the Soviet attitude during the Taiwan crises to Mao:

> Between us, in a confidential way, we say that we will not fight over Taiwan, but for outside consumption, so to say, we state on the contrary, that in case of an aggravation of the situation because of Taiwan the USSR will defend the PRC. In its turn, the US declare that they will defend Taiwan. Therefore, a kind of pre-war situation emerges.[50]

Khrushchev had enabled Mao to lure him into so futile a course by trying to be both clever and cynical. Especially when ultimate decisions of peace and war are involved, a strategist must be aware that bluffs may be called and must take into account the impact on his future credibility of an empty threat. On Taiwan, Mao used Khrushchev's ambivalence to entice him into making a nuclear threat that he had admitted he had no intention of carrying out, straining Moscow's relationship with the United States on behalf of an issue Khrushchev considered unimportant and of an allied leader who despised him.

One can only imagine Mao's bemusement: he had goaded Moscow and Washington into threatening nuclear war against each other over some of the world's least vital geopolitical real estate in what was an essentially nonmilitary piece of Chinese political theater. Moreover, Mao had done so at a time of his choosing, while China remained vastly weaker than the United States or the USSR, and in a manner that allowed him to claim a significant propaganda victory and rejoin Sino-U.S. ambassadorial talks from what his propaganda would claim was a position of strength.

Having triggered the crisis and brought it to a close, Mao asserted that he had achieved his objectives:

> We fought this campaign, which made the United States willing to talk. The United States has opened the door. The situation seems to be no good for them, and they will feel nervous day in and day out if they don't hold talks with us now. OK, then let's talk. For the overall situation, it is better to settle disputes with the United States through talks, or peaceful means, because we are all peace-loving people.[51]

Zhou Enlai offered an even more complicated assessment. He saw the second Taiwan Strait Crisis as a demonstration of the ability of the two Chinese parties to engage in tacit bargaining with each other across the barriers of opposing ideologies and even while the nuclear powers were fencing about nuclear war. Nearly fifteen years later, Zhou recounted Beijing's strategy to Richard Nixon during the President's 1972 visit to Beijing:

> In 1958, then Secretary Dulles wanted Chiang Kai-shek to give up the islands of Quemoy and Matsu so as to completely sever Taiwan and the mainland and draw a line there. Chiang Kai-shek was not willing to do this.[52] We also advised him not to withdraw from Quemoy and Matsu. We advised him not to withdraw by firing artillery shells at them—that is, on odd days we would shell them, and not shell them on even days, and on holidays we would not shell them. So they understood our intentions and didn't withdraw. No other means or messages were required; just by this method of shelling they understood."[53]

These brilliant achievements must be balanced against the global impact of the crisis, however. The ambassadorial talks deadlocked almost as soon as they resumed. Mao's ambiguous maneuvers, in fact, froze Sino-American relations into an adversarial posture from which they did not recover for over a decade. The notion that China was determined to eject the United States from the Western Pacific grew into an article of faith in Washington that deprived both sides of options for a more flexible diplomacy.

The impact on the Soviet leadership was the opposite of what Mao had intended. Far from abandoning the policy of peaceful coexistence, Moscow was panicked by Mao's rhetoric and unsettled by his nuclear brinkmanship, his repeated musing on the likely positive effects of nuclear war for world socialism, and his failure to consult Moscow. In the aftermath of the crisis, Moscow suspended nuclear cooperation with Beijing, and in June of 1959 withdrew its commitment to provide China with a model atomic bomb. In 1960, Khrushchev withdrew Russian technicians from China and canceled all aid projects, claiming that "[we] couldn't simply stand by, allowing some of our best-qualified specialists—people who'd been trained in our own agriculture and industry—to receive nothing but harassment in exchange for their help."[54]

Internationally Mao achieved another demonstration of China's hair-trigger response to perceived threats to its national security or territorial integrity. This would discourage attempts by China's neighbors to exploit the domestic upheaval into which Mao was about to plunge his society. But it also started a process of progressive isolation that would cause Mao to rethink his foreign policy a decade later.

CHAPTER 7

A Decade of Crises

DURING THE FIRST DECADE of the People's Republic of China's existence, its tough leaders navigated the decrepit empire they had conquered and turned it into a major power internationally. The second decade was dominated by Mao's attempt to accelerate the continuous revolution at home. The driving force of continuous revolution was Mao's maxim that moral and ideological vigor would overcome physical limitations. The decade began and ended amidst domestic turmoil that was ordered by China's own leaders. So encompassing was this crisis that China shut itself off from the rest of the world; almost all its diplomats were recalled to Beijing. Two complete overhauls of China's domestic structure took place: first of the economy, with the Great Leap Forward at the beginning of the decade; and second, of the social order, with the Cultural Revolution at the end. Diplomacy was out of fashion; but war was not. When Mao felt the national interest challenged, in the midst of all its self-inflicted travail, China stood up once again, to go to war at its furthest western frontier in the inhospitable Himalayas.

The Great Leap Forward

China's leaders had felt obliged by Khrushchev's Secret Speech to confront the issue of what, absent claims to a Party Chairman's godlike infallibility, constituted Communist political legitimacy. In the months following the February 1956 speech, they seemed to feel their way toward making their own governance more transparent, presumably to avoid the need for periodic shocks of rectification. Worshipful references to Mao Zedong were deleted from the Communist Party constitution. The Party adopted resolutions cautioning against "rash advance" in the economic field and suggesting that the main phase of "class struggle" would now draw to a close.[1]

But such a prosaic approach quickly clashed with Mao's vision of continuous revolution. Within months Mao proposed an alternative route to political rectification: the Chinese Communist Party would invite debate and criticism of its methods and open up China's intellectual and artistic life to let "one hundred flowers bloom and one hundred schools of thought contend." Mao's exact motives in issuing this call remain a subject of debate. The Hundred Flowers Campaign has been explained as either a sincere call for the Party to cut through its bureaucratic isolation to hear directly from the people or a stratagem to coax enemies into identifying themselves. Whatever the motive, popular criticism quickly moved beyond suggestions for tactical adjustments into criticisms of the Communist system. Students set up a "democracy wall" in Beijing. Critics protested the abuses of local officials and the privations imposed by Soviet-style economic policies; some contrasted the first decade of Communist rule unfavorably with the Nationalist era that preceded it.[2]

Whatever the original intention, Mao never brooked a challenge to his authority for long. He executed a sharp about-face and justified it as an aspect of his dialectic approach. The Hundred Flowers movement was transformed into an "Anti-Rightist Campaign" to deal with those who had misunderstood the limits of the earlier invitation to debate. A massive purge led to the imprisonment, reeducation, or internal exile of thousands of intellectuals. At the end of the process, Mao stood again as China's unchallenged leader, having cleared the field of his critics. He used his preeminence to accelerate the continuous revolution, turning it into the Great Leap Forward.

The 1957 Moscow conference of socialist parties had found Mao issuing a fateful claim about Chinese economic development. Responding to Khrushchev's prediction that the Soviet Union would surpass the United States economically in fifteen years, Mao delivered an impromptu speech proclaiming that China would surpass Great Britain in steel production in the same interval.[3]

This comment soon acquired the status of a directive. The fifteen-year steel target—subsequently reduced, in a series of largely extemporaneous remarks, to *three* years[4]—was matched by a series of similarly ambitious agricultural goals. Mao was preparing to launch China's continuous revolution into a more active phase and to confront the Chinese people with its most stupendous challenge yet.

Like many of Mao's undertakings, the Great Leap Forward combined aspects of economic policy, ideological exaltation, and foreign policy. For Mao, these were not distinct fields of endeavor but interrelated strands of the grand project of the Chinese revolution.[5]

In its most literal sense, the Great Leap Forward was designed to carry out Mao's sweeping ideas of industrial and agricultural development. Much of China's remaining private property and individual incentives were eliminated as the country was reorganized into "people's communes" pooling possessions, food, and labor. Peasants were conscripted in quasi-military brigades for massive public works projects, many improvised.

These projects had international as well as domestic implications—especially with respect to the conflict with Moscow. If successful, the Great Leap Forward would rebut Moscow's prescriptions of gradualism and effectively relocate the ideological center of the Communist world to China. When Khrushchev visited Beijing in 1958, Mao insisted that China would achieve full Communism before the Soviet Union did, while the Soviet Union had opted for a slower, more bureaucratic, and less inspirational route of development. To Soviet ears, this was a shocking ideological heresy.

But for once, Mao had set a challenge so far outside the realm of objective reality that even the Chinese people fell short of its achievement. The Great Leap Forward's production goals were exorbitant, and the prospect of dissent or failure was so terrifying that local cadres took to falsifying their output figures and reporting inflated totals to Beijing. Taking these reports literally, Beijing continued to export grain to the Soviet Union in exchange for heavy industry and weaponry. Compounding the disaster was that Mao's steel targets had been implemented so literally as to encourage the melting down of useful implements as scrap to fulfill the quotas. Yet, in the end, the laws of nature and economics could not be abrogated, and the Great Leap Forward's reckoning was brutal. From 1959 to 1962, China experienced one of the worst famines in human history, leading to the deaths of over twenty million people.[6] Mao had again called on the Chinese people to move mountains, but this time the mountains had not moved.

The Himalayan Border Dispute and the 1962 Sino-Indian War

By 1962, barely a decade after the establishment of the People's Republic of China, China had fought a war with the United States in Korea and engaged in two military confrontations involving the United States over the offshore islands of Taiwan. It had restored Chinese authority to imperial China's historic frontiers (with the exception of Mongolia and Taiwan) by reoccupying Xinjiang and Tibet. The famine triggered by the Great Leap Forward had barely been overcome. Nevertheless, Mao did not shrink from another military conflict when he considered China's definition of its historic borders was being challenged by India.

The Sino-Indian border crisis concerned two territories located in the high Himalayas in the trackless and largely uninhabitable region of plateaus amidst forbidding mountains between Tibet and India. Fundamentally, the issue arose over the interpretation of colonial history.

China claimed the imperial boundaries along the southern foothills of the Himalayas, encompassing what China considered "South Tibet" but which India administered as the state of Arunachal Pradesh. The Indian perception was of relatively recent vintage. It had evolved out of the British effort to demarcate a dividing line with the Russian Empire advancing toward Tibet. The final relevant document was between Britain and Tibet, signed in 1914, that delineated the border in the eastern sector, called the McMahon Line after the principal British negotiator.

China had a long relationship with Tibet. The Mongols had conquered both Tibet and the Chinese agricultural heartland in the same wave of conquest in the thirteenth century, bringing them into close political contact. Later the Qing Dynasty had regularly intervened in Tibet to expel the forces of other non-Han peoples making incursions into Tibet from the north and west. Eventually Beijing settled into a form of suzerainty exercised by "imperial residents" in Lhasa. Beijing, since the Qing Dynasty, treated Tibet as part of the All Under Heaven ruled by the Chinese Emperor and reserved the right to eject hostile interlopers; but distance and the Tibetans' nomadic culture made full Sinicization impractical. In this manner, Tibetans were afforded a substantial degree of autonomy over their day-to-day life.

By the end of the Qing Dynasty in 1912, with China's governance severely strained, the Chinese governmental presence in Tibet had shrunk. Shortly after the collapse of the dynasty, British authorities in India convened a conference in the hill station of Simla with Chinese and Tibetan representatives, with the goal of demarcating the borders between India and Tibet. The Chinese government, having no effective force with which to contest these developments, objected on principle to the cession of any territory to which China had a historic claim. Beijing's attitude to the conference was reflected by its representative in Calcutta—then the seat of Britain's Indian administration—Lu Hsing-chi: "Our country is at present in an enfeebled condition; our external relations are involved and difficult and our finances embarrassed. Nevertheless, Tibet is of paramount importance to both [Sichuan and Yunnan, provinces in southwest China] and we must exert ourselves to the utmost during this conference."[7]

The Chinese delegate at the conference solved their dilemma by initialing, but not signing, the resulting document. Tibetan and British delegates signed the document. In diplomatic practice, initialing freezes the text; it signifies that the negotiations have been concluded. Signing the document puts it into force. China maintained that the Tibetan representatives lacked the legal standing to sign the border agreement, since Tibet was part of China and not entitled to the exercise of sovereignty. It refused to recognize the validity of Indian administration of the territory south of the McMahon Line, although it initially made no overt attempt to contest it.

In the western sector, the disputed territory was known as Aksai Chin. It is nearly inaccessible from India, which is why it took some months for India to realize, in 1955, that China was building a road across it linking Xinjiang and Tibet. The historical provenance of the region was also problematic. Britain claimed it on most official maps, though never seems to have administered it. When India proclaimed its independence from Britain, it did not proclaim its independence from British territorial claims. It included the Aksai Chin territory as well as the line demarcated by McMahon on all of its maps.

Both demarcation lines were of strategic consequence. In the 1950s, a certain balance existed between the positions of the two sides. China viewed the McMahon Line as a symbol of British plans to loosen China's control over Tibet or perhaps to dominate it. Indian Prime Minister Jawaharlal Nehru claimed a cultural and sentimental interest in Tibet based on historical links between India's classical Buddhist culture and Tibetan Buddhism. But he was prepared to acknowledge Chinese sovereignty in Tibet so long as substantial autonomy was maintained. In pursuit of this policy, Nehru declined to support petitions to table the issue of Tibet's political status at the U.N.

But when the Dalai Lama fled in 1959 and was granted asylum in India, China began to treat the issue of demarcation lines increasingly in strategic terms. Zhou offered a deal trading Chinese claims in the eastern part of the line for Indian claims in the west, in other words, acceptance of the McMahon Line as a basis for negotiations in return for recognition of Chinese claims to Aksai Chin.

Almost all postcolonial countries have insisted on the borders within which they achieved independence. To throw them open to negotiations invites unending controversies and domestic pressure. On the principle that he was not elected to bargain away territory that he considered indisputably Indian, Nehru rejected the Chinese proposal by not answering it.

In 1961, India adopted what it called the Forward Policy. To overcome the impression that it was not contesting the disputed territory, India moved its outposts forward, close to Chinese outposts previously established across the existing line of demarcation. Indian commanders were given the authority to fire on Chinese forces at their discretion, on the theory that the Chinese were intruders on Indian territory. They were reinforced in that policy after the first clashes in 1959 when Mao, in order to avoid a crisis, ordered Chinese forces to withdraw some twenty kilometers. Indian planners drew the conclusion that Chinese forces would not resist a forward movement by India; rather they would use it as an excuse to disengage. Indian forces were ordered to, in the words of the official Indian history of the war, "patrol as far forward as possible from our [India's] present position toward the International Border as recognized by us . . . [and] prevent the Chinese from advancing further and also to dominate any Chinese posts already established on our territory."[8]

It proved a miscalculation. Mao at once canceled the previous withdrawal orders. But he was still cautious, telling a meeting of the Central Military Commission in Beijing: "Lack of forbearance in small matters upsets great plans. We must pay attention to the situation."[9] It was not yet an order for military confrontation; rather a kind of alert to prepare a strategic plan. As such, it triggered the familiar Chinese style of dealing with strategic decisions: thorough analysis; careful preparation; attention to psychological and political factors; quest for surprise; and rapid conclusion.

In meetings of the Central Military Commission and of top leaders, Mao commented on Nehru's Forward Policy with one of his epigrams: "A person sleeping in a comfortable bed is not easily roused by someone else's snoring."[10] In other words, Chinese forces in the Himalayas had been too passive in responding to the Indian Forward Policy—which, in the Chinese perception, was taking place on Chinese soil. (That, of course, was the essence of the dispute: each side argued that its adversary had ventured onto its own soil.)

The Central Military Commission ordered an end of Chinese withdrawals, declaring that any new Indian outposts should be resisted by building Chinese outposts near them, encircling them. Mao summed it up: "You wave a gun, and I'll wave a gun. We'll stand face to face and can each practice our courage." Mao defined the policy as "armed coexistence."[11] It was, in effect, the exercise of *wei qi* in the Himalayas.

Precise instructions were issued. The goal was still declared to be to avoid a larger conflict. Chinese troops were not authorized to fire unless Indian forces came closer than fifty meters to their positions. Beyond that, military actions could be initiated only on orders from higher authorities.

Indian planners noted that China had stopped withdrawals but also observed Chinese restraint in firing. They concluded that another probe would do the trick. Rather than contest empty land, the goal became "to push back the Chinese posts they already occupied."[12]

Since the two objectives of China's stated policy—to prevent further Indian advances and to avoid bloodshed—were not being met, Chinese leaders began to consider whether a sudden blow might force India to the negotiating table and end the tit for tat.

In pursuit of that objective, Chinese leaders were concerned that the United States might use the looming Sino-Indian conflict to unleash Taiwan against the mainland. Another worry was that the American diplomacy seeking to block Hanoi's effort to turn Laos into a base area for the war in Vietnam might be a forerunner of an eventual American attack on southern China via Laos. Chinese leaders could not believe that America would involve itself to the extent it did in Indochina (even then, before the major escalation had started) for local strategic stakes.

The Chinese leaders managed to obtain reassurance on both points, in the process demonstrating the comprehensive way in which Chinese policy was being planned. The Warsaw talks were the venue chosen to determine American intentions in the Taiwan Strait. The Chinese ambassador to these talks was recalled from vacation and instructed to ask for a meeting. There he claimed that Beijing had noted preparations in Taiwan for a landing on the mainland. The American ambassador, who had not heard of any such preparations—since they were not, in fact, taking place—was instructed to reply that the United States desired peace and "under present circumstances" would not support a Nationalist offensive. The Chinese ambassador at these talks, Wang Bingnan, noted in his memoirs that this information played a "very big role" in Beijing's final decision to proceed with operations in the Himalayas.[13] There is no evidence that the United States government asked itself what policy might have produced the request for a special meeting. It was the difference between a segmented and a comprehensive approach to policymaking.

The Laotian problem solved itself. At the Geneva Conference of 1962, the neutralization of Laos and withdrawal of American forces from it removed Chinese concerns.

With these reassurances in hand, Mao, in early October 1962, assembled Chinese leaders to announce the final decision, which was for war:

> We fought a war with old Chiang [Kai-shek]. We fought a war with Japan, and with America. With none of these did we fear. And in each case we won. Now the Indians want to fight a war with us. Naturally, we don't have fear. We cannot give ground, once we give ground it would be tantamount to letting them seize a big piece of land equivalent to Fujian province. . . . Since Nehru sticks his head out and insists on us fighting him, for us not to fight with him would not be friendly enough. Courtesy emphasizes reciprocity.[14]

On October 6, a decision in principle was taken. The strategic plan was for a massive assault to produce a shock that would impel a negotiation or at least an end to the Indian military probing for the foreseeable future.

Before the final decision to order the offensive, word was received from Khrushchev that, in case of war, the Soviet Union would back China under the provisions of the Treaty of Friendship and Alliance of 1950. It was a decision totally out of keeping with Soviet-Chinese relations in the previous years and the neutrality heretofore practiced by the Kremlin on the issue of Indian relations with China. A plausible explanation is that Khrushchev, aware of the imminence of a showdown over Soviet deployment of nuclear weapons to Cuba, wanted to assure himself of Chinese support in the Caribbean crisis.[15] He never returned to the offer once the Cuban crisis was over.

The Chinese attack took place in two stages: a preliminary offensive starting on October 20 lasting four days, followed by a massive assault in the middle of November, which reached the foothills of the Himalayas in the vicinity of the traditional imperial demarcation line.

At this point, the PLA stopped and returned to its starting point well behind the line it was claiming. The disputed territory has remained disputed until today, but neither side has sought to enforce its claims beyond the existing lines of control.

The Chinese strategy was similar to that of the offshore islands crises. China did not conquer any territory in the 1962 Sino-Indian War—although it continued to claim the territory south of the McMahon Line. This may have reflected a political judgment or a recognition of logistical realities. The conquered eastern sector territory could be held only over seriously extended supply lines across forbidding terrain.

At the end of the war, Mao had withstood—and in this case, prevailed in—another major crisis, even while a famine was barely ended in China. It was in a way a replay of the American experience in the Korean War: an underestimation of China by its adversary; unchallenged intelligence estimates about Chinese capabilities; and coupled with grave errors in grasping how China interprets its security environment and how it reacts to military threats.

At the same time, the 1962 war added another formidable adversary for China at a moment when relations with the Soviet Union had gone beyond the point of no return. For the Soviet offer of support proved as fleeting as the Soviet nuclear presence in Cuba.

As soon as military clashes in the Himalayas escalated, Moscow adopted a posture of neutrality. To rub salt into Chinese wounds, Khrushchev justified his neutrality with the proposition that he was promoting the loathed principle of peaceful coexistence. A December 1962 editorial in the *People's Daily,* the official newspaper of the Chinese Communist Party, angrily noted that this marked the first time a Communist state had not sided with another Communist state against a "bourgeois" country: "For a communist the minimum requirement is that he should make a clear distinction between the enemy and ourselves, that he should be ruthless towards the enemy and kind to his own comrades."[16] The editorial added a somewhat plaintive call for

China's allies to "examine their conscience and ask themselves what has become of their Marxism-Leninism and what has become of their proletarian internationalism."[17]

By 1964, the Soviets dropped even the pretense of neutrality. Referring to the Cuban Missile Crisis, Mikhail Suslov, a member of the Politburo and party ideologist, accused the Chinese of aggression against India at a moment of maximum difficulty for the Soviet Union:

> It is a fact that precisely at the height of the Caribbean crisis the Chinese People's Republic extended the armed conflict on the Chinese-Indian border. No matter how the Chinese leaders have tried since then to justify their conduct at the time they cannot escape the responsibility for the fact that through their actions they in effect aided the most reactionary circles of imperialism.[18]

China, having barely overcome a vast famine, now had declared adversaries on all frontiers.

The Cultural Revolution

At this moment of potential national emergency, Mao chose to smash the Chinese state and the Communist Party. He launched what he hoped would prove a final assault on the stubborn remnants of traditional Chinese culture—from the rubble of which, he prophesied, would rise a new, ideologically pure generation better equipped to safeguard the revolutionary cause from its domestic and foreign foes. He propelled China into the decade of ideological frenzy, vicious factional politics, and near civil war known as the Great Proletarian Cultural Revolution.

No institution was spared from the ensuing waves of upheaval.

Across the country, local governments were dissolved in violent confrontations with "the masses," urged on by propaganda from Beijing. Distinguished Communist Party and People's Liberation Army leaders, including leaders of the revolutionary wars, were purged and subjected to public humiliation. China's education system—so long the backbone of the Chinese social order—ground to a halt, with classes suspended indefinitely so that the younger generation could wander the country and follow Mao's exhortation to "learn revolution by making revolution."[19]

Many of these suddenly unconstrained youths joined factions of the Red Guards, youth militias bonded by ideological fervor, operating above the law and outside of (and often in explicit opposition to) ordinary institutional structures. Mao endorsed their efforts with vague but incendiary slogans, such as "To rebel is justified" and "Bombard the headquarters."[20] He approved their violent attacks on the existing Communist Party bureaucracy and traditional social mores and encouraged them not to fear "disorder" as they fought to eradicate the dreaded "Four Olds"—old ideas, old culture, old customs, and old habits—that, in Maoist thinking, had kept China weak.[21] The *People's Daily* fanned the flames by editorializing "In Praise of Lawlessness"—an explicit, government-sanctioned rebuke to China's millennial tradition of harmony and order.[22]

The result was a spectacular human and institutional carnage, as one by one China's organs of power and authority—including the highest ranks of the Communist Party—succumbed to the assaults of teenage ideological shock troops. China—a civilization heretofore known for its respect for learning and erudition—became an upside-down world, with children turning on parents, students brutalizing teachers and burning books, and professionals and high officials sent down to farms and factories to learn revolutionary practice from illiterate peasants. Scenes of cruelty unfolded across the country, as Red Guards and citizens allied to them—some simply picking a faction at random in the hope of surviving the storm—turned their fury on any target that might conceivably augur a return of the old "feudal" order to China.

That some of these targets were individuals who had been dead for centuries did not diminish the fury of the assault. Revolutionary students and teachers from Beijing descended on Confucius's home village, vowing to put an end to the old sage's influence on Chinese society once and for all by burning ancient books, smashing memorial tablets, and razing the gravesites of Confucius and his descendants. In Beijing, Red Guard assaults destroyed 4,922 of the capital's 6,843 designated "places of cultural or historical interest." The Forbidden City itself was reportedly saved only by Zhou Enlai's personal intervention.[23]

A society traditionally governed by an elite of Confucian literati now looked to uneducated peasants as its source of wisdom. Universities were closed. Anyone identified as an "expert" was suspect, professional competence being a dangerously bourgeois concept.

China's diplomatic posture came unhinged. The world was treated to the nearly incomprehensible sight of a China raging with indiscriminate fury against the Soviet bloc, the Western powers, and its own history and culture. Chinese diplomats and support staffs abroad harangued the citizens of their host countries with calls to revolution and lectures on "Mao Zedong Thought." In scenes reminiscent of the Boxer Uprising seventy years earlier, throngs of Red Guards attacked foreign embassies in Beijing, including a sack of the British mission complete with the beating and molestation of its fleeing staff. When the British Foreign Secretary wrote to Foreign Minister Marshal Chen Yi, suggesting that Britain and China, "while maintaining diplomatic relations . . . withdr[a]w their mission and personnel from each other's capital for the time being," he was met by silence: the Chinese Foreign Minister was himself being "struggled" against and could not reply.[24] Eventually all but one of China's ambassadors—the able and ideologically unimpeachable Huang Hua in Cairo—and roughly two-thirds of embassy staffs were called home for reeducation in the countryside or participation in revolutionary activities.[25] China was actively embroiled in disputes with the governments of several dozen countries during this time. It had genuinely positive relations with just one—the People's Republic of Albania.

Emblematic of the Cultural Revolution was the "Little Red Book" of Mao quotations, compiled in 1964 by Lin Biao, later designated as Mao's successor and killed while fleeing the country in an obscure airline crash, allegedly after attempting a coup. All Chinese were required to carry a copy of the "Little Red Book." Red Guards brandishing copies conducted "seizures" of public buildings throughout China under the authorization—or at least toleration—of Beijing, violently challenging the provincial bureaucracies.

But the Red Guards were no more immune to the dilemma of revolutions turning on themselves than the cadres they were supposed to purify. Bonded by ideology rather than formal training, the Red Guards became factions pursuing their own ideological and personal preferences. Conflict between them became so intense that, by 1968, Mao officially disbanded the Red Guards and placed loyal Party and military leaders in charge of reestablishing provincial governments.

A new policy of "sending down" a generation of youths to remote parts of the countryside to learn from the peasantry was enunciated. By this point, the military was the last major Chinese institution whose command structure remained standing, and it assumed roles far outside its ordinary competencies. Military personnel ran the gutted government ministries, tended fields, and administered factories—all in addition to their original mission of defending the country from attack.

The immediate impact of the Cultural Revolution was disastrous. After the death of Mao, the assessment by the second and third generations of leaders—almost all of whom were victims at one time or another—has been condemnatory. Deng Xiaoping, the principal leader of China from 1979 to 1991, argued that the Cultural Revolution had nearly destroyed the Communist Party as an institution and wrecked its credibility at least temporarily.[26]

In recent years, as personal memories have faded, another perspective is beginning to make a tentative appearance. This view acknowledges the colossal wrongs committed during the Cultural Revolution, but it begins to inquire whether perhaps Mao raised an important question, even if his answer to it proved disastrous. The problem Mao is said to have identified is the relationship of the modern state—especially the Communist state—to the people it governs. In largely agricultural—and even incipient industrial—societies, governance concerns issues within the capacity of the general public to understand. Of course, in aristocratic societies, the relevant public is limited. But whatever the formal legitimacy, some tacit consensus by those who are to carry out directives is needed—unless governance is to be entirely by imposition, which is usually unsustainable over a historic period.

A challenge of the modern period is that issues have become so complex that the legal framework is increasingly impenetrable. The political system issues directives but the execution is left, to an ever larger degree, to bureaucracies separated from both the political process and the public, whose only control is periodic elections, if that. Even in the United States, major legislative acts often comprise thousands of pages that, to put it mildly, only the fewest legislators have read in detail. Especially in Communist states, bureaucracies operate in self-contained units with their own rules in pursuance of procedures they often define for themselves. Fissures open up between the political and the bureaucratic classes and between both of those and the general public. In this manner, a new mandarin class risks emerging by bureaucratic momentum. Mao's attempt to solve the problem in one grand assault nearly wrecked Chinese society. A recent book by the Chinese scholar and government advisor Hu Angang argues that the Cultural Revolution, while a failure, set the stage for Deng's reforms of the late

1970s and 1980s. Hu now proposes using the Cultural Revolution as a case study for ways in which the "decision-making systems" in China's existing political system could become "more democratic, scientific, and institutionalized."[27]

Was There a Lost Opportunity?

In retrospect, one wonders whether the United States was in a position to start a dialogue with China perhaps a decade earlier than it did. Could the turmoil in China have become the starting point for a serious dialogue? In other words, were the 1960s a lost opportunity for Sino-American rapprochement? Could the opening to China have occurred earlier?

In truth, the fundamental obstacle to a more imaginative American foreign policy was Mao's concept of continuous revolution. Mao was determined at this stage to forestall any moment of calm. Attempts at reconciliation with the capitalist archenemy were not conceivable while the blood feud with Moscow revolved around Mao's adamant rejection of Khrushchev's commitment to peaceful coexistence.

There were some tentative gropings on the American side toward a more flexible perception of China. In October 1957, Senator John F. Kennedy published an article in *Foreign Affairs* remarking on "the fragmentation of authority within the Soviet orbit" and calling American policy in Asia "probably too rigid." He argued that the policy of not recognizing the People's Republic should be continued but that America should be prepared to revisit the "brittle conception of a shiftless totalitarian China" as circumstances developed. He counseled that "we must be very careful not to strait-jacket our policy as a result of ignorance and fail to detect a change in the objective situation when it comes."[28]

Kennedy's perception was subtle—but by the time he became President, the next change in Mao's dialectic was in the opposite direction:

toward *more* hostility, not less; and toward the increasingly violent elimination of domestic opponents and countervailing institutional structures, not moderate reform.

In the years immediately following Kennedy's article, Mao launched the Anti-Rightist Campaign in 1957, a second crisis in the Taiwan Strait in 1958 (which he described as an attempt to "teach the Americans a lesson"[29]), and the Great Leap Forward. When Kennedy became President, China undertook a military attack in its border conflict with India, a country that the Kennedy administration had conceived of as offering an Asian alternative to Communism. These were not the signs of conciliation and change for which Kennedy had advised Americans to stay attuned.

The Kennedy administration did offer a humanitarian gesture to alleviate China's precarious agricultural condition during the famine triggered by the Great Leap Forward. Described as an effort to secure "food for peace," the offer required, however, a specific Chinese request acknowledging a "serious desire" for assistance. Mao's commitment to self-reliance precluded any admission of dependence on foreign assistance. China, its representative at the Warsaw ambassadorial talks replied, was "overcoming its difficulties by its own efforts."[30]

In the last years of Lyndon Johnson's presidency, senior staff members and eventually the President himself began considering a move toward a less confrontational course. In 1966, the State Department instructed its negotiators to take a more forthcoming attitude at the Warsaw ambassadorial talks and authorized them to initiate informal social contacts on the sidelines of negotiations. In March 1966, the American representative at the talks offered an olive branch by stating that "the United States government was willing to develop further relations with the People's Republic of China"—the first time an American official had used the official post-1949 appellation for China in any formal capacity.

Finally, Johnson himself held out a peaceful option in a July 1966 speech on Asia policy. "Lasting peace," he observed, "can never come to Asia as long as the 700 million people of mainland China are isolated by their rulers from the outside world." While pledging to resist China's "policy of aggression by proxy" in Southeast Asia, he looked forward to an eventual era of "peaceful cooperation" and of "reconciliation between nations that now call themselves enemies."[31]

These views were put forward as abstract hopes geared to some undefined change in Chinese attitudes. No practical conclusion followed. Nor could it have. For these statements coincided almost exactly with the onset of the Cultural Revolution, when China swung back to a stance of defiant hostility.[32]

China's policies during this period did little to invite—and may have been designed to dissuade—a conciliatory approach from the United States. For its part, Washington exhibited considerable tactical skill in resisting military challenges, as in the two Taiwan Strait Crises, but showed much less imagination in shaping foreign policy in an evolving, fluid political framework.

An American National Intelligence Estimate of 1960 expressed, and perhaps helped shape, the underlying assessment:

> A basic tenet of Communist China's foreign policy—to establish Chinese hegemony in the Far East—almost certainly will not change appreciably during the period of this estimate. The regime will continue to be violently anti-American and to strike at US interests wherever and whenever it can do so without paying a disproportionate price. . . . Its arrogant self-confidence, revolutionary fervor and distorted view of the world may lead Peiping to miscalculate risks.[33]

There was much evidence to support the prevailing view. But the analysis left open the question as to what extent China could possibly achieve such sweeping objectives. Wracked by the catastrophic consequences of the Great Leap Forward, the China of the 1960s was exhausted. By 1966, it was embarking on the Cultural Revolution, which spelled a de facto retreat from the world with most diplomats recalled to Beijing, many for reeducation. What were the implications for American foreign policy? How was it possible to speak of a unified Asian bloc? What about the basic premise of America's Indochina policy that the world was facing a conspiracy directed from Moscow and Beijing? The United States, preoccupied with Vietnam and its own domestic turmoil, found few occasions to address these issues.

Part of the reason for American single-mindedness was that, in the 1950s, many of the leading China experts had left the State Department during the various investigations into who "lost" China. As a result, a truly extraordinary group of Soviet experts—including George Kennan, Charles "Chip" Bohlen, Llewellyn Thompson, and Foy Kohler—dominated State Department thinking without counterpoise, and they were convinced that any rapprochement with China risked war with the Soviet Union.

But even had the right questions been asked, there would have been no opportunity to test the answers. Some Chinese policymakers urged Mao to adapt his policies to new conditions. In February 1962, Wang Jiaxiang, head of the International Liaison Department of the Central Committee of the Communist Party, addressed a memorandum to Zhou urging that a peaceful international environment would more effectively assist China to build a stronger socialist state and a more rapidly growing economy than the prevailing posture of confrontation in all directions.[34]

Mao would not hear of it, declaring:

> In our Party there are some who advocate the "three moderations and one reduction." They say we should be more moderate toward the imperialist, more moderate toward the reactionaries, and more moderate toward the revisionists,

> while toward the struggle of the peoples of Asia, Africa and Latin-America, we should reduce assistance. This is a revisionist line.[35]

Mao insisted on the policy of challenging all potential adversaries simultaneously. He countered that "China should struggle against the imperialists, the revisionists, and the reactionaries of all countries," and that "more assistance should be given to anti-imperialist, revolutionary, and Marxist-Leninist political parties and factions."[36]

In the end, as the 1960s progressed, even Mao began to recognize that potential perils to China were multiplying. Along its vast borders, China faced a potential enemy in the Soviet Union; a humiliated adversary in India; a massive American deployment and an escalating war in Vietnam; self-proclaimed governments-in-exile in Taipei and the Tibetan enclave of northern India; a historic opponent in Japan; and, across the Pacific, an America that viewed China as an implacable adversary. Only the rivalries between these countries had prevented a common challenge so far. But no prudent statesman could gamble forever that this self-restraint would last—especially as the Soviet Union seemed to be preparing to put an end to the mounting challenges from Beijing. The Chairman would soon be obliged to prove that he knew how to be prudent as well as daring.

CHAPTER 8

The Road to Reconciliation

BY THE TIME the improbable pair of Richard Nixon and Mao Zedong decided to move toward each other, both of their countries were in the midst of upheaval. China was nearly consumed by the turmoil of the Cultural Revolution; America's political consensus was strained by the growing protest movement against the Vietnam War. China faced the prospect of war on all its frontiers—especially its northern border, where actual clashes between Soviet and Chinese forces were taking place. Nixon inherited a war in Vietnam and a domestic imperative to end it, and entered the White House at the end of a decade marked by assassinations and racial conflict.

Mao tried to address China's peril by returning to a classical Chinese stratagem: pitting the barbarians against each other, and enlisting faraway enemies against those nearby. Nixon, true to the values of his society, invoked Wilsonian principles in proposing to invite China to reenter the community of nations: "We simply cannot afford," he wrote in an article in *Foreign Affairs* in October 1967, "to leave China forever outside the family of nations, there to nurture its fantasies, cherish its hates and threaten its neighbors. There is no place on this small planet for a billion of its potentially most able people to live in angry isolation."[1]

Nixon went beyond a call for a diplomatic adjustment to an appeal for a reconciliation. He likened the diplomatic challenge to the problem of social reform in American inner cities: "In each case dialogues have to be opened; in each case aggression has to be restrained while education proceeds; and, not least, in neither case can we afford to let those now self-exiled from society stay exiled forever."[2]

Necessity may provide the impetus for policy; it does not, however, automatically define the means. And both Mao and Nixon faced huge obstacles in initiating a dialogue, not to speak of a reconciliation between the United States and China. Their countries had, for twenty years, considered each other implacable enemies. China had classified America as a "capitalist-imperialist" country—in Marxist terms, the ultimate form of capitalism, which, it was theorized, would be able to overcome its "contradictions" only by war. Conflict with the United States was unavoidable; war was probable.

America's perception was the mirror image of China's. A decade of military conflicts and near conflicts seemed to bear out the national assessment that China, acting as the fount of world revolution, was determined to expel the United States from the Western Pacific. To Americans, Mao seemed even more implacable than the Soviet leaders.

For all these reasons, Mao and Nixon had to move cautiously. First steps were likely to offend basic domestic constituencies and unnerve allies. This was a particular challenge for Mao in the midst of the Cultural Revolution.

The Chinese Strategy

Though few observers noticed it at the time, starting in 1965, Mao began slightly altering his tone toward America—and given his nearly divine status, even a nuance had vast implications. One of Mao's favorite vehicles for conveying his thinking to the United States was through interviews with the American journalist Edgar Snow. The two had met in the Communist base area of Yan'an in the 1930s. Snow had distilled his experience in a book called *Red Star over China,* which presented Mao as a kind of romantic agrarian guerrilla.

In 1965, during the preliminaries of the Cultural Revolution, Mao invited Snow to Beijing and made some startling comments—or they would have been startling had anyone in Washington paid attention to them. As Mao told Snow: "Naturally I personally regret that forces of history have divided and separated the American and Chinese peoples from virtually all communication during the past 15 years. Today the gulf seems broader than ever. However, I myself do not believe it will end in war and one of history's major tragedies."[3]

This from the leader who, for a decade and a half, had proclaimed his readiness for nuclear war with the United States in so graphic a manner that he scared both the Soviet Union and its European allies into dissociation from China. But with the Soviet Union in a menacing posture, Mao was more ready than anyone realized at the time to consider applying the maxim of moving closer to his distant adversary, the United States.

At the time of the Snow interview an American army was being built up on China's borders in Vietnam. Though the challenge was comparable to the one Mao had faced in Korea a decade and a half earlier, this time he opted for restraint. Limiting itself to noncombat support, China supplied matériel, strong moral encouragement, and some 100,000 Chinese logistical troops to work on communications and infrastructure in North Vietnam.[4] To Snow, Mao was explicit that China would fight the United States only in China, not in Vietnam: "We are not going to start the war from our side; only when the United States attacks shall we fight back. . . . As I've already said, please rest assured that we won't attack the United States."[5]

Lest the Americans miss the point, Mao reiterated that, as far as China was concerned, the Vietnamese had to cope with "their situation" by their own efforts: "The Chinese were very busy with their internal affairs. Fighting beyond one's own borders was criminal. Why should the Chinese do that? The Vietnamese could cope with their situation."[6]

Mao went on to speculate on various possible outcomes of the Vietnam War in the manner of a scientist analyzing some natural event, not as a leader dealing with military conflict along his borders. The contrast with Mao's reflections during the Korean War—when he consistently linked Korean and Chinese security concerns—could not have been more marked. Among the possible outcomes seemingly acceptable to the Chairman was that a "conference might be held, but United States troops might stay around Saigon, as in the case of South Korea"—in other words, a continuation of two Vietnam states.[7] Every American President dealing with the Vietnam War would have been willing to settle for such an outcome.

There is no evidence that the interview with Snow was ever the subject of high-level policy discussions in the Johnson administration, or that the historical tensions between China and Vietnam were considered relevant in any of the administrations (including Nixon's) that pursued the Vietnam War. Washington continued to describe China as a threat even greater than the Soviet Union. In 1965, McGeorge Bundy, who was President Johnson's National Security Advisor, made a statement typical of American views of China in the 1960s: "Communist China is quite a different problem [from the Soviet Union], and both her nuclear explosion [a reference to China's first nuclear test in October 1964] and her aggressive attitudes toward her neighbors make her a major problem for all peaceful people."[8]

On April 7, 1965, Johnson justified American intervention in Vietnam primarily on the grounds of resisting a combined design of Beijing and Hanoi: "Over this war—and all Asia—is another reality: the deepening shadow of Communist China. The rulers in Hanoi are urged on by Peking. . . . The contest in Viet-Nam is part of a wider pattern of aggressive purposes."[9] Secretary of State Dean Rusk repeated the same theme before the House Foreign Relations Committee a year later.[10]

What Mao had described to Snow was a kind of resignation from the traditional Communist doctrine of world revolution: "Wherever there is revolution, we will issue statements and hold meetings to support it. This is exactly what imperialists resent. We like to say empty words and fire empty cannons, but we will not send in troops."[11]

When reviewing Mao's statements in retrospect, one wonders whether taking them seriously might have affected the Johnson administration strategy on Vietnam. On the other hand, Mao never translated them into formal official policy partly because to do so would have required reversing a decade and a half of ideological indoctrination at a moment when ideological purity was his domestic battle cry and the conflict with the Soviet Union was based on a rejection of Khrushchev's policy of peaceful coexistence. Mao's words to Snow were almost certainly a tentative reconnaissance. But Snow was not an ideal vehicle for such a sortie. He was trusted in Beijing—at least as far as any American could be. But in Washington, Snow was considered a propagandist for Beijing. The normal Washington instinct would have been—as it was again five years later—to wait for some more concrete evidence of a Chinese shift in policy.

By any sober strategic calculations, Mao had maneuvered China into great peril. If either the United States or the Soviet Union attacked China, the other might stand aside. Logistics favored India in the two countries' border dispute, since the Himalayas were far from China's centers of strength. The United States was establishing a military presence in Vietnam. Japan, with all its historical baggage, was unfriendly and economically resurgent.

It was one of the few periods in which Mao seemed uncertain about his options on foreign policy issues. In a November 1968 meeting with the Australian Communist leader E. F. Hill, he displayed perplexity rather than his customary assurance in the guise of homilies. (Since

Mao's maneuvers were always complex, it is also possible that one of his targets was the rest of the leadership who would read the transcript and that he wanted to convey to them that he was exploring new options.) Mao seemed concerned that since a longer period had passed since the end of the Second World War than in the interwar period between the first two world wars, some global catastrophe might be imminent: "All in all, now there is neither war nor revolution. Such a situation will not last long."[12] He posed a question: "Do you know what the imperialists will do? I mean, are they going to start a world war? Or maybe they will not start the war at this moment, but will start it after a while? According to your experience in your own country and in other countries, what do you feel?"[13] In other words, does China have to choose now, or is waiting on developments the wiser course?

Above all, what is the significance, Mao wanted to know, of what he later called "turmoil under the heavens"?

> [W]e must take people's consciousness into our consideration. When the United States stopped bombing North Vietnam, American soldiers in Vietnam were very glad, and they even cheered. This indicates that their morale is not high. Is the morale of American soldiers high? Is the morale of Soviet soldiers high? Is the morale of the French, British, German, and Japanese soldiers high? The student strike is a new phenomenon in European history. Students in the capitalist countries usually do not strike. But now, all under the heaven is great chaos.[14]

What, in short, was the balance of forces between China and its potential adversaries? Did the queries about the morale of American and European soldiers imply doubts about their capacities to perform the role assigned to them in Chinese strategy—paradoxically very similar to their role in American strategy—to contain Soviet expansionism?

But if American troops were demoralized and student strikes a symptom of a general political collapse of will, the Soviet Union might emerge as the dominant world power. Some in the Chinese leadership were already arguing for an accommodation with Moscow.[15] Whatever the outcome of the Cold War, perhaps the low morale in the West proved that revolutionary ideology was at last prevailing. Should China rely on a revolutionary wave to overthrow capitalism, or should it concentrate on manipulating the rivalry of the capitalists?

It was highly unusual for Mao to ask questions that did not imply either that he was testing his interlocutor or that he knew the answer but had chosen not to reveal it yet. After some more general talk, he concluded the meeting with the query that was haunting him:

> Let me put forward a question, I will try to answer it, and you will try to answer it. I will consider it, and I ask you also to consider it. This is an issue with worldwide significance. This is the issue about war. The issue about war and peace. Will we see a war, or will we see a revolution? Will the war give rise to revolution, or will revolution prevent war?[16]

If war was imminent, Mao needed to take a position—indeed he might be its first target. But if revolution would sweep the world, Mao had to implement his life's convictions, which was revolution. Until the end of his life, Mao never fully resolved his choice.

A few months later, Mao had chosen his course for the immediate future. His doctor reported a conversation from 1969: "Mao presented me with a riddle. 'Think about this,' he said to me one day. 'We have the Soviet Union to the north and the west, India to the south, and Japan to the east. If all our enemies were to unite, attacking us from the north, south, east, and west, what do you think we should do?'" When Mao's interlocutor responded with perplexity, the Chairman continued: "Think again. . . . Beyond Japan is the United States. Didn't our ancestors counsel negotiating with faraway countries while fighting with those that are near?"[17]

Mao tiptoed into the reversal of two decades of Communist governance by two acts: one symbolic, the other practical. He used Nixon's inaugural address on January 20, 1969, as an opportunity to hint to the Chinese public that new thinking about America was taking place. On that occasion, Nixon had made a subtle reference to an opening to China, paraphrasing the language of his earlier *Foreign Affairs* article: "Let all nations know that during this administration our lines of communication will be open. We seek an open world—open to ideas, open to the exchange of goods and people—a world in which no people, great or small, will live in angry isolation."[18]

The Chinese response hinted that Beijing was interested in ending its isolation but was in no hurry to abandon its anger. Chinese newspapers reprinted Nixon's speech; since the Communist takeover, no speech of an American President had received such attention. That did not soften the invective. An article in the *People's Daily* of January 27 mocked the American President: "Although at the end of his rope, Nixon had the cheek to speak about the future. . . . A man with one foot in the grave tries to console himself by dreaming of paradise. This is the delusion and writhing of a dying class."[19]

Mao had noted Nixon's offer and taken it sufficiently seriously to put it before his public. He was not open to contact by exhortation, however. Something more substantive would be needed—especially since a Chinese move toward America might escalate the weekly military clashes along the Sino-Soviet border into something far more menacing.

Almost at the same time, Mao started to explore the practical implications of his general decision by recalling four PLA marshals—Chen Yi, Nie Rongzhen, Xu Xiangqian, and Ye Jianying—who had been purged during the Cultural Revolution and assigned to "investigation and study" at factories in the provinces, a euphemism for manual labor.[20] Mao asked the marshals to undertake an analysis of China's strategic options.

It required reassurance from Zhou Enlai to convince the marshals that this was not a maneuver to make them indict themselves as part of the self-rectification campaign of the Cultural Revolution. After a month, they demonstrated how much China had lost by depriving itself of their talents. They produced a thoughtful assessment of the international situation. Reviewing the capabilities and intentions of key countries, they summed up China's strategic challenge as follows:

> For the U.S. imperialists and the Soviet revisionists, the real threat is the one existing between themselves. For all other countries, the real threat comes from U.S. imperialists and Soviet revisionists. Covered by the banner of opposing China, U.S. imperialists and Soviet revisionists collaborate with each other while at the same time fighting against each other. The contradictions between them, however, are not reduced because of the collaboration between them; rather, their hostilities toward each other are more fierce than ever before.[21]

This might mean an affirmation of existing policy: Mao would be able to continue to challenge both superpowers simultaneously. The marshals argued that the Soviet Union would not dare to invade because of the difficulties it would face: lack of popular support for a war, long supply lines, insecure rear areas, and doubts about the attitude of the United States. The marshals summed up the American attitude in a Chinese proverb of "sitting on top of the mountain to watch a fight between two tigers."[22]

But a few months later, in September, they modified this judgment to one reached nearly simultaneously by Nixon. In the marshals' new view, the United States, in the event of a Soviet invasion, would not be able to confine its role to that of a spectator. It would have to take a stand: "The last thing the U.S. imperialists are willing to see is a victory by the Soviet revisionists in a Sino-Soviet war, as this would [allow the Soviets] to build up a big empire more powerful than the American empire in resources and manpower."[23] In other words, contact with the United States, however much assailed in Chinese media at the moment, was needed for the defense of the country.

The astute analysis ended with what reads like a rather cautious conclusion in substance—though it was daring in terms of its challenge to the basic premises of Chinese foreign policy during the Cultural Revolution. The marshals urged, in March 1969, that China should end its isolation and that it should discourage Soviet or American adventurism by "adopt[ing] a military strategy of active defense and a political strategy of active offense"; "actively carry[ing] out diplomatic activities"; and "expand[ing] the international united front of anti-imperialism and anti-revisionism."[24]

These general suggestions that Mao allow China to reenter international diplomacy proved insufficient for his larger vision. In May 1969, Mao sent the marshals back to the drawing board for further analysis and recommendations. By now, clashes along the Sino-Soviet border had multiplied. How was China to respond to the growing peril? A later account by Xiong Xianghui, a veteran intelligence operative and diplomat assigned by Mao to serve as the marshals' private secretary, recorded that the group deliberated the question of "whether, from a strategic perspective, China should play the American card in case of a large-scale Soviet attack on China."[25] Searching for precedents for such an unorthodox move, Chen Yi suggested that the group study the modern example of Stalin's nonaggression pact with Hitler.

Ye Jianying proposed a far older precedent from China's own Three Kingdoms period, when, following the collapse of the Han Dynasty, the empire split into three states striving for dominance. The states' contests were recounted in a fourteenth-century epic novel, *The Romance of the Three Kingdoms*, then banned in China. Ye cited the strategy pursued by one of its central characters as a template: "We can consult the example of Zhuge Liang's strategic guiding principle, when the three states of Wei, Shu, and Wu confronted each other: 'Ally with Wu in the east to oppose Wei in the north.'"[26] After decades of vilifying China's past, Mao was invited by the purged marshals to look to China's "ancestors" for strategic inspiration by means of a strategy amounting to a reversal of alliances.

The marshals went on to describe potential relations with the United States as a strategic asset: "To a large extent, the Soviet revisionists' decision to launch a war of aggression against China depends on the attitude of the U.S. imperialists."[27] In a move that was intellectually brave and politically risky, the marshals recommended the resumption of the deadlocked ambassadorial talks with the United States. Though they made a bow to established doctrine, which treated both superpowers as equal threats to peace, the marshals' recommendation left little doubt that they considered the Soviet Union the principal danger. Marshal Chen Yi submitted an addendum to the views of his colleagues. He pointed out that while the United States had in the past rejected Chinese overtures, the new President, Richard Nixon, seemed eager "to win over China." He proposed what he called "'wild' ideas"[28]: to move the U.S.-China ambassadorial dialogue to a higher level—at least ministerial and perhaps higher. Most revolutionary was the proposal to drop the precondition that the return of Taiwan had to be settled first:

> First, when the meetings in Warsaw [the ambassadorial talks] are resumed, we may take the initiative in proposing to hold Sino-American talks at the ministerial or even higher levels, so that basic and related problems in Sino-American relations can be solved. . . . Second, a Sino-American meeting at higher levels holds strategic significance. We should not raise any prerequisite. . . . The Taiwan question can be gradually

> solved by talks at higher levels. Furthermore, we may discuss with the Americans other questions of strategic significance.[29]

Soviet pressure supplied a growing impetus. In the face of increasing Soviet troop concentrations and a major battle at the border of Xinjiang, on August 28 the Central Committee of the Chinese Communist Party ordered a mobilization of all Chinese military units along all of China's borders. Resumption of contact with the United States had become a strategic necessity.

The American Strategy

When Richard Nixon took his oath of office, China's anxieties presented him with an extraordinary strategic opportunity, though this was not at first obvious to an administration divided over Vietnam. Many of the policy elites who had made the decision to defend Indochina against what they had conceived as a concerted assault from Moscow and Beijing had had second thoughts. A significant segment of the Establishment—significant enough to complicate an effective policy—had come to the view that the Vietnam War was not only unwinnable, but that it reflected a congenital moral failure of the American political system.

Nixon did not believe that one could end a war into which his predecessors had sent 500,000 American soldiers halfway across the world by pulling out unconditionally—as many of his critics demanded. And he took seriously the commitments of his predecessors from both parties, whose decisions had led to the dilemmas he now faced. Nixon knew that whatever the agony of its involvement in Vietnam, the United States remained the strongest country in an alliance against Communist aggression around the world, and American credibility was critical. The Nixon administration—in which I served as National

Security Advisor and later as Secretary of State—therefore sought a staged withdrawal from Indochina to give the people of the region an opportunity to shape their own future and to sustain the world's faith in America's role.

Nixon's critics equated a new approach to foreign policy with a single issue: in effect, the unconditional withdrawal from the Vietnam War, ignoring the millions of Indochinese who had engaged themselves in reliance on America's word and the scores of countries who had joined the effort at America's behest. Nixon was committed to ending the war, but equally strongly to giving America a dynamic role in reshaping the international order just emerging piece by piece. Nixon intended to free American policy from the oscillations between extremes of commitment and withdrawal and ground it in a concept of the national interest that could be sustained as administrations succeeded each other.

In this design, China played a key role. The leaders of the two countries viewed their common goals from different perspectives. Mao treated the rapprochement as a strategic imperative, Nixon as an opportunity to redefine the American approach to foreign policy and international leadership. He sought to use the opening to China to demonstrate to the American public that, even in the midst of a debilitating war, the United States was in a position to bring about a design for long-term peace. He and his associates strove to reestablish contact with one-fifth of the world's population to place in context and ease the pain of an inevitably imperfect withdrawal from a corner of Southeast Asia.

This is where the paths of Mao, the advocate of continuous revolution, and Nixon, the pessimistic strategist, converged. Mao was convinced that vision and willpower would overcome all obstacles. Nixon was committed to careful planning, though ridden by the fear that even the best-laid plans would go awry as a result of fate intervening in an unforeseen and unforeseeable manner. But he carried out his plans anyway. Mao and Nixon shared one overriding trait: a willingness to follow the global logic of their reflections and instincts to ultimate conclusions. Nixon tended to be the more pragmatic. One of his frequently expressed maxims was "You pay the same price for doing something halfway as for doing it completely. So you might as well do it completely." What Mao carried out with elemental vitality, Nixon pursued as a resigned recognition of the workings and obligations of fate. But once launched on a course, he followed it with comparable determination.

That China and the United States would find a way to come together was inevitable given the necessities of the time. It would have happened sooner or later whatever the leadership in either country. That it took place with such decisiveness and proceeded with so few detours is a tribute to the leadership that brought it about. Leaders cannot create the context in which they operate. Their distinctive contribution consists in operating at the limit of what the given situation permits. If they exceed these limits, they crash; if they fall short of what is necessary, their policies stagnate. If they build soundly, they may create a new set of relationships that sustains itself over a historical period because all parties consider it in their own interest.

First Steps—Clashes at the Ussuri River

Though reconciliation was the eventual result, it was not easy for the United States and China to find their way to a strategic dialogue. Nixon's article in *Foreign Affairs* and the study by the four marshals for Mao had produced parallel conclusions, but the actual movement of the two sides was inhibited by domestic complexities, historical experience, and cultural perceptions. The publics on both sides had been exposed to two decades of hostility and suspicion; they had to be prepared for a diplomatic revolution.

Nixon's tactical problem was more complicated than Mao's. Once

Mao had made a decision, he was in a position to implement it ruthlessly. And opponents would remember the fate of Mao's previous critics. But Nixon had to overcome a legacy of twenty years of American foreign policy based on the assumption that China would use every opportunity to weaken the United States and to expel it from Asia. By the time he entered the White House, this view had congealed into established doctrine.

Nixon therefore had to tread carefully lest China's diplomatic overtures turn out to be propaganda with no serious change of approach in Beijing. That was a distinct possibility given that the only point of contact Americans had had with the Chinese in twenty years had been the ambassadorial talks in Warsaw, whose 136 meetings were distinctive only for their monotonously sterile rhythm. Two dozen members of Congress had to be briefed on every step, and new approaches were bound to be lost in the conflicting pressures of briefings of some fifteen countries, which were being kept informed about the Warsaw talks and included Taiwan—still recognized by most of them, and especially the United States, as the legitimate government of China.

Nixon's general design was turned into an opportunity as a result of a clash between Soviet and Chinese forces on Zhenbao (or Damansky) Island in the Ussuri River, where Siberia abuts the Chinese frontier. The clash might not have attracted the White House's attention so quickly had the Soviet ambassador, Anatoly Dobrynin, not come to my office repeatedly to brief me on the Soviet version of what had happened. It was unheard of in that cold period of the Cold War for the Soviet Union to brief us on an event so remote from our usual dialogue—or on any event for that matter. We drew the conclusion that the Soviet Union was the probable aggressor and that the briefing, less than a year after the occupation of Czechoslovakia, hid a larger design. This suspicion was confirmed by a study on the border clashes by Allen Whiting of the RAND Corporation. Whiting concluded that because the incidents took place close to Soviet supply bases and far from Chinese ones, the Soviets were the probable aggressors, and that the next step might well be an attack on China's nuclear facilities. If a Sino-Soviet war was imminent, some American governmental position needed to be developed. In my capacity as National Security Advisor, I ordered an interdepartmental review.

As it turned out, the analysis of the immediate causes of the clashes was mistaken, at least regarding the Zhenbao incident. It was a case of mistaken analysis leading to a correct judgment. Recent historical studies have revealed that the Zhenbao incident had in fact been initiated by the Chinese as Dobrynin claimed; they had laid a trap in which a Soviet border patrol suffered heavy casualties.[30] But the Chinese purpose was defensive, in keeping with the Chinese concept of deterrence described in the previous chapter. The Chinese planned the particular incident to shock the Soviet leadership into putting an end to a series of clashes along the border, probably initiated by the Soviets, and which in Beijing were treated as Soviet harassment. The offensive deterrence concept involves the use of a preemptive strategy not so much to defeat the adversary militarily as to deal him a psychological blow to cause him to desist.

The Chinese action in fact had the opposite effect. The Soviets stepped up harassment all along the frontier, resulting in the wiping out of a Chinese battalion at the Xinjiang border. In this atmosphere, beginning in the summer of 1969, the United States and China began to exchange deniable signals. The United States eased some minor trade restrictions with China. Zhou Enlai released two American yachtsmen who had been detained since straying into Chinese waters.

During the summer of 1969, the signals of a possible war between China and the Soviet Union multiplied. Soviet troops along the Chinese border grew to some forty-two divisions—over a million men. Middle-level Soviet officials began to inquire of acquaintances at comparable levels around the world how their governments would react to a Soviet preemptive attack on Chinese nuclear installations.

These developments caused the United States government to speed up its consideration of a potential large-scale Soviet attack on China. The very query ran counter to the experience of those who had conducted Cold War foreign policy. For a generation, China had been viewed as the more bellicose of the two Communist giants. That the United States might take sides in a war between them had never been considered; the fact that Chinese policymakers compulsively studied America's likely attitudes demonstrated the extent to which long isolation had dulled their understanding of the American decision-making process.

But Nixon was determined to define policy by geopolitical considerations, and in these terms, any fundamental change in the balance of power had to evoke at least an American attitude, and, if significant, a policy. Even if we decided to stay aloof, it should be by conscious decision, not by default. At a National Security Council meeting in August 1969, Nixon chose an attitude, if not yet a policy. He put forward the then shocking thesis that, in the existing circumstances, the Soviet Union was the more dangerous party and that it would be against American interests if China were "smashed" in a China-Soviet war.[31] What this meant practically was not discussed then. What it should have implied for anyone familiar with Nixon's thinking was that, on the issue of China, geopolitics trumped other considerations. In pursuit of this policy, I issued a directive that in case of conflict between the Soviet Union and China the United States would adopt a posture of neutrality but within that framework tilt to the greatest extent possible toward China.[32]

It was a revolutionary moment in U.S. foreign policy: an American President declared that we had a strategic interest in the survival of a major Communist country with which we had had no meaningful contact for twenty years and against which we had fought a war and engaged in two military confrontations. How to communicate this decision? The Warsaw ambassadorial talks had not been convened for months and would have been too low-level to present a view of such magnitude. The administration therefore decided to go to the other extreme and go public with the American decision to view a conflict between the two Communist giants as a matter affecting the American national interest.

Amidst a drumbeat of bellicose Soviet statements in various forums threatening war, American officials were instructed to convey that the United States was not indifferent and would not be passive. Central Intelligence Agency Director Richard Helms was asked to give a background briefing in which he disclosed that Soviet officials seemed to be sounding out other Communist leaders about their attitude toward a preemptive attack on Chinese nuclear installations. On September 5, 1969, Undersecretary of State Elliot Richardson became explicit in a speech to the American Political Science Association: "Ideological differences between the two Communist giants are not our affair. We could not fail to be deeply concerned, however, with an escalation of this quarrel into a massive breach of international peace and security."[33] In the code of the Cold War, Richardson's statement warned that, whatever course the United States adopted, it would not be indifference; that it would act according to its strategic interests.

When these measures were being designed, the principal goal was to create a psychological framework for an opening to China. Having since seen many documents published by the main parties, I now lean toward the view that the Soviet Union was much closer to a preemptive attack than we realized and that uncertainty about American reactions proved to be a principal reason for postponing that project. It is now clear for example that in October 1969 Mao thought an attack so imminent that he ordered all leaders (except Zhou, needed to run the government) to disperse across the country and to alert China's nuclear forces, tiny as they were then.

Whether as a result of American warnings or of the Communist world's own inner dynamics, the tensions between the two Communist giants eased over the course of the year, and the immediate threat of war diminished. Soviet Prime Minister Aleksei Kosygin, who had flown to Hanoi for Ho Chi Minh's funeral in September via India rather than China—a much longer route—suddenly altered his return trip while en route and turned his plane toward Beijing, the kind of dramatic action countries take when they want either to issue an ultimatum or to usher in a new phase. Neither happened or, depending on one's perspective, both did. Kosygin and Zhou met for three hours at the Beijing airport—hardly a warm welcome for the prime minister of a country that was still technically an ally. Zhou Enlai produced a draft understanding providing for mutual withdrawals at contested positions on the northern frontier and other measures to ease tensions. The document was supposed to be co-signed on Kosygin's return to Moscow. It did not happen. Tensions reached a high point in October when Mao ordered China's top leadership to evacuate Beijing and Defense Minister Lin Biao placed the military on "first-degree combat readiness" alert.[34]

Space was thereby created for the unfolding of Sino-American contacts. Each side leaned over backward to avoid being perceived as having made the first public move—the United States because it had no forum to translate the presidential strategy into a formal position, China because it did not want to show weakness in the face of threats. The result was a minuet so intricate that both sides could always claim that they were not in contact, so stylized that neither country needed to bear the onus of an initiative that might be rejected, and so elliptical that existing political relations could be continued without the need for consultation on a script that had yet to be written. Between November 1969 and February 1970, there were at least ten occasions when American and Chinese diplomats in various capitals around the world had exchanged words—an event remarkable primarily because, before then, the diplomats had always avoided each other. The deadlock was broken when we ordered Walter Stoessel, the U.S. ambassador in

Warsaw, to approach Chinese diplomats at the next social function and express the desire for a dialogue.

The setting for this encounter was a Yugoslav fashion show in the Polish capital. The Chinese diplomats in attendance, who were without instructions, fled the scene. The Chinese attaché's account of the incident shows how constrained relations had become. Interviewed years later, he recalled seeing two Americans talking and pointing at the Chinese contingent from across the room; this prompted the Chinese to stand up and leave, lest they be drawn into conversation. The Americans, determined to carry out their instructions, followed the Chinese. When the desperate Chinese diplomats speeded up, the Americans started running after them, shouting in Polish (the only mutually intelligible language available), "We are from American embassy. We want to meet your ambassador . . . President Nixon said he wanted to resume his talk with Chinese."[35]

Two weeks later, the Chinese ambassador in Warsaw invited Stoessel to a meeting at the Chinese Embassy, to prepare for a resumption of the Warsaw talks. Reopening the forum inevitably raised the fundamental issues. What were the two sides going to talk about? And to what end?

This brought into the open the differences in negotiating tactics and style between the Chinese and American leadership—at least with the American diplomatic establishment that had supervised the Warsaw talks through over a hundred abortive meetings. The differences had been obscured so long as both sides believed deadlock served their purposes: the Chinese would demand the return of Taiwan to Chinese sovereignty; the Americans would propose a renunciation of force over what was presented as a dispute between two Chinese parties.

Now that both sides sought progress, the difference in negotiating style became important. Chinese negotiators use diplomacy to weave together political, military, and psychological elements into an overall strategic design. Diplomacy to them is the elaboration of a strategic principle. They ascribe no particular significance to the process of negotiation as such; nor do they consider the opening of a particular negotiation a transformational event. They do not think that personal relations can affect their judgments, though they may invoke personal ties to facilitate their own efforts. They have no emotional difficulty with deadlocks; they consider them the inevitable mechanism of diplomacy. They prize gestures of goodwill only if they serve a definable objective or tactic. And they patiently take the long view against impatient interlocutors, making time their ally.

The attitude of the American diplomat varies substantially. The prevalent view within the American body politic sees military force and diplomacy as distinct, in essence separate, phases of action. Military action is viewed as occasionally creating the conditions for negotiations, but once negotiations begin, they are seen as being propelled by their own internal logic. This is why, at the start of negotiations, the United States reduced military operations in Korea and agreed to a bombing halt in Vietnam, in each case substituting reassurance for pressure and reducing material incentives on behalf of intangible ones. American diplomacy generally prefers the specific over the general, the practical over the abstract. It is urged to be "flexible"; it feels an obligation to break deadlocks with new proposals—unintentionally inviting new deadlocks to elicit new proposals. These tactics often can be used by determined adversaries in the service of a strategy of procrastination.

In the case of the Warsaw talks, American proclivities had the opposite effect. China had returned to the Warsaw talks because Mao had made a strategic decision to follow the four marshals' recommendations to seek a high-level dialogue with the United States. But American diplomats (in contrast to their President) did not envisage—or even imagine—such a breakthrough; or rather, they defined a breakthrough as breathing life into a process they had been nursing through 134 meetings to date. On that journey, they had developed an agenda reflecting the pragmatic issues that had accumulated between the two countries: settlement of financial claims the two sides had against each other; prisoners held in each other's jails; trade; arms control; cultural exchanges. The negotiators' idea of a breakthrough was China's readiness to discuss this agenda.

A dialogue of the deaf developed at the two meetings of the resumed Warsaw talks on February 20 and March 20, 1970. As National Security Advisor in the White House, I had urged the negotiating team to repeat what our envoys had tried to say to the fleeing Chinese diplomats, that the United States "would be prepared to consider sending a representative to Peking for direct discussions with your officials, or receiving a representative from your government to Washington." Chinese negotiators formally repeated the standard position on Taiwan albeit in a mild form. But wrapped inside the formulaic response on Taiwan was an unprecedented move: China was willing to consider talks outside the Warsaw channels at the ambassadorial level or through other channels "to reduce tensions between China and the US and fundamentally improve relations."[36] It did not make such talks conditional on the settlement of the Taiwan issue.

The American negotiators in Warsaw sought to avoid this broader approach. The first time it was made, they did not respond at all. Afterward they developed talking points to deflect the Chinese proposition of an overall review of relationships into an opportunity to address the American agenda developed over two decades of desultory conversations.[37]

Nixon was no less impatient with this approach than Mao must have been. "They will kill this baby before it is born," Nixon said when confronted with a plan put forward by the negotiating team. But he was reluctant to order them to engage in a geopolitical dialogue for fear that the briefing system would produce a firestorm and a need for multiple reassurances, all before the Chinese attitude was clear. Mao's attitude was more ambivalent. On the one hand, he wanted to explore rapprochement with the United States. But these exchanges were taking place in early 1970, when the Nixon administration faced massive demonstrations protesting the decision to send forces into Cambodia to disrupt the bases and supply chains supporting Hanoi's offensives into South Vietnam. The question for Mao was whether the demonstrations marked the beginning of the genuine world revolution so long expected by the Marxists and as often disappointed. If China moved closer to the United States, would it be doing it just when the world revolutionary agenda was being fulfilled? To wait out these prospects consumed much of Mao's planning in 1970.[38] He used the American military incursion into Cambodia as a pretext to cancel the next session of Warsaw talks scheduled for May 20, 1970. They were never resumed.

Nixon was looking for a forum less bureaucratically constraining and more under his direct control. Mao sought for a way to break through to the highest levels of the United States government whenever he had made a firm decision. Both had to move carefully lest a premature disclosure trigger a Soviet onslaught or a rejection by the other side thwart the entire initiative. When the Warsaw talks foundered, the operating level of the U.S. government seemed relieved to be freed of the perplexities and domestic risks of a negotiation with Beijing. During the year that Nixon and Mao were searching for venues for a high-level dialogue, lower levels of the American diplomatic establishment never raised the question at the White House of what had happened to the Warsaw talks or suggested reconvening them.

For nearly a year after the Chinese cancellation of the proposed May 20 meeting, both the American and Chinese leaders agreed on the objective but found themselves thwarted by the gulf of twenty years of isolation. The problem was no longer simply the cultural differences between the Chinese and the American approaches to negotiations. It was that Nixon's approach differed more from that of his own diplomats than from Mao's. He and I wanted to explore the strategic situation produced by the triangular relationship between the Soviet Union,

China, and the United States. We strove for an occasion not so much to remove irritants as to conduct a geopolitical dialogue.

As the two sides were circling each other, their choice of intermediaries conveyed a great deal about their perceptions of the task at hand. Nixon used the occasion of an around-the-world trip in July 1970 to tell his hosts in Pakistan and Romania that he sought high-level exchanges with Chinese leaders and that they were free to communicate this to Beijing. As National Security Advisor, I mentioned the same point to Jean Sainteny, the former French ambassador in Hanoi, a friend of many years who was acquainted with the Chinese ambassador in Paris, Huang Zhen. In other words, the White House chose a nonaligned friend of China (Pakistan), a member of the Warsaw Pact known for its quest for independence from Moscow (Romania), and a member of NATO distinguished by its commitment to strategic independence (France—on the assumption that Sainteny was bound to pass our message to the French government). Beijing passed hints to us via its embassy in Oslo, Norway (a NATO ally), and, strangely enough, in Kabul, Afghanistan (perhaps on the theory that the venue was so improbable as to be sure to gain our attention). We ignored Oslo because our embassy was not equipped for the necessary staff support; Kabul, of course, was even more remote. And we did not want to conduct the dialogue once again through embassies.

China ignored the direct approach via Paris but eventually responded to the overtures via Romania and Pakistan. Before that, however, Mao communicated with us but so subtly and indirectly that we missed the point. In October 1970 Mao granted another interview to Edgar Snow, considered by the Nixon White House to be a Mao sympathizer. To demonstrate the importance Mao attached to the occasion, he placed Snow next to him on the reviewing stand during the parade celebrating the Communist victory in the civil war on October 8, 1970. The mere presence of an American standing next to the Chairman symbolized—or was intended to symbolize to the Chinese people—that contact with America was not only permissible but a high priority.

The interview proceeded in a complex manner. Snow was given a transcript of the interview with the restriction that he could use only indirect quotations. He was also instructed to delay any publication for three months. The Chinese reasoning must have been that Snow would submit the actual text to the U.S. government and that the published summary would then reinforce a process already in train.

It did not work out that way for the same reason that the 1965 interview failed to influence the U.S. government. Snow was a friend of the PRC of long standing; that very fact caused him to be written off in the American foreign policy establishment as a Beijing propagandist. No transcript of his interview reached high levels of government, still less the White House, and by the time the article appeared months later, it had been overtaken by other communications.

It was a pity the transcript did not reach us, because the Chairman had made some revolutionary pronouncements. For nearly a decade, China had cut itself off from the outside world. Now Mao announced that he would soon start inviting Americans of all political persuasions to visit China. Nixon would be welcome "either as a tourist or as President" because the Chairman had concluded that "the problems between China and the U.S.A. would have to be solved with Nixon"—because of the upcoming presidential election within two years.[39]

Mao had moved from vilifying the United States to inviting a dialogue with the American President. And he added a startling comment about the Chinese domestic situation, which hinted that the dialogue would take place with a new China.

Mao told Snow that he was ending the Cultural Revolution. What he had intended as a moral and intellectual renovation had turned into coercion, he said. "When foreigners reported that China was in great chaos, they were not telling lies. It had been true. Fighting [between

Chinese] was going on . . . first with spears, then rifles, then mortars."[40] Mao, as Snow reported, now deplored the cult of personality built around his person: "It was hard, the chairman said, for people to overcome the habits of 3,000 years of emperor-worshipping tradition." The titles ascribed to him such as "Great Helmsman . . . would all be eliminated sooner or later." The sole title he wished to retain was "teacher."[41]

These were extraordinary assertions. After having convulsed his country with upheavals that destroyed even the Communist Party so that only a cult of personality was left for cohesion, Mao now pronounced the end of the Cultural Revolution. It had been proclaimed so that the Chairman could govern without doctrinal or bureaucratic inhibitions. It had been sustained by shredding existing structures and by what Mao now described as "maltreatment of 'captives'—party members and others removed from power and subjected to reeducation."[42]

Where did all this leave Chinese governance? Or was it being told to a foreign journalist in Mao's characteristic elliptically wandering way, in pursuit of its principal purpose, to encourage a new phase in the relationship between China and the United States and the world by conveying an altered governance? As Snow recorded, Mao announced that "between Chinese and Americans there need be no prejudices. There could be mutual respect and equality. He said he placed high hopes on the peoples of the two countries."[43]

Nixon, in a break with American foreign policy tradition, had urged a relaxation of tensions on the basis of geopolitical considerations in order to return China to the international system. But to the China-centered Mao, the principal vision was not the international system so much as the future of China. To achieve its security, he was willing to shift the center of gravity of Chinese policy and bring about a reversal of the alliances—not, however, in the name of a theory of international relations but rather of a new direction for Chinese society in which China could even learn from the United States:

> China should learn from the way America developed, by decentralizing and spreading responsibility and wealth among the 50 states. A central government could not do everything. China must depend upon regional and local initiatives. It would not do [*spreading his hands*] to leave everything up to him [Mao].[44]

Mao, in short, reaffirmed classic principles of Chinese governance cast in Confucian principles of moral rectitude. He devoted a part of his interview to castigating the habit of lying, which he blamed not on the Americans but on the recently disempowered Red Guards. "If one did not speak the truth, Mao concluded, how could he gain the confidence of others? Who would trust one?"[45] Snow recorded. The fire-breathing, radical ideologist of yesterday now appeared in the garb of a Confucian sage. His concluding sentence seemed to express a sense of resignation to new circumstance if not without, as always, taunting double meanings: "He was, he said, only a lone monk walking the world with a leaky umbrella."[46]

There was more to the last line than Mao's habitual mockery in presenting the creator of the Great Leap Forward and the Cultural Revolution as returning to his original philosophic vocation as a lonely teacher. For as several Chinese commentators later noted, the quotation in Snow's English text was but the first line of a familiar Chinese couplet.[47] If completed, the couplet is not so much mocking as ominous. Left unspoken, or at least untranslated, was the second line of the couplet: "*wu fa wu tian.*" As written, the Chinese characters mean "without hair, without sky"—that is, the monk is bald, and because he holds an umbrella, he does not see the sky above him. But in the tonal Chinese language, the line is a pun. Pronounced slightly differently, the line takes on a new meaning: "without law, without heaven"—or, less literally: "defying laws both human and divine"; "neither God-fearing nor law-abiding"; "trampling law underfoot without batting an eyelid."[48]

Mao's closing salvo was, in other words, even further reaching and more subtle than initially apparent. Mao cast himself as a wandering classical sage but also as a law unto himself. Was Mao toying with his English-speaking interviewer? Could he possibly think Snow would understand the pun, which is, for a Western ear, almost impossibly obscure? (Mao did sometimes overestimate Western subtlety even as the West sometimes exaggerated his.) Given the context, the probability is that Mao's pun was directed to his domestic audience, particularly those leaders who might oppose rapprochement with the heretofore hated United States and whose opposition later culminated in the crisis—and alleged coup—of Lin Biao shortly after the U.S. opening to China. Mao was effectively announcing that he was about to turn the world upside down again. In that mission, he would not be bound by "laws human or divine," not even the laws of his own ideology. It warned doubters to get out of the way.

The text of Mao's interview was surely circulated in high levels of Beijing even as it was being ignored in Washington. Snow had been asked to delay publication so that China could develop an official initiative. Mao decided to cut through the minuet of third-party communications by addressing the American administration directly at the highest level. On December 8, 1970, a message was delivered to my office in the White House from Zhou Enlai. Reviving a diplomatic practice of previous centuries, the Pakistani ambassador brought it from Islamabad, where it had been delivered as a handwritten communication. Beijing's missive formally acknowledged the messages received through intermediaries. It noted a comment made by Nixon to President Agha Muhammad Yahya Khan of Pakistan, when Yahya called at the White House a few weeks earlier, to the effect that America, in its negotiations with the Soviet Union, would not participate in a "condominium against China" and would be prepared to send an emissary to a mutually convenient place to arrange high-level contacts with China.[49]

Zhou Enlai replied as he had not to previous messages because, he said, this was the first time a message had "come from a Head, through a Head, to a Head."[50] Emphasizing that his reply had been approved by Mao and Lin Biao, then Mao's designated heir, Zhou invited a special emissary to Beijing to discuss "the vacation [*sic*] of Chinese territories called Taiwan" which "have now been occupied by foreign troops of the United States for the last fifteen years."[51]

It was an artful document. For what exactly was Zhou Enlai proposing to discuss? The reversion of Taiwan to China or the presence of American troops on the island? There was no reference to the treaty of mutual assistance. Whatever it meant, it was the mildest formulation on Taiwan that had been received from Beijing for twenty years. Did it apply only to American forces stationed in Taiwan, most of whom were support forces for Vietnam? Or did it imply a more sweeping demand? In any event, to invite the representative of the reviled "monopoly capitalists"[52] to Beijing had to reflect some deeper imperative than the desire to discuss Taiwan, for which a forum already existed; it had to involve the security of China.

The White House opted to leave the answer open for actual direct contacts. Our reply accepted the principle of an emissary but defined his mission as "the broad range of issues which lie between the People's Republic of China and the U.S."—in other words, the U.S. emissary would not agree to confine the agenda to Taiwan.[53]

Leaving nothing to the chance that the Pakistan channel might not work efficiently, Zhou Enlai sent a parallel message via Romania, which, for some never explained reason, arrived a month after the Pakistani message, in January. This message, too, we were told, had been "reviewed by Chairman Mao and Lin Piao [Lin Biao]."[54] It described Taiwan as the one outstanding issue between China and the United States and added an entirely new element: since President Nixon had already visited Belgrade and Bucharest—capitals of Communist countries—he would also be welcome in Beijing. In light of the military clashes of the past decade and a half, it was significant that Taiwan was listed as the *only* issue between China and the United States; in other words, Vietnam clearly was not an obstacle to reconciliation.

We replied through the Romanian channel, accepting the principle of an emissary but ignoring the invitation to the President. At this early stage of contacts, accepting a presidential visit seemed too importuning, not to mention too risky. We conveyed our definition of an appropriate agenda phrased, to avoid confusion, identically with the message via Pakistan, to the effect that the United States was prepared to discuss all issues of concern to both sides, including Taiwan.

Zhou Enlai had seen Yahya in October and the Romanian Vice Premier in November. Mao had received Snow in early October. That all these messages emerged within a few weeks of each other reflected the fact that diplomacy had gone beyond the tactical and was being orchestrated for a major denouement.

But to our surprise—and no little uneasiness—there was no response for three months. Probably it was because of the South Vietnamese offensive, backed by U.S. airpower, on the Ho Chi Minh Trail through southern Laos, the principal supply route for North Vietnamese forces in the South. Mao also seems to have had second thoughts about the prospects of an American revolution based on the anti–Vietnam War demonstrations.[55] Perhaps it was because Beijing prefers to move at a pace that demonstrates its imperviousness to mere tactical considerations and precludes any demonstration of Chinese eagerness, much less of weakness. Most likely, Mao needed time to align his own domestic constituencies.

It was not until the beginning of April that we heard from China again. It chose none of the channels we had established but a method of its own, which forced into the open the issue of the Chinese desire to achieve a better relationship with America and was less dependent on actions of the United States government.

This is the background to the episode that has entered folklore as

Ping-Pong diplomacy. A Chinese Ping-Pong team participated in an international tournament in Japan, the first time a Chinese sports team had competed outside China since the beginning of the Cultural Revolution. In recent years, it has emerged that the impending encounter between the Chinese and American teams caused considerable internal debate in the Chinese leadership. The Chinese Foreign Ministry initially recommended avoiding the tournament entirely, or at least remaining aloof from the American team. Zhou forwarded the matter for reconsideration by Mao, who deliberated for two days. Late one night, after one of his periodic bouts of insomnia, Mao lay "slumped over the table" in a sleeping-pill-induced haze. Suddenly he croaked to his nurse, telling her to phone the Foreign Ministry—"to invite the American team to visit China." The nurse recalled asking him, "Does your word count after taking sleeping pills?" Mao replied, "Yes, it counts, every word counts. Act promptly, or it will be too late!"[56]

This order from Mao in hand, the Chinese players used the occasion to invite the American team to visit China. On April 14, 1971, the amazed young Americans found themselves at the Great Hall of the People in the presence of Zhou Enlai, which was more than had ever been achieved by the vast majority of the foreign ambassadors stationed in Beijing.

"You have opened a new chapter in the relations of the American and Chinese people," affirmed the Chinese Premier. "I am confident that the beginning of our friendship will certainly find support with the majority of our peoples." The athletes, stunned by the fact that they were being propelled into high-level diplomacy, did not respond, causing Zhou Enlai to end with a sentence we later came to recognize as characteristic: "Don't you think so?"—evoking a round of applause.[57]

As usual with Chinese diplomacy, Mao and Zhou were operating on many levels. On one level, the Ping-Pong diplomacy constituted an answer to the American messages of January. It committed China publicly to the course heretofore confined to the most secret diplomatic channels. In that sense, it was reassurance. But it was also a warning of what course China could pursue were the secret communications thwarted. Beijing could then undertake a public campaign—what would today be called "people-to-people diplomacy"—much as Hanoi was doing in pressing its objectives on Vietnam, and appeal to the growing protest movement in American society on the basis of another "lost chance for peace."

Zhou soon conveyed that the diplomatic channel remained his preferred option. On April 29, the Pakistani ambassador brought another handwritten message from Beijing dated April 21. It explained the long silence by "the situation of the time"[58] without explaining whether this referred to domestic or international conditions but reiterating the willingness to receive a special envoy. Zhou was specific about the emissary Beijing had in mind, naming me or Secretary of State William Rogers or "even the President of the U.S. himself."[59] As a condition of restoration of the relations, Zhou mentioned only the withdrawal of American armed forces from Taiwan and the Taiwan Strait—by far the least contentious issue—and omitted the reversion of Taiwan.

At that point, the secrecy with which the diplomacy had been conducted nearly derailed the enterprise and would have in any previous period of dealing with Beijing. Nixon had decided that the channel to Beijing should be confined to the White House. No other agency had been told of the two communications from Zhou Enlai in December and January. Thus in a public briefing on April 28, a State Department spokesman declared as the American position that sovereignty over Taiwan was "an unsettled question subject to future international resolution." And when the Secretary of State, attending a diplomatic meeting in London, appeared on television the next day, he commented on the Snow interview and dismissed the invitation to Nixon as "fairly casually made" and not "serious." He described Chinese foreign policy as "expansionist" and "rather paranoiac." Progress in negotiations—and a possible Nixon trip to China—would be possible only if China decided to join the international community in some unspecified way and complied "with the rules of international law."[60]

It was a measure of China's strategic imperatives that progress toward resumption of the dialogue continued. The reference to Taiwan as an unsettled question was denounced as "fraudulent" and a "brazen intervention in the affairs of the Chinese people" by the governmental spokesman. But the invective was coupled with a reaffirmation that the visit of the table tennis team was a new development in the friendship between the Chinese and American peoples.

On May 10, we accepted Zhou's invitation to Nixon but reiterated our insistence on a broad agenda. Our communication read: "At such a meeting each side would be free to raise the issue of principal concern to it."[61] To prepare for the summit, the President proposed that as his assistant for national security I should represent him at a preliminary secret meeting with Zhou. We indicated a specific date. The reason for the date was not high policy. During the late spring and early summer, the Cabinet and White House had planned a series of travels, and it was the first time a high-level plane became available.

On June 2, we received the Chinese reply. Zhou informed us that he had reported Nixon's acceptance of the Chinese invitation to Mao "with much pleasure"[62] and that he would welcome me to Beijing for preliminary conversations on the proposed date. We paid little attention to the fact that Lin Biao's name was dropped from this communication.

Within a year, Sino-American diplomacy had moved from irreconcilable conflict to a visit to Beijing by a presidential emissary to prepare a visit by the President himself. It did so by sidestepping the rhetoric of two decades and staying focused on the fundamental strategic objective of a geopolitical dialogue leading to a recasting of the Cold War international order. Had Nixon followed professional advice, he would have used the Chinese invitation to return to the traditional agenda and speed up its consideration as a condition for higher-level talks. Not only might this have been treated as a rejection, the whole process of intensified Sino-U.S. contact would almost certainly have been overwhelmed by domestic and international pressures in both countries. Nixon's contribution to the emerging Sino-American understanding was not so much that he understood its desirability but that he was able to give it a conceptual foundation to which Chinese thinking could relate. To Nixon, the opening to China was part of an overall strategic design, not a shopping list of mutual irritations.

Chinese leaders pursued a parallel approach. Invocations of returning to an existing international order were meaningless to them, if only because they did not consider the existing international system, which they had no hand in forming, as relevant to them. They had never conceived their security to reside in the legal arrangement of a community of sovereign states. Americans to this day often treat the opening to China as ushering in a static condition of friendship. But the Chinese leaders were brought up on the concept of *shi*—the art of understanding matters in flux.

When Zhou wrote about reestablishing friendship between the Chinese and American peoples, he described an attitude needed to foster a new international equilibrium, not a final state of the relationship between peoples. In Chinese writings, the hallowed words of the American vocabulary of a legal international order are rarely to be found. What was sought, rather, was a world in which China could find security and progress through a kind of combative coexistence, in which readiness to fight was given equal pride of place to the concept of coexistence. Into this world, the United States entered with its first diplomatic mission to Communist China.

CHAPTER 9

Resumption of Relations: First Encounters with Mao and Zhou

THE MOST DRAMATIC EVENT of the Nixon presidency occurred in near obscurity. For Nixon had decided that for the mission to Beijing to succeed, it would have to take place in secrecy. A public mission would have set off a complicated internal clearance project within the U.S. government and insistent demands for consultations from around the world, including Taiwan (still recognized as the government of China). This would have mortgaged our prospects with Beijing, whose attitudes we were being sent to discover. Transparency is an essential objective, but historic opportunities for building a more peaceful international order have imperatives as well.

So my team set off to Beijing via Saigon, Bangkok, New Delhi, and Rawalpindi on an announced fact-finding journey on behalf of the President. My party included a broader set of American officials, as well as a core group destined for Beijing—myself, aides Winston Lord, John Holdridge, and Dick Smyser, and Secret Service agents Jack Ready and Gary McLeod. The dramatic denouement required us to go through tiring stops at each city designed to be so boringly matter-of-fact that the media would stop tracking our movements. In Rawalpindi, we disappeared for forty-eight hours for an ostensible rest (I had feigned illness) in a Pakistani hill station in the foothills of the

Himalayas. In Washington, only the President and Colonel Alexander Haig (later General), my top aide, knew our actual destination.

When the American delegation arrived in Beijing on July 9, 1971, we had experienced the subtlety of Chinese communication but not the way Beijing conducted actual negotiations, still less the Chinese style of receiving visitors. American experience with Communist diplomacy was based on contacts with Soviet leaders, principally Andrei Gromyko, who had a tendency to turn diplomacy into a test of bureaucratic will; he was impeccably correct in negotiation but implacable on substance—sometimes, one sensed, straining his self-discipline.

Strain was nowhere apparent in the Chinese reception of the secret visit or during the dialogue that followed. In all the preliminary maneuvers, we had been sometimes puzzled by the erratic pauses between their messages, which we assumed had something to do with the Cultural Revolution. Nothing now seemed to disturb the serene aplomb of our hosts, who acted as if welcoming the special emissary of the American President for the first time in the history of the People's Republic of China was the most natural occurrence.

For in fact what we encountered was a diplomatic style closer to traditional Chinese diplomacy than to the pedantic formulations to which we had become accustomed during our negotiations with other Communist states. Chinese statesmen historically have excelled at using hospitality, ceremony, and carefully cultivated personal relationships as tools of statecraft. It was a diplomacy well suited to China's traditional security challenge—the preservation of a sedentary and agricultural civilization surrounded by peoples who, if they combined, wielded potentially superior military capacity. China survived, and generally prevailed, by mastering the art of fostering a calibrated combination of rewards and punishments and majestic cultural performance. In this context, hospitality becomes an aspect of strategy.

In our case, the ministrations began not when our delegation reached

Beijing but en route from Islamabad. To our surprise, a group of English-speaking Chinese diplomats had been sent to Pakistan to escort us on the journey and ease any tension we might have felt on a five-hour flight to an unfamiliar destination. They had boarded the plane before us, shocking our accompanying security people, who had been trained to treat Mao suits as enemy uniforms. On the journey, the team was also able to test some of their research, practice aspects of their conduct, and collect information about their visitors' personal characteristics for their Premier.

The team had been selected by Zhou two years earlier when the idea of opening with the United States first was mooted in the aftermath of the report of the four marshals. It included three members of the Foreign Ministry, one of whom, Tang Longbin, later was part of the protocol team for the Nixon visit; another was Zhang Wenjin, a former ambassador and specialist in what the Chinese termed "West European, American, and Oceania Affairs" and, as it turned out, an awesome linguist. Two younger members of the delegation, in effect, represented Mao and reported directly to him. They were Wang Hairong, his grand-niece, and Nancy Tang, an exceptionally capable Brooklyn-born interpreter, whose family had emigrated to China to join the revolution and who also acted as a kind of political advisor. All this we learned later, as well as the fact that, when first approached, the Foreign Ministry officials reacted like the marshals had. They needed Zhou's personal reassurance that the assignment represented a Mao directive rather than a test of their revolutionary loyalty.

Marshal Ye Jianying, the Vice Chairman of the Military Commission—one of the four marshals who had been seconded by Mao to analyze China's strategic options—welcomed us at the Beijing airport when we landed at noon, a symbol of the support of the People's Liberation Army for the new Sino-U.S. diplomacy. The marshal took me in a long Chinese-made limousine with drawn blinds to Diaoyutai, the State Guesthouse in a walled-off park in the western part of the city. The compound had formerly served as an imperial fishing lake. Ye suggested that the delegation take a rest until Premier Zhou would come to the guesthouse four hours later to welcome us and for a first round of discussions.

Zhou's coming to call on us was a gesture of considerable courtesy. The normal diplomatic procedure is for a visiting delegation to be received in a public building of the host country, especially when the difference in protocol rank of the head of the two delegations is so great. (In contrast to Zhou, the Premier, my protocol rank as National Security Advisor was equivalent to that of a deputy Cabinet secretary, three levels down.)

We soon discovered that our Chinese hosts had designed an almost improbably leisurely schedule—as if to signal that after surviving more than two decades of isolation, they were in no particular hurry to conclude a substantive agreement now. We were scheduled to be in Beijing for almost exactly forty-eight hours. We could not extend our stay because we were expected in Paris for talks on Vietnam; nor did we control the schedule of the presidential plane of Pakistan, which had taken us to Beijing.

When we saw our program, we realized that, in addition to this pause before Zhou's arrival, a four-hour visit to the Forbidden City had been planned. Thus eight hours of the available forty-eight hours had been provided for. As it turned out, Zhou would be unavailable for the next evening, which had been reserved for a visit by a North Korean Politburo member, which could not be rescheduled—or perhaps was not as a cover for the secret trip. If one allowed for sixteen hours for two nights' rest, there would be less than twenty-four hours left for the first dialogue between countries that had been at war, near war, and without significant diplomatic contact for twenty years.

In fact only two formal negotiating sessions were available: seven hours on the day of my arrival, from 4:30 P.M. to 11:20 P.M.; and six hours on the next, from noon until about 6:30 P.M. The first meeting was at the State Guesthouse—the United States acting as host by the conceit of Chinese protocol. The second was at the Great Hall of the People, where the Chinese government would receive us.

It could be argued that the apparent Chinese nonchalance was a form of psychological pressure. To be sure, had we left without progress, it would have been a major embarrassment to Nixon, who had not shared my mission with any other Cabinet member. But if the calculations of two years of China diplomacy were correct, the exigencies that had induced Mao to extend the invitation might turn unmanageable by a rebuff of an American mission to Beijing.

Confrontation made no sense for either side; that is why we were in Beijing. Nixon was eager to raise American sights beyond Vietnam. Mao's decision had been for a move that might force the Soviets to hesitate before taking on China militarily. Neither side could afford failure. Each side knew the stakes.

In a rare symbiosis of analyses, both sides decided to spend most of the time on trying to explore each other's perception of the international order. Since the ultimate purpose of the visit was to start the process of determining whether the previously antagonistic foreign policies of the two countries could be aligned, a conceptual discussion—at some points sounding more like a conversation between two professors of international relations than a working diplomatic dialogue—was, in fact, the ultimate form of practical diplomacy.

When the Premier arrived, our handshake was a symbolic gesture—at least until Nixon could arrive in China for a public repetition—since Secretary of State John Foster Dulles had refused to shake hands with Zhou at the Geneva Conference in 1954, a slight that rankled, despite the frequent Chinese protestations that it made no difference. We then repaired to a conference room in the guesthouse and faced each other across a green baize table. Here the American delegation had its first personal experience with the singular figure who had worked by Mao's side through nearly a half century of revolution, war, upheaval, and diplomatic maneuver.

Zhou Enlai

In some sixty years of public life, I have encountered no more compelling figure than Zhou Enlai. Short, elegant, with an expressive face framing luminous eyes, he dominated by exceptional intelligence and capacity to intuit the intangibles of the psychology of his opposite number. When I met him, he had been Premier for nearly twenty-two years and an associate of Mao for forty. He had made himself indispensable as the crucial mediator between Mao and the people who formed the raw material for the Chairman's vast agenda, translating Mao's sweeping visions into concrete programs. At the same time, he had earned the gratitude of many Chinese for moderating the excesses of these visions, at least wherever Mao's fervor gave scope for moderation.

The difference between the leaders was reflected in their personalities. Mao dominated any gathering; Zhou suffused it. Mao's passion strove to overwhelm opposition; Zhou's intellect would seek to persuade or outmaneuver it. Mao was sardonic; Zhou penetrating. Mao thought of himself as a philosopher; Zhou saw his role as an administrator or a negotiator. Mao was eager to accelerate history; Zhou was content to exploit its currents. A saying he often repeated was "The helmsman must ride with the waves." When they were together, there was no question of the hierarchy, not simply in the formal sense but in the deeper aspect of Zhou's extraordinarily deferential conduct.

Later on, Zhou was criticized for having concentrated on softening some of Mao's practices rather than resisting them. When the American delegation met Zhou, China had just undergone the Cultural Revolution, of which he was—as a cosmopolitan, foreign-educated advocate for pragmatic engagement with the West—an obvious target. Was he its enabler or a brake on it? Surely Zhou's methods of political survival involved lending his administrative skill to the execution of policies that he may well have found personally distasteful; perhaps because of this, however, he was spared the purges that were the fate of most of his contemporary leaders in the 1960s (until he eventually came under increasing attack and was in effect removed from office in late 1973).

The advisor to the prince occasionally faces the dilemma of balancing the benefits of the ability to alter events against the possibility of exclusion, should he bring his objections to any one policy to a head. How does the ability to modify the prince's prevailing conduct weigh against the moral onus of participation in his policies? How does one measure the element of nuance over time against the claims of absolutes in the immediate? What is the balance between the cumulative impact of moderating trends against that of a grand (and probably doomed) gesture?

Deng Xiaoping cut to the heart of these dilemmas in his subsequent assessment of Zhou's role in the Cultural Revolution, in which Deng and his family suffered considerably: "Without the premier the Cultural Revolution would have been much worse. And without the premier the Cultural Revolution wouldn't have dragged on for such a long time."[1] Publicly at least, Deng resolved these issues on behalf of Zhou. In an interview Deng gave to the Italian journalist Oriana Fallaci in 1980, after his return from exile, he stated:

> Premier Zhou was a man who worked hard and uncomplainingly all his life. He worked 12 hours a day, and sometimes 16 hours or more, throughout his life. We got to know each other quite early, that is, when we were in France on a work-study programme during the 1920s. I have always looked upon him as my elder brother. We took the revolutionary road at about the same time. He was much respected by his comrades and all the people. Fortunately he survived during the "Cultural

> Revolution" when we were knocked down. He was in an extremely difficult position then, and he said and did many things that he would have wished not to. But the people forgave him because, had he not done and said those things, he himself would not have been able to survive and play the neutralizing role he did, which reduced losses. He succeeded in protecting quite a number of people.[2]

Contrary views have had their hearing; not all analysts share Deng's ultimate appraisal of the exigencies of Zhou's political survival.[3]

In my dealings with him, Zhou's subtle and sensitive style helped overcome many pitfalls of an emerging relationship between two previously hostile major countries. The Sino-U.S. rapprochement started as a tactical aspect of the Cold War; it evolved to where it became central to the evolution of the new global order. Neither of us had any illusion of changing the basic convictions of the other. It was precisely the absence of any such illusion that facilitated our dialogue. But we articulated common purposes that survived both our periods in office— one of the highest rewards to which statesmen can lay claim.

All that was still in the distant future when Zhou and I sat down around the baize table to explore whether a beginning of reconciliation was truly possible at all. Zhou invited me, as the guest, to make the opening statement. I had decided not to detail the issues that had divided the two countries but rather to concentrate on the evolution of Sino-U.S. relations from a philosophical perspective. My opening remarks included the somewhat florid phrase "Many visitors have come to this beautiful and, to us, mysterious land . . ." At this point, Zhou interrupted: "You will find it not mysterious. When you have become familiar with it, it will not be so mysterious as before."[4]

Unraveling each other's mysteries was a good way of defining our challenge, but Zhou went further. In his first comments to an

American envoy in twenty years, he stated that restoring friendship was one of the principal goals of the emerging relationship—a point he had already made when he met with the American Ping-Pong team.

On my second visit three months later, Zhou greeted my delegation as if the friendship were already an established fact:

> So it's only the second meeting, and I am saying what I want to you. You and Mr. [Winston] Lord are familiar with this but not Miss [Diane] Matthews [my secretary] and our new friend [referring to Commander Jon Howe, my military assistant]. You probably thought the Chinese Communist Party has three heads and six arms. But, lo and behold, I am like you. Someone you can talk reason with and talk honestly.[5]

In February 1973, Mao made the same point: the United States and China had once been "two enemies," he offered in welcoming me to his study, but "[n]ow we call the relationship between ourselves a friendship."[6]

It was, however, a hardheaded, unsentimental perception of friendship. The Chinese Communist leadership retained some of the traditional approach to barbarian management. In it, the other side is flattered by being admitted to the Chinese "club" as an "old friend," a posture that makes disagreement more complicated and confrontations painful. When they conduct Middle Kingdom diplomacy, Chinese diplomats maneuver to induce their opposite numbers to propose the Chinese preference so that acquiescence can appear as the granting of a personal favor to the interlocutor.

At the same time, the emphasis on personal relationships goes beyond the tactical. Chinese diplomacy has learned from millennia of experience that, in international issues, each apparent solution is generally an admission ticket to a new set of related problems. Hence Chinese diplomats consider continuity of relationships an important task and perhaps more important than formal documents. By comparison, American diplomacy tends to segment issues into self-contained units to be dealt with on their own merits. In this task, American diplomats also prize good personal relations. The difference is that Chinese leaders relate the "friendship" less to personal qualities and more to long-term cultural, national, or historic ties; Americans stress the individual qualities of their counterparts. Chinese protestations of friendship seek durability for long-term relationships through the cultivation of intangibles; American equivalents attempt to facilitate ongoing activities by emphasis on social contact. And Chinese leaders will pay some (though not unlimited) price for the reputation of standing by their friends—for example, Mao's invitation to Nixon shortly after his resignation, when he was being widely ostracized. The same gesture was made to former Prime Minister Kakuei Tanaka of Japan, when he retired due to a scandal in 1974.

A good illustration of the Chinese emphasis on intangibles is an exchange I had with Zhou during my October 1971 visit. I presented the proposals of our advance team for the presidential visit with the reassurance that, since we had so many substantive issues to deal with, technical problems would not be permitted to stand in the way. Zhou replied by turning my operational point into a cultural paradigm: "Right. Mutual trust and mutual respect. These two points." I had emphasized functionality; Zhou stressed context.

One cultural trait regularly invoked by Chinese leaders was their historic perspective—the ability, indeed the necessity, to think of time in categories different from the West's. Whatever an individual Chinese leader achieves is brought about in a time frame that represents a smaller fraction of his society's total experience than any other leader in the world. The duration and scale of the Chinese past allow Chinese leaders to use the mantle of an almost limitless history to evoke a certain modesty in their opposite numbers (even if, in the retelling, what is presented as history is occasionally defined by a metaphorical interpretation). The foreign interlocutor can be made to feel that he is standing against the way of nature and that his actions are already destined to be written as a footnoted aberration in the grand sweep of Chinese history.

In those first exchanges with us on our arrival in Beijing, Zhou made a valiant effort to confer on America a history longer than China's as a kind of welcoming present. In the next sentence, however, he was back to the traditional perspective:

> We are two countries on two sides of the Pacific Ocean, yours with a history of 200 years, and ours with a history of only 22 years, dating from the founding of New China. Therefore, we are younger than you. As for our ancient culture, every country has it—the Indians in the U.S. and Mexico, the Inca Empire in South America, which was even more ancient than China. It's a pity that their scriptures were not preserved, but were lost. With respect to China's long history, there's one good point, the written language, which contains a heritage of 4,000 years based on historical relics. This is beneficial to the unification and development of our nation.[7]

Altogether, Zhou sought to outline a new approach to international relations, claiming a special moral quality that had evolved under Confucianism and was now ascribed to Communism:

> Chairman Mao on many occasions has said that we would absolutely not become a superpower. What we strive for is that all countries, big or small, be equal. It is not just a question of equality for two countries. Of course, it's a good thing for our two countries to negotiate on the basis of equality to exchange views, and to seek to find common points as well as putting on the table our differences. In order to really gain a relaxation

> in the international arena over a comparatively long period of time, one must deal with one another on the basis of equality. That is not easy to achieve.[8]

Machiavelli would have argued that it is in the interest of the country in need of reassurance yet unwilling to ask for it to strive for a general proposition that could then be applied to specific cases. This was one reason why Zhou insisted that, however strong it became, China would maintain a unique approach to international affairs that eschewed the traditional concept of power:

> We do not consider ourselves a power. Although we are developing our economy, in comparison to others we are comparatively backward. Of course, your President also mentioned that in the next five to ten years, China will speedily develop. We think it will not be so soon, although we will try to go all out, aim high, and develop our socialist construction in a better, faster, and more economical way.
>
> The second part of our answer is that when our economy is developed, we will still not consider ourselves a superpower and will not join in the ranks of the superpowers.[9]

The proposition that all that China sought was equality among nations would surely have marked a departure from an imperial history in which China is described as the Middle Kingdom. It was also a way of reassuring the United States that China was not a potential threat requiring countervailing force. The principle that Chinese international conduct was based on norms transcending the assertion of power went back to Confucius. As a basis for a new relationship, the test would be the compatibility of these norms with the pressures of a period of upheaval.

The underlying challenge of the secret visit was to establish enough confidence to turn a first meeting into a process. Almost invariably, high-level diplomatic exchanges begin by clearing away the underbrush of day-to-day issues. The unusual aspect of the secret visit was that, in the absence of any contact for twenty years, there were no day-to-day problems to clear away except two, which were recognized as insoluble in the short term: Taiwan and Vietnam. The problem was how to put them aside.

Both of these issues were anomalies. In 1971—it is hard to remember—the United States did not recognize Beijing as the capital of China. China and America had no diplomats in each other's capitals and had no direct way to communicate with each other. The U.S. ambassador to China was assigned to Taipei, and the Chinese ambassador to the United States represented Taiwan. No U.S. diplomats or officials were assigned to Beijing. (So-called liaison offices were not established until eighteen months later.)

The second anomaly was the Vietnam War. Part of my task was to achieve Chinese understanding for a war America was fighting on China's border against an ally of China. Both Zhou and I knew that my very presence in Beijing was a grievous blow to Hanoi, raising the implication of its isolation—though neither Zhou nor I ever discussed the issue in these terms.[10]

The Taiwan issue had become deeply embedded in the domestic attitudes of both countries, defined by two preconditions that had so far stymied diplomatic movement. Beijing's position had been that American acceptance of the "one China principle" was the precondition of any progress. The American precondition was that China commit itself to peaceful resolution of the issue before the United States would discuss it.

In the first exchange over the agenda, Zhou cut that Gordian knot. In the exchanges before the meeting, he had already accepted the principle that both sides would be free to raise any topic, but he had not yet abandoned the condition that the Taiwan issue needed to be discussed and presumably settled first. In the initial exchange, Zhou indicated that he was open to any sequence of discussion I might suggest—in other words, Taiwan no longer needed to be discussed, much less settled first. He also accepted linkage in reverse—that is, to make a settlement of issues relating to Taiwan dependent on the solution of other issues, for example, Indochina:

> KISSINGER: I wanted to ask the Prime Minister how he proposes to proceed. We can do it in one of two ways—each stating the problems which concern us, reserving its answers until later, or proceeding with the issues one at a time. Which do you prefer?
>
> ZHOU: What is your opinion?
>
> KISSINGER: I have no strong opinion. One possible way is that since Prime Minister Zhou has stated his views on Taiwan, we could state our views on Indochina. Then I could tell him of my reaction to his statement on Taiwan, and he could tell me of his reaction to mine on Indochina. Or we could take each issue one at a time.
>
> ZHOU: Either way, it's your decision. You can say whatever you like. You could speak first on the Taiwan question or Indochina, or together, because you may think they are linked.
>
> KISSINGER: I believe they are linked to some extent.[11]

In the event, we made the withdrawal of our military forces from Taiwan conditional on the settlement of the Indochina war.

Zhou's substantive position on Taiwan, which he articulated during the long opening discussion on the first day, was familiar; we had heard it at 136 Warsaw meetings. The United States needed to "recognize the PRC as the sole legitimate government of China and not make any exceptions" and accept that Taiwan was "an inalienable part of China."[12]

"The natural logic of the matter" dictated that the United States must "withdraw all its armed forces and dismantle all its military installations on Taiwan and in the Taiwan Straits within a limited time period."[13] As these processes unfolded, eventually the U.S.–Republic of China defense treaty—whose legality Beijing did not recognize—"would not exist."[14]

At the time of the secret trip to China, there was no difference between Beijing and Taipei as to the nature of the Chinese state. Both Chinese sides subscribed to the one China principle; the Taiwanese authorities forbade agitation for independence. Therefore for the United States, the issue was not agreeing to the one China principle so much as putting the recognition of Beijing as the capital of a united China into a time frame compatible with American domestic necessities. The secret trip began the delicate process by which the United States has step by step accepted a one China concept, and China has been extremely flexible about the timing of its implementation. Successive American Presidents of both parties have skillfully pursued a balancing act. They have progressively deepened relations with Beijing while creating conditions in which Taiwan's economy and democracy have flourished. Successive Chinese leaders, while vigorously insisting on their perception of one China, have not pushed it to a showdown.

Zhou followed the same pattern on Vietnam that I had on Taiwan in the sense of avoiding any immediate commitment but also any sense of urgency. Zhou listened to my presentation and asked penetrating questions; yet he stopped far short of even moral pressure, much less threats. Whatever support China gave Vietnam had a historical, not an ideological or strategic, origin, he explained. "The debt we owe them was incurred by our ancestors. We have since liberation no responsibility because we overthrew the old system. Yet we still feel a deep and full sympathy for them."[15] Sympathy, of course, was not the same as political or military support; it was a delicate way to convey that China would not become involved militarily or press us diplomatically.

At lunch on the second day, at the Great Hall of the People, Zhou suddenly raised the issue of the Cultural Revolution. We had undoubtedly observed it from outside, he said, but he wanted his guests to understand the road that had led China—however circuitously—to where Chinese and American leaders could now meet.

Mao had sought to purify the Communist Party and break through the bureaucratic structures, Zhou explained. To this end, he had created the Red Guards as an institution outside the Party and the government, whose task was to return the system to the true ideology and ideological purity. The decision turned out to produce turmoil, as various Red Guard units pursued increasingly autonomous and incompatible policies. Indeed a point was reached, according to Zhou's account, where various organizations or even regions created their own Red Guard units to protect themselves in the spreading chaos. The spectacle of these splinter Red Guard units fighting each other was truly shocking for a people brought up on the universal truth of Communist beliefs and faith in China's unity. At that point, Chairman Mao had asked the PLA to restore order after the country on the whole had made progress in defeating bureaucracy and clarifying its convictions.

Zhou was in a delicate position in presenting this account, which he must have been instructed to do by Mao. He clearly sought to distinguish himself from the Cultural Revolution and yet remain loyal to Mao, who would read the transcript. At the time I tried to sum up Zhou's main point to myself as indicating a measure of disassociation from Mao by means of an expression of qualified support as follows: There was much chaos during the Cultural Revolution. At one point, the Red Guards locked Zhou up in his own office. On the other hand, Zhou had not been as farsighted as Chairman Mao, who saw the need to inject new vigor into the revolution.[16]

Why present such a narrative to an American delegation on the first visit from the United States in two decades? Because the objective was to go beyond normalization to what our interlocutors called friendship, but which would be more accurately described as strategic cooperation. For that, it was important to define China as a country that had overcome its turmoil and was therefore reliable. Having navigated the Cultural Revolution, Zhou implied, it was able to face any foreign foe as a united country and was therefore a potential partner against the Soviet threat. Zhou made the theme explicit in the formal session that immediately followed. It was held in the Fujian Hall of the Great Hall of the People, where each hall is named after a Chinese province. Fujian is the province to which, in both Beijing's and Taipei's administrative divisions, Taiwan and the so-called offshore islands belonged.[17] Zhou did not make a point of the symbolism, and the Americans ignored it.

Zhou began by outlining China's defiance, even should all conceivable enemies unite against it:

> You like to talk about philosophy. The worst would be that China would be carved up once again. You could unite, with the USSR occupying all areas north of the Yellow River, and you occupying all the areas south of the Yangtze River, and the eastern section between these two rivers could be left to Japan. . . .
>
> If such a large maneuver should occur, what would the Chinese Communist Party and Chairman Mao be prepared to do? We would be prepared to resist for a protracted period by people's warfare, engaging in a long-term struggle until final victory. This would take time and, of course, we would have to sacrifice lives, but this is something which we would have to contemplate.[18]

According to recent Chinese historical accounts, Zhou had been specifically instructed by Mao to "brag" that "although all under the heaven[s] is in great chaos, the situation is wonderful."[19] Mao was worried about Soviet aggression, but he did not want to express concern, even less appear to ask for help. The narrative of turmoil under the heavens was his way of eliciting American attitudes without the implication of concern involved in asking for them: to sketch both the maximum conceivable threat and China's fortitude in resisting even it. No American intelligence estimate had ever conceived so cataclysmic a contingency; no American policymaker had considered so global a confrontation. Yet its sweep did not specify the specific dominant concern—which was a Soviet attack—and thus China avoided appearing as a supplicant.

Despite its apparent explicitness, Zhou's presentation was a subtle approach to a discussion of strategic cooperation. In the Atlantic region we were allied with friendly countries under a looming threat. They would seek reassurance by transforming oral pledges into a legal obligation. The Chinese leaders took the opposite course. How China was prepared to stand alone, even in the face of a nuclear threat, and fight a protracted guerrilla war on its own against a coalition of all major powers became a standard Chinese narrative over the next decade. Its underlying purpose was to turn self-reliance into a weapon and into a method of mutual assistance based on parallel perceptions. Reciprocal obligations between China and the United States would not be established in a legal document but in a shared perception of a common threat. Though China made no claim for outside assistance, it would spontaneously arise from shared perceptions; it would be dispensed with if the other party did not share—or no longer shared—the Chinese view of the challenge.

At the very end of the second day's session and with the evening blocked for Zhou by the visit of the North Korean dignitary—with about eighteen hours before our unbreakable departure deadline—Zhou raised the issue of a visit by President Nixon. Both Zhou and I had made glancing references to it but had avoided being specific because neither of us wanted to deal with a rebuff or to appear as a supplicant. Zhou finally adopted the elegant solution of moving into the topic as a procedural issue:

> ZHOU: What is your thinking on an announcement of the visit?
>
> KISSINGER: What visit?
>
> ZHOU: Would it cover only your visit or also President Nixon's visit?
>
> KISSINGER: We could announce my visit and say that Chairman Mao has extended an invitation to President Nixon and he has accepted, either in principle or at a fixed time, next spring. What is your pleasure? I think there are advantages in doing both together.
>
> ZHOU: Then would it be possible for the two sides to designate some of our men to draft an announcement?
>
> KISSINGER: We should draft in the context we have been discussing.
>
> ZHOU: Both visits.
>
> KISSINGER: That would be all right.
>
> ZHOU: We shall try it. . . . I have an appointment at six o'clock that will last until ten o'clock. My office is free to you. Or you can go to your residence for discussions. You can have supper and rest and a film.
>
> KISSINGER: We will meet at 10:00.
>
> ZHOU: Yes, I will come to your residence. We will work deep into the night.[20]

As it happened, the communiqué could not be finished that night because of a deadlock over who would be said to have invited whom. Each side wanted the other to look more eager. We split the difference. The draft needed the Chairman's approval, and Mao had gone to bed. Mao finally approved a formulation in which Zhou, "[k]nowing of President Nixon's expressed desire to visit the People's Republic of China," was said to have "extended an invitation," which Nixon had then accepted "with pleasure."

We finished drafting the terms of a statement for the visit of President Nixon just before the deadline for our departure on the afternoon of Sunday, July 11. "Our announcement will shake the world," said Zhou, and the delegation flew back, concealing its excitement for the hours before the world could be shaken. I briefed Nixon at his San Clemente "Western White House." Then, simultaneously on July 15, from Los Angeles and Beijing, the secret trip and the invitation were both made public.

Nixon in China: The Meeting with Mao

Seven months after the secret visit, on February 21, 1972, President Nixon arrived in Beijing on a raw winter day. It was a triumphant moment for the President, the inveterate anti-Communist who had seen a geopolitical opportunity and seized it boldly. As a symbol of the fortitude with which he had navigated to this day and of the new era he was inaugurating, he wanted to descend alone from Air Force One to meet Zhou Enlai, who was standing on the windy tarmac in his immaculate Mao jacket as a Chinese military band played "The Star-Spangled Banner." The symbolic handshake that erased Dulles's snub duly took place. But for a historic occasion, it was strangely muted. When Nixon's motorcade drove into Beijing, the streets had been cleared of onlookers. And his arrival was played as the last item on the evening news.[21]

As revolutionary as the opening itself had been, the final communiqué had not yet been fully agreed—especially in the key paragraph on Taiwan. A celebration would have been premature and perhaps weakened the Chinese negotiating position of studied equanimity. Too, the Chinese leaders knew that their Vietnamese allies were furious that China had given Nixon an opportunity to rally the American public.

A public demonstration for their enemy in the capital of their ally would have proved too great a strain on the ever-tenuous Sino-Vietnamese relationship.

Our hosts made up for the missing demonstrations by inviting Nixon to a meeting with Mao within hours of our arrival. "Inviting" is not the precise word for how meetings with Mao occurred. Appointments were never scheduled; they came about as if events of nature. They were echoes of emperors granting audiences. The first indication of Mao's invitation to Nixon occurred when, shortly after our arrival, I received word that Zhou needed to see me in a reception room. He informed me that "Chairman Mao would like to see the President." To avoid the impression that Nixon was being summoned, I raised some technical issues about the order of events at the evening banquet. Uncharacteristically impatient, Zhou responded: "Since the Chairman is inviting him, he wants to see him fairly soon." In welcoming Nixon at the very outset of his visit, Mao was signaling his authoritative endorsement to domestic and international audiences before talks had even begun. Accompanied by Zhou, we set off for Mao's residence in Chinese cars. No American security personnel were permitted, and the press could be notified only afterward.

Mao's residence was approached through a wide gate on the east–west axis carved from where the ancient city walls stood before the Communist revolution. Inside the Imperial City, the road hugged a lake, on the other side of which stood a series of residences for high officials. All had been built in the days of Sino-Soviet friendship and reflected the heavy Stalinist style of the period similar to the State Guesthouses.

Mao's residence appeared no different, though it stood slightly apart from the others. There were no visible guards or other appurtenances of power. A small anteroom was almost completely dominated by a Ping-Pong table. It did not matter because we were taken directly to Mao's study, a room of modest size with bookshelves lining three walls filled with manuscripts in a state of considerable disarray. Books covered the tables and were piled up on the floor. A simple wooden bed stood in a corner. The all-powerful ruler of the world's most populous nation wished to be perceived as a philosopher-king who had no need to buttress his authority with traditional symbols of majesty.

Mao rose from an armchair in the middle of a semicircle of armchairs with an attendant close by to steady him if necessary. We learned later that he had suffered a debilitating series of heart and lung ailments in the weeks before and that he had difficulty moving. Overcoming his handicaps, Mao exuded an extraordinary willpower and determination. He took Nixon's hands in both of his and showered his most benevolent smile on him. The picture appeared in all Chinese newspapers. The Chinese were skillful in using Mao photographs to convey a mood and a direction of policy. When Mao scowled, storms were approaching. When he was photographed wagging a finger at a visitor, it indicated reservations of a somewhat put-upon teacher.

The meeting provided us our first introduction to Mao's bantering and elliptical style of conversation. Most political leaders present their thoughts in the form of bullet points. Mao advanced his ideas in a Socratic manner. He would begin with a question or an observation and invite comment. He would then follow with another observation. Out of this web of sarcastic remarks, observations, and queries would emerge a direction, though rarely a binding commitment.

From the outset, Mao abjured any intention to conduct either a philosophical or strategic dialogue with Nixon. Nixon had mentioned to the Chinese Vice Foreign Minister, Qiao Guanhua, who had been sent to escort the presidential party from Shanghai to Beijing (Air Force One had stopped in Shanghai to take a Chinese navigator aboard), that he was looking forward to discussing philosophy with the Chairman. Mao would have none of it. Asserting that I was the only doctor of philosophy available, he added: "What about asking him to be the main speaker today?" As if by habit, Mao was playing at the "contradictions" between his guests: this sarcastic evasion could have served the purpose of creating a potential for a rift between the President and the National Security Advisor—presidents being generally unappreciative of being upstaged by their security advisor.

Nor was Mao willing to take a Nixon hint to discuss challenges posed by a number of countries he enumerated. Nixon framed the main issues as follows:

> We, for example, must ask ourselves—again in the confines of this room—why the Soviets have more forces on the border facing you than on the border facing Western Europe. We must ask ourselves, what is the future of Japan? Is it better—here I know we have disagreements—is it better for Japan to be neutral, totally defenseless, or is it better for a time for Japan to have some relations with the United States? . . . The question is which danger the People's Republic faces, whether it is the danger of American aggression or Soviet aggression.[22]

Mao refused the bait: "All those troublesome questions I don't want to get into very much." He suggested they be discussed with the Premier.

What, then, did Mao wish to convey through his apparently meandering dialogue? The perhaps most important messages were things that did not happen. First, after decades of mutual recrimination over Taiwan, the subject in effect did not come up. The sum total of discussions devoted to it was as follows:

> MAO: Our common old friend, Generalissimo Chiang Kai-shek, doesn't approve of this. He calls us Communist bandits. He recently issued a speech. Have you seen it?
>
> NIXON: Chiang Kai-shek calls the Chairman a bandit. What does the Chairman call Chiang Kai-shek?

> ZHOU: Generally speaking we call them Chiang Kai-shek's clique. In the newspapers sometimes we call him a bandit; we are also called bandits in turn. Anyway, we abuse each other.
>
> MAO: Actually, the history of our friendship with him is much longer than the history of your friendship with him.[23]

No threats, no demands, no deadlines, no references to past deadlock. After a war, two military confrontations, and 136 deadlocked ambassadorial meetings, the Taiwan issue had lost its urgency. It was being put aside, at least for the time being, as first suggested by Zhou at the secret meeting.

Second, Mao wanted to convey that Nixon was a welcome visitor. The photograph had taken care of that. Third, Mao was eager to remove any threat from China to the United States:

> At the present time, the question of aggression from the United States or aggression from China is relatively small; that is, it could be said that this is not a major issue, because the present situation is one in which a state of war does not exist between our two countries. You want to withdraw some of your troops back on your soil; ours do not go abroad.[24]

This cryptic sentence that Chinese troops stayed at home removed the concern that Vietnam might end like Korea with massive Chinese intervention.

Fourth, Mao wanted to convey that he had encountered a challenge in pursuing the opening to America but that he had overcome it. He offered a sardonic epitaph to Lin Biao, who had fled the capital in September 1971 in a military airplane that crashed in Mongolia, in what was reportedly an abortive coup:

> In our country also there is a reactionary group which is opposed to our contact with you. The result was that they got on an airplane and fled abroad. . . . As for the Soviet Union, they finally went to dig out the corpses, but they didn't say anything about it.[25]

Fifth, Mao favored accelerated bilateral cooperation and urged technical talks on the subject:

> Our side also is bureaucratic in dealing with matters. For example, you wanted some exchange of persons on a personal level, things like that; also trade. But rather than deciding that we stuck with our stand that without settling major issues there is nothing to do with smaller issues. I myself persisted in that position. Later on I saw you were right, and we played table tennis.[26]

Sixth, he stressed his personal goodwill to Nixon, both personally and because he said he preferred dealing with right-wing governments on the grounds that they were more reliable. Mao, the author of the Great Leap Forward and the Anti-Rightist Campaign, made the astonishing remark that he had "voted for" Nixon, and that he was "comparatively happy when these people on the right come into power" (in the West at least):

> NIXON: When the Chairman says he voted for me, he voted for the lesser of two evils.
>
> MAO: I like rightists. People say you are rightists, that the Republican Party is to the right, that Prime Minister Heath[27] is also to the right.
>
> NIXON: And General De Gaulle.[28]
>
> MAO: De Gaulle is a different question. They also say the

> Christian Democratic Party of West Germany is also to the right. I am comparatively happy when these people on the right come into power.[29]

Nevertheless, he warned that if the Democrats gained power in Washington, China would establish contacts with them, too.

At the beginning of the Nixon visit, Mao was prepared to commit himself to the direction it implied though not yet to the details of the specific negotiations about to begin. It was not clear whether a formula on Taiwan could be found (all other issues having been essentially settled). But he was ready to endorse a substantial agenda of cooperation in the fifteen hours of dialogue that had been scheduled between Nixon and Zhou. The basic direction having been set, Mao counseled patience and hedged should we fail to come up with an agreed communiqué. Rather than treat that setback as a failure, Mao argued it should spur renewed efforts. The impending strategic design overrode all other concerns—even deadlock over Taiwan. Mao advised both sides not to stake too much on one set of negotiations:

> It is alright to talk well and also alright if there are no agreements, because what use is there if we stand in deadlock? Why is it that we must be able to reach results? People will say . . . if we fail the first time, then people will talk why are we not able to succeed the first time? The only reason would be that we have taken the wrong road. What will they say if we succeed the second time?[30]

In other words, even if for some unforeseen reason the talks about to begin were to deadlock, China would persevere to achieve the desired result of a strategic cooperation with America in the future.

As the meeting was breaking up, Mao, the prophet of continuous revolution, emphasized to the President of the heretofore vilified capitalist-imperialist society that ideology was no longer relevant to relations between the two countries:

> MAO: [*pointing to Dr. Kissinger*] "Seize the hour and seize the day." I think that, generally speaking, people like me sound a lot of big cannons. [*Zhou laughs.*] That is, things like "the whole world should unite and defeat imperialism, revisionism, and all reactionaries, and establish socialism."[31]

Mao laughed uproariously at the implication that anyone might have taken seriously a slogan that had been scrawled for decades on public surfaces all over China. He ended the conversation with a comment characteristically sardonic, mocking, and reassuring:

> But perhaps you as an individual may not be among those to be overthrown. They say that he [Dr. Kissinger] is also among those not to be overthrown personally. And if all of you are overthrown we wouldn't have any more friends left.[32]

With our long-term personal safety thus assured and the nonideological basis of their relationship certified by the highest authority on that subject, the two sides commenced five days of dialogue and banquets interspersed with sightseeing trips.

The Nixon-Zhou Dialogue

The substantive issues had been divided into three categories, the first being the long-term objectives of the two sides and their cooperation against hegemonic powers—a shorthand for the Soviet Union without the invidiousness of naming it. This would be conducted by

Zhou and Nixon and restricted staffs, which included me. We met for at least three hours every afternoon.

Second, a forum for discussing economic cooperation and scientific and technical exchanges was headed by the foreign ministers of the two sides. Lastly, there was a drafting group for the final communiqué headed by Vice Foreign Minister Qiao Guanhua and myself. The drafting meetings took place late at night after the banquets.

The meetings between Nixon and Zhou were unique in encounters between heads of government (Nixon, of course, was also head of state) in that they did not deal with *any* contemporary issues; these were left to the communiqué drafters and the foreign ministers' panel. Nixon concentrated on placing a conceptual roadmap of American policy before his counterpart. Given the starting point of the two sides, it was important that our Chinese interlocutors would hear an authoritative and reliable guide to American purposes.

Nixon was extraordinarily well equipped for this role. As a negotiator, his reluctance to engage in face-to-face confrontations—and indeed his evasion of them—tended to produce vagueness and ambiguity. But he was a great briefer. Among the ten American Presidents I have known, he had a unique grasp of long-term international trends. He used the fifteen hours of meetings with Zhou to put before him a vision of U.S.-China relations and their impact on world affairs.

While I was en route to China, Nixon had outlined his perspective to the U.S. ambassador in Taipei, who would have the painful task of explaining to his hosts that America in the years ahead would be shifting the emphasis of its China policy to Beijing from Taipei:

> We must have in mind, and they [Taipei] must be prepared for the fact, that there will continue to be a step-by-step, a more normal relationship with the other—the Chinese mainland. Because our interests require it. Not because we love them, but

> because they're there. . . . And because the world situation has so drastically changed.[33]

Nixon forecast that despite China's turmoil and privation, its people's outstanding abilities would eventually propel China to the first rank of world powers:

> Well, you can just stop and think of what could happen if anybody with a decent system of government got control of that mainland. Good God. . . . There'd be no power in the world that could even—I mean, you put 800 million Chinese to work under a decent system . . . and they will be the leaders of the world.[34]

Now in Beijing, Nixon was in his element. Whatever his long-established negative views on Communism as a system of governance, he had not come to China to convert its leaders to American principles of democracy or free enterprise—judging it to be useless. What Nixon sought throughout the Cold War was a stable international order for a world filled with nuclear weapons. Thus in his first meeting with Zhou, Nixon paid tribute to the sincerity of the revolutionaries whose success he had earlier decried as a signal failure of American policy: "We know you believe deeply in your principles, and we believe deeply in our principles. We do not ask you to compromise your principles, just as you would not ask us to compromise ours."[35]

Nixon acknowledged that his principles had earlier led him—like many of his countrymen—to advocate policies in opposition to Chinese aims. But the world had changed, and now the American interest required that Washington adapt to these changes:

> [M]y views, because I was in the Eisenhower Administration, were similar to those of Mr. Dulles at that time. But the world

> has changed since then, and the relationship between the People's Republic and the United States must change too. As the Prime Minister has said in a meeting with Dr. Kissinger, the helmsman must ride with the waves or he will be submerged with the tide.[36]

Nixon proposed to base foreign policy on the reconciliation of interests. Provided the national interest was clearly perceived and that it took into account the mutual interest in stability, or at least in avoiding catastrophe, this would introduce predictability into Sino-U.S. relations:

> [S]peaking here, the Prime Minister knows and I know that friendship—which I feel we do have on a personal basis—cannot be the basis on which an established relationship must rest, not friendship alone. . . . As friends, we could agree to some fine language, but unless our national interests would be served by carrying out agreements set forward in that language, it would mean very little.[37]

For such an approach, candor was the precondition of genuine cooperation. As Nixon told Zhou: "It is important that we develop complete candor and recognize that neither of us would do anything unless we considered it was in our interests."[38] Nixon's critics often decried these and similar statements as a version of selfishness. Yet Chinese leaders reverted to them frequently as guarantors of American reliability—because they were precise, calculable, and reciprocal.

On this basis, Nixon put forward a rationale for an enduring American role in Asia, even after the withdrawal of the bulk of U.S. forces from Vietnam. What was unusual about it was that he presented it as being in the *mutual* interest. For decades, Chinese propaganda had assailed the American presence in the region as a form of colonialist oppression and called upon "the people" to rise up against it. But Nixon in Beijing insisted that geopolitical imperatives transcended ideology—his very presence in Beijing testified to that. With one million Soviet troops on China's northern border, Beijing would no longer be able to base its foreign policy on slogans about the need to strike down "American imperialism." He had stressed America's essential world role to me before the trip:

> We cannot be too apologetic about America's world role. We cannot, either in the past, or in the present, or in the future. We cannot be too forthcoming in terms of what America will do. Well, in other words, beat our breasts, wear a hair shirt, and well, we'll withdraw, and we'll do this, and that, and the other thing. Because I think we have to say that, well, "Who does America threaten? Who would you rather have playing this role?"[39]

The invocation of the national interest in the absolute form as put forward by Nixon is difficult to apply as the sole organizing concept of international order. Conditions by which to define the national interest vary too widely, and the possible fluctuations in interpretation are too great, to provide a reliable single guide to conduct. Some congruence on values is generally needed to supply an element of restraint.

When China and the United States first began to deal with each other after a hiatus of two decades, the values of the two sides were different, if not opposed. A consensus on national interest with all its difficulties was the most meaningful element of moderation available. Ideology would drive the two sides toward confrontation, tempting tests of strength around a vast periphery.

Was pragmatism enough? It can sharpen clashes of interests as easily as resolve them. Every side will know its objectives better than the other side's. Depending on the solidity of its domestic position, concessions that are necessary from the pragmatic point of view can be used by domestic opponents as a demonstration of weakness. There is therefore a constant temptation to raise the stakes. In the first dealings with China, the issue was how congruent the definitions of interests were or could be made to be. The Nixon-Zhou conversations provided the framework of congruence, and the bridge to it was the Shanghai Communiqué and its much debated paragraph about the future of Taiwan.

The Shanghai Communiqué

Normally, communiqués have a short shelf life. They define a mood rather than a direction. This was not the case with the communiqué that summed up Nixon's visit to Beijing.

Leaders like to create the impression that communiqués emerge full-blown from their minds and conversations with their counterparts. The popular idea that the leaders write and agree on every comma is not one they discourage. Experienced and wise leaders know better. Nixon and Zhou understood the danger of obliging leaders into drafting sessions on the short deadlines inherent in a summit. Usually men of strong will—why else would they find themselves where they are—may not be able to resolve deadlocks when time is short and the media insistent. As a result, diplomats frequently arrive at major meetings with communiqués already largely drafted.

I had been sent to Beijing by Nixon in October 1971—on a second visit—for that purpose. In subsequent exchanges, it was decided that the code name for this trip would be Polo II, our imaginations having been exhausted by naming the first secret trip Polo I. The chief purpose of Polo II was to agree on a communiqué that the Chinese leadership and the President could endorse at the conclusion of Nixon's trip four months later.

We arrived in Beijing during a time of upheaval in the Chinese governmental structure. A few weeks earlier, Mao's appointed successor, Lin Biao, had been accused of a plot whose full dimensions have never been officially revealed. Different explanations exist. The prevalent view at the time was that Lin Biao, the compiler of the "Little Red Book" of Mao's sayings, seemed to have concluded that China's security would be better assured by returning to the principles of the Cultural Revolution than by maneuvering with America. It has also been suggested that, by this point, Lin actually opposed Mao from something closer to the pragmatist position of Zhou and Deng, and that his outward ideological zealotry was a defensive tactic.[40]

Vestiges of the crisis were still all around us when my associates and I arrived on October 20. On the way from the airport, we passed posters that proclaimed the familiar slogan "Down with American Imperial Capitalism and its Running Dogs." Some of the posters were in English. Leaflets with similar themes had been left in our rooms at the State Guesthouse. I asked my staff assistant to collect and return them to the Chinese protocol officer, saying that they had been left behind by a previous occupant.

The next day, the acting Foreign Minister escorting me to a meeting with Zhou at the Great Hall of the People took note of the potential embarrassment. He called my attention to a wall poster that had replaced an offending one, which said in English: "Welcome to the Afro-Asian Ping Pong Tournament." All other posters we passed had been painted over. Zhou mentioned as if in passing that we should observe China's actions, not its "empty cannons" of rhetoric—a forerunner of what Mao would say to Nixon a few months later.

The discussion on the communiqué began conventionally enough. I tabled a draft communiqué that my staff and I had prepared and Nixon had approved. In it, both sides affirmed their devotion to peace and pledged cooperation on outstanding issues. The section on Taiwan was left blank. Zhou accepted the draft as a basis for discussion and promised to present Chinese modifications and alternatives the next morning. All this was conventional communiqué drafting.

What happened next was not. Mao intervened by telling Zhou to stop the drafting of what he called a "bullshit communiqué." He might call his exhortations of Communist orthodoxy "empty cannons"; he was not prepared to abandon them as guidelines for Communist cadres. He instructed Zhou to produce a communiqué that would restate Communist orthodoxies as the Chinese position. Americans could state their view as they chose. Mao had based his life on the proposition that peace could emerge only out of struggle, not as an end in itself. China was not afraid to avow its differences with America. Zhou's draft (and mine) was the sort of banality the Soviets would sign but neither mean nor implement.[41]

Zhou's presentation followed his instructions from Mao. He put forward a draft communiqué that stated the Chinese position in uncompromising language. It left blank pages for our position, which was expected to be comparably strong to the contrary. There was a final section for common positions.

At first, I was taken aback. But as I reflected, the unorthodox format appeared to solve both sides' problem. Each could reaffirm its fundamental convictions, which would reassure domestic audiences and uneasy allies. The differences had been known for two decades. The contrast would highlight the agreements being reached, and the positive conclusions would be far more credible. Without the ability to communicate with Washington in the absence of diplomatic representation or adequate secure communication, I was confident enough of Nixon's thinking to proceed.

In this manner, a communiqué issued on Chinese soil and published by Chinese media enabled America to affirm its commitment to "individual freedom and social progress for all the peoples of the world"; proclaim its close ties with allies in South Korea and Japan; and articulate a view of an international order that rejected infallibility for any country and permitted each nation to develop free of foreign interference.[42] The Chinese draft of the communiqué was, of course, equally expressive of contrary views. These could not have come as a surprise to the Chinese population; they heard and saw them all day in their media. But by signing a document containing both perspectives, each side was effectively calling an ideological truce and underscoring where our views converged.

By far the most significant of these convergences was the article on hegemony. It read:

> —Neither [side] should seek hegemony in the Asia-Pacific region and each is opposed to efforts by any other country or group of countries to establish such hegemony.[43]

Alliances have been founded on far less. For all its pedantic phraseology, it was a stunning conclusion. The enemies of a little more than six months earlier were announcing their joint opposition to any further expansion of the Soviet sphere. It was a veritable diplomatic revolution, for the next step would inevitably be to discuss a strategy to counter Soviet ambitions.

The sustainability of the strategy depended on whether progress could be made on Taiwan. By the time Taiwan was discussed during the Nixon trip, the parties had already explored the subject, starting with the secret visit seven months earlier.

Negotiations had now reached the point where the diplomat has a choice to make. One tactic—and indeed the traditional approach—is to outline one's maximum position and gradually retreat to a more attainable stance. Such a tactic is much beloved by negotiators eager to protect their domestic standing. Yet while it appears "tough" to start with an extreme set of demands, the process amounts to a progressive weakening ushered in by the abandonment of the opening move. The other party is tempted to dig in at each stage to see what the next modification will bring and to turn the negotiating process into a test of endurance.

Rather than exalting process over substance, the preferable course is to make opening proposals close to what one judges to be the most sustainable outcome, a definition of "sustainable" in the abstract being one that both sides have an interest in maintaining. This was a particular challenge with respect to Taiwan, where the margin for concession for both sides was narrow. We therefore from the beginning put forward views on Taiwan we judged necessary for a constructive evolution. Nixon advanced these on February 22 as five principles distilled from previous exchanges during my July and October meetings. They were comprehensive and at the same time also the limit of American concessions. The future would have to be navigated within their framework. They were: an affirmation of a one China policy; that the United States would not support internal Taiwan independence movements; that the United States would discourage any Japanese move into Taiwan (a matter, given history, of special concern to China); support for any peaceful resolution between Beijing and Taipei; and commitment to continued normalization.[44] On February 24, Nixon explained how the Taiwan issue might evolve domestically as the United States pursued these principles. His intention, he affirmed, was to complete the normalization process in his second term and withdraw American troops from Taiwan in that time frame—though he warned that he was in no position to make any formal commitments. Zhou responded that both sides had "difficulties" and that there was "no time limit."

Principle and pragmatism thus existing in ambiguous equilibrium, Qiao Guanhua and I drafted the last remaining section of the Shanghai Communiqué. The key passage was only one paragraph, but it took two nearly all-night sessions to produce. It read:

> The U.S. side declared: The United States acknowledges that all Chinese on either side of the Taiwan Strait maintain there is but one China and that Taiwan is a part of China. The United States Government does not challenge that position. It reaffirms its interest in a peaceful settlement of the Taiwan

> question by the Chinese themselves. With this prospect in mind, it affirms the ultimate objective of the withdrawal of all U.S. forces and military installations from Taiwan. In the meantime, it will progressively reduce its forces and military installations on Taiwan as the tension in the area diminishes.[45]

This paragraph folded decades of civil war and animosity into an affirmative general principle to which Beijing, Taipei, and Washington could all subscribe. The United States dealt with the one China policy by acknowledging the convictions of Chinese on either side of the Chinese dividing line. The flexibility of this formulation permitted the United States to move from "acknowledge" to "support" in its own position in the decades since. Taiwan has been given an opportunity to develop economically and internally. China achieved recognition of its "core interest" in a political connection between Taiwan and the mainland. The United States affirmed its interest in a peaceful resolution.

Despite occasional tensions, the Shanghai Communiqué has served its purpose. In the forty years since it was signed, neither China nor the United States has allowed the issue to interrupt the momentum of their relationship. It has been a delicate and occasionally tense process. Throughout, the United States has affirmed its view of the importance of a peaceful settlement and China its conviction of the imperative of ultimate unification. Each side has acted with restraint and sought to avoid obliging the other side to a test of wills or strength. China has invoked core principles but has been flexible as to the timing of their implementation. The United States has been pragmatic, moving from case to case, sometimes heavily influenced by domestic American pressures. On the whole, Beijing and Washington have given priority to the overriding importance of the Chinese-American relationship.

Still, one must not confuse a modus vivendi with a permanent state of affairs. No Chinese leader has ever abandoned the insistence on ultimate unification or can be expected to do so. No foreseeable American leader will jettison the American conviction that this process should be peaceful or alter the American view on that subject. Statesmanship will be needed to prevent a drift toward a point where both sides feel obliged to test the firmness and nature of each other's convictions.

The Aftermath

The reader should keep in mind that the kind of protocol and hospitality described here has evolved substantially in the decades since. Ironically, the style of hospitality practiced by the early Communist leaders was more comparable to that of the Chinese imperial tradition than of contemporary practice, which is less elaborate, with fewer toasts and a less effusive tone on the governmental side. What has not changed significantly is the meticulous preparation, the complexity of argumentation, the capacity for long-range planning, and the subtle sense for the intangible.

Nixon's visit to China is one of the few occasions where a state visit brought about a seminal change in international affairs. The reentry of China into the global diplomatic game, and the increased strategic options for the United States, gave a new vitality and flexibility to the international system. Nixon's visit was followed by comparable visits by the leaders of other Western democracies and Japan. The adoption of the anti-hegemony clauses in the Shanghai Communiqué signified a de facto shift of alliances. Though at first confined to Asia, the undertaking was expanded a year later to include the rest of the world. Consultation between China and the United States reached a level of intensity rare even among formal allies.

For a few weeks, there was a mood of exaltation. Many Americans greeted the China initiative as enabling China to return to the community of nations to which it originally belonged (which was true), and treated the new state of affairs as a permanent feature of international politics (which was not). Neither Nixon, by nature skeptical, nor I forgot that the Chinese policies described in the earlier chapters had been carried out with the same conviction as the current ones, or that the leaders who greeted us so charmingly and elegantly had, not too long ago, been equally insistent and plausible in their diametrically different course. Nor could it be assumed that Mao—or his successors—would jettison the convictions that had seen them through a lifetime.

The direction of Chinese policy in the future would be a composite of ideology and national interest. What the opening to China accomplished was an opportunity to increase cooperation where interests were congruent and to mitigate differences where they existed. At the time of the rapprochement, the Soviet threat had provided an impetus, but the deeper challenge was the need to establish a belief in cooperation over the decades, so that a new generation of leaders would be motivated by the same imperatives. And to foster the same kind of evolution on the American side. The reward for Sino-American rapprochement would not be a state of perpetual friendship or a harmony of values, but a rebalancing of the global equilibrium that would require constant tending and perhaps, in time, produce a greater harmony of values.

In that process, each side would be the guardian of its own interests. And each would seek to use the other as a source of leverage in its relations with Moscow. As Mao never tired of stressing, the world would not remain static; contradiction and disequilibrium were a law of nature. Reflecting this view, the Chinese Communist Party's Central Committee issued a document describing Nixon's visit as an instance of China "utilizing contradictions, dividing up enemies, and enhancing ourselves."[46]

Would the interests of the two sides ever be truly congruent? Could they ever separate them from prevalent ideologies sufficiently to avoid tumults of conflicting emotions? Nixon's visit to China had opened the door to dealing with these challenges; they are with us still.

CHAPTER 10

The Quasi-Alliance: Conversations with Mao

THE SECRET TRIP to China reestablished the Sino-American relationship. The Nixon visit began a period of strategic cooperation. But while the principles of that cooperation were emerging, its framework remained to be settled. The language of the Shanghai Communiqué implied a kind of alliance. The reality of China's self-reliance made it difficult to relate form to substance.

Alliances have existed as long as history records international affairs. They have been formed for many reasons: to pool the strength of individual allies; to provide an obligation of mutual assistance; to supply an element of deterrence beyond the tactical considerations of the moment. The special aspect of Sino-American relations was that the partners sought to coordinate their actions without creating a formal obligation to do so.

Such a state of affairs was inherent in the nature of China's perception of international relations. Having proclaimed that China had "stood up," Mao would reach out to the United States but never admit that China's strength might not be adequate for whatever challenge it might confront. Nor would he accept an abstract obligation to render assistance beyond the requirements of the national interest as it appeared at any given moment. China in the early stages of Mao's leadership made only one alliance: that with the Soviet Union at the very beginning of the People's Republic, when China needed support as it felt its way toward international status. It entered into a Treaty of Friendship, Cooperation, and Mutual Assistance with North Korea in 1961, containing a clause on mutual defense against outside attack that is still in force at this writing. But that was more in the nature of the tributary relationship familiar from Chinese history: Beijing offered protection; North Korean reciprocity was irrelevant to the relationship. The Soviet alliance frayed from the very outset largely because Mao would not accept even the hint of subordination.

After Nixon's visit to China, there emerged a partnership not by way of formal reciprocal assurances enshrined in documentation. It was not even a tacit alliance, based on informal agreements. It was a kind of quasi-alliance, growing out of understandings that emerged from conversations with Mao—in February and November of 1973—and long meetings with Zhou—hours of them in 1973. From then on, Beijing no longer sought to constrain or check the projection of American power—as it had before President Nixon's visit. Instead China's avowed goal became to enlist the United States as a counterweight to the "polar bear" by means of an explicit strategic design.

This parallelism depended on whether Chinese and American leaders could come to share common geopolitical aims, especially with regard to the Soviet Union. American leaders were treated by their Chinese counterparts to private seminars on Soviet intentions—often in uncharacteristically blunt language, as if the Chinese feared this topic was too important to be left to their customary subtlety and indirection. The United States reciprocated with extensive briefings about its strategic design.

In the early years of the new relationship, Chinese leaders would continue occasionally to fire ideological "cannons" against American imperialism—some of them involving well-practiced rhetoric—but in private, they would criticize U.S. officials for being, if anything, too restrained in foreign policy. In fact, throughout the 1970s, Beijing was more in favor of the United States acting robustly against Soviet designs than much of the American public or Congress.

The "Horizontal Line": Chinese Approaches to Containment

For a year what was lacking in this design was Mao's imprimatur. He had blessed the general direction in the conversations with Nixon but he had ostentatiously refused to discuss either strategy or tactics, probably because what became the Shanghai Communiqué was still unsettled.

Mao filled this gap in two extensive conversations with me: the first one, late at night on February 17, 1973, lasted from 11:30 P.M. to 1:20 A.M. The second occurred on November 12, 1973, and lasted from 5:40 P.M. to 8:25 P.M. The context of the conversations explains their scope. The first took place less than a month after Le Duc Tho—the principal North Vietnamese negotiator—and I had initialed the Paris Peace Accords to end the Vietnam War. This freed China from any further need to demonstrate Communist solidarity with Hanoi. The second occurred following the decisive U.S. role during the 1973 Arab-Israeli War and the resulting switch in Arab reliance from the Soviet Union to the United States, especially in Egypt.

On both occasions, Mao warmly endorsed the Sino-American relationship in front of assembled media. In February he noted that the United States and China had once been "two enemies," but that "[n]ow we call the relationship between ourselves a friendship."[1] Having proclaimed the new relationship as friendship Mao proceeded to give it an operational definition. Since he liked to speak in parables, he chose a subject that we were least worried about, possible Chinese intelligence operations against American officials visiting China. It was an indirect way of proclaiming a kind of partnership without making a request for reciprocity:

> But let us not speak false words or engage in trickery. We don't steal your documents. You can deliberately leave them somewhere and try us out. Nor do we engage in eavesdropping and bugging. There is no use in those small tricks. And some of the big maneuvering, there is no use to them too. I said that to your correspondent, Mr. Edgar Snow. . . . We also have our intelligence service and it is the same with them. They do not work well [*Prime Minister Zhou laughs*]. For instance, they didn't know about Lin Biao [*Prime Minister Zhou laughs.*] Then again they didn't know you wanted to come.[2]

The least plausible prospect was that China and the United States would abandon collecting intelligence on each other. If the United States and China were indeed entering a new era in their relationship, it was important for each side to be transparent with the other and to elaborate parallel calculations. But limiting the activities of their intelligence services was an unlikely way to start. The Chairman was conveying an offer of transparency but also a warning that he was beyond being tricked—a point with which Mao led into the November conversation as well. As an introduction he recounted with a blend of humor, contempt, and strategy how he had amended his promise to wage ten thousand years of ideological struggle against the Soviets:

> MAO: They tried to make peace through [Communist leader Nicolae] Ceauşescu of Romania, and they tried to persuade us not to continue the struggle in the ideological field.
>
> KISSINGER: I remember he was here.
>
> MAO/ZHOU: That was long ago.
>
> ZHOU: The first time he came to China. [*Said in English.*]
>
> MAO: And the second time [Soviet Prime Minister Aleksei]

Kosygin came himself, and that was in 1960. I declared to him that we were going to wage a struggle against him for ten thousand years [*laughter*].

INTERPRETER: The Chairman was saying ten thousand years of struggle.

MAO: And this time I made a concession to Kosygin. I said that I originally said this struggle was going to go on for ten thousand years. On the merit of his coming to see me in person, I will cut it down by one thousand years [*laughter*]. And you must see how generous I am. Once I make a concession, it is for one thousand years.[3]

The basic message was the same: cooperation if possible and no tactical maneuvering, for it would not prove possible to deceive this veteran of every kind of conflict imaginable. On a deeper level, it was also a warning that, if thwarted in conciliation, China would turn into a tenacious and forbidding enemy.

When talking to Nixon a year earlier Mao had omitted any substantive reference to Taiwan. Now to remove any element of threat Mao explicitly delinked the issue of Taiwan from the overall U.S.-China relationship: "The question of the U.S. relations with us should be separate from that of our relations with Taiwan." The United States, Mao suggested, should "sever the diplomatic relations with Taiwan" as Japan had done (while maintaining unofficial social and economic ties); "then it is possible for our two countries to solve the issue of diplomatic relations." But as for the question of Beijing's relations with Taiwan, Mao warned, "[T]hat is quite complex. I do not believe in a peaceful transition." Mao then turned to Foreign Minister Ji Pengfei and asked, "Do you believe in it?" After further colloquy with the other Chinese in the room, Mao made his principal point—that there were no time pressures of any kind:

MAO: They are a bunch of counterrevolutionaries. How could they cooperate with us? I say that we can do without Taiwan for the time being, and let it come after one hundred years. Do not take matters on this world so rapidly. Why is there need to be in such great haste? It is only such an island with a population of a dozen or more million.

ZHOU: They now have 16 million.

MAO: As for your relations with us, I think they need not take a hundred years.

KISSINGER: I would count on that. I think they should come much faster.

MAO: But that is to be decided by you. We will not rush you. If you feel the need, we can do it. If you feel it cannot be done now, then we can postpone it to a later date.

. . .

KISSINGER: It isn't a question of needing it; it is a question of practical possibilities.

MAO: That's the same [*laughter*].[4]

In Mao's typical paradoxical style, there were two principal points here of equal importance: first, that Beijing would not foreclose its option to use force over Taiwan—and indeed expected to have to use force someday; but second, for the time being at least, Mao was putting off this day, indeed he spoke of being willing to wait for a hundred years. The banter was designed to clear the way for the dominant theme, which was a militant application of the containment theory of George Kennan to the effect that the Soviet system, if prevented from expanding, would collapse as a result of its internal tensions.[5] But while Kennan applied his principles primarily to the conduct of diplomacy and domestic policy, Mao argued for direct confrontation across the range of available pressures.

The Soviet Union, Mao told me, represented a global threat that needed to be resisted globally. Whatever any other nation might do, China would resist an attack, even if its forces had to retire into the interior of the country to fight a guerrilla war. But cooperation with the United States and other likeminded countries would speed the victory in the struggle whose outcome was predetermined by the long-term weakness of the Soviet Union. China would not ask for help nor make its cooperation conditional on the cooperation of others. But it was prepared to adopt parallel strategies, especially with the United States. The bond would be common convictions, not formal obligations. A policy of determined global containment of the Soviets, Mao argued, was bound to prevail because Soviet ambitions were beyond their capacities:

> MAO: They have to deal with so many adversaries. They have to deal with the Pacific. They have to deal with Japan. They have to deal with China. They have to deal with South Asia which also consists of quite a number of countries. And they only have a million troops here—not enough even for the defense of themselves and still less for attack forces. But they can't attack unless you let them in first, and you first give them the Middle East and Europe so they are able to deploy troops eastward. And that would take over a million troops.
>
> KISSINGER: That will not happen. I agree with the Chairman that if Europe and Japan and the U.S. hold together—and we are doing in the Middle East what the Chairman discussed with me last time—then the danger of an attack on China will be very low.
>
> MAO: We are also holding down a portion of their troops which is favorable to you in Europe and the Middle East. For instance, they have troops stationed in Outer Mongolia, and that had not happened as late as Khrushchev's time. At that time they had still not stationed troops

in Outer Mongolia, because the Zhenbao Island incident occurred after Khrushchev. It occurred in Brezhnev's time.

KISSINGER: It was 1969. That is why it is important that Western Europe and China and the U.S. pursue a coordinated course in this period.

MAO: Yes.[6]

The cooperation Mao encouraged was not limited to Asian issues. With no trace of irony, Mao encouraged U.S. military involvement in the Middle East to counter the Soviets—exactly the type of "imperialist aggression" that Chinese propaganda had traditionally thundered against. Shortly after the 1973 Arab-Israeli War, and following Saddam Hussein's visit to Moscow, Iraq attracted Mao's attention and was presented as part of his global strategy:

MAO: And now there is a crucial issue, that is the question of Iraq, Baghdad. We don't know if it is possible for you to do some work in that area. As for us, the possibilities are not so very great.

ZHOU: It is relatively difficult to do that. It is possible to have contacts with them, but it takes a period of time for them to change their orientation. It is possible they would change their orientation after they have suffered from them.[7]

Zhou was suggesting that it was necessary for a coordinated policy to make Iraq's reliance on the Soviet Union so costly that it would have to change its orientation—much as Egypt was doing. (It may also have been a wry comment on how allies would eventually tire of Moscow's overbearing treatment, as China had.) In this manner Mao reviewed the strengths and weaknesses of various states in the Middle East, almost country by country. He stressed the importance of Turkey, Iran, and Pakistan as barriers to Soviet expansion. In addition to Iraq, he was uneasy about South Yemen.[8] He urged the United States to increase its strength in the Indian Ocean. He was the quintessential Cold Warrior; American conservatives would have approved of him.

Japan was to be a principal component for Mao's coordinated strategy. At the secret meeting in 1971, the Chinese leaders still professed considerable suspicion about U.S.-Japanese collusion. Zhou warned us to beware of Japan; the existing friendship, he said, would wither once economic recovery had put Japan into a position to challenge us. In October 1971 he stressed that Japan's "feathers have grown on its wings and it is about to take off."[9] I replied, and Nixon elaborated during his visit, that Japan would be much more problematical if isolated than as part of an international order, including an alliance with the United States. By the time of our conversations in November 1973, Mao had accepted that point of view. He was now urging me to pay *more* attention to Japan and spend more time cultivating Japanese leaders:

> MAO: Let's discuss something about Japan. This time you are going to Japan to stay a few more days there.
>
> KISSINGER: The Chairman always scolds me about Japan. I'm taking the Chairman very seriously, and this time I'm staying two and a half days. And he's quite right. It is very important that Japan does not feel isolated and left alone. And we should not give them too many temptations to maneuver.
>
> MAO: That is not to force them over to the Soviet side.[10]

How would global coordination between the United States and China be implemented? Mao suggested that each side develop a clear concept of its national interest and cooperate out of its own necessity:

MAO: We also say in the same situation [*gesturing with his hand*] that's what your President said when he was sitting here, that each side has its own means and acted out of its own necessity. That resulted in the two countries acting hand-in-hand.

KISSINGER: Yes, we both face the same danger. We may have to use different methods sometimes but for the same objectives.

MAO: That would be good. So long as the objectives are the same, we would not harm you nor would you harm us. And we can work together to commonly deal with a bastard. [*Laughter*] Actually it would be that sometime we want to criticize you for a while and you want to criticize us for a while. That, your President said, is the ideological influence. You say, away with you Communists. We say, away with you imperialists. Sometimes we say things like that. It would not do not to do that.[11]

In other words, each side could arm itself with whatever ideological slogans fulfilled its own domestic necessities, so long as it did not let them interfere with the need for cooperation against the Soviet danger. Ideology would be relegated to domestic management; it took a leave from foreign policy. The ideological armistice was, of course, valid only so long as objectives remained compatible.

In the execution of policy, Mao could be pragmatic; in the conception of it, he always strove for some overriding principles. Mao had not been the leader of an ideological movement for half a century to turn suddenly to pure pragmatism. Kennan's containment theory applied primarily to Europe and Atlantic relations; Mao's was global. In Mao's concept, countries threatened by Soviet expansionism "should draw a horizontal line—the U.S.–Japan–Pakistan–Iran . . . Turkey and Europe."[12] (This is why Iraq had appeared in the earlier dialogue.) Mao put forward his concept to me in February 1973, explaining how this grouping should conduct the struggle with the Soviet Union. Later, he canvassed it with the Japanese foreign minister in terms of a "big terrain" composed of countries along the frontal line.[13]

We agreed with the substance of the analysis. But the differences between the Chinese and American domestic systems that it sought to skirt reemerged over issues of implementation. How were two such different political systems to carry out the same policy? For Mao, conception and execution were identical. For the United States, the difficulty lay in building a supportive consensus among our public and among our allies at a time when the Watergate scandal threatened the authority of the President.

The strategy of holding a horizontal line against the Soviet Union reflected China's dispassionate analysis of the international situation. Its strategic necessity would be its own justification. But it raised the inherent ambiguities of a policy based largely on national interest. It depended on the ability of all sides to sustain comparable calculations from case to case. A coalition of the United States, China, Japan, and Europe was bound to prevail against the Soviet Union. But what if some partners calculated differently—especially in the absence of formal obligations? What if, as the Chinese feared, some partners concluded that the best means to create a balance was for the United States or Europe or Japan, instead of confronting the Soviet Union, to conciliate it? What if one of the components of the triangular relationship perceived an opportunity to alter the nature of the triangle rather than stabilize it? What, in short, might other countries do if they applied the Chinese principle of aloof self-reliance to themselves? Thus the moment of greatest cooperation between China and the United States also led to discussions between their leaders over how the various elements of the quasi-alliance might be tempted to exploit it for their own purposes. China's concept of self-reliance had the paradoxical consequence of making it difficult for Chinese leaders to believe in the willingness of their partners to run the same risks they were.

In applying his horizontal line concept, Mao, the specialist in contradictions, confronted an inevitable series of them. One was that the concept was difficult to reconcile with the Chinese idea of self-reliance. Cooperation depended on a merging of independent analyses. If they all coincided with China's, there was no problem. But in the event of disagreement between the parties, China's suspicions would become sui generis and grow difficult to overcome.

The horizontal line concept implied a muscular version of the Western concept of collective security. But in practice collective security is more likely to operate by the least common denominator than on the basis of the convictions of the country with the most elaborate geopolitical design. This surely has been the experience of America in the alliances it has sought to lead.

These difficulties, inherent in any global system of security, were compounded for Mao because the opening with America did not have the impact on U.S.-Soviet relations he had originally calculated. Mao's turn toward the United States was based on the belief that U.S.-Soviet differences would, in the end, prevent any substantial compromises between the two nuclear superpowers. It was, in a sense, an application of the Communist "united front" strategies of the 1930s and 1940s, as expressed in the slogan promulgated after Nixon's visit: "utilizing contradictions and defeating enemies one by one." Mao had assumed that America's opening to China would multiply Soviet suspicions and magnify tensions between the United States and the Soviet Union. The former happened; the latter did not. After the opening to China, Moscow started to compete for Washington's favor. Contacts between the nuclear superpowers multiplied. While the United States clearly signaled that it considered China an essential component of the international order and would support it if threatened, the mere fact that

America had a separate and more strategic option ran against the old revolutionary's strategic instincts.

The trouble with the horizontal line concept, as Mao began to examine it, was that, if calculations of power determined all conduct, the relative military weakness of China would make it somewhat dependent on American support, at least for an interim period.

This is why, at every stage of the dialogue about cooperation, Mao and other Chinese leaders insisted on a proposition designed to preserve Chinese freedom of maneuver and self-respect: that they did not need protection and that China was able to handle all foreseeable crises, alone if necessary. They used the rhetoric of collective security but reserved the right to prescribe its content.

In each of the conversations with Mao in 1973 he made a point of conveying China's imperviousness to any form of pressure, even and perhaps especially nuclear pressure. If a nuclear war killed all Chinese above the age of thirty, he said in February, it might prove of long-term benefit to China by helping unify it linguistically: "[I]f the Soviet Union would throw its bombs and kill all those over 30 who are Chinese, that would solve the problem [of the complexity of China's many dialects] for us. Because the old people like me can't learn [Mandarin] Chinese."[14]

When Mao described in detail how deep into China he might retreat to lure the aggressor into the trap of an engulfing hostile population, I asked, "But if they use bombs and do not send armies?" To which Mao replied, "What should we do? Perhaps you can organize a committee to study the problem. We'll let them beat us up and they will lose any resources."[15] The innuendo that Americans were prone to indulge in study while Chinese acted explains why Mao, even while advocating his horizontal line theory, inevitably included dramatic details on how China would be prepared to stand alone if the quasi-alliance failed. Mao and Zhou (and later Deng) stressed that China was "digging tunnels" and was equipped to survive for decades on "rifles and millet" alone. In a way, the bombast was likely calculated to mask China's vulnerability—but it reflected as well a serious analysis about how it would confront the existential nightmare of a global war.

Mao's repeated musings about China's ability to survive a nuclear war, sometimes with breezy humor—because there were simply too many Chinese to kill even with nuclear weapons—were treated as a sign of derangement by some Western observers and, in a sense, weakened Western determination because they stirred the fear of nuclear war.

What Mao was really worried about, however, was facing the implications of the doctrine on which the United States and the Western world was basing its concept of security. The dominant theory of Mutual Assured Destruction deterrence depended on the ability to inflict a given percentage of total devastation. The adversary presumably had a comparable capability. How could a threat of global suicide be kept from turning into a bluff? Mao interpreted the U.S. reliance on Mutual Assured Destruction as reflecting a lack of confidence in its other armed forces. It was the subject of a conversation in 1975, in which Mao penetrated to the heart of our Cold War nuclear dilemma: "You have confidence in, you believe in, nuclear weapons. You do not have confidence in your own army."[16]

What about China, exposed to nuclear threat without, for some time, adequate means of retaliation? Mao's answer was that it would create a narrative based on historical performance and biblical endurance. No other society could imagine that it would be able to achieve a credible security policy by a willingness to prevail after casualties in the hundreds of millions and the devastation or occupation of most of its cities. That gap alone defined the difference between Western and Chinese perceptions of security. Chinese history testified to the ability to overcome depredations inconceivable anywhere else and, at the end, to prevail by imposing its culture or its vastness on the would-be conqueror. That faith in his own people and culture was the reverse side of Mao's sometimes misanthropic reflections on their day-to-day performance. It was not only that there were so many Chinese; it was also the tenacity of their culture and the cohesiveness of their relationships.

But Western leaders, more attuned and responsive to their populations, were not prepared to offer them in so categorical a manner (though they did it indirectly via their strategic doctrine). For them, nuclear war had to be a demonstrated last resort, not a standard operating procedure.

The Chinese almost obsessive self-reliance was not always fully understood on the American side. Accustomed to strengthening our European ties by a ritual of reassurance, we did not always judge correctly the impact of comparable statements on Chinese leaders. When Colonel Alexander Haig, leading the American advance team for the Nixon trip, met with Zhou in January 1972, he used standard NATO phraseology when he said that the Nixon administration would resist Soviet efforts to encircle China. Mao's reaction was emphatic: "Encircling China? I need them to rescue me, how could that be? . . . They are concerned about me? That is like 'the cat weeping over the dead mouse'!"[17]

At the end of my November 1973 visit, I suggested to Zhou a hotline between Washington and Beijing as part of an agreement on reducing the risks of accidental war. My purpose was to take account of Chinese suspicions that arms control negotiations were part of a joint U.S.-Soviet design to isolate China by giving China an opportunity to participate in the process. Mao saw it differently. "Someone wants to lend us an umbrella," he said. "We don't want it, a protective nuclear umbrella."[18]

China did not share our strategic view on nuclear weapons, much less our doctrine of collective security; it was applying the traditional maxim of "using barbarians against barbarians" in order to achieve a divided periphery. China's historic nightmare had been that the barbarians would decline to be so "used," would unite, and would then use their superior force to either conquer China outright or divide it into separate fiefdoms. From the Chinese perspective, that nightmare never completely disappeared, locked as China was in an antagonistic relationship with the Soviet Union and India and not without suspicions of its own toward the United States.

There was a difference in underlying approach toward the Soviet Union. China favored a posture of uncompromising confrontation. The United States was equally uncompromising in resisting threats to the international equilibrium. But we insisted on keeping open the prospect of improved relations on other issues. The opening to China shook up Moscow; this was one of our reasons for undertaking it. In fact, during the months of preparation for the secret trip we were simultaneously exploring a summit between Nixon and Brezhnev. That the Beijing summit came first was due in large part to the Soviet attempt to make the Moscow visit dependent on conditions, a tactic quickly abandoned once the Nixon visit to Beijing was announced. The Chinese of course noticed that we were closer to Moscow and Beijing than they were to each other. It elicited caustic comments about détente from Chinese leaders.

Even at the high point of Sino-U.S. relations, Mao and Zhou would occasionally express their concern about how the United States might implement its strategic flexibility. Was the intention of the United States to "reach out to the Soviet Union by standing on Chinese shoulders"?[19] Was America's commitment to "anti-hegemony" a ruse, and once China let its guard down, would Washington and Moscow collude in Beijing's destruction? Was the West deceiving China, or was the West deceiving itself? In either case, the practical consequence could be to push the "ill waters of the Soviet Union" eastward toward China. This was Zhou's theme in February 1973:

ZHOU: Perhaps they [the Europeans] want to push the ill waters of the Soviet Union in another direction—eastward.

KISSINGER: Whether the Soviet Union attacks eastward or westward is equally dangerous for the U.S. The U.S. gains no advantage if the Soviet Union attacks eastward. In fact, if the Soviet Union attacks it is more convenient if it attacks westward because we have more public support for resistance.

ZHOU: Yes, therefore, we believe that the Western European aspiration to push the Soviet Union eastward is also an illusion.[20]

Mao, ever carrying ideas to their ultimate conclusion, sometimes ascribed to the United States a dialectical strategy as he might have practiced it. He argued that America might think of solving the problem of Communism once and for all by applying the lesson of Vietnam: that involvement in local wars drains the big power participant. In that interpretation, the horizontal line theory or the Western concept of collective security might turn into a trap for China:

MAO: Because since in being bogged down in Vietnam you met so many difficulties, do you think they [the Soviets] would feel good if they were bogged down in China?

KISSINGER: The Soviet Union?

NANCY TANG: The Soviet Union.

MAO: And then you can let them get bogged down in China, for half a year, or one, or two, or three, or four years. And then you can poke your finger at the Soviet back. And your slogan then will be for peace, that is you must bring down Socialist imperialism for the sake of peace. And perhaps you can begin to help them in doing business, saying whatever you need we will help against China.

KISSINGER: Mr. Chairman, it is really very important that we understand each other's motives. We will never knowingly cooperate in an attack on China.

MAO: [*Interrupting*] No, that's not so. Your aim in doing that would be to bring the Soviet Union down.[21]

Mao had a point. This was a theoretically feasible strategy for the United States. All it lacked was a leader to conceive it or a public to support it. Its abstract manipulation was not attainable in the United States, nor was it desirable; American foreign policy can never be based on power politics alone. The Nixon administration was serious about the importance it attached to China's security. In practice the United States and China exchanged a great deal of information and were cooperating in many fields. But Washington could not abdicate the right to determine the tactics of how to achieve its security to another country, however important.

The Impact of Watergate

At a point when American and Chinese strategic thinking was striving for congruence, the Watergate crisis threatened to derail the progress of the relationship by enfeebling the American capacity to manage the geopolitical challenge. The destruction of the President who had conceived the opening to China was incomprehensible in Beijing. Nixon's resignation on August 8, 1974, and the assumption of the presidency by Vice President Gerald Ford led to a collapse of congressional support for an activist foreign policy in the subsequent congressional elections in November 1974. The military budget became controversial. Embargoes were placed on a key ally (Turkey); a public investigation of the intelligence community was launched by two congressional committees (the Church Committee in the Senate and the Pike Committee in the House), hemorrhaging classified intelligence information. The American capacity to prevent Soviet adventures in the developing world was reduced by the passage of the War Powers Act. The United States was sliding into a position of domestic paralysis—with an unelected President facing a hostile Congress—producing an opportunity for the Soviets that some Chinese leaders were tempted to believe had been our design in the first place. In early 1975 the congressional action that stopped a joint U.S.-China effort to establish a coalition government in Cambodia came to be interpreted in Beijing as weakness in the face of the Soviet encirclement of China.[22] In that atmosphere, in the Chinese view, the policy of détente threatened to turn into what Mao called shadowboxing, creating the illusion, not the reality, of diplomatic progress. Chinese leaders lectured the Americans (and many other Western leaders) about the dangers of appeasement. The Helsinki Conference on Security and Cooperation was a special candidate for Chinese criticism on the grounds that it created the illusion of stability and peace.[23]

The basis for the quasi-alliance had been the Chinese conviction that the United States's contribution to global security was indispensable. Beijing had entered the relationship looking to Washington as a bulwark against Soviet expansionism. Now Mao and Zhou began to hint that what looked like feebleness in Washington was in reality a deep game—trying to set the Soviets and Chinese against each other in a war designed to destroy them both. Increasingly, however, the Chinese accused the United States of something worse than treachery: ineffectualness. This is where matters stood when, at the end of 1973, China's domestic travail began to parallel our own.

CHAPTER 11

The End of the Mao Era

AT EVERY STAGE of China's diplomatic revolution, Mao was torn between Sinocentrist pragmatism and revolutionary fervor. He made the necessary choices and opted for pragmatism cold-bloodedly though never happily. When we first met Mao in 1972, he was already ill and speaking—with some irony for an avowed atheist—about having received an "invitation from God." He had destroyed or radicalized most of the country's institutions, including even the Communist Party, increasingly ruling by personal magnetism and the manipulation of opposing factions. Now, as his rule was nearing its end, Mao's grip on power—and his capacity to manipulate—were both slipping away. The crisis over Lin Biao had destroyed Mao's designated successor. Now Mao had no accepted heir, and there was no blueprint for a post-Mao China.

The Succession Crisis

Instead of choosing a new successor, Mao attempted to institutionalize his own ambivalence. He bequeathed to China an extraordinarily complex set of political rivalries by promoting officials from both sides of his vision of China's destiny. With characteristic convolution, he fostered each camp and then set them against each other—all while fomenting "contradictions" within each faction (such as between Zhou and Deng) to make sure no one person became dominant enough to emerge with authority approaching his own. On the one side stood a camp of practical administrators led by Zhou and subsequently Deng; on the other were the ideological purists around Jiang Qing and her faction of Shanghai-based radicals (to whom Mao later applied the derisive label "the Gang of Four"). They insisted on a literal application of Mao Zedong Thought. Between them stood Hua Guofeng, Mao's immediate successor—to whom fell the awesome (and eventually unmanageable) task of mastering the "contradictions" that Mao had enshrined (and with whose brief career the next chapter will deal).

The two principal factions engaged in numerous disputes over culture, politics, economic policy, and the perquisites of power—in short, on how to run the country. But a fundamental subtext concerned the philosophical questions that had occupied China's best minds in the nineteenth and early twentieth centuries: how to define China's relationship with the outside world and what, if anything, it could learn from foreigners.

The Gang of Four advocated turning inward. They sought to purify Chinese culture and politics of suspect influences (including anything deemed foreign, "revisionist," bourgeois, traditional, capitalist, or potentially anti-Party), to reinvigorate China's ethic of revolutionary struggle and radical egalitarianism, and to reorient social life around an essentially religious worship of Mao Zedong. Mao's wife, Jiang Qing, a former actress, oversaw the reform and radicalization of traditional Beijing opera and the development of revolutionary ballets—including *The Red Detachment of Women,* performed for President Nixon in 1972, to the American delegation's general stupefaction.

After Lin fell from grace, Jiang Qing and the Gang of Four survived. Ideologues under their sway dominated much of the Chinese press, universities, and the cultural sphere, and they used this influence to vilify Zhou, Deng, and China's supposed tendency toward "revisionism." Their conduct during the Cultural Revolution had made them a number of powerful enemies, however, and they were unlikely contenders for succession. Lacking association with the military establishment or the Long March veterans, they were unlikely aspirants for the top position: an actress and theatrical producer seeking posts that only a small handful of women had reached in all of Chinese history (Jiang Qing); a journalist and political theorist (Zhang Chunqiao); a leftist literary critic (Yao Wenyuan); and a former security guard, plucked from obscurity after agitating against his factory's management and possessing no power base of his own (Wang Hongwen).[1]

The Gang of Four stood opposite a camp of relative pragmatists associated with Zhou Enlai and, increasingly, Deng Xiaoping. Though Zhou himself was a dedicated Communist with decades of devoted service to Mao, for many Chinese he had come to represent order and moderation. Both to his critics and to his admirers, Zhou was a symbol of China's long tradition of mandarin gentleman-officials—urbane, highly educated, restrained in his personal habits and, within the spectrum of Chinese Communism, his political preferences.

Deng possessed a blunter and less refined personal style than Zhou; he punctuated his conversations by spitting loudly into a spittoon, producing occasional incongruous moments. Yet he shared, and went beyond, Zhou's vision of a China that balanced its revolutionary principles with order and a quest for prosperity. Eventually he was to resolve Mao's ambivalence between radical ideology and a more strategically based reform approach. Neither man was a believer in Western principles of democracy. Both had been uncritical participants in Mao's first waves of upheaval. But in contrast to Mao and the Gang of Four, Zhou and Deng were reluctant to mortgage China's future to continuous revolution.

Accused by their critics of "selling out" China to foreigners, both the nineteenth- and twentieth-century sets of reformers sought to use Western technology and economic innovations to bolster China's strength while preserving China's essence.[2] Zhou was closely identified with the Sino-U.S. rapprochement and with the attempt to return Chinese domestic affairs to a more normal pattern in the wake of the Cultural Revolution, both of which the Gang of Four opposed as a betrayal of revolutionary principles. Deng and likeminded officials, such as Hu Yaobang and Zhao Ziyang, were associated with economic pragmatism, which the Gang of Four attacked as the restoration of aspects of the capitalist system.

As Mao grew increasingly frail, the Chinese leadership was locked in a power struggle and a debate over China's destiny, profoundly affecting Sino-U.S. relations. When China's radicals gained in relative power, the U.S.-China relationship cooled; when America's freedom of action was limited by domestic upheavals, it strengthened the radicals' arguments that China was unnecessarily compromising its ideological purity by tying its foreign policy to a country itself riven by domestic disputes and incapable of assisting China's security. To the end, Mao attempted to manage the contradiction of preserving his legacy of continuous revolution while safeguarding the strategic rapprochement with the United States, which he continued to deem important for China's security. He left the impression that he sympathized with the radicals even as the national interest impelled him to sustain the new relationship with America, which, in turn, frustrated him with its own domestic divisions.

Mao, in his prime, could have overcome internal conflicts, but the aging Mao was increasingly torn by the complexities he had created. Zhou, the Mao loyalist for forty years, became a victim of this ambivalence.

The Fall of Zhou Enlai

Political survival for the second man in an autocracy is inherently difficult. It requires being close enough to the leader to leave no space for a competitor but not so close as to make the leader feel threatened. None of Mao's number twos had managed that tightrope act: Liu Shaoqi, who served as number two with the title of President from 1959 to 1967 and was imprisoned during the Cultural Revolution, and Lin Biao had both been destroyed politically and lost their lives in the process.

Zhou had been our principal interlocutor at all meetings. We noticed on the visit in November 1973 that he was a shade more tentative than usual and even more deferential to Mao than customarily. But it was compensated for by a conversation of nearly three hours with Mao, the most comprehensive review of foreign policy strategy we had had yet. It ended with Mao escorting me to the anteroom and an official release announcing that the Chairman and I had had "a far-ranging discussion in a friendly atmosphere."

With Mao's apparent imprimatur, all negotiations ended rapidly and favorably. The final communiqué extended the joint opposition to hegemony from "the Asia-Pacific region" (as in the Shanghai Communiqué of 1972) to the global plane. It affirmed the need to deepen consultations between the two countries at "authoritative levels" even further. Exchanges and trade were to be increased. The scope of the liaison offices was to be expanded. Zhou said he would recall the head of the Chinese Liaison Office from Washington to instruct him on the nature of the agreed intensified dialogue.

Contemporary Chinese historians point out that the criticisms of the Gang of Four against Zhou were reaching a crisis point at this time. We were aware from the media that an anti-Confucian campaign was taking place but did not consider that it had any immediate relevance to foreign policy or Chinese leadership issues. In his dealings with Americans, Zhou continued to exhibit unflappable self-assurance. On only one occasion did his serenity leave him. At a banquet in the Great Hall of the People in November 1973, in a general conversation, I made the observation that China seemed to me to have remained essentially

Confucian in its belief in a single, universal, generally applicable truth as the standard of individual conduct and social cohesion. What Communism had done, I suggested, was to establish Marxism as the content of that truth.

I cannot recall what possessed me to make this statement, which, however accurate, surely did not take into account Mao's attacks on Confucians who were alleged to be impeding his policies. Zhou exploded, the only time I saw him lose his temper. Confucianism, he said, was a doctrine of class oppression while Communism represented a philosophy of liberation. With uncharacteristic insistence, he kept up the argument, no doubt to some degree so as to have it on record for the benefit of Nancy Tang, the interpreter who was close to Jiang Qing, and Wang Hairong, the grand-niece of Mao, who was always in Zhou's entourage.

Shortly afterward, we learned that Zhou was stricken with cancer and that he was withdrawing from the day-to-day management of affairs. A dramatic upheaval followed. The visit to China had ended on a dramatic high. The meeting with Mao was not only the most substantive of all previous dialogues; its symbolism—its length, the demonstrative courtesies such as escorting me to the anteroom, the warm communiqué—was designed to emphasize its significance. As I was leaving, Zhou told me that he thought the dialogue had been the most significant since the secret visit:

> ZHOU: We wish you success and also success to the President.
>
> KISSINGER: Thank you and thank you for the reception we have received as always.
>
> ZHOU: It is what you deserve. And once the course has been set, as in 1971, we will persevere in the course.
>
> KISSINGER: So will we.
>
> ZHOU: That is why we use the term farsightedness to describe your meeting with the Chairman.[3]

The dialogue provided for in the communiqué never got underway. The nearly completed negotiations on financial issues languished. The head of the liaison office returned to Beijing but did not come back for four months. The National Security Council officer in charge of China reported that bilateral relations were "immobilized."[4] Within a month, the change in Zhou's fortunes—though not its extent—became visible.

It has since emerged that in December 1973, less than a month after the events described here, Mao obliged Zhou to undergo "struggle sessions" in front of the Politburo to justify his foreign policy, described as too accommodating by Nancy Tang and Wang Hairong, the Mao loyalists in his entourage. In the course of the sessions, Deng, who had been brought back from exile as a possible alternative to Zhou, summed up the prevailing criticism as follows: "Your position is just one step away from [the] Chairman. . . . To others, the Chairmanship is within sight, but beyond reach. To you, however, it is within sight and within reach. I hope you will always keep this in mind."[5] Zhou was, in effect, accused of overreaching.

When the session ended, a Politburo meeting criticized Zhou openly:

> Generally speaking, [Zhou] forgot about the principle of preventing "rightism" while allying with [the United States]. This is mainly because [he] forgot about the Chairman's instructions. [He] over-estimated the power of the enemy and devaluated the power of the people. [He] also failed to grasp the principle of combining the diplomatic line with supporting revolution.[6]

By early 1974, Zhou disappeared as a policymaker, ostensibly on account of his cancer. But illness was not a sufficient explanation for the oblivion into which he fell. No Chinese official referred to him again. In my first meeting with Deng in early 1974, he mentioned Mao repeatedly and ignored any reference I made to Zhou. If a negotiating record was needed, our Chinese opposite numbers would cite the two conversations with Mao in 1973. I saw Zhou only one more time, in December 1974, when I had taken some members of my family to Beijing with me on an official visit. My family was invited to the meeting. In what was described as a hospital but looked like a State Guesthouse, Zhou avoided any political or diplomatic subjects by saying his doctors had forbidden any exertions. The meeting lasted a little more than twenty minutes. It was carefully staged to symbolize that dialogue about Sino-American relations with Zhou had come to an end.

There was no little poignancy at such an end to a career defined by ultimate loyalty to Mao. Zhou had stood by the aging Chairman through crises that obliged him to balance his admiration for Mao's revolutionary leadership against the pragmatic and more humane instincts of his own nature. He had survived because he was indispensable and, in an ultimate sense, loyal—too loyal, his critics argued. Now he was removed from authority when the storms seemed to be subsiding and with the reassuring shore within sight. He had not differed from Mao's policies as Deng had done a decade earlier. No American dealing with him noted any departure from what Mao had said (and in any event, the Chairman seemed to be monitoring the meetings by reading the transcripts every evening). True, Zhou treated the American delegations with consummate—though aloof—courtesy; that was the prerequisite for moving toward partnership with America, which China's difficult security situation required. I interpreted his conduct as a way to facilitate Chinese imperatives, not as concessions to my or any other American's personality.

It is conceivable that Zhou may have begun to view the American relationship as a permanent feature, while Mao treated it as a tactical phase. Zhou may have concluded that China, emerging from the wreckage of the Cultural Revolution, would not be able to thrive in the world unless it ended its isolation and became a genuine part of the international order. But this is something I surmise from Zhou's conduct, not his words. Our dialogue never reached an exchange of personal comments. Some of Zhou's successors tend to refer to him as "your friend, Zhou." To the extent that they mean this literally—and even if it has a sardonic undertone—I consider it an honor.

Politically hobbled, emaciated, and terminally ill, Zhou surfaced in January 1975 for one last public gesture. The occasion was a meeting of China's National People's Congress, the first convocation of its kind since the start of the Cultural Revolution. Zhou was still technically Premier. He opened with a declaration of carefully worded praise for the Cultural Revolution and the anti-Confucius campaign, both of which had nearly destroyed him and both of which he now hailed as "great," "important," and "far-reaching" in their influence. It was the last public declaration of loyalty to the Chairman whom he had served for forty years. But then halfway through the speech, Zhou presented, as if it were simply the logical continuation of this program, a completely new direction. He revisited a long dormant proposal from before the Cultural Revolution—that China should strive to achieve "comprehensive modernization" in four key sectors: agriculture; industry; national defense; and science and technology. Zhou noted that he was issuing this call—effectively a repudiation of the goals of the Cultural Revolution—"on Chairman Mao's instructions," though when and how these were issued was left unclear.[7]

Zhou exhorted China to achieve the "Four Modernizations" "before the end of the century." Zhou's listeners could not fail to note that he would never live to see this goal realized. And as the first half of Zhou's speech attested, such modernization would be achieved, if at all, only after further ideological struggle. But Zhou's audience would remember his assessment—part forecast, part challenge—that by the end of the twentieth century, China's "national economy will be advancing in the front ranks of the world."[8] In the years to come, some of them would heed this call and champion the cause of technological advancement and economic liberalization, even at serious political and personal risk.

Final Meetings with Mao: The Swallows and the Coming of the Storm

After the disappearance of Zhou, in early 1974, Deng Xiaoping became our interlocutor. Though he had only recently returned from exile, he conducted affairs with the aplomb and self-assurance with which Chinese leaders seem naturally endowed, and he was soon named Executive Vice Premier.

By that time, the horizontal line concept was abandoned—after only one year—because it was too close to traditional alliance concepts, thus limiting China's freedom of action. In its place Mao put forward the vision of the "Three Worlds," which he ordered Deng to announce at a special session of the United Nations General Assembly in 1974. The new approach replaced the horizontal line with a vision of three worlds: The United States and the Soviet Union belonged to the first world. Countries such as Japan and Europe were part of the second world. All the underdeveloped countries constituted the Third World, to which China belonged as well.[9]

According to that vision, world affairs were conducted in the shadow of the conflict of the two nuclear superpowers. As Deng argued in his U.N. speech:

> Since the two superpowers are contending for world hegemony, the contradiction between them is irreconcilable; one either overpowers the other, or is overpowered. Their compromise and collusion can only be partial, temporary and

> relative, while their contention is all-embracing, permanent and absolute. . . . They may reach certain agreements, but their agreements are only a facade and a deception.[10]

The developing world should use this conflict for its own purposes: the two superpowers had "created their own antithesis" by "arous[ing] strong resistance among the Third World and the people of the whole world."[11] Real power lay not with the United States or the Soviet Union; instead "the really powerful are the Third World and the people of all countries uniting together and daring to fight and daring to win."[12]

The Three Worlds theory restored China's freedom of action at least from the ideological point of view. It permitted differentiation between the two superpowers for temporary convenience. It provided a vehicle for an active, independent role for China through its role in the developing world, and it gave China tactical flexibility. Still, it could not solve China's strategic challenge, as Mao had described it in his two long conversations in 1973: the Soviet Union was threatening in both Asia and Europe; China needed to participate in the world if it wanted to speed its economic development; and a quasi-alliance between China and the United States had to be sustained even as the domestic evolution in both countries pressed their governments in the opposite direction.

Had the radical element achieved enough influence with Mao to lead to the removal of Zhou? Or had Mao used the radicals to overthrow his number two associate just as he had done with Zhou's predecessors? Whatever the answer, Mao needed to triangulate. He sympathized with the radicals, but he was too significant a strategist to abandon the American safety net; on the contrary, he sought to strengthen it so long as America appeared as an effective partner.

A clumsy American agreement to a summit between President Ford and Soviet Premier Brezhnev in Vladivostok in November 1974 complicated U.S.-Chinese relations. The decision had been made for purely practical reasons. Ford, as a new President, wanted to meet his Soviet counterpart. It was determined that he could not go to Europe without meeting some European leaders eager to establish their relations with the new President, which would crowd Ford's schedule. A presidential trip to Japan and Korea had already been scheduled during the Nixon presidency; a twenty-four-hour side trip to Vladivostok would make the least demand on presidential time. In the process, we overlooked that Vladivostok was acquired by Russia only a century earlier in one of the "unequal treaties" regularly castigated in China and that it was located in the Russian Far East, where military clashes between China and the Soviet Union had triggered the reassessment of our China policy just a few years earlier. Technical convenience had been allowed to override common sense.

Chinese irritation with Washington in the wake of the Vladivostok meeting was evident when I traveled to Beijing from Vladivostok in December 1974. It was the only visit during which Mao did not receive me. (Since one could never request a meeting, the slight could be presented as an omission rather than a rebuff.)

Misstep aside, the United States remained committed to the strategy inaugurated in the Nixon administration, whatever the fluctuations of internal Chinese and American politics. Should the Soviets have attacked China, both Presidents I served, Richard Nixon and Gerald Ford, would have strongly supported China and done their utmost to defeat such a Soviet adventure. We were also determined to defend the international equilibrium. But we judged the American national interest and global peace best served if the United States maintained the capacity for dialogue with *both* Communist giants. By being closer to each of them than they were to each other, we would achieve the maximum diplomatic flexibility. What Mao described as "shadowboxing" was what both Nixon and Ford were convinced was required to build a consensus for foreign policy in the aftermath of the Vietnam War, Watergate, and the coming into office of a nonelected President.

In this international and domestic environment, my last two conversations with Mao took place in October and December 1975. The occasion was the first visit to China of President Ford. The initial meeting was to prepare the summit between the two leaders; the second concerned their actual conversation. In addition to providing a summary of the dying Chairman's last views, they demonstrated Mao's colossal willpower. He had not been well when he met Nixon; now he was desperately ill. He needed the assistance of two nurses to rise from the chair. He could barely speak. Chinese being a tonal language, the stricken Mao made his interpreter write down her interpretation of the wheezes issuing from his broken hulk. She would then show them to him, and Mao would nod or shake his head before the translation. In the face of his infirmities, Mao conducted both conversations with extraordinary lucidity.

Even more remarkable was the way these conversations at the edge of the grave exhibited the turmoil within Mao. Sarcastic and penetrating, taunting and cooperative, they distilled one final time revolutionary conviction grappling with a complex sense of strategy. Mao began the conversation of October 21, 1975, by challenging a banality I had uttered to Deng the day before to the effect that China and the United States wanted nothing from each other: "If neither side had anything to ask from the other, why would you be coming to Beijing? If neither side had anything to ask, then why did you want to come to Beijing, and why would we want to receive you and the President?"[13] In other words, abstract expressions of goodwill were meaningless to the apostle of continuous revolution. He was still in quest of a common strategy, and as a strategist he recognized the need for priorities even at the temporary sacrifice of some of China's historic goals. Therefore he volunteered an assurance from a previous meeting: "The small issue is Taiwan, the big issue is the world."[14] As was his habit, Mao pushed the necessary to its extreme with his characteristic combination of whimsy, aloof patience, and implicit threat—at times in elusive, if not unfathomable, phrasing. Not only would Mao continue to be patient as he had indicated he would be in the meeting with Nixon and the follow-up meetings with me, he did not want to confuse the debate about Taiwan with the strategy for protecting the global equilibrium. Therefore he made what would have seemed an incredible assertion two years earlier—that China did not want Taiwan at this moment:

> MAO: It's better for it to be in your hands. And if you were to send it back to me now, I would not want it, because it's not wantable. There are a huge bunch of counter-revolutionaries there. A hundred years hence we will want it [*gesturing with his hand*], and we are going to fight for it.
>
> KISSINGER: Not a hundred years.
>
> MAO: [*Gesturing with his hand, counting*] It is hard to say. Five years, ten, twenty, a hundred years. It's hard to say. [*Points toward the ceiling*] And when I go to heaven to see God, I'll tell him it's better to have Taiwan under the care of the United States now.
>
> KISSINGER: He will be very astonished to hear that from the Chairman.
>
> MAO: No, because God blesses you, not us. God does not like us [*waves his hands*] because I am a militant warlord, also a communist. That's why he doesn't like me. [*Pointing to the three Americans*][15] He likes you and you and you.[16]

There was an urgency, however, in getting the issue of international security right: China, Mao argued, had slid to last place in American priorities among the five power centers of the world, with the Soviet

Union having pride of place, followed by Europe and Japan: "We see that what you are doing is leaping to Moscow by way of our shoulders, and these shoulders are now useless. You see, we are the fifth. We are the small finger."[17] Moreover, Mao claimed, the European countries, though outranking China in terms of power, were overwhelmed by their fear of the Soviet Union, summed up in an allegory:

> MAO: This world is not tranquil, and a storm—the wind and rain—are coming. And at the approach of the rain and wind the swallows are busy.
>
> TANG: He [the Chairman] asks me how one says "swallow" in English and what is "sparrow." Then I said it is a different kind of bird.
>
> KISSINGER: Yes, but I hope we have a little more effect on the storm than the swallows do on the wind and rain.
>
> MAO: It is possible to postpone the arrival of the wind and rain, but it's difficult to obstruct the coming.[18]

When I replied that we agreed about the coming of the storm but maneuvered to be in the best position to survive it, Mao answered with a lapidary word: "Dunkirk."[19]

Mao elaborated that the American army in Europe was not strong enough to resist the Soviet ground forces there, and public opinion would prevent the use of nuclear weapons. He rejected my assertion that the United States would surely use nuclear weapons in defense of Europe: "There are two possibilities. One is your possibility, the other is that of *The New York Times*"[20] (referring to the book *Can America Win the Next War?*, by *New York Times* reporter Drew Middleton, which doubted whether America could prevail in a general war with the Soviet Union over Europe). At any rate, added the Chairman, it did not matter, because in neither case would China rely on the decisions of other countries:

> We adopt the Dunkirk strategy, that is we will allow them to occupy Beijing, Tianjin, Wuhan, and Shanghai, and in that way through such tactics we will become victorious and the enemy will be defeated. Both world wars, the first and the second, were conducted in that way and victory was obtained only later.[21]

In the meantime, Mao sketched the place of some pieces of his international vision of the *wei qi* board. Europe was "too scattered, too loose";[22] Japan aspired to be hegemonial; German unification was desirable but achievable only if the Soviet Union grew weaker and "without a fight the Soviet Union cannot be weakened."[23] As for the United States, "it was not necessary to conduct the Watergate affair in that manner"[24]—in other words, destroy a strong President over domestic controversies. Mao invited Secretary of Defense James Schlesinger to visit China—perhaps as part of the entourage of President Ford's visit—where he could tour the frontier regions near the Soviet Union like Xinjiang and Manchuria. Presumably this was to demonstrate American willingness to risk confrontation with the Soviet Union. It also was a not very subtle attempt to interject China into the American domestic discussions, since Schlesinger had been reported as having challenged the prevailing détente policy.

Part of the difficulty was a problem of perspective. Mao was aware that he did not have long to live and was anxious to ensure that his vision would prevail afterward. He spoke with the melancholy of old age, intellectually aware of limits, not yet fully prepared to face that, for him, the range of choices was fading and the means to implement them disappearing.

> MAO: I'm 82 years old now. [*Points toward Secretary Kissinger*] And how old are you? 50 maybe.
>
> KISSINGER: 51.

MAO: [*Pointing toward Vice Premier Deng*] He's 71. [*Waving his hands*] And after we're all dead, myself, him [Deng], Zhou Enlai, and Ye Jianying, you will still be alive. See? We old ones will not do. We are not going to make it out.[25]

He added, "You know I'm a showcase exhibit for visitors."[26] But whatever his physical decrepitude, the frail Chairman could never remain in a passive position. As the meeting was breaking up—a point usually inviting a gesture of conciliation—he suddenly spewed defiance, affirming the immutability of his revolutionary credentials:

MAO: You don't know my temperament. I like people to curse me [*raising his voice and hitting his chair with his hand*]. You must say that Chairman Mao is an old bureaucrat and in that case I will speed up and meet you. In such a case I will make haste to see you. If you don't curse me, I won't see you, and I will just sleep peacefully.

KISSINGER: That is difficult for us to do, particularly to call you a bureaucrat.

MAO: I ratify that [*slamming his chair with his hand*]. I will only be happy when all foreigners slam on tables and curse me.

Mao escalated the element of menace even further by taunting me about Chinese intervention in the Korean War:

MAO: The UN passed a resolution which was sponsored by the U.S. in which it was declared that China committed aggression against Korea.

KISSINGER: That was 25 years ago.

MAO: Yes. So it is not directly linked to you. That was during Truman's time.

KISSINGER: Yes. That was a long time ago, and our perception has changed.

MAO: [*Touching the top of his head*] But the resolution has not yet been cancelled. I am still wearing this hat "aggressor." I equally consider that the greatest honor which no other honor could excel. It is good, very good.

KISSINGER: But then we shouldn't change the UN resolution?

MAO: No, don't do that. We have never put forward that request. . . . We have no way to deny that. We have indeed committed aggression against China [Taiwan], and also in Korea. Will you please assist me on making that statement public, perhaps in one of your briefings? . . .

KISSINGER: I think I will let you make that public. I might not get the historically correct statement.[27]

Mao was making at least three points: First, China was prepared to stand alone, as it had in the Korean War against America and in the 1960s against the Soviet Union. Second, he reaffirmed the principles of permanent revolution advanced in these confrontations, however unattractive they might be to the superpowers. Finally, he was prepared to return to them if thwarted on his current course. The opening to America did not, for Mao, imply an end of ideology.

Mao's prolix comments reflected a deep ambivalence. No one understood China's geopolitical imperatives better than the dying Chairman. At that point in history, they clashed with the traditional concept of self-reliance for China. Whatever Mao's criticisms of the policy of détente, the United States bore the brunt of confrontation with the Soviets and most of the military expenditures for the non-Communist world. These were the prerequisites of China's security. We were in the fourth year of reestablishing relations with China. We agreed with Mao's general view on strategy. It was not possible to delegate its execution to China, and Mao knew it. But it was precisely that margin of flexibility to which Mao was objecting.

At the same time, to make sure that the world understood the continuing ties and distilled the correct conclusions, a Chinese statement announced that Mao "had a conversation with Dr. Kissinger in a friendly atmosphere." This positive statement was given a subtle perspective in the accompanying picture: it showed a smiling Mao next to my wife and me but wagging a finger, suggesting that perhaps the United States was in need of some benevolent tutoring.

It was always difficult to sum up Mao's elliptical and aphoristic comments and sometimes even to understand them. In an oral report to President Ford, I described Mao's stance as "sort of admirable" and reminded him that these were the same people who had led the Long March (the yearlong strategic retreat, across arduous terrain and under frequent attack, that had preserved the Chinese Communist cause in the civil war).[28] The thrust of Mao's comment was not about détente but about which of the three parties of the triangular relationship could avoid being engulfed at the beginning of evolving crises. As I told President Ford:

> I guarantee you that if we do go into confrontation with the Soviet Union, they will attack us and the Soviet Union and draw the Third World around them. Good relations with the Soviet Union are the best for our Chinese relations—and vice versa. Our weakness is the problem—they see us in trouble with SALT and détente. That plays into their hands.[29]

Winston Lord, then head of the Policy Planning Staff of the State Department and my principal planner for the secret visit as well as later China policy, added a subtle interpretation of ambiguous Mao comments, which I passed on to the President:

> The Chairman's basic message and principal themes were clear. They clearly formed the strategic framework for the Kissinger visit, indeed for the evolution in our relations in the past couple of years. But there were several cryptic passages that are unclear. The tendency is to dig for the subtleties, the deeper meanings behind the Chairman's laconic, earthy prose. In most instances the larger meaning is apparent. In others, however, there may be nothing particularly significant, or a somewhat senile man might have been wandering aimlessly for a moment. . . . To cite just one example of ambiguity: "Do you have any way to assist me in curing my present inability to speak clearly?" The odds are that this was basically small talk about his own health. It is very doubtful that he was seriously asking for medical assistance. But was the Chairman saying that his voice within China (or in the world) was not being heard, that his influence is being circumscribed, and that he wants U.S. help to strengthen his position through our policies? Does he want us to help him "speak clearly" in the larger sense?[30]

At the time, I thought Lord's comments probably farfetched. Having since learned more about internal Chinese maneuvering, I now consider that Mao meant it in the larger sense.

In any event, the October trip to pave the way for Ford's visit took place in a very chilly atmosphere, reflecting the internal Chinese tensions. It seemed so unpromising that we reduced the presidential visit from five to three days, eliminating two stops outside Beijing and replacing them with brief visits to the Philippines and Indonesia.

On the day I returned from China, Schlesinger had been dismissed as Secretary of Defense and replaced by Donald Rumsfeld. I was advised about it after the fact and would indeed have preferred it not happen; I was sure it would generate controversy over foreign policy in Washington, with arguments challenging the diplomatic process in which we were currently engaged. In fact, the dismissal had nothing to do with Mao's invitation that Schlesinger visit China. Ford's move was an attempt to batten down the hatches for the imminent political campaign, and he had always been uncomfortable with the acerbic Schlesinger. But, undoubtedly, some in the Chinese leadership read the Schlesinger dismissal as a demonstrative rebuff of the Chinese taunt.

A few weeks later, the first week of December, President Ford paid his inaugural visit to China. During Ford's visit, the internal Chinese split was evident. Mao's wife, Jiang Qing, one of the architects of the Cultural Revolution, appeared only once for a few minutes at a reception during a sporting event. Still powerful, she conducted herself with aloof, icy politeness during her demonstratively brief stay. (Her one appearance during the Nixon visit had been to host her revolutionary ballet.)

Mao chose a nearly two-hour meeting with Ford to make the split within the Chinese leadership explicit. Mao's condition had deteriorated somewhat from when he had received me five weeks earlier. However, he had decided that relations with America needed some warming up and conveyed this by a jocular beginning:

> MAO: Your Secretary of State has been interfering in my internal affairs.
>
> FORD: Tell me about it.
>
> MAO: He does not allow me to go and meet God. He even tells me to disobey the order that God has given to me. God has sent me an invitation, yet he [Kissinger] says, don't go.
>
> KISSINGER: That would be too powerful a combination if he went there.
>
> MAO: He is an atheist [Kissinger]. He is opposed to God. And he is also undermining my relations with God. He is a

> very ferocious man and I have no other recourse than to obey his orders.[31]

Mao went on to observe that he expected "nothing great" to occur in U.S.-Chinese relations for the next two years, that is, during the period of the 1976 presidential election and its aftermath. "Perhaps afterwards, the situation might become a bit better."[32] Did he mean that a more united America might emerge or that, by then, Chinese internal struggles would have been overcome? His words implied that he expected the shaky relationship to last through the Ford presidency.

The more significant explanation for the hiatus in the U.S.-China relationship concerned China's internal situation. Mao seized on a comment by Ford that he appreciated the work of the head of the Beijing Liaison Office in Washington (Huang Zhen) and hoped he would stay:

> There are some young people who have some criticism about him [Ambassador Huang].[33] And these two [Wang and Tang][34] also have some criticism of Lord Qiao.[35] And these people are not to be trifled with. Otherwise, you will suffer at their hands—that is, a civil war. There are now many big character posters out. And you perhaps can go to Tsinghua University and Peking University to have a look at them.[36]

If Mao's interpreters—Nancy Tang and Wang Hairong, who was close to Mao's wife—were opposing the Foreign Minister and the de facto ambassador to Washington, matters had reached a fraught moment, and the internal split had reached the highest levels. Mao's calling the Foreign Minister "Lord Qiao"—implying that the Foreign Minister was a Confucian—was another danger sign of the domestic rift. If there were big character posters—the large-font declarations by which the ideological campaigns were conducted during the Cultural

Revolution—being put up at the universities, some of the methods and surely some of the arguments of the Cultural Revolution were beginning to reappear. In that case, Mao's reference to a possible civil war could have been more than a figure of speech.

Ford, who obscured his shrewdness behind a facade of Midwestern simplicity and directness, chose to ignore the signs of division. Instead, he conducted himself as if the premises of the Zhou era of Sino-U.S. relations were still valid and launched himself into a case-by-case discussion of issues around the world. His basic theme was the measures America was taking to prevent Soviet hegemony, and he invited specific Chinese cooperation, especially in Africa. Mao had rebuffed Nixon for attempting much less in their conversation three years earlier. Whether Ford's seeming guilelessness disarmed Mao or Mao had planned a strategic dialogue all along, this time he joined in, adding characteristically mordant comments, especially about Soviet moves in Africa, that proved that he had maintained his mastery of detail.

At the very end of the conversation, there was a strange appeal by Mao for help on presenting a better public posture on U.S.-China relations:

> MAO: . . . [T]here are now some newspaper reports that describe relations between us two as being very bad. Perhaps you should let them in on the story a bit and maybe brief them.
>
> KISSINGER: On both sides. They hear some of it in Peking.
>
> MAO: But that is not from us. Those foreigners give that briefing.[37]

There was no time to inquire which foreigners were in a position to give briefings that the media would believe. It was a problem Mao traditionally could have solved by ordering up a positive communiqué, assuming he still had the power to impose his will on his factions.

Mao did not do so. No practical consequences followed. We found the draft communiqué, presumably overseen by Foreign Minister Qiao Guanhua, to be unhelpful, if not provocative, and refused to accept it. Clearly, a significant power struggle was taking place inside China. Deng, though critical of our tactics with the Soviets, was eager to maintain the relationship with America established by Zhou and Mao. Equally obviously, some groups in the power structure were challenging this course. Deng overcame the impasse by issuing a statement, in his capacity as a member of the Politburo Standing Committee (the executive committee of the Communist Party), affirming the usefulness of Ford's visit and the importance of Sino-U.S. friendship.

For months following the meetings, the Chinese split was in plain view. Deng, who had replaced Zhou without being given the title of Premier, was once more under attack, presumably from the same forces that had exiled him a decade earlier. Zhou had disappeared from the scene. The conduct of the Foreign Minister, Qiao Guanhua, turned confrontational. The silken style with which Zhou had eased the road toward collaboration was replaced by a taunting insistence.

The potential for confrontation was kept in check because Deng sought occasions to demonstrate the importance of close relations with the United States. For example, at the welcoming dinner for my visit in October 1975, Qiao had delivered a fire-breathing toast in front of American television castigating U.S. policy toward the Soviet Union—a violation of diplomatic protocol at total variance with the sensitive handling of American delegations heretofore. When I responded sharply, the television lights were turned off so that my words could not be broadcast.

The next day, Deng invited the American delegation to a picnic in the Western Hills near Beijing where the Chinese leaders live, which had not been on the schedule originally, and conducted it with the solicitude that had characterized all meetings since the opening to China.

Matters came to a head when Zhou died on January 8, 1976. Roughly coincident with the Qingming Festival (Tomb-Sweeping Day) in April, hundreds of thousands of Chinese visited the Monument to the People's Heroes in Tiananmen Square to pay tribute to Zhou's memory, leaving wreaths and poems. The memorials revealed a deep admiration for Zhou and a hunger for the principles of order and moderation he had come to represent. Some poems contained thinly veiled criticism of Mao and Jiang Qing (again using the favored technique of historical analogy).[38] The memorials were cleared overnight, leading to a standoff between police and mourners (known as the "Tiananmen Incident" of 1976). The Gang of Four persuaded Mao that Deng's reforming tendencies had led to counterrevolutionary protests. The next day, the Gang of Four organized counterdemonstrations. Two days after the mourning for Zhou, Mao dismissed Deng from all Party posts. The position of acting Premier went to a little-known provincial party secretary from Hunan named Hua Guofeng.

Chinese relations with the United States became increasingly distant. George H. W. Bush having been named CIA Director, Tom Gates, a former Secretary of Defense, was appointed head of the Beijing Liaison Office. Hua Guofeng did not receive him for four months and, when he did, stuck to established, if formal, phraseology. A month later in mid-July, Vice Premier Zhang Chunqiao, generally regarded as the strongest man in the leadership and a key member of the Gang of Four, took the occasion of a visit by Senate Minority Leader Hugh Scott to put forward an extremely bellicose position regarding Taiwan, quite at odds with what Mao had told us:

> We are very clear on Taiwan. Since the issue of Taiwan has arisen, this is a noose around the neck of the U.S. It is in the interests of the American people to take it off. If you don't, the PLA will cut it off. This will be good both for the American and Chinese peoples—we are generous—we are ready to help

> the U.S. solve the problem by our bayonets—perhaps that doesn't sound pleasant, but that is the way it is.[39]

The Gang of Four was pushing China in a direction reminiscent of the Cultural Revolution and of the provocative Maoist style toward Khrushchev.

On September 9, 1976, Mao succumbed to his illness, leaving his successors with his achievements and premonitions, with the legacy of his grandiosity and brutality, of great vision distorted by self-absorption. He left behind a China unified as it had not been for centuries, with most vestiges of the original regime eliminated, clearing away the underbrush for reforms never intended by the Chairman. If China remains united and emerges as a twenty-first-century superpower, Mao may hold, for many Chinese, the same ambiguous yet respected role in Chinese history as Qin Shihuang, the Emperor he personally revered: the dynasty-founding autocrat who dragged China into the next era by conscripting its population for a massive national exertion, and whose excesses were later acknowledged by some as a necessary evil. For others, the tremendous suffering Mao inflicted on his people will dwarf his achievements.

Two strands of policy had been competing with each other through the turbulences of Mao's rule. There was the revolutionary thrust that saw China as a moral and political force, insisting on dispensing its unique precepts by example to an awestruck world. There was the geopolitical China coolly assessing trends and manipulating them to its own advantage. There was a China seeking coalitions for the first time in its history but also the one defiantly challenging the entire world. Mao had taken a war-wracked country and maneuvered it between competing domestic factions, hostile superpowers, an ambivalent Third World, and suspicious neighbors. He managed to have China participate in each overlapping concentric circle but commit itself to none. China had survived wars, tensions, and doubts while its influence grew, and in the end, it became an emerging superpower whose Communist form of government survived the collapse of the Communist world. Mao achieved this at horrendous cost by relying on the tenacity and perseverance of the Chinese people, using their endurance and cohesion, which so often exasperated him, as the bedrock of his edifice.

Approaching the end of his life, Mao was edging toward a challenge to the American design of world order, insisting on defining tactics and not only strategy. His successors shared his belief in Chinese strengths, but they did not think China capable of achieving its unique potential by willpower and ideological commitment alone. They sought self-reliance but knew that inspiration was not enough, and so they devoted their energies to domestic reform. This new wave of reform would bring China back to the foreign policy conducted by Zhou—characterized by an effort to connect China to global economic and political trends for the first time in its long history. This policy would be embodied by a leader purged twice in a decade and returned from internal exile for the third time: Deng Xiaoping.

CHAPTER 12

The Indestructible Deng

ONLY THOSE WHO experienced Mao Zedong's China can fully appreciate the transformations wrought by Deng Xiaoping. China's bustling cities, the construction booms, the traffic gridlocks, the un-Communist dilemma of a growth rate occasionally threatened by inflation and, at other times, looked to by the Western democracies as a bulwark against global recession—all of these were inconceivable in Mao's drab China of agricultural communes, a stagnant economy, and a population wearing standard jackets while professing ideological fervor from the "Little Red Book" of Mao quotations.

Mao destroyed traditional China and left its rubble as building blocks for ultimate modernization. Deng had the courage to base modernization on the initiative and resilience of the individual Chinese. He abolished the communes and fostered provincial autonomy to introduce what he called "socialism with Chinese characteristics." The China of today—with the world's second-largest economy and largest volume of foreign exchange reserves, and with multiple cities boasting skyscrapers taller than the Empire State Building—is a testimonial to Deng's vision, tenacity, and common sense.

Deng's First Return to Power

Deng's was a fitful and improbable road to power. In 1974, when Deng Xiaoping became America's principal interlocutor, we knew very little about him. He had been General Secretary of the Communist Party's powerful Central Committee until he was arrested in 1966, charged with being a "capitalist roader." We learned that, in 1973, he had been restored to the Central Committee through Mao's personal intervention and against the opposition of the radicals in the Politburo. Though Jiang Qing had publicly snubbed Deng shortly after his return to Beijing, he was clearly important to Mao. Uncharacteristically, Mao apologized for Deng's humiliation during the Cultural Revolution. The same reports also told us that, in speaking to a delegation of Australian scientists, Deng had struck themes that were to become his trademark. China was a poor country, he had said, in need of scientific exchanges and learning from advanced countries such as Australia—the sort of admission China's leaders had never made heretofore. Deng advised the Australian visitors to look at the backward side of China in their travels and not only at its achievements, another unprecedented comment for a Chinese leader.

Deng arrived in New York in April 1974 as part of a Chinese delegation, technically headed by the Foreign Minister, to a special session of the U.N. General Assembly dealing with economic development. When I invited the Chinese delegation to dinner, it became immediately evident who its senior member was and, even more important, that far from being restored to ease Zhou's burden, as our intelligence reports claimed, Deng was, in fact, assigned to replace Zhou and, in a way, to exorcise him. Several friendly references to Zhou were ignored; allusions to remarks of the Premier were answered by comparable quotes from Mao's conversations with me.

Shortly afterward, Deng was made Vice Premier in charge of foreign policy, and only a little later, he emerged as Executive Vice Premier with a supervisory role over domestic policy—an informal replacement for Zhou, who was, however, left with the now largely symbolic title of Premier.

Soon after Mao initiated the Cultural Revolution in 1966, Deng had been stripped of his Party and government positions. He had spent the next seven years first on an army base, then in exile in Jiangxi province, growing vegetables and working a half-day shift as a manual laborer in a tractor repair plant. His family was deemed ideologically incorrect and received no protection from the Red Guards. His son, Deng Pufang, was tormented by Red Guards and pushed off the top of a building at Beijing University. Though he broke his back, Deng Pufang was denied admission to a hospital. He emerged from the ordeal a paraplegic.[1]

Among the many extraordinary aspects of the Chinese people is the manner in which many of them have retained a commitment to their society regardless of how much agony and injustice it may have inflicted on them. None of the victims of the Cultural Revolution I have known has ever volunteered his suffering to me or responded to queries with more than minimal information. The Cultural Revolution is treated, sometimes wryly, as a kind of natural catastrophe that had to be endured but is not dwelt on as defining the person's life afterward.

For his part, Mao seems to have reflected much of the same attitude. Suffering inflicted by him or on his orders was not necessarily his final judgment on the victim but a necessity, potentially temporary, for his view of the purification of society. Mao seems to have considered many of those exiled as available for service as a kind of strategic reserve. He recalled the four marshals from exile when he needed advice on how to position China in the face of the international crisis of 1969. This, too, is how Deng returned to high office. When Mao decided to drop Zhou, Deng was the best—perhaps the only—strategic reserve available to run the country.

Having grown accustomed to Mao's philosophical disquisitions and indirect allusions and to Zhou's elegant professionalism, I needed some time to adjust to Deng's acerbic, no-nonsense style, his occasional sarcastic interjections, and his disdain of the philosophical in favor of the eminently practical. Compact and wiry, he entered a room as if propelled by some invisible force, ready for business. Deng rarely wasted time on pleasantries, nor did he feel it necessary to soften his remarks by swaddling them in parables as Mao was wont to do. He did not envelop one with solicitude as Zhou did, nor did he treat me, as Mao had, as a fellow philosopher from among whose ranks only a select few were worthy of his personal attention. Deng's attitude was that we were both there to do our nations' business and adult enough to handle the rough patches without taking them personally. Zhou understood English without translation and would occasionally speak it. Deng described himself to me as a "rustic person" and confessed, "Languages are hard. When I was a student in France, I never learned French."

As time went on, I developed enormous regard for this doughty little man with the melancholy eyes who had maintained his convictions and sense of proportion in the face of extraordinary vicissitudes and who would, in time, renew his country. After 1974, out of the wreckage of the Cultural Revolution, Deng, at some personal risk since Mao was still in charge, began to fashion a modernization that during the twenty-first century was to turn China into an economic superpower.

In 1974, when Deng returned from his first exile, he conveyed little sense that he would be a figure of historic consequence. He articulated no grand philosophy; unlike Mao, he made no sweeping claims about the Chinese people's unique destiny. His pronouncements seemed pedestrian, and many were concerned with practical details. Deng spoke on the importance of discipline in the military and the reform of the Ministry of Metallurgical Industry.[2] He issued a call to increase the number of railway cars loaded per day, to bar conductors from drinking on the job, and to regularize their lunch breaks.[3] These were technical, not transcendent, speeches.

In the wake of the Cultural Revolution and given the hovering presence of Mao and the Gang of Four, workaday pragmatism was a bold statement in itself. For a decade, Mao and the Gang of Four had advocated anarchy as a means of social organization, endless "struggle" as a means of national purification, and a sort of violent amateurism in economic and academic endeavors. The Cultural Revolution having elevated the pursuit of ideological fervor as a badge of authenticity, Deng's call for a return to order, professionalism, and efficiency—almost boilerplate in the developed world—was a daring proposition. China had endured a decade of rampaging youth militias that had come close to destroying Deng's career and family. His pragmatic, matter-of-fact style recalled China from the dream of cutting short history to a world where history is fulfilled by sweeping ambitions but in practical stages.

On September 26, 1975, in remarks entitled "Priority Should Be Given to Scientific Research," Deng sounded several of the themes that would become his trademarks: the need to emphasize science and technology in Chinese economic development; the reprofessionalization of the Chinese workforce; and the encouragement of individual talent and initiative—precisely the qualities that had been paralyzed by political purges, the shuttering of the universities during the Cultural Revolution, and the promotion of incompetent individuals on ideological grounds.

Above all, Deng sought to end once and for all the debate about what, if anything, China could learn from foreigners that had been raging since the nineteenth century. Deng insisted that China emphasize professional competence above political correctness (even to the point of encouraging "eccentric" individuals' professional pursuits) and to reward individuals for excelling in their chosen fields. This was a radical shift of emphasis for a society in which government officials and work units had dictated the most minute details of individuals' educational, professional, and personal lives for decades. Where Mao took issues into the stratosphere of ideological parables, Deng subordinated ideological pursuits to professional competence:

> Presently, some scientific research personnel are involved in factional struggles and pay little or no attention to research. A few of them are engaged in research privately, as if they were committing crimes. . . . It would be advantageous for China to have one thousand such talented people whose authority is generally recognized by the world. . . . As long as they are working in the interest of the People's Republic of China, these people are much more valuable than those who are engaged in factionalism and thereby obstruct others from working.[4]

Deng defined traditional Chinese priorities as "the need to achieve consolidation, stability and unity."[5] Though not in the position of supreme power with Mao still active and the Gang of Four remaining influential, Deng spoke bluntly about the need to overcome the prevailing chaos and "put things in order":

> There is at present a need to put things in order in every field. Agriculture and industry must be put in order, and the policies on literature and art need to be adjusted. Adjustment, in fact, also means putting things in order. By putting things in order, we want to solve problems in rural areas, in factories, in science and technology, and in all other spheres. At Political Bureau meetings I have discussed the need for doing so in several fields, and when I reported to Comrade Mao Zedong, he gave his approval.[6]

What Mao was, in fact, approving when he had given his "approval" was left vague. If Deng was brought back to supply a more ideological alternative to Zhou, the opposite was the result. How Deng defined order and stability remained the subject of intense challenge from the Gang of Four.

The Death of Leaders—Hua Guofeng

Before Deng could fully launch his reform program, China's power structure underwent an upheaval, and he himself was purged a second time.

On January 8, 1976, Zhou Enlai succumbed to his long battle with cancer. His death evoked an outpouring of public grief unprecedented in the history of the People's Republic. Deng used the occasion of Zhou's funeral on January 15 to eulogize him for his human qualities:

> He was open and aboveboard, paid attention to the interests of the whole, observed Party discipline, was strict in "dissecting" himself and good at uniting the mass of cadres, and upheld the unity and solidarity of the Party. He maintained broad and close ties with the masses and showed boundless warmheartedness toward all comrades and the people. . . . We should learn from his fine style—being modest and prudent, unassuming and approachable, setting an example by his conduct, and living in a plain and hard-working way.[7]

Almost all of these qualities—especially the devotion to unity and discipline—had been criticized at the Politburo meeting of December 1973, after which Zhou's powers were removed (though he kept a title). Deng's eulogy was thus an act of considerable courage. After the demonstrations in memory of Zhou, Deng was purged again from all his offices. He avoided being arrested only because the PLA protected him on military bases, first in Beijing, then in southern China.

Five months later, Mao died. His death was preceded by (and in the view of some Chinese, augured by) a catastrophic earthquake in the city of Tangshan.

With the downfall of Lin Biao and the passing of Zhou and Mao in such close succession, the future of the Party and the country was thrown wide open. After Mao, no other figure came close to commanding comparable authority.

As Mao came to distrust the ambitions and probably the suitability of the Gang of Four, he had engineered the rise of Hua Guofeng. Hua has remained something of a cipher; he was not in office long enough to stand for anything in particular except succeeding Mao. Mao first appointed Hua as Premier when Zhou died. And when Mao died shortly thereafter, Hua Guofeng inherited his positions as Chairman and head of the Central Military Commission, though not necessarily his authority. As he rose through the ranks of the Chinese leadership, Hua adopted Mao's personality cult, but he exhibited little of his predecessor's personal magnetism. Hua named his economic program the "Great Leap Outward," in an unfortunate echo of Mao's disastrous industrial and agricultural policy of the 1950s.

Hua's chief contribution to post-Mao Chinese political theory was his February 1977 promulgation of what came to be known as the "Two Whatevers": "We will resolutely uphold whatever policy decisions Chairman Mao made, and unswervingly follow whatever instructions Chairman Mao gave."[8] This was hardly the type of principle that inspired a rush to the ramparts.

I met Hua only twice—the first time in Beijing in April 1979, and the second in October 1979 when he was on a state visit to France. Both occasions revealed a considerable gap between Hua's performance and the oblivion into which he eventually disappeared. The same must be said about the records of his conversations with Zbigniew Brzezinski, National Security Advisor during the administration of Jimmy

Carter. Hua conducted each conversation with the assurance that senior Chinese officials invariably display in meetings with foreigners. He was well briefed and confident, if less polished than Zhou and with none of the biting sarcasm of Mao. There was no reason to suppose that Hua would vanish as suddenly as he had emerged.

What Hua lacked was a political constituency. He had been projected into power because he belonged to neither of the principal contending factions, the Gang of Four or the Zhou/Deng moderate faction. But once Mao had disappeared, Hua fell over the supreme contradiction of attempting to combine uncritical adherence to Maoist precepts of collectivization and class struggle with Deng's ideas of economic and technological modernization. The Gang of Four adherents opposed Hua for insufficient radicalism; Deng and his supporters would in time reject Hua, increasingly openly, for insufficient pragmatism. Outmaneuvered by Deng, he became increasingly irrelevant to the fate of the nation whose primary leadership posts he still technically held.

But before slipping from the pinnacle, Hua performed an act of transcendent consequence. Within a month of Mao's death, Hua Guofeng allied himself with the moderates—and high-level victims of the Cultural Revolution—to arrest the Gang of Four.

Deng's Ascendance—"Reform and Opening Up"

In this highly fluid environment, Deng Xiaoping emerged from his second exile in 1977 and began to articulate a vision of Chinese modernity.

Deng started from a position that in a bureaucratic sense could not have been more disadvantageous. Hua held all the key offices, which he had inherited from Mao and Zhou: he was Chairman of the Communist Party, Premier, and Chairman of the Central Military Commission. He had the benefit of Mao's explicit endorsement. (Mao had famously told Hua, "With you in charge, I'm at ease.")[9] Deng was restored to his former posts in the political and military establishment, but in every aspect of formal hierarchy he was Hua's subordinate.

Their views on foreign policy were relatively parallel, but they were strikingly different in their visions of China's future. In April 1979 on a visit to Beijing, I had separate meetings with the two leaders. Both put forward their ideas for economic reform. For the only time in my experience with Chinese leaders, philosophical and practical disagreements were made explicit. Hua described an economic program to spur production by traditional Soviet methods, emphasizing heavy industry, improvements in agricultural production based on communes, increased mechanization, and use of fertilizers within the framework of a ubiquitous Five-Year Plan.

Deng rejected all these orthodoxies. The people, he said, needed to be given a stake in what they produced. Consumer goods had to have priority over heavy industry, the ingenuity of Chinese farmers had to be liberated, the Communist Party needed to become less intrusive, and government would have to be decentralized. The conversation continued over a banquet, with a number of round tables. I was seated next to Deng. In what was essentially a dinner conversation, I raised the question of the balance between centralization and decentralization. Deng stressed the importance of decentralization in a vast country with a huge population and significant regional differences. But this was not the principal challenge, he said. Modern technology had to be introduced to China, tens of thousands of Chinese students would be sent abroad ("We have nothing to fear from Western education"), and the abuses of the Cultural Revolution would be ended once and for all. While Deng had not raised his voice, the tables around us had fallen silent. The other Chinese present were sitting at the edge of their seats, not even pretending not to be listening in on the old man as he outlined his vision of their future. "We have to get it right this time," concluded Deng. "We have made too many mistakes already." Soon after, Hua faded from the leadership. Over the course of the next decade, Deng implemented what he had described at the banquet in 1979.

Deng prevailed because he had over the decades built connections within the Party and especially in the PLA, and operated with far greater political dexterity than Hua. As a veteran of decades of internal Party struggles, he had learned how to make ideological arguments serve political purposes. Deng's speeches during this period were masterpieces of ideological flexibility and political ambiguity. His main tactic was to elevate the concepts of "seeking truth from facts" and "integrating theory with practice" to "the fundamental principle of Mao Zedong Thought"—a proposition seldom advanced before Mao's death.

Like every Chinese contender for power, Deng was careful to present his ideas as elaborations of statements by Mao, quoting liberally (if sometimes artfully out of context) from the Chairman's speeches. Mao had not placed any particular emphasis on practical domestic precepts, at least since the mid-1960s. And he would in general have held that ideology overrode and could overwhelm practical experience. Marshaling disparate fragments of Maoist orthodoxy, Deng abandoned Mao's continuous revolution. In Deng's account, Mao emerged as a pragmatist:

> Comrades, let's think it over: Isn't it true that seeking truth from facts, proceeding from reality and integrating theory with practice form the fundamental principle of Mao Zedong Thought? Is this fundamental principle outdated? Will it ever become outdated? How can we be true to Marxism-Leninism and Mao Zedong Thought if we are against seeking truth from facts, proceeding from reality and integrating theory with practice? Where would that lead us?[10]

On the basis of defending Maoist orthodoxy, Deng criticized Hua Guofeng's Two Whatevers statement because it implied that Mao was infallible, which even the Great Helmsman had not claimed. (On the other hand, the fallibility of Mao was rarely asserted while he was living.) Deng invoked the formula by which Mao had judged Stalin—that he had been 70 percent correct and 30 percent wrong—suggesting that Mao himself might deserve a "70-30" rating (this would soon become official Party policy and remains so to this day). In the process, he managed to accuse the heir appointed by Mao, Hua Guofeng, of falsifying Mao's legacy in his insistence on its literal application:

> [T]he "two whatevers" are unacceptable. If this principle were correct, there could be no justification for my rehabilitation, nor could there be any for the statement that the activities of the masses at Tiananmen Square in 1976 [that is, the mourning and demonstrations following the death of Zhou Enlai] were reasonable. We cannot mechanically apply what Comrade Mao Zedong said about a particular question to another question. . . . Comrade Mao Zedong himself said repeatedly . . . that if one's work was rated as consisting 70 per cent of achievements and 30 per cent of mistakes, that would be quite all right, and that he himself would be very happy and satisfied if future generations could give him this "70-30" rating after his death.[11]

In short, there was no unchangeable orthodoxy. Chinese reform would be based to a large extent on what worked.

Deng sounded his basic themes with increasing urgency. In a May 1977 speech, he challenged China to "do better" than the Meiji Restoration, Japan's dramatic modernization drive of the nineteenth century. Invoking Communist ideology to encourage what amounted to a market economy, Deng suggested that "as proletarians," the Chinese would be able to exceed a program engineered by the "emerging Japanese bourgeoisie" (though one suspects that this was really an attempt to mobilize Chinese national pride). Unlike Mao, who appealed to his people by the vision of a transcendent, glorious future, Deng challenged them into a major commitment to overcome their backwardness:

> The key to achieving modernization is the development of science and technology. And unless we pay special attention to education, it will be impossible to develop science and technology. Empty talk will get our modernization programme nowhere; we must have knowledge and trained personnel. . . . Now it appears that China is fully 20 years behind the developed countries in science, technology and education.[12]

As Deng consolidated power, these principles turned into the operational maxims of China's efforts to become a world power. Mao had shown little interest in increasing China's international trade or making its economy internationally competitive. On Mao's death, America's total trade with China amounted to $336 million, slightly lower than the level of America's trade with Honduras and one-tenth of America's trade with Taiwan, which had approximately 1.6 percent of China's population.[13]

China as the present-day economic superpower is the legacy of Deng Xiaoping. It is not that he designed specific programs to accomplish his ends. Rather, he fulfilled the ultimate task of a leader—of taking his society from where it is to where it has never been. Societies operate by standards of average performance. They sustain themselves by practicing the familiar. But they progress through leaders with a vision of the necessary and the courage to undertake a course whose benefits at first reside largely in their vision.

Deng's political challenge was that, in the first thirty years of Communist rule, China had been governed by a dominating leader who propelled it toward unity and international respect but also toward unsustainable domestic and social goals. Mao had unified the country and, except for Taiwan and Mongolia, restored it to its historic limits.

But he demanded of it efforts contrary to its historic distinctiveness. China had achieved greatness by developing a cultural model in rhythm with the pace its society could sustain. Mao's continuous revolution had driven China to the limits of even its vast endurance. It had produced pride in the reemergence of a national identity taken seriously by the international community. But it had not discovered how China could progress other than through fits of ideological exaltation.

Mao had governed as a traditional emperor of a majestic and awe-inspiring kind. He embodied the myth of the imperial ruler supplying the link between heaven and earth and closer to the divine than the terrestrial. Deng governed in the spirit of another Chinese tradition: basing omnipotence on the ubiquitousness but also the invisibility of the ruler.

Many cultures, and surely all Western ones, buttress the authority of the ruler by demonstrative contact of some kind with the ruled. This is why in Athens, Rome, and most Western pluralistic states, oratory was considered an asset in government. There is no general tradition of oratory in China (Mao was somewhat of an exception). Chinese leaders traditionally have not based their authority on rhetorical skills or physical contact with the masses. In the mandarin tradition, they operate essentially out of sight, legitimized by performance. Deng held no major office; he refused all honorific titles; he almost never appeared on television, and practiced politics almost entirely behind the scenes. He ruled not like an emperor but as the principal mandarin.[14]

Mao had governed by counting on the endurance of the Chinese people to sustain the suffering his personal visions would impose on them. Deng governed by liberating the creativeness of the Chinese people to bring about their own vision of the future. Mao strove for economic advancement with mystical faith in the power of the Chinese "masses" to overcome any obstacle by sheer willpower and ideological purity. Deng was forthright about China's poverty and the vast gaps that separated its standard of living from that of the developed world.

Decreeing that "poverty is not socialism," Deng proclaimed that China needed to obtain foreign technology, expertise, and capital to remedy its deficiencies.

Deng culminated his return at the December 1978 Third Plenum of the Eleventh Central Committee of the Chinese Communist Party. The Plenum promulgated the slogan that would characterize all of Deng's subsequent policies: "Reform and Opening Up." Marking a break with Maoist orthodoxy, the Central Committee approved pragmatic "socialist modernization" policies echoing Zhou Enlai's Four Modernizations. Private initiative in agriculture was again permitted. The verdict on the crowds mourning Zhou (which had earlier been deemed "counterrevolutionary") was reversed, and the veteran military commander Peng Dehuai—who had commanded during the Korean War and was later purged by Mao for criticizing the Great Leap Forward—was posthumously rehabilitated. At the close of the conference, Deng issued a clarion call in a speech on "how to emancipate our minds, use our heads, seek truth from facts and unite as one in looking to the future." After a decade in which Mao Zedong had prescribed the answer to virtually all of life's questions, Deng stressed the need to loosen ideological constraints and encourage "thinking things out for yourself."[15]

Using Lin Biao as a metaphor for the Gang of Four and aspects of Mao, Deng condemned "intellectual taboos" and "bureaucratism." Merit needed to replace ideological correctness; too many took the road of least resistance and fell in with the prevalent stagnation:

> In fact, the current debate about whether practice is the sole criterion for testing truth is also a debate about whether people's minds need to be emancipated. . . . When everything has to be done by the book, when thinking turns rigid and blind faith is the fashion, it is impossible for a party or a nation to make progress. Its life will cease and that party or nation will perish.[16]

Independent creative thinking was to be the principal guideline of the future:

> The more Party members and other people there are who use their heads and think things through, the more our cause will benefit. To make revolution and build socialism we need large numbers of pathbreakers who dare to think, explore new ways and generate new ideas. Otherwise, we won't be able to rid our country of poverty and backwardness or to catch up with—still less surpass—the advanced countries.[17]

The break with Maoist orthodoxy, at the same time, revealed the reformer's dilemma. The revolutionary's dilemma is that most revolutions occur in opposition to what is perceived as abuse of power. But the more existing obligations are dismantled, the more force must be used to re-create a sense of obligation. Hence the frequent outcome of revolution is an increase in central power; the more sweeping the revolution, the more this is true.

The dilemma of reform is the opposite. The more the scope of choice is expanded, the harder it becomes to compartmentalize it. In pursuit of productivity, Deng stressed the importance of "thinking things out for yourself" and advocated the "complete" emancipation of minds. Yet what if those minds, once emancipated, demanded political pluralism? Deng's vision called for "large numbers of pathbreakers who dare to think, explore new ways and generate new ideas," but it assumed that these pathbreakers would limit themselves to exploring practical ways to build a prosperous China and stay away from exploration of ultimate political objectives. How did Deng envision reconciling emancipation of thought with the imperative for political stability? Was this a calculated risk, based on the assessment that China had no better alternative? Or did he, following Chinese tradition, reject the likelihood of any challenge to political stability, especially as Deng was making the Chinese people better off and considerably freer? Deng's vision of economic liberalization and national revitalization did not include a significant move toward what would be recognized in the West as pluralistic democracy. Deng sought to preserve one-party rule not so much because he reveled in the perquisites of power (he famously abjured many of the luxuries of Mao and Jiang Qing), but because he believed the alternative was anarchy.

Deng was soon forced to confront these issues. In the 1970s, he had encouraged individuals to air their grievances about suffering during the Cultural Revolution. But when this newfound openness developed into nascent pluralism, Deng in 1979 found himself obliged to discuss in detail how he understood the nature of freedom as well as its limits:

> In the recent period a small number of persons have provoked incidents in some places. Instead of accepting the guidance, advice, and explanations of leading officials of the Party and government, certain bad elements have raised sundry demands that cannot be met at present or are altogether unreasonable. They have provoked or tricked some of the masses into raiding Party and government organizations, occupying offices, holding sit-down and hunger strikes and obstructing traffic, thereby seriously disrupting production, other work and public order.[18]

That these incidents were not isolated or rare events was demonstrated by the catalogue of them presented by Deng. He described the China Human Rights Group, which had gone so far as to request that the President of the United States show concern for human rights in China: "Can we permit such an open call for intervention in China's internal affairs?"[19] Deng's catalogue included the Shanghai Democracy Forum, which, according to Deng, advocated a turn to capitalism. Some of these groups, according to Deng, had made clandestine contact with the Nationalist authorities in Taiwan, and others were talking of seeking political asylum abroad.

This was an astonishing admission of political challenge. Deng was clearer about its scope than about how to deal with it:

> [T]he struggle against these individuals is no simple matter that can be settled quickly. We must strive to clearly distinguish between people (many of them innocent young people) and the counter-revolutionaries and bad elements who have hoodwinked them, and whom we must deal with sternly and according to law. . . .
>
> What kind of democracy do the Chinese people need today? It can only be socialist democracy, people's democracy, and not bourgeois democracy, individualist democracy.[20]

Though he was insistent on authoritarian conduct of politics, Deng abandoned the personality cult, declined to purge his predecessor Hua Guofeng (instead allowing him to fade into insignificance), and began planning for an orderly succession for himself. After consolidating power, Deng declined to occupy most of the top formal positions in the Party hierarchy.[21] As he explained to me in 1982, when I met with him in Beijing:

> DENG: . . . I am approaching the stage when I will become outmoded.
>
> KISSINGER: It doesn't appear so from reading the documents of the Party Congress.
>
> DENG: I am now on the Advisory Commission.
>
> KISSINGER: I consider that a sign of self-confidence.
>
> . . .
>
> DENG: The aging of our leadership has compelled us to this so we have historical experience and lessons. . . .

KISSINGER: I do not know what title to use for you.

DENG: I have several hats. I am a member of the Standing Committee of the Politburo and Chairman of the Advisory Commission and also Chairman of the People's Political Consultative Conference. I would like to give this out to others. I have too many titles. . . . I have so many titles. I want to do as less as possible. My colleagues also hope I will take care of less routine affairs. The only purpose is that I can live longer.

Deng broke with the precedent set by Mao by downplaying his own expertise rather than presenting himself as a genius in any particular field. He entrusted his subordinates to innovate, then endorsed what worked. As he explained, with typical directness, in a 1984 conference on foreign investment: "I am a layman in the field of economics. I have made a few remarks on the subject but all from a political point of view. For example, I proposed China's economic policy of opening to the outside world, but as for the details or specifics of how to implement it, I know very little indeed."[22]

As he elaborated his domestic vision, Deng grew into China's face to the world. By 1980, his ascendance was complete. At the Fifth Plenum of the Central Committee of the Communist Party in February 1980, Hua Guofeng's supporters were demoted or relieved of their posts; Deng's allies, Hu Yaobang and Zhao Ziyang, were appointed to the Politburo Standing Committee. Deng's massive changes were not achieved without significant social and political tensions, ultimately culminating in the Tiananmen Square crisis of 1989. But a century after the thwarted promise of China's self-strengthening nineteenth-century reformers, Deng had tamed and reinvented Mao's legacy, launching China headlong on a course of reform that was, in time, to reclaim the influence to which its performance and history entitled it.

CHAPTER 13

"Touching the Tiger's Buttocks"

The Third Vietnam War

IN APRIL 1979, Hua Guofeng, still China's Premier, summed up the results of the Third Vietnam War, in which China had invaded Vietnam and withdrawn after six weeks, in a contemptuous dig at the Soviet role: "They did not dare to move. So after all we could still touch the buttocks of the tiger."[1]

China had invaded Vietnam to "teach it a lesson" after Vietnamese troops had occupied Cambodia in response to a series of border clashes with the Khmer Rouge, which had taken over Cambodia in 1975, and in ultimate pursuit of Hanoi's goal of creating an Indochinese Federation. China had done so in defiance of a mutual defense treaty between Hanoi and Moscow, signed less than a month earlier. The war had been extremely costly to the Chinese armed forces, not yet fully restored from the depredations of the Cultural Revolution.[2] But the invasion served its fundamental objective: when the Soviet Union failed to respond it demonstrated the limitations of its strategic reach. From that point of view, it can be considered a turning point of the Cold War, though it was not fully understood as such at the time. The Third Vietnam War was also the high point of Sino-American strategic cooperation during the Cold War.

Vietnam: Confounder of Great Powers

China found itself involved in the Third Vietnam War by factors comparable to what had drawn the United States into the second one. Something in the almost maniacal Vietnamese nationalism drives other societies to lose their sense of proportion and to misapprehend Vietnamese motivations and their own possibilities. That certainly was America's fate in what is now treated by historians as the Second Vietnam War (the first being Vietnam's anticolonial war with France). Americans found it difficult to accept that a medium-sized developing nation could cultivate such a fierce commitment only for its own parochial causes. Hence they interpreted Vietnamese actions as symbols of a deeper design. Hanoi's combativeness was treated as a vanguard of a Sino-Soviet coordinated conspiracy to dominate at least Asia. And Washington believed as well that once the initial thrust by Hanoi was blocked, some diplomatic compromise might emerge.

The assessment was wrong on both grounds. Hanoi was not any other country's proxy. It fought for its vision of independence and, ultimately, for an Indochinese Federation, which assigned to Hanoi in Southeast Asia the dominant role Beijing had historically played in East Asia. To these single-minded survivors of centuries of conflict with China, compromise was inconceivable between their idea of independence and any outsider's conception of stability. The poignancy of the Second Vietnam War in Indochina was the interaction between the American yearning for compromise and the North Vietnamese insistence on victory.

In that sense, America's overriding mistake in the Vietnam War was not what divided the American public: whether the U.S. government was sufficiently devoted to a diplomatic outcome. Rather, it was the inability to face the fact that a so-called diplomatic outcome, so earnestly—even desperately—sought by successive administrations of both American political parties, required pressures equivalent to what amounted to the total defeat of Hanoi—and that Moscow and Beijing had only a facilitating, not a directive, role.

In a more limited way, Beijing fell into a parallel misconception. When the U.S. buildup in Vietnam began, Beijing interpreted it in *wei qi* terms: as another example of American bases surrounding China from Korea to the Taiwan Strait and now to Indochina. China supported the North Vietnamese guerrilla war, partly for reasons of ideology, partly in order to push American bases as far from Chinese borders as possible. Zhou Enlai told North Vietnamese Prime Minister Pham Van Dong in April 1968 that China supported North Vietnam to prevent the strategic encirclement of China, to which Pham Van Dong gave an equivocal reply—largely because preventing the encirclement of China was not a Vietnamese objective and Vietnamese objectives were national ones:

> ZHOU: For a long time, the United States has been half-encircling China. Now the Soviet Union is also encircling China. The circle is getting complete, except [the part of] Vietnam.
>
> PHAM: We are all the more determined to defeat the US imperialists in all of Vietnamese territory.
>
> ZHOU: That is why we support you.
>
> PHAM: That we are victorious will have a positive impact in Asia. Our victory will bring about unforeseeable outcomes.
>
> ZHOU: You should think that way.[3]

In pursuit of a Chinese strategy from which Pham Van Dong had been careful to stay aloof, China sent over 100,000 noncombat military personnel to support North Vietnamese infrastructure and logistics. The United States opposed North Vietnam as the spearhead of a

Soviet-Chinese design. China supported Hanoi to blunt a perceived American thrust to dominate Asia. Both were mistaken. Hanoi fought only for its own national account. And a unified Communist-led Vietnam, victorious in its second war in 1975, would turn out to be a far greater strategic threat to China than to the United States.

The Vietnamese eyed their northern neighbor with suspicion approaching paranoia. During long periods of Chinese domination, Vietnam had absorbed the Chinese writing system and political and cultural forms (evidenced, most spectacularly, in the imperial palace and tombs at the former capital of Hue). Vietnam had used these "Chinese" institutions, however, to build a separate state and bolster its own independence. Geography did not allow Vietnam to retreat into isolation as Japan had at a comparable period in its history. From the second century B.C. through the tenth century, Vietnam was under more or less direct Chinese rule, reemerging fully as an independent state only with the collapse of the Tang Dynasty in the year 907.

Vietnamese national identity came to reflect the legacy of two somewhat contradictory forces: on the one hand, absorption of Chinese culture; on the other, opposition to Chinese political and military domination. Resistance to China helped produce a passionate pride in Vietnamese independence and a formidable military tradition. Absorption of Chinese culture provided Vietnam with a Chinese-style Confucian elite who possessed something of a regional Middle Kingdom complex of their own vis-à-vis their neighbors. During the Indochina wars of the twentieth century, Hanoi displayed its sense of political and cultural entitlement by availing itself of Lao and Cambodian neutral territory as if by right and, after the war, extending "special relationships" with the Communist movements in each of these countries, amounting to Vietnamese dominance.

Vietnam confronted China with an unprecedented psychological and geopolitical challenge. Hanoi's leaders were familiar with Sun Tzu's *Art of War* and employed its principles to significant effect against both France and the United States. Even before the end of the long Vietnam wars, first with the French seeking to reclaim their colony after World War II, and then with the United States from 1963 to 1975, both Beijing and Hanoi began to realize that the next contest would be between themselves for dominance in Indochina and Southeast Asia.

Cultural proximity may account for the relative absence of the sure touch in strategic analysis that usually guided Chinese policy during America's Vietnam War. Ironically, Beijing's long-term strategic interest was probably parallel to Washington's: an outcome in which four Indochinese states (North and South Vietnam, Cambodia, and Laos) balanced each other. This may explain why Mao, in outlining possible outcomes of the war to Edgar Snow in 1965, listed an outcome preserving South Vietnam as possible and, therefore, presumably acceptable.[4]

During my secret trip to Beijing in 1971, Zhou explained China's objectives in Indochina as being neither strategic nor ideological. According to Zhou, Chinese policy in Indochina was based entirely on a historical debt incurred by ancient dynasties. China's leaders probably assumed that America could not be defeated and that the north of a divided Vietnam would come to depend on Chinese support much as North Korea did after the end of the Korean War.

As the war evolved, there were several signs that China was preparing itself—albeit reluctantly—for Hanoi's victory. Intelligence noticed Chinese road building in northern Laos that had no relevance to the ongoing conflict with the United States but would be useful for postwar strategy to balance Hanoi or even a possible conflict over Laos. In 1973, after the Paris Agreement to end the Vietnam War, Zhou and I were negotiating a postwar settlement for Cambodia based on a coalition among Norodom Sihanouk (the exiled former ruler of Cambodia residing in Beijing), the existing Phnom Penh government, and the Khmer Rouge. Its main purpose was to create an obstacle to a takeover of Indochina by Hanoi. The agreement ultimately aborted when the

U.S. Congress in effect prohibited any further military role for America in the region, making the American role irrelevant.[5]

Hanoi's latent hostility to its then ally was brought home to me on a visit to Hanoi in February 1973 designed to work out the implementation of the Paris Agreement, which had been initialed two weeks earlier. Le Duc Tho took me on a visit to Hanoi's national museum primarily to show me the sections devoted to Vietnam's historic struggles against China—still formally an ally of Vietnam.

With the fall of Saigon in 1975, the inherent and historic rivalries burst into the open, leading to a victory of geopolitics over ideology. It proved that the United States was not alone in wrongly assessing the significance of the Vietnam War. When the United States had first intervened, China viewed it as a kind of last gasp of imperialism. It had—almost routinely—cast its lot with Hanoi. It interpreted the American intervention as another step toward the encirclement of China—much as it had viewed the U.S. intervention in Korea a decade earlier.

Ironically, from a geopolitical point of view, Beijing's and Washington's long-term interests should have been parallel. Both should have preferred the status quo, which was an Indochina divided among four states. Washington resisted Hanoi's domination of Indochina because of the Wilsonian idea of global order—the right of self-determination of existing states—and the notion of a global Communist conspiracy. Beijing had the same general objective, but from the geopolitical point of view, because it wanted to avoid the emergence of a Southeast Asia bloc on its southern border.

For a while, Beijing seemed to believe that Communist ideology would trump a thousand-year history of Vietnamese opposition to Chinese predominance. Or else it did not think it possible that the United States could be brought to total defeat. In the aftermath of the fall of Saigon, Beijing was obliged to face the implications of its own policy. And it recoiled before them. The outcome in Indochina merged with the permanent Chinese fear of encirclement. Preventing an Indochina bloc linked to the Soviet Union became the dominant preoccupation of Chinese foreign policy under Deng and a link to increased cooperation with the United States. Hanoi, Beijing, Moscow, and Washington were playing a quadripartite game of *wei qi*. Events in Cambodia and in Vietnam would determine who would wind up surrounded and neutralized: Beijing or Hanoi.

Beijing's nightmare of encirclement by a hostile power appeared to be coming true. Vietnam alone was formidable enough. But if it realized its aim of an Indochinese Federation, it would approach a bloc of 100 million in population and be in a position to bring significant pressure on Thailand and other Southeast Asian states. In this context, the independence of Cambodia as a counterweight to Hanoi became a principal Chinese objective. As early as August 1975—three months after the fall of Saigon—Deng Xiaoping told the visiting Khmer Rouge leader Khieu Samphan: "[W]hen one superpower [the United States] was compelled to withdraw its forces from Indochina, the other superpower [the Soviet Union] seized the opportunity . . . to extend its evil tentacles to Southeast Asia . . . in an attempt to carry out expansion there."[6] Cambodia and China, Deng said, "both . . . face the task of combating imperialism and hegemonies. . . . We firmly believe that . . . our two peoples will unite even more closely and march together towards new victories in the common struggle."[7] During a March 1976 visit of Lao Prime Minister Kaysone Phomvihane to Beijing, Hua Guofeng, then Premier, warned of the Soviet Union to the effect that: "In particular, the superpower that hawks 'détente' while extending its grabbing claws everywhere is stepping up its armed expansion and war preparations and attempting to bring more countries into its sphere of influence and play the hegemonic overlord."[8]

Freed from the necessity of feigning Communist solidarity in the face of the American "imperialist" threat, the adversaries moved into open opposition to each other soon after the fall of Saigon in April 1975.

Within six months of the fall of all of Indochina, 150,000 Vietnamese were forced to leave Cambodia. A comparable number of ethnically Chinese Vietnamese citizens were obliged to flee Vietnam. By February 1976, China ended its aid program to Vietnam, and a year later, it cut off any deliveries based on existing programs. Concurrently, Hanoi moved toward the Soviet Union. At a meeting of the Vietnamese Politburo in June 1978, China was identified as Vietnam's "principal enemy." The same month, Vietnam joined Comecon, the Soviet-led trade bloc. In November 1978, the Soviet Union and Vietnam signed the Treaty of Friendship and Cooperation, which contained military clauses. In December 1978, Vietnamese troops invaded Cambodia, overthrowing the Khmer Rouge and installing a pro-Vietnamese government.

Ideology had disappeared from the conflict. The Communist power centers were conducting a balance-of-power contest based not on ideology but on national interest.

Viewed from Beijing, a strategic nightmare was evolving along China's borders. In the north, the Soviet buildup continued unabated: Moscow still maintained nearly fifty divisions along the border. To China's west, Afghanistan had undergone a Marxist coup and was subjected to increasingly overt Soviet influence.[9] Beijing also saw Moscow's hand in the Iranian revolution, which culminated with the flight of the Shah on January 16, 1979. Moscow continued to push an Asian collective security system with no other plausible purpose than to contain China. Meanwhile, Moscow was negotiating the SALT II treaty with Washington. In Beijing's perception, such agreements served to "push the ill waters of the Soviet Union eastward" toward China. China seemed to be in an exceptionally vulnerable position. Now Vietnam had joined the Soviet camp. The "unforeseeable outcomes" predicted by Pham Van Dong to Zhou in 1968 appeared to include Soviet encirclement of China. An additional complication was that all these challenges occurred while Deng was still consolidating his position in his second return to power—a process not completed until 1980.

A principal difference between Chinese and Western diplomatic strategy is the reaction to perceived vulnerability. American and Western diplomats conclude that they should move carefully to avoid provocation; Chinese response is more likely to magnify defiance. Western diplomats tend to conclude from an unfavorable balance of forces an imperative for a diplomatic solution; they urge diplomatic initiatives to place the other side in the "wrong" to isolate it morally but to desist from the use of force—this was essentially the American advice to Deng after Vietnam invaded Cambodia and occupied it. Chinese strategists are more likely to increase their commitment to substitute courage and psychological pressure against the material advantage of the adversary. They believe in deterrence in the form of preemption. When Chinese planners conclude that their opponent is gaining unacceptable advantage and that the strategic trend is turning against them, they respond by seeking to undermine the enemy's confidence and allow China to reclaim the psychological, if not material, upper hand.

Faced with a threat on all fronts, Deng decided to go on the diplomatic and strategic offensive. Though not yet in complete control in Beijing, he moved daringly on several levels abroad. He changed the Chinese position toward the Soviet Union from containment to explicit strategic hostility and, in effect, to roll-back. China would no longer confine itself to advising the United States on how to contain the Soviet Union; it would now play an active role in constructing an anti-Soviet and anti-Vietnam coalition, especially in Asia. It would put the pieces in place for a possible showdown with Hanoi.

Deng's Foreign Policy—Dialogue with America and Normalization

When Deng returned from his second exile in 1977, he reversed Mao's domestic policy but left Mao's foreign policy largely in place. This was because both shared strong national feelings and had parallel views of the Chinese national interest. It was also because foreign policy had set more absolute limits to Mao's revolutionary impulses than domestic policy.

There was, however, a significant difference in style between Mao's criticism and Deng's. Mao had questioned the strategic intentions of America's Soviet policy. Deng assumed an identity of strategic interests and concentrated on achieving a parallel implementation. Mao dealt with the Soviet Union as a kind of abstract strategic threat whose menace was no more applicable to China than to the rest of the world. Deng recognized the special danger to China, especially an immediate threat at China's southern border compounding a latent threat in the north. Dialogue therefore took on a more operational character. Mao acted like a frustrated teacher, Deng as a demanding partner.

In the face of actual peril, Deng ended the ambivalence about the American relationship of Mao's last year. There was no longer any Chinese nostalgia for opportunities on behalf of world revolution. Deng, in all conversations after his return, argued that, in resisting the thrust of Soviet policy toward Europe, China and Japan needed to be brought into a global design.

However close the consultation had become between China and the United States, the anomaly continued that America still formally recognized Taiwan as the legitimate government of China and Taipei as the capital of China. China's adversaries along its northern and southern borders might misconstrue the absence of recognition as an opportunity.

Normalization of relations moved to the top of the Sino-American agenda as Jimmy Carter took office. The first visit to Beijing of the new Secretary of State, Cyrus Vance, in August 1977 did not turn out well. "I left Washington," he wrote in his memoirs,

> believing it would be unwise to take on an issue as politically controversial as normalization with China until the Panama

> issue [referring to the ratification of the Panama Canal treaty turning over operation of the canal] was out of the way, unless—and I did not expect it to happen—the Chinese were to accept our proposal across the board. For political reasons, I intended to represent a maximum position to the Chinese on the Taiwan issue. . . . Accordingly, I did not expect the Chinese to accept our proposal, but I felt it wise to make it, even though we might eventually have to abandon it.[10]

The American proposal on Taiwan contained a series of ideas involving retention of some limited American diplomatic presence on Taiwan that had been put forward and rejected during the Ford administration. The proposals were rejected again by Deng, who called them a step backward. A year later, the internal American debate ended when President Carter decided to assign high priority to the relationship with China. Soviet pressures in Africa and the Middle East convinced the new President to opt for rapid normalization with China, by what amounted to the quest for a de facto strategic alliance with China. On May 17, 1978, Carter sent his National Security Advisor, Zbigniew Brzezinski, to Beijing with these instructions:

> You should stress that I see the Soviet Union as essentially in a competitive relationship with the United States, though there are also some cooperative aspects. . . .
>
> To state it most succinctly, my concern is that the combination of increasing Soviet military power and political shortsightedness, fed by big-power ambitions, might tempt the Soviet Union both to exploit local turbulence (especially in the Third World) and to intimidate our friends in order to seek political advantage and eventually even political preponderance.[11]

Brzezinski was also authorized to reaffirm the five principles enunciated by Nixon to Zhou in 1972.[12] Long a strong advocate of strategic cooperation with China, Brzezinski carried out his instructions with enthusiasm and skill. When he visited Beijing in May 1978 in pursuit of normalizing relations, Brzezinski found a receptive audience. Deng was eager to proceed with normalization to enlist Washington more firmly in a coalition to oppose, by means of what he called "real, solid, down-to-earth work,"[13] Soviet advances in every corner of the globe.

The Chinese leaders were deeply aware of the strategic dangers surrounding them; but they presented their analysis less as a national concern than as a broader view of global conditions. "Turmoil under heaven," the "horizontal line," the "Three Worlds": all represented general theories of international relations, not distinct national perceptions.

Foreign Minister Huang Hua's analysis of the international situation displayed a remarkable self-confidence. Rather than appearing as a supplicant in what was, after all, a very difficult situation for China, Huang struck the attitude of a Confucian teacher, lecturing on how to conduct a comprehensive foreign policy. He opened with a general assessment of the "contradictions" between the two superpowers, the futility of negotiations with the Soviet Union, and the inevitability of a world war:

> [T]he Soviet Union is the most dangerous source of war. Your excellency has mentioned that the Soviet Union is confronted with many difficulties. That is true. To strive for world hegemony is the fixed strategic goal of Soviet socialist imperialism. Although it may suffer a lot of setbacks, it will never give up its ambition.[14]

Huang raised concerns that also bothered American students of strategy—especially those which tried to relate nuclear weapons to traditional ways of thinking about strategy. Reliance on nuclear weapons would open up a gap between deterrent threats and the willingness to implement them: "As for the argument that the Soviet Union would not dare to use conventional arms for fear of nuclear attack from the West, this is only wishful thinking. To base a strategic stance on this thinking is not only dangerous but also unreliable."[15]

In the Middle East—"the flank of Europe" and a "source of energy in a future war"—the United States had failed to check Soviet advances. It had issued a joint statement on the Middle East with the Soviet Union (inviting regional states to a conference to explore the prospect of a comprehensive Palestinian settlement), "thus opening the door wide for the Soviet Union to further infiltrate the Middle East." Washington had left President Anwar Sadat of Egypt—whose "bold action" had "created a situation unfavorable to the Soviet Union"—in a dangerous position and allowed the Soviet Union to "seize the chance to raise serious division among the Arab countries."[16]

Huang summed up the situation by invoking an old Chinese proverb: "appeasement" of Moscow, he said, was "like giving wings to a tiger to strengthen it." But a policy of coordinated pressure would prevail, since the Soviet Union was "only outwardly strong but inwardly weak. It bullies the weak and fears the strong."[17]

All this was to supply the context for Indochina. Huang addressed "the problem of regional hegemony." America, of course, had trod this path a good ten years earlier. Vietnam aimed to dominate Cambodia and Laos and establish an Indochinese Federation—and "behind that there lies the Soviet Union." Hanoi had already achieved a dominant position in Laos, stationing troops there and maintaining "advisors in every department and in every level in Laos." But Hanoi had encountered resistance in Cambodia, which opposed Vietnamese regional ambitions. Vietnamese-Cambodian tension represented "not merely some sporadic skirmishes along the borders" but a major conflict which "may last for a long time." Unless Hanoi gave up its goal of dominating Indochina, "the problem will not be solved in a short period."[18]

Deng followed up the Huang Hua critique later that day. Concessions and agreements had never produced Soviet restraint, he warned Brzezinski. Fifteen years of arms control agreements had allowed the Soviet Union to achieve strategic parity with the United States. Trade with the Soviet Union meant that "the U.S. is helping the Soviet Union overcome its weaknesses." Deng offered a mocking assessment of American responses to Soviet adventurism in the Third World and chided Washington for trying to "please" Moscow:

> Your spokesmen have constantly justified and apologized for Soviet actions. Sometimes they say there are no signs to prove that there is the meddling of the Soviet Union and Cuba in the case of Zaire or Angola. It is of no use for you to say so. To be candid with you, whenever you are about to conclude an agreement with the Soviet Union it is the product of [a] concession on the U.S. side to please the Soviet side.[19]

It was an extraordinary performance. The country which was the principal target of the Soviet Union was proposing joint action as a conceptual obligation, not a bargain between nations, much less as a request. At a moment of great national danger—which its own analysis demonstrated—China nevertheless acted as an instructor on strategy, not as a passive consumer of American prescriptions, as America's European allies frequently did.

The staples of much of the American debate—international law, multilateral solutions, popular consensus—were absent from the Chinese analysis except as practical tools to an agreed objective. And that objective, as Deng pointed out to Brzezinski, was "coping with the polar bear and that's that."[20]

But for Americans there is a limit to the so-called realist approach in the fundamental values of American society. And the murderous Khmer Rouge governing Cambodia represented such a limit. No American President could treat the Khmer Rouge as another stone in the *wei qi* strategy. Its genocidal conduct—driving the population of Phnom Penh into the jungle, mass killings of designated categories of civilians—could not simply be ignored (though as we shall see necessity did on occasion abort principle).

Hua Guofeng, still Premier, was even more emphatic in a meeting the next day:

> [W]e have also told a lot of our friends that the main danger of war comes from the Soviet Union. Then how should we deal with it? The first thing is one should make preparations. . . . If one is prepared and once a war breaks out, one will not find himself in a disadvantageous position. The second thing is that it is imperative to try to upset the strategic deployment of Soviet aggression. Because in order to obtain hegemony in the world the Soviet Union has first to obtain air and naval bases throughout the world, so it has to make [a] strategic deployment. And we must try to upset its plans for global deployment.[21]

No member of the Atlantic Alliance had put forward a comparably sweeping call to joint—essentially preemptive—action or had indicated that it was prepared to act alone on its assessment.

Operationally the Chinese leaders were proposing a kind of cooperation in many ways more intimate and surely more risk taking than the Atlantic Alliance. They sought to implement the strategy of offensive deterrence described in earlier chapters. Its special feature was that Deng proposed no formal structure or long-term obligation. A common assessment would supply the impetus for common action, but the de facto alliance would not survive if the assessments began to diverge—China insisted on being self-reliant even when in extreme danger. That China was so insistent on joint action despite the scathing criticism of specific American policies demonstrated that cooperation with the United States for security was perceived as imperative.

Normalization emerged as a first step toward a common global policy. From the time of the secret visit in July 1971, the Chinese conditions for normalization had been explicit and unchanging: withdrawal of all American forces from Taiwan; ending the defense treaty with Taiwan; and establishing diplomatic relations with China exclusively with the government in Beijing. It had been part of the Chinese position in the Shanghai Communiqué. Two Presidents—Richard Nixon and Gerald Ford—had agreed to these conditions. Nixon had indicated he would realize them in his second term. Both Nixon and Ford had emphasized America's concern for a peaceful solution to the issue, including continuation of some security assistance for Taiwan. They had not been able to fulfill these promises because of the impact of Watergate.

In an unusual act of nonpartisan foreign policy, President Carter early in his term reaffirmed all the undertakings regarding Taiwan that Nixon had made to Zhou in February 1972. In 1978, he put forward a specific formula for normalization to enable both sides to maintain their established principles: reaffirmation of the principles accepted by Nixon and Ford; an American statement stressing the country's commitment to peaceful change; Chinese acquiescence to some American arms sales to Taiwan. Carter advanced these ideas personally in a conversation with the Chinese ambassador, Chai Zemin, in which he threatened that, in the absence of American arms sales, Taiwan would be obliged to resort to developing nuclear weapons—as if the United States had no influence over Taiwan's plans or actions.[22]

In the end, normalization came about when Carter supplied a deadline by inviting Deng to visit Washington. Deng agreed with unspecified arms sales to Taiwan and did not contradict an American declaration that Washington expected the ultimate solution of the Taiwan issue to be peaceful—even though China had established an extended record that it would undertake no formal obligation to that effect. Beijing's position remained, as Deng had stressed to Brzezinski, that "the liberation of Taiwan is an internal affair of China in which no foreign country has the right to interfere."[23]

Normalization meant that the American Embassy would move from Taipei to Beijing; a diplomat from Beijing would replace Taipei's representative in Washington. In response the U.S. Congress passed the Taiwan Relations Act in April 1979, which expressed the American concerns regarding the future as a binding law for Americans. It could not, of course, bind China.

This balance between American and Chinese imperatives illustrates why ambiguity is sometimes the lifeblood of diplomacy. Much of normalization has been sustained for forty years by a series of ambiguities. But it cannot do so indefinitely. Wise statesmanship on both sides is needed to move the process forward.

Deng's Journeys

As Deng moved from exhortation to implementation, he saw to it that China would not wait passively for American decisions. Wherever possible—especially in Southeast Asia—he would create the political framework he was advocating.

Where Mao had summoned foreign leaders to his residence like an emperor, Deng adopted the opposite approach—touring Southeast Asia, the United States, and Japan and practicing his own brand of highly visible, blunt, and occasionally hectoring diplomacy. In 1978 and 1979, Deng undertook a series of journeys to change China's image abroad from revolutionary challenger to fellow victim of Soviet and Vietnamese geopolitical designs. China had been on the other side during the Vietnam War. In Thailand and Malaysia, China had previously encouraged revolution among the overseas Chinese and minority populations.[24] All this was now subordinated to dealing with the immediate threat.

In an interview with *Time* magazine in February 1979, Deng advertised the Chinese strategic design to a large public: "If we really want to be able to place curbs on the polar bear, the only realistic thing for us is to unite. If we only depend on the strength of the U.S., it is not enough. If we only depend on the strength of Europe, it is not enough. We are an insignificant, poor country, but if we unite, well, it will then carry weight."[25]

Throughout his trips, Deng stressed China's relative backwardness and its desire to acquire technology and expertise from advanced industrial nations. But he maintained that China's lack of development did not alter its determination to resist Soviet and Vietnamese expansion, if necessary by force and alone.

Deng's overseas travel—and his repeated invocations of China's poverty—were striking departures from the tradition of Chinese statecraft. Few Chinese rulers had ever gone abroad. (Of course, since in the traditional conception they ruled all under heaven, there technically was no "abroad" to go to.) Deng's willingness openly to emphasize China's backwardness and need to learn from others stood in sharp contrast to the aloofness of China's Emperors and officialdom in dealing with foreigners. Never had a Chinese ruler proclaimed to foreigners a need for foreign goods. The Qing court had accepted foreign innovations in limited doses (for example, in its welcoming attitude to Jesuit astronomers and mathematicians) but had always insisted that foreign trade was an expression of Chinese goodwill, not a necessity for China. Mao, too, had stressed self-reliance, even at the price of impoverishment and isolation.

Deng began his travels in Japan. The occasion was the ratification of the treaty by which normalization of diplomatic relations between Japan and China had been negotiated. Deng's strategic design required reconciliation, not simply normalization, so that Japan could help isolate the Soviet Union and Vietnam.

For this objective Deng was prepared to bring to a close half a century of suffering inflicted on China by Japan. Deng conducted himself exuberantly, declaring "My heart is full of joy," and hugging his Japanese counterpart, a gesture for which his host could have found few precedents in his own society or, for that matter, in China's. Deng made no attempt to hide China's economic lag: "If you have an ugly face, it is no use pretending that you are handsome." When asked to sign a visitors' book, he wrote an unprecedented appreciation of Japanese accomplishments: "We learn from and pay respect to the Japanese people, who are great, diligent, brave and intelligent."[26]

In November 1978, Deng visited Southeast Asia, traveling to Malaysia, Singapore, and Thailand. He branded Vietnam the "Cuba of the East" and spoke of the newly signed Soviet-Vietnamese treaty as a threat to world peace.[27] In Thailand on November 8, 1978, Deng stressed that the "security and peace of Asia, the Pacific and the whole world are threatened" by the Soviet-Vietnamese treaty: "This treaty is not directed against China alone. . . . It is a very important worldwide Soviet scheme. You may believe that the meaning of the treaty is to encircle China. I have told friendly countries that China is not afraid of being encircled. It has a most important meaning for Asia and the Pacific. The security and peace of Asia, the Pacific and the whole world are threatened."[28]

On his visit to Singapore, Deng met a kindred spirit in the extraordinary Prime Minister Lee Kuan Yew and glimpsed a vision of China's possible future—a majority-Chinese society prospering under what Deng would later describe admiringly as "strict administration" and "good public order."[29] At the time, China was still desperately poor, and its own "public order" had barely survived the Cultural Revolution. Lee Kuan Yew recounted a memorable exchange:

> He invited me to visit China again. I said I would when China had recovered from the Cultural Revolution. That, he said, would take a long time. I countered that they should have no problem getting ahead and doing much better than Singapore because we were the descendants of illiterate, landless peasants from Fujian and Guangdong while they had the progeny of the scholars, mandarins and literati who had stayed at home. He was silent.[30]

Lee paid tribute to Deng's pragmatism and willingness to learn from experience. Lee also used the opportunity to express some of Southeast Asia's concerns that might not filter through the Chinese bureaucratic and diplomatic screen:

> China wanted Southeast Asian countries to unite with it to isolate the "Russian bear"; the fact was that our neighbors wanted us to unite and isolate the "Chinese dragon." There were no "overseas Russians" in Southeast Asia leading communist insurgencies supported by the Soviet Union, as there were "overseas Chinese" encouraged and supported by the Chinese Communist Party and government, posing threats to Thailand, Malaysia, the Philippines, and, to a lesser extent, Indonesia. Also, China was openly asserting a special relationship with the overseas Chinese because of blood ties, and was making direct appeals to their patriotism over the heads of the governments of these countries of which they were citizens. . . . [I] suggested that we discuss how to resolve this problem.[31]

In the event, Lee proved correct. The Southeast Asian countries, with the exception of Singapore, behaved with great caution in confronting either the Soviet Union or Vietnam. Nevertheless, Deng achieved his fundamental objectives: his many public statements constituted a warning of a possible Chinese effort to remedy the situation. And they were bound to be noted by the United States, which was a key building block for Deng's design. That strategic design needed a more firmly defined relationship with America.

Deng's Visit to America and the New Definition of Alliance

Deng's visit to the United States was announced to celebrate the normalization of relations between the two countries and to inaugurate a common strategy that, elaborating on the Shanghai Communiqué, applied primarily to the Soviet Union.

It also demonstrated a special skill of Chinese diplomacy: to create the impression of support by countries that have not in fact agreed to that role or even been asked to play it. The pattern began in the crisis over the offshore islands twenty years earlier. Mao had begun the 1958 shelling of Quemoy and Matsu three weeks after Khrushchev's tense visit to Beijing, creating the impression that Moscow had agreed to Beijing's actions in advance, which was not the case. Eisenhower had gone so far as to accuse Khrushchev of helping to instigate the crisis.

Following the same tactic, Deng preceded the war with Vietnam with a high-profile visit to the United States. In neither case did China ask for assistance for its impending military endeavor. Khrushchev was apparently not informed of the 1958 operation and resented being faced with the risk of nuclear war; Washington was informed of the 1979 invasion after Deng's arrival in America but gave no explicit support and limited the U.S. role to intelligence sharing and diplomatic coordination. In both cases, Beijing succeeded in creating the impression that its actions enjoyed the blessing of one superpower, thus discouraging the other superpower from intervening. In that subtle and daring strategy, the Soviet Union in 1958 had been powerless to prevent the Chinese attack on the offshore islands; with respect to Vietnam, it was left guessing as to what had been agreed during Deng's visit and was likely to assume the worst from its point of view.

In that sense, Deng's visit to the United States was a kind of shadow play, one of whose purposes was to intimidate the Soviet Union. Deng's week-long tour of the United States was part diplomatic summit, part business trip, part barnstorming political campaign, and part psychological warfare for the Third Vietnam War. The trip included stops in Washington, D.C., Atlanta, Houston, and Seattle, and produced scenes unimaginable under Mao. At a state dinner at the White House on January 29, the leader of "Red China" dined with the heads of Coca-Cola, PepsiCo, and General Motors. At a gala event at the Kennedy Center, the diminutive Vice Premier shook hands with members of the Harlem Globetrotters basketball team.[32] Deng played to the crowd at a rodeo and barbecue in Simonton, Texas, donning a ten-gallon hat and riding in a stagecoach.

Throughout the visit, Deng stressed China's need to acquire foreign technology and develop its economy. At his request, he toured manufacturing and technology facilities, including a Ford assembly plant in Hapeville, Georgia; the Hughes Tool Company in Houston (where Deng inspected drill bits for use in offshore oil exploration); and the Boeing plant outside Seattle. On his arrival in Houston, Deng avowed his desire to "learn about your advanced experience in the petroleum industry and other fields."[33] Deng offered a hopeful assessment of Sino-U.S. relations, proclaiming his desire to "get to know all about American life" and "absorb everything of benefit to us."[34] At the Johnson Space Center in Houston, Deng lingered in the space shuttle flight simulator. One news report captured the scene:

> Deng Xiaoping, who is using his trip to the United States to dramatize China's eagerness for advanced technology, climbed into the cockpit of a flight simulator here today to discover what it would be like to land this newest American spacecraft from an altitude of 100,000 feet.
>
> China's senior Deputy Prime Minister [Deng] seemed to be so fascinated by the experience that he went through a second landing and even then seemed reluctant to leave the simulator.[35]

This was worlds away from the Qing Emperor's studied indifference to Macartney's gifts and promises of trade or Mao's rigid insistence on economic autarky. At his meeting with President Carter on January 29, Deng explained China's Four Modernizations policy, put forward by Zhou in his last public appearance, which promised to modernize the fields of agriculture, industry, science and technology, and national defense. All this was subordinate to the overriding purpose of Deng's trip: to develop a de facto alliance between the United States and China. He summed up:

> Mr. President, you asked for a sketch of our strategy. To realize our Four Modernizations, we need a prolonged period of a peaceful environment. But even now we believe the Soviet Union will launch a war. But if we act well and properly, it is possible to postpone it. China hopes to postpone a war for twenty-two years.[36]
>
> Under such a premise, we are not recommending the establishment of a formal alliance, but each should act on the basis of our standpoint and coordinate our activities and adopt necessary measures. This aim could be attained. If our efforts are to no avail, then the situation will become more and more empty.[37]

To act as allies without forming an alliance was pushing realism to extremes. If all leaders were competent strategists and thought deeply and systematically about strategy, they would all come to the same conclusions. Alliances would be unnecessary; the logic of their analysis would impel parallel directions.

But differences of history and geography apart, even similarly situated leaders do not necessarily come to identical conclusions—especially under stress. Analysis depends on interpretation; judgments differ as to what constitutes a fact, even more about its significance. Countries have therefore made alliances—formal instruments that insulate the common interest, to the extent possible, from extraneous circumstances or domestic pressures. They create an additional obligation to calculations of national interest. They also provide a legal obligation to justify common defense, which can be appealed to in a crisis. Finally, alliances reduce—to the extent that they are seriously pursued—the danger of miscalculation by the potential adversary and thereby inject an element of calculability into the conduct of foreign policy.

Deng—and most Chinese leaders—considered a formal alliance unnecessary in the U.S.-Chinese relationship and, on the whole, redundant in the conduct of their foreign policy. They were prepared to rely on tacit understandings. But there was also an implied warning in Deng's last sentence. If it was not possible to define or implement parallel interests, the relationship would turn "empty," that is to say, would wither, and China would presumably return to Mao's Three Worlds concept—which was still official policy—to enable China to navigate between the superpowers.

The parallel interests, in Deng's view, would express themselves in an informal global arrangement to contain the Soviet Union in Asia by political/military cooperation with parallel objectives to NATO in Europe. It was to be less structured and depended largely on the bilateral Sino-U.S. political relationship. It was also based on a different geopolitical doctrine. NATO sought to unite its partners, above all, in resistance against actual Soviet aggression. It demonstratively avoided any concept of military preemption. Concerned with avoiding diplomatic confrontation, the strategic doctrine of NATO has been exclusively defensive.

What Deng was proposing was an essentially preemptive policy; it was an aspect of China's offensive deterrence doctrine. The Soviet Union was to be pressured along its entire periphery and especially in regions to which it had extended its presence only recently, notably in Southeast Asia and even in Africa. If necessary, China would be prepared to initiate military action to thwart Soviet designs—especially in Southeast Asia.

The Soviet Union would never be bound by agreements, Deng warned; it understood only the language of countervailing force. The Roman statesman Cato the Elder is reputed to have ended all his speeches with the clarion call *"Carthago delenda est"* ("Carthage must be destroyed"). Deng had his own trademark exhortation: that the Soviet Union must be resisted. He included in all his presentations some variation on the admonition that Moscow's unchanging nature was to "squeeze in wherever there is an opening,"[38] and that, as Deng told President Carter, "[w]herever the Soviet Union sticks its fingers, there we must chop them off."[39]

Deng's analysis of the strategic situation included a notification to the White House that China intended to go to war with Vietnam because it had concluded that Vietnam would not stop at Cambodia. "[T]he so-called Indochinese Federation is to include more than three states," Deng warned. "Ho Chi Minh cherished this idea. The three states is only the first step. Then Thailand is to be included."[40] China had an obligation to act, Deng declared. It could not await developments; once they had occurred, it would be too late.

Deng told Carter that he had considered the "worst possibility"—massive Soviet intervention, as the new Moscow-Hanoi defense treaty seemingly required. Indeed, reports indicated that Beijing had evacuated up to 300,000 civilians from its northern border territories and put its forces along the Sino-Soviet border on maximum alert.[41] But, Deng told Carter, Beijing judged that a brief, limited war would not give Moscow time for "a large reaction" and that winter conditions would make a full-scale Soviet attack on northern China difficult. China was "not afraid," Deng stated, but it needed Washington's "moral support,"[42] by which he meant sufficient ambiguity about American designs to give the Soviets pause.

A month after the war, Hua Guofeng explained to me the careful strategic analysis that had preceded it:

> We also considered this possibility of a Soviet reaction. The first possibility was a major attack on us. That we considered a low possibility. A million troops are along the border, but for a major attack on China, that is not enough. If they took back some of the troops from Europe, it would take time and they would worry about Europe. They know a battle with China would be a major matter and could not be concluded in a short period of time.

Deng confronted Carter with a challenge to both principle and public attitude. In principle, Carter did not approve preemptive strategies, especially since they involved military movements across sovereign borders. At the same time, he took seriously, even when he did not fully share, National Security Advisor Zbigniew Brzezinski's view of the strategic implications of the Vietnamese occupation of Cambodia, which was parallel to Deng's. Carter resolved his dilemma by invoking principle but leaving scope for adjustment to circumstance. Mild disapproval shaded into vague, tacit endorsement. He called attention to the favorable moral position that Beijing would forfeit by attacking Vietnam. China, now widely considered a peaceful country, would run the risk of being accused of aggression:

> This is a serious issue. Not only do you face a military threat from the North, but also a change in international attitude. China is now seen as a peaceful country that is against aggression. The ASEAN countries, as well as the UN, have condemned the Soviet Union, Vietnam, and Cuba. I do not need to know the punitive action being contemplated, but it could result in escalation of violence and a change in the world posture from being against Vietnam to partial support for Vietnam.
>
> It would be difficult for us to encourage violence. We can give you intelligence briefings. We know of no recent movements of Soviet troops towards your borders.
>
> I have no other answer for you. We have joined in the condemnation of Vietnam, but invasion of Vietnam would be [a] very serious destabilizing action.[43]

To refuse to endorse violence but to offer intelligence about Soviet troop movements was to give a new dimension to ambivalence. It might mean that Carter did not share Deng's view of an underlying Soviet threat. Or, by reducing Chinese fears of a possible Soviet reaction, it might be construed as an encouragement to invasion.

The next day, Carter and Deng met alone, and Carter handed Deng a note (as yet unpublished) summarizing the American position. According to Brzezinski: "The President himself drafted by hand a letter to Deng, moderate in tone and sober in content, stressing the importance of restraint and summarizing the likely adverse international consequences. I felt that this was the right approach, for we could not collude formally with the Chinese in sponsoring what was tantamount to overt military aggression."[44] Informal collusion was another matter.

According to a memorandum recounting the private conversation (at which only an interpreter was present), Deng insisted that strategic analysis overrode Carter's invocation of world opinion. Above all,

China must not be thought of as pliable: "China must still teach Vietnam a lesson. The Soviet Union can use Cuba, Vietnam, and then Afghanistan will evolve into a proxy [for the Soviet Union]. The PRC is approaching this issue from a position of strength. The action will be very limited. If Vietnam thought the PRC soft, the situation will get worse."[45]

Deng left the United States on February 4, 1979. On his return trip from the United States, he completed placing the last *wei qi* piece on the board. He stopped off in Tokyo for the second time in six months, to assure himself of Japanese support for the imminent military action and to isolate the Soviet Union further. To Prime Minister Masayoshi Ohira, Deng reiterated China's position that Vietnam had to be "punished" for its invasion of Cambodia, and he pledged: "To uphold the long-term prospects of international peace and stability . . . [the Chinese people] will firmly fulfill our internationalist duties, and will not hesitate to even bear the necessary sacrifices."[46]

After having visited Burma, Nepal, Thailand, Malaysia, Singapore, Japan twice, and the United States, Deng had accomplished his objective of drawing China into the world and isolating Hanoi. He never left China again, adopting in his last years the remoteness and inaccessibility of traditional Chinese rulers.

The Third Vietnam War

On February 17, China mounted a multipronged invasion of northern Vietnam from southern China's Guangxi and Yunnan provinces. The size of the Chinese force reflected the importance China attached to the operation; it has been estimated to have numbered more than 200,000 and perhaps as many as 400,000 PLA soldiers.[47] One historian has concluded that the invasion force, which included "regular ground forces, militia, and naval and air force units . . . was similar in scale to the assault with which China made such an impact on its entry into the

Korean War in November 1950."[48] The official Chinese press accounts called it the "Self-Defensive Counterattack Against Vietnam" or the "Counterattack in Self-Defense on the Sino-Vietnamese Border." It represented the Chinese version of deterrence, an invasion advertised in advance to forestall the next Vietnamese move.

The target of China's military was a fellow Communist country, recent ally, and longtime beneficiary of Chinese economic and military support. The goal was to preserve the strategic equilibrium in Asia, as China saw it. Further, China undertook the campaign with the moral support, diplomatic backing, and intelligence cooperation of the United States—the same "imperialist power" that Beijing had helped eject from Indochina five years earlier.

The stated Chinese war aim was to "put a restraint on the wild ambitions of the Vietnamese and to give them an appropriate limited lesson."[49] "Appropriate" meant to inflict sufficient damage to affect Vietnamese options and calculations for the future; "limited" implied that it would be ended before outside intervention or other factors drove it out of control. It was also a direct challenge to the Soviet Union.

Deng's prediction that the Soviet Union would not attack China was borne out. The day after China launched its invasion, the Soviet government released a lukewarm statement that, while condemning China's "criminal" attack, emphasized that "the heroic Vietnamese people . . . is capable of standing up for itself this time again[.]"[50] The Soviet military response was limited to sending a naval task force to the South China Sea, undertaking a limited arms airlift to Hanoi, and stepping up air patrols along the Sino-Soviet border. The airlift was constrained by geography but also by internal hesitations. In the end, the Soviet Union gave as much support in 1979 to its new ally, Vietnam, as it had extended twenty years earlier to its then ally, China, in the Taiwan Strait Crises. In neither case would the Soviet Union run any risks of a wider war.

Shortly after the war, Hua Guofeng summed up the outcome in a pithy phrase contemptuous of Soviet leaders: "As for threatening us, they did that by maneuvers near the border, sending ships to the South China Sea. But they did not dare to move. So after all we could still touch the buttocks of the tiger."

Deng sarcastically rejected American advice to be careful. During a late February 1979 visit of Treasury Secretary Michael Blumenthal to Beijing, Blumenthal called for Chinese troops to withdraw from Vietnam "as quickly as possible" because Beijing "ran risks that were unwarranted."[51] Deng demurred. Speaking to American reporters just before his meeting with Blumenthal, Deng displayed his disdain for equivocation, mocking "some people" who were "afraid of offending" the "Cuba of the Orient."[52]

As in the Sino-Indian War, China executed a limited "punitive" strike followed immediately by a retreat. It was over in twenty-nine days. Shortly after the PLA captured (and reportedly laid waste to) the capitals of the three Vietnamese provinces along the border, Beijing announced that Chinese forces would withdraw from Vietnam, save for several disputed pieces of territory. Beijing made no attempt to overthrow the Hanoi government or to enter Cambodia in any overt capacity.

A month after the Chinese troops had withdrawn, Deng explained the Chinese strategy to me on a visit to Beijing:

> DENG: After I came back [from the United States], we immediately fought a war. But we asked you for your opinion beforehand. I talked it over with President Carter and then he replied in a very formal and solemn way. He read a written text to me. I said to him: China will handle this question independently and if there is any risk, China will take on the risk alone. In retrospect, we think if we had driven deeper into Vietnam in our punitive action, it would have been even better.

KISSINGER: It could be.

DENG: Because our forces were sufficient to drive all the way to Hanoi. But it wouldn't be advisable to go that far.

KISSINGER: No, it would probably have gone beyond the limits of calculation.

DENG: Yes, you're right. But we could have driven 30 kilometers deeper into Vietnam. We occupied all the defensive areas of fortification. There wasn't a defense line left all the way to Hanoi.

The conventional wisdom among historians is that the war was a costly Chinese failure.[53] The effects of the PLA's politicization during the Cultural Revolution became apparent during the campaign: hampered by outdated equipment, logistical problems, personnel shortages, and inflexible tactics, Chinese forces advanced slowly and at great cost. By some analysts' estimates, the PLA suffered as many killed in action in one month of fighting the Third Vietnam War as the United States suffered in the most costly years of the second one.[54]

Conventional wisdom is based, however, on a misapprehension of the Chinese strategy. Whatever the shortcomings of its execution, the Chinese campaign reflected a serious long-term strategic analysis. In the Chinese leadership's explanations to their American counterparts, they described the consolidation of Soviet-backed Vietnamese power in Indochina as a crucial step in the Soviet Union's worldwide "strategic deployment." The Soviet Union had already concentrated troops in Eastern Europe and along China's northern border. Now, the Chinese leaders warned, Moscow was "beginning to get bases" in Indochina, Africa, and the Middle East.[55] If it consolidated its position in these areas, it would control vital energy resources and be able to block key sea lanes—most notably the Malacca Strait connecting the Pacific Ocean and the Indian Ocean. This would give Moscow the strategic initiative in any future conflict. In a broader sense, the war resulted from Beijing's analysis of Sun Tzu's concept of *shi*—the trend and "potential energy" of the strategic landscape. Deng aimed to arrest and, if possible, reverse what he saw as an unacceptable momentum of Soviet strategy.

China achieved this objective in part by its military daring, in part by drawing the United States into unprecedentedly close cooperation. China's leaders had navigated the Third Vietnam War by meticulous analysis of their strategic choices, daring execution, and skillful diplomacy. With all these qualities, they would not have been able to "touch the buttocks of the tiger" but for the cooperation of the United States.

The Third Vietnam War ushered in the closest collaboration between China and the United States for the period of the Cold War. Two trips to China by American emissaries established an extraordinary degree of joint action. Vice President Walter "Fritz" Mondale visited China in August 1979 to devise a diplomacy for the aftermath of the Deng visit, especially with respect to Indochina. It was a complex problem in which strategic and moral considerations were in severe conflict. The United States and China agreed that it was in each country's national interest to prevent the emergence of an Indochinese Federation under Hanoi's control. But the only part of Indochina that was still contested was Cambodia, which had been governed by the execrable Pol Pot, who had murdered millions of his compatriots. The Khmer Rouge constituted the best organized element of Cambodia's anti-Vietnam resistance.

Carter and Mondale took a long and dedicated record of devotion to human rights into government; indeed they had, in their presidential campaign, attacked Ford on the ground of insufficient attention to the issue of human rights.

Deng had first raised the issue of aid to the Cambodian guerrilla resistance against the Vietnamese invaders during the private conversation with Carter about the invasion of Vietnam. According to the official report: "The President asked if the Thais could accept and relay it to the Cambodians. Deng said yes and that he has in mind light weapons. The Thais are now sending a senior officer to the Thai-Cambodian border to keep communications more secure."[56] The de facto cooperation between Washington and Beijing on aid to Cambodia through Thailand had the practical effect of indirectly assisting the remnants of the Khmer Rouge. American officials were careful to stress to Beijing that the United States "cannot support Pol Pot" and welcomed China's assurances that Pol Pot no longer exercised full control over the Khmer Rouge. This sop to conscience did not change the reality that Washington provided material and diplomatic support to the "Cambodian resistance" in a manner that the administration must have known would benefit the Khmer Rouge. Carter's successors in Ronald Reagan's administration followed the same strategy. America's leaders undoubtedly expected that if the Cambodian resistance prevailed, they or their successors would oppose the Khmer Rouge element of it in the aftermath—which is what in effect happened after the Vietnamese withdrawal over a decade later.

American ideals had encountered the imperatives of geopolitical reality. It was not cynicism, even less hypocrisy, that forged this attitude: the Carter administration had to choose between strategic necessities and moral conviction. They decided that for their moral convictions to be implemented ultimately they needed first to prevail in the geopolitical struggle. The American leaders faced the dilemma of statesmanship. Leaders cannot choose the options history affords them, even less that they be unambiguous.

The visit of Secretary of Defense Harold Brown marked a further step toward Sino-American cooperation unimaginable only a few years earlier. Deng welcomed him: "Your coming here itself is of major significance," he noted to Brown, "because you are the Secretary of Defense."[57] A few veterans of the Ford administration understood this hint about the invitation to Secretary Schlesinger, aborted when Ford dismissed him.

The main agenda was to define the United States' military relationship with China. The Carter administration had come to the conclusion that an increase in China's technological and military capacity was important for global equilibrium and American national security. Washington had "drawn a distinction between the Soviet Union and China," Secretary Brown explained, and was willing to transfer some military technology to China that it would not make available to the Soviets.[58] Further, the United States was willing to sell "military equipment" to China (such as surveillance equipment and vehicles), though not "arms." It would not, moreover, interfere in decisions by NATO allies to sell arms to China. As President Carter explained in his instructions to Brzezinski:

> [T]he United States does not object to the more forthcoming attitude which our allies are adopting in regard to trade with China in technology-sensitive areas. We have an interest in a strong and secure China—and we recognize and respect this interest.[59]

In the end, China was not able to rescue the Khmer Rouge or force Hanoi to withdraw its troops from Cambodia for another decade; perhaps recognizing this, Beijing framed its war aims in much more limited terms. However, Beijing did impose heavy costs on Vietnam. Chinese diplomacy in Southeast Asia before, during, and after the war worked with great determination and skill to isolate Hanoi. China maintained a heavy military presence along the border, retained several disputed pieces of territory, and continued to hold out the threat of a "second lesson" to Hanoi. For years afterward, Vietnam was forced to support considerable forces on its northern border to defend against another possible Chinese attack.[60] As Deng had told Mondale in August 1979:

> For a country of that size to keep a standing force of more than one million, where will you find enough work force? A standing force of one million needs a lot of logistical support. Now they depend on the Soviet Union. Some estimates say they are getting $2 million a day from the Soviet Union, some estimates say $2½ million. . . . [I]t will increase difficulties, and this burden on the Soviet Union will grow heavier and heavier. Things will become more difficult. In time the Vietnamese will come to realize that not all their requests to the Soviet Union can be met. In those circumstances perhaps a new situation will emerge.[61]

That situation did, in fact, occur over a decade later when the collapse of the Soviet Union and of Soviet financial support brought about a retrenchment in Vietnamese deployment in Cambodia. Ultimately over a time period more difficult to sustain for democratic societies, China achieved a considerable part of its strategic objectives in Southeast Asia. Deng achieved sufficient maneuvering room to meet his objective of thwarting Soviet domination of Southeast Asia and the Malacca Strait.

The Carter administration performed a tightrope act that maintained an option toward the Soviet Union via negotiations over the limitations of strategic arms while basing its Asian policy on the recognition that Moscow remained the principal strategic adversary.

The ultimate loser in the conflict was the Soviet Union, whose global ambitions had caused alarm around the world. A Soviet ally had been attacked by the Soviet Union's most vocal and strategically most explicit adversary, which was openly agitating for a containment alliance against Moscow—all this within a month of the conclusion of the Soviet-Vietnamese alliance. In retrospect, Moscow's relative passivity in the Third Vietnam War can be seen as the first symptom of the decline of the Soviet Union. One wonders whether the Soviets' decision a year later to intervene in Afghanistan was prompted in part by an attempt to compensate for their ineffectuality in supporting Vietnam against the Chinese attack. In either case, the Soviets' miscalculation in both situations was in not realizing the extent to which the correlation of global forces had shifted against them. The Third Vietnam War may thus be counted as another example in which Chinese statesmen succeeded in achieving long-term, big-picture strategic objectives without the benefit of a military establishment comparable to that of their adversaries. Though providing breathing space for the remnants of the Khmer Rouge can hardly be counted as a moral victory, China achieved its larger geopolitical aims vis-à-vis the Soviet Union and Vietnam—both of whose militaries were better trained and equipped than China's.

Equanimity in the face of materially superior forces has been deeply ingrained in Chinese strategic thinking—as is apparent from the parallels with China's decision to intervene in the Korean War. Both Chinese decisions were directed against what Beijing perceived to be a gathering danger—a hostile power's consolidation of bases at multiple points along the Chinese periphery. In both cases, Beijing believed that if the hostile power were allowed to complete its design, China would be encircled and thus remain in a permanent state of vulnerability. The adversary would be in a position to launch a war at a time of its choosing, and knowledge of this advantage would allow it to act, as Hua Guofeng told President Carter when they met in Tokyo, "without scruples."[62] Therefore, a seemingly regional issue—in the first case the American rebuff of North Korea, in the second case Vietnam's occupation of Cambodia—was treated as "the focus of the struggles in the world" (as Zhou described Korea).[63]

Both interventions set China against a stronger power that threatened its perception of its security; each, however, did so on terrain and at a time of Beijing's choosing. As Vice Premier Geng Biao later told Brzezinski: "The Soviet Union's support for Vietnam is a component of its global strategy. It is directed not just at Thailand, but at Malaysia, Singapore, Indonesia, and the Straits of Malacca. If they succeeded, it would be a fatal blow to ASEAN and would also interdict the lines of communications for Japan and the United States. We are committed to do something about this. We may have no capability to cope with the Soviet Union, but we have the capability to cope with Vietnam."[64]

These were not elegant affairs: China threw troops into immensely costly battles and sustained casualties on a scale that would have been unacceptable in the Western world. In the Sino-Vietnam War, the PLA seems to have pursued its task with many shortcomings, significantly increasing the scale of Chinese losses. But both interventions achieved noteworthy strategic goals. At two key moments in the Cold War, Beijing applied its doctrine of offensive deterrence successfully. In Vietnam, China succeeded in exposing the limits of the Soviet defense commitment to Hanoi and, more important, of its overall strategic reach. China was willing to risk war with the Soviet Union to prove that it refused to be intimidated by the Soviet presence on its southern flank.

Singapore's Prime Minister Lee Kuan Yew has summed up the ultimate result of the war: "The Western press wrote off the Chinese punitive action as a failure. I believe it changed the history of East Asia."[65]

CHAPTER 14

Reagan and the Advent of Normalcy

ONE OF THE obstacles to continuity in America's foreign policy is the sweeping nature of its periodic changes of government. As a result of term limits, every presidential appointment down to the level of Deputy Assistant Secretary is replaced at least every eight years—a change of personnel involving as many as five thousand key positions. The successors have to undergo a prolonged vetting process. In practice, a vacuum exists for the first nine months or so of the incoming administration, in which it is obliged to act by improvisation or on the recommendations of holdover personnel, as it gradually adjusts to exercising its own authority. The inevitable learning period is complicated by the desire of the new administration to legitimize its rise to office by alleging that all inherited problems are the policy faults of its predecessor and not inherent problems; they are deemed soluble and in a finite time. Continuity of policy becomes a secondary consideration if not an invidious claim. Since new Presidents have just won an election campaign, they may also overestimate the range of flexibility that objective circumstances permit or rely excessively on their persuasive power. For countries relying on American policy, the perpetual psychodrama of democratic transitions is a constant invitation to hedge their bets.

These tendencies were a special challenge to the relationship with China. As these pages show, the early years of rapprochement between the United States and the People's Republic of China involved a period of mutual discovery. But later decades depended importantly on the two countries' ability to develop parallel assessments of the international situation.

Harmonizing intangibles becomes especially difficult when leadership is in constant flux. And both China and the United States witnessed dramatic leadership changes in the decade of the 1970s. The Chinese transitions have been described in earlier chapters. In the United States, the President who opened relations with China resigned eighteen months later, but the key foreign policy remained in place.

The Carter administration represented the first change in political parties for the Chinese leadership. They had observed statements by Carter as a candidate promising a transformation of American foreign policy to embrace a new openness and emphasis on human rights. He had said little about China. There was some concern in Beijing whether Carter would maintain the "anti-hegemony" dimension of the established relationship.

As it turned out, Carter and his top advisors reaffirmed the basic principles of the relationship—including those with respect to Taiwan personally affirmed by Nixon during his visit to Beijing. At the same time, the advent of Deng and the collapse of the Gang of Four gave the dialogue between China and the United States a new pragmatic dimension.

The most intense strategic dialogue between the United States and China had barely been established when another change of administrations brought in a new Republican President with a landslide win. For China, the new President was an unsettling prospect. Ronald Reagan was difficult to analyze even for China's meticulous researchers. He did not fit any established category. A former movie star and president of the Screen Actors Guild who had willed himself to political prominence, Reagan represented a dramatically different kind of American conservatism than the withdrawn and cerebral Nixon or the serene

Midwestern Ford. Defiantly optimistic about American possibilities in a period of crisis, Ronald Reagan, more than any high American official since John Foster Dulles, attacked Communism as an evil to be eradicated within a finite period of time, not a threat to be contained over generations. Yet he focused his critique of Communism almost entirely on the Soviet Union and its satellite states. In 1976, Reagan had campaigned against Gerald Ford for the Republican presidential nomination by attacking the détente policy with the Soviet Union, but had, on the whole, avoided criticizing the rapprochement with China. Reagan's critique of Soviet intentions—which he continued with renewed vigor in the 1980 campaign—had much in common with the lectures Deng had been delivering to top American officials since his first return from exile. Yet in Reagan's case, it was paired with a strong personal attachment to the prevailing political order in Taiwan.

In October 1971, Nixon had encouraged Reagan, then Governor of California, to visit Taiwan as a special emissary to affirm that the improvement of relations between Washington and Beijing had not altered the basic American interest in Taiwan's security. Reagan left the island with warm personal feelings toward its leaders and a profound commitment to the relationship of the peoples of America and Taiwan. Subsequently, while Reagan stopped short of challenging the existing understanding with Beijing, he was highly critical of the Carter administration's move to sever formal diplomatic ties with Taipei and downgrade the American Embassy in Taiwan to an unofficial "American Institute." In his 1980 presidential campaign against Carter, he pledged that under a Reagan administration there would be "no more Vietnams," "no more Taiwans," and "no more betrayals."

Technically, the embassy in Taipei had been the American Embassy to *China*; the American decision, culminated under the Carter administration, to relocate this embassy to Beijing was a belated recognition that the Nationalists were no longer poised to "recover the mainland." Reagan's implicit critique was that the United States should have retained a full embassy in Taipei as part of a two China solution recognizing both sides of the Taiwan Strait as separate independent states. Yet in its negotiations with the Nixon, Ford, and Carter administrations (and with all other governments negotiating the terms of diplomatic recognition), this was the one outcome that Beijing consistently and adamantly refused to consider.

Ronald Reagan thus embodied the existing American ambivalence. A powerful commitment to the new relationship with Beijing coexisted with a strong residue of emotional support for Taiwan.

One of Reagan's themes was to advocate "official relations" with Taiwan, though he never explained publicly exactly what this meant. During the 1980 presidential campaign, Reagan decided to try to square the circle. He sent his vice presidential candidate, George H. W. Bush, to Beijing, where he had served with distinction as head of the U.S. Liaison Office, which functioned in lieu of an embassy. Bush told Deng that Reagan did not mean to imply that he endorsed formal diplomatic relations with Taiwan; nor did Reagan intend to move toward a two China solution.[1] Deng's frosty reply—surely not unaffected by the fact that Reagan repeated his advocacy of formal relations with Taiwan while Bush was in Beijing—induced Reagan to ask me, in September 1980, to serve as an intermediary in delivering a similar, somewhat more detailed, message on his behalf to the Chinese ambassador, Chai Zemin. It was a tall order.

Meeting with Chai in Washington, I affirmed that, despite his campaign rhetoric, candidate Reagan intended to uphold the general principles of U.S.-Chinese strategic cooperation established during the Nixon, Ford, and Carter administrations and outlined in the Shanghai Communiqué and the 1979 communiqué announcing normalization of diplomatic relations. Specifically, Reagan had asked me to convey that he would not pursue a two China policy, or a "one China, one Taiwan" policy. I added that I was sure that the ambassador and his government had studied Governor Reagan's career, and that in doing so they would have noted that he had many close friends on Taiwan. Attempting to put this in a human context, I argued that Reagan could not abandon personal friendships and that Chinese leaders would lose respect for him if he did so. As President, however, Reagan would be committed to the existing framework of U.S.–People's Republic relations, which provided a basis for shared Chinese and American efforts to prevent "hegemony" (that is, Soviet dominance). In other words, Reagan, as President, would stand by his friends but also by America's commitments.

It cannot be said that the Chinese ambassador received this information with unrelieved enthusiasm. Conscious of the favorable public opinion polls projecting Reagan's victory in November, he took no chances in expressing an opinion.

Taiwan Arms Sales and the Third Communiqué

The early phase of the Reagan administration was marked by its chief's faith that his persuasiveness could bridge the gap between two, on the face, incompatible positions. In practice, it meant that both positions were carried out simultaneously. The issue had some urgency because normalization had taken precedence over resolving a final legal status for Taiwan. Carter had stated that America intended to continue to supply arms to Taiwan. Deng, eager to complete the normalization process so that he could confront Vietnam with at least the appearance of American support, proceeded with normalization, in effect ignoring Carter's unilateral statement on arms supply. In the meantime, in 1979 the U.S. Congress had responded to the winding down of the official American diplomatic presence in Taipei by passing the Taiwan Relations Act. This legislation outlined a framework for continued robust economic, cultural, and security ties between the United States and Taiwan, and declared that the United States "will make available to Taiwan such defense articles and defense services in such quantity as may be necessary to enable it to maintain a sufficient self-defense capacity."[2] As soon as the Reagan administration took office, Chinese leaders raised the Taiwan arms issue again, treating it as an unfinished aspect of normalization and bringing to a head the American internal contradictions. Reagan made no secret of his wish that some arms sales to Taiwan go forward. His Secretary of State, Alexander Haig, had a contrary view. Haig had been my deputy on the Nixon White House staff that planned the secret visit in 1971. He had led the technical team that advanced Nixon's visit, during which he had a substantive conversation with Zhou. As a member of the generation that had experienced the start of the Cold War, Haig was keenly aware of how the addition of China to the anti-Soviet camp altered the strategic equilibrium. Haig treated the potential role of China as a de facto American ally as a breakthrough to be preserved as a top priority. As a result, Haig sought for ways to come to an understanding with Beijing whereby the United States would supply arms to both China and Taiwan.

That scheme foundered on both sides. Reagan would not agree to formal arms sales to China, and Beijing would not consider a deal that implied a trade of principle for military hardware. Matters threatened to get out of hand. Haig, conducting arduous negotiations both within the U.S. government and with his counterparts in Beijing, achieved an agreement that permitted both sides to postpone a final resolution, while establishing a roadmap for the future. That Deng acquiesced in so indefinite and partial an outcome demonstrates the importance he attached to maintaining close relations with the United States (as well as his confidence in Haig).

The so-called Third Communiqué of August 17, 1982, has become part of the basic architecture of the U.S.-China relationship, regularly reaffirmed as part of the sacramental language of subsequent high-level dialogues and joint communiqués. It is odd that the Third

Communiqué should have achieved such a status together with the Shanghai Communiqué of Nixon's visit and the normalization agreement of the Carter period. For the communiqué is quite ambiguous, hence a difficult roadmap for the future.

Each side, as before, restated its basic principles: China affirmed its position that Taiwan was a domestic Chinese affair in which foreigners had no legitimate role; America restated its concern for a peaceful resolution, going so far as to claim that it "appreciates the Chinese policy of striving for a peaceful resolution." This formulation evaded the consistent and frequently repeated Chinese assertion that it reserved its freedom of action to use force if a peaceful resolution proved unfeasible. The key operative paragraph concerned arms sales to Taiwan. It read:

> [T]he United States Government states that it does not seek to carry out a long-term policy of arms sales to Taiwan, that its arms sales to Taiwan will not exceed, either in qualitative or in quantitative terms, the level of those supplied in recent years since the establishment of diplomatic relations between the United States and China, and that it intends to reduce gradually its sales of arms to Taiwan, leading over a period of time to a final resolution. In so stating, the United States acknowledges China's consistent position regarding the thorough settlement of this issue.[3]

None of these terms was precisely defined—or, for that matter, defined at all. What was meant by "gradually" was left open; nor was the "level" reached in the Carter period, which was to be the benchmark, ever specified. While the United States abjured a policy of long-term arms sales, it gave no indication of what it understood by "long-term." While China reaffirmed its insistence on a final settlement, it established no deadline and submitted no threat. Domestic imperatives on both sides dictated the limits: China would not accept the principle of a foreign arms supplier on what it considered its own territory. American politics, underscored by the passage of the Taiwan Relations Act by wide margins in the U.S. Congress, did not permit any cutoff of arms for Taiwan. It is a tribute to the statesmanship on both sides that this state of affairs has been continued for nearly thirty years since the events discussed in these pages.

The immediate aftermath of the Third Communiqué showed that its meaning was not self-evident to the President of the United States. He told the publisher of the *National Review*: "You can tell your friends there I have not changed my mind one damn bit about Taiwan. Whatever weapons they need to defend themselves against attacks or invasion by Red China, they will get from the United States."[4] Reagan felt so strongly on this subject that he called Dan Rather, then the anchor on the *CBS Evening News,* to deny reports that he no longer backed Taiwan, declaring: "There has been no retreat by me. . . . We will continue to arm Taiwan."[5]

To carry out the President's conviction, the White House secretly negotiated the so-called Six Assurances with Taiwan to restrict the implementation of the communiqué it had just signed with China. The assurances affirmed that the United States had not set a specific date to end arms sales to Taiwan, had not committed to consulting with Beijing on such sales, had not committed to amend the Taiwan Relations Act, had not altered its position regarding Taiwan's political status, and would neither pressure Taipei to negotiate with Beijing nor serve as a mediator.[6] The assurances were reinforced by a memorandum placed in the files of the National Security Council that tied observance of the communiqué to the peaceful solution of the differences between the People's Republic and Taiwan. The administration also proceeded to give a liberal interpretation to the Third Communiqué's concept of "reducing" "arms sales" to Taiwan. Through technology transfers (technically not "arms sales") and an inventive interpretation of the "level" of various weapons programs, Washington extended a program of military support to Taiwan whose duration and substance Beijing seems not to have anticipated.

The Taiwan Relations Act, of course, binds the President; it has never been acknowledged by China's leaders, who do not accept the premise that American legislation can create an obligation with respect to arms sales to Taiwan or condition American diplomatic recognition on the peaceful resolution of the Taiwan issue. It would be dangerous to equate acquiescence to circumstance with agreement for the indefinite future. That a pattern of action has been accepted for a number of years does not obviate its long-term risks, as Beijing's heated reaction to the arms sale of the spring of 2010 demonstrates.

The Reagan administration's China and Taiwan policy during the first term was therefore a study in almost incomprehensible contradictions—between competing personalities, conflicting policy goals, contradictory assurances to Beijing and Taipei, and incommensurable moral and strategic imperatives. Reagan gave the impression of supporting all of them at once, all as a matter of deep conviction.

To the scholar or the traditional policy analyst, the Reagan administration's early approach to the People's Republic and Taiwan violated every ground rule of coherent policy. However, as with many other controversial and unconventional Reagan policies, it worked out quite well in the following decades.

The remarkable aspect of Reagan's presidency was his ability to blunt the edges of controversy even while affirming his own essentially unchanging convictions. Whatever his disagreements, Reagan never turned them into personal confrontations; nor did he transform his strong ideological convictions into crusades other than rhetorical. He was therefore in a position to reach across ideological gulfs on the basis of practicality and even goodwill—as Reagan and his subsequent Secretary of State George Shultz's remarkable series of negotiations with their Soviet counterparts Mikhail Gorbachev and Eduard

Shevardnadze over nuclear arms limitations would demonstrate. With respect to China, its leaders came to understand that Reagan had gone as far as his convictions permitted and to the utmost limit of what he was able to accomplish within the American political context. He would therefore gain credit for goodwill even while taking positions that would have been rejected—perhaps even indignantly—had they been put forward in a more formal setting or by a different President.

The seeming contradictions in the end established two timelines: what would be done immediately and what might be left to the future. Deng seems to have understood that the communiqué established a general direction. It could be traveled once conditions had altered the context that prevented it at the beginning of the Reagan administration.

After Shultz took over the State Department in 1982, despite some uncomfortable conversations and bruised egos, the United States, the People's Republic, and Taiwan all emerged from the early 1980s with their core interests generally fulfilled. Beijing was disappointed with Washington's flexible interpretation of the communiqué; but on the whole, the People's Republic achieved another decade of American assistance as it built its economic and military power and its capacity to play an independent role in world affairs. Washington was able to pursue amicable relations with both sides of the Taiwan Strait and to cooperate with China on common anti-Soviet imperatives, such as intelligence sharing and support for the Afghan insurgency. Taiwan obtained a bargaining position from which to negotiate with Beijing. When the dust eventually settled, the most vocally anti-Communist and pro-Taiwan President since Nixon had been able to preside over a "normal" relationship with the People's Republic of China without any major crisis.

China and the Superpowers—The New Equilibrium

The real drama of the 1980s was not in Washington's and Beijing's relations with each other, but in their respective relationships with Moscow. The impetus was a series of significant shifts in the strategic landscape.

In assessing China's policies, one contingency can generally be excluded: that Chinese policymakers overlooked a set of discoverable facts. So when China went along with the ambiguous language and the flexible interpretation of the Taiwan clause in the Third Communiqué, it can only have been because it thought cooperation with the United States would fulfill its other national purposes.

When Ronald Reagan came into office, the strategic offensive started by the Soviet Union in the late 1970s had not yet run its course. In the years since the collapse of the American position in Indochina, the Soviet Union and its proxies had embarked on an unprecedented (and nearly indiscriminate) series of advances in the developing world: in Angola, Ethiopia, Afghanistan, and Indochina. But the U.S.-China rapprochement had set up a significant bulwark against further expansion. Powered by the convictions of Deng and his colleagues and skillful cooperation by American officials of both political parties, the horizontal line Mao envisioned had, in fact, taken shape.

By the mid-1980s, the Soviet Union faced coordinated defense—and, in many cases, active resistance—on almost all of its borders. In the United States, Western Europe, and East Asia, a loose coalition of nearly all the industrial countries had formed against the Soviet Union. In the developed world, the Soviet Union's only remaining allies were the Eastern European satellites in which it stationed troops. Meanwhile, the developing world had proven skeptical about the benefits of popular "liberation" under Soviet and Cuban arms. In Africa, Asia, and Latin America, Soviet expansionist efforts were turning into costly stalemates or discredited failures. In Afghanistan, the Soviet Union experienced many of the same trials America had undergone in Vietnam—in this case, backed by coordinated efforts of the United States, China, the Gulf States, and Pakistan to sponsor and train an armed resistance. In Vietnam itself, Moscow's attempt to bring Indochina united under Hanoi into the Soviet orbit met a forceful rebuff from China, facilitated by American cooperation. Beijing and Washington were—as Deng had so vividly described it to Carter—"chopping off" Soviet fingers. At the same time, the American strategic buildup, especially the Strategic Defense Initiative championed by Reagan, posed a technological challenge that the stagnant and overburdened Soviet economy—already bearing a defense burden three times that of the United States as a percentage of each country's respective GDP—could not begin to meet.[7]

At this high point in Sino-American cooperation, the Reagan White House and the top Chinese leadership had roughly congruent assessments of Soviet weakness; but they drew significantly different conclusions about the policy implications of this new state of affairs. Reagan and his top officials perceived Soviet disarray as an opportunity to go on the offensive. Pairing a major military buildup with a new ideological assertiveness, they sought to pressure the Soviet Union both financially and geopolitically and drive for what amounted to victory in the Cold War.

The Chinese leaders had a similar conception of Soviet weakness, but they drew the opposite lesson: they saw it as an invitation to recalibrate the global equilibrium. Beginning in 1969, they had tacked toward Washington to redress China's precarious geopolitical position; they had no interest in the global triumph of American values and Western liberal democracy that Reagan proclaimed as his ultimate goal. Having "touched the buttocks of the tiger" in Vietnam, Beijing concluded that it had withstood the high point of the Soviet threat. It now behooved China to tack back toward an enhanced freedom of maneuver.

In the 1980s, therefore, the euphoria of the original opening had run its course; the overriding Cold War concerns of the recent past were being overcome. Sino-American relations settled into the sort of interactions major powers have with each other more or less routinely with fewer high points or troughs. The beginning of the decline of Soviet power played a role although the chief actors on both the American and the Chinese side had become so used to Cold War patterns that it took them a while to recognize it. The weak Soviet response to the Chinese invasion of Vietnam marked the beginning of an at first gradual, then accelerating, Soviet decline. The three transitions in Moscow—from Leonid Brezhnev to Yuri Andropov in 1982, from Andropov to Konstantin Chernenko in 1984, and from Chernenko to Mikhail Gorbachev in 1985—at a minimum signified that the Soviet Union would be preoccupied with its domestic crises. The American rearmament begun under Carter and accelerated under Reagan gradually altered the balance of power and constrained the Soviet readiness to intervene around its periphery.

Most of the Soviet gains of the 1970s were reversed—though several of these retreats did not take place until the George H. W. Bush administration. The Vietnamese occupation of Cambodia was ended in 1990, elections were held in 1993, and refugees prepared to return home; Cuban troops withdrew from Angola by 1991; the Communist-backed government in Ethiopia collapsed in 1991; in 1990, the Sandinistas in Nicaragua were brought to accept free elections, a risk no governing Communist Party had ever before been prepared to take; perhaps the most important, Soviet armies withdrew from Afghanistan in 1989.

Soviet retreats gave Chinese diplomacy a new flexibility to maneuver. Chinese leaders spoke less of military containment and began to explore their scope for a new diplomacy with Moscow. They continued to list three conditions for improving relations with the Soviets: evacuation of Cambodia; ending Soviet troop concentrations in Siberia and Mongolia along the northern Chinese border; and evacuation of Afghanistan. These demands were in the process of being fulfilled largely by changes in the balance of power that made Soviet forward positions untenable and the decisions to withdraw inevitable. The United States received reassurances that China was not ready to move toward Moscow—the Chinese proving that two sides could play at triangular diplomacy. The reassurances, in any event, had a dual purpose: they affirmed continued adherence to the established strategy of preventing Soviet expansion, but they also served to bring China's growing options before the United States.

China soon began to exercise its new options globally. In a conversation I had with Deng in September 1987, he applied the new framework of analysis to the Iran-Iraq War, then raging in its fifth year. The United States was backing Iraq—at least enough to prevent its being defeated by the revolutionary regime in Tehran. Deng argued that China needed "leeway" to take a more "flexible position" toward Iran so that it could play a more significant role in the diplomacy to end the war.

Deng had been carrying out Mao's horizontal line concept during the confrontation with the Soviet Union. It was now being transformed back into a Three Worlds approach in which China stood apart from superpower competition and in which adherence to an independent foreign policy would allow it to pursue its preferences in all three circles: the superpowers; the developed country circle; and the Third World.

Hu Yaobang, a Deng protégé and Party Secretary, outlined the prevailing Chinese foreign policy concept to the Communist Party's Twelfth National Congress in September 1982. Its key provision was a reprise of Mao's "China has stood up": "China never attaches itself to any big power or group of powers, and never yields to pressure from any big power."[8] Hu began with a tour d'horizon outlining China's critical assessment of American *and* Soviet foreign policies and a list of demands for actions by which each power could demonstrate its good faith. The failure to resolve the Taiwan issue meant that "a cloud has all along hung over the relations" between China and the United States. Relations would "develop soundly" only if the United States ceased interfering in what China regarded as its purely internal affair. Meanwhile, Hu commented loftily, "We note that Soviet leaders have expressed more than once the desire to improve relations with China. But deeds, rather than words, are important."[9]

China, for its part, was solidifying its position in the Third World, standing apart from and to some degree against both superpowers: "The main forces jeopardizing peaceful coexistence among nations today are imperialism, hegemonism and colonialism. . . . The most important task for the people of the world today is to oppose hegemonism and safeguard world peace."[10]

In effect, China claimed a unique moral stature as the largest of the "neutral" powers, standing above superpower contests:

> We have always firmly opposed the arms race between the superpowers, stood for the prohibition of the use of nuclear weapons and for their complete destruction and demanded that the superpowers be the first to cut their nuclear and conventional arsenals drastically. . . .
>
> China regards it as her sacred international duty to struggle resolutely against imperialism, hegemonism and colonialism together with the other third world countries.[11]

It was traditional Chinese foreign policy served up at a Communist Party Congress: self-reliance, moral aloofness, and superiority, coupled with a commitment to negate superpower aspirations.

A 1984 State Department memorandum sent to President Reagan explained that China had positioned itself

> both to support [the American] military buildup against Soviet expansionism and to attack superpower rivalry as the major cause of global tension. As a result, China is able to pursue parallel strategic interests with the US and, at the same time, to strengthen its relations with what it perceives to be an ascendant Third World bloc.[12]

In 1985 a CIA report described China as "maneuvering in the triangle" by cultivating closer ties with the Soviet Union through a series of high-level meetings and inter–Communist Party exchanges of a protocol level and frequency not seen since the Sino-Soviet split. The analysis noted that Chinese leaders had resumed referring to their Soviet counterparts as "comrade," and calling the Soviet Union a "socialist" (as opposed to "revisionist") country. Top Chinese and Soviet officials had held substantive consultations on arms control—an unthinkable concept in the previous two decades—and during a week-long 1985 visit by the Chinese Vice Premier Yao Yilin to Moscow, the two sides signed a landmark agreement on bilateral trade and economic cooperation.[13]

The notion of overlapping circles was more or less what Mao had been advancing toward the end of his life. But the practical consequence was limited. The Third World defined itself by its distinction from the two superpowers. It would lose this status if it shifted definitively to one side or another, even in the guise of admitting a superpower to its ranks. As a practical matter, China was on the way to becoming a superpower, and it was acting like one even now, when it was just beginning its reforms. The Third World, in short, would exercise major influence only if one of the superpowers joined, and then, by definition, it would stop being a Third World. So long as the Soviet Union was a nuclear superpower and relations with it were precarious, China would have no incentive to move away from the United States. (After the Soviet Union's collapse, there were only two circles left, and the question would be whether China would step into the place vacated by the Soviet Union as a challenger or opt for cooperation with the United States.) The Sino-American relationship of the 1980s was, in short, in transition from a Cold War pattern to a global international order that created new challenges for China-U.S. partnership. All this assumed that the Soviet Union remained the basic security threat.

The architect of the opening to China, Richard Nixon, understood the world in the same way. In a memorandum to President Reagan after a private visit to China in late 1982, Nixon wrote:

> I believe it is very much in our interest to encourage the Chinese to play a greater role in the third world. The more successful they are, the less successful the Soviet Union will be....
>
> What brought us together primarily in 1972 was our common concern about the threat of Soviet aggression. While that threat is far greater today than it was in 1972, the major unifying factor which will draw us closer together in the next decade could well be our economic interdependence.[14]

Nixon went on to urge that, for the next decade, the United States, its Western allies, and Japan should work jointly to speed the economic development of China. He had a vision of an entirely new international order emerging based essentially on using China's influence to build the Third World into an anti-Soviet coalition. But not even Nixon's prescience extended to a world in which the Soviet Union had collapsed and, within a generation, China would be in a position where much of the world's economic health depended on its economic performance. Or where the question would be raised whether China's rise would make international relations bipolar again.

George Shultz, Reagan's redoubtable Secretary of State and a trained economist, came up with another, American conception of concentric circles, which placed the Sino-U.S. relationship into a context beyond the Soviet-American conflict. He argued that overemphasis on China's indispensability for dealing with the Soviet threat gave China an excessive bargaining advantage.[15] Relations with it should be on the basis of strict reciprocity. In such a diplomacy, China would play its role for its own national reasons. Chinese goodwill should result from common projects in the joint interest. The purpose of China policy should be to elaborate these common interests. Simultaneously, the United States would seek to reinvigorate its alliance with Japan—the country in which Mao, a few years earlier, had urged American officials to "spend more time"—a fellow democracy, and now, after decades of rapid growth in the aftermath of the Second World War, a major global economic player. (Decades of intervening economic malaise have obscured the fact that in the 1980s Japan's economic capacity not only vastly outmatched China's, but was assumed by many analysts to be on the verge of surpassing that of the United States.) This relationship was given a new footing by the personal camaraderie that developed between Reagan and Japan's Prime Minister Yasuhiro Nakasone—or, as it came to be known in the media, the "Ron and Yasu show."

Both the United States and China were edging away from the previous alignment in which they saw themselves as strategic partners facing a common existential threat. Now that the Soviet menace had begun to recede, China and the United States were in effect partners of convenience on selected issues on which their interests aligned.

During the Reagan period, no fundamental new tensions developed, and inherited issues like Taiwan were handled undramatically. Reagan performed with characteristic vitality during a 1984 state visit to China—at several points even conjuring up phrases from classical Chinese poetry and the ancient divination manual the *I Ching* or *Book of Changes* to describe the cooperative relationship between the United States and China. Attempting more Mandarin Chinese than any of his predecessors, Reagan even invoked the Chinese idioms *"tong li he zuo"* ("connect strength, work together") and *"hu jing hu hui"* ("mutual respect, mutual benefit") to describe the U.S.-China relationship.[16] Yet Reagan never developed a record of close exchanges with any Chinese counterpart as he had with Nakasone—for that matter, no American President did with his Chinese counterpart—and his visit was given no major issues to settle and confined itself to a review of the world situation. When Reagan criticized a certain unnamed "major power" for massing troops on China's borders and threatening its neighbors, this portion of his speech was omitted from the Chinese broadcast.

As the Reagan years ended, the situation in Asia was the most tranquil it had been in decades. A half century of war and revolution in China, Japan, Korea, Indochina, and maritime Southeast Asia had given way to a system of Asian states on essentially Westphalian lines—following the pattern of sovereign states emerging in Europe at the end of the Thirty Years' War in 1648. With the exception of periodic provocations from the impoverished and isolated North Korea and the insurgency against the Soviet occupation in Afghanistan, Asia was now a world of discrete states with sovereign governments, recognized borders, and a nearly universal tacit agreement to refrain from involvement in each other's domestic political and ideological alignments. The project of exporting Communist revolution—taken up eagerly in turn by Chinese, North Korean, and North Vietnamese proponents—had drawn to a close. An equilibrium between the various centers of power had been preserved, in part due to the exhaustion of the parties and in part due to American (and subsequently Chinese) efforts to turn back various contestants for dominance. Within this context, a new era of Asian economic reform and prosperity was taking root—one that in the twenty-first century may well return the region to its historic role as the world's most productive and prosperous continent.

Deng's Reform Program

What Deng labeled "Reform and Opening Up" was not only an economic but also a spiritual endeavor. It involved, first, the stabilization of a society at the edge of economic collapse and, then, a search for the inner strength to advance by new methods for which there was no precedent in either Communist or Chinese history.

The economic situation inherited by Deng was close to desperate. China's collectivized agricultural structure was barely keeping pace with the needs of its massive population. Per capita food consumption was roughly the same as it had been in the early Mao period. One Chinese leader was reported to have admitted that 100 million Chinese peasants—the equivalent of nearly half the entire American population in 1980—went without sufficient food.[17] The closing of the school system during the Cultural Revolution had produced calamitous conditions. In 1982, 34 percent of China's workforce had only a primary school education, and 28 percent were considered "illiterates or semi-illiterates"; just 0.87 percent of China's workforce was college-educated.[18] Deng had called for a period of rapid economic growth; but he faced the challenge of how to transform an uneducated, isolated, and still largely impoverished general population into a workforce able to assume a productive and competitive role in the world economy and to withstand its occasional strains.

The traditional tools available to those undertaking the reform compounded the challenge. Deng's insistence on modernizing China by opening it to the outside world was the same kind of effort that had thwarted reformers since it was first attempted in the second half of the nineteenth century. Then the obstacle was the reluctance to abandon a way of life Chinese associated with what defined China's special identity. Now it was how to overturn the practices on which all Communist societies had been operating while maintaining the philosophical principles on which the cohesion of the society had been based since Mao's time.

At the beginning of the 1980s, central planning was still the operating mode of all Communist societies. Its failures were apparent, but remedies had proved elusive. In its advanced stage, Communism's incentives were all counterproductive, rewarding stagnation and discouraging initiative. In a centrally planned economy, goods and services are allocated by bureaucratic decision. Over a period of time, prices established by administrative fiat lose their relationship to costs. The pricing system becomes a means of extorting resources from the population and establishing political priorities. As terror by which authority was established eases, prices turn into subsidies and are transformed into a method of gaining public support for the Communist Party.

Reform Communism proved unable to abolish the laws of economics. Somebody had to pay for real costs. The penalty of central planning and subsidized pricing was poor maintenance, lack of innovation, and overemployment—in other words, stagnation and falling per capita income.

Central planning, moreover, provided few incentives to emphasize quality or innovation. Since all a manager produced would be bought by a relevant ministry, quality was not a consideration. And innovation was, in effect, discouraged lest it throw the whole planning edifice out of kilter.

In the absence of markets that balanced preferences, the planner was obliged to impose more or less arbitrary judgments. As a result, the goods that were wanted were not produced, and the goods that were produced were not wanted.

Above all, the centrally planned state, far from creating a classless society, ended up by enshrining class stratification. Where goods were allocated rather than bought, the real rewards were perquisites of office: special stores, hospitals, educational opportunities for cadres.

Enormous discretion in the hands of officials inevitably led to corruption. Jobs, education, and most perquisites depended on some kind of personal relationship. It is one of history's ironies that Communism, advertised as bringing a classless society, tended to breed a privileged class of feudal proportions. It proved impossible to run a modern economy by central planning, but no Communist state had ever been run without central planning.

Deng's Reform and Opening Up was designed to overcome this built-in stagnation. He and his associates embarked on market economics, decentralized decision making, and opening to the outside world—all unprecedented changes. They based their revolution on releasing the talents of the Chinese people, whose natural economic vitality and entrepreneurial spirit had long been constrained by war, ideological dogma, and severe strictures on private investment.

Deng had two principal collaborators on the reforms—Hu Yaobang and Zhao Ziyang—though he later fell out with both when they attempted to carry the principles of economic reform into the political field.

One of the youngest participants in the Long March, Hu Yaobang emerged as a Deng protégé and later fell with Deng in the Cultural Revolution; when Deng returned to power, he elevated Hu to some of the highest leadership posts in the Communist Party, culminating in his appointment as General Secretary. During his tenure, Hu was associated with relatively liberal stances on political and economic issues. With his forthright manner, he consistently pushed the limits of what his party and society were willing to accept. He was the first Communist Party leader to appear regularly in Western suits and provoked controversy by suggesting that Chinese abandon chopsticks for knives and forks.[19]

Zhao Ziyang, appointed Premier in 1980 and General Secretary of the Communist Party in January 1987, had pioneered agricultural decollectivization while Party Secretary in Sichuan. His success in producing a significant rise in living standards earned him the approbation of rural Chinese, as expressed in a pithy pun on his last name (a near homonym for the Chinese word "look for"): "If you want to eat grain, *Zhao* (look for) Ziyang." Like Hu Yaobang, he was politically unorthodox. He was ultimately removed as General Secretary by Deng at the height of the Tiananmen crisis.

Deng and his colleagues were impelled, above all, by the shared rejection of the Cultural Revolution. All the leaders who governed China had survived degradation, and many of them physical abuse. The experiences of the Cultural Revolution permeated the conversation of Chinese leaders. I had a wistful conversation with Deng in September 1982 when I was in China on a private visit:

KISSINGER: I met you in April 1974 when you came to the 6th Special [U.N. General] Assembly and then with Mao and you did not speak a word.

DENG: Then in November of 1974 [in Beijing] we were the two persons who talked the most because that time Zhou was sick and I was in charge of the State Council, and in 1975 I was in charge of the workings of the Party and the government. Only for one year I was struck down. When we look back to this period of history it was very interesting. It was such setbacks which enlightened us. . . . Our experience from 1979 to 1981 proved that our policies are correct. You have not been here for 3½ years. Do you see any changes?

KISSINGER: When I was here last time—it may be due to my ignorance—I had the sense that the Chairman of the Advisory Commission [Deng] had many opponents in high position. . . .

DENG: . . . People abroad often wonder if there is political stability in China. To judge if there is political stability in

> China one must see if there is stability in areas where 800 million Chinese live. Today the peasants are most happy. There are also some changes in the cities but not as much as in the countryside. . . . [People] have greater confidence in the socialist economic institutions and greater trust in the Party and government. This is of far reaching significance. Before the Cultural Revolution the Party and the government had high prestige but the prestige was destroyed in the Cultural Revolution.

There was little experience on which to draw for the reform effort. When I returned in 1987, Zhao Ziyang gave me an advance explanation of a program to be submitted to the Party Congress that October. He emphasized that China was on a complicated and very long course of meshing capitalism with socialism:

> A key question being addressed is how to rationalize the relationship between socialism and market forces. The report will state that planning for socialism should include use of market forces and not exclude them. Since [John Maynard] Keynes all countries, including capitalist ones, have practiced some degree of government interference in economic activities. The U.S. and South Korea are examples. Governments regulate either through planning or the market; China will use both methods. Enterprises will make full use of market forces and the State will guide the economy through macroeconomic policies. There also will be planning where necessary, but future regulation by planning will be one means and will not be viewed as the very nature of socialism.

In pursuing these objectives, Deng would move gradually. In Chinese terms, the leadership would "cross the river by feeling the stones," charting a path in part on the basis of what worked. Mao's continuous revolution was, in effect, jettisoned together with visions of utopian transformation. The Chinese leadership would not let ideology constrain their reforms; they would instead redefine "socialism with Chinese characteristics" so that "Chinese characteristics" were whatever brought greater prosperity to China.

To facilitate the process, China welcomed foreign investment, in part through Special Economic Zones on the coast, where enterprises were given wider latitude and investors were granted special conditions. Given China's previous negative experience with "foreign investors" on its coast in the nineteenth century—and the prominent role this experience played in the Chinese nationalist narrative—this was an act of considerable boldness. It also showed a willingness—to some degree unprecedented—to abandon the centuries-old vision of Chinese economic self-sufficiency by joining an international economic order. By 1980, the People's Republic of China had joined the IMF and the World Bank, and foreign loans were beginning to flow into the country.

Systematic decentralization followed. Agricultural communes were abandoned by encouraging the so-called responsibility centers, which, in practice, amounted to family farming. For other enterprises, a distinction was elaborated between ownership and management. Ownership would remain in the hands of the state; management would be left largely to managers. Agreements between the authorities and the managers would define the function of each, with substantial latitudes for managers.

The results of these changes were spectacular. Between 1978—the year the first economic reforms were promulgated—and 1984, the income of Chinese peasants doubled. The private sector, driven by the renewal of individual economic incentives, rose to constitute nearly 50 percent of the gross industrial output in an economy that had been ordered almost entirely by government fiat. China's Gross Domestic Product grew at an average rate of over 9 percent annually throughout the 1980s—an unprecedented and nearly uninterrupted period of economic growth that continues as of this writing.[20]

An effort of such scope depended, above all, on the quality of the officials charged with carrying out the reforms. This was the subject of an exchange with Deng in 1982. In response to my question as to whether the rejuvenation of personnel was moving in the desired direction, Deng replied:

> DENG: Yes. I think I can say so. But it is not over yet. We have to continue. The agricultural problem has not been solved. We have to be patient. Two years ago we put Premier Zhao Ziyang and Hu Yaobang in jobs of the first line. Perhaps you have noticed that 60% of the members of the Party Committee are below age 60 and many are about 40.
>
> KISSINGER: I have noticed this.
>
> DENG: This is not enough. We have to make arrangements for return of old comrades. That is how we set up the Advisory Commission. I recommended myself to be the Chairman of the Advisory Commission. It means that personally I want to gradually shake off the official positions and put myself in the position of advisor.
>
> KISSINGER: I have noticed some colleagues who are older than the Chairman and they have not joined the Advisory Commission.
>
> DENG: That is because our party is very old. And it is necessary to keep some old people in the first line. But this problem will be gradually solved.
>
> KISSINGER: I was told that the problem of the Cultural Revolution was that many people became cadres who did not have the same high level of education that is customary. Is that a problem and will you be able to deal with it?

DENG: Yes. Our criteria to select those to be responsible cadres are as follows: They must be revolutionaries. They must be younger. Better educated. Professionally competent. As I said, the 12th Party Congress has not only shown the continuity of the new policies but also insured continuity and the personnel arrangements have also assured continuity.

Five years later, Deng was still concerned with how to rejuvenate the Party. In September 1987, he gave me a preview of what he was planning for the upcoming Party Congress scheduled for October. Tanned, rested, and at eighty-three displaying undiminished vigor, Deng said that he would like to entitle the forthcoming congress "A Conference of Reform and Opening to the Outside World." Zhao Ziyang would be given the key position of General Secretary of the Communist Party, replacing Hu Yaobang and necessitating the selection of a new Premier. Hu Yaobang had "made some errors," Deng said—presumably in letting a set of 1986 student protests go too far—but he would remain in the Politburo (a distinction from previous periods when individuals removed from high office would also be removed from the policy process). No member of the Standing Committee (the executive committee of the Communist Party) would retain a dual position, speeding up the transition to the next generation of top officials. Other "senior people" would retire.

Deng would, he explained, now move from economic to political structural reforms. It would be much more complicated than economic reform because "it would involve the interests of millions of people." The divisions of work between the Communist Party and government would change. Many Party members would have to change jobs when professional managers took over for Party Secretaries.

But where was the line that separated policymaking from

administration? Deng replied that ideological issues would be for the Party, operational policy for managers. Asked for an example, Deng indicated that a shift of alliance toward the Soviet Union would be clearly an ideological issue. From my many conversations with him, I concluded that this would not be a frequent subject. On further reflection, I wonder whether by merely broaching such a previously unthinkable concept, Deng was not serving notice that China was weighing tacking back to greater freedom of diplomatic maneuver.

What Deng was proposing politically had no precedent in Communist experience. The Communist Party, he seemed to suggest, would maintain an overall supervisory role in the nation's economy and political structure. But it would steadily withdraw from its previous position of controlling the detailed aspects of Chinese daily life. The initiatives of individual Chinese would be given wide scope. These sweeping reforms, Deng maintained, would be carried out "in an orderly manner." China was stable now, and "must remain so if it is to develop." Its government and people "recall[ed] the chaos of the Cultural Revolution," and they would never allow it to recur. China's reforms were "unprecedented"; this would inevitably mean that "some mistakes will be made." The vast majority of people supported the current reforms, he said, but "courage" and "prudence" would be required to ensure their success.

As it turned out, these were not abstract issues: Deng would soon be forced to confront the tensions inherent in his program of "orderly" reform. While most of the world was marveling at the surging Chinese economic growth rate, the tens of thousands of students being sent abroad, and the changes in the standard of living inside the country, there emerged significant indications that new currents were churning within.

The early stages of the reform process tended to merge the problems of planning with those of the market. The attempt to make prices reflect real costs inevitably led to price increases, at least in the short term. Price reform caused a run on savings to buy up goods before prices went even higher, creating a vicious cycle of hoarding and greater inflation.

In a September 1987 meeting, Zhao Ziyang outlined a shift toward reliance on market forces for about 50 percent of GDP. Beyond the technical economic issues, this required a substantial recasting of the command system. There was to be greater emphasis, as in European states, on indirect control of the economy through manipulation of the money supply and intervention to forestall depression. Many central institutions in China would have to be dismantled and the functions of others redefined. To facilitate this process, a review of Party membership and a streamlining of the bureaucracy was ordered. Since this involved thirty million individuals and was carried out by the very people whose activities needed to be modified, the review faced many obstacles.

The relative success of economic reform produced constituencies at the core of the later discontent. And the government would face declining loyalty from the political cadres whose jobs the reforms threatened.

Administering a two-price system opened many avenues for corruption and nepotism. The shift to market economics actually increased opportunities for corruption, at least for an interim period. The fact that two economic sectors coexisted—a shrinking but still very large public sector and a growing market economy—produced two sets of prices. Unscrupulous bureaucrats and entrepreneurs were thus in a position to shift commodities back and forth between the two sectors for personal gain. Undoubtedly some of the profits in the private sector in China were the result of widespread graft and nepotism.

Nepotism is a special problem, in any event, in a culture as family-oriented as the Chinese. In times of turmoil, Chinese turn to their families. In all Chinese societies—whether it is mainland China,

Taiwan, Singapore, or Hong Kong—ultimate reliance is placed on family members, who in turn benefit in ways determined by family criteria rather than abstract market forces.

The marketplace created its own discontent. A market economy will, in time, enhance general well-being, but the essence of competition is that somebody wins and somebody loses. In the early stages of a market economy, the winnings are likely to be disproportionate. The losers are tempted to blame the "system" rather than their own failure. Often they are right.

On the popular level, economic reform had raised Chinese expectations about living standards and personal liberties, while at the same time creating tensions and inequities that many Chinese felt could only be redressed by a more open and participatory political system. The Chinese leadership was also increasingly divided about China's political and ideological course. The example of Gorbachev's reforms in the Soviet Union raised the stakes of the debate. To some in the Chinese leadership, *glasnost* and *perestroika* were dangerous heresies, akin to Khrushchev's throwing away the "sword of Stalin." To others, including many in China's younger generation of students and Party officials, Gorbachev's reforms were a possible model for China's own path.

The economic reforms overseen by Deng, Hu, and Zhao had transformed the face of Chinese daily life. At the same time, the reappearance of phenomena eradicated during the Mao years—income disparities, colorful and even provocative clothing, and an open celebration of "luxury" items—prompted traditional Communist cadres to complain that the People's Republic was succumbing to the dreaded "peaceful evolution" to capitalism once projected by John Foster Dulles.

While Chinese officials and intellectuals often framed this debate in terms of Marxist dogma—such as a high-profile campaign against the threat of "bourgeois liberalization"—the split ultimately went back to the questions that had divided China since the nineteenth century. By turning outward, was China fulfilling its destiny, or was it compromising its moral essence? What, if anything, should it aim to learn from Western social and political institutions?

In 1988, the debate crystallized around a seemingly esoteric television miniseries. Broadcast on Chinese Central Television, the six-part documentary *River Elegy* adopted the metaphor of China's turbid, slow-moving Yellow River to argue that Chinese civilization itself had grown insular and stagnant. Blending indictments of traditional Confucian culture with a veiled critique of more recent political developments, the film suggested that China needed to renew itself by looking outward to the "blue ocean" of the outside world, including Western culture. The series catalyzed a national debate, including discussion at the highest levels of China's government. Traditional Communists considered the film "counterrevolutionary" and succeeded in having it banned, albeit after it had first been broadcast.[21] The generations-long debate over China's destiny and its relationship with the West was active again.

CHAPTER 15

Tiananmen

CRACKS IN THE Soviet monolith began to emerge in Eastern Europe at the start of 1989, leading to the fall of the Berlin Wall in November and the eventual dissolution of the Soviet Union itself. But China seemed stable, and its relations with the rest of the world were the best since the Communist victory in 1949 and the proclamation of the People's Republic. Relations with the United States especially had made major progress. The two countries were cooperating in thwarting the Soviet occupation of Afghanistan; the United States was selling significant levels of arms to China; trade was increasing; and exchanges, from cabinet members to naval vessels, were flourishing.

Mikhail Gorbachev, still presiding over the Soviet Union, was planning a visit to Beijing in May. Moscow had met to a significant extent the three conditions put forward by Beijing for an improvement in Sino-Soviet relations: withdrawal of Soviet forces from Afghanistan; redeployment of Soviet forces away from the Chinese border; and a Vietnamese withdrawal from Cambodia. International conferences were routinely scheduled for Beijing—including a meeting that April of the board of directors of the Asian Development Bank, a multilateral development organization that China had joined three years earlier, which unexpectedly provided a backdrop for the unfolding drama.

It all began with the death of Hu Yaobang. Deng had overseen his rise in 1981 to General Secretary, the highest leadership post of the Communist Party. In 1986, when conservative critics blamed Hu for indecisiveness in the face of student demonstrations, he was replaced as General Secretary by Zhao Ziyang, another protégé of Deng, while remaining a member of the ruling Politburo. During a Politburo meeting on April 8, 1989, the seventy-three-year-old Hu suffered a heart attack. His stunned colleagues revived him and rushed him to the hospital. He suffered another heart attack there and died on April 15.

As with Zhou Enlai's passing in 1976, Hu's death was the occasion for politically charged mourning. However, in the intervening years, the restrictions on permissible speech had been relaxed. While Zhou's mourners in 1976 had veiled their criticisms of Mao and Jiang Qing in allegorical references to ancient dynastic court politics, the demonstrators over Hu in 1989 named their targets. The atmosphere was already tense due to the upcoming seventieth anniversary of the May Fourth Movement, a 1919 campaign by nationalist-minded Chinese protesting the weakness of the Chinese government and perceived inequities in the Treaty of Versailles.[1]

Hu's admirers laid wreaths and elegiac poems at the Monument to the People's Heroes in Tiananmen Square, many praising the former General Secretary's dedication to political liberalization and calling for his spirit to live on in further reforms. Students in Beijing and other cities took the opportunity to voice their frustration with corruption, inflation, press restrictions, university conditions, and the persistence of Party "elders" ruling informally behind the scenes. In Beijing, seven demands were put forward by various student groups, which threatened to demonstrate until the government had implemented them. Not all the groups supported every demand; an unprecedented confluence of disparate resentments escalated into upheaval. What had started as a demonstration evolved into an occupation of Tiananmen Square challenging the authority of the government.

Events escalated in a manner neither observers nor participants thought conceivable at the beginning of the month. By June, antigovernment protests of various sizes had spread nationwide to 341 cities.[2] Protesters had taken over trains and schools, and main roads in the capital were blocked. In Tiananmen Square, students declared a hunger strike, attracting widespread attention from both local and international observers and other nonstudent groups, which began to join the protesters. Chinese leaders were obliged to move Gorbachev's welcoming ceremony from Tiananmen Square. Humiliatingly, a muted ceremony was held at the Beijing airport without public attendance. Some reports held that elements of the People's Liberation Army defied orders to deploy to the capital and quell the demonstrations, and that government employees were marching with the protesters in the street. The political challenge was underscored by developments in China's far west, where Tibetans and members of China's Uighur Muslim minority had begun to agitate based on their own cultural issues (in the Uighur case, the recent publication of a book claimed to offend Islamic sensibilities).[3]

Uprisings generally develop their own momentum as developments slide out of the control of the principal actors, who become characters in a play whose script they no longer know. For Deng, the protests stirred the historical Chinese fear of chaos and memories of the Cultural Revolution—whatever the stated goals of the demonstrators. The scholar Andrew J. Nathan has summed up the impasse eloquently:

> The students did not set out to pose a mortal challenge to what they knew was a dangerous regime. Nor did the regime relish the use of force against the students. The two sides shared many goals and much common language. Through miscommunication and misjudgment, they pushed one another into positions in which options for compromise became less and less available. Several times a solution seemed just within reach, only to dissolve at the last moment. The slide to calamity seemed

> slow at first but then accelerated as divisions deepened on both sides. Knowing the outcome, we read the story with a sense of horror that we receive from true tragedy.[4]

This is not the place to examine the events that led to the tragedy at Tiananmen Square; each side has different perceptions depending on the various, often conflicting, origins of their participation in the crisis. The student unrest started as a demand for remedies to specific grievances. But the occupation of the main square of a country's capital, even when completely peaceful, is also a tactic to demonstrate the impotence of the government, to weaken it, and to tempt it into rash acts, putting it at a disadvantage.

There is no dispute about the denouement, however. After hesitating for seven weeks and exhibiting serious divisions within its ranks over the use of force, the Chinese leadership cracked down decisively on June 4. The General Secretary of the Communist Party, Zhao Ziyang, was dismissed. After weeks of internal debates, Deng and a majority of the Politburo ordered the PLA to clear Tiananmen Square. A harsh suppression of the protest followed—all seen on television, broadcast by media that had come from all over the world to record the momentous meeting between Gorbachev and the Chinese leadership.

American Dilemmas

The international reaction was stark. The People's Republic of China had never claimed to function as a Western-style democracy (and indeed had consistently rejected the insinuation). Now it emerged in the media of the world as an arbitrary authoritarian state crushing popular aspirations to human rights. Deng, heretofore widely lauded as a reformer, was criticized as a tyrant.

In this atmosphere, the entire Sino-U.S. relationship, including the established practice of regular consultations between the two countries, came under attack from across a wide political spectrum. Traditional conservatives saw themselves vindicated in their conviction that China, under the leadership of the Communist Party, would never be a reliable partner. Human rights activists across the entire political spectrum were outraged. Liberals argued that the aftermath of Tiananmen imposed on America the obligation to fulfill its ultimate mission to spread democracy. However varied their objectives, the critics converged on the need for sanctions to pressure Beijing to alter its domestic institutions and encourage human rights practices.

President George H. W. Bush, who had assumed the presidency less than five months earlier, was uncomfortable with the long-range consequences of sanctions. Both Bush and his National Security Advisor, General Brent Scowcroft, had served in the Nixon administration. They had met Deng when they were in office; they remembered how he had preserved the relationship with America against the machinations of the Gang of Four and on behalf of greater scope for the individual. They admired his economic reforms, and they balanced their distaste of the repression against their respect for the way the world had been transformed since the opening to China. They had participated in the conduct of foreign policy when every opponent of the United States could count on Chinese support, when all the nations of Asia feared a China isolated from the world, and when the Soviet Union could conduct a policy of pressure against the West, unrestrained by concerns over its other flanks.

President Bush had served in China as head of the American Liaison Office in Beijing ten years earlier during tense periods. Bush had enough experience to understand that the leaders who had been on the Long March, survived in the caves of Yan'an, and confronted both the United States and the Soviet Union simultaneously in the 1960s would not submit to foreign pressures or the threat of isolation. And what was the objective? To overthrow the Chinese government? To change its structure toward what alternative? How could the process of intervention be ended once it was started? And what would be the costs?

Before Tiananmen, America had become familiar with the debate about the role of its diplomacy in promoting democracy. In simplified form, the debate pitted idealists against realists—idealists insisting that domestic systems affect foreign policy and are therefore legitimate items on the diplomatic agenda, realists arguing that such an agenda is beyond any country's capacity and that diplomacy should therefore focus primarily on external policies. The absolutes of moral precept were weighed against the contingencies of deducing foreign policy from the balancing of national interests. The actual distinctions are more subtle. Idealists, when they seek to apply their values, will be driven to consider the world of specific circumstance. Thoughtful realists understand that values are an important component of reality. When decisions are made, the distinction is rarely absolute; often it comes down to a question of nuance.

With respect to China, the issue was not whether America preferred democratic values to prevail. By a vast majority, the American public would have answered in the affirmative, as would have all the participants in the debate on China policy. The issue was what price they would be prepared to pay in concrete terms over what period of time and what their capacity was, in any circumstances, to bring about their desired outcome.

Two broad operational policies appeared in the public debate over the tactics of dealing with authoritarian regimes. One group argued for confrontation, urging the United States to resist undemocratic behavior or human rights violations by withholding any benefit America might afford, whatever the price for America. In the extreme, it pressed for change of offending regimes; in the case of China, it insisted on an unambiguous move toward democracy as a condition for any mutual benefit.[5]

The contrary view argued that human rights progress is generally better reached by a policy of engagement. Once enough confidence has been established, changes in civil practice can be advocated in the name of common purposes or at least the preservation of a common interest.

Which method is appropriate depends in part on circumstances. There are instances of violations of human rights so egregious that it is impossible to conceive of benefit in a continuing relationship; for example the Khmer Rouge in Cambodia, and the genocide in Rwanda. Since public pressure shades either into regime change or a kind of abdication, it is difficult to apply to countries with which a continuous relationship is important for American security. This is especially the case with China, so imbued with the memory of humiliating intervention by Western societies.

China would be a major factor in world politics, whatever the immediate outcome of the Tiananmen crisis. If the leadership consolidated itself, China would resume its economic reform program and grow increasingly strong. America and the world would then be faced with deciding whether to move to restore a cooperative relationship with an emerging great power or to seek to isolate China so as to induce it to adopt domestic policies in keeping with American values. Isolating China would usher in a prolonged period of confrontation with a society that did not buckle when the Soviet Union, its only source of outside help, withdrew assistance in 1959. The Bush administration, in its first months, was still operating on the premises of the Cold War, in which China was needed to balance the Soviet Union. But as the Soviet threat declined, China would emerge in an increasingly strong position to go it alone because the fear of the Soviet Union, which had brought China and the United States together, would recede.

There were objective limits to American influence on China's domestic institutions, whether confrontation or engagement was pursued. Did we have the knowledge to shape the internal developments of a country of the size, mass, and complexity of China? Was there a risk that a collapse of central authority might trigger a recurrence of the civil wars that were at least compounded by nineteenth-century foreign interventions?

President Bush was in a delicate position after Tiananmen. As former head of the United States Liaison Office in Beijing, he had gained an appreciation for Chinese sensitivities about perceived foreign interference. With his long career in U.S. politics, he also had an astute understanding of American domestic political realities. He was aware that most Americans believed that Washington's China policy should seek—as Nancy Pelosi, the then junior Democratic representative from California, termed it—"to send a clear and principled message of outrage to the leaders in Beijing."[6] But Bush had also come to know that the United States' relationship with China served vital American interests independent of the People's Republic's system of governance. He was wary of antagonizing a government that had cooperated with the United States for nearly two decades on some of the most fundamental security issues of the Cold War world. As he later wrote: "For this understandably proud, ancient, and inward-looking people, foreign criticism (from peoples they still perceived as 'barbarians' and colonialists untutored in Chinese ways) was an affront, and measures taken against them a return to the coercions of the past."[7] Facing pressure for stronger measures from both the right and the left, Bush maintained that

> we could not look the other way when it came to human rights or political reforms: but we could make plain our views in terms of encouraging their strides of progress (which were many since the death of Mao) rather than unleashing an endless barrage of criticism. . . . The question for me was how to condemn what we saw as wrong and react appropriately while also remaining engaged with China, even if the relationship must now be "on hold."[8]

Bush walked this tightrope with skill and elegance. When Congress imposed punitive measures on Beijing, he softened some of the edges. At the same time, to express his convictions, on June 5 and June 20, he suspended high-level government exchanges; halted military cooperation and sales of police, military, and dual-use equipment; and announced opposition to new loans to the People's Republic by the World Bank and other international financial institutions. American sanctions dovetailed with comparable steps undertaken by the European Community, Japan, Australia, and New Zealand, and with expressions of regret and condemnation from governments around the world. Congress, reflecting popular pressure, pushed for even stronger measures, including legislative sanctions (which would be more difficult to lift than administrative sanctions imposed by the President, which were at the chief executive's discretion) and a law automatically extending the visas of all Chinese students currently in the United States.[9]

The U.S. and Chinese governments—which had acted as de facto allies for much of the previous decade—were drifting apart, with resentment and recrimination building on both sides in the absence of high-level contacts. Determined to avoid an irreparable break, Bush appealed to his long-standing relationship with Deng. He drafted a long and personal letter on June 21, addressing Deng "as a friend" and bypassing the bureaucracy and his own ban on high-level exchanges.[10] In a deft diplomatic performance, Bush expressed his "great reverence for Chinese history, culture and tradition" and avoided any terms that might suggest he was dictating to Deng how to govern China. At the same time, Bush urged China's paramount leader to understand popular outrage in the United States as a natural outgrowth of American idealism:

> I ask you as well to remember the principles on which my young country was founded. Those principles are democracy and freedom—freedom of speech, freedom of assemblage,

> freedom from arbitrary authority. It is reverence for those principles which inevitably affects the way Americans view and react to events in other countries. It is not a reaction of arrogance or of a desire to force others to our beliefs but of simple faith in the enduring value of those principles and their universal applicability.[11]

Bush suggested that he himself was operating at the limits of his domestic political influence:

> I will leave what followed to the history books, but again, with their own eyes the people of the world saw the turmoil and the bloodshed with which the demonstrations were ended. Various countries reacted in various ways. Based on the principles I have described above, the actions that I took as President of the United States could not be avoided.[12]

Bush appealed to Deng to exercise compassion because of the effect this would have on the American public—and, implicitly, on Bush's own freedom of maneuver:

> Any statement that could be made from China that drew from earlier statements about peacefully resolving further disputes with protestors would be very well received here. Any clemency that could be shown the student demonstrators would be applauded worldwide.[13]

To explore these ideas, Bush proposed sending a high-level emissary to Beijing "in total confidence" to "speak with total candor to you representing my heartfelt convictions on these matters." Though he had not shied from expressing the differences in perspectives between the two nations, Bush closed with an appeal for a continuation of the existing cooperation: "We must not let the aftermath of the tragic recent events undermine a vital relationship patiently built up over the past seventeen years."[14]

Deng responded to Bush's overture the next day, welcoming an American envoy to Beijing. It was a measure of the importance Bush attached to the relationship with China and his confidence in Deng that, on July 1, he sent National Security Advisor Brent Scowcroft and Deputy Secretary of State Lawrence Eagleburger to Beijing three weeks after the violence in Tiananmen Square. The mission was a closely guarded secret, known only to a handful of high-level officials in Washington and Ambassador James Lilley, who was recalled from Beijing to be briefed in person about the impending visit.[15] Scowcroft and Eagleburger flew into Beijing in an unmarked C-141 military transport plane; news of their arrival was so tightly held that Chinese air defense forces allegedly called President Yang Shangkun to inquire whether they should shoot down the mystery plane.[16] The plane was equipped for refueling in midair to avoid the need for a stopover along the route and carried its own communications equipment so the party could communicate directly with the White House. No flags were displayed at the meetings or banquets, and the visit was not reported in the news.

Scowcroft and Eagleburger met with Deng, Premier Li Peng, and Foreign Minister Qian Qichen. Deng praised Bush and reciprocated his expressions of friendship but placed the blame for the strain in relations on the United States:

> This was an earthshaking event and it is very unfortunate that the United States is too deeply involved in it. . . . We have been feeling since the outset of these events more than two months ago that the various aspects of US foreign policy have actually cornered China. That's the feeling of us here . . . because the aim of the counterrevolutionary rebellion was to overthrow

> the People's Republic of China and our socialist system. If they should succeed in obtaining that aim the world would be a different one. To be frank, this could even lead to war.[17]

Did he mean civil war or war by disgruntled or revanche-seeking neighbors or both? "Sino-US relations," Deng warned, "are in a very delicate state and you can even say that they are in a dangerous state." Punitive American policies were "leading to the breakup of the relationship," he argued, although he held out hope that it could be preserved.[18] Then, falling back on the traditional stance of defiance, Deng spoke at length of China's imperviousness to outside pressure and its leadership's unique, battle-hardened determination. "We don't care about the sanctions," Deng told the American envoys. "We are not scared by them."[19] Americans, he said, "must understand history":

> [W]e have won the victory represented by the founding of the People's Republic of China by fighting a twenty-two-year war with the cost of more than twenty million lives, a war fought by the Chinese people under the leadership of the Communist Party. . . . There is no force whatsoever that can substitute for the People's Republic of China represented by the Communist Party of China. This is not an empty word. It is something which has been proven and tested over several decades of experience.[20]

It was up to the United States to improve relations, Deng stressed, quoting a Chinese proverb: "[I]t is up to the person who tied the knot to untie it."[21] For its part, Beijing would not waver in "punishing those instigators of the rebellion," Deng vowed. "Otherwise how can the PRC continue to exist?"[22]

Scowcroft replied by stressing the themes that Bush had emphasized in his letters to Deng. Close ties between the United States and

China reflected both countries' strategic and economic interests. But they also brought into close contact societies with "two different cultures, backgrounds, and perceptions." Now Beijing and Washington found themselves in a world in which Chinese domestic practices, broadcast on television, could have a profound effect on American public opinion.

This U.S. reaction, Scowcroft argued, reflected deeply held values. These American values "reflect our own beliefs and traditions," which were just as much a part of the "diversity between our two societies" as Chinese sensitivities regarding foreign interference: "What the American people perceived in the demonstrations they saw—rightly or wrongly—[as] an expression of values which represent their most cherished beliefs, stemming from the American Revolution."[23]

The Chinese government's treatment of demonstrators was, Scowcroft conceded, a "wholly internal affair of China." Yet it was "an obvious fact" that such treatment produced an American popular reaction, "which is real and with which the President must cope." Bush believed in the importance of preserving the long-term relationship between the United States and China. But he was obliged to respect "the feelings of the American people," which demanded some concrete expression of disapproval from its government. Sensitivity by both sides would be required to navigate the impasse.[24]

The difficulty was that both sides were right. Deng felt his regime under siege; Bush and Scowcroft considered America's deepest values challenged.

Premier Li Peng and Qian Qichen stressed similar points, and the two sides parted without reaching any concrete agreement. Scowcroft explained the impasse, as diplomats often do to explain deadlock, as a successful enterprise in keeping open lines of communication: "Both sides had been frank and open. We had aired our differences and listened to each other, but we still had a distance to go before we bridged the gap."[25]

Matters could not rest there. By the fall of 1989, relations between China and the United States were at their most fraught point since contact had been resumed in 1971. Neither government wanted a break, but neither seemed in a position to avoid it. A break, once it occurred, could develop its own momentum, much as the Sino-Soviet controversy evolved from a series of tactical disputes into a strategic confrontation. America would have lost diplomatic flexibility. China would have had to slow down its economic momentum or perhaps even abandon it for a substantial period with serious consequences for its domestic stability. Both would have lost the opportunity to build on the many areas of bilateral cooperation that had greatly increased in the late 1980s and to work together to overcome the upheavals threatening in different parts of the world.

Amidst these tensions, I accepted an invitation from China's leaders to come to Beijing that November to form my own views. The President and General Scowcroft were told of the planned private visit. Before I left for Beijing, Scowcroft gave me a briefing on the status of our relations with China—a procedure that due to the long history of my involvement with China has been followed also by every other administration. Scowcroft informed me of the discussions with Deng. He gave me no specific message to convey, but if the occasion arose, he hoped I would reinforce the administration's views. I would as usual report my impressions to Washington.

Like most Americans, I was shocked by the way the Tiananmen protest was ended. But unlike most Americans, I had had the opportunity to observe the Herculean task Deng had undertaken for a decade and a half to remold his country: moving Communists toward acceptance of decentralization and reform; traditional Chinese insularity toward modernity and a globalized world—a prospect China had often rejected. And I had witnessed his steady efforts to improve Sino-American ties.

The China I saw on this occasion had lost the self-assurance of my previous visits. In the Mao period, Chinese leaders represented by Zhou had acted with the self-confidence conferred by ideology and a judgment on international affairs seasoned by a historical memory extending over millennia. The China of the early Deng period exhibited an almost naive faith that overcoming the memory of the suffering of the Cultural Revolution would provide the guide toward economic and political progress based on individual initiative. But in the decade since Deng had first promulgated his reform program in 1978, China had experienced, together with the exhilaration of success, some of its penalties. The movement from central planning to more decentralized decision making turned out to be in constant jeopardy from two directions: the resistance of an entrenched bureaucracy with a vested interest in the status quo; and the pressures from impatient reformers for whom the process was taking too long. Economic decentralization led to demands for pluralism in political decision making. In that sense, the Chinese upheaval reflected the intractable dilemmas of reform Communism.

Over Tiananmen, the Chinese leaders had opted for political stability. They had done so hesitantly after nearly six weeks of internal controversy. I heard no emotional justification of the events of June 4; they were treated like an unfortunate accident that had descended as if from nowhere. The Chinese leaders, stunned by the reactions of the outside world and their own divisions, were concerned with reestablishing their international standing. Even allowing for China's traditional skill in putting the foreigner on the defensive, my opposite numbers had a genuine difficulty; they could not understand why the United States took umbrage at an event that had injured no American material interests and for which China claimed no validity outside its own territory. Explanations of America's historic commitment to human rights were dismissed, either as a form of Western "bullying" or as a sign of the unwarranted righteousness of a country that had its own human rights problems.

In our conversations, the Chinese leaders pursued their basic strategic objective, which was to restore a working relationship with the United States. In a sense, the conversation returned to the pattern of the early meetings with Zhou. Would the two societies find a way to cooperate? And, if so, on what basis? Roles were now reversed. In the early meetings Chinese leaders emphasized the distinctiveness of Communist ideology. Now they sought a rationale for compatible views.

Deng established the basic theme, which was that peace in the world depended to a considerable extent on order in China:

> It is very easy for chaos to come overnight. It will not be easy to maintain order and tranquility. Had the Chinese government not taken resolute steps in Tiananmen, there would have been a civil war in China. And because China has one fifth of the world's population, instability in China would cause instability in the world which could even involve the big powers.

The interpretation of history expresses the memory of a nation. And for this generation of China's leaders, the traumatic event of China's history was the collapse of central authority in China in the nineteenth century, which tempted the outside world into invasion, quasi-colonialism, or colonial competition and produced genocidal levels of casualties in civil wars, as in the Taiping Rebellion.

The purpose of a stable China, Deng said, was to contribute constructively to a new international order. Relations with the United States were central: "This is one thing," Deng said to me,

> I have to make clear to others after my retirement.[26] The first thing I did after my release from prison was to devote attention to furthering Sino-US relations. It is also my desire to put an end to the recent past, to enable Sino-US relations to return

> to normal. I hope to tell my friend President Bush that we will see a furthering of Sino-US relations during his term as President.

The obstacle, according to Li Ruihuan (Party ideologist and considered by analysts as among the liberal element) was that "Americans think they understand China better than the Chinese people themselves." What China could not accept was dictation from abroad:

> Since 1840 the Chinese people have been subjected to foreign bullying; it was a semi-feudal society then. . . . Mao fought all of his life to say that China should be friendly to countries that treat us with equality. In 1949 Mao said "the Chinese people have stood up." By standing up he meant the Chinese people were going to enjoy equality with other nations. We don't like to hear that others ask us what to do. But Americans tend to like to ask others to do this or that. The Chinese people do not want to yield to the instructions of others.

I tried to explain to the Vice Premier in charge of foreign policy, Qian Qichen, the domestic pressures and the values compelling American actions. Qian would not hear of it. China would act at its own pace based on its determination of its national interest, which could not be prescribed by foreigners:

> QIAN: We are trying to maintain political and economic stability and push ahead with reform and contact with the outside world. We can't move under US pressure. We are moving in that direction anyway.
>
> KISSINGER: But that's what I mean. As you move in that direction it could have presentational aspects that would be beneficial.

> QIAN: China started economic reform out of China's own interest not because of what the US wanted.

International relations, in the Chinese view, were determined by the national interest and the national purpose. If national interests were compatible, cooperation was possible, even necessary. There was no substitute for a congruence of interests. Domestic structures were irrelevant to this process—an issue we had already encountered in the differing views regarding attitudes toward the Khmer Rouge. According to Deng, the U.S.-China relationship had thrived when this principle had been observed:

> At the time that you and President Nixon decided to reestablish relations with China, China was not only striving for socialism but also for Communism. The Gang of Four preferred a system of communist poverty. You accepted our communism then. There is therefore no reason not to accept Chinese socialism now. The days are gone when state to state relations are handled on the basis of social systems. Countries with different social systems can have friendly relations now. We can find many common interests between China and the U.S.

There was a time when a Chinese leader's abjuring a crusading role for Communist ideology would have been greeted by the democratic world as proof of a beneficent evolution. Now that the heirs of Mao were arguing that the age of ideology was over and that national interest was the determinant, eminent Americans were insisting that democratic institutions were required to guarantee a compatibility of national interests. That proposition—verging on an article of faith for many American analysts—would be difficult to demonstrate from historical experience. When World War I started, most governments in Europe (including Britain, France, and Germany) were governed by essentially democratic institutions. Nevertheless, World War I—a catastrophe from which Europe has never fully recovered—was enthusiastically approved by all elected parliaments.

But neither is the calculation of national interest self-evident. National power or national interest may be the most complicated elements of international relations to calculate precisely. Most wars occur as the result of a combination of misjudgment of the power relationships and domestic pressures. In the period under discussion, different American administrations have come up with varying solutions to the conundrum of balancing a commitment to American political ideals with the pursuit of peaceful and productive U.S.-China relations. The administration of George H. W. Bush chose to advance American preferences through engagement; that of Bill Clinton, in its first term, would attempt pressure. Both had to face the reality that in foreign policy, a nation's highest aspirations tend to be fulfilled only in imperfect stages.

The basic direction of a society is shaped by its values, which define its ultimate goals. At the same time, accepting the limits of one's capacities is one of the tests of statesmanship; it implies a judgment of the possible. Philosophers are responsible to their intuition. Statesmen are judged by their ability to sustain their concepts over time.

The attempt to alter the domestic structure of a country of the magnitude of China from the outside is likely to involve vast unintended consequences. American society should never abandon its commitment to human dignity. It does not diminish the importance of that commitment to acknowledge that Western concepts of human rights and individual liberties may not be directly translatable, in a finite period of time geared to Western political and news cycles, to a civilization for millennia ordered around different concepts. Nor can the traditional Chinese fear of political chaos be dismissed as an anachronistic irrelevancy needing only "correction" by Western enlightenment. Chinese history, especially in the last two centuries, provides numerous examples in which a splintering of political authority—sometimes inaugurated with high expectations of increased liberties—tempted social and ethnic upheaval; frequently it was the most militant, not the most liberal, elements that prevailed.

By the same principle, countries dealing with America need to understand that the basic values of our country include an inalienable concept of human rights and that American judgments can never be separated from America's perceptions of the practice of democracy. There are abuses bound to evoke an American reaction, even at the cost of an overall relationship. Such events can drive American foreign policy beyond national interest calculations. No American President can ignore them, but he must be careful to define them and be aware of the principle of unintended consequences. No foreign leader should dismiss them. How to define and how to establish the balance will determine the nature of America's relationship to China and perhaps the peace of the world.

The statesmen on both sides faced this choice in November 1989. Deng, as always practical, suggested an effort to develop a new concept of international order, which established nonintervention in domestic affairs into a general principle of foreign policy: "I believe we should propose the establishment of a new international political order. We have not made much headway in establishing a new international economic order. So at present we should work on a new political order which would abide by the five principles of peaceful coexistence." One of which, of course, was to proscribe intervention in the domestic affairs of other states.[27]

Beyond all these strategic principles loomed a crucial intangible. Calculation of national interest was not simply a mathematical formula. Attention had to be paid to national dignity and self-respect. Deng urged me to convey to Bush his desire to come to an agreement with the United States, which, as the stronger country, should make the first move.[28] The quest for a new phase of cooperation would not be able to avoid human rights issues altogether. Deng's query of who should initiate a new dialogue was, in the end, answered by Deng himself, who began a dialogue over the fate of a single individual: a dissident named Fang Lizhi.

The Fang Lizhi Controversy

By the time of my visit in November 1989, the dissident physicist Fang Lizhi had become a symbol of the divide between the United States and China. Fang was an eloquent proponent of Western-style parliamentary democracy and individual rights with a long history of pushing at the boundaries of official tolerance. In 1957, he had been expelled from the Communist Party as part of the Anti-Rightist Campaign, and during the Cultural Revolution he was imprisoned for a year for "reactionary" activities. Rehabilitated after Mao's death, Fang pursued a successful academic career, speaking out in favor of increased political liberalization. Following the pro-democracy demonstrations of 1986, Fang was again reprimanded, though he continued to circulate calls for reform.

When President Bush visited China in February 1989, Fang was included on the list the U.S. Embassy had recommended to the White House to be invited to a state dinner hosted by the President in Beijing. The Embassy followed what they thought was the precedent of Reagan's visit to Moscow during which he met self-declared dissidents. The White House approved the list—though probably unaware of the intensity of the Chinese views with respect to Fang. Fang's inclusion on the invitation list provoked a contretemps between the United States and the Chinese government and within the new Bush administration.[29] Eventually it was agreed between the Embassy and the Chinese government that Fang would be seated far from Chinese government officials. On the night of the event, Chinese security services stopped Fang's car and blocked him from reaching the venue.

Though Fang did not personally participate in the Tiananmen Square demonstrations, the student protesters were in sympathy with the principles he advocated, and Fang was believed to be a likely target for government reprisal. In the immediate wake of the June 4 crackdown, Fang and his wife sought refuge at the American Embassy. Several days later, the Chinese government issued an arrest warrant for Fang and his wife for "crimes of counter-propaganda and instigation before and after the recent turmoil." Government publications demanded that the United States turn over the "criminal who created this violence" or face a deterioration of U.S.-China relations.[30] "We had no choice but to take him in," Bush concluded in his diary, "but it's going to be a real stick in the eye to the Chinese."[31]

Fang's presence in the Embassy was a source of constant tension: the Chinese government was unwilling to let its most prominent critic leave the country for fear that he would agitate from abroad; Washington was unwilling to turn over a dissident espousing liberal democracy to face what was certain to be harsh retribution. In a cable to Washington, Ambassador James Lilley noted of Fang, "He is with us as a constant reminder of our connection to 'bourgeois liberalism' and puts us at odds with the regime here. He is a living symbol of our conflict with China over human rights."[32]

In his June 21 letter to Deng Xiaoping, Bush raised "the matter of Fang Lizhi," regretting that it was a "high-profile wedge driven between us." Bush defended the American decision to grant Fang refuge—based on, he asserted, "our widely-accepted interpretation of international law"—and averred that "[w]e cannot now put Fang out of the Embassy without some assurance that he will not be in physical danger." Bush offered the possibility of settling the matter discreetly, noting that other governments had solved similar issues by "quietly permitting departure through expulsion."[33] But the issue proved resistant to negotiation, and Fang and his wife remained in the Embassy.

During the briefing General Scowcroft had given me prior to my departure for Beijing he familiarized me with the case. He urged me not to raise it, since the administration had said all it could say. But I could respond to Chinese initiatives within the framework of existing policy. I had followed his advice. I had not raised the Fang Lizhi issue, nor had any of my Chinese interlocutors. During my farewell call on Deng, he suddenly introduced the subject after a few desultory comments on the reform problem and used it to suggest a package deal. An extended summary of the relevant exchange will give the flavor of the mood in Beijing six months after Tiananmen:

> DENG: I talked with President Bush about the Fang Lizhi case.
>
> KISSINGER: As you know, the President did not know about the invitation to the banquet until it was already public.
>
> DENG: He told me that.
>
> KISSINGER: Since you have raised Fang, I would like to express a consideration to you. I did not raise the issue in any of my other conversations here because I know that it is a matter of great delicacy and affects Chinese dignity. But I think your best friends in America would be relieved if some way could be found to get him out of the Embassy and let him leave the country. There is no other single step which would so impress the American public as having it happen before there is too much agitation.

At this point, Deng got up from his seat and unscrewed the microphones between his seat and mine as a symbol that he wanted to talk privately.

> DENG: Can you make a suggestion?
>
> KISSINGER: My suggestion would be that you expel him from

> China and we agree that as a government we will make no political use of him whatsoever. Perhaps we would encourage him to go to some country like Sweden where he would be far away from the US Congress and our press. An arrangement like this could make a deep impression on the American public, more than a move on any technical subject.

Deng wanted more specific assurances. Was it possible for the American government to "require Fang to write a confession" to crimes under Chinese law; or for Washington to guarantee that "after his expulsion [from China] . . . Fang will say and do nothing opposing China"? Deng broadened this to a request that Washington "undertake the responsibility that it prevent further nonsense being uttered by Fang and by [other Chinese] demonstrators" currently in the United States. Deng was looking for a way out. But the measures he proposed were outside the legal authority of the American government.

> DENG: What would you think if we were to expel him after he has written a paper confessing to his crimes?
>
> KISSINGER: I would be surprised if he would do this. I was at the Embassy this morning, but I did not see Fang.
>
> DENG: But he would have to do it if the US side insists. This issue was started by people at the US Embassy including some good friends of yours and including people I thought of as friends.[34]
>
> What if the American side required Fang to write a confession and after that we could expel him as an ordinary criminal and he can go where he wants. If this won't do, what about another idea: The US undertakes the responsibility after his expulsion that Fang will say and do

nothing opposing China. He should not use the US or another country to oppose the PRC.

KISSINGER: Let me comment on the first proposal. If we ask him to sign a confession, assuming we could even do that, what matters is not what he says in the Embassy but what he says when he gets out of China. If he says that the American government forced him to confess, it will be worse for everyone than if he did not confess. The importance of releasing him is as a symbol of the self-confidence of China. To contradict the caricatures that many of your opponents have made of China in the US.

DENG: Then let's consider the second proposal. The US would say that after he leaves China, he will make no remarks opposing the PRC. Can the US give such a guarantee?

KISSINGER: Well, I am speaking to you as a friend.

DENG: I know. I am not asking you to undertake the agreement.

KISSINGER: What might be possible is that the US government agrees that the US government will make no use of Fang in any way, for example on the Voice of America or in any way which the President can control. Also we could promise to advise him not to do it on his own. We could agree that he would not be received by the President or given any official status by any US governmental organization.

This led Deng to tell me about a letter he had just received from Bush proposing the visit of a special envoy to brief him on the forthcoming U.S. summit with Gorbachev and to review the Sino-American relationship. Deng accepted the idea and connected it with the Fang discussions as a way to find an overall solution:

> In the process of solving the Fang issue, other issues may also be put forward in order to achieve a package solution to all the issues. Now things are like this. I asked Bush to move first; he asks me to move first. I think if we can get a package then there is no question of the order of the steps.

The "package deal" was described by Chinese Foreign Minister Qian Qichen in his memoirs:

> (1) China would permit Fang Lizhi and his wife to leave the U.S. embassy in Beijing to go to the United States or a third country, (2) The United States, in ways that suited itself, should make an explicit announcement that it would lift the sanctions on China, (3) Both sides should make efforts to conclude deals on one or two major economic cooperation projects, (4) The United States should extend an invitation to Jiang Zemin [just appointed as General Secretary of the Communist Party to replace Zhao Ziyang] to pay an official visit the following year.[35]

After a further exchange on the modalities of Fang's possible exile, Deng ended this part of the conversation:

> DENG: Will Bush be pleased and agree to this proposal?
>
> KISSINGER: My opinion is that he will be pleased with it.

I expected Bush to welcome the demonstration of Chinese concern and flexibility, but I doubted that the pace of improving relations could be as rapid as Deng envisaged.

A renewed understanding between China and the United States had become all the more important because the growing upheaval in the Soviet Union and Eastern Europe seemed to undermine the premises of the existing triangular relationship. With the Soviet empire disintegrating, what had become of the motive for the original rapprochement between the United States and China? The urgency was underlined as I left Beijing the evening of my meeting with Deng and learned, at my first stop in the United States, that the Berlin Wall had fallen, shattering the premises of Cold War foreign policy.

The political revolutions in Eastern Europe nearly engulfed the package deal. When I returned to Washington three days later, I reported my conversation with Deng to Bush, Scowcroft, and Secretary of State James Baker at a dinner in the White House. As it turned out, China was not the principal subject. The subject of overriding importance for my hosts at that moment was the impact of the fall of the Berlin Wall and an imminent meeting between Bush and Gorbachev—set for December 2–3, 1989, in Malta. Both issues required some immediate decision about tactics and long-term strategy. Were we heading for the collapse of the East German satellite where twenty Soviet divisions were still stationed? Would there now be two German states, albeit a non-Communist East German one? If unification became the goal, by what diplomacy should it be sought? And what should America's attitude be in foreseeable contingencies?

Amidst the drama surrounding the Soviet collapse in Eastern Europe, Deng's package deal could not receive the priority it would have elicited in less tumultuous times.

The special mission I discussed with Deng did not take place until mid-December, when Brent Scowcroft and Lawrence Eagleburger visited Beijing for the second time in six months. The visit was not secret as the July trip had been (and at this point, still remained) but was intended to be low-profile to avoid congressional and media controversy. However, the Chinese side engineered a photo op of Scowcroft toasting Qian Qichen, provoking considerable consternation in the United States. Scowcroft would later recount:

> [A]s the ritual toasts began at the end of the welcoming dinner given by the foreign minister, the television crews reappeared. It was an awkward situation for me. I could go through with the ceremony and be seen as toasting those the press was labeling "the butchers of Tiananmen Square," or refuse to toast and put in jeopardy the whole purpose of the trip. I chose the former and became, to my deep chagrin, an instant celebrity—in the most negative sense of the term.[36]

The incident demonstrated the conflicting imperatives of the two sides. China wanted to demonstrate to its public that its isolation was ending; Washington sought to draw a minimum of attention, to avoid a domestic controversy until an agreement had been reached.

Inevitably, discussion of the Soviet Union occupied much of Scowcroft and Eagleburger's trip, though in quite the opposite direction from what had become traditional: the subject now was no longer the military menace of the USSR, but its growing weakness. Qian Qichen predicted the disintegration of the Soviet Union and described Beijing's surprise when Gorbachev, on his visit in May, at the height of the Tiananmen demonstrations, asked China for economic assistance. Scowcroft later recounted the Chinese version of these events:

> The Soviets did not grasp the economy very well and Gorbachev often did not grasp what he was asking of it. Qian predicted the collapsing economy and the nationalities problems would result in turmoil. "I have not seen Gorbachev taking any measures," he added. "Gorbachev has called on the Chinese side to provide consumer necessities," he told us. ". . . [W]e can provide consumer goods and they will pay back in raw materials. They also want loans. We were quite taken

> aback when they first raised this. We have agreed to extend some money to them."[37]

The Chinese leaders put forward their "package" solution to Scowcroft and linked the release of Fang Lizhi to the removal of American sanctions. The administration preferred to treat the Fang case as a separate humanitarian issue to be settled in its own right.

Further upheavals in the Soviet bloc—including the bloody overthrow of Romania's Communist leader, Nicolae Ceauşescu—bolstered the sense of siege in the Chinese Communist Party. The disintegration of the Eastern European Communist states also strengthened the hand of those in Washington who argued that the United States should wait for what they saw as the seemingly inevitable collapse of the Beijing government. In this atmosphere, neither side was in a position to depart from its established positions. Negotiations over Fang's release would continue through the American Embassy, and the two sides would not reach a deal until June 1990—over a year after Fang and his wife first sought refuge and eight months after Deng had put forward his package proposal.[38]

In the meantime, the annual reauthorization of China's Most Favored Nation trade status—required for "nonmarket" countries under the terms of the 1974 Jackson-Vanik Amendment, which made Most Favored Nation treatment conditional on emigration practices—was transformed into a forum for congressional condemnation of China's human rights record. The underlying assumption of the debate was that any agreement with China was a favor, and under the circumstances repugnant to American democratic ideals; trade privileges should thus be predicated on China's moving toward an American conception of human rights and political liberties. A sense of isolation began to descend on Beijing and a mood of triumphalism on Washington. In the spring of 1990, as Communist governments collapsed in East Germany,

Czechoslovakia, and Romania, Deng circulated a stark warning to Party members:

> Everyone should be very clear that, in the present international situation, all the attention of the enemy will be concentrated on China. It will use every pretext to cause trouble, to create difficulties and pressures for us. [China therefore needs] stability, stability, and still more stability. The next three to five years will be extremely difficult for our party and our country, and extremely important. If we stand fast and survive them, our cause will develop quickly. If we collapse, China's history will regress for several tens of years, even for a hundred years.[39]

The 12- and 24-Character Statements

At the close of the dramatic year, Deng chose to carry out his long-planned retirement. During the 1980s, he had taken many steps to end the traditional practice of centralized power ending only by the death of the incumbent or the loss of the Mandate of Heaven—criteria both indefinite and inviting chaos. He had established an advisory council of elders to which he retired leaders who were holding on to lifetime tenure. He had told visitors—including me—that he himself intended to retire soon to the chairmanship of that body.

Starting in early 1990, Deng began a gradual withdrawal from high office—the first Chinese leader to have done so in the modern period. Tiananmen may have accelerated the decision so that Deng could oversee the transition while a new leader was establishing himself. In December 1989, Brent Scowcroft proved to be the last foreign visitor to be received by Deng. At the same time, Deng stopped attending public functions. By the time of his death in 1997, he had become a recluse.

As he receded from the scene, Deng decided to buttress his successor by leaving behind a set of maxims for his guidance and that of the next generation of leaders. In issuing these instructions to Communist Party officials, Deng chose a method from Chinese classical history. The instructions were stark and succinct. Written in classical Chinese poetic style, they embraced two documents: a 24-character instruction and a 12-character explanation restricted to high officials. The 24-character instruction read:

> Observe carefully; secure our position; cope with affairs calmly; hide our capacities and bide our time; be good at maintaining a low profile; and never claim leadership.[40]

The 12-character policy explanation followed with an even more restricted circulation among the leaders. It read:

> Enemy troops are outside the walls. They are stronger than we. We should be mainly on the defensive.[41]

Against whom and what? The multiple-character statements were silent on that issue, probably because Deng could assume that his audience would understand instinctively that their country's position had grown precarious, both domestically and even more so internationally.

Deng's maxims were, on one level, an evocation of historic China surrounded by potentially hostile forces. In periods of resurgence, China would dominate its environs. In periods of decline, it would play for time, confident that its culture and political discipline would enable it to reclaim the greatness that was its due. The 12-character statement told China's leaders that perilous times had arrived. The outside world had always had difficulty dealing with this unique organism, aloof yet universal, majestic yet given over to occasional bouts of chaos. Now the aged leader of an ancient people was giving a last instruction to his society, feeling besieged as it was attempting to reform itself.

Deng sought to rally his people not by appealing to its emotions or to Chinese nationalism, as he easily could have. Instead he invoked its ancient virtues: calm in the face of adversity; high analytical ability to be put in the service of duty; discipline in pursuit of a common purpose. The deepest challenge, he saw, was less to survive the trials sketched in the 12-character statement than to prepare for the future, when the immediate danger had been overcome.

Was the 24-character statement intended as guidance for a moment of weakness or a permanent maxim? At the moment, China's reform was threatened by the consequences of internal turmoil and the pressure of foreign countries. But at the next stage, when reform had succeeded, China's growth might trigger another aspect of the world's concern. Then the international community might seek to resist China's march to becoming a dominant power. Did Deng, at the moment of great crisis, foresee that the gravest danger to China might arise upon its eventual resurgence? In that interpretation, Deng urged his people to "hide our capacities and bide our time" and "never claim leadership"—that is to say, do not evoke unnecessary fears by excessive assertiveness.

At its low point of turmoil and isolation, Deng may well have feared both that China might consume itself in its contemporary crisis and also that its future might depend on whether the leaders of the next generation could gain the perspective needed to recognize the perils of excessive self-confidence. Was the statement addressed to China's immediate travail, or to whether it could practice the 24-character principle when it was strong enough to no longer have to observe it? On China's answer to these questions depends much of the future of Sino-American relations.

CHAPTER 16

What Kind of Reform?

Deng's Southern Tour

IN JUNE 1989, with the Communist Party leadership divided on what to do, the Party General Secretary Zhao Ziyang, appointed by Deng three years earlier, was purged over his handling of the crisis. The Party Secretary of Shanghai, Jiang Zemin, was elevated to head the Communist Party.

The crisis confronting Jiang was one of the most complex in the history of the People's Republic. China was isolated, challenged abroad by trade sanctions and at home by the aftermath of nationwide unrest. Communism was in the process of disintegrating in every other country in the world except North Korea, Cuba, and Vietnam. Prominent Chinese dissidents had fled abroad, where they received asylum, a sympathetic ear, and freedom to organize. Tibet and Xinjiang were restive. The Dalai Lama was feted abroad; in the same year as Tiananmen, he won the Nobel Peace Prize amidst an upsurge of international attention to the cause of Tibetan autonomy.

After every social and political upheaval, the most serious challenge for governance is how to restore a sense of cohesion. But in the name of what principle? The domestic reaction to the crisis was more threatening to reform in China than the sanctions from abroad. Conservative members of the Politburo, whose support Deng had needed during the Tiananmen crisis, blamed Deng's "evolutionary policy" for the crisis and pressured Jiang to return to traditional Maoist verities. They went so far as to seek to reverse seemingly well-established policies such as the condemnation of the Cultural Revolution. A Politburo member named Deng Liqun (also known as "Little Deng") asserted: "If we fail to wage a resolute struggle against liberalization or [against] capitalistic reform and opening up, our socialist cause will be ruined."[1] Deng and Jiang held exactly the opposite view. The Chinese political structure, in their perception, could be given a new impetus only by accelerating the reform program. They saw in improving the standard of living and enhancing productivity the best guarantee of social stability.

In this atmosphere Deng, in early 1992, emerged from retirement for his last great public gesture. He chose the medium of an "inspection tour" through southern China to urge continued economic liberalization and build public support for Jiang's reform leadership. With reform efforts stagnating and his protégés losing ground to traditionalists in the Party hierarchy, the eighty-seven-year-old Deng set out with his daughter Deng Nan and several close associates on a tour through economic hubs in southern China, including Shenzhen and Zhuhai, two of the Special Economic Zones established under the 1980s reform program. It was a crusade for reform on behalf of "socialism with Chinese characteristics," which meant a role for free markets, scope for foreign investment, and appeal to individual initiative.

Deng, at this point, had no official title or formal function. Nevertheless, like an itinerant preacher, he turned up at schools, high-technology facilities, model businesses, and other symbols of his vision of Chinese reform, challenging his countrymen to redouble their efforts and setting far-reaching goals for China's economic and intellectual development. The national press (which was, at the time, controlled by conservative elements) initially ignored the speeches. But accounts in the Hong Kong press eventually filtered back to mainland China.

In time, Deng's "Southern Tour" would take on an almost mythical significance, and his speeches would serve as the blueprint for another two decades of Chinese political and economic policy. Even today, billboards in China portray images and quotations from Deng's Southern Tour, including his famous dictum that "development is the absolute principle."

Deng set out to vindicate the program of reform against the charge that it was betraying China's socialist heritage. Economic reform and development, he argued, were fundamentally "revolutionary" acts. Abandoning reform, Deng warned, would lead China down a "blind alley." To "win the trust and support of the people," the program of economic liberalization must continue for "a hundred years." Reform and opening up, Deng insisted, had allowed the People's Republic to avoid civil war in 1989. He reiterated his condemnation of the Cultural Revolution, describing it as beyond failure, a kind of civil war.[2]

The heir of Mao's China was advocating market principles, risk taking, private initiative, and the importance of productivity and entrepreneurship. The profit principle, according to Deng, reflected not an alternative theory to Marxism but an observation of human nature. Government would lose popular support if it punished entrepreneurs for their success. Deng's advice was that China should "be bolder," that it should redouble its efforts and "dare to experiment": "We must not act like women with bound feet. Once we are sure that something should be done, we should dare to experiment and break a new path. . . . Who dares claim that he is 100 percent sure of success and that he is taking no risks?"[3]

Deng dismissed criticism that his reforms were leading China down the "capitalist road." Rejecting decades of Maoist indoctrination, he invoked his familiar maxim that what mattered was the result, not the doctrine under which it was achieved. Nor should China be afraid of foreign investment:

> At the current stage, foreign-funded enterprises in China are allowed to make some money in accordance with existing laws

> and policies. But the government levies taxes on those enterprises, workers get wages from them, and we learn technology and managerial skills. In addition, we can get information from them that will help us open more markets.[4]

In the end, Deng attacked the "left" of the Communist Party, which was in a sense part of his own early history, when he had been Mao's "enforcer" in creating agricultural communes: "At present, we are being affected by both Right and 'Left' tendencies. But it is the 'Left' tendencies that have the deepest roots. . . . In the history of the Party, those tendencies have led to dire consequences. Some fine things were destroyed overnight."[5]

Prodding his countrymen by appealing to their national pride, Deng challenged China to match the growth rates of neighboring countries. In a sign of how far China has come in less than twenty years since the Southern Tour, Deng, in 1992, extolled the "four big items" it was essential to make available to consumers in the countryside: a bicycle, a sewing machine, a radio, and a wristwatch. China's economy could "reach a new stage every few years," he declared, and China would succeed if the Chinese dared to "emancipate our minds and act freely" in responding to challenges as they arose.[6]

Science and technology were the key. Echoing his pathbreaking speeches from the 1970s, Deng insisted that "intellectuals are part of the working class"; in other words, they were eligible for Communist Party membership. In an overture to Tiananmen supporters, Deng urged intellectuals who were in exile to return to China. If they possessed specialized knowledge and skills, they would be welcomed regardless of their previous attitudes: "They should be told that if they want to make their contributions, it would be better for them to come home. I hope that concerted efforts will be made to accelerate progress in China's scientific, technological and educational undertakings. . . . We should all love our country and help to develop it."[7]

What an extraordinary reversal in the convictions of the octogenarian revolutionary who had helped build, often ruthlessly, the economic system he was now dismantling. When serving in Yan'an with Mao during the civil war, Deng gave no indication that he would, fifty years later, be traveling around his country, urging reform of the very revolution he had enforced. Until he ran afoul of the Cultural Revolution, he had been one of Mao's principal aides, distinguished by his single-mindedness.

Over the decades, a gradual shift had taken place. Deng had come to redefine the criteria of good governance in terms of the well-being and development of the ordinary person. A considerable amount of nationalism was also involved in this dedication to rapid development, even if that required adopting methods prevalent in the previously reviled capitalist world. As one of Deng's children later told the American scholar and head of the National Committee on United States–China Relations David Lampton:

> In the mid-1970s, my father looked around China's periphery, to the small dragon economies [Singapore, Hong Kong, Taiwan, and South Korea]. They were growing at eight to ten percent per year and these economies had a considerable technological lead over China. If we were to surpass them and resume our rightful place in the region and ultimately the world, China would have to grow faster than them.[8]

In the service of this vision, Deng was advocating many American economic and social principles as part of his reform program. But what he called socialist democracy was vastly different from pluralistic democracy. He remained convinced that, in China, Western political principles would produce chaos and thwart development.

Yet even as he espoused the need for an authoritarian government, Deng saw his ultimate mission as passing on power to another generation, which, if his development plan succeeded, was bound to develop its own conception of political order. Deng hoped that the success of his reform program would remove the incentive for a democratic evolution. But he must have understood that the change he was bringing about was bound eventually to lead to political consequences of as yet unpredictable dimensions. These are the challenges now facing his successors.

For the immediate future, Deng, in 1992, stated relatively modest goals:

> We shall push ahead along the road to Chinese-style socialism. Capitalism has been developing for several hundred years. How long have we been building socialism? Besides, we wasted twenty years. If we can make China a moderately developed country within a hundred years from the founding of the People's Republic, that will be an extraordinary achievement.[9]

That would have been in 2049. In fact, China has done much better—by a generation.

Over a decade after Mao's death, his vision of continuous revolution was reappearing. But it was a different kind of continuous revolution based on personal initiative, not ideological exaltation; connection with the outside world, not autarky. And it was to change China as fundamentally as the Great Helmsman sought, albeit in a direction opposite of what he had conceived. This is why, at the end of the Southern Tour, Deng sketched his hope for the emergence of a new generation of leaders with their own new viewpoints. The existing leadership of the Communist Party, he said, was too old. Now over sixty, they were better suited for conversation than for decisions. People of his age needed to stand aside—a painful confession for someone who had been such an activist.

> The reason I insisted on retiring was that I didn't want to make mistakes in my old age. Old people have strengths but also great weaknesses—they tend to be stubborn, for example—and they should be aware of that. The older they are, the more modest they should be and the more careful not to make mistakes in their later years. We should go on selecting younger comrades for promotion and helping train them. Don't put your trust only in old age. . . . When they reach maturity, we shall rest easy. Right now we are still worried.[10]

For all the matter-of-factness of Deng's prescriptions, there was about them the melancholy of old age, conscious that he would miss the fruition of what he was advocating and planning. He had seen—and, at times, generated—so much turmoil that he needed his legacy to be a period of stability. For all his show of assurance, a new generation was needed to enable him, in his words, "to sleep soundly."

The Southern Tour was Deng's last public service. The implementation of its principles became the responsibility of Jiang Zemin and his associates. Afterward Deng retired into increasing inaccessibility. He died in 1997, and by then Jiang had solidified his position. Aided by the extraordinary Premier Zhu Rongji, Jiang carried out the legacy of Deng's Southern Tour with such skill that, by the end of his term in office in 2002, the debate was no longer over whether this was the proper course but rather over the impact of an emerging, dynamic China on world order and the global economy.

CHAPTER 17

A Roller Coaster Ride Toward Another Reconciliation

The Jiang Zemin Era

IN THE WAKE of Tiananmen, Sino-U.S. relations found themselves practically back to their starting point. In 1971–72, the United States had sought rapprochement with China, then in the final phases of the Cultural Revolution, convinced that relations with China were central to the establishment of a peaceful international order and transcended America's reservations about China's radical governance. Now the United States had imposed sanctions, and the dissident Fang Lizhi was in the sanctuary of the U.S. Embassy in Beijing. And with liberal democratic institutions being embraced across the world, reform of China's domestic structure was turning into a major American policy goal.

I had met Jiang Zemin when he served as Mayor of Shanghai. I would not have expected him to emerge as the leader who would—as he did—guide his country from disaster to the stunning explosion of energy and creativity that has marked China's rise. Though initially doubted, he oversaw one of the greatest per capita GDP increases in human history, consummated the peaceful return of Hong Kong, reconstituted China's relations with the United States and the rest of the world, and launched China on the road to becoming a global economic powerhouse.

Shortly after Jiang's elevation, in November 1989, Deng was at pains to emphasize to me his high regard for the new General Secretary:

DENG: You have met the General Secretary Jiang Zemin and in the future you will have other chances to meet him. He is a man of his own ideas and of high caliber.

KISSINGER: I was very impressed with him.

DENG: He is a real intellectual.

Few outside observers imagined that Jiang would succeed. As Shanghai's Party Secretary, he had won praise for his measured handling of his city's protests: he had closed an influential liberal newspaper early in the crisis but declined to impose martial law, and Shanghai's demonstrations were quelled without bloodshed. But as General Secretary he was widely assumed to be a transitional figure—and may well have been a compromise candidate halfway between the relatively liberal element (including the Party ideologist, Li Ruihuan) and the conservative group (such as Li Peng, the Premier). He lacked a significant power base of his own, and, in contrast to his predecessors, he did not radiate an aura of command. He was the first Chinese Communist leader without revolutionary or military credentials. His leadership, like that of his successors, arose from bureaucratic and economic performance. It was not absolute and required a measure of consensus in the Politburo. He did not, for example, establish his dominance in foreign policy until 1997, eight years after he became General Secretary.[1]

Previous Chinese Party leaders had conducted themselves with the aloof aura appropriate to the priesthood of a mixture of the new Marxist materialism and vestiges of China's Confucian tradition. Jiang set a different pattern. Unlike Mao the philosopher-king, Zhou the mandarin, or Deng the battle-hardened guardian of the national interest, Jiang behaved more like an affable family member. He was warm and informal. Mao would deal with his interlocutors from Olympian heights, as if they were graduate students undergoing an examination into the adequacy of their philosophical insights. Zhou conducted conversations with the effortless grace and superior intelligence of the Confucian sage. Deng cut through discussions to their practical aspects, treating digressions as a waste of time.

Jiang made no claim to philosophical preeminence. He smiled, laughed, told anecdotes, and touched his interlocutors in order to establish a bond. He took pride, sometimes exuberantly so, in his talent for foreign languages and knowledge of Western music. With non-Chinese visitors, he regularly incorporated English or Russian or even Romanian expressions into his presentations to emphasize a point—shifting without warning between a rich store of Chinese classical idioms and such American colloquialisms as "It takes two to tango." When the occasion allowed it, he might punctuate social meetings—and occasionally official ones—by bursting into song, either to deflect an uncomfortable point or to emphasize camaraderie.

Chinese leaders' dialogues with foreign visitors usually occur in the presence of an entourage of advisors and note takers who do not speak and very rarely pass notes to their chiefs. Jiang, on the contrary, tended to turn his phalanx into a Greek chorus; he would begin a thought, then throw it to an advisor to conclude in a manner so spontaneous as to leave the impression that one was dealing with a team of which Jiang was the captain. Well read and highly educated, Jiang sought to draw his interlocutor into the atmosphere of goodwill that seemed to envelop him, at least in dealing with foreigners. He would generate a dialogue in which the views of his opposite number, and even his colleagues, were treated as deserving of the same importance he was claiming for his own. In that sense, Jiang was the least Middle Kingdom–type of personality that I have encountered among Chinese leaders.

Upon Jiang's elevation to the top ranks of China's national leadership, an internal State Department report described him as "[u]rbane, energetic, and occasionally flamboyant," and related "an incident in 1987 when he rose from the VIP rostrum at Shanghai National Day festivities to conduct a symphony orchestra in a rousing version of the Internationale, complete with flashing lights and clouds of smoke."[2]

During a private visit by Nixon to Beijing in 1989, Jiang had, unannounced, sprung to his feet to recite the Gettysburg Address in English.

There was little precedent for this brand of informality with either Chinese or Soviet Communist leaders. Many outsiders underestimated Jiang, mistaking his avuncular style for lack of seriousness. The opposite was true. Jiang's bonhomie was designed to define the line, when he drew it, that much more definitively. When he believed his country's vital interests were involved, he could be determined in the mold of his titanic predecessors.

Jiang was cosmopolitan enough to understand that China would have to operate *within* an international system rather than through Middle Kingdom remoteness or dominance. Zhou had understood that as well, as had Deng. But Zhou could implement his vision only fragmentally because of Mao's suffocating presence, and Deng's was aborted by Tiananmen. Jiang's affability was the expression of a serious and calculating attempt to build China into a new international order and to restore international confidence, both to help heal China's domestic wounds and to soften its international image. Disarming critics with his occasional flamboyance, Jiang presented an effective face for a government working to break out of international isolation and to spare its system the fate of its Soviet counterpart.

In his international goals, Jiang was blessed with one of the most skillful foreign ministers I have known, Qian Qichen, and a chief economic policymaker of exceptional intelligence and tenacity, the Vice Premier (and eventual Premier) Zhu Rongji. Both men were unapologetic proponents of the notion that China's prevailing political institutions best served its interests. Both also believed that China's continued development required deepening its links to international institutions and the world economy—including a Western world often vocal in its criticism of Chinese domestic political practices. Following Jiang's course of defiant optimism, Qian and Zhu launched themselves into extensive foreign travel, international conferences, interviews, and diplomatic and economic dialogues, facing often skeptical and critical audiences with determination and good humor. Not all Chinese observers relished the project of engaging with a Western world perceived as dismissive of Chinese realities; not all Western observers approved of the effort to engage with a China falling short of Western political expectations. Statesmanship needs to be judged by the management of ambiguities, not absolutes. Jiang, Qian, Zhu, and their senior associates managed to navigate their country out of isolation, and to restore the fragile links between China and a skeptical Western world.

Shortly after his appointment in November 1989, Jiang invited me for a conversation in which he cast events through the lens of returning to traditional diplomacy. He could not understand why China's reaction to a domestic challenge had caused a rupture of relations with the United States. "There are no big problems between China and the U.S. except Taiwan," he insisted. "We have no border disputes; on the Taiwan issue the Shanghai Communiqué established a good formula." China, he stressed, made no claim that its domestic principles were applicable abroad: "We do not export revolution. But the social system of each country must be chosen by that country. The socialist system in China comes from our own historical position."

In any event, China would continue its economic reforms: "So far as China is concerned the door is always open. We are ready to react to any positive gesture by the U.S. We have many common interests." But reform would have to be voluntary; it could not be dictated from the outside:

> Chinese history proves that greater pressure only leads to greater resistance. Since I am a student of natural sciences I try to interpret things according to laws of natural sciences. China has 1.1 billion people. It is large and has lots of momentum. It is not easy to push it forward. As an old friend, I speak frankly with you.

Jiang shared his reflections on the Tiananmen Square crisis. The Chinese government had not been "mentally prepared for the event," he explained, and the Politburo had initially been split. There were few heroes in his version of events—not the student leaders, nor the Party, whom he described ruefully as ineffective and divided in the face of an unprecedented challenge.

When I saw Jiang again nearly a year later, in September 1990, relations with the United States were still tense. The package deal tying our easing of sanctions to the release of Fang Lizhi had been slow in implementation. In a sense, the disappointments were not surprising given the definition of the problem. The American advocates of human rights insisted on values they considered universal. The Chinese leaders were making some adjustments based on their perceptions of Chinese interests. The American activists, especially some NGOs (nongovernmental organizations), were not inclined to declare their goals fulfilled by partial measures. To them, what Beijing considered concessions implied that their objectives were subject to bargaining and hence not universal. The activists emphasized moral, not political, goals; the Chinese leaders were focused on a continuing political process—above all, in ending the immediate tensions and returning to "normal" relationships. That return to normalcy was exactly what the activists either rejected or sought to make conditional.

Lately a pejorative adjective has been entered into the debate, dismissing traditional diplomacy as "transactional." In that view, a constructive long-term relationship with nondemocratic states is not sustainable almost by definition. The advocates of this course start from the premise that true and lasting peace presupposes a community of democratic states. This is why both the Ford administration and the Clinton administration twenty years later failed in obtaining a compromise on the implementation of the Jackson-Vanik Amendment from Congress, even when the Soviet Union and China seemed prepared to make concessions. The activists rejected partial steps and argued that persistence would achieve their ultimate goals. Jiang raised this issue with me in 1990. China had recently "adopted a lot of measures," motivated importantly by a desire to improve relations with the United States:

> Some of them are matters that even concern purely Chinese domestic issues such as the lifting of martial law in Beijing and in Tibet. We proceeded on these matters from two considerations. The first is that they are testimony to the Chinese domestic stability. Second, we don't hide the fact that we use these measures to provide a better understanding for U.S.-China relations.

These moves, in Jiang's view, had not been reciprocated. Beijing had fulfilled its side of Deng's proposed package deal but had been met by escalating demands from Congress.

Democratic values and human rights are the core of America's belief in itself. But like all values they have an absolute character, and this challenges the element of nuance by which foreign policy is generally obliged to operate. If adoption of American principles of governance is made the central condition for progress in all other areas of the relationship, deadlock is inevitable. At that point, both sides are obliged to balance the claims of national security against the imperatives of their principles of governance. Faced with adamant rejection of the principle in Beijing, the Clinton administration chose to modify its position, as we shall see later in this chapter. The problem then returns to the adjustment of priorities between the United States and its interlocutor—in other words, to "transactional" traditional diplomacy. Or else to a showdown.

It is a choice that needs to be made and cannot be fudged. I respect those who are prepared to battle for their views of the imperatives of spreading American values. But foreign policy must define means as well as objectives, and if the means employed grow beyond the tolerance of the international framework or of a relationship considered essential for national security, a choice must be made. What we must not do is to minimize the nature of the choice. The best outcome in the American debate would be to combine the two approaches: for the idealists to recognize that principles need to be implemented over time and hence must be occasionally adjusted to circumstance; and for the "realists" to accept that values have their own reality and must be built into operational policies. Such an approach would recognize the many gradations that exist in each camp, which an effort should be made to shade into each other. In practice this goal has often been overwhelmed by the passions of the controversy.

In the 1990s, American domestic debates were replicated in the discussions with Chinese leaders. Forty years after the victory of Communism in their country, China's leaders would argue on behalf of an international order that rejected the projection of values across borders (once a hallowed principle of Communist policy) while the United States would insist on the universal applicability of its values to be achieved by pressure and incentives, that is, by intervention in another country's domestic politics. There was no little irony in the fact that Mao's heir would lecture me about the nature of an international system based on sovereign states about which I, after all, had written several decades earlier.

Jiang used my 1990 visit for precisely such a discourse. He and other Chinese leaders kept insisting on what would have been conventional wisdom as late as five years earlier: that China and the United States should work together on a new international order—based on principles comparable to those of the traditional European state system since 1648. In other words, domestic arrangements were beyond the scope of foreign policy. Relations between states were governed by principles of national interest.

That proposition was exactly what the new political dispensation in the West was jettisoning. The new concept insisted that the world was entering a "post-sovereign" era, in which international norms of human rights would prevail over the traditional prerogatives of sovereign governments. By contrast Jiang and his associates sought a multipolar world that accepted China's brand of hybrid socialism and "people's democracy," and in which the United States treated China on equal terms as a great power.

During my next visit to Beijing in September 1991, Jiang returned to the theme of the maxims of traditional diplomacy. The national interest overrode the reaction to China's domestic conduct:

> There is no fundamental conflict of interest between our two countries. There is no reason not to bring relations back to normal. If there can be mutual respect and if we refrain from interference in internal affairs, and if we can conduct our relations on the basis of equality and mutual benefit, then we can find a common interest.

With Cold War rivalries ebbing, Jiang argued that "in today's situation ideological factors are not important in state relations."

Jiang used my September 1990 visit to convey that he had taken over all of Deng's functions—this had not yet become obvious, since the precise internal arrangements of the Beijing power structure are always opaque:

> Deng Xiaoping knows of your visit. He expresses his welcome to you through me and expresses his greetings to you. Second, he mentioned the letter which President Bush has written to him and in this respect he made two points. First, he has requested me as General Secretary to extend his greetings through you to President Bush. Second, after his retirement last year he has entrusted all of the administration of these

> affairs to me as General Secretary. I do not intend to write a letter in response to President Bush's letter to Deng Xiaoping but what I am saying to you, although I put it in my words, conforms to the thinking and spirit of what Deng wants to say.

What Jiang asked me to convey was that China had conceded enough, and now the onus was on Washington to improve relations. "So far as China is concerned," Jiang said, "it has always cherished the friendship between our two countries." Now, Jiang declared, China was finished with concessions: "The Chinese side has done enough. We have exerted ourselves and we have done the best we can."

Jiang repeated the by now traditional theme of Mao and Deng—China's imperviousness to pressure and its fearsome resistance to any hint of foreign bullying. And he argued that Beijing, like Washington, faced political pressure from its people: "Another point, we hope the U.S. side takes note of this fact. If China takes unilateral steps without corresponding U.S. moves that would go beyond the tolerance of the Chinese people."

China and the Disintegrating Soviet Union

An undercurrent of all the discussions was the disintegration of the Soviet Union. Mikhail Gorbachev had been in Beijing at the beginning of the Tiananmen crisis, but even while China was being rent by domestic controversy, the basis of Soviet rule was collapsing in real time on television screens all across the world as if in slow motion.

Gorbachev's dilemmas were even more vexing than Beijing's. The Chinese controversies were about how the Communist Party should govern. The Soviet disputes were about whether the Communist Party should govern at all. By giving political reform (*glasnost*) priority over economic restructuring (*perestroika*), Gorbachev had made inevitable a controversy over the legitimacy of Communist rule. Gorbachev had recognized the pervasive stagnation but lacked the imagination or skill to break through its built-in rigidities. The various supervisory bodies of the system had, with the passage of time, turned into part of the problem. The Communist Party, once the instrument of revolution, had no function in an elaborated Communist system other than to supervise what it did not understand—the management of a modern economy, a problem it solved by colluding with what it was allegedly controlling. The Communist elite had become a mandarin class of the privileged; theoretically in charge of the national orthodoxy, it concentrated on preserving its perquisites.

Glasnost clashed with *perestroika*. Gorbachev wound up ushering in the collapse of the system that had shaped him and to which he owed his eminence. But before he did, he redefined the concept of peaceful coexistence. Previous leaders had affirmed it, and Mao had quarreled with Khrushchev over it. But Gorbachev's predecessors had advocated peaceful coexistence as a temporary respite on the way to ultimate confrontation and victory. Gorbachev, at the Twenty-seventh Party Congress in 1986, proclaimed it as a *permanent* fixture in the relationship between Communism and capitalism. It was his way of recentering the international system in which Russia had participated in the pre-Soviet period.

On my visits, Chinese leaders were at pains to distinguish China from the Russian model, especially Gorbachev. In our meeting in September 1990, Jiang stressed:

> Efforts to find a Chinese Gorbachev will be of no avail. You can see that from your discussions with us. Your friend Zhou Enlai used to talk about our five principles of peaceful coexistence. Well they are still in existence today. It won't do that there should only be a single social system in the world. We don't want to impose our system on others and we don't want others to impose theirs on us.

The Chinese leaders affirmed the same principles of coexistence as Gorbachev. But they used them not to conciliate the West, as Gorbachev did, but to wall themselves off from it. Gorbachev was treated in Beijing as irrelevant, not to mention misguided. His modernization program was rejected as ill conceived because it put political reform before economic reform. In the Chinese view, political reform might be needed over time, but economic reform had to precede it. Li Ruihuan explained why price reform could not work in the Soviet Union: when almost all commodities were in short supply, price reform was bound to lead to inflation and panic. Zhu Rongji, visiting the United States in 1990, was repeatedly lauded as "China's Gorbachev"; he took pains to emphasize, "I'm not China's Gorbachev. I'm China's Zhu Rongji."[3]

When I visited China again in 1992, Qian Qichen described the collapse of the Soviet Union as "like the aftermath of an explosion—shock waves in all directions." The collapse of the Soviet Union had indeed created a new geopolitical context. As Beijing and Washington assessed the new landscape, they found their interests no longer as evidently congruent as in the days of near alliance. Then, disagreements had been mainly over the tactics of resisting Soviet hegemony. Now, as the common opponent withered, it was inevitable that the differences in the two leaderships' values and worldviews would come to the fore.

In Beijing, the end of the Cold War produced a mixture of relief and dread. On one level, Chinese leaders welcomed the disintegration of the Soviet adversary. Mao's and Deng's strategy of active, even offensive, deterrence had prevailed. At the same time, Chinese leaders could not avoid comparisons between the unraveling of the Soviet Union and their own domestic challenge. They, too, had inherited an ancient multiethnic empire and sought to administer it as a modern socialist state. Though the percentage of non-Han population was much smaller in China (about 10 percent) than the share of non-Russians in the Soviet empire (about 50 percent), ethnic minorities with distinct traditions existed. Moreover, these minorities lived in regions that were strategically sensitive, bordering Vietnam, Russia, and India.

No American president in the 1970s would have risked confrontation with China so long as the Soviet Union loomed as a strategic threat. On the American side, however, the disintegration of the Soviet Union was seen as representing a kind of permanent and universal triumph of democratic values. A bipartisan sentiment held that traditional "history" was being superseded: allies and adversaries alike were moving inexorably toward adopting multiparty parliamentary democracy and open markets (institutions that, in the American view, were inevitably linked). Any obstacle standing in the way of this wave would be swept aside.

A new concept had evolved to the effect that the nation-state was declining in importance and the international system would henceforth be based on transnational principles. Since it was assumed that democracies were inherently peaceful while autocracies tended toward violence and international terrorism, promoting regime change was considered a legitimate act of foreign policy, not an intervention into domestic affairs.

China's leaders rejected the American prediction of the universal triumph of Western liberal democracy, but they also understood that their reform program needed America's cooperation. So in September 1990 they sent an "oral message" through me to President Bush, which ended with an appeal to the American President:

> For over a century, the Chinese people were all along subjected to bullying and humiliation by foreign powers. We do not want to see this wound reopened. I believe that as an old friend of China, Mr. President, you understand the sentiments of the Chinese people. China cherishes Sino-U.S. friendly relations and cooperation which did not come easily, but it cherishes its independence, sovereignty and dignity even more.

> Against the new background, there is all the more need for Sino-U.S. relations to return to normal without delay. I am sure that you can find a way leading to that goal. And we will make the necessary response to any positive actions that you may take in the interest of better Sino-U.S. relations.

To reinforce what Jiang had told me personally, Chinese Foreign Ministry officials gave me a written message to transmit to President Bush. Unsigned, it was described as a written oral communication—more formal than a conversation, less explicit than an official note. In addition, the Vice Minister of Foreign Affairs escorting me to the airport handed me written replies to clarifying questions I had raised during the meeting with Jiang. Like the message, they had already been conveyed at the meeting; they were given to me in writing for emphasis:

Question: What is the significance of Deng not answering the President's letter?
Answer: Deng retired last year. He already sent the President an oral message saying that all administrative authority over such affairs has been given to Jiang.

Question: Why is the answer oral rather than written?
Answer: Deng has read the letter. But since he entrusted these matters to Jiang, he asked Jiang to reply. We wanted to give Dr. Kissinger the opportunity to convey an oral message to the President because of the role Dr. Kissinger played in favor of U.S.-Chinese relations.

Question: Is Deng aware of the content of your reply?
Answer: Of course.

Question: When you mention U.S. failure to take "corresponding measures," what do you have in mind?
Answer: Biggest problem is continued U.S. sanctions on China. Would be

> best if the President could lift them or even lift de facto. Also the U.S. has a decisive say in World Bank loans. Another point concerns high-level visits which was part of the package.
>
> . . .

Question: Would you be willing to consider another package deal?
Answer: It is illogical since the first package never materialized.

President George H. W. Bush believed from personal experience that to carry out a policy of intervention in the most populous nation and the state with the longest continuous history of self-government was inadvisable. Prepared to intervene in special circumstances and on behalf of individuals or specific groups, he thought an across-the-board confrontation over China's domestic structure would jeopardize a relationship vital to American national security.

In response to Jiang's oral message, Bush made an exception to the ban on high-level visits to China and encouraged his Secretary of State, James Baker, to visit Beijing for consultations. Relations steadied for a brief interval. But when the Clinton administration came into office eighteen months later they returned, for most of the new administration's first term, to a roller coaster ride.

The Clinton Administration and China Policy

On the campaign trail in September 1992, Bill Clinton had challenged China's governmental principles and criticized the Bush administration for "coddling" Beijing in the wake of Tiananmen. "China cannot withstand forever the forces of democratic change," Clinton argued. "One day it will go the way of Communist regimes in Eastern Europe and the former Soviet Union. The United States must do what it can to encourage that process."[4]

After Clinton took office in 1993, he adopted "enlargement" of democracies as a principal foreign policy objective. The goal was, he proclaimed to the U.N. General Assembly in September 1993, to "expand and strengthen the world's community of market-based democracies" and to "enlarge the circle of nations that live under those free institutions" until humanity achieved "a world of thriving democracies that cooperate with each other and live in peace."[5]

The new administration's aggressive human rights posture was not intended as a strategy for weakening China or gaining a strategic edge for the United States. It reflected a general concept of world order in which China was expected to participate as a respected member. From the Clinton administration's point of view, it was a sincere attempt to support practices that the President and his advisors believed would serve China well.

In Beijing, however, the American pressures, which were reinforced by other Western democracies, were seen as a design to keep China weak by interfering in its domestic issues in the manner of the nineteenth-century colonialists. The Chinese leaders interpreted the new administration's pronouncements as a capitalist attempt to overthrow Communist governments all over the world. They harbored a deep suspicion that, with the Soviet Union disintegrating, the United States might do as Mao had predicted: turn from the destruction of one Communist giant to "poke its finger" in the back of the other.

In his confirmation hearings as Secretary of State, Warren Christopher phrased the goal of transforming China in more limited terms: that the United States would "seek to facilitate a peaceful evolution of China from communism to democracy by encouraging the forces of economic and political liberalization in that great country."[6] But Christopher's reference to "peaceful evolution" revived, whether intentionally or not, the term used by John Foster Dulles to project the eventual collapse of Communist states. In Beijing, it signaled not a hopeful trend, but perceived Western designs to convert China to capitalist democracy without recourse to war.[7] Neither Clinton's nor Christopher's statements were regarded as controversial in the United States; both were anathema in Beijing.

Having thrown down the gauntlet—without perhaps fully recognizing the magnitude of its challenge—the Clinton administration proclaimed that it was ready to "engage" China on a broad range of issues. These included the conditions of China's domestic reform and its integration with the broader world economy. That the Chinese leaders might have qualms about entering into a dialogue with the same high American officials who had just called for the replacement of their political system was apparently not considered an insuperable obstacle. The fate of this initiative illustrates the complexities and ambiguities of such a policy.

Chinese leaders no longer made any claim to represent a unique revolutionary truth available for export. Instead, they espoused the essentially defensive aim of working toward a world not overtly hostile to their system of governance or territorial integrity and buying time to develop their economy and work out their domestic problems at their own pace. It was a foreign policy posture arguably closer to Bismarck's than Mao's: incremental, defensive, and based on building dams against unfavorable historical tides. But even as tides were shifting, Chinese leaders projected a fiery sense of independence. They masked their concern by missing no opportunity to proclaim that they would resist outside pressure to the utmost. As Jiang insisted to me in 1991: "[W]e never submit to pressure. This is very important [*spoken in English*]. It is a philosophical principle."

Nor did China's leaders accept the interpretation of the end of the Cold War as ushering in a period of America as a hyperpower. In a 1991 conversation, Qian Qichen cautioned that the new international order could not remain unipolar indefinitely and that China would work toward a multipolar world—which meant that it would work to counter American preeminence. He cited demographic realities—including a somewhat threatening reference to China's massive population advantage—to bolster his point:

> We believe it is impossible that such a unipolar world would come into existence. Some people seem to believe that after the end of the Gulf War and the Cold War, the U.S. can do anything. I don't think that is correct. . . . In the Muslim world there are over 1 billion people. China has a population of 1.1 billion. The population of South Asia is over 1 billion. The population of China is more than the populations of the U.S., the Soviet Union, Europe and Japan combined. So it is still a diverse world.

Premier Li Peng delivered possibly the most frank assessment of the human rights issue. In reply to my delineation of three policy areas in need of improvement—human rights, weapons technology transfer, and trade—he stated in December 1992:

> With regard to the three areas you mentioned, we can talk about human rights. But because of major differences between us, I doubt major progress is possible. The concept of human rights involves traditions and moral and philosophical values. These are different in China than in the West. We believe that the Chinese people should have more democratic rights and play a more important role in domestic politics. But this should be done in a way acceptable to the Chinese people.

Coming from a representative of the conservative wing of the Chinese leadership, Li Peng's affirmation of the need for progress toward democratic rights was unprecedented. But so was the frankness with which he delineated the limits of Chinese flexibility: "Naturally in issues like human rights, we can do some things. We can have discussions and without compromising our principles, we can take flexible measures. But we cannot reach a full agreement with the West. It would shake the basis of our society."

A signature China initiative of Clinton's first term brought matters to a head: the administration's attempt to condition China's Most Favored Nation trade status on improvements in China's human rights record. "Most Favored Nation" is a somewhat misleading phrase: since a significant majority of countries enjoy the status, it is less a special mark of favor than an affirmation that a country enjoys normal trade privileges.[8] The concept of MFN conditionality presented its moral purpose as a typically American pragmatic concept of rewards and penalties (or "carrots" and "sticks"). As Clinton's National Security Advisor Anthony Lake explained it, the United States would withhold a benefit until it produced results, "providing penalties that raise the costs of repression and aggressive behavior" until the Chinese leadership made a rational interest-based calculation to liberalize its domestic institutions.[9]

In May 1993, Winston Lord, then Assistant Secretary of State for East Asian and Pacific Affairs, and in the 1970s my indispensable associate during the opening to China, visited Beijing to brief Chinese officials on the new administration's thinking. At the close of his trip, Lord warned that "dramatic progress" on human rights, nonproliferation, and other issues was necessary if China were to avoid suspension of its MFN status.[10] Caught between a Chinese government rejecting any conditionality as illegitimate and American politicians demanding ever more stringent conditions, he made no headway at all.

I visited Beijing shortly after Lord's trip, where I encountered a Chinese leadership struggling to chart a course out of the MFN conditionality impasse. Jiang offered a "friendly suggestion":

> China and the U.S. as two big countries should see problems in the long-term perspective. China's economic development and social stability serve China's interests but also turn China into a major force for peace and stability, in Asia and elsewhere. I think that in looking at other countries, the U.S. should take into account their self-esteem and sovereignty. That is a friendly suggestion.

Jiang again attempted to dissuade the United States from thinking of China as a potential threat or competitor, thereby to reduce American incentives to try to hold China down:

> Yesterday at a symposium I spoke about this issue. I also mentioned an article in *The Times* which suggested China will one day be a superpower. I've said over and over that China will never be a threat to any country.

Against the backdrop of Clinton's tough rhetoric and the belligerent mood in Congress, Lord negotiated a compromise with Senate Majority Leader George Mitchell and Representative Nancy Pelosi that extended MFN for a year. It was expressed in a flexible executive order rather than binding legislation. It confined conditionality to human rights rather than including other areas of democratization that many in Congress urged. But to the Chinese, conditionality was a matter of principle—just as it had been for the Soviet Union when they rejected the Jackson-Vanik Amendment. Beijing objected to the fact of conditions, not their content.

On May 28, 1993, President Clinton signed the executive order extending China's MFN status for twelve months, after which it would be either renewed or canceled based on China's conduct in the interim Clinton stressed that the "core" of the administration's China policy would be "a resolute insistence upon significant progress on human rights in China."[11] He explained MFN conditionality in principle as an expression of American outrage over Tiananmen and continuing "profound concerns" about the manner in which China was governed.[12]

The executive order was accompanied by a rhetoric more pejorative about China than that of any administration since the 1960s. In September 1993, National Security Advisor Lake suggested in a speech that unless China acceded to American demands, it would be counted among what he called "reactionary 'backlash' states" clinging to outmoded forms of governance by means of "military force, political imprisonment and torture," as well as "the intolerant energies of racism, ethnic prejudice, religious persecution, xenophobia, and irredentism."[13]

Other events combined to deepen the Chinese suspicions. Negotiations over China's accession to GATT, the General Agreement on Tariffs and Trade (later subsumed into the World Trade Organization, or WTO), deadlocked over substantive issues. Beijing's bid for the 2000 Olympics came under attack. Majorities in both houses of Congress voiced their disapproval of the bid; the U.S. government maintained a cautious silence.[14] China's application for hosting the Olympics was narrowly defeated. Tensions were further inflamed by an intrusive (and ultimately unsuccessful) American inspection of a Chinese ship suspected of carrying chemical weapons components to Iran. All of these incidents, each of which had its own rationale, were analyzed in China in terms of the Chinese style of Sun Tzu strategy, which knows no single events, only patterns reflecting an overall design.

Matters came to a head with the visit of Secretary of State Warren Christopher to Beijing in March 1994. The purpose of Christopher's visit, he later recounted, was to achieve a resolution of the MFN issue by the time the deadline for the one-year extension of MFN would expire in June, and to "underscore to the Chinese that under the president's policy they had only limited time to mend their human rights record. If they wanted to keep their low-tariff trading privileges, there had to be significant progress, and soon."[15]

Chinese officials had suggested that the timing of the visit was inopportune. Christopher was scheduled to arrive the day of the opening of the annual session of China's legislature, the National People's Congress. The presence of an American Secretary of State challenging the Chinese government on human rights issues promised either to overshadow the body's deliberations or to tempt Chinese officials to take the offensive to prove their imperviousness to outside pressure. It was, Christopher later conceded, "a perfect forum for them to demonstrate that they intended to stand up to America."[16]

And so they did. The result was one of the most pointedly hostile diplomatic encounters since the U.S.-China rapprochement. Lord, who accompanied Christopher, described Christopher's session with Li Peng as "the most brutal diplomatic meeting he'd ever attended"[17]—and he had been at my side during all the negotiations with the North Vietnamese. Christopher related in his memoirs the reaction of Li Peng, who held that

> China's human rights policy was none of our business, noting that the United States had plenty of human rights problems of its own that needed attention. . . . To ensure that I had not failed to appreciate the depth of their unhappiness, the Chinese abruptly canceled my meeting later in the day with President Jiang Zemin.[18]

These tensions, which seemed to undo two decades of creative China policy, led to a split in the administration between the economic departments and the political departments charged with pressing the human rights issues. Faced with Chinese resistance and American domestic pressures from companies doing business in China, the administration began to find itself in the demeaning position of pleading with

Beijing in the final weeks before the MFN deadline to make enough modest concessions to justify extending MFN.

Shortly after Christopher's return, and with the self-imposed deadline for MFN renewal at hand, the administration quietly abandoned its policy of conditionality. On May 26, 1994, Clinton announced that the policy's usefulness had been exhausted and that China's MFN status would be extended for another year essentially without conditions. He pledged to pursue human rights progress by other means, such as support for NGOs in China and encouraging best business practices.

Clinton, it must be repeated, throughout had every intention to support the policies that had sustained relations with China for five administrations of both parties. But as a recently elected President he was also sensitive to domestic American opinion, more so than to the intangibles of the Chinese approach to foreign policy. He put forward conditionality out of conviction and, above all, because he sought to protect China policy from the swelling congressional onslaught that was attempting to deny MFN to China altogether. Clinton believed that the Chinese "owed" the U.S. administration human rights concessions in return for restoring high-level contacts and putting forward MFN. But the Chinese considered that they were "entitled" to the same unconditional high-level contacts and trade terms extended to them by all other nations. They did not view the removal of a unilateral threat as a concession, and they were extraordinarily touchy regarding any hint of intervention in their domestic affairs. So long as human rights remained the principal subject of the Sino-American dialogue, deadlock was inevitable. This experience should be studied carefully by advocates of a confrontational policy in our day.

During the remainder of his first term, Clinton toned down the confrontational tactics and emphasized "constructive engagement." Lord assembled America's Asian ambassadors in Hawaii to discuss a comprehensive Asia policy balancing the administration's human rights goals with its geopolitical imperatives. Beijing committed itself to renewed dialogue, essential for the success of China's reform program and membership in the WTO.

Clinton, as George H. W. Bush had before him, sympathized with the concerns of the advocates for democratic change and human rights. But like all his predecessors and successors, he came to appreciate the strength of Chinese leaders' convictions and their tenacity in the face of public challenge.

Relations between China and the United States rapidly mended. A long-sought visit by Jiang to Washington took place in 1997 and was reciprocated by an eight-day visit by Clinton to Beijing in 1998. Both Presidents performed ebulliently. Extended communiqués were published. They established consultative institutions, dealt with a host of technical issues, and ended the atmosphere of confrontation of nearly a decade.

What the relationship lacked was a defining shared purpose such as had united Beijing and Washington in resistance to Soviet "hegemonism." American leaders could not remain oblivious to the various pressures regarding human rights that were generated by their own domestic politics and convictions. The Chinese leaders continued to see American policy as at least partially designed to keep China from reaching great power status. In a 1995 conversation Li Peng sounded a theme of reassurance, which amounted to calming presumed American fears over what objectives a resurgent China might seek: "[T]here is no need for some people to worry about the rapid development. China will take 30 years to catch up with the medium level countries. Our population is too big." The United States, in turn, made regular pledges that it had not changed its policy to containment. The implication of both assurances was that each side had the capability of implementing what it reassured the other about and was in part restraining itself. Reassurance thus merged with threat.

The Third Taiwan Strait Crisis

The tensions surrounding the granting of Most Favored Nation status were in the process of being overcome when the issue of Taiwan reemerged. Within the framework of the tacit bargain undergirding the three communiqués on which the normalization of relations had been based, Taiwan had established a vibrant economy and democratic institutions. It had joined the Asian Development Bank and APEC (Asian Pacific Economic Cooperation) and participated in the Olympic Games with Beijing's acquiescence. For its part, Beijing had put forward, beginning in the 1980s, proposals for unification in which Taiwan was to be given total internal autonomy. So long as Taiwan accepted its status as a "Special Administrative Region" of the People's Republic (the same legal status that Hong Kong and Macao were to have), Beijing pledged, it would be permitted to retain its own distinct political institutions and even its own armed forces.[19]

Taipei's reaction to these proposals was circumspect. But it benefitted from the People's Republic's economic transformation and became increasingly economically interdependent with it. Following the loosening of restrictions on bilateral trade and investment in the late 1980s, many Taiwanese companies shifted production to the mainland. By the end of 1993, Taiwan had surpassed Japan to become the second-largest source of overseas investment in China.[20]

While economic interdependence developed, the two sides' political paths diverged significantly. In 1987, Taiwan's aging leader, Chiang Ching-kuo, had lifted martial law. A dramatic liberalization of Taiwan's domestic institutions followed: press restrictions were lifted; rival political parties were allowed to stand for legislative elections. In 1994, a constitutional amendment laid the groundwork for the direct election of the Taiwanese President by universal suffrage. New voices in Taiwan's political arena that had had their activities circumscribed by the martial law–era restrictions now began advocating a distinct

Taiwanese national identity and potentially formal independence. Chief among them was Lee Teng-hui, the mercurial agricultural economist who had worked his way up the ranks of the Nationalist Party and was appointed its chairman in 1988.

Lee incarnated everything Beijing detested in a Taiwanese official. He had grown up during the Japanese colonization of Taiwan, taken a Japanese name, studied in Japan, and served in the Imperial Japanese Army during World War II. Later he had received advanced education in the United States, at Cornell University. Unlike most Nationalist Party officials, Lee was a native Taiwanese; he was outspoken about regarding himself as "a Taiwan person first and a Chinese person second," and was a proud and insistent proponent of Taiwan's distinct institutions and historical experience.[21]

As the 1996 election drew nearer, Lee and his Cabinet engaged in a series of acts designed step by step to increase what they described as Taiwan's "international living space." To the discomfort of Beijing (and many in Washington), Lee and other senior ministers embarked on a course of "vacation diplomacy" that found large delegations of Taiwanese officials traveling "unofficially" to world capitals, occasionally during meetings of international organizations, and then maneuvering to be received with as many of the formal trappings of statehood as possible.

The Clinton administration attempted to stand apart from these developments. In a November 1993 meeting and press conference with Jiang Zemin in Seattle, on the occasion of an APEC summit of nations from both sides of the Pacific, Clinton stated:

> In our meeting I reaffirmed the United States support for the three joint communiqués as the bedrock of our one China policy. . . .
>
> The policy of the United States on one China is the right policy for the United States. It does not preclude us from

> following the Taiwan Relations Act, nor does it preclude us from the strong economic relationship we enjoy with Taiwan. There's a representative [of Taiwan], as you know, here at this meeting. So I feel good about where we are on that. But I don't think that will be a major stumbling block in our relationship with China.[22]

For Clinton's approach to work, Taiwan's leaders needed to exercise restraint. But Lee was determined to push the principle of Taiwan's national identity. In 1994, he sought permission to stop in Hawaii to refuel his plane en route to Central America—the first time a Taiwanese President had landed on American soil. Lee's next target was the 1995 reunion at Cornell, where he had obtained his economics PhD in 1958. Vigorously urged by the newly elected Speaker of the House, Newt Gingrich, Congress voted unanimously in the House and with only one dissenting vote in the Senate to support Lee's visit. Warren Christopher had assured the Chinese Foreign Minister in April that approving Lee's visit would be "inconsistent with American policy." But in the face of such formidable pressure, the administration reversed itself and granted the request for a personal and unofficial visit.

Once at Cornell, Lee delivered a speech straining the definition of "unofficial." After a brief nod to fond memories of his time at Cornell, Lee launched into a rousing talk on the aspirations of Taiwan's people for formal recognition. Lee's elliptical phrasings, frequent references to his "country" and "nation," and blunt discussion of the imminent demise of Communism all exceeded Beijing's tolerance.

Beijing recalled its ambassador from Washington, delayed the approval of the American ambassadorial nominee, James Sasser, and canceled other official contacts with the American government. Then, following the script of the Taiwan Strait Crises of the 1950s, Beijing began military exercises and missile tests off the coast of southeast China that were equal parts military deterrent and political theater.

In a series of threatening moves, China fired missiles into the Taiwan Strait—to demonstrate its military capabilities and to warn Taiwan's leaders. But it used dummy warheads, thus signaling that the launches had a primarily symbolic quality.

Quiescence on Taiwan could be maintained only so long as none of the parties challenged the three communiqués. For they contained so many ambiguities that an effort by any party to alter the structure or to impose its interpretation of the clauses would upend the entire framework. Beijing had not pressed for the clarification, but once it was challenged, it felt compelled to demonstrate at a minimum how seriously China took the issue.

In early July 1995, as the crisis was still gathering momentum, I was in Beijing with a delegation from the America-China Society, a bipartisan group of former high officials dealing with China. On July 4, we met with then Vice Premier Qian Qichen and the Chinese ambassador to the United States, Li Daoyu. Qian laid out the Chinese position. Sovereignty was nonnegotiable:

> Dr. Kissinger, you must be aware that China attaches great importance to Sino-U.S. relations, despite our occasional quarrels. We hope to see Sino-U.S. relations restored to normal and improved. But the U.S. government should be clear about the point: we have no maneuver-room on the Taiwan question. We will never give up our principled position on Taiwan.

Relations with China had reached a point where the weapon of choice of both the United States and China was the suspension of high-level contacts, creating the paradox that both sides were depriving themselves of the mechanism for dealing with a crisis when it was most needed. After the disintegration of the Soviet Union, each side proclaimed friendship with the other less to pursue a common strategic objective than to find a way to symbolize cooperation—at that moment, in defiance of its actuality.

The Chinese leaders conveyed shortly after my arrival their desire for a peaceful outcome by one of the subtle gestures at which they are so adept. Before the formal schedule of the America-China Society began, I was invited to give a talk at a secondary school in Tianjin that Zhou Enlai had once attended. Accompanied by a senior Foreign Ministry official, I was photographed near a statue of Zhou, and the official introducing me used the occasion to recall the heyday of close Sino-American cooperation.

Another sign that matters would not get out of hand came from Jiang. While the rhetoric on all sides was intense, I asked Jiang whether Mao's statement that China could wait one hundred years for Taiwan still stood. No, replied Jiang. When I asked in what way not, Jiang responded, "The promise was made twenty-three years ago. Now only seventy-seven years are left."

The professed mutual desire to ease tensions ran up, however, against the aftermath of the Tiananmen crisis. There had been no high-level dialogue, nor a ministerial visit, since 1989; the only high-level discussion for six years had been at the sidelines of international meetings or at the U.N. Paradoxically, in the aftermath of military maneuvers in the Taiwan Strait, the immediate issue resolved itself into a partly procedural problem of how a meeting between leaders could be arranged.

Ever since Tiananmen, the Chinese had sought an invitation for a presidential visit to Washington. Both Presidents Bush and Clinton had evaded the prospect. It rankled. The Chinese, too, were refusing high-level contacts until assurances were given to forestall a repetition of the visit to America by the Taiwanese President.

Matters were back to the discussions at the end of the secret visit twenty-five years earlier, which had briefly stalemated over the issue of who was inviting whom—a deadlock broken by a formula by Mao, which could be read as implying that each side had invited the other.

A solution of sorts was found when Secretary of State Christopher and the Chinese Foreign Minister met on the occasion of an ASEAN meeting in Brunei, obviating the need of determining who had made the first move. Secretary Christopher conveyed an assurance—including a still classified presidential letter defining American intentions—regarding visits to America by Taiwanese senior officials and an invitation for a meeting of Jiang with the President.

The summit between Jiang and Clinton materialized in October, though not in a manner that took full account of China's amour propre. It was not a state visit nor in Washington; rather, it was scheduled for New York, in the context of the fiftieth anniversary celebration of the United Nations. Clinton met with Jiang at Lincoln Center, as part of a series of similar meetings with the most important leaders attending the U.N. session. A Washington visit by a Chinese President in the aftermath of Chinese military exercises in the Taiwan Strait would have encountered too hostile a reception.

In this atmosphere of inconclusive ambivalence—of veiled overtures and tempered withdrawals—Taiwan's parliamentary elections, scheduled for December 2, 1995, raised the temperature again. Beijing began a new round of military exercises off the Fujian coast, with air, naval, and ground forces conducting joint maneuvers to simulate an amphibious landing on hostile territory. This was accompanied by an equally aggressive campaign of psychological warfare. The day before the December legislative election, the PLA announced a further round of exercises to take place in March 1996, just prior to the Taiwanese presidential election.[23]

As the election approached, missile tests "bracketing" Taiwan hit points just off key port cities in the island's northeast and southwest. The United States responded with the most significant American show of force directed at China since the 1971 rapprochement, sending two aircraft carrier battle groups with the carrier *Nimitz* through the Taiwan Strait on the pretext of avoiding "bad weather." At the same time, walking a narrow passage, Washington assured China that it was not changing its one China policy and warned Taiwan not to engage in provocative acts.

Approaching the precipice, both Washington and Beijing recoiled, realizing that they had no war aims over which to fight or terms to impose which would alter the overriding reality, which was (in Madeleine Albright's description) that China "is in its own category—too big to ignore, too repressive to embrace, difficult to influence, and very, very proud."[24] For its part, America was too powerful to be coerced and too committed to constructive relations with China to need to be. A superpower America, a dynamic China, a globalized world, and the gradual shift of the center of gravity of world affairs from the Atlantic Ocean to the Pacific required a peaceful and cooperative relationship. In the wake of the crisis, relations between China and the United States improved markedly.

As relations began to approach previous highs, yet another crisis shook the relationship as suddenly as a thunderclap at the end of a summer day. During the Kosovo war, at what was otherwise a high point in U.S.-Chinese relations, in May 1999, an American B-2 bomber originating in Missouri destroyed the Chinese Embassy in Belgrade. A firestorm of protests swept over China. Students and the government seemed united in their outrage at what was assumed to be another demonstration of American disrespect for China's sovereignty. Jiang spoke of "deliberate provocation." He elaborated with defiance revealing a latent disquiet: "The great People's Republic of China will never be bullied, the great Chinese nation will never be humiliated, and the great Chinese people will never be conquered."[25]

As soon as Secretary of State Madeleine Albright was informed, she asked the Deputy Chairman of the Joint Chiefs of Staff to accompany her to the Chinese Embassy in Washington, though it was the middle of the night, to express the regrets of the U.S. government.[26] Jiang felt obliged by the public mood, however, to express his own outrage but then to use that expression to restrain his public (a pattern similar to that of American Presidents on the human rights issue).

Chinese indignation was matched on the American side by arguments that China needed to be faced down. Both viewpoints reflected serious convictions, and illustrated the potential for confrontation in a relationship in which both sides were drawn by the nature of modern foreign policy into tensions with each other around the world. The governments on both sides remained committed to the need for cooperation, but they could not control all the ways the countries impinged on each other. It is the unsolved challenge of Chinese-American relations.

China's Resurgence and Jiang's Reflections

In the midst of the periodic crises recounted above, the 1990s witnessed a period of stunning economic growth in China, and with it a transformation of the country's broader world role. In the 1980s, China's "Reform and Opening Up" had remained partly a vision: its effects were noticeable, but their depth and longevity were open to debate. Within China itself the direction was still contested; in the wake of Tiananmen some of the country's academic and political elites advocated an inward turn and a scaling back of China's economic links with the West (a trend Deng ultimately felt obliged to challenge through his Southern Tour). When Jiang assumed national office, a largely unreformed sector of state-owned enterprises on the Soviet model still constituted over 50 percent of the economy.[27] China's links to the world trade system were tentative and partial. Foreign companies still were skeptical about investing in China; Chinese companies rarely ventured abroad.

By the end of the decade, what had once seemed an improbable prospect had become a reality. Throughout the decade China grew at a rate of no lower than 7 percent per year, and often in the double digits, continuing an increase in per capita GDP that ranks as one of the most sustained and powerful in history.[28] By the end of the 1990s average income was approximately three times what it had been in 1978; in urban areas the income level rose even more dramatically, to roughly five times the 1978 level.[29]

Throughout these changes, China's trade with neighboring countries was burgeoning, and it played an increasingly central regional economic role. It tamed a period of dangerously escalating inflation in the early 1990s, implementing capital controls and a fiscal austerity program that were later credited with sparing China the worst of the Asian financial crisis in 1997–98. Standing, for the first time, as a bulwark of economic growth and stability in a time of economic crisis, China found itself in an unaccustomed role: once the recipient of foreign, often Western, economic policy prescriptions, it was now increasingly an independent proponent of its own solutions—and a source of emergency assistance to other economies in crisis. By 2001, China's new status was cemented with a successful application to host the 2008 Olympics in Beijing, and the conclusion of negotiations making China a member of the WTO.

Fueling this transformation was a recalibration of China's domestic political philosophy. Traveling further along the reformist road Deng had first charted, Jiang undertook to broaden the concept of Communism by opening it from an exclusive class-based elite to a wider spectrum of society. He spelled out his philosophy, which became known as the "Three Represents," at the Sixteenth Party Congress in 2002—the last Congress he would attend as President on the eve of the first peaceful transfer of power in China's modern history. It laid out why the Party that had won support through revolution needed now to represent as well the interests of its former ideological foes, including entrepreneurs.

Jiang opened the Communist Party to business leaders, democratizing the internal governance of the Communist Party in what remained a one-party state.

Throughout this process, China and the United States were becoming increasingly intertwined economically. At the beginning of the 1990s the total volume of U.S. trade with mainland China was still only half the volume of American trade with Taiwan. By the end of the decade U.S.-China trade had quadrupled, and Chinese exports to the United States had increased sevenfold.[30] American multinationals viewed China as an essential component of their business strategies, both as a locus of production and as an increasingly monetary market in its own right. China in turn was using its increasing cash reserves to invest in U.S. Treasury bonds (and in 2008 would become the largest foreign holder of American debt).

In all this China was surging toward a new world role, with interests in every corner of the globe and integrated to an unprecedented degree with broader political and economic trends. Two centuries after the first mutually miscomprehending negotiations over trade and diplomatic recognition between Macartney and the Chinese court, there was a recognition in both China and the West that they were arriving at a new stage in their interactions, whether or not they were prepared for the challenges it would pose. As China's then Vice Premier Zhu Rongji observed in 1997: "Never before in history has China had such frequent exchanges and communications with the rest of the world."[31]

In earlier eras—such as Macartney's or even the Cold War era—a "Chinese world" and a "Western world" had interacted in limited instances and at a stately pace. Now modern technology and economic interdependence made it impossible, for better or for worse, to manage relations in such a measured manner. As a result, the two sides confronted a somewhat paradoxical situation in which they had vastly more opportunities for mutual understanding, but, at the same time, new opportunities to impinge on each other's sensitivities. A globalized world had brought them together, but also risked more frequent and rapid exacerbation of tensions in times of crisis.

As his period in office moved toward its conclusion, Jiang expressed his recognition of this danger in a personal, almost sentimental, way not generally found in the aloof, conceptual, self-contained manner of the Chinese leadership. The occasion was a meeting in 2001 with some members of the America-China Society. Jiang was in the last year of his twelve-year tenure but already seized by the nostalgia of those who are leaving activity in which, by definition, every action made a difference for a world in which they will soon be largely spectators. He had presided over a turbulent period, which had begun with China substantially isolated internationally, at least among the advanced democratic states, the countries China most needed to implement its reform program.

Jiang had surmounted these challenges. Political cooperation with America had been reestablished. The reform program was accelerating and producing the extraordinary growth rate that would, within another decade, turn China into a financial and economic global power. A decade that began in turbulence and doubt had turned into a period of extraordinary achievement.

In all of China's extravagant history, there was no precedent for how to participate in a global order, whether in concert with—or opposition to—another superpower. As it turned out, that superpower, the United States, also lacked the experience for such a design—if indeed it had the inclination for it. A new international order was bound to emerge, whether by design or by default. Its nature and the measures for bringing it about were the unsolved challenges for both countries. They would interact, either as partners or as adversaries. Their contemporary leaders professed partnership, but neither had yet managed to define it or build shelters against the possible storms ahead.

Now Jiang was encountering a new century and a different generation of American leaders. The United States had a new President, the son of George H. W. Bush, who had been in office when Jiang was elevated so unexpectedly by events no one could have foreseen. The relationship with the new President started with another unsought military clash. On April 1, 2001, an American reconnaissance plane flying along the Chinese coast just outside Chinese territorial waters was being tailed by a Chinese military aircraft, which then crashed into it near Hainan Island off China's southern coast. Neither Jiang nor Bush permitted the incident to torpedo the relationship. Two days later, Jiang left on a long-planned trip to South America, signaling that he, as head of the Central Military Commission, did not expect crisis action. Bush expressed regret, not for the reconnaissance flight but for the death of the Chinese pilot.

Some foreboding of the danger of drifting events seems to have been in Jiang's mind during the meeting with America-China Society members, as he meandered on in a seemingly discursive statement quoting classical Chinese poetry, interjecting English phrases, extolling the importance of U.S.-Chinese cooperation. Prolix as his utterances were, they reflected a hope and a dilemma: the hope that the two countries would find a way to work together to avoid the storms generated by the very dynamism of their societies—and the fear that they might miss their chance to do so.

The key theme of Jiang's opening remarks was the importance of the Sino-American relationship: "I am not trying to exaggerate our self-importance, but good cooperation between the U.S. and China is important for the world. We will do our best to do that [*said in English*]. This is important for the whole world." But if the whole world was the subject, were any leaders really qualified to deal with it? Jiang pointed out that his education had started with traditional Confucianism on a trajectory that included Western education, then schools in the former Soviet Union. Now he was leading the transition of a country that dealt with all these cultures.

China and the United States were confronting an immediate issue, the future of Taiwan. Jiang did not use the familiar rhetoric to which we had become accustomed. Rather, his remarks concerned the internal dynamics of the dialogue and how it might be driven out of control, whatever the intention of the leaders, who might be urged by their publics to actions they would prefer to avoid: "The biggest issue between the U.S. and China is the Taiwan issue. For example, we often say 'peaceful resolution' and 'one country, two systems.' Generally speaking, I limit myself to saying these two things. But sometimes I add that we cannot undertake not to use force."

Jiang could not avoid, of course, the issue that had caused a deadlock in over 130 meetings between Chinese and American diplomats before the opening to China or the deliberate ambiguities since. But while China refused to abjure the use of force because it would imply a limitation of its sovereignty, it had in practice refrained from it for thirty years by the time of the conversation with Jiang. And Jiang had put forward the sacramental language in the gentlest of manners.

Jiang did not insist on an immediate change. Rather, he pointed out that the American position contained an anomaly. The United States did not support independence for Taiwan nor, on the other hand, did it promote reunification. The practical consequence was to turn Taiwan into "an unsinkable aircraft carrier" for America. In such a situation, whatever the intentions of the Chinese government, the convictions of its population might generate their own momentum toward confrontation:

> [I]n the nearly twelve years I've been in the Central government, I've felt very strongly the sentiments of the 1.2 billion Chinese people. Of course we have the best aspirations toward you, but if a spark flares up it will be hard to control the emotions of 1.2 billion people.

I felt obliged to reply to this threat of force, however regretfully and indirectly formulated:

> [I]f the discussion concerns use of force it will strengthen all the forces that want to use Taiwan to harm our relationship. In a military confrontation between the U.S. and China, even those of us who would be heartbroken would be obliged to support our own country.

Jiang replied not by repeating the by now traditional invocation of the imperviousness of China to the danger of war. He took the perspective of a world whose future depended on Sino-American cooperation. He spoke of compromise—a word almost never used by Chinese leaders about Taiwan, even when it was practiced. He avoided making either a proposal or a threat. And he was no longer in a position to shape the outcome. He called for a global perspective—precisely what was most needed and what each nation's history made most difficult:

> It is not clear whether China and the U.S. can find common language and resolve the Taiwan question. I have remarked that if Taiwan were not under U.S. protection, we would have been able to liberate it. Therefore, the question is how we can compromise and get a satisfactory solution. This is the most sensitive part of our relations. I am not suggesting anything here. We are old friends. I do not need to use diplomatic language. In the final analysis, I hope that with Bush in office our two countries can approach U.S.-China relations from a strategic and global perspective.

The Chinese leaders I had previously met had a long-range perspective, but it drew a great deal from lessons of the past. They also were in the process of undertaking great projects with significance for a distant future. But they rarely described the shape of the middle-term future, assuming that its character would emerge from the vast efforts in which they were involved. Jiang asked for something less dramatic but perhaps even deeper. At the end of his presidency, he addressed the need to redefine the philosophical framework of each side. Mao had urged ideological rigor even while making tactical maneuvers. Jiang seemed to be saying that each side should realize that if they were to cooperate genuinely, they needed to understand the modifications they were obliged to make in their traditional attitudes. He urged each side to reexamine its own internal doctrines and be open to reinterpreting them—including socialism:

> The world should be a rich, colorful, diversified place. For example, in China in 1978 we made a decision for reform and opening up. . . . In 1992 in the Fourteenth National Congress I stated that China's development model should be in the direction of a socialist market economy. For those who are accustomed to the West, you think the market is nothing strange, but in 1992 to say "market" here was a big risk.

For that reason, Jiang argued that both sides should adapt their ideologies to the necessities of their interdependence:

> Simply put, the West is best advised to set aside its past attitude toward communist countries, and we should stop taking communism in naive or simplistic ways. Deng famously said in his 1992 trip to the South that socialism will take generations, scores of generations. I am an engineer. I calculated that there have been 78 generations from Confucius until now. Deng said socialism will take so long. Deng, I now think, created very good environmental conditions for me. On your point about value systems, East and West must improve mutual understanding. Perhaps I am being a bit naive.

The reference to seventy-eight generations was intended to reassure the United States that it should not be alarmed at the rise of a powerful China. It would need that many generations to fulfill itself. But political circumstances in China had certainly changed when a successor of Mao could say Communists should stop talking about their ideology in naive and simplistic ways. Or speak of the need for a dialogue between the Western world and China over how to adjust their philosophical frameworks to each other.

On the American side, the challenge was to find a way through a series of divergent assessments. Was China a partner or an adversary? Was the future cooperation or confrontation? Was the American mission the spread of democracy to China, or cooperation with China to bring about a peaceful world? Or was it possible to do both?

Both sides have been obliged ever since to overcome their internal ambivalences and to define the ultimate nature of their relationship.

CHAPTER 18

The New Millennium

THE END OF the Jiang Zemin presidency marked a turning point in Sino-American relations. Jiang was the last President with whom the principal subject of the Sino-American dialogue was the relationship itself. After that, both sides merged if not their convictions then their practice into a pattern of cooperative coexistence. China and the United States no longer had a common adversary, but neither had they yet developed a joint concept of world order. Jiang's mellow reflections in the long conversation with him, described in the last chapter, illustrated the new reality: the United States and China perceived that they needed each other because both were too large to be dominated, too special to be transformed, and too necessary to each other to be able to afford isolation. Beyond that, were common purposes attainable? And to what end?

The millennium was the symbolic beginning of that new relationship. A new generation of leaders had come into office in China and the United States: on the Chinese side, a "fourth generation" headed by President Hu Jintao and Premier Wen Jiabao; on the American side, administrations led by Presidents George W. Bush and, beginning in 2009, Barack Obama. Both sides had an ambivalent attitude toward the turmoil of the decades that preceded them.

Hu and Wen brought an unprecedented perspective to the task of managing China's development and defining its world role. They represented the first generation of top officials without personal experience of the revolution, the first leaders in the Communist period to take office through constitutional processes—and the first to assume positions of national responsibility in a China unambiguously emerging as a great power.

Both men had direct experience of their country's fragility and its complex domestic challenges. As young cadres during the 1960s, Hu and Wen were among the last students to receive formal higher education before the chaos of the Cultural Revolution closed the universities. Educated at Qinghua University in Beijing—a hub of Red Guard activity—Hu stayed at the university as a political counselor and research assistant, able to observe the chaos of the warring factions and, on occasion, becoming their target as allegedly "too individualistic."[1] When Mao decided to put an end to Red Guard depredations by sending the young generation to the countryside, Hu nevertheless shared their fate. He was dispatched to Gansu province, one of China's more desolate and rebellious regions, to work at a hydraulic power plant. Wen, a recent graduate of the Beijing Institute of Geology, received a similar assignment, and was sent to work on mineralogical projects in Gansu, where he would remain for more than a decade. There in the far northwestern reaches of their turmoil-stricken country, Hu and Wen undertook a slow climb up the internal ranks of the Communist Party hierarchy. Hu rose to the position of secretary of the Communist Youth League for Gansu province. Wen became the deputy director of the provincial geological bureau. In an era of upheaval and revolutionary fervor, both men distinguished themselves by their steadiness and competency.

For Hu, the next advancement took place at the Central Party School in Beijing, where, in 1982, he came to the attention of Hu Yaobang, then General Secretary of the Party. It led to a rapid promotion to the position of Party Secretary for Guizhou, in China's remote southwest; at forty-three, Hu Jintao was the youngest provincial Party Secretary in Communist Party history.[2] His experience in Guizhou, a poor province with a substantial number of minorities, prepared Hu for his next assignment in 1988, as Party Secretary for the autonomous region of Tibet. Wen, meanwhile, was transferred to Beijing, where he served in a series of positions of increasing responsibility in the Communist Party's Central Committee. He established himself as a trusted top aide to three successive Chinese leaders: Hu Yaobang, Zhao Ziyang, and, later, Jiang Zemin.

Both Hu and Wen had close personal experience with China's 1989 unrest—Hu in Tibet, where he arrived in December 1988, just as a major Tibetan uprising was unfolding; Wen in Beijing, where as deputy to Zhao Ziyang he was at the General Secretary's side during his last forlorn expedition among the students in Tiananmen Square.

Thus by the time they assumed the top national leadership posts in 2002–2003, Hu and Wen had gained a distinctive perspective on China's resurgence. Trained in its rugged, unstable frontiers and serving at a middle level during Tiananmen, they were conscious of the complexity of China's domestic challenges. Coming to power during a long period of sustained domestic growth and in the wake of China's entry into the international economic order, they assumed the helm of a China undeniably "arriving" as a world power, with interests in every corner of the globe.

Deng had called a truce in the Maoist war on Chinese tradition and allowed the Chinese to reconnect with their historic strengths. But as other Chinese leaders occasionally hinted, the Deng era was an attempt to make up for lost time. There was in this period a sense of special exertion and a subtext of almost innocent embarrassment at China's missteps. Jiang projected unshakable confidence and bonhomie, but he assumed the helm of a China still recovering from domestic crisis and endeavoring to regain its international standing.

It was at the turn of the century that the efforts of the Deng and Jiang periods were coming to fruition. Hu and Wen presided over a country that no longer felt constrained by the sense of apprenticeship to Western technology and institutions. The China they governed was confident enough to reject, and even on occasion subtly mock, American lectures on reform. It was now in a position to conduct its foreign policy not based on its long-term potential or its ultimate strategic role but in terms of its actual power.

Power to what end? Beijing's initial approach to the new era was largely incremental and conservative. Jiang and Zhu had negotiated China's entry into the World Trade Organization and full participation in the international economic order. China under Hu and Wen aspired first of all to normalcy and stability. Its goals, in the official formulations, were a "harmonious society" and a "harmonious world." Its domestic agenda centered on continued economic development, and the preservation of social harmony within a vast population experiencing both unprecedented prosperity and unaccustomed levels of inequality. Its foreign policy avoided dramatic moves, and its chief policymakers responded circumspectly to appeals from abroad for China to play a more visible international leadership role. China's foreign policy aimed primarily for a peaceful international environment (including good relations with the United States) and access to raw materials to ensure continued economic growth. And it retained a special interest in the developing world—a legacy of Mao's Three Worlds theory—even as it moved into the rank of economic superpower.

As Mao had feared, the Chinese DNA had reasserted itself. Confronting the new challenges of the twenty-first century, and in a world where Leninism had collapsed, Hu and Wen turned to traditional wisdom. They described their reform aspirations not in terms of the utopian visions of Mao's continuous revolution, but by the goal of building a "*xiaokang*" ("moderately well-off") society—a term with distinctly

Confucian connotations.[3] They oversaw a revival of the study of Confucius in Chinese schools and a celebration of his legacy in popular culture. And they enlisted Confucius as a source of Chinese soft power on the world stage—in the official "Confucius Institutes" established in cities worldwide, and in the 2008 Beijing Olympics opening ceremony, which featured a contingent of traditional Confucian scholars. In a dramatic symbolic move, in January 2011, China marked the rehabilitation of the ancient moral philosopher by installing a statue of Confucius at the center of the Chinese capital, Tiananmen Square, within sight of Mao's mausoleum—the only other personality so honored.[4]

The new American administration signified a comparable change of generations. Both Hu and Bush were the first Presidents who had been bystanders at their nations' traumatic experiences of the 1960s: for China, the Cultural Revolution; for the United States, the Vietnam War. Hu drew the conclusion that social harmony should be a guideline of his presidency. Bush came into office in the aftermath of the collapse of the Soviet Union amidst an American triumphalism that believed America capable of reshaping the world in its image. The younger Bush did not hesitate to conduct foreign policy under the banner of America's deepest values. He spoke passionately about individual liberties and religious freedom, including on his visits to China.

Bush's freedom agenda projected what seemed improbably fast evolutions for non-Western societies. Nevertheless, in the practice of his diplomacy, Bush overcame the historic ambivalence between America's missionary and pragmatic approaches. He did so not through a theoretical construct but by means of a sensible balance of strategic priorities. He left no doubt about America's commitment to democratic institutions and human rights. At the same time, he paid attention to the national security element without which moral purpose operates in a vacuum. Though criticized in the American debate for his alleged espousal of unilateralism, Bush, in dealing with China, Japan, and India simultaneously—countries that based their policy on national interest calculations—managed to improve relations with each—a model for a constructive Asian policy for the United States. In Bush's presidency, U.S.-China relations were the matter-of-fact dealings of two major powers. Neither side supposed the other shared all of its aims. On some issues, like domestic governance, their goals were not compatible. Still, they found their interests intersecting in enough areas to confirm the emerging sense of partnership.

Washington and Beijing inched closer to each other's positions on Taiwan in 2003, after Taiwan's President Chen Shui-bian proposed a referendum on applying for U.N. representation under the name "Taiwan." Since such a move would have been a violation of American undertakings in the three communiqués, Bush administration officials conveyed their opposition to Taipei. During Wen Jiabao's December 2003 visit to Washington, Bush reaffirmed the three communiqués and added that Washington "opposes any unilateral decision by China or Taiwan to change the status quo"; he suggested that a referendum raising Taiwan's political status would not find support in the United States. Wen responded with a notably forthcoming formulation on the desirability of peaceful reunification: "Our fundamental policy on the settlement of the question of Taiwan is peaceful reunification, and one country–two systems. We would do our utmost with utmost sincerity to bring about national unity and peaceful reunification through peaceful means."[5]

One of the reasons for renewed cooperation was the attacks of September 11, which redirected America's primary strategic focus away from East Asia to the Middle East and Southwest Asia, with wars in Iraq and Afghanistan and a program to combat terrorist networks. China, no longer a revolutionary challenger of the international order and concerned about the impact of global terrorism within its own minority regions, especially Xinjiang, was quick to condemn the 9/11 attacks and offer intelligence and diplomatic support. In the lead-up to the Iraq war, it was notably less confrontational against the United States in the United Nations than some of America's European allies were.

On a perhaps more fundamental level, however, the period began a process of divergence in Chinese and American assessments of how to deal with terrorism. China remained an agnostic bystander to the American projection of power across the Muslim world and above all to the Bush administration's proclamation of ambitious goals of democratic transformation. Beijing retained its characteristic willingness to adjust to changes in alignments of power and in the composition of foreign governments without passing a moral judgment. Its main concerns were continued access to oil from the Middle East and (after the fall of the Taliban) protection of Chinese investments in Afghanistan's mineral resources. With these interests generally fulfilled, China did not contest American efforts in Iraq and Afghanistan (and may well have welcomed them in part because they represented a diversion of American military capabilities from East Asia).

The range of interaction between China and the United States signified the reestablishment of a central role for China in regional and world affairs. China's quest for equal partnership was no longer the outsized claim of a vulnerable country; it was increasingly a reality backed by financial and economic capacities. At the same time, impelled by new security challenges and changing economic realities, and not least a new alignment of relative political and economic influence between them, both countries were engaged in searching debates about their domestic purposes, their world roles—and ultimately their relation to each other.

Differences in Perspective

As the new century progressed, two trends emerged, in some respects working against each other. On many issues, Sino-American relations evolved in a largely cooperative manner. At the same time, differences rooted in history and geopolitical orientation began to be apparent. Economic issues and the proliferation of weapons of mass destruction are good examples.

Economic Issues: When China was a minor player in the world economy, the exchange rate for its currency was not an issue; even during the 1980s and 1990s, it would have seemed improbable that the value of the yuan would become a daily point of dispute in American political debate and media analysis. But China's economic rise and growing U.S.-China economic interdependence turned the once arcane issue into a daily controversy, with American frustrations—and Chinese suspicions about American intentions—expressed in increasingly insistent language.

The fundamental difference arises over the concept underlying the two sides' respective currency policies. In the American view, the low value of the yuan (also known as the renminbi) is treated as currency manipulation favoring Chinese companies and, by extension, harming American companies operating in the same general industries. An undervalued yuan is said to contribute to the loss of American jobs—a point of serious political and emotional consequence in an age of incipient American austerity. In the Chinese view, the pursuit of a currency policy that favors domestic manufacturers is not an economic policy so much as an expression of China's need for political stability. Thus in explaining to an American audience in September 2010 why China would not drastically revalue its currency, Wen Jiabao used social, not financial, arguments: "You don't know how many Chinese companies would go bankrupt. There would be major disturbances. Only the Chinese premier has such pressure on his shoulders. This is the reality."[6]

The United States treats economic issues from the point of view of the requirements of global growth. China considers the political implications, both domestic and international. When America urges China to consume more and export less, it puts forward an economic maxim. But for China, a shrinking export sector means a perhaps significant increase in unemployment with political consequences. Ironically, from the long-range point of view, were China to adopt the American conventional wisdom, it might reduce its incentives for ties with America because it would be less dependent on exports and foster the development of an Asian bloc because it would imply enhanced economic ties with neighboring countries.

The underlying issue is therefore political not economic. A concept of mutual benefit rather than recriminations over alleged misconduct must emerge. This makes it important to evolve the concept of co-evolution and of Pacific Community discussed in the epilogue.

Nonproliferation and North Korea: Throughout the Cold War, nuclear weapons were in the possession primarily of the United States and the Soviet Union. For all their ideological and geopolitical hostility, their calculation of risk was essentially parallel, and they possessed the technical means to protect themselves against accident, unauthorized launches, and, to a considerable extent, surprise attack. But as nuclear weapons spread, this balance is in jeopardy: the calculation of risk is no longer symmetrical; and technical safeguards against accidental launch or even theft will be much more difficult, if not impossible, to implement—especially for countries without the expertise of the superpowers.

As proliferation accelerates, the calculus of deterrence grows increasingly abstract. It becomes ever more difficult to decide who is deterring whom and by what calculations. Even if it is assumed that new nuclear countries have the same reluctance as the established ones with respect to initiating nuclear hostilities against each other—an extremely dubious judgment—they may use their weapons to protect terrorist or rogue state assaults on the international order. Finally, the experience with the "private" proliferation network of apparently friendly Pakistan with North Korea, Libya, and Iran demonstrates the vast consequences to the international order of the spread of nuclear weapons, even when the proliferating country does not meet the formal criteria of a rogue state.

The spread of these weapons into hands not restrained by the historical and political considerations of the major states augurs a world of devastation and human loss without precedent even in our age of genocidal killings.

It is ironic that nuclear proliferation in North Korea should emerge on the agenda of the dialogue between Washington and Beijing, for it is over Korea that the United States and the People's Republic of China first encountered each other on the battlefield sixty years ago. In 1950, the just established People's Republic went to war with the United States because it saw in a permanent American military presence on its border with Korea a threat to Chinese long-term security. Sixty years later, the commitment of North Korea to a military nuclear program has created a new challenge re-creating some of the same geopolitical issues.

For the first ten years of North Korea's nuclear program, China took the position that it was a matter for the United States and North Korea to settle between themselves. Because North Korea felt threatened primarily by the United States, so the Chinese argument went, it was chiefly up to the United States to provide it with the requisite sense of security to substitute for nuclear weapons. With the passage of time it became obvious that nuclear proliferation into North Korea would sooner or later affect China's security. If North Korea were to be accepted as a nuclear power, it is highly likely that Japan and South Korea, and possibly other Asian countries such as Vietnam and Indonesia, would ultimately also join the nuclear club, altering the strategic landscape of Asia.

China's leaders oppose such an outcome. But equally, China fears a catastrophic collapse of North Korea, since that could re-create at its borders the very conditions it fought to prevent sixty years ago.

The internal structure of the Korean regime compounds the problem. Though it proclaims itself to be a Communist state, its actual authority is in the hands of a single family. In 2011, at this writing, the head of the ruling family is in the process of devolving his power to a twenty-seven-year-old son with no previous experience of even Communist management, much less international relations. The possibility of an implosion from unpredictable or unknowable elements is ever present. Affected countries might then feel obliged to protect their vital interests by unilateral measures. By that time, it would be too late or perhaps too complicated to coordinate action. To prevent such an outcome must be an essential part of a Sino-American dialogue and of the Six Party Talks involving the United States, China, Russia, Japan, and the two Koreas.

How to Define Strategic Opportunity

In the pursuit of dealing with a growing list of issues, Beijing and Washington during the 2000s searched for an overall framework to define their relationship. The effort was symbolized by the inauguration of the U.S.-China Senior Dialogue and the U.S.-China Strategic Economic Dialogue (now merged into one Strategic and Economic Dialogue) during George W. Bush's second term. This was in part an attempt to revitalize the spirit of candid exchange on conceptual issues that prevailed between Washington and Beijing during the 1970s, as described in earlier chapters.

In China, the search for an organizing principle for the era took the form of a government-endorsed analysis that the first twenty years of the twenty-first century represented a distinct "strategic opportunity period" for China. The concept reflected both a recognition of China's progress and potential for strategic gains, and—paradoxically—an apprehension about its continuing vulnerabilities. Hu Jintao gave voice to this theory at a November 2003 meeting of the Communist Party Central Committee's Political Bureau, where he suggested that a unique convergence of domestic and international trends put China in the position to advance its development by "leaps and bounds." Opportunity was linked to danger, according to Hu Jintao; like other rising powers before it, if China "lost the opportunity" presented, "it might become a straggler."[7]

Wen affirmed the same assessment in a 2007 article, in which he warned that "[o]pportunities are rare and fleeting," and recalled that China had missed an earlier opportunity period because of "major mistakes, especially the ten-year catastrophe of the 'great cultural revolution.'" The first fifth of the new century was an opportunity period "which we must tightly grasp and in which we can get much accomplished." Making good use of this window, Wen assessed, would be "of extreme importance and significance" for China's development goals.[8]

What did China have the strategic opportunity to accomplish? To the extent the Chinese debate on this question can be said to have had a formal beginning, it may be found in a series of special lectures and study sessions convened by Chinese academics and the country's top leadership between 2003 and 2006. The program concerned the rise and fall of great powers in history: the means of their rise; the causes of their frequent wars; and whether, and how, a modern great power might rise without recourse to military conflict with the dominant actors in the international system. These lectures were subsequently elaborated into *The Rise of Great Powers,* a twelve-part film series aired on Chinese national television in 2006 and watched by hundreds of millions of viewers. As the scholar David Shambaugh has noted, this may have been a uniquely philosophical moment in the history of great power politics: "Few, if any, other major or aspiring powers engage in such self-reflective discourse."[9]

What lessons could China draw from these historical precedents? In one of the first and most comprehensive attempts at an answer, Beijing sought to allay foreign apprehensions over its growing power by articulating the proposition of China's "peaceful rise." A 2005 *Foreign Affairs* article by the influential Chinese policy figure Zheng Bijian served as a quasi-official policy statement. Zheng offered the assurance that China had adopted a "strategy . . . to transcend the traditional ways for great powers to emerge." China sought a "new international political and economic order," but it was "one that can be achieved through incremental reforms and the democratization of international relations." China, Zheng wrote, would "not follow the path of Germany leading up to World War I or those of Germany and Japan leading up to World War II, when these countries violently plundered resources and pursued hegemony. Neither will China follow the path of the great powers vying for global domination during the Cold War."[10]

Washington's response was to articulate the concept of China as a "responsible stakeholder" in the international system, abiding by its norms and limits and shouldering additional responsibilities in line with its rising capabilities. In a 2005 speech at the National Committee on United States–China Relations, Robert Zoellick, then Deputy Secretary of State, put forward this American response to Zheng's article. While Chinese leaders may have hesitated to grant the implication that they had ever been an "irresponsible" stakeholder, Zoellick's speech amounted to an invitation to China to become a privileged member, and shaper, of the international system.

Almost concurrently, Hu Jintao delivered a speech at the United Nations General Assembly, entitled "Build Towards a Harmonious World of Lasting Peace and Common Prosperity," on the same theme as Zheng Bijian's article. Hu reaffirmed the importance of the United Nations system as a framework for international security and development and outlined "what China stands for." While reiterating that China favored the trend toward democratization of world affairs—in practice, of course, a relative diminution of American power in the direction of a multipolar world—Hu insisted that China would pursue its goals peacefully and within the framework of the U.N. system:

> China will, as always, abide by the purposes and principles of the U.N. charter, actively participate in international affairs and fulfill its international obligations, and work with other countries in building towards a new international political and economic order that is fair and rational. The Chinese nation loves peace. China's development, instead of hurting or threatening anyone, can only serve peace, stability, and common prosperity in the world.[11]

The "peaceful rise" and "harmonious world" theories evoked the principles of the classical era that had secured China's greatness: gradualist; harmonizing with trends and eschewing open conflict; organized as much around moral claims to a harmonious world order as actual physical or territorial domination. They also described a route to great power status plausibly attractive to a generation of leadership that had come of age during the social collapse of the Cultural Revolution, that knew its legitimacy now depended in part on delivering China's people a measure of wealth and comfort and a respite from the previous century's upheavals and privations. Reflecting an even more measured posture, the phrase "peaceful rise" was amended in official Chinese pronouncements to "peaceful development," on the reported grounds that the notion of a "rise" was too threatening and triumphalist.

Over the next three years, through one of the periodic confluences of random events by which historical tides shift, the worst financial crisis since the Great Depression coincided with a period of protracted ambiguity and stalemate in the wars in Iraq and Afghanistan, the awe-inspiring 2008 Beijing Olympic Games, and a continued period of robust Chinese economic growth. The confluence of events caused some of China's elites, including portions of the upper echelons of China's government, to revisit the assumptions underlying the gradualist position articulated in 2005 and 2006.

The causes of the financial crisis and its worst effects were primarily in the United States and Europe. It led to unprecedented emergency infusions of Chinese capital to Western countries and companies, and appeals by Western policymakers for China to change the value of its currency and increase its domestic consumption to foster the health of the world economy.

Ever since Deng's call to "reform and open up," China had seen the West as a model of economic prowess and financial expertise. It was assumed that whatever the Western countries' ideological or political shortcomings, they knew how to manage their economies and the world's financial system in a uniquely productive manner. While China refused to acquire this knowledge at the cost of Western political tutelage, the implicit assumption among many Chinese elites was that the West had a kind of knowledge worthy of diligent study and adaptation.

The collapse of American and European financial markets in 2007 and 2008—and the spectacle of Western disarray and miscalculation contrasted with Chinese success—seriously undermined the mystique of Western economic prowess. It prompted a new tide of opinion in China—among the vocal younger generation of students and Internet users and quite possibly in portions of the political and military leadership—to the effect that a fundamental shift in the structure of the international system was taking place.

The symbolic culmination of this period was the drama of the Beijing Olympics, which took place just as the economic crisis was beginning to tear at the West. Not purely a sporting event, the Games were conceived as an expression of China's resurgence. The opening ceremony was symbolic. The lights in the vast stadium were darkened. At exactly eight minutes after eight o'clock (China time), on the eighth day of the eighth month of the year, taking advantage of the auspicious number that had caused that day to be selected for the opening,[12] two thousand drums broke the silence with one huge sound and continued playing for ten minutes, as if to say: "We have arrived. We are a fact of life, no longer to be ignored or trifled with but prepared to contribute our civilization to the world." After that, the global audience saw an hour of tableaux on themes of China's civilization. China's period of weakness and underachievement—one might call it China's "long nineteenth century"—was officially drawn to a close. Beijing was once again a center of the world, its civilization the focus of awe and admiration.

At a conference of the World Forum on China Studies held in Shanghai in the aftermath of the Olympics, Zheng Bijian, the author of the "peaceful rise" concept, told a Western reporter that China had at last overcome the legacy of the Opium War and China's century of struggles with foreign intrusion, and that it was now engaged in a historic process of national renewal. The reforms initiated by Deng Xiaoping, Zheng said, had allowed China to solve the "riddle of the century," developing rapidly and lifting millions out of poverty. As it emerged as a major power, China would rely on the attraction of its model of development, and relations with other countries would be "open, non-exclusive and harmonious," aiming to "mutually open up the route to world development."[13]

The cultivation of harmony did not preclude the pursuit of strategic advantage. At a July 2009 conference of Chinese diplomats, Hu Jintao delivered a major speech assessing the new trends. He affirmed that the first twenty years of the twenty-first century were still a "strategic opportunity period" for China; this much, he said, had not changed. But in the wake of the financial crisis and other seismic shifts, Hu suggested that the *shi* was now in flux. In light of the "complex and deep changes" now underway, "there have been some new changes in the opportunities and challenges we are facing." The opportunities ahead would be "important"; the challenges would be "severe." If China guarded against potential pitfalls and managed its affairs diligently, the period of upheaval might be turned to its advantage:

> Since entering the new century and the new stage, internationally there has been a series of major events of a comprehensive and strategic nature, which have had a significant and far-reaching influence on all aspects of the international political and economic situation. Looking at the world, peace and development are still the main theme of the times, but the competition for comprehensive national power is becoming more intense; the demands of an expanding number of developing countries to participate equally in international affairs are growing stronger by the day; calls to bring about the democratization of international relations are becoming louder; the international financial crisis has caused the current world economic and financial system and the world economic governance structure to receive a major shock; the prospects for global multipolarity have grown clearer; the international situation has produced some new features and trends worthy of extremely close attention.[14]

With world affairs in a state of flux, China's task was to dispassionately analyze and navigate the new configuration. Out of the crisis, opportunities might arise. But what were these opportunities?

The National Destiny Debate—The Triumphalist View

China's encounter with the modern, Western-designed international system has evoked in the Chinese elites a special tendency in which they debate—with exceptional thoroughness and analytical ability—their national destiny and overarching strategy for achieving it. The world is witnessing, in effect, a new stage in a national dialogue about the nature of Chinese power, influence, and aspirations that has gone on fitfully since the West first pried open China's doors. China's previous national-destiny debates occurred during periods of exceptional Chinese vulnerability; the current debate is occasioned not by China's peril but by its strength. After an uncertain and sometimes harrowing journey, China is finally arriving at the vision cherished by reformers and revolutionaries over the past two centuries: a prosperous China wielding modern military capacities while preserving its distinctive values.

The previous stages of the national-destiny debate asked whether China should reach outward for knowledge to rectify its weakness or turn inward, away from an impure if technologically stronger world. The current stage of the debate is based on the recognition that the great project of self-strengthening has succeeded and China is catching up with the West. It seeks to define the terms on which China should interact with a world that—in the view of even many of China's contemporary liberal internationalists—gravely wronged China and from whose depredations China is now recovering.

As the economic crisis spread across the West in the period after the Olympics, new voices—both unofficial and quasi-official—began to challenge the thesis of China's "peaceful rise." In this view, Hu's analysis of strategic trends was correct, but the West remained a dangerous force that would never allow China to rise harmoniously. It thus behooved China to consolidate its gains and assert its claims to world power and even superpower status.

Two widely read Chinese books symbolize that trend: an essay collection titled *China Is Unhappy: The Great Era, the Grand Goal, and Our Internal Anxieties and External Challenges* (2009), and *China Dream: Great Power Thinking and Strategic Posture in the Post-American Era*

(2010). Both books are deeply nationalistic. Both start from the assumption that the West is much weaker than previously thought, but that "some foreigners have not yet woken up; they have not truly understood that a power shift is taking place in Sino-Western relations."[15] In this view, it is thus up to China to shake off its self-doubt and passivity, abandon gradualism, and recover its historic sense of mission by means of a "grand goal."

Both books have been criticized in the Chinese press and in anonymous postings on Chinese websites as irresponsible and not reflecting the views of the great majority of Chinese. But both books made it past governmental review and became best-sellers in China, so they presumably reflect the views of at least some portion of China's institutional structure. This is particularly true in the case of *China Dream,* written by Liu Mingfu, a PLA Senior Colonel and professor at China's National Defense University. The books are presented here not because they represent official Chinese government policy—indeed, they are contrary to what President Hu has strongly affirmed in his U.N. address and during his January 2011 state visit in Washington—but because they crystallize certain impulses to which the Chinese government has felt itself obliged to respond.

A representative essay in *China Is Unhappy* sets out the basic thesis. Its title posits that "America is not a paper tiger"—as Mao tauntingly used to call it—but rather "an old cucumber painted green."[16] The author, Song Xiaojun, starts from the premise that even under the present circumstances, the United States and the West remain a dangerous and fundamentally adversarial force:

> Countless facts have already proven that the West will never abandon its treasured technique of "commerce at bayonet-point," which it has refined over the course of several hundred years. Do you think it is possible that if you "return the

> weapons to the storehouse and put the war-horses out to pasture"[17] that this will convince [the West] to simply drop their weapons and trade with you peacefully?[18]

After thirty years of rapid Chinese economic development, Song urges, China is in a position of strength: "more and more of the masses and the youth" are realizing that "now the opportunity is coming."[19] After the financial crisis, he writes, Russia has become more interested in fostering its relations with China; Europe is moving in a similar direction. American export controls are now essentially irrelevant because China already possesses most of the technology it needs to become a comprehensively industrialized power and will soon have an agricultural, industrial, and "post-industrial" economic base of its own—in other words, it will no longer be reliant on the products or the goodwill of others.

The author appeals to the nationalist youth and masses to rise to the occasion, and he contrasts the current elites unfavorably with them: "What a good opportunity to become a comprehensively industrialized country, to become known as a country that wants to rise and change the world's unjust and irrational political and economic system—how is it that there are no elites to think of it!"[20]

PLA Senior Colonel Liu Mingfu's 2010 *China Dream* defines a national "grand goal": to "become number one in the world," restoring China to a modern version of its historic glory. This, he writes, will require displacing the United States.[21]

China's rise, Liu prophesies, will usher in a golden age of Asian prosperity in which Chinese products, culture, and values set the standard for the world. The world will be harmonious because China's leadership will be wiser and more temperate than America's, and because China will eschew hegemony and limit its role to acting as *primus inter pares* of the nations of the world.[22] (In a separate passage, Liu comments favorably on the role of traditional Chinese Emperors, whom he describes as acting as a kind of benevolent "elder brother" to smaller and weaker countries' kings.)[23]

Liu rejects the concept of a "peaceful rise," arguing that China cannot rely solely on its traditional virtues of harmony to secure the new international order. Due to the competitive and amoral nature of great power politics, he writes, China's rise—and a peaceful world—can be safeguarded only if China nurtures a "martial spirit" and amasses military force sufficient to deter or, if necessary, defeat its adversaries. Therefore, he posits, China needs a "military rise" in addition to its "economic rise."[24] It must be prepared, both militarily and psychologically, to struggle and prevail in a contest for strategic preeminence.

The publication of these books coincided with a series of crises and tensions in the South China Sea, with Japan, and over the borders of India, in such close succession and of a sufficiently common character as to prompt speculation whether the episodes were the product of a deliberate policy. Though in each case there is a version of events in which China is the wronged party, the crises themselves constitute a stage in the ongoing Chinese debate about China's regional and world role.

The books discussed here, including the criticisms of China's supposedly passive "elites," could not have been published or become a national cause célèbre had the elites prohibited publication. Was this one ministry's way of influencing policy? Does it reflect the attitudes of the generation too young to have lived through the Cultural Revolution as adults? Did the leadership allow the debate to drift as a kind of psychological gambit, so that the world would understand China's internal pressures and begin to take account of them? Or is this just an example of China becoming more pluralistic, allowing a greater multiplicity of voices, and of the reviewers happening to be generally more tolerant of nationalist voices?[25]

Dai Bingguo—A Reaffirmation of Peaceful Rise

China's leaders decided to take a hand in the debate at this point, to demonstrate that the published triumphalism is far from the mood of the leadership. In December 2010, State Councilor Dai Bingguo (the highest-ranking official overseeing China's foreign policy) entered the lists with a comprehensive statement of policy.[26] With the title "Persisting with Taking the Path of Peaceful Development," Dai's article may be seen as a response both to foreign observers concerned that China harbors aggressive intentions, and to those within China—including, one posits, some in the Chinese leadership structure—who argue that China *should* adopt a more insistent posture.

Peaceful development, Dai argues, is neither a ruse by which China "hides its brightness and bides its time" (as some non-Chinese now suspect) nor a naive delusion that forfeits China's advantages (as some within China now charge). It is China's genuine and enduring policy because it best serves Chinese interests and comports with the international strategic situation:

> Persisting with taking the path of peaceful development is not the product of a subjective imagination or of some kind of calculations. Rather, it is the result of our profound recognition that both the world today and China today have undergone tremendous changes as well as that China's relations with the world today have also undergone great changes; hence it is necessary to make the best of the situation and adapt to the changes.[27]

The world, Dai observes, has grown smaller, and major issues now require an unprecedented degree of global interaction. Global cooperation is, therefore, in China's self-interest; it is not a strategy for advancing a purely national policy. Dai continues with what could be read as a standard affirmation of the demand of the people of the world for peace and cooperation—though in context, it is more likely a warning about the obstacles a militant China would face (probably it is addressed to both audiences):

> Because of economic globalization and the in-depth development of informatization, as well as the rapid advances in science and technology, the world has become increasingly "smaller" and has turned into a "global village." With the interaction and interdependence of all countries as well as the intersection of interests reaching an unprecedented level, their common interests have become more extensive, the problems which require them joining hands to address them have multiplied, and the aspirations for mutually beneficial cooperation have grown stronger.[28]

China, he writes, can thrive in such a situation because it is broadly integrated into the world. In the past thirty years it has grown by linking its talents and resources to a broader international system, not as a tactical device but as a means of fulfilling the necessities of the contemporary period:

> Contemporary China is undergoing broad and profound changes. Following more than 30 years of reform and opening up, we have shifted from "class struggle as the key" to economic construction as the central task as we comprehensively carry out the cause of socialist modernization. We have shifted from engaging in a planned economy to promoting reform in all aspects as we build a socialist market economic system. We have shifted from a state of isolation and one-sided emphasis on self-reliance to opening up to the outside world and development of international cooperation.[29]

These "earthshaking" changes require that China abandon the vestiges of Mao's doctrine of absolute self-reliance, which would isolate China. If China fails to correctly analyze the situation and, as Dai insists, "very satisfactorily manage our relations with the external world," then the chances offered by the current strategic opportunity period "may likely be lost." China, Dai emphasizes, "is a member of the big international family." Beyond representing simply moral aspirations, China's harmonious and cooperative policies "are what are most compatible with our interests and those of other countries."[30] Lingering beneath the surface of this analysis, though never stated directly, is the recognition that China has a host of neighbors with significant military and economic capacities of their own, and that China's relations with almost all of them have deteriorated over the past one to two years—a trend the Chinese leadership is seeking to reverse.

With leaders of any country describing their strategies, a tactical element can never be excluded, as there was with the amendment of the phrase "peaceful rise" to the blander "peaceful development." In Dai's article, he specifically addresses foreign skepticism that his arguments may be largely tactical:

> Internationally, there are some people who say: China has a saying: "Hide one's capabilities and bide one's time, and endeavor to achieve something." So they speculate that China's declaration of taking a path of peaceful development is a secret conspiracy carried out under circumstances in which it is still not powerful.

But this, Dai writes, is "groundless suspicion":

> This statement was first made by Comrade Deng Xiaoping in the late 1980s, early 1990s. Its main connotation is: China should remain humble and cautious as well as refrain from

> taking the lead, from waving the flag, from seeking expansion, and from claiming hegemony; this is consistent with the idea of taking the path of peaceful development.[31]

Peaceful development, Dai stresses, is a task for many generations. The importance of the task is underscored by the suffering of generations past. China does not want revolution; it does not want war or revenge; it simply wants the Chinese people to "bid farewell to poverty and enjoy a better life" and for China to become—in contrast to the taunting rejectionism of Mao—"the most responsible, the most civilized, and the most law abiding and orderly member of the international community."[32]

Of course, however much grander goals might be disclaimed, countries in the region—those that have seen the waxing and waning of previous Chinese empires, some of them stretching further than the current political borders of the People's Republic of China—find such disclaimers difficult to reconcile with China's growing power and historical record. Will a country that, for most of its modern period—which in China starts two thousand years ago—regarded itself as the pinnacle of civilization, and that for nearly two centuries has regarded its uniquely moral world leadership position to have been usurped by the rapaciousness of Western and Japanese colonial powers, be content to limit its strategic goals to "build[ing] a moderately prosperous society in all aspects"?[33]

It must, Dai answers. China is "not in a position to be arrogant and boastful" because it still faces tremendous challenges domestically. The Gross Domestic Product of China, no matter how large in absolute numbers, has to be spread over a population of 1.3 billion, of whom 150 million live below the poverty line; therefore "the economic and social problems that we encounter can be said to be the biggest and thorniest issues in the world; hence we are not in a position to be arrogant and boastful."[34]

Dai rejects claims that China will seek to dominate Asia or to displace the United States as the world's preeminent power as "pure myths" that contradict China's historical record and its current policies. He includes a striking invitation from Deng Xiaoping—so contrary to China's usual insistence on self-reliance—to the effect that the world would be allowed to "supervise" China to confirm it would never seek hegemony: "Comrade Deng Xiaoping once stated: If one day China should seek to claim hegemony in the world, then the people of the world should expose, oppose and even fight against it. On this point, the international community can supervise us."[35]

Dai's is a powerful and eloquent statement. Having spent many hours over a decade with this thoughtful and responsible leader, I do not question his sincerity or intent. Still, granting that Hu, Dai, and their colleagues are stating in full candor their perspective for the next stage in Chinese policy, it is difficult to imagine that this will be the last word on China's world role or that it will remain uncontested. A new generation of younger Chinese and rising Party and PLA elites will come into office in 2012—the first generation since the early nineteenth century to have grown up in a China that is at peace, and politically unified, that did not experience the Cultural Revolution, and whose economic performance outstrips that of most of the rest of the world. The fifth generation of Chinese leaders since the creation of the People's Republic, they will, as did their predecessors, distill their experiences into a view of the world and a vision of national greatness. It is on the dialogue with this generation that American strategic thinking needs to occupy itself.

By the time the Obama administration took office, relations had fallen into a distinct pattern. Both Presidents proclaimed their commitment to consultation, even to partnership. But their media and much elite opinion increasingly affirmed a different view.

During Hu Jintao's state visit in January 2011, extensive consultation procedures were reinforced. They will permit increased U.S.-China dialogue on issues as they arise, such as the Korea problem, and attempts to overcome some lingering issues, such as the exchange rate and differing views on the definition of freedom of navigation in the South China Sea.

What remains to be dealt with is to move from crisis management to a definition of common goals, from the solution of strategic controversies to their avoidance. Is it possible to evolve a genuine partnership and a world order based on cooperation? Can China and the United States develop genuine strategic trust?

EPILOGUE

Does History Repeat Itself?

The Crowe Memorandum

A NUMBER OF COMMENTATORS, including some in China, have revisited the example of the twentieth-century Anglo-German rivalry as an augury of what may await the United States and China in the twenty-first century. There are surely strategic comparisons to be made. At the most superficial level, China is, as was imperial Germany, a resurgent continental power; the United States, like Britain, is primarily a naval power with deep political and economic ties to the continent. China, throughout its history, was more powerful than any of the plethora of its neighbors, but they, when combined, could—and did—threaten the security of the empire. As in the case of Germany's unification in the nineteenth century, the calculations of all of these countries are inevitably affected by the reemergence of China as a strong, united state. Such a system has historically evolved into a balance of power based on equilibrating threats.

Can strategic trust replace a system of strategic threats? Strategic trust is treated by many as a contradiction in terms. Strategists rely on the intentions of the presumed adversary only to a limited extent. For intentions are subject to change. And the essence of sovereignty is the right to make decisions not subject to another authority. A certain amount of threat based on capabilities is therefore inseparable from the relations of sovereign states.

It is possible—though it rarely happens—that relations grow so close that strategic threats are excluded. In relations between the states bordering the North Atlantic, strategic confrontations are not conceivable. The military establishments are not directed against each other. Strategic threats are perceived as arising outside the Atlantic region, to be dealt with in an alliance framework. Disputes between the North Atlantic states tend to focus on divergent assessments of international issues and the means of dealing with them; even at their most bitter, they retain the character of an interfamily dispute. Soft power and multilateral diplomacy are the dominant tools of foreign policy, and for some Western European states, military action is all but excluded as a legitimate instrument of state policy.

In Asia, by contrast, the states consider themselves in potential confrontation with their neighbors. It is not that they necessarily plan on war; they simply do not exclude it. If they are too weak for self-defense, they seek to make themselves part of an alliance system that provides additional protection, as in the case with ASEAN, the Association of Southeast Asian Nations. Sovereignty, in many cases regained relatively recently after periods of foreign colonization, has an absolute character. The principles of the Westphalian system prevail, more so than on their continent of origin. The concept of sovereignty is considered paramount. Aggression is defined as the movement of organized military units across borders. Noninterference in domestic affairs is taken as a fundamental principle of interstate relations. In a state system so organized, diplomacy seeks to preserve the key elements of the balance of power.

An international system is relatively stable if the level of reassurance required by its members is achievable by diplomacy. When diplomacy no longer functions, relationships become increasingly concentrated on military strategy—first in the form of arms races, then as a maneuvering for strategic advantage even at the risk of confrontation, and, finally, in war itself.

A classic example of a self-propelling international mechanism is European diplomacy prior to World War I, at a time when world policy was European policy because much of the world was in colonial status. By the second half of the nineteenth century, Europe had been without a major war since the Napoleonic period had ended in 1815. The European states were in rough strategic equilibrium; the conflicts between them did not involve their existence. No state considered another an irreconcilable enemy. This made shifting alliances feasible. No state was considered powerful enough to establish hegemony over the others. Any such effort triggered a coalition against it.

The unification of Germany in 1871 brought about a structural change. Until that time, Central Europe contained—it is hard to imagine today—thirty-nine sovereign states of varying size. Only Prussia and Austria could be considered major powers within the European equilibrium. The multiple small states were organized within Germany in an institution that operated like the United Nations in the contemporary world, the so-called German Confederation. Like the United Nations, the German Confederation found it difficult to take initiatives but occasionally came together for joint action against what was perceived as overwhelming danger. Too divided for aggression, yet sufficiently strong for defense, the German Confederation made a major contribution to the European equilibrium.

But equilibrium was not what motivated the changes of the nineteenth century in Europe. Nationalism did. The unification of Germany reflected the aspirations of a century. It also led over time to a crisis atmosphere. The rise of Germany weakened the elasticity of the diplomatic process, and it increased the threat to the system. Where once there had been thirty-seven small states and two relatively major ones, a single political unit emerged uniting thirty-eight of them. Where previously European diplomacy had achieved a certain flexibility through the shifting alignments of a multiplicity of states, the unification of Germany reduced the possible combinations and led to the creation of a state stronger than each of its neighbors alone. This is why Prime Minister Benjamin Disraeli of Britain called the unification of Germany an event more significant than the French Revolution.

Germany was now so strong that it could defeat each of its neighbors singly, though it would be in grave peril if all the major European states combined against it. Since there were only five major states now, the combinations were limited. Germany's neighboring states had an incentive to form a coalition with each other—especially France and Russia, which did so in 1892—and Germany had a built-in incentive to break the alliances.

The crisis of the system was inherent in its structure. No single country could avoid it, least of all the rising power Germany. But they could avoid policies that exacerbated latent tensions. This no country did—least of all, once again, the German empire. The tactics chosen by Germany to break up hostile coalitions proved unwise as well as unfortunate. It sought to use international conferences to demonstratively impose its will on the participants. The German theory was that the humiliated target of German pressure would feel abandoned by its allies and, leaving the alliance, would seek security within the German orbit. The consequences proved the opposite of what was intended. The humiliated countries (France, in the Moroccan crisis in 1905; and Russia, over Bosnia-Herzegovina in 1908) were reinforced in their determination not to accept subjugation, thereby tightening the alliance system that Germany had sought to weaken. The Franco-Russian alliance was, in 1904, joined (informally) by Britain, which Germany had offended by demonstratively sympathizing with Britain's Dutch settler adversaries in the Boer War (1899–1902). In addition, Germany challenged Britain's command of the seas by building a large navy to complement what was already the most powerful land army on the continent. Europe had slipped into, in effect, a bipolar system with no diplomatic flexibility. Foreign policy had become a zero-sum game.

Will history repeat itself? No doubt were the United States and China to fall into strategic conflict, a situation comparable to the pre–World War I European structure could develop in Asia, with the formation of blocs pitted against each other and with each seeking to undermine or at least limit the other's influence and reach. But before we surrender to the presumed mechanism of history, let us consider how the United Kingdom and German rivalry actually operated.

In 1907, a senior official in the British Foreign Office, Eyre Crowe, wrote a brilliant analysis of the European political structure and Germany's rise. The key question he raised, and which has acute relevance today, is whether the crisis that led to World War I was caused by Germany's rise, evoking a kind of organic resistance to the emergence of a new and powerful force, or whether it was caused by specific and, hence, avoidable German policies.[1] Was the crisis caused by German capabilities or German conduct?

In his memorandum, submitted on New Year's Day 1907, Crowe opted for the conflict being inherent in the relationship. He defined the issue as follows:

> For England particularly, intellectual and moral kinship creates a sympathy and appreciation of what is best in the German mind, which has made her naturally predisposed to welcome, in the interest of the general progress of mankind, everything tending to strengthen that power and influence—on one condition: there must be respect for the individualities of other nations, equally valuable coadjutors, in their way, in the work of human progress, equally entitled to full elbow-room in which to contribute, in freedom, to the evolution of a higher civilization.[2]

But what was Germany's real goal? Was it natural evolution of German cultural and economic interests across Europe and the world, to which German diplomacy was giving traditional support? Or did Germany seek "a general political hegemony and maritime ascendancy, threatening the independence of her neighbours and ultimately the existence of England"?[3]

Crowe concluded that it made no difference what goal Germany avowed. Whichever course Germany was pursuing, "Germany would clearly be wise to build as powerful a navy as she can afford." And once Germany achieved naval supremacy, Crowe assessed, this *in itself*—regardless of German intentions—would be an objective threat to Britain, and "incompatible with the existence of the British Empire."[4]

Under those conditions, formal assurances were meaningless. No matter what the German government's professions were, the result would be "as formidable a menace to the rest of the world as would be presented by any deliberate conquest of a similar position by 'malice aforethought.'"[5] Even if moderate German statesmen were to demonstrate their bona fides, moderate German foreign policy could "at any stage merge into" a conscious scheme for hegemony.

Thus structural elements, in Crowe's analysis, precluded cooperation or even trust. As Crowe wryly observed: "It would not be unjust to say that ambitious designs against one's neighbours are not as a rule openly proclaimed, and that therefore the absence of such proclamation, and even the profession of unlimited and universal political benevolence, are not in themselves conclusive evidence for or against the existence of unpublished intentions."[6] And since the stakes were so high, it was "not a matter in which England can safely run any risks."[7] London was obliged to assume the worst, and act on the basis of its assumptions—at least so long as Germany was building a large and challenging navy.

In other words, already in 1907 there was no longer any scope for diplomacy; the issue had become who would back down in a crisis, and whenever that condition was not fulfilled, war was nearly inevitable. It took seven years to reach the point of world war.

Were Crowe to analyze the contemporary scene, he might emerge with a judgment comparable to his 1907 report. I will sketch that interpretation, though it differs substantially from my own, because it approximates a view widely held on both sides of the Pacific. The United States and China have been not so much nation-states as continental expressions of cultural identities. Both have historically been driven to visions of universality by their economic and political achievements and their people's irrepressible energy and self-confidence. Both Chinese and American governments have frequently assumed a seamless identity between their national policies and the general interests of mankind. Crowe might warn that when two such entities encounter each other on the world stage significant tension is probable.

Whatever China's intentions, the Crowe school of thought would treat a successful Chinese "rise" as incompatible with America's position in the Pacific and by extension the world. Any form of cooperation would be treated as simply giving China scope to build its capacities for an eventual crisis. Thus the entire Chinese debate recounted in chapter 18, and the question of whether China might stop "hiding its brightness," would be immaterial for purposes of a Crowe-type analysis: someday it will (the analysis would posit), so America should act now as if it already had.

The American debate adds an ideological challenge to Crowe's balance-of-power approach. Neoconservatives and other activists would argue that democratic institutions are the prerequisite to relations of trust and confidence. Nondemocratic societies, in this view, are inherently precarious and prone to the exercise of force. Therefore the United States is obliged to exercise its maximum influence (in its polite expression) or pressure to bring about more pluralistic institutions where they do not exist, and especially in countries capable of threatening American security. In these conceptions, regime change is the ultimate goal of American foreign policy in dealing with nondemocratic societies; peace with China is less a matter of strategy than of change in Chinese governance.

Nor is the analysis, interpreting international affairs as an unavoidable struggle for strategic preeminence, confined to Western strategists. Chinese "triumphalists" apply almost identical reasoning. The principal difference is that their perspective is that of the rising power, while Crowe represented the United Kingdom, defending its patrimony as a status quo country. An example of this genre is Colonel Liu Mingfu's *China Dream,* discussed in chapter 18. In Liu's view, no matter how much China commits itself to a "peaceful rise," conflict is inherent in U.S.-China relations. The relationship between China and the United States will be a "marathon contest" and the "duel of the century."[8] Moreover, the competition is essentially zero-sum; the only alternative to total success is humiliating failure: "If China in the 21st century cannot become world number one, cannot become the top power, then inevitably it will become a straggler that is cast aside."[9]

Neither the American version of the Crowe Memorandum nor the more triumphalist Chinese analyses have been endorsed by either government, but they provide a subtext of much current thought. If the assumptions of these views were applied by either side—and it would take only one side to make it unavoidable—China and the United States could easily fall into the kind of escalating tension described earlier in this epilogue. China would try to push American power as far away from its borders as it could, circumscribe the scope of American naval power, and reduce America's weight in international diplomacy. The United States would try to organize China's many neighbors into a counterweight to Chinese dominance. Both sides would emphasize their ideological differences. The interaction would be even more complicated because the notions of deterrence and preemption are not symmetrical between these two sides. The United States is more focused on overwhelming military power, China on decisive psychological impact. Sooner or later, one side or the other would miscalculate.

Once such a pattern has congealed, it becomes increasingly difficult to overcome. The competing camps achieve identity by their definition of themselves. The essence of what Crowe described (and the Chinese triumphalists and some American neoconservatives embrace) is its seeming automaticity. Once the pattern was created and the alliances were formed, no escape was possible from its self-imposed requirements, especially not from its internal assumptions.

The reader of the Crowe Memorandum cannot fail to notice that the specific examples of mutual hostility being cited were relatively trivial compared to the conclusions drawn from them: incidents of colonial rivalry in Southern Africa, disputes about the conduct of civil servants. It was not what either side had already done that drove the rivalry. It was what it might do. Events had turned into symbols; symbols developed their own momentum. There was nothing left to settle because the system of alliances confronting each other had no margin of adjustment.

That must not happen in the relations of the United States and China insofar as American policy can prevent it. Of course, were Chinese policy to insist on playing by Crowe Memorandum rules, the United States would be bound to resist. It would be an unfortunate outcome.

I have described the possible evolution at such length to show that I am aware of the realistic obstacles to the cooperative U.S.-China relationship I consider essential to global stability and peace. A cold war between the two countries would arrest progress for a generation on both sides of the Pacific. It would spread disputes into internal politics of every region at a time when global issues such as nuclear proliferation, the environment, energy security, and climate change impose global cooperation.

Historical parallels are by nature inexact. And even the most precise analogy does not oblige the present generation to repeat the mistakes of its predecessors. After all, the outcome was disaster for all involved, victors as well as defeated. Care must be taken lest both sides analyze themselves into self-fulfilling prophecies. This will not be an easy task.

For, as the Crowe Memorandum has shown, mere reassurances will not arrest the underlying dynamism. For were any nation determined to achieve dominance, would it not be offering assurances of peaceful intent? A serious joint effort involving the continuous attention of top leaders is needed to develop a sense of genuine strategic trust and co-operation.

Relations between China and the United States need not—and should not—become a zero-sum game. For the pre–World War I European leader, the challenge was that a gain for one side spelled a loss for the other, and compromise ran counter to an aroused public opinion. This is not the situation in the Sino-American relationship. Key issues on the international front are global in nature. Consensus may prove difficult, but confrontation on these issues is self-defeating.

Nor is the internal evolution of the principal players comparable to the situation before World War I. When China's rise is projected, it is assumed that the extraordinary thrust of the last decades will be projected into the indefinite future and that the relative stagnation of America is fated. But no issue preoccupies Chinese leaders more than the preservation of national unity. It permeates the frequently proclaimed goal of social harmony, which is difficult in a country where its coastal regions are on the level of the advanced societies but whose interior contains some of the world's most backward areas.

The Chinese national leadership has put forward to its people a catalogue of tasks to be accomplished. These include combating corruption, which President Hu Jintao has called an "unprecedentedly grim task" and in the fight against which Hu has been involved at various stages of his career.[10] They involve as well a "Western development campaign," designed to lift up poor inland provinces, among them the three in which Hu once lived. Key proclaimed tasks also include establishing additional ties between the leadership and the peasantry, including fostering village-level democratic elections, and enhanced transparency of the political process as China evolves into an urbanized society. In his

December 2010 article, discussed in chapter 18, Dai Bingguo outlined the scope of China's domestic challenge:

> According to the United Nations' living standard of $1 per day, China today still has 150 million people living below the poverty line. Even based on the poverty standard of per capita income of 1,200 yuan, China still has more than 40 million people living in poverty. At present, there are still 10 million people without access to electricity and the issue of jobs for 24 million people has to be resolved every year. China has a huge population and a weak foundation, the development between the cities and the countryside is uneven, the industrial structure is not rational, and the underdeveloped state of the forces of production has not been fundamentally changed.[11]

The Chinese domestic challenge is, by the description of its leaders, far more complex than can be encompassed in the invocation of the phrase "China's inexorable rise."

Amazing as Deng's reforms were, part of China's spectacular growth over the initial decades was attributable to its good fortune that there existed a fairly easy correspondence between China's huge pool of young, then largely unskilled labor—which had been "unnaturally" cut off from the world economy during the Mao years—and the Western economies, which were on the whole wealthy, optimistic, and highly leveraged on credit, with cash to buy Chinese-made goods. Now that China's labor force is becoming older and more skilled (causing some basic manufacturing jobs to move to lower-wage countries such as Vietnam and Bangladesh) and the West is entering a period of austerity, the picture is far more complicated.

Demography will compound that task. Propelled by increasing standards of living and longevity combined with the distortions of the one-child policy, China has one of the world's most rapidly aging populations. The country's total working-age population is expected to peak in 2015.[12] From this point on, a shrinking number of Chinese citizens aged fifteen to sixty-four need to support an increasingly large elderly population. The demographic shifts will be stark: by 2030, the number of rural workers between the ages of twenty and twenty-nine is estimated to be half its current level.[13] By 2050, one-half of China's population is projected to be forty-five or older, with a full quarter of China's population—roughly equivalent to the entire current population of the United States—sixty-five and older.[14]

A country facing such large domestic tasks is not going to throw itself easily, much less automatically, into strategic confrontation or a quest for world domination. The existence of weapons of mass destruction and modern military technologies of unknowable ultimate consequences define a key distinction from the pre–World War I period. The leaders who started that war had no understanding of the consequences of the weapons at their disposal. Contemporary leaders can have no illusions about the destructive potential they are capable of unleashing.

The crucial competition between the United States and China is more likely to be economic and social than military. If present trends in the two countries' economic growth, fiscal health, infrastructure spending, and educational infrastructure continue, a gap in development—and in third-party perceptions of relative influence—may take hold, particularly in the Asia-Pacific region. But this is a prospect it is in the capacity of the United States to arrest or perhaps reverse by its own efforts.

The United States bears the responsibility to retain its competitiveness and its world role. It should do this for its own traditional convictions, rather than as a contest with China. Building competitiveness is a largely American project, which we should not ask China to solve for us. China, fulfilling its own interpretation of its national destiny, will continue to develop its economy and pursue a broad range of interests in Asia and beyond. This is not a prospect that dictates the confrontations that led to the First World War. It suggests an evolution in many aspects of which China and the United States cooperate as much as they compete.

The issue of human rights will find its place in the total range of interaction. The United States cannot be true to itself without affirming its commitment to basic principles of human dignity and popular participation in government. Given the nature of modern technology, these principles will not be confined by national borders. But experience has shown that to seek to impose them by confrontation is likely to be self-defeating—especially in a country with such a historical vision of itself as China. A succession of American administrations, including the first two years of Obama's, has substantially balanced long-term moral convictions with case-to-case adaptations to requirements of national security. The basic approach—discussed in previous chapters—remains valid; how to achieve the necessary balance is the challenge for each new generation of leaders on both sides.

The question ultimately comes down to what the United States and China can realistically ask of each other. An explicit American project to organize Asia on the basis of containing China or creating a bloc of democratic states for an ideological crusade is unlikely to succeed—in part because China is an indispensable trading partner for most of its neighbors. By the same token, a Chinese attempt to exclude America from Asian economic and security affairs will similarly meet serious resistance from almost all other Asian states, which fear the consequences of a region dominated by a single power.

The appropriate label for the Sino-American relationship is less partnership than "co-evolution." It means that both countries pursue their domestic imperatives, cooperating where possible, and adjust their relations to minimize conflict. Neither side endorses all the aims of the other or presumes a total identity of interests, but both sides seek to identify and develop complementary interests.[15]

The United States and China owe it to their people and to global well-being to make the attempt. Each is too big to be dominated by the other. Therefore neither is capable of defining terms for victory in a war or in a Cold War type of conflict. They need to ask themselves the question apparently never formally posed at the time of the Crowe Memorandum: Where will a conflict take us? Was there a lack of vision on all sides, which turned the operation of the equilibrium into a mechanical process, without assessing where the world would be if the maneuvering colossi missed a maneuver and collided? Which of the leaders who operated the international system that led to the First World War would not have recoiled had he known what the world would look like at its end?

Toward a Pacific Community?

Such an effort at co-evolution must deal with three levels of relationships. The first concerns problems that arise in the normal interactions of major power centers. The consultation system evolved over three decades has proved largely adequate to that task. Common interests—such as trade ties and diplomatic cooperation on discrete issues—are pursued professionally. Crises, when they arise, are generally resolved by discussion.

The second level would be to attempt to elevate familiar crisis discussions into a more comprehensive framework that eliminates the underlying causes of the tensions. A good example would be to deal with the Korea problem as part of an overall concept for Northeast Asia. If North Korea manages to maintain its nuclear capability through the inability of the negotiating parties to bring matters to a head, the proliferation of nuclear weapons throughout Northeast Asia and the Middle East becomes likely. Has the time come to take the next step and deal with the Korea proliferation issue in the context of an agreed peaceful order for Northeast Asia?

An even more fundamental vision would move the world to a third level of interaction—one that the leaders prior to the catastrophes of the First World War never reached.

The argument that China and the United States are condemned to collision assumes that they deal with each other as competing blocs across the Pacific. But this is the road to disaster for both sides.

An aspect of strategic tension in the current world situation resides in the Chinese fear that America is seeking to contain China—paralleled by the American concern that China is seeking to expel the United States from Asia. The concept of a Pacific Community—a region to which the United States, China, and other states all belong and in whose peaceful development all participate—could ease both fears. It would make the United States and China part of a common enterprise. Shared purposes—and the elaboration of them—would replace strategic uneasiness to some extent. It would enable other major countries such as Japan, Indonesia, Vietnam, India, and Australia to participate in the construction of a system perceived as joint rather than polarized between "Chinese" and "American" blocs. Such an effort could be meaningful only if it engaged the full attention, and above all the conviction, of the leaders concerned.

One of the great achievements of the generation that founded the world order at the end of the Second World War was the creation of the concept of an Atlantic Community. Could a similar concept replace or at least mitigate the potential tensions between the United States and China? It would reflect the reality that the United States is an Asian power, and that many Asian powers demand it. And it responds to China's aspiration to a global role.

A common regional political concept would also in large part answer China's fear that the United States is conducting a containment policy toward China. It is important to understand what one means by the term "containment." Countries on China's borders with substantial resources, such as India, Japan, Vietnam, and Russia, represent realities not created by American policy. China has lived with these countries throughout its history. When Secretary of State Hillary Clinton rejected the notion of containing China, she meant an American-led effort aimed at creating a strategic bloc on an anti-Chinese basis. In a Pacific Community effort, both China and the United States would have constructive relations with each other and all other participants, not as part of confronting blocs.

The future of Asia will be shaped to a significant degree by how China and America envision it, and by the extent to which each nation is able to achieve some congruence with the other's historic regional role. Throughout its history, the United States has often been motivated by visions of the universal relevance of its ideals and of a proclaimed duty to spread them. China has acted on the basis of its singularity; it expanded by cultural osmosis, not missionary zeal.

For these two societies representing different versions of exceptionalism, the road to cooperation is inherently complex. The mood of the moment is less relevant than the ability to develop a pattern of actions capable of surviving inevitable changes of circumstance. The leaders on both sides of the Pacific have an obligation to establish a tradition of consultation and mutual respect so that, for their successors, jointly building a shared world order becomes an expression of parallel national aspirations.

When China and the United States first restored relations forty years ago, the most significant contribution of the leaders of the time was their willingness to raise their sights beyond the immediate issues of the day. In a way, they were fortunate in that their long isolation from each other meant that there were no short-term day-to-day issues between them. This enabled the leaders of a generation ago to deal with their future, not their immediate pressures, and to lay the basis for a world unimaginable then but unachievable without Sino-American cooperation.

In pursuit of understanding the nature of peace, I have studied the construction and operation of international orders ever since I was a graduate student well over half a century ago. On the basis of these studies, I am aware that the cultural, historic, and strategic gaps in perception that I have described will pose formidable challenges for even the best-intentioned and most far-sighted leadership on both sides. On the other hand, were history confined to the mechanical repetition of the past, no transformation would ever have occurred. Every great achievement was a vision before it became a reality. In that sense, it arose from commitment, not resignation to the inevitable.

In his essay "Perpetual Peace," the philosopher Immanuel Kant argued that perpetual peace would eventually come to the world in one of two ways: by human insight or by conflicts and catastrophes of a magnitude that left humanity no other choice. We are at such a juncture.

When Premier Zhou Enlai and I agreed on the communiqué that announced the secret visit, he said: "This will shake the world." What a culmination if, forty years later, the United States and China could merge their efforts not to shake the world, but to build it.

Notes

Prologue

1. John W. Garver, "China's Decision for War with India in 1962," in Alastair Iaian Johnston and Robert S. Ross, eds., *New Directions in the Study of China's Foreign Policy* (Stanford: Stanford University Press, 2006), 116, citing Sun Shao and Chen Zibin, *Ximalaya shan de xue: Zhong Yin zhanzheng shilu [Snows of the Himalaya Mountains: The True Record of the China-India War]* (Taiyuan: Bei Yue Wenyi Chubanshe, 1991), 95; Wang Hongwei, *Ximalaya shan qingjie: Zhong Yin guanxi yanjiu [The Himalayas Sentiment: A Study of China-India Relations]* (Beijing: Zhongguo Zangxue Chubanshe, 1998), 228–30.
2. *Huaxia* and *Zhonghua,* other common appellations for China, have no precise English meaning, but carry similar connotations of a great and central civilization.

Chapter 1: The Singularity of China

1. "Ssuma Ch'ien's Historical Records—Introductory Chapter," trans. Herbert J. Allen, *The Journal of the Royal Asiatic Society of Great Britain and Ireland* (London: Royal Asiatic Society, 1894), 278–80 ("Chapter I: Original Records of the Five Gods").
2. Abbé Régis-Evariste Huc, *The Chinese Empire* (London: Longman, Brown, Green & Longmans, 1855), as excerpted in Franz Schurmann and Orville Schell, eds., *Imperial China: The Decline of the Last Dynasty and the Origins of Modern China—The 18th and 19th Centuries* (New York: Vintage, 1967), 31.
3. Luo Guanzhong, *The Romance of the Three Kingdoms*, trans. Moss Roberts (Beijing: Foreign Languages Press, 1995), 1.
4. Mao used this example to demonstrate why China would survive even a nuclear war. Ross Terrill, *Mao: A Biography* (Stanford: Stanford University Press, 2000), 268.
5. John King Fairbank and Merle Goldman, *China: A New History*, 2nd enlarged ed. (Cambridge: Belknap Press, 2006), 93.
6. F. W. Mote, *Imperial China: 900–1800* (Cambridge: Harvard University Press, 1999), 614–15.
7. Ibid., 615.
8. Thomas Meadows, *Desultory Notes on the Government and People of China* (London: W. H. Allen & Co., 1847), as excerpted in Schurmann and Schell, eds., *Imperial China*, 150.
9. Lucian Pye, "Social Science Theories in Search of Chinese Realities," *China Quarterly* 132 (1992): 1162.
10. Anticipating that his colleagues in Washington would object to this proclamation of Chinese universal jurisdiction, the American envoy in Beijing obtained an alternate translation and textual exegesis from a local British

expert. The latter explained that the offending expression—literally "to soothe and bridle the world"—was a standard formulation, and that the letter to Lincoln was in fact a (by the Chinese court's standards) particularly modest document whose phrasing indicated genuine goodwill. *Papers Relating to Foreign Affairs Accompanying the Annual Message of the President to the First Session of the Thirty-eighth Congress*, vol. 2 (Washington, D.C.: U.S. Government Printing Office, 1864), Document No. 33 ("Mr. Burlingame to Mr. Seward, Peking, January 29, 1863"), 846–48.

11. For a brilliant account of these achievements by a Western scholar deeply (and perhaps excessively) enchanted by China, see Joseph Needham's encyclopedic multivolume *Science and Civilisation in China* (Cambridge: Cambridge University Press, 1954).
12. Fairbank and Goldman, *China*, 89.
13. Angus Maddison, *The World Economy: A Millennial Perspective* (Paris: Organisation for Economic Co-operation and Development, 2006), Appendix B, 261–63. It must be allowed that until the Industrial Revolution, total GDP was tied more closely to population size; thus China and India outstripped the West in part by virtue of their larger populations. I would like to thank Michael Cembalest for bringing these figures to my attention.
14. Jean-Baptiste Du Halde, *Description géographique, historique, chronologique, politique, et physique de l'empire de la Chine et de la Tartarie chinoise* (La Haye: H. Scheurleer, 1736), as translated and excerpted in Schurmann and Schell, eds., *Imperial China*, 71.
15. François Quesnay, *Le despotisme de la Chine*, as translated and excerpted in Schurmann and Schell, eds., *Imperial China*, 115.
16. For an exploration of Confucius's political career synthesizing classical Chinese accounts, see Annping Chin, *The Authentic Confucius: A Life of Thought and Politics* (New York: Scribner, 2007).
17. See Benjamin I. Schwartz, *The World of Thought in Ancient China* (Cambridge: Belknap Press, 1985), 63–66.
18. Confucius, *The Analects,* trans. William Edward Soothill (New York: Dover, 1995), 107.
19. See Mark Mancall, "The Ch'ing Tribute System: An Interpretive Essay," in John King Fairbank, ed., *The Chinese World Order* (Cambridge: Harvard University Press, 1968), 63–65; Mark Mancall, *China at the Center: 300 Years of Foreign Policy* (New York: Free Press, 1984), 22.
20. Ross Terrill, *The New Chinese Empire* (New York: Basic Books, 2003), 46.
21. Fairbank and Goldman, *China*, 28, 68–69.
22. Masataka Banno, *China and the West, 1858–1861: The Origins of the Tsungli Yamen* (Cambridge: Harvard University Press, 1964), 224–25; Mancall, *China at the Center,* 16–17.
23. Banno, *China and the West,* 224–28; Jonathan Spence, *The Search for Modern China* (New York: W. W. Norton, 1999), 197.
24. Owen Lattimore, "China and the Barbarians," in Joseph Barnes, ed., *Empire in the East* (New York: Doubleday, 1934), 22.
25. Lien-sheng Yang, "Historical Notes on the Chinese World Order," in Fairbank, ed., *The Chinese World Order,* 33.
26. As excerpted in G. V. Melikhov, "Ming Policy Toward the Nüzhen (1402–1413)," in S. L. Tikhvinsky, ed., *China and Her Neighbors: From Ancient*

Times to the Middle Ages (Moscow: Progress Publishers, 1981), 209.

27. Ying-shih Yü, *Trade and Expansion in Han China: A Study in the Structure of Sino-Barbarian Economic Relations* (Berkeley: University of California Press, 1967), 37.
28. Immanuel C. Y. Hsü, *China's Entrance into the Family of Nations: The Diplomatic Phase, 1858–1880* (Cambridge: Harvard University Press, 1960), 9.
29. Thus the extension of Chinese sovereignty over Mongolia (both "Inner" and, at various points of Chinese history, "Outer") and Manchuria, the respective founts of the foreign conquerors that founded the Yuan and Qing Dynasties.
30. For enlightening discussions of these themes, and a fuller explanation of the rules of *wei qi,* see David Lai, "Learning from the Stones: A *Go* Approach to Mastering China's Strategic Concept, *Shi*" (Carlisle, Pa.: United States Army War College Strategic Studies Institute, 2004); and David Lai and Gary W. Hamby, "East Meets West: An Ancient Game Sheds New Light on U.S.-Asian Strategic Relations," *Korean Journal of Defense Analysis* 14, no. 1 (Spring 2002).
31. A convincing case has been made that *The Art of War* is the work of a later (though still ancient) author during the Warring States period, and that he sought to imbue his ideas with greater legitimacy by backdating them to the era of Confucius. These arguments are summarized in Sun Tzu, *The Art of War,* trans. Samuel B. Griffith (Oxford: Oxford University Press, 1971), Introduction, 1–12; and Andrew Meyer and Andrew Wilson, "*Sunzi Bingfa* as History and Theory," in Bradford A. Lee and Karl F. Walling, eds., *Strategic Logic and Political Rationality: Essays in Honor of Michael Handel* (London: Frank Cass, 2003).
32. Sun Tzu, *The Art of War,* trans. John Minford (New York: Viking, 2002), 3.
33. Ibid., 87–88.
34. Ibid., 14–16.
35. Ibid., 23.
36. Ibid., 6.
37. In Mandarin Chinese, "*shi*" is pronounced roughly the same as "sir" with a "sh." The Chinese character combines the elements of "cultivate" and "strength."
38. Kidder Smith, "The Military Texts: The *Sunzi,*" in Wm. Theodore de Bary and Irene Bloom, eds., *Sources of Chinese Tradition,* vol. 1, *From Earliest Times to 1600*, 2nd ed. (New York: Columbia University Press, 1999), 215. The Chinese author Lin Yutang explained *shi* as an aesthetic and philosophic notion of what a situation "is going to become . . . the way the wind, rain, flood or battle looks for the future, whether increasing or decreasing in force, stopping soon or continuing indefinitely, gaining or losing, in what direction [and] with what force." Lin Yutang, *The Importance of Living* (New York: Harper, 1937), 442.
39. See Joseph Needham and Robin D. S. Yates, *Science and Civilisation in China*, vol. 5, part 6: "Military Technology Missiles and Sieges" (Cambridge: Cambridge University Press, 1994), 33–35, 67–79.
40. See Lai and Hamby, "East Meets West," 275.
41. Georg Wilhelm Friedrich Hegel, *The Philosophy of History*, trans. E. S. Haldane and Frances Simon, as quoted in Spence, *The Search for Modern China*, 135–36.

Chapter 2: The Kowtow Question and the Opium War

1. The story of Qing expansion in "inner Asia" under a series of exceptionally able Emperors is related in rich detail in Peter Perdue, *China Marches West: The Qing Conquest of Central Eurasia* (Cambridge: Belknap Press, 2005).
2. See J. L. Cranmer-Byng, ed., *An Embassy to China: Being the journal kept by Lord Macartney during his embassy to the Emperor Ch'ien-lung, 1793–1794* (London: Longmans, Green, 1962), Introduction, 7–9 (citing the *Collected Statutes* of the Qing dynasty).
3. "Lord Macartney's Commission from Henry Dundas" (September 8, 1792), in Pei-kai Cheng, Michael Lestz, and Jonathan Spence, eds., *The Search for Modern China: A Documentary Collection* (New York: W. W. Norton, 1999), 93–96.
4. Ibid., 95.
5. Macartney's Journal, in *An Embassy to China,* 87–88.
6. Ibid., 84–85.
7. Alain Peyrefitte, *The Immobile Empire* (New York: Alfred A. Knopf, 1992), 508.
8. Macartney's Journal, in *An Embassy to China*, 105.
9. Ibid., 90.
10. Ibid., 123.
11. Ibid.
12. See Chapter 1, "The Singularity of China," page 21.
13. Macartney's Journal, in *An Embassy to China*, 137.
14. Qianlong's First Edict to King George III (September 1793), in Cheng, Lestz, and Spence, eds., *The Search for Modern China: A Documentary Collection*, 104–6.
15. Qianlong's Second Edict to King George III (September 1793), in Cheng, Lestz, and Spence, eds., *The Search for Modern China: A Documentary Collection*, 109.
16. Macartney's Journal, in *An Embassy to China,* 170.
17. Angus Maddison, *The World Economy: A Millennial Perspective* (Paris: Organisation for Economic Co-operation and Development, 2006), Appendix B, 261, Table B–18, "World GDP, 20 Countries and Regional Totals, 0–1998 A.D."
18. See Jonathan Spence, *The Search for Modern China* (New York: W. W. Norton, 1999), 149–50; Peyrefitte, *The Immobile Empire*, 509–11; Dennis Bloodworth and Ching Ping Bloodworth, *The Chinese Machiavelli: 3000 Years of Chinese Statecraft* (New York: Farrar, Straus & Giroux, 1976), 280.
19. Peter Ward Fay, *The Opium War, 1840–1842* (Chapel Hill: University of North Carolina Press, 1975), 68.
20. Peyrefitte, *The Immobile Empire*, xxii.
21. "Lin Tse-hsü's Moral Advice to Queen Victoria, 1839," in Ssu-yü Teng and John K. Fairbank, eds., *China's Response to the West: A Documentary Survey, 1839–1923* (Cambridge: Harvard University Press, 1979), 26.
22. Ibid., 26–27.
23. Ibid., 25–26.
24. "Lord Palmerston to the Minister of the Emperor of China" (London, February 20, 1840), as reprinted in Hosea Ballou Morse, *The International Relations of the Chinese Empire*, vol. 1, *The Period of Conflict, 1834–1860*, part 2 (London: Longmans, Green, 1910), 621–24.
25. Ibid., 625.
26. Memorial to the Emperor, as translated and excerpted in Franz Schurmann and Orville Schell, eds., *Imperial China: The*

Decline of the Last Dynasty and the Origins of Modern China, the 18th and 19th Centuries (New York: Vintage, 1967), 146–47.

27. E. Backhouse and J. O. P. Bland, *Annals and Memoirs of the Court of Peking* (Boston: Houghton Mifflin, 1914), 396.
28. Tsiang Ting-fu, *Chung-kuo chin tai shih* [*China's Modern History*] (Hong Kong: Li-ta Publishers, 1955), as translated and excerpted in Schurmann and Schell, eds., *Imperial China*, 139.
29. Ibid., 139–40.
30. Maurice Collis, *Foreign Mud: Being an Account of the Opium Imbroglio at Canton in the 1830s and the Anglo-Chinese War That Followed* (New York: New Directions, 1946), 297.
31. See Teng and Fairbank, eds., *China's Response to the West*, 27–29.
32. Immanuel C. Y. Hsü, *The Rise of Modern China*, 6th ed. (Oxford: Oxford University Press, 2000), 187–88.
33. Spence, *The Search for Modern China*, 158.
34. John King Fairbank, *Trade and Diplomacy on the China Coast: The Opening of the Treaty Ports, 1842–1854* (Stanford: Stanford University Press, 1969), 109–12.
35. "Ch'i-ying's Method for Handling the Barbarians, 1844," as translated in Teng and Fairbank, eds., *China's Response to the West*, 38–39.
36. Ibid., 38. See also Hsü, *The Rise of Modern China*, 208–9. A copy of this memorial was discovered years later in the British capture of an official residence in Guangzhou. Disgraced by its revelation during an 1858 negotiation with British representatives, Qiying fled. For fleeing an official negotiation without authorization, Qiying was sentenced to death. Deference to his elite stature was made, and he was "permitted" to perform the deed himself with a silken bowstring.
37. Meadows, *Desultory Notes on the Government and People of China*, in Schurmann and Schell, eds., *Imperial China*, 148–49.
38. See Morse, *The International Relations of the Chinese Empire*, vol. 1, part 2, 632–36.
39. See ibid., part 1, 309–10; Qianlong's Second Edict to King George III, in Cheng, Lestz, and Spence, *The Search for Modern China: A Documentary Collection*, 109.

Chapter 3: From Preeminence to Decline

1. "Wei Yuan's Statement of a Policy for Maritime Defense, 1842," in Ssu-yü Teng and John K. Fairbank, eds., *China's Response to the West: A Documentary Survey, 1839–1923* (Cambridge: Harvard University Press, 1979), 30.
2. Ibid., 31–34.
3. Ibid., 34.
4. Opinion differs as to whether the inclusion of Most Favored Nation clauses in these initial treaties represented a concerted Chinese strategy or a tactical oversight. One scholar notes that in some respects it curtailed the Qing court's scope of maneuver in subsequent negotiations with the foreign powers, since any Western power could be sure it would gain the benefits afforded to its rivals. On the other hand, the practical effect was to prevent any one colonizer from attaining a dominant economic position—a contrast to the experience of many neighboring countries during this period. See Immanuel C. Y. Hsü, *The Rise of*

Modern China, 6th ed. (Oxford: Oxford University Press, 2000), 190–92.

5. "Wei Yuan's Statement of a Policy for Maritime Defense," in Teng and Fairbank, eds., *China's Response to the West*, 34.
6. Prince Gong (Yixin), "The New Foreign Policy of January 1861," in Teng and Fairbank, eds., *China's Response to the West*, 48.
7. Macartney's Journal, in J. L. Cranmer-Byng, ed., *An Embassy to China: Being the journal kept by Lord Macartney during his embassy to the Emperor Ch'ien-lung, 1793–1794* (London: Longmans, Green, 1962), 191, 239.
8. John King Fairbank and Merle Goldman, *China: A New History*, 2nd enlarged ed. (Cambridge: Belknap Press, 2006), 216. For an account of the Taiping Rebellion and the career of its charismatic leader Hong Xiuquan, see Jonathan Spence, *God's Chinese Son* (New York: W. W. Norton 1996).
9. Hsü, *The Rise of Modern China*, 209.
10. Ibid., 209–11.
11. Bruce Elleman, *Modern Chinese Warfare, 1795–1989* (New York: Routledge, 2001), 48–50; Hsü, *The Rise of Modern China*, 212–15.
12. Mary C. Wright, *The Last Stand of Chinese Conservatism: The T'ung-Chih Restoration, 1862–1874*, 2nd ed. (Stanford: Stanford University Press, 1962), 233–36.
13. Hsü, *The Rise of Modern China*, 215–18.
14. Commenting acidly on the loss of Vladivostok 115 years later (and on President Ford's summit with Soviet General Secretary Leonid Brezhnev in that city), Deng Xiaoping told me that the different names given to the city by the Chinese and the Russians reflected their respective purposes: the Chinese name translated roughly as "Sea Slug," while the Russian name meant "Rule of the East." "I don't think it has any other meaning except what it means at face value," he added.
15. "The New Foreign Policy of January 1861," in Teng and Fairbank, eds., *China's Response to the West*, 48. For consistency within the present volume, the spelling of "Nian" has been changed in this passage from "Nien," the spelling more common at the time of the quoted book's publication. The underlying Chinese word is the same.
16. Ibid.
17. Ibid.
18. Ibid.
19. Christopher A. Ford, *The Mind of Empire: China's History and Modern Foreign Relations* (Lexington: University of Kentucky Press, 2010), 142–43.
20. I am indebted to my associate, Ambassador J. Stapleton Roy, for bringing this linguistic point to my attention.
21. This account of Li's career draws on events related in William J. Hail, "Li Hung-Chang," in Arthur W. Hummel, ed., *Eminent Chinese of the Ch'ing Period* (Washington, D.C.: U.S. Government Printing Office, 1943), 464–71; J. O. P. Bland, *Li Hung-chang* (New York: Henry Holt, 1917); and Edgar Sanderson, ed., *Six Thousand Years of World History*, vol. 7, *Foreign Statesmen* (Philadelphia: E. R. DuMont, 1900), 425–44.
22. Hail, "Li Hung-Chang," in Hummel, ed., *Eminent Chinese of the Ch'ing Period*, 466.
23. "Excerpts from Tseng's Letters, 1862," as translated and excerpted in Teng and Fairbank, eds., *China's Response to the West*, 62.
24. Li Hung-chang, "Problems of Industrialization," in Franz Schurmann

and Orville Schell, *Imperial China: The Decline of the Last Dynasty and the Origins of Modern China, the 18th and 19th Centuries* (New York: Vintage, 1967), 238.

25. Teng and Fairbank, eds., *China's Response to the West*, 87.
26. "Letter to Tsungli Yamen Urging Study of Western Arms," in ibid., 70–72.
27. "Li Hung-chang's Support of Western Studies," in ibid., 75.
28. Ibid.
29. Ibid.
30. As cited in Wright, *The Last Stand of Chinese Conservatism*, 222.
31. As cited in Jerome Ch'en, *China and the West: Society and Culture, 1815–1937* (Bloomington: Indiana University Press, 1979), 429.
32. According to the fourteenth-century "Records of the Legitimate Succession of the Divine Sovereigns" (a work later widely distributed in the 1930s by the Thought Bureau of Japan's Ministry of Education): "Japan is the divine country. The heavenly ancestor it was who first laid its foundations, and the Sun Goddess left her descendants to reign over it forever and ever. This is true only of our country, and nothing similar may be found in foreign lands. That is why it is called the divine country." John W. Dower, *War Without Mercy: Race and Power in the Pacific War* (New York: Pantheon, 1986), 222.
33. See Kenneth B. Pyle, *Japan Rising* (New York: PublicAffairs, 2007), 37–38.
34. See Karel van Wolferen, *The Enigma of Japanese Power: People and Politics in a Stateless Nation* (London: Macmillan, 1989), 13.
35. On the classical conception of a Japan-centered tributary order, see Michael R. Auslin, *Negotiating with Imperialism: The Unequal Treaties and the Culture of Japanese Diplomacy* (Cambridge: Harvard University Press, 2004), 14; and Marius B. Jansen, *The Making of Modern Japan* (Cambridge: Belknap Press, 2000), 69.
36. Jansen, *The Making of Modern Japan*, 87.
37. Cited in Ch'en, *China and the West*, 431.
38. Masakazu Iwata, *Okubo Toshimichi: The Bismarck of Japan* (Berkeley: University of California Press, 1964), citing Wang Yusheng, *China and Japan in the Last Sixty Years* (Tientsin: Ta Kung Pao, 1932–34).
39. The occasion of the 1874 crisis was a shipwreck of a Ryukyu Islands crew on the far southeast coast of Taiwan, and the murder of the sailors by a Taiwanese tribe. When Japan demanded a harsh indemnity, Beijing initially responded that it had no jurisdiction over un-Sinicized tribes. In the traditional Chinese view, this had a certain logic: "barbarians" were not Beijing's responsibility. Seen in modern international legal and political terms, it was almost certainly a miscalculation, since it signaled that China did not exert full authority over Taiwan. Japan responded with a punitive expedition against the island, which Qing authorities proved powerless to stop. Tokyo then prevailed on Beijing to pay an indemnity, which one contemporary observer called "a transaction which really sealed the fate of China, in advertising to the world that here was a rich Empire which was ready to pay, but not ready to fight." (Alexander Michie, *An Englishman in China During the Victorian Era,* vol. 2 [London: William Blackwood & Sons, 1900], 256.) What made the crisis additionally damaging to China was that until that point, both Beijing and Tokyo had laid claim to the Ryukyu Islands as a tribute state; after

the crisis, the islands fell under Japan's sway. See Hsü, *The Rise of Modern China*, 315–17.

40. Teng and Fairbank, eds., *China's Response to the West,* 71.
41. As quoted in Bland, *Li Hung-chang,* 160.
42. Ibid., 160–61.
43. "Text of the Sino-Russian Secret Treaty of 1896," in Teng and Fairbank, eds., *China's Response to the West,* 131.
44. Bland, *Li Hung-chang,* 306.
45. For an account of these events and of the Chinese court's internal deliberations, see Hsü, *The Rise of Modern China,* 390–98.
46. In contrast with earlier indemnities, most of the Boxer indemnity was later renounced or redirected by the foreign powers to charitable enterprises within China. The United States directed a portion of its indemnity to the construction of Tsinghua University in Beijing.
47. These strategies are recounted in compelling detail in Scott A. Boorman, *The Protracted Game: A Wei-ch'i Interpretation of Maoist Revolutionary Strategy* (New York: Oxford University Press, 1969).
48. Jonathan Spence, *The Search for Modern China* (New York: W. W. Norton, 1999), 485.

Chapter 4: Mao's Continuous Revolution

1. For Mao on Qin Shihuang, see, for example, "Talks at the Beidaihe Conference: August 19, 1958," in Roderick MacFarquhar, Timothy Cheek, and Eugene Wu, eds., *The Secret Speeches of Chairman Mao: From the Hundred Flowers to the Great Leap Forward* (Cambridge: Harvard University Press, 1989), 405; "Talks at the First Zhengzhou Conference: November 10, 1958," in MacFarquhar, Cheek, and Wu, eds., *The Secret Speeches of Chairman Mao,* 476; Tim Adams, "Behold the Mighty Qin," *The Observer* (August 19, 2007); and Li Zhisui, *The Private Life of Chairman Mao*, trans. Tai Hung-chao (New York: Random House, 1994), 122.
2. André Malraux, *Anti-Memoirs,* trans. Terence Kilmartin (New York: Henry Holt, 1967), 373–74.
3. "Speech at the Supreme State Conference: Excerpts, 28 January 1958," in Stuart Schram, ed., *Mao Tse-tung Unrehearsed: Talks and Letters: 1956–71* (Harmondsworth: Penguin, 1975), 92–93.
4. "On the People's Democratic Dictatorship: In Commemoration of the Twenty-eighth Anniversary of the Communist Party of China: June 30, 1949," *Selected Works of Mao Tse-tung,* vol. 4 (Peking: Foreign Languages Press, 1969), 412.
5. "Sixty Points on Working Methods—A Draft Resolution from the Office of the Centre of the CPC: 19.2.1958," in Jerome Ch'en, ed., *Mao Papers: Anthology and Bibliography* (London: Oxford University Press, 1970), 63.
6. Ibid., 66.
7. "The Chinese People Have Stood Up: September 1949," in Timothy Cheek, ed., *Mao Zedong and China's Revolutions: A Brief History with Documents* (New York: Palgrave, 2002), 126.
8. See M. Taylor Fravel, "Regime Insecurity and International Cooperation: Explaining China's Compromises in Territorial Disputes," *International Security* 30, no. 2 (Fall 2005): 56–57; "A Himalayan Rivalry: India and China," *The Economist* 396, no. 8696 (August 21, 2010), 17–20.

9. Zhang Baijia, "Zhou Enlai—The Shaper and Founder of China's Diplomacy," in Michael H. Hunt and Niu Jun, eds., *Toward a History of Chinese Communist Foreign Relations, 1920s–1960s: Personalities and Interpretive Approaches* (Washington, D.C.: Woodrow Wilson International Center for Scholars, Asia Program, 1992), 77.
10. Charles Hill, *Grand Strategies: Literature, Statecraft, and World Order* (New Haven: Yale University Press, 2010), 2.
11. "Memorandum of Conversation: Beijing, July 10, 1971, 12:10–6 p.m.," in Steven E. Phillips, ed., *Foreign Relations of the United States (FRUS), 1969–1976*, vol. 17, *China 1969–1972*, (Washington, D.C.: U.S. Government Printing Office, 2006), 404. Zhou Enlai recited these lines during one of our first meetings in Beijing in July 1971.
12. John W. Garver, "China's Decision for War with India in 1962," in Alastair Iain Johnston and Robert S. Ross, eds., *New Directions in the Study of China's Foreign Policy* (Stanford: Stanford University Press, 2006), 107.
13. Li, *The Private Life of Chairman Mao*, 83.
14. "On the Correct Handling of Contradictions Among the People: February 27, 1957," *Selected Works of Mao Tse-tung,* vol. 5 (Peking: Foreign Languages Press, 1977), 417.
15. Edgar Snow, *The Long Revolution* (New York: Random House, 1972), 217.
16. Lin Piao [Lin Biao], *Long Live the Victory of People's War!* (Peking: Foreign Languages Press, 1967), 38 (originally published September 3, 1965, in the *Renmin Ribao* [*People's Daily*]).
17. Kuisong Yang and Yafeng Xia, "Vacillating Between Revolution and Détente: Mao's Changing Psyche and Policy Toward the United States, 1969–1976," *Diplomatic History* 34, no. 2 (April 2010).
18. Chen Jian and David L. Wilson, eds., "All Under the Heaven Is Great Chaos: Beijing, the Sino-Soviet Border Clashes, and the Turn Toward Sino-American Rapprochement, 1968–69," *Cold War International History Project Bulletin* 11 (Washington, D.C.: Woodrow Wilson International Center for Scholars, Winter 1998), 161.
19. Michel Oksenberg, "The Political Leader," in Dick Wilson, ed., *Mao Tse-tung in the Scales of History* (Cambridge: Cambridge University Press, 1978), 90.
20. Stuart Schram, *The Thought of Mao Tse-Tung* (Cambridge: Cambridge University Press, 1989), 23.
21. "The Chinese Revolution and the Chinese Communist Party: December 1939," *Selected Works of Mao Tse-tung,* vol. 2, 306.
22. John King Fairbank and Merle Goldman, *China: A New History,* 2nd enlarged edition (Cambridge: Belknap Press, 2006), 395.
23. "Memorandum of Conversation: Beijing, Feb. 21, 1972, 2:50–3:55 pm.," *FRUS* 17, 678.
24. "The Foolish Old Man Who Removed the Mountains," *Selected Works of Mao Tse-tung,* vol. 3, 272.

Chapter 5: Triangular Diplomacy and the Korean War

1. "Conversation Between I. V. Stalin and Mao Zedong: Moscow, December 16, 1949," Archive of the President of the Russian Federation (APRF), fond 45, opis 1, delo 329, listy 9–17, trans. Danny Rozas, from *Cold War International History Project: Virtual Archive,* Woodrow Wilson International Center

for Scholars, accessed at www.cwihp.org.

2. Strobe Talbott, trans. and ed., *Khrushchev Remembers: The Last Testament* (Boston: Little, Brown, 1974), 240.
3. "Conversation Between I. V. Stalin and Mao Zedong," www.cwihp.org.
4. Ibid.
5. Ibid.
6. Ibid.
7. See Chapter 6, "China Confronts Both Superpowers," page 170.
8. "Appendix D to Part II—China: The Military Situation in China and Proposed Military Aid," in *The China White Paper: August 1949,* vol. 2 (Stanford: Stanford University Press, 1967), 814.
9. "Letter of Transmittal: Washington, July 30, 1949," in *The China White Paper: August 1949,* vol. 1 (Stanford: Stanford University Press, 1967), xvi.
10. Dean Acheson, "Crisis in Asia—An Examination of U.S. Policy," *Department of State Bulletin* (January 23, 1950), 113.
11. Sergei N. Goncharov, John W. Lewis, and Xue Litai, *Uncertain Partners: Stalin, Mao, and the Korean War* (Stanford: Stanford University Press, 1993), 98.
12. Acheson, "Crisis in Asia—An Examination of U.S. Policy," 115.
13. Ibid.
14. Ibid., 118.
15. The results of postwar Sino-Soviet negotiations still rankled four decades later. In 1989, Deng Xiaoping urged President George H. W. Bush to "look at the map to see what happened after the Soviet Union severed Outer Mongolia from China. What kind of strategic situation did we find ourselves in? Those over fifty in China remember that the shape of China was like a maple leaf. Now, if you look at a map, you see a huge chunk of the north cut away." George H. W. Bush and Brent Scowcroft, *A World Transformed* (New York: Alfred A. Knopf, 1998), 95–96. Deng's reference to China's strategic situation must be understood also in light of the significant Soviet military presence in Mongolia, which began during the Sino-Soviet split and lasted throughout the Cold War.
16. Goncharov, Lewis, and Xue, *Uncertain Partners,* 103.
17. Stuart Schram, *The Thought of Mao Tse-Tung* (Cambridge: Cambridge University Press, 1989), 153.
18. "Conversation Between I. V. Stalin and Mao Zedong," at www.cwihp.org.
19. Soviet forces had initially advanced further south, past the 38th parallel, but heeded a call from Washington to return north and divide the peninsula roughly halfway.
20. Chen Jian, *China's Road to the Korean War: The Making of the Sino-American Confrontation* (New York: Columbia University Press, 1994), 87–88 (citing author interview with Shi Zhe).
21. Kathryn Weathersby, "'Should We Fear This?': Stalin and the Danger of War with America," Cold War International History Project Working Paper Series, working paper no. 39 (Washington, D.C.: Woodrow Wilson International Center for Scholars, July 2002), 9–11.
22. "M'Arthur Pledges Defense of Japan," *New York Times* (March 2, 1949), from *New York Times* Historical Archives.
23. Acheson, "Crisis in Asia—An Examination of U.S. Policy," 116.
24. Ibid.
25. Weathersby, "'Should We Fear This?'" 11.
26. Goncharov, Lewis, and Xue, *Uncertain Partners,* 144.

27. Ibid.
28. Ibid., 145.
29. Chen, *China's Road to the Korean War,* 112.
30. Shen Zhihua, *Mao Zedong, Stalin, and the Korean War,* trans. Neil Silver (forthcoming), Chapter 6 (originally published in Chinese as *Mao Zedong, Sidalin yu Chaoxian zhanzheng* [Guangzhou: Guangdong Renmin Chubanshe, 2003]).
31. Ibid.
32. Ibid.
33. Yang Kuisong, Introduction to ibid. (as adapted from Yang Kuisong, "Sidalin Weishenma zhichi Chaoxian zhanzheng—du Shen Zhihua zhu '*Mao Zedong, Sidalin yu Chaoxian zhanzheng*'" ["Why Did Stalin Support the Korean War—On Reading Shen Zhihua's 'Mao Zedong, Stalin and the Korean War'"], *Ershiyi Shiji* [*Twentieth Century*], February 2004).
34. Harry S. Truman, "Statement by the President on the Situation in Korea, June 27, 1950," no. 173, *Public Papers of the Presidents of the United States* (Washington, D.C.: U.S. Government Printing Office, 1965), 492.
35. Gong Li, "Tension Across the Taiwan Strait in the 1950s: Chinese Strategy and Tactics," in Robert S. Ross and Jiang Changbin, eds., *Re-examining the Cold War: U.S.-China Diplomacy, 1954–1973* (Cambridge: Harvard University Press, 2001), 144.
36. United Nations General Assembly Resolution 376(V), "The Problem of the Independence of Korea" (October 7, 1950), accessed at http://daccess-dds-ny.un.org/doc/RESOLUTION/GEN/NR0/059/74/IMG/NR005974.pdf?OpenElement.
37. For a fascinating discussion of these principles as applied to the Ussuri River clashes, see Michael S. Gerson, *The Sino-Soviet Border Conflict: Deterrence, Escalation, and the Threat of Nuclear War in 1969* (Alexandria, Va.: Center for Naval Analyses, 2010).
38. On Mao's war aims, see for example Shu Guang Zhang, *Mao's Military Romanticism: China and the Korean War, 1950–1953* (Lawrence: University Press of Kansas, 1995), 101–7, 123–25, 132–33; and Chen Jian, *Mao's China and the Cold War* (Chapel Hill: University of North Carolina Press, 2001), 91–96.
39. Chen, *China's Road to the Korean War,* 137.
40. Shen, *Mao Zedong, Stalin, and the Korean War,* Chapter 7.
41. Ibid.
42. Chen, *China's Road to the Korean War,* 143.
43. Ibid., 143–44.
44. Ibid., 144.
45. Goncharov, Lewis, and Xue, *Uncertain Partners,* 164–67.
46. Chen, *China's Road to the Korean War,* 149–50.
47. Ibid., 150.
48. Ibid., 164.
49. "Doc. 64: Zhou Enlai Talk with Indian Ambassador K. M. Panikkar, Oct. 3, 1950," in Goncharov, Lewis, and Xue, *Uncertain Partners,* 276.
50. Ibid., 278.
51. Ibid. Prime Minister Jawaharlal Nehru had written to Zhou, as well as to U.S. and British representatives, regarding prospects for limiting the Korean conflict.
52. "Letter from Fyn Si [Stalin] to Kim Il Sung (via Shtykov): October 8, 1950," APRF, fond 45, opis 1, delo 347, listy 65–67 (relaying text asserted to be Stalin's cable to Mao), from *Cold War International History Project: Virtual Archive,* Woodrow Wilson International

Center for Scholars, accessed at www.cwihp.org.

53. Goncharov, Lewis, and Xue, *Uncertain Partners,* 177.
54. Ibid.
55. Ibid.
56. See Shen Zhihua, "The Discrepancy Between the Russian and Chinese Versions of Mao's 2 October 1950 Message to Stalin on Chinese Entry into the Korean War: A Chinese Scholar's Reply," *Cold War International History Project Bulletin* 8/9 (Washington, D.C.: Woodrow Wilson International Center for Scholars, Winter 1996), 240.
57. Goncharov, Lewis, and Xue, *Uncertain Partners,* 200–201, citing Hong Xuezhi and Hu Qicai, "Mourn Marshal Xu with Boundless Grief," *People's Daily* (October 16, 1990), and Yao Xu, *Cong Yalujiang dao Banmendian* [*From the Yalu River to Panmunjom*] (Beijing: People's Press, 1985).
58. Goncharov, Lewis, and Xue, *Uncertain Partners,* 195–96.

Chapter 6: China Confronts Both Superpowers

1. "Assistant Secretary Dean Rusk addresses China Institute in America, May 18, 1951," as reproduced in "Editorial Note," Fredrick Aandahl, ed., *Foreign Relations of the United States (FRUS), 1951,* vol. 7, *Korea and China: Part 2* (Washington, D.C.: U.S. Government Printing Office, 1983), 1671–72.
2. Due to differences in dialect and methods of transliteration, Quemoy is elsewhere known as "Jinmen," "Kinmen," or "Ch'in-men." Matsu is also known as "Mazu."
3. Xiamen was then known in the Western press as "Amoy"; Fuzhou was "Foochow."
4. Dwight D. Eisenhower, "Annual Message to the Congress on the State of the Union: February 2, 1953," no. 6, *Public Papers of the Presidents of the United States* (Washington, D.C.: U.S. Government Printing Office, 1960), 17.
5. John Lewis Gaddis, *The Cold War: A New History* (New York: Penguin, 2005), 131.
6. Robert L. Suettinger, "U.S. 'Management' of Three Taiwan Strait 'Crises,'" in Michael D. Swaine and Zhang Tuosheng with Danielle F. S. Cohen, eds., *Managing Sino-American Crises: Case Studies and Analysis* (Washington, D.C.: Carnegie Endowment for International Peace, 2006), 254.
7. Ibid., 255.
8. "The Chinese People Cannot Be Cowed by the Atom Bomb: January 28th, 1955 (Main points of conversation with Ambassador Carl-Johan [Cay] Sundstrom, the first Finnish envoy to China, upon presentation of his credentials in Beijing)," *Mao Tse-tung: Selected Works,* vol. 5 (Peking: Foreign Languages Press, 1977), 152–53.
9. "Text of the Joint Resolution on the Defense of Formosa: February 7, 1955," *Department of State Bulletin,* vol. 32, no. 815 (Washington, D.C.: U.S. Government Printing Office, 1955), 213.
10. "Editorial Note," in John P. Glennon, ed., *Foreign Relations of the United States (FRUS),* vol. 19, *National Security Policy, 1955–1957* (Washington, D.C.: U.S. Government Printing Office, 1990), 61.
11. Suettinger, "U.S. 'Management' of Three Taiwan Strait 'Crises,'" 258.
12. Strobe Talbott, trans. and ed., *Khrushchev Remembers: The Last Testament* (Boston: Little, Brown, 1974), 263.
13. "Memorandum of Conversation of N. S. Khrushchev with Mao Zedong, Beijing:

2 October 1959," *Cold War International History Project Bulletin* 12/13 (Washington, D.C.: Woodrow Wilson International Center for Scholars, Fall/Winter 2001), 264.

14. Jung Chang and Jon Halliday, *Mao: The Unknown Story* (New York: Random House, 2005), 389–90.
15. Zhang Baijia and Jia Qingguo, "Steering Wheel, Shock Absorber, and Diplomatic Probe in Confrontation: Sino-American Ambassadorial Talks Seen from the Chinese Perspective," in Robert S. Ross and Jiang Changbin, eds., *Re-examining the Cold War: U.S.-China Diplomacy, 1954–1973* (Cambridge: Harvard University Press, 2001), 185.
16. Steven Goldstein, "Dialogue of the Deaf? The Sino-American Ambassadorial-Level Talks, 1955–1970," in Ross and Jiang, eds., *Re-examining the Cold War*, 200. For a compelling history of the talks making use of both Chinese and American sources, see Yafeng Xia, *Negotiating with the Enemy: U.S.-China Talks During the Cold War, 1949–1972* (Bloomington: Indiana University Press, 2006).
17. "Text of Rusk's Statement to House Panel on U.S. Policy Toward Communist China," *New York Times* (April 17, 1966), accessed at ProQuest Historical Newspapers (1851–2007).
18. Ibid.
19. Talbott, trans. and ed., *Khrushchev Remembers,* 249.
20. Lorenz M. Lüthi, *The Sino-Soviet Split: Cold War in the Communist World* (Princeton: Princeton University Press, 2008), 38.
21. The October Revolution refers to the Bolshevik seizure of power in October 1917.
22. Stuart Schram, *The Thought of Mao Tse-Tung* (Cambridge: Cambridge University Press, 1989), 113.
23. Ibid., 149.
24. Lüthi, *The Sino-Soviet Split,* 50, citing author examination of 1956 Chinese "Internal Reference Reports" and Wu Lengxi, *Shinian lunzhan, 1956–1966: ZhongSu guanxi huiyilu* [*Ten Years of Debate, 1956–1966: Recollections of Sino-Soviet Relations*] (Beijing: Zhongyang wenxian, 1999), (memoirs of the former head of China's official Xinhua news agency).
25. Ibid., 62–63.
26. Li Zhisui, *The Private Life of Chairman Mao,* trans. Tai Hung-chao (New York: Random House, 1994), 261–62.
27. Talbott, trans. and ed., *Khrushchev Remembers,* 255.
28. Ibid.
29. Ibid., 260.
30. "Playing for High Stakes: Khrushchev speaks out on Mao, Kennedy, Nixon and the Cuban Missile Crisis," *LIFE* 69, no. 25 (December 18, 1970), 25.
31. The Nationalist Party, also known as the Kuomintang.
32. "First conversation between N. S. Khrushchev and Mao Zedong: 7/31/1958," *Cold War International History Project: Virtual Archive,* Woodrow Wilson International Center for Scholars, accessed at www.cwihp.org.
33. Ibid.
34. Ibid.
35. William Taubman, *Khrushchev: The Man and His Era* (New York: W. W. Norton, 2003), 392.
36. "Discussion Between N. S. Khrushchev and Mao Zedong: October 03, 1959," Archive of the President of the Russian Federation (APRF), fond 52, opis 1, delo 499, listy 1–33, trans. Vladislav M. Zubok, *Cold War International History*

Project: Virtual Archive, Woodrow Wilson International Center for Scholars, accessed at www.cwihp.org.

37. Ibid.
38. Lüthi, *The Sino-Soviet Split,* 101; Wu Lengxi, "Inside Story of the Decision Making During the Shelling of Jinmen" (*Zhuanji wenxue* [*Biographical Literature*], Beijing, no. 1, 1994), as translated and reproduced in Li Xiaobing, Chen Jian, and David L. Wilson, eds., "Mao Zedong's Handling of the Taiwan Straits Crisis of 1958: Chinese Recollections and Documents," *Cold War International History Project Bulletin* 6/7 (Washington, D.C.: Woodrow Wilson International Center for Scholars, Winter 1995), 213–14.
39. Wu, "Inside Story of the Decision Making During the Shelling of Jinmen," 208.
40. Ibid., 209–10.
41. Gong Li, "Tension Across the Taiwan Strait in the 1950s: Chinese Strategy and Tactics," in Ross and Jiang, eds., *Re-examining the Cold War,* 157–58; Chen Jian, *Mao's China and the Cold War* (Chapel Hill: University of North Carolina Press, 2001), 184.
42. Chen, *Mao's China and the Cold War,* 184–85.
43. "Statement by the Secretary of State, September 4, 1958," in Harriet Dashiell Schwar, ed., *Foreign Relations of the United States (FRUS), 1958–1960,* vol. 19, *China* (Washington, D.C.: U.S. Government Printing Office, 1996), 135.
44. "Telegram from the Embassy in the Soviet Union to the Department of State, Moscow, September 7, 1958, 9 p.m.," *FRUS* 19, 151.
45. Dwight D. Eisenhower, "Letter to Nikita Khrushchev, Chairman, Council of Ministers, U.S.S.R., on the Formosa Situation: September 13, 1958," no. 263, *Public Papers of the Presidents of the United States* (Washington, D.C.: U.S. Government Printing Office, 1960), 702.
46. Andrei Gromyko, *Memoirs* (New York: Doubleday, 1990), 251–52.
47. Lüthi, *The Sino-Soviet Split,* 102.
48. Ibid., 102–3.
49. "Telegram from the Embassy in the Soviet Union to the Department of State, September 19, 1958, 8 p.m.," *FRUS* 19, 236.
50. "Discussion Between N. S. Khrushchev and Mao Zedong: October 03, 1959."
51. Xia, *Negotiating with the Enemy,* 98–99.
52. On September 30, 1958, six weeks into the second offshore islands crisis, Dulles gave a press conference in which he questioned the utility of stationing so many Nationalist troops on Quemoy and Matsu, and noted that the United States bore "no legal responsibility to defend the coastal islands." Chiang Kai-shek responded the next day by dismissing Dulles's remarks as a "unilateral statement" that Taipei "had no obligation to abide by," and Taipei continued to defend and fortify the islands. Li, "Tension Across the Taiwan Strait in the 1950s: Chinese Strategy and Tactics," 163.
53. "Memorandum of Conversation, Beijing, February 24, 1972, 5:15–8:05 p.m.," in Steven E. Phillips, ed., *Foreign Relations of the United States (FRUS), 1969–1976,* vol. 17, *China 1969–1972* (Washington, D.C.: U.S. Government Printing Office, 2006), 766.
54. Talbott, trans. and ed., *Khrushchev Remembers,* 265.

Chapter 7: A Decade of Crises

1. Frederick C. Teiwes, "The Establishment and Consolidation of the New Regime, 1949–1957," in Roderick

MacFarquhar, ed., *The Politics of China: The Eras of Mao and Deng,* 2nd ed. (Cambridge: Cambridge University Press, 1997), 74.

2. Jonathan Spence, *The Search for Modern China* (New York: W. W. Norton, 1999), 541–42.
3. Lorenz M. Lüthi, *The Sino-Soviet Split: Cold War in the Communist World* (Princeton: Princeton University Press, 2008), 76.
4. Ibid., 84.
5. For an elaboration of this point, and of the links between Mao's foreign and domestic policies, see Chen Jian, *Mao's China and the Cold War* (Chapel Hill: University of North Carolina Press, 2001), 6–15.
6. Grim accounts of this singularly destructive episode are available in Jasper Becker, *Hungry Ghosts: Mao's Secret Famine* (New York: Henry Holt, 1998); and Frederick C. Teiwes, *China's Road to Disaster: Mao, Central Politicians, and Provincial Leaders in the Unfolding of the Great Leap Forward, 1955–1959* (Armonk, N.Y.: East Gate, 1998).
7. Neville Maxwell, *India's China War* (Garden City, NY: Anchor, 1972), 37.
8. John W. Garver, "China's Decision for War with India in 1962," in Alastair Iain Johnston and Robert S. Ross, eds., *New Directions in the Study of China's Foreign Policy* (Stanford: Stanford University Press, 2006), 106.
9. Ibid., 107.
10. Ibid.
11. Ibid., 108.
12. Ibid., 109.
13. Ibid., 110.
14. Ibid., 115.
15. Ibid., 120–21.
16. "Workers of All Countries Unite, Oppose Our Common Enemy: December 15, 1962" (Peking: Foreign Languages Press, 1962) (reprint of editorial from *Renmin Ribao* [*People's Daily*]).
17. Ibid.
18. *Pravda,* April 5, 1964, as quoted in Hemen Ray, *Sino-Soviet Conflict over India: An Analysis of the Causes of Conflict Between Moscow and Beijing over India Since 1949* (New Delhi: Abhinav Publications, 1986), 106.
19. John King Fairbank and Merle Goldman, *China: A New History,* 2nd enlarged edition (Cambridge: Belknap Press, 2006), 392.
20. Roderick MacFarquhar and Michael Schoenals, *Mao's Last Revolution* (Cambridge: Belknap Press, 2006), 87–91.
21. Mark Gayn, "China Convulsed," *Foreign Affairs* 45, issue 2 (January 1967): 247, 252.
22. *Renmin Ribao* [*People's Daily*] (Beijing), January 31, 1967, at 6, as cited in Tao-tai Hsia and Constance A. Johnson, "Legal Developments in China Under Deng's Leadership" (Washington, D.C.: Library of Congress, Far Eastern Law Division, 1984), 9.
23. Anne F. Thurston, *Enemies of the People* (New York: Alfred A. Knopf, 1987), 101–3; MacFarquhar and Schoenals, *Mao's Last Revolution,* 118–20.
24. MacFarquhar and Schoenals, *Mao's Last Revolution,* 224–27.
25. Ibid., 222–23.
26. See Chapter 14, "Reagan and the Advent of Normalcy," page 400.
27. See Yafeng Xia, moderator, *H-Diplo Roundtable Review* 11, no. 43 (Hu Angang, *Mao Zedong yu wenge* [*Mao Zedong and the Cultural Revolution*]) (October 6, 2010), 27–33, accessed at http://www.h-net.org/~diplo/roundtables/PDF/Roundtable-XI-43.pdf.

28. John F. Kennedy, "A Democrat Looks at Foreign Policy," *Foreign Affairs* 36, no. 1 (October 1957): 50.
29. Wu Lengxi, "Inside Story of the Decision Making During the Shelling of Jinmen," in Li, Chen, and Wilson, eds., "Mao Zedong's Handling of the Taiwan Straits Crisis of 1958," *CWIHP Bulletin* 6/7, 208.
30. Yafeng Xia, *Negotiating with the Enemy: U.S.-China Talks During the Cold War, 1949–1972* (Bloomington: Indiana University Press, 2006), 109–14, 234; Noam Kochavi, *A Conflict Perpetuated: China Policy During the Kennedy Years* (Westport, Conn.: Praeger, 2002), 101–14.
31. Lyndon B. Johnson, "Remarks to the American Alumni Council: United States Asian Policy: July 12, 1966," no. 325, *Public Papers of the Presidents of the United States* (Washington, D.C.: U.S. Government Printing Office, 1967), book 2, 719–20.
32. Xia, *Negotiating with the Enemy,* 117–31.
33. "Communist China: 6 December 1960," *National Intelligence Estimate,* no. 13–60, 2–3.
34. Li Jie, "Changes in China's Domestic Situation in the 1960s and Sino-U.S. Relations," in Robert S. Ross and Jiang Changbin, eds., *Re-examining the Cold War: US-China Diplomacy, 1954–1973* (Cambridge: Harvard University Press, 2001), 302.
35. Ibid., 304.
36. Ibid., 185, 305.

Chapter 8: The Road to Reconciliation

1. Richard M. Nixon, "Asia After Viet Nam," *Foreign Affairs* 46, no. 1 (October 1967): 121.
2. Ibid., 123.
3. Edgar Snow, "Interview with Mao," *The New Republic* 152, no. 9, issue 2623 (February 27, 1965): 21–22.
4. The extent of Chinese support is shown in the records of recently declassified conversations between Chinese and Vietnamese leaders. For a compilation of key conversations with editorial commentary, see Odd Arne Westad, Chen Jian, Stein Tønnesson, Nguyen Vu Tung, and James G. Hershberg, eds., "77 Conversations Between Chinese and Foreign Leaders on the Wars in Indochina, 1964–1977," Cold War International History Project Working Paper Series, working paper no. 22 (Washington, D.C.: Woodrow Wilson International Center for Scholars, May 1998). For an analysis of the People's Republic's involvement in Hanoi's wars with France and the United States, see Qiang Zhai, *China and the Vietnam Wars, 1950–1975* (Chapel Hill: University of North Carolina Press, 2000).
5. Zhang Baijia, "China's Role in the Korean and Vietnam Wars," in Michael D. Swaine and Zhang Tuosheng with Danielle F. S. Cohen, eds., *Managing Sino-American Crises: Case Studies and Analysis* (Washington, D.C.: Carnegie Endowment for International Peace, 2006), 201.
6. Snow, "Interview with Mao," 22.
7. Ibid., 23.
8. Yawei Liu, "Mao Zedong and the United States: A Story of Misperceptions," in Hongshan Li and Zhaohui Hong, eds., *Image, Perception, and the Making of U.S.-China Relations* (Lanham: University Press of America, 1998), 202.
9. Lyndon B. Johnson, "Address at Johns Hopkins University: Peace Without Conquest: April 7, 1965," no. 172, *Public*

Papers of the Presidents of the United States (Washington, D.C.: U.S. Government Printing Office, 1966), 395.

10. "Text of Rusk's Statement to House Panel on U.S. Policy Toward Communist China," *New York Times* (April 17, 1966), accessed at ProQuest Historical Newspapers (1851–2007).
11. Liu, "Mao Zedong and the United States," 203.
12. Chen Jian and David L. Wilson, eds., "All Under the Heaven Is Great Chaos: Beijing, the Sino-Soviet Border Clashes, and the Turn Toward Sino-American Rapprochement, 1968–69," *Cold War International History Project Bulletin* 11 (Washington, D.C.: Woodrow Wilson International Center for Scholars, Winter 1998), 161.
13. Ibid., 158.
14. Ibid.
15. As described by Donald Zagoria in a farsighted article in 1968, an influential cross-section of the Chinese leadership, including Deng Xiaoping and Liu Shaoqi, favored a conditional reconciliation with Moscow. In a conclusion that outpaced the analysis of many observers, Zagoria suggested that strategic necessities would ultimately drive China toward reconciliation with the United States. Donald S. Zagoria, "The Strategic Debate in Peking," in Tang Tsou, ed., *China in Crisis*, vol. 2 (Chicago: University of Chicago Press, 1968).
16. Chen and Wilson, eds., "All Under the Heaven Is Great Chaos," 161.
17. Li Zhisui, *The Private Life of Chairman Mao,* trans. Tai Hung-chao (New York: Random House, 1994), 514.
18. Richard Nixon, "Inaugural Address: January 20, 1969," no. 1, *Public Papers of the Presidents of the United States* (Washington, D.C.: U.S. Government Printing Office, 1971), 3.
19. See Henry Kissinger, *White House Years* (Boston: Little, Brown, 1979), 168.
20. Chen Jian, *Mao's China and the Cold War* (Chapel Hill: University of North Carolina Press, 2001), 245–46.
21. Chen and Wilson, eds., "All Under the Heaven Is Great Chaos," 166.
22. Ibid., 167.
23. Ibid., 170.
24. Ibid., 168.
25. Xiong Xianghui, "The Prelude to the Opening of Sino-American Relations," *Zhonggong dangshi ziliao* [CCP History Materials], no. 42 (June 1992), 81, as excerpted in William Burr, ed., "New Documentary Reveals Secret U.S., Chinese Diplomacy Behind Nixon's Trip," National Security Archive Electronic Briefing Book, no. 145 (December 21, 2004), http://www.gwu.edu/~nsarchiv/NSAEBB/NSAEBB145/index.htm.
26. Ibid.
27. Chen and Wilson, eds., "All Under the Heaven Is Great Chaos," 170.
28. Ibid., 171.
29. Ibid.
30. For an account of the incident synthesizing recent scholarship, see Michael S. Gerson, *The Sino-Soviet Border Conflict: Deterrence, Escalation, and the Threat of Nuclear War in 1969* (Alexandria, Va.: Center for Naval Analyses, 2010), 23–24.
31. See Kissinger, *White House Years,* 182.
32. "Minutes of the Senior Review Group Meeting, Subject: U.S. Policy on Current Sino-Soviet Differences (NSSM 63)," 134–35. See also Gerson, *The Sino-Soviet Border Conflict,* 37–38.
33. Elliot L. Richardson, "The Foreign Policy of the Nixon Administration: Address to the American Political

Science Association, September 5, 1969," *Department of State Bulletin* 61, no. 1567 (September 22, 1969), 260.

34. Gerson, *The Sino-Soviet Border Conflict,* 49–52.
35. "Jing Zhicheng, Attaché, Chinese Embassy, Warsaw on: The Fashion Show in Yugoslavia," *Nixon's China Game*, pbs.org, September 1999, accessed at http://www.pbs.org/wgbh/amex/china/filmmore/reference/interview/zhicheng01.html.
36. Ibid.
37. "Memorandum from Secretary of State Rogers to President Nixon, March 10, 1970," in Steven E. Phillips, ed., *Foreign Relations of the United States (FRUS), 1969–1976,* vol. 17, *China 1969–1972* (Washington, D.C.: U.S. Government Printing Office 2006). 188–91.
38. See Kuisong Yang and Yafeng Xia, "Vacillating Between Revolution and Détente: Mao's Changing Psyche and Policy Toward the United States, 1969–1976," *Diplomatic History* 34, no. 2 (April 2010).
39. Edgar Snow, "A Conversation with Mao Tse-Tung," *LIFE* 70, no. 16 (April 30, 1971), 47.
40. Ibid., 48.
41. Ibid., 46.
42. Ibid., 48.
43. Ibid., 47.
44. Ibid., 48.
45. Ibid.
46. Ibid.
47. See Zhengyuan Fu, *Autocratic Tradition and Chinese Politics* (New York: Cambridge University Press, 1993), 188; and Li, *The Private Life of Chairman Mao*, 120. Mao's physician surmised that Mao's translator, who lacked a background in literary Chinese, missed the hidden meaning and translated the phrase literally. Another possibility is that Mao's translator understood the expression quite well, but was too terrified to translate a pun that Mao had merely implied, and that—if volunteered in English—would have seemed dangerously disrespectful. Mao's wife, Jiang Qing, shouted the same line in defiance at the close of her trial in 1980. Ross Terrill, *Madame Mao: The White-Boned Demon* (Stanford: Stanford University Press, 1999), 344.
48. *Oxford Concise English-Chinese/Chinese-English Dictionary,* 2nd ed. (Hong Kong: Oxford University Press, 1999), 474. I am indebted to my research assistant, Schuyler Schouten, for the linguistic analysis.
49. "Editorial Note," *FRUS* 17, 239–40.
50. "Tab B.," *FRUS* 17, 250.
51. Ibid.
52. Snow, "A Conversation with Mao Tse-Tung," 47.
53. "Tab A.," *FRUS* 17, 249.
54. "Memorandum from the President's Assistant for National Security Affairs (Kissinger) to President Nixon, Washington, January 12, 1971," *FRUS* 17, 254.
55. Yang and Xia, "Vacillating Between Revolution and Détente," 401–2.
56. Ibid., 405, citing Lin Ke, Xu Tao, and Wu Xujun, *Lishi de zhenshi—Mao Zedong shenbian gongzuo renyuan de zhengyan* [*The True Life of Mao Zedong—Eyewitness Accounts by Mao's Staff*] (Hong Kong, 1995), 308. See also Yafeng Xia, "China's Elite Politics and Sino-American Rapprochement, January 1969–February 1972," *Journal of Cold War Studies* 8, no. 4 (Fall 2006): 13–17.
57. See Kissinger, *White House Years,* 710.
58. "Message from the Premier of the People's Republic of China Chou En-lai to President Nixon, Beijing, April 21, 1971," *FRUS* 17, 301.

59. Ibid.
60. See Kissinger, *White House Years*, 720.
61. "Message from the Government of the United States to the Government of the People's Republic of China, Washington, May 10, 1971," *FRUS* 17, 318.
62. "Message from the Premier of the People's Republic of China Chou En-lai to President Nixon, Beijing, May 29, 1971," *FRUS* 17, 332.

Chapter 9: Resumption of Relations: First Encounters with Mao and Zhou

1. Gao Wenqian, *Zhou Enlai: The Last Perfect Revolutionary,* trans. Peter Rand and Lawrence R. Sullivan (New York: PublicAffairs, 2007), 162.
2. "Answers to the Italian Journalist Oriana Fallaci: April 21 and 23, 1980," in *Selected Works of Deng Xiaoping (1975–1982)*, vol. 2, trans. The Bureau for the Compilation and Translation of Works of Marx, Engels, Lenin and Stalin Under the Central Committee of the Communist Party of China (Beijing: Foreign Languages Press, 1984), 326–27.
3. Gao Wenqian's *Zhou Enlai: The Last Perfect Revolutionary* offers a complex and at many points admiring portrait of Zhou. It ultimately adopts a different conclusion than Deng about Zhou's participation in Mao's domestic upheavals. A recent work on the Cultural Revolution by Hu Angang, *Mao Zedong yu wenge* [*Mao Zedong and the Cultural Revolution*] (Hong Kong: Da Feng Chubanshe, 2008), passes a somewhat harsher verdict on Zhou's role in this period. For an English-language discussion, see Yafeng Xia, moderator, *H-Diplo Roundtable Review* 11, no. 43 (October 6, 2010), http://www.h-net.org/~diplo/roundtables/PDF/Roundtable-XI-43.pdf.
4. "Memorandum of Conversation: Beijing, July 9, 1971, 4:35–11:20 p.m.," in Steven E. Phillips, ed., *Foreign Relations of the United States (FRUS), 1969–1976,* vol. 17, *China 1969–1972* (Washington, D.C.: U.S. Government Printing Office, 2006), 363.
5. "Memorandum of Conversation: Beijing, October 21, 1971, 10:30 a.m.–1:45 p.m.," *FRUS* 17, 504. The original American records of these conversations list the name "Zhou" using the then-prevalent Wade-Giles transliteration "Chou." To avoid frequent shifts in spelling between the present volume's main text and the quoted conversations, in passages excerpted from American transcripts the names of Chinese interlocutors, as well as Chinese-language words originally spoken by Chinese parties, have been rendered using pinyin spellings.
6. "Memorandum of Conversation: Beijing, February 17–18, 1973, 11:30 p.m.–1:20 a.m.," in David P. Nickles, ed., *Foreign Relations of the United States (FRUS), 1969–1976,* vol. 18, *China 1973–1976* (Washington, D.C.: U.S. Government Printing Office, 2007), 124.
7. "Memorandum of Conversation: Beijing, July 9, 1971, 4:35–11:20 p.m.," *FRUS* 17, 367.
8. Ibid., 390.
9. "Memorandum of Conversation: Beijing, July 10, 1971, 12:10–6:00 p.m.," *FRUS* 17, 400.
10. Shortly after my July 1971 visit, Zhou flew to Hanoi to brief North Vietnamese leaders on China's new diplomatic posture. By most accounts, these talks did not proceed smoothly; nor did Zhou's subsequent discussions with Madame Nguyen Thi Binh, the implacable shadow foreign minister

of the Hanoi front "Provisional Revolutionary Government" of South Vietnam. See Chen Jian, "China, Vietnam and Sino-American Rapprochement," in Odd Arne Westad and Sophie Quinn-Judge, eds., *The Third Indochina War: Conflict Between China, Vietnam and Cambodia, 1972–1979* (London: Routledge, 2006), 53–54; and Qiang Zhai, *China and the Vietnam Wars, 1950–1975* (Chapel Hill: University of North Carolina Press, 2000), 196–97.

11. "Memorandum of Conversation: Beijing, July 9, 1971, 4:35–11:20 p.m.," *FRUS* 17, 367–68.
12. Ibid., 367.
13. Ibid.
14. Ibid., 369.
15. "Memorandum of Conversation: Shanghai, February 28, 1972, 8:30–9:30 a.m.," *FRUS* 17, 823.
16. A partial record of this luncheon discussion is available in *FRUS* 17, 416.
17. In the years since, Fujian has become a center of cross-Strait trade and tourism links, including via Quemoy and Matsu.
18. "Memorandum of Conversation: Beijing, July 10, 1971, 12:10–6:00 p.m.," *FRUS* 17, 403–4.
19. Chen Jian, *Mao's China and the Cold War* (Chapel Hill: University of North Carolina Press, 2001), 267.
20. "Memorandum of Conversation: Beijing, July 10, 1971, 12:10–6:00 p.m.," *FRUS* 17, 430–31.
21. Margaret MacMillan, *Nixon and Mao: The Week That Changed the World* (New York: Random House, 2007), 22.
22. "Memorandum of Conversation: Beijing, February 21, 1972, 2:50–3:55 p.m.," *FRUS* 17, 681.
23. Ibid., 678–79.
24. Ibid., 681.
25. Ibid., 680.
26. Ibid., 681–82.
27. Edward (Ted) Heath, British Prime Minister from 1970 to 1974. Heath would later visit Beijing and meet with Mao in 1974 and 1975.
28. Charles de Gaulle, French resistance leader and President from 1959 to 1969. Paris had recognized the People's Republic of China in 1964.
29. "Memorandum of Conversation: Beijing, February 21, 1972, 2:50–3:55 p.m.," *FRUS* 17, 679–80.
30. Ibid., 684.
31. Ibid., 683.
32. Ibid.
33. "Conversation Between President Nixon and the Ambassador to the Republic of China (McConaughy): Washington, June 30, 1971, 12:18–12:35 p.m.," *FRUS* 17, 349.
34. Ibid., 351–52.
35. "Memorandum of Conversation: Beijing, February 21, 1972, 5:58–6:55 p.m.," *FRUS* 17, 688.
36. Ibid., 689.
37. "Memorandum of Conversation: Beijing, February 22, 1972, 2:10–6:00 p.m.," *FRUS* 17, 700.
38. "Memorandum of Conversation: Beijing, February 24, 1972, 5:15–8:05 p.m.," *FRUS* 17, 770.
39. "Memorandum of Conversation: Washington, February 14, 1972, 4:09–6:19 p.m.," *FRUS* 17, 666.
40. See, for example, Gao Wenqian, *Zhou Enlai*, 151–53, 194–200.
41. See Kuisong Yang and Yafeng Xia, "Vacillating Between Revolution and Détente: Mao's Changing Psyche and Policy Toward the United States, 1969–1976," *Diplomatic History* 34, no. 2 (April 2010): 407.
42. "Joint Statement Following Discussions with Leaders of the People's Republic of

China: Shanghai, February 27, 1972," *FRUS* 17, 812–16.
43. Ibid., 814.
44. "Memorandum of Conversation: Beijing, February 22, 1972, 2:10–6:00 p.m.," *FRUS* 17, 697.
45. "Joint Statement Following Discussions with Leaders of the People's Republic of China: Shanghai, February 27, 1972," *FRUS* 17, 815.
46. CCP Central Committee, "Notice on the Joint Sino-American Communiqué, March 7, 1972," as translated and quoted in Yang and Xia, "Vacillating Between Revolution and Détente," 395.

Chapter 10: The Quasi-Alliance: Conversations with Mao

1. "Memorandum of Conversation: Beijing, February 17–18, 1973, 11:30 p.m.–1:20 a.m.," in David P. Nickles, ed., *Foreign Relations of the United States (FRUS), 1969–1976,* vol. 18, *China 1973–1976* (Washington, D.C.: U.S. Government Printing Office, 2007), 124.
2. Ibid., 124–25.
3. Ibid., 381.
4. Ibid., 387–88.
5. George Kennan's 1946 "Long Telegram" from Moscow and his nominally anonymous 1947 *Foreign Affairs* article, "The Sources of Soviet Conduct," argued that the Soviet Union was driven by ideology to implacable hostility to the United States and the West, and that Soviet-led Communism would expand wherever not met by a resolute response. Though Kennan posited that Soviet pressure could be "contained by the adroit and vigilant application of counter-force at a series of constantly shifting geographical and political points," his theory of containment was not primarily a military doctrine; it placed significant weight on the use of diplomatic pressure and the power of internal political and social reform in the non-Communist world as a bulwark against Soviet expansion.
6. "Memorandum of Conversation: Beijing, November 12, 1973, 5:40–8:25 p.m.," *FRUS* 18, 385.
7. Ibid., 389.
8. The People's Democratic Republic of Yemen, then a separate state aligned with Moscow.
9. "Memorandum from the President's Assistant for National Security Affairs (Kissinger) to President Nixon: Washington, November 1971," in Steven E. Phillips, *Foreign Relations of the United States (FRUS), 1969–1976,* vol. 17, *China 1969–1972* (Washington, D.C.: U.S. Government Printing Office, 2006), 548.
10. "Memorandum of Conversation: Beijing, November 12, 1973, 5:40–8:25 p.m.," *FRUS* 18, 391.
11. "Memorandum of Conversation: Beijing, February 17–18, 1973, 11:30 p.m.–1:20 a.m.," *FRUS* 18, 125.
12. "Memorandum of Conversation: Beijing, November 12, 1973, 5:40–8:25 p.m.," *FRUS* 18, 131. According to some accounts, Mao's list of the countries in the horizontal line included China. The word was not translated and did not appear in the American transcript of the conversation. China's inclusion was at least implied by the presence of countries to China's east and west.
13. Kuisong Yang and Yafeng Xia, "Vacillating Between Revolution and Détente: Mao's Changing Psyche and Policy Toward the United States, 1969–1976," *Diplomatic History* 34, no. 2 (April 2010): 408.
14. "Memorandum of Conversation: Beijing, February 17–18, 1973, 11:30 p.m.–1:20 a.m.," *FRUS* 18, 134.

15. Ibid., 136.
16. "Memorandum of Conversation: Beijing, October 21, 1975, 6:25–8:05 p.m.," *FRUS* 18, 794.
17. Yang and Xia, "Vacillating Between Revolution and Détente," 413.
18. Ibid., 414.
19. "Memorandum of Conversation: Beijing, February 15, 1973, 5:57–9:30 p.m.," *FRUS* 18, 38.
20. Ibid., 32.
21. "Memorandum of Conversation: Beijing, February 17–18, 1973, 11:30 p.m.–1:20 a.m.," *FRUS* 18, 137.
22. See Chapter 13, "'Touching the Tiger's Buttocks': The Third Vietnam War," and Henry Kissinger, *Years of Upheaval* (Boston: Little, Brown, 1982), 16–18, 339–67.
23. The Chinese analysis proved less accurate than usual for the long term, since the Helsinki Accords, signed in 1975, are now generally recognized as having been a major element in weakening Soviet control of Eastern Europe.

Chapter 11: The End of the Mao Era

1. Roderick MacFarquhar, "The Succession to Mao and the End of Maoism, 1969–1982," in Roderick MacFarquhar, ed., *The Politics of China: The Eras of Mao and Deng,* 2nd ed. (Cambridge: Cambridge University Press, 1997), 278–81, 299–301. In quest of finding a successor among China's "pure" young generation, Mao elevated the thirty-seven-year-old Wang Hongwen, previously distinguished only as a provincial-level leftist organizer, to the third-ranking position in the Communist Party hierarchy. His meteoric rise baffled many observers. Closely aligned with Jiang Qing, Wang never achieved an independent political identity or authority commensurate with his formal position. He fell with the rest of the Gang of Four in October 1976.
2. This comparison is elaborated, among other places, in David Shambaugh, "Introduction: Assessing Deng Xiaoping's Legacy" and Lucian W. Pye, "An Introductory Profile: Deng Xiaoping and China's Political Culture," in David Shambaugh, ed., *Deng Xiaoping: Portrait of a Chinese Statesman* (Oxford: Clarendon Press, 2006), 1–2, 14.
3. "Memorandum of Conversation: Beijing, November 14, 1973, 7:35–8:25 a.m.," in David P. Nickles, ed., *Foreign Relations of the United States (FRUS), 1969–1976,* vol. 18, *China 1973–1976* (Washington, D.C.: U.S. Government Printing Office, 2007), 430.
4. "Memorandum from Richard H. Solomon of the National Security Council Staff to Secretary of State Kissinger, Washington, January 25, 1974," *FRUS* 18, 455.
5. Gao Wenqian, *Zhou Enlai: The Last Perfect Revolutionary,* trans. Peter Rand and Lawrence R. Sullivan (New York: Public Affairs, 2007), 246.
6. Kuisong Yang and Yafeng Xia, "Vacillating Between Revolution and Détente: Mao's Changing Psyche and Policy Toward the United States, 1969–1976," *Diplomatic History* 34, no. 2 (April 2010): 414. The proceedings of this meeting have not been published. The quotation draws on an unpublished memoir by the senior Chinese diplomat Wang Youping, who was privy to Foreign Minister Qiao Guanhua's summary of the Politburo meeting.
7. Chou Enlai, "Report on the Work of the Government: January 13, 1975," *Peking Review* 4 (January 24, 1975), 21–23.

8. Ibid, 23.
9. "Speech by Chairman of the Delegation of the People's Republic of China, Teng Hsiao-Ping, at the Special Session of the U.N. General Assembly: April 10, 1974" (Peking: Foreign Languages Press, 1974).
10. Ibid., 5.
11. Ibid., 6.
12. Ibid., 8.
13. "Memorandum of Conversation: Beijing, October 21, 1975, 6:25–8:05 p.m.," *FRUS* 18, 788–89.
14. Ibid., 788.
15. George H. W. Bush, Chief of the U.S. Liaison Office in Beijing; Winston Lord, Director of the State Department Policy Planning Staff; and myself.
16. "Memorandum of Conversation: Beijing, October 21, 1975, 6:25–8:05 p.m.," *FRUS* 18, 789–90.
17. Ibid., 789.
18. Ibid., 793.
19. Ibid. In 1940, Britain withdrew its expeditionary force after the Battle of France.
20. Ibid., 794.
21. Ibid.
22. Ibid., 791.
23. Ibid., 792.
24. Ibid.
25. Ibid., 790.
26. Ibid., 791.
27. Ibid.
28. "Memorandum of Conversation: Beijing, October 25, 1975, 9:30 a.m.," *FRUS* 18, 832.
29. Ibid.
30. "Paper Prepared by the Director of Policy Planning Staff (Lord), Washington, undated," *FRUS* 18, 831.
31. "Memorandum of Conversation: Beijing, December 2, 1975, 4:10–6:00 p.m.," *FRUS* 18, 858.
32. Ibid., 859.
33. A companion of Mao's in Yan'an during the civil war; a former general, now ambassador in Washington.
34. Wang Hairong and Nancy Tang.
35. Qiao Guanhua, Foreign Minister.
36. "Memorandum of Conversation: Beijing, December 2, 1975, 4:10–6:00 p.m.," *FRUS* 18, 859.
37. Ibid., 867.
38. Some of the texts leveled harsh criticism against the excesses of Qin Shihuang and the Tang Dynasty Empress Wu Zetian, rhetorical stand-ins for Mao and Jiang Qing respectively.
39. See Henry Kissinger, *Years of Renewal* (New York: Simon & Schuster, 1999), 897.

Chapter 12: The Indestructible Deng

1. Richard Evans, *Deng Xiaoping and the Making of Modern China* (New York: Viking, 1993), 186–87.
2. See, for example, "The Army Needs to Be Consolidated: January 25, 1975," *Selected Works of Deng Xiaoping: 1975–1982,* vol. 2, trans. The Bureau for the Compilation and Translation of Works of Marx, Engels, Lenin and Stalin Under the Central Committee of the Communist Party of China (Beijing: Foreign Languages Press, 1984), 11–13; and "Some Problems Outstanding in the Iron and Steel Industry: May 29, 1975," in ibid., 18–22.
3. "The Whole Party Should Take the Overall Interest into Account and Push the Economy Forward: March 5, 1975," in ibid., 14–17.
4. "Priority Should Be Given to Scientific Research: September 26, 1975," http://web.peopledaily.com.cn/english/dengxp/vol2/text/b1080.html.
5. "The Army Needs to Be Consolidated: January 25, 1975," in *Selected Works of Deng Xiaoping,* 13.

6. "Things Must Be Put in Order in All Fields: September 27 and October 4, 1975," in ibid., 47.
7. Deng Xiaoping, "Memorial Speech," as reproduced in *China Quarterly* 65 (March 1976): 423.
8. "The 'Two Whatevers' Do Not Accord with Marxism: May 24, 1977," in *Selected Works of Deng Xiaoping,* vol. 2, 51, note 1 (quoting February 1977 editorial advancing the principle); see also Roderick MacFarquhar, "The Succession to Mao and the End of Maoism, 1969–1982," in Roderick MacFarquhar, ed., *The Politics of China: The Eras of Mao and Deng,* 2nd ed. (Cambridge: Cambridge University Press, 1997), 312–13.
9. MacFarquhar, "The Succession to Mao and the End of Maoism, 1969–1982," in MacFarquhar, ed., *The Politics of China,* 312.
10. "Speech at the All-Army Conference on Political Work: June 2, 1978," in *Selected Works of Deng Xiaoping,* vol. 2, 132.
11. "The 'Two Whatevers' Do Not Accord with Marxism: May 24, 1977," in ibid., 51.
12. "Respect Knowledge, Respect Trained Personnel: May 24, 1977," in ibid., 53.
13. Stanley Karnow, "Our Next Move on China," *New York Times* (August 14, 1977); Jonathan Spence, *The Search for Modern China* (New York: W. W. Norton, 1999), 632.
14. See Lucian W. Pye, "An Introductory Profile: Deng Xiaoping and China's Political Culture," in David Shambaugh, ed., *Deng Xiaoping: Portrait of a Chinese Statesman* (Oxford: Clarendon Press, 2006).
15. "Emancipate the Mind, Seek Truth from Facts and Unite As One in Looking into the Future: December 13, 1978," in *Selected Works of Deng Xiaoping,* vol. 2, 152.
16. Ibid., 154.
17. Ibid.
18. "Uphold the Four Cardinal Principles: March 30, 1979," in *Selected Works of Deng Xiaoping,* vol. 2, 181.
19. Ibid., 181.
20. Ibid., 182–83.
21. Until 1983, Deng was Vice Premier and Chairman of the Chinese People's Political Consultative Congress. From 1981 to 1989, he was Chairman of the Central Military Commission and Chairman of the Advisory Commission.
22. Evans, *Deng Xiaoping and the Making of Modern China,* 256.

Chapter 13: "Touching the Tiger's Buttocks": The Third Vietnam War

1. "Touch the tiger's buttocks" is a Chinese idiom popularized by Mao, meaning to do something daring or dangerous. The occasion of this remark was my meeting with Hua Guofeng in Beijing in April 1979.
2. During the Cultural Revolution, then Defense Minister Lin Biao abolished all ranks and insignia and ordered extensive ideological training for Chinese troops using the "Little Red Book" of Mao's aphorisms. The PLA was called on to play social and ideological roles far outside the mission of an ordinary military. A penetrating account of the toll these developments took on the PLA during the conflict with Vietnam may be found in Edward O'Dowd, *Chinese Military Strategy in the Third Indochina War* (New York: Routledge, 2007).
3. "Zhou Enlai, Kang Sheng, and Pham Van Dong: Beijing, 29 April 1968," in Odd Arne Westad, Chen Jian, Stein Tønnesson, Nguyen Vu Tung, and

James G. Hershberg, eds., "77 Conversations Between Chinese and Foreign Leaders on the Wars in Indochina, 1964–1977," Cold War International History Project Working Paper Series, working paper no. 22 (Washington, D.C.: Woodrow Wilson International History Project, May 1998), 127–28. (Brackets in original.)

4. See Chapter 8, "The Road to Reconciliation," page 205.
5. I have always believed that having been willing to force the—to Mao—ideologically correct Khmer Rouge into a compromise, unnecessarily as it turned out, contributed to Zhou's fall. See also Kissinger, *Years of Upheaval* (Boston: Little, Brown, 1982), 368.
6. Robert S. Ross, *The Indochina Tangle: China's Vietnam Policy, 1975–1979* (New York: Columbia University Press, 1988), 74, quoting Xinhua news report (August 15, 1975), as translated in Foreign Broadcast Information Service (FBIS) Daily Report, People's Republic of China (August 18, 1975), A7.
7. Ibid.
8. Ibid., 98, quoting Xinhua news report (March 15, 1976), as translated in FBIS Daily Report, People's Republic of China (March 16, 1976), A13.
9. In April 1978, the Afghan President was assassinated and his government was replaced; on December 5, 1978, the Soviet Union and the new government of Afghanistan entered into a Treaty of Friendship, Good-Neighborliness and Cooperation; and on February 19, 1979, the U.S. ambassador to Afghanistan was assassinated.
10. Cyrus Vance, *Hard Choices: Critical Years in America's Foreign Policy* (New York: Simon & Schuster, 1983), 79.
11. "President Carter's Instructions to Zbigniew Brzezinski for His Mission to China, May 17, 1978," in Zbigniew Brzezinski, *Power and Principle: Memoirs of the National Security Adviser, 1977–1981* (New York: Farrar, Straus & Giroux, 1985), Annex I, 2.
12. The five principles were: affirmation of a one China policy; a commitment not to offer American support to Taiwan independence movements; American discouragement of a hypothetical Japanese deployment into Taiwan; support for any peaceful resolution between Beijing and Taipei; and a commitment to continued normalization. See Chapter 9, "Resumption of Relations: First Encounters with Mao and Zhou," page 271.
13. "Memorandum of Conversation, Summary of the President's Meeting with the People's Republic of China Vice Premier Deng Xiaoping: Washington, January, 29th 1979, 3:35–4:59 p.m.," Jimmy Carter Presidential Library (JCPL), Vertical File—China, item no. 270, 10–11.
14. "Summary of Dr. Brzezinski's Meeting with Foreign Minister Huang Hua: Beijing, May 21st, 1978," JCPL, Vertical File—China, item no. 232, 3.
15. Ibid., 6–7.
16. Ibid. Sadat served as President of Egypt from 1970 until his assassination in 1981. The "bold action" referred to included Sadat's expulsion of over twenty thousand Soviet military advisors from Egypt in 1972, the launching of the October 1973 War, and the subsequent entry into a peace process with Israel.
17. Ibid., 4.
18. Ibid., 10–11.
19. "Memorandum of Conversation, Meeting with Vice Premier Teng Hsiao P'ing: Beijing, May 21st, 1978," JCPL, Vertical File—China, item no. 232-e, 16.

20. Ibid., 5–6.
21. "Summary of Dr. Brzezinski's Meeting with Chairman Hua Kuo-feng: Beijing, May 22nd, 1978," JCPL, Vertical File—China, item no. 233c, 4–5.
22. "Memorandum of Conversation, Summary of the President's Meeting with Ambassador Ch'ai Tse-min: Washington, September 19, 1978," JCPL, Vertical File—China, item no. 250b, 3.
23. "Memorandum of Conversation, Meeting with Vice Premier Teng Hsiao P'ing: Beijing, May 21st 1978," JCPL, Vertical File—China, item no. 232-e, 6.
24. In recent years, Chinese leaders and policy analysts have introduced the phrase "peaceful rise" to describe China's foreign policy aspiration to achieve major-power status within the framework of the existing international system. In a thoughtful article synthesizing both Chinese and Western scholarship on the concept, the scholar Barry Buzan raises the prospect that China's "peaceful rise" began in the late 1970s and early 1980s, as Deng increasingly aligned China's domestic development and foreign policy to the nonrevolutionary world and sought out common interests with the West. Deng's trips abroad offered dramatic proof of this realignment. See Barry Buzan, "China in International Society: Is 'Peaceful Rise' Possible?" *The Chinese Journal of International Politics* 3 (2010): 12–13.
25. "An Interview with Teng Hsiao P'ing," *Time* (February 5, 1979), http://www.time.com/time/magazine/article/0,9171,946204,00.html.
26. "China and Japan Hug and Make Up," *Time* (November 6, 1978), http://www.time.com/time/magazine/article/0,9171,948275-1,00.html.
27. Henry Kamm, "Teng Begins Southeast Asian Tour to Counter Rising Soviet Influence," *New York Times* (November 6, 1978), A1.
28. Henry Kamm, "Teng Tells the Thais Moscow-Hanoi Treaty Perils World's Peace," *New York Times* (November 9, 1978), A9.
29. "Excerpts from Talks Given in Wuchang, Shenzhen, Zhuhai and Shanghai: January 18–February 21, 1992," in *Selected Works of Deng Xiaoping,* vol. 3, trans., The Bureau for the Compilation and Translation of Works of Marx, Engels, Lenin and Stalin Under the Central Committee of the Communist Party of China (Beijing: Foreign Languages Press, 1994), 366.
30. Lee Kuan Yew, *From Third World to First: The Singapore Story—1965–2000* (New York: HarperCollins, 2000), 597.
31. Ibid., 598–99.
32. Fox Butterfield, "Differences Fade as Rivals Mingle to Honor Teng," *New York Times* (January 30, 1979), A1.
33. Joseph Lelyveld, "'Astronaut' Teng Gets New View of World in Houston," *New York Times* (February 3, 1979), A1.
34. Fox Butterfield, "Teng Again Says Chinese May Move Against Vietnam," *New York Times* (February 1, 1979), A16.
35. Joseph Lelyveld, "'Astronaut' Teng Gets New View of World in Houston," A1. For consistency with the main text of the present volume, the quoted passage's original spelling "Teng Hsiao-p'ing" has been rendered as "Deng Xiaoping."
36. Twenty-two years represented the interval between the two world wars. Since more than twenty-two years had elapsed since the end of the Second World War, Chinese leaders were nervous that a certain historical rhythm

was moving events. Mao had made the same point to the Australian Communist leader E. F. Hill a decade earlier. See also Chapter 8, "The Road to Reconciliation," page 207; and Chen Jian and David L. Wilson, eds., "All Under the Heaven Is Great Chaos: Beijing, the Sino-Soviet Border Clashes, and the Turn Toward Sino-American Rapprochement, 1968–69," *Cold War International History Project Bulletin* 11 (Washington, D.C.: Woodrow Wilson International Center for Scholars, Winter 1998), 161.

37. "Memorandum of Conversation, Summary of the President's First Meeting with PRC Vice Premier Deng Xiaoping: Washington, January 29th, 1979," JCPL, Vertical File—China, item no. 268, 8–9.
38. "Memorandum of Conversation, Meeting with Vice Premier Teng Hsiao P'ing: Beijing, May 21st, 1978," JCPL, Vertical File—China, item no. 232-e, 14.
39. "Memorandum of Conversation, Summary of the President's Meeting with the People's Republic of China Vice Premier Deng Xiaoping: Washington, January 29th, 1979, 3:35–4:59 p.m.," JCPL, Vertical File—China, item no. 270, 10–11.
40. "Memorandum of Conversation, Carter–Deng, Subject: Vietnam: Washington, January 29th, 1979, 5:00 p.m.–5:40 p.m.," JCPL, Brzezinski Collection, China [PRC] 12/19/78–10/3/79, item no. 007, 2.
41. Ross, *The Indochina Tangle,* 229.
42. "Memorandum of Conversation, Carter–Deng, Washington, January 29th, 1979, 5:00 p.m.–5:40 p.m.," JCPL, Brzezinski Collection, China [PRC] 12/19/78–10/3/79, item no. 007, 2.
43. Ibid., 5.
44. Brzezinski, *Power and Principle,* 410.
45. "President Reporting on His Conversations with Deng: January 30th, 1979," JCPL, Brzezinski Collection, China [PRC] 12/19/78–10/3/79, item no. 009, 1.
46. Henry Scott-Stokes, "Teng Criticizes the U.S. for a Lack of Firmness in Iran," *New York Times* (February 8, 1979), A12.
47. The lower figure appears in Bruce Elleman, *Modern Chinese Warfare, 1795–1989* (New York: Routledge, 2001), 285. The higher figure is the estimate of Edward O'Dowd in *Chinese Military Strategy in the Third Indochina War,* 3, 45–55.
48. O'Dowd, *Chinese Military Strategy in the Third Indochina War,* 45.
49. Deng Xiaoping to Jimmy Carter on January 30, 1979, as quoted in Brzezinski, *Power and Principle,* 409–10.
50. "Text of Declaration by Moscow," *New York Times* (February 19, 1979); Craig R. Whitney, "Security Pact Cited: Moscow Says It Will Honor Terms of Treaty—No Direct Threat Made," *New York Times* (February 19, 1979), A1.
51. Edward Cowan, "Blumenthal Delivers Warning," *New York Times* (February 28, 1979), A1.
52. Ibid.
53. One of the few scholars to challenge this conventional wisdom—and to emphasize the conflict's anti-Soviet dimension—is Bruce Elleman, in his *Modern Chinese Warfare,* 284–97.
54. For a review of various estimates of PLA casualties, see O'Dowd, *Chinese Military Strategy in the Third Indochina War,* 45.
55. "Memorandum of Conversation, Summary of the President's First Meeting with PRC Vice Premier Deng Xiaoping: Washington, January 29th, 1979," JCPL, Vertical File—China, item no. 268, 8.

56. "Memorandum, President Reporting on His Conversations with Deng: January 30th, 1979," JCPL, Brzezinski Collection, China [PRC] 12/19/78–10/3/79, item no. 009, 2.
57. "Memorandum of Conversation with Vice Premier Deng Xiaoping: Beijing, January 8th, 1980," JCPL, NSA Brzez. Matl. Far East, Box No. 69, Brown (Harold) Trip Memcons, 1/80, File, 16.
58. "Memorandum of Conversation with Vice Premier Deng Xiaoping: Beijing, January 8th, 1980," JCPL, NSA Brzez. Matl. Far East, Box No. 69, Brown (Harold) Trip Memcons, 1/80, File, 15.
59. "President Carter's Instructions to Zbigniew Brzezinski for His Mission to China, May 17, 1978," in Brzezinski, *Power and Principle,* Annex I, 4.
60. By one estimate, as of 1986 Vietnam stationed "700,000 combat troops in the northern portion of the country." Karl D. Jackson, "Indochina, 1982–1985: Peace Yields to War," in Solomon and Kosaka, eds., *The Soviet Far East Military Buildup,* as cited in Elleman, *Modern Chinese Warfare,* 206.
61. "Memorandum of Conversation, Summary of the Vice President's Meeting with People's Republic of China Vice Premier Deng Xiaoping: Beijing, August 28th, 1979, 9:30 a.m.–12:00 noon," JCPL, Vertical File—China, item no. 279, 9.
62. "Memorandum of Conversation Between President Carter and Premier Hua Guofeng of the People's Republic of China: Tokyo, July 10th, 1980," JCPL, NSA Brzez. Matl. Subj. File, Box No. 38, "Memcons: President, 7/80."
63. As quoted in Chen Jian, *China's Road to the Korean War* (New York: Columbia University Press, 1994), 149.
64. "Memorandum of Conversation, Summary of Dr. Brzezinski's Conversation with Vice Premier Geng Biao of the People's Republic of China: Washington, May 29th, 1980," JCPL, NSA Brzez. Matl. Far East, Box No. 70, "Geng Biao Visit, 5/23–31/80," Folder, 5.
65. Lee, *From Third World to First,* 603.

Chapter 14: Reagan and the Advent of Normalcy

1. George H. W. Bush and Brent Scowcroft, *A World Transformed* (New York: Alfred A. Knopf, 1998), 93–94.
2. Taiwan Relations Act, Public Law 96-8, § 3.1.
3. Joint Communiqué Issued by the Governments of the United States and the People's Republic of China (August 17, 1982), as printed in Alan D. Romberg, *Rein In at the Brink of the Precipice: American Policy Toward Taiwan and U.S.-PRC Relations* (Washington, D.C.: Henry L. Stimson Center, 2003), 243.
4. Nancy Bernkopf Tucker, *Strait Talk: United States–Taiwan Relations and the Crisis with China* (Cambridge: Harvard University Press, 2009), 151.
5. Ibid.
6. Ibid., 148–50.
7. John Lewis Gaddis, *The Cold War: A New History* (New York: Penguin, 2005), 213–14, note 43.
8. Hu Yaobang, "Create a New Situation in All Fields of Socialist Modernization—Report to the 12th National Congress of the Communist Party of China: September 1, 1982," *Beijing Review* 37 (September 13, 1982): 29.
9. Ibid., 30–31.
10. Ibid.
11. Ibid.

12. Charles Hill, "Shifts in China's Foreign Policy: The US and USSR" (April 21, 1984), Ronald Reagan Presidential Library (hereafter RRPL), 90946 (Asian Affairs Directorate, NSC).
13. Directorate of Intelligence, Central Intelligence Agency, "China-USSR: Maneuvering in the Triangle" (December 20, 1985), RRPL, 007-R.
14. "Memorandum to President Reagan from Former President Nixon," as appended to Memorandum for the President from William P. Clark, re: Former President Nixon's Trip to China (September 25, 1982), RRPL, William Clark Files, 002.
15. George P. Shultz, *Turmoil and Triumph: My Years as Secretary of State* (New York: Charles Scribner's Sons, 1993), 382.
16. Ronald Reagan, "Remarks at Fudan University in Shanghai, April 30, 1984," *Public Papers of the Presidents of the United States* (Washington, D.C.: U.S. Government Printing Office, 1986), book 1, 603–8; "Remarks to Chinese Community Leaders in Beijing, April 27, 1984," *Public Papers of the Presidents of the United States*, book 1, 579–84.
17. Donald Zagoria, "China's Quiet Revolution," *Foreign Affairs* 62, no. 4 (April 1984): 881.
18. Jonathan Spence, *The Search for Modern China* (New York: W. W. Norton, 1999), 654–55.
19. Nicholas Kristof, "Hu Yaobang, Ex-Party Chief in China, Dies at 73," *New York Times* (April 16, 1989), http://www.nytimes.com/1989/04/16/obituaries/hu-yaobang-ex-party-chief-in-china-dies-at-73.html?pagewanted=1.
20. Christopher Marsh, *Unparalleled Reforms* (New York: Lexington, 2005), 41.
21. Richard Baum, *Burying Mao: Chinese Politics in the Age of Deng Xiaoping* (Princeton: Princeton University Press, 1994), 231–32.

Chapter 15: Tiananmen

1. Jonathan Spence notes that 1989 represented a convergence of several politically charged anniversaries: it was "the two hundredth anniversary of the French Revolution, the seventieth anniversary of the May Fourth movement, the fortieth birthday of the People's Republic itself, and the passage of ten years since formal diplomatic relations with the United States had been reinstituted." Spence, *The Search for Modern China* (New York: W. W. Norton, 1999), 696.
2. Andrew J. Nathan, "Preface to the Paperback Edition: The Tiananmen Papers—An Editor's Reflections," in Zhang Liang, Andrew Nathan, and Perry Link, eds., *The Tiananmen Papers* (New York: Public Affairs, 2001), viii.
3. Richard Baum, *Burying Mao: Chinese Politics in the Age of Deng Xiaoping* (Princeton: Princeton University Press, 1994), 254.
4. Nathan, Introduction to *The Tiananmen Papers*, "The Documents and Their Significance," lv.
5. An example of one such attempt to implement conditionality was the Clinton administration's policy of conditioning China's Most Favored Nation trade status on changes in its human rights record, to be discussed more fully in Chapter 17, "A Roller Coaster Ride Toward Another Reconciliation: The Jiang Zemin Era."
6. David M. Lampton, *Same Bed, Different Dreams: Managing U.S.-China Relations, 1989–2000* (Berkeley: University of California Press, 2001), 305.
7. George H. W. Bush and Brent Scowcroft, *A World Transformed* (New York: Alfred A. Knopf, 1998), 89–90.
8. Ibid., 97–98.
9. Congress and the White House shared a

concern that visiting students who had publicly protested in the United States would be subject to punishment on their return to China. The President had signaled that applications for visa extensions would be treated favorably, while Congress sought to grant the extensions without requiring an application.

10. Bush and Scowcroft, *A World Transformed,* 100.
11. Ibid., 101.
12. Ibid.
13. Ibid., 102.
14. Ibid.
15. Lampton, *Same Bed, Different Dreams,* 302.
16. Bush and Scowcroft, *A World Transformed,* 105–6. Chinese Foreign Minister Qian Qichen disputes this account in his memoirs, averring that the plane was never in any danger. Qian Qichen, *Ten Episodes in China's Diplomacy* (New York: HarperCollins, 2005), 133.
17. Bush and Scowcroft, *A World Transformed,* 106.
18. Ibid.
19. Qian, *Ten Episodes in China's Diplomacy,* 134.
20. Bush and Scowcroft, *A World Transformed,* 109.
21. Ibid., 107.
22. Ibid.
23. Ibid., 107–8.
24. Ibid., 107–9.
25. Ibid., 110.
26. Deng had made clear that he intended to retire very shortly. He did, in fact, do so in 1992, though he continued to be regarded as an influential arbiter of policy.
27. The five principles of peaceful coexistence were negotiated by India and China in 1954. They concerned coexistence and mutual noninterference between countries with different ideological orientations.
28. Deng made a similar point to Richard Nixon during the latter's October 1989 private visit to Beijing: "Please tell President Bush let's end the past, the United States ought to take the initiative, and only the United States can take the initiative. The United States is able to take the initiative. . . . China is unable to initiate. This is because the stronger is America, the weaker is China, the injured is China. If you want China to beg, it cannot be done. If it drags on a hundred years, the Chinese people can't beg [you] to end sanctions [against China]. . . . Whatever Chinese leader makes a mistake in this respect would surely fall, the Chinese people will not forgive him." As quoted in Lampton, *Same Bed, Different Dreams,* 29.
29. Some in the White House maintained that it was unnecessarily provocative to invite Fang Lizhi to attend a presidential banquet with the same Chinese authorities he was criticizing. They blamed the American Embassy in Beijing for failing to forewarn them of the impending controversy. In including Fang on the list of potential invitees, the American ambassador in Beijing, Winston Lord, had in fact flagged him as an outspoken dissident whose inclusion might provoke Chinese government consternation, but who nonetheless merited an invitation.
30. "Cable, From: U.S. Embassy Beijing, To: Department of State, Wash DC, SITREP No. 49, June 12, 0500 Local (June 11, 1989)," in Jeffrey T. Richardson and Michael L. Evans, eds., *Tiananmen*

Square, 1989: The Declassified History, National Security Archive Electronic Briefing Book no. 16 (June 1, 1999), Document 26.

31. Bush and Scowcroft, *A World Transformed,* 99.
32. U.S. Embassy Beijing Cable, "China and the U.S.—A Protracted Engagement," July 11, 1989, SECRET, in Michael L. Evans, ed., *The U.S. Tiananmen Papers: New Documents Reveal U.S. Perceptions of 1989 Chinese Political Crisis,* National Security Archive Electronic Briefing Book (June 4, 2001), Document 11.
33. Bush and Scowcroft, *A World Transformed,* 101–2.
34. Deng's reference was to Winston Lord.
35. Qian, *Ten Episodes in China's Diplomacy,* 140.
36. Bush and Scowcroft, *A World Transformed,* 174.
37. Ibid., 176–77.
38. Fang and his wife would ultimately depart China for the U.K. on an American military transport plane. They subsequently relocated to the United States, where Fang became a professor of physics at the University of Arizona.
39. Richard Evans, *Deng Xiaoping and the Making of Modern China* (London: Hamish Hamilton, 1993), 304 (quoting *Zheng Ming*, Hong Kong, May 1, 1990).
40. "Deng Initiates New Policy 'Guiding Principle,'" FBIS-CHI-91-215; see also United States Department of Defense, Office of the Secretary of Defense, "Military Power of the People's Republic of China: A Report to Congress Pursuant to the National Defense Authorization Act Fiscal Year 2000" (2007), 7, http://www.defense.gov/pubs/pdfs/070523-china-military-power-final.pdf.
41. "Deng Initiates New Policy 'Guiding Principle,'" FBIS-CHI-91-215.

Chapter 16: What Kind of Reform? Deng's Southern Tour

1. Richard Baum, *Burying Mao: Chinese Politics in the Age of Deng Xiaoping* (Princeton: Princeton University Press, 1994), 334.
2. "Excerpts from Talks Given in Wuchang, Shenzhen, Zhuhai and Shanghai: January 18–February 21, 1992," *Selected Works of Deng Xiaoping,* vol. 3, trans., The Bureau for the Compilation and Translation of Works of Marx, Engels, Lenin and Stalin Under the Central Committee of the Communist Party of China (Beijing: Foreign Languages Press, 1994), 359.
3. Ibid., 360.
4. Ibid., 361.
5. Ibid., 362–63.
6. Ibid, 364–65.
7. Ibid., 366.
8. David M. Lampton, *Same Bed, Different Dreams: Managing U.S.-China Relations, 1989–2000* (Berkeley: University of California Press, 2001), xi.
9. "Excerpts from Talks Given in Wuchang, Shenzhen, Zhuhai and Shanghai: January 18—February 21, 1992," *Selected Works of Deng Xiaoping,* vol. 3, 370.
10. Ibid., 369.

Chapter 17: A Roller Coaster Ride Toward Another Reconciliation: The Jiang Zemin Era

1. See David M. Lampton, *Same Bed, Different Dreams: Managing U.S.-China Relations, 1989–2000* (Berkeley: University of California Press, 2001), 293, 308.
2. State Department Bureau of Intelligence and Research, "China: Aftermath of the

Crisis" (July 27, 1989), 17, in Jeffrey T. Richardson and Michael L. Evans, eds., "Tiananmen Square, 1989: The Declassified History," National Security Archive Electronic Briefing Book no. 16 (June 1, 1999), Document 36.

3. Steven Mufson, "China's Economic 'Boss': Zhu Rongji to Take Over as Premier," *Washington Post* (March 5, 1998), A1.
4. September 14, 1992, statement, as quoted in A. M. Rosenthal, "On My Mind: Here We Go Again," *New York Times* (April 9, 1993); on divergent Chinese and Western interpretations of this statement, see also Lampton, *Same Bed, Different Dreams,* 32.
5. "Confronting the Challenges of a Broader World," President Clinton Address to the United Nations General Assembly, New York City, September 27, 1993, from *Department of State Dispatch* 4, no. 39 (September 27, 1993).
6. Robert Suettinger, *Beyond Tiananmen: The Politics of U.S.-China Relations, 1989–2000* (Washington, D.C.: The Brookings Institution, 2003), 161.
7. Deng Xiaoping had given a speech in November 1989 calling on China to "Adhere to Socialism and Prevent Peaceful Evolution toward Capitalism." Mao had warned repeatedly against "peaceful evolution" as well. See "Mao Zedong and Dulles's 'Peaceful Evolution' Strategy: Revelations from Bo Yibo's Memoirs," *Cold War International History Project Bulletin* 6/7 (Washington, D.C.: Woodrow Wilson International Center for Scholars, Winter 1996/1997), 228.
8. Reflecting this fact, "Most Favored Nation" has since been technically renamed "Permanent Normal Trade Relations," although the "MFN" label remains in use.
9. Anthony Lake, "From Containment to Enlargement," address at the Nitze School of Advanced International Studies, Johns Hopkins University, Washington, D.C., September 21, 1993, from *Department of State Dispatch* 4, no. 39 (September 27, 1993).
10. Suettinger, *Beyond Tiananmen,* 165.
11. William J. Clinton, "Statement on Most-Favored-Nation Trade Status for China" (May 28, 1993), *Public Papers of the Presidents of the United States* (Washington, D.C.: U.S. Government Printing Office, 1994), book 1, 770–71.
12. Ibid., 770–72.
13. Lake, "From Containment to Enlargement."
14. Suettinger, *Beyond Tiananmen,* 168–71.
15. Warren Christopher, *Chances of a Lifetime* (New York: Scribner, 2001), 237.
16. Ibid.
17. Ibid., 238.
18. Ibid., 238–39.
19. See, for example, Deng Xiaoping, "An Idea for the Peaceful Reunification of the Chinese Mainland and Taiwan: June 26, 1983," *Selected Works of Deng Xiaoping,* vol. 3, 40–42.
20. John W. Garver, *Face Off: China, the United States, and Taiwan's Democratization* (Seattle: University of Washington Press, 1997), 15; James Carman, "Lee Teng-Hui: A Man of the Country," *Cornell Magazine* (June 1995), accessed at http://www.news.cornell.edu/campus/Lee/Cornell_Magazine_Profile.html.
21. Lampton, *Same Bed, Different Dreams,* 101.
22. William J. Clinton, "Remarks and an Exchange with Reporters Following Discussions with President Jiang Zemin of China in Seattle: November 19, 1993," *Public Papers of the Presidents of the United States* (Washington, D.C.: U.S.

Government Printing Office, 1994), 2022–25.

23. Garver, *Face Off,* 92–97; Robert Suettinger, "U.S. 'Management' of Three Taiwan Strait 'Crises,'" in Michael D. Swaine and Zhang Tuosheng with Danielle F. S. Cohen, eds., *Managing Sino-American Crises: Case Studies and Analysis* (Washington, D.C.: Carnegie Endowment for International Peace, 2006), 278.
24. Madeleine Albright, *Madam Secretary* (New York: Hyperion, 2003), 546.
25. Robert Lawrence Kuhn, *The Man Who Changed China: The Life and Legacy of Jiang Zemin* (New York: Crown Publishers, 2004), 2.
26. Albright, *Madam Secretary,* 531.
27. Christopher Marsh, *Unparalleled Reforms* (New York: Lexington, 2005), 72.
28. Barry Naughton, *The Chinese Economy: Transitions and Growth* (Cambridge: MIT Press, 2007), 142–43.
29. Michael P. Riccards, *The Presidency and the Middle Kingdom: China, the United States, and Executive Leadership* (New York: Lexington Books, 2000), 12.
30. Lampton, *Same Bed, Different Dreams,* Appendix A, 379–80.
31. Zhu Rongji, "Speech and Q&A at the Advanced Seminar on China's Economic Development in the Twenty-first Century" (September 22, 1997), in *Zhu Rongji's Answers to Journalists' Questions* (Oxford: Oxford University Press, 2011) (forthcoming), Chapter 5.

Chapter 18: The New Millennium

1. Richard Daniel Ewing, "Hu Jintao: The Making of a Chinese General Secretary," *China Quarterly* 173 (March 2003): 19.
2. Ibid., 21–22.
3. *Xiaokang*, now a widely used official policy term, is a 2,500-year-old Confucian phrase suggesting a moderately well-off population with a modest amount of disposable income. See "Confucius and the Party Line," *The Economist* (May 22, 2003); "Confucius Makes a Comeback," *The Economist* (May 17, 2007).
4. "Rectification of Statues," *The Economist* (January 20, 2011).
5. George W. Bush, "Remarks Following Discussions with Premier Wen Jiabao and an Exchange with Reporters: December 9, 2003," *Public Papers of the Presidents of the United States* (Washington, D.C.: U.S. Government Printing Office, 2006), 1701.
6. David Barboza, "Chinese Leader Fields Executives' Questions," *New York Times* (September 22, 2010).
7. Cui Changfa and Xu Mingshan, eds., *Gaoceng Jiangtan [Top-leaders' Rostrums]* (Beijing: Hongqi Chubanshe, 2007), 165–82, as cited in Masuda Masayuki, "China's Search for a New Foreign Policy Frontier: Concept and Practice of 'Harmonious World,'" 62, in Masafumi Iida, ed., *China's Shift: Global Strategy of the Rising Power* (Tokyo: NIDS Joint Research Series, 2009).
8. Wen Jiabao, "A Number of Issues Regarding the Historic Tasks in the Initial Stage of Socialism and China's Foreign Policy," *Xinhua* (February 26, 2007), as cited in Masuda, "China's Search for a New Foreign Policy Frontier: Concept and Practice of 'Harmonious World,'" 62–63.
9. David Shambaugh, "Coping with a Conflicted China," *The Washington Quarterly* 34, no. 1 (Winter 2011): 8.
10. Zheng Bijian, "China's 'Peaceful Rise' to Great-Power Status," *Foreign Affairs* 84, no. 5 (September/October 2005): 22.

11. Hu Jintao, "Build Towards a Harmonious World of Lasting Peace and Common Prosperity," speech at the United Nations Summit (New York, September 15, 2005).
12. The number eight is regarded as auspicious in Chinese numerology. It is a near homonym for the word "to prosper" in some Chinese dialects.
13. Nathan Gardels, "Post-Olympic Powershift: The Return of the Middle Kingdom in a Post-American World," *New Perspectives Quarterly* 25, no. 4 (Fall 2008): 7–8.
14. "Di shi yi ci zhuwaishi jie huiyi zhao kai, Hu Jintao, Wen Jiabao jianghua" ["Hu Jintao and Wen Jiabao speak at the 11th meeting of overseas envoys"], website of the Central People's Government of the People's Republic of China, accessed at http://www.gov.cn/ldhd/2009-07/20/content_1370171.html.
15. Wang Xiaodong, "Gai you xifang zhengshi zhongguo 'bu gaoxing' le" ["It is now up to the West to face squarely that China is unhappy"], in Song Xiaojun, Wang Xiaodong, Huang Jisu, Song Qiang, and Liu Yang, *Zhongguo bu gaoxing: da shidai, da mubiao ji women de neiyou waihuan* [*China Is Unhappy: The Great Era, the Grand Goal, and Our Internal Anxieties and External Challenges*] (Nanjing: Jiangsu Renmin Chubanshe, 2009), 39.
16. Song Xiaojun, "Meiguo bu shi zhilaohu, shi 'lao huanggua shua lü qi'" ["America is not a paper tiger, it's an 'old cucumber painted green'"] in Song, Wang, et al., *Zhongguo bu gaoxing*, 85.
17. A classical Chinese expression signifying a postconflict return to peace with no expectation of recommencing hostilities.
18. Song, "Meiguo bu shi zhilaohu," 86.
19. Ibid., 92.
20. Ibid.
21. Liu Mingfu, *Zhongguo meng: hou meiguo shidai de daguo siwei yu zhanlüe dingwei* [*China Dream: Great Power Thinking and Strategic Posture in the Post-American Era*] (Beijing: Zhongguo Youyi Chuban Gongsi, 2010).
22. Ibid., 69–73, 103–17.
23. Ibid., 124.
24. Ibid., 256–62.
25. Some analyses posit that while the sentiments expressed in these books are real and may be common in much of the Chinese military establishment, they partly reflect a profit motive: provocative books sell well in any country, and nationalist tracts such as *China Is Unhappy* and *China Dream* are published by private publishing companies. See Phillip C. Saunders, "Will *China's Dream* Turn into America's Nightmare?" *China Brief* 10, no. 7 (Washington, D.C.: Jamestown Foundation, April 1, 2010): 10–11.
26. Dai Bingguo, "Persisting with Taking the Path of Peaceful Development" (Beijing: Ministry of Foreign Affairs of the People's Republic of China, December 6, 2010).
27. Ibid.
28. Ibid.
29. Ibid.
30. Ibid.
31. Ibid.
32. Ibid.
33. Hu Jintao, "Speech at the Meeting Marking the 30th Anniversary of Reform and Opening Up" (December 18, 2008), accessed at http://www.bjreview.com.cn/Key_Document_Translation/2009-04/27/content_194200.htm.
34. Dai, "Persisting with Taking the Path of Peaceful Development."
35. Ibid.

Epilogue: Does History Repeat Itself? The Crowe Memorandum

1. Crowe knew the issue from both sides. Born in Leipzig to a British diplomat father and a German mother, he had moved to England only at the age of seventeen. His wife was of German origin, and even as a loyal servant of the Crown, Crowe retained a cultural and familial connection to the European continent. Michael L. Dockrill and Brian J. C. McKercher, *Diplomacy and World Power: Studies in British Foreign Policy, 1890–1951* (Cambridge: Cambridge University Press, 1996), 27.
2. Eyre Crowe, "Memorandum on the Present State of British Relations with France and Germany" (Foreign Office, January 1, 1907), in G. P. Gooch and Harold Temperley, eds., *British Documents on the Origins of the War,* vol. 3: *The Testing of the Entente* (London: H.M. Stationery Office, 1928), 406.
3. Ibid., 417.
4. Ibid., 416.
5. Ibid., 417.
6. Ibid., 407.
7. Ibid.
8. Phillip C. Saunders, "Will *China's Dream* Turn into America's Nightmare?" *China Brief* 10, no. 7 (Washington, D.C.: Jamestown Foundation, April 1, 2010): 10 (quoting Liu Mingfu *Global Times* article).
9. Liu Mingfu, *Zhongguo meng: hou meiguo shidai de daguo siwei yu zhanlüe dingwei* [*China Dream: Great Power Thinking and Strategic Posture in the Post-American Era*] (Beijing: Zhongguo Youyi Chuban Gongsi, 2010), 24; Chris Buckley, "China PLA Officer Urges Challenging U.S. Dominance," Reuters, February 28, 2010, accessed at http://www.reuters.com/article/2010/03/01/us-china-usa-military-exclusive-idUSTRE6200P620100301.
10. Richard Daniel Ewing, "Hu Jintao: The Making of a Chinese General Secretary," *China Quarterly* 173 (March 2003): 29–31.
11. Dai Bingguo, "Persisting with Taking the Path of Peaceful Development" (Beijing: Ministry of Foreign Affairs of the People's Republic of China, December 6, 2010).
12. Adele Hayutin, "China's Demographic Shifts: The Shape of Things to Come" (Stanford: Stanford Center on Longevity, October 24, 2008), 7.
13. Ethan Devine, "The Japan Syndrome," *Foreign Policy* (September 30, 2010), accessed at http://www.foreignpolicy.com/articles/2010/09/30/the_japan_syndrome.
14. Hayutin, "China's Demographic Shifts," 3.
15. See Joshua Cooper Ramo, "Hu's Visit: Finding a Way Forward on U.S.-China Relations," *Time* (April 8, 2010). Ramo adopts the concept of co-evolution from the field of biology as an interpretive framework for U.S.-China relations.

Index